YESTERDAY AND TODAY

YESTERDAY

AND TODAY

A Dictionary of Recent American History

Stanley Hochman

McGRAW-HILL BOOK COMPANY

New York   St. Louis   San Francisco   Auckland
Bogotá   Düsseldorf   Johannesburg   London
Madrid   Mexico   Montreal   New Delhi
Panama   São Paulo   Singapore
Sidney   Tokyo   Toronto

Library of Congress Cataloging in Publication Data

Hochman, Stanley.
  Yesterday and today.

  Includes index.
  1. United States—History—1945-   —Dictionaries.
I. Title.
E838.6.H62   973.9   79-12265
  ISBN 0-07-029103-9

1234567890   KPKP   7865432109

*The editors for this book were Robert A. Rosenbaum, Patricia Allen-Browne,
and Carolyn Nagy, the designer was Naomi Auerbach, and the production supervisor
was Thomas G. Kowalczyk. It was set in Illumna by KBC/Rocappi, Inc.*

Printed and bound by The Kingsport Press.

07992

To Lee—

"My head, my heart, mine Eyes, nay more
My joy, my Magazine of earthly store."
—Anne Bradstreet

T.I.M.

Contents

Preface

The alphabetically arranged entries that follow cover a range of major and minor topical events and institutions in our national political and cultural life since the end of World War II. Here is what was happening in our legislatures, courts, schools, entertainment media, intellectual and political lives, and on our cities' streets. At one time the focus of national attention, these controversies, organizations, tragedies, books, movies, and fads were featured in our morning newspapers, nightly news roundups, and weekly magazines. They were what Americans talked about with friends, neighbors, and co-workers; they provided the material and themes for the imaginative creations of our artists. Significant or ephemeral in terms of our national development, they entered our national awareness, however briefly, and references to them have become a shorthand by which those who share a common culture and history tend to communicate.

However, though they are part of our history, these events and institutions are often not yet part of our *histories*, the texts used in our institutions of formal education. Casual references to them appearing in our newspapers, books, and movies tend to be confusing to those who have not lived through the national experience involved. Yet most contemporary writers of fact and fiction assume that some knowledge of them is a portion of the intellectual equipment of their readers. For example, at the time this was being written, the morning newspapers reported with little or no explanatory comment the continuing effect of the **Bakke Case** on **Affirmative Action** and noted current doubts about the accuracy of the **Warren Report** on President John F. Kennedy's assassination in Dallas, Texas, on **November 22, 1963;** an editorial attacked increased federal subsidies for **Amtrak;** and a feature article on this country's establishment of formal diplomatic relations with Red China after some thirty years referred to an earlier crisis over **Quemoy and Matsu,** and the U.S. government's **Two-Chinas Policy,** the stage of **Ping-Pong Diplomacy,** etc. Additional stories on the Carter administration's response to the Vietnamese invasion of Cambodia assumed that the reader had in mind the events and the emotional atmosphere of the **Vietnam War** and the **Cambodian "Incursion"**; the same was true of an item on Ohio's decision to compensate the families of the victims of the **Kent State Tragedy,** and of editorial comment on the failure of Mississippi officials to make any attempt to compensate the families of victims of the **Jackson State Tragedy.**

In a lighter vein, this book hopes to reduce the blank looks indicating an attack of **Generation Gap** when there is mention of the **Hula-Hoop Craze,** the **Davy Crockett Craze,** or **The Man in the Gray Flannel Suit;** or of the slogans and bywords that once studded our postwar political life: **"Dump the Hump," "Eight Millionaires and a Plumber," "I am not a crook,"** and a **"Republican Cloth Coat."**

The emphasis in this "dictionary" is on the events and initiatives that have affected the course of American civilization and society during the last thirty-five years. For example, while no attempt is made to comment on the continuing development of the Democratic and Republican parties, there are entries on the **States' Rights Party** and the **Progressive Party of America,** both of which are products of the postwar period. There are no entries on individuals as such, but by consulting the index the reader can easily trace the important roles played in recent American society by political personalities such as Hubert H. Humphrey, Robert A. Taft, Margaret Chase Smith, George C. Marshall, John Foster Dulles, and the various Presidents they served—if sometimes only as members of a loyal opposition—and by intellectual leaders and thinkers like Martin Luther King, Jr., C. Wright Mills, Rachel Carson, John Kenneth Galbraith, Herbert Marcuse, Michael Harrington, Betty Friedan, and Erik H. Erikson. Information on influential events, institutions, books, and organizations not given an individual entry in the main text can therefore often be found by using the comprehensive Index of Names in the News.

Yesterday and Today: A Dictionary of Recent American History was planned and compiled in dictionary form to aid in its use as a quick reference. Boldface cross-references in the alphabetically arranged entries direct the reader to other articles that can provide additional or related information on the topic. This book is not intended as a comprehensive history of the times, but the author fondly hopes that readers will be sufficiently seduced by the interest of some of the entries to indulge in the casual browsing that will build up an overall picture of American life in the postwar era.

The facts have been culled from daily newspapers, specialized journals, published accounts by men and women in public life, government documents, and current books covering a variety of topics about how America lives, works, plays, and is governed. The author wishes to thank the overworked members of the New York Public Library for their help in suggesting sources of material.

Stanley Hochman

A

Attica

ABMS *See* **Antiballistic Missile System.**

Abominable No Man Name applied in White House circles to H. R. Haldeman, Chief of Staff to President Richard M. Nixon during most of the latter's term in office. Haldeman saw his job as "protecting" the President from interruptions and "trivia," among which he included visits from congressmen and members of the Cabinet. He was fond of saying that "every President needs an S.O.B.—and I'm Nixon's."

Implicated by White House Counsel John W. Dean III in the cover-up that followed the break-in of Democratic National Committee headquarters in Washington's Watergate complex on June 17, 1972 (*see* **Watergate Scandal**), Haldeman resigned from office on April 30, 1973, along with John D. Erlichman, Assistant to the President for Domestic Affairs, and Dean himself. He was indicted on March 1, 1974, along with other members of the White House staff, on charges of conspiring to obstruct the investigation of the break-in. Found guilty on January 1, 1975, he initially remained loyal to the former President and went to prison in stony silence. However, in *The Ends of Power* (1978) he wrote:

I believe that Richard Nixon himself caused those burglars to break into Democratic Chairman Lawrence O'Brien's office in the Watergate. I believe Nixon told Charles Colson to get the goods on O'Brien's connection with Howard Hughes [as a secret lobbyist]. He lit the match and handed it to Colson, who in turn touched off the fuse.

Among other things, the former Chief of Staff said that President Nixon was in on the cover-up that followed "from Day One."

In December 1978, Haldeman was paroled from a prison camp at Lompoc, Calif., after serving eighteen months of his one-to-four-year sentence—reduced from an original two-and-a-half-to-eight-year sentence. Of the more than twenty men originally sentenced to prison as a result of Watergate, only former Attorney General John N. Mitchell was in jail by the end of the year, and he was released on parole on January 19, 1979 (*see* **"White House Horrors"**).

During the incumbency of President Dwight D. Eisenhower, the Assistant to the President, Sherman Adams, was also known as the Abominable No Man and was similarly accused of isolating the Chief Executive. When, in 1958, Adams became implicated on charges of having interceded with the Federal Trade Commission on behalf of textile manufacturer Bernard Goldfine, President Eisenhower strongly resisted pressure to force Adams' resignation.
See **Adams-Goldfine Scandal.**

Abstract Expressionism *See* **Action Painting.**

Acheson-Lilienthal Report *See* **Baruch Plan.**

Acheson Plan *See* **"Uniting for Peace."**

ACTION Not an acronym but the name given to the umbrella agency set up by President Richard M. Nixon on July 1, 1971, to coordinate six volunteer programs that had previously been administered by separate federal agencies. Originally, ACTION included: **Volunteers in Service to America** (VISTA), the **Peace Corps,** the Foster Grandparents Program, the Retired Senior Volunteer Program (RSVP), the Active Corps of Executives (ACE), and the **Service Corps of Retired Executives** (SCORE). These programs, which were administered from Washington and ten regional offices established throughout the nation, involved approximately 23,000 volunteers. Three years later that number had grown to 127,000, and ACTION included new programs such as University Year for ACTION (UYA), in which universities cooperated in a program under which student volunteers spent a year living and working in low-income communities; the Senior Companion Program, under which retired adults could supplement their income by helping needy adults; and ACTION Cooperative Volunteers (ACV), under which community groups were able to share with ACTION the costs of one-year volunteer programs.

In spring 1978, ACTION sponsored a one-year national demonstration project in Syracuse, N.Y., that provided more than 1,600 youths between the ages of 16 and 21 with paid opportunities to participate in community services projects. Funded with a grant from the Department of Labor's Youth Employment Program, the newly established Youth Community Service (YCS) was to test the possibility of a national youth service.

In December 1978, Rep. Robert H. Michel (R.-Ill.) charged in a draft report of a congressional investigation of ACTION that under the directorship of Samuel W. Brown, Jr., who was widely known in the 1960s as an anti-**Vietnam War** activist, the agency had suffered from "widespread mismanagement and a blatant disregard for the agency's mission by its senior executives." Mr. Brown countercharged that "the right is looking for a hit and I'm it." He welcomed an investigation of the charges and noted that he had President Jimmy Carter's full support.

ACTION requested a $231 million budget for fiscal 1979.

Action Painting The term was originally used by art critic Harold Rosenberg in the 1940s and 1950s to denote the form of abstract expressionism by which the "New York School" of painters rejected traditional techniques in an attempt to give direct and fuller expression to the immediacy of feeling. Perhaps the work that best exemplifies this approach to painting is that of Jackson Pollock, a former student of the realist painter Thomas Hart Benton. Sometimes known as "Jack the Dripper," Pollock noted in 1947 that he had abandoned the traditional painter's easel, preferring to tack his canvas to the wall or spread it on the floor, where he was free to walk around it, "work from the four sides and literally be *in* the painting. . . . I continue to get further away from the usual painter's tools such as easel, palette, brushes, etc. I prefer sticks, trowels, knives, and dripping fluid paint or heavy impasto with sand, broken glass and other foreign matter added."

Other representative painters who attempted to capture feelings by the use of rapid and free techniques were Hans Hofmann, Willem de Kooning, Adolph Gottlieb, and Clyfford Still. The work of Franz Kline and Mark Rothko emphasized classical form to a greater extent.

Pop Art, which used a hard-edged technique, was a reaction to action painting.

Acupuncture Although the origins of the Chinese medical therapy called acupuncture go back some 5,000 years, the technique did not receive much attention in the United States until *New York Times* journalist James Reston reported on his experiences with it in China, where it was used to relieve his postsurgical pain. At present, there are acupuncture clinics all over the country, although in some states the legal status of the technique is in question.

The philosophical and religious basis for acupuncture is the belief in traditional Chinese cosmography that all that comes to be is the result of the interaction between the forces of Yin (the feminine and negative principle: passivity, depth, darkness, cold, wetness) and Yang (the masculine and positive principle: activity, height, light, heat, dryness). When there is an upset of this equilibrium in the body, the desired balance can be restored by using long, fine needles to allow excesses of one or the other force to escape. The number of insertion

points accepted by authorities varies from 295 to 365.

ADA *See* **Americans for Democratic Action.**

Adams-Goldfine Scandal Testifying before a House Special Subcommittee on Legislative Oversight on June 17, 1958, Sherman Adams, assistant to President Dwight D. Eisenhower, denied that he had ever interceded with the Federal Trade Commission (FTC) or the Securities and Exchange Commission (SEC) in behalf of New Hampshire textile manufacturer Bernard Goldfine.

The former governor of New Hampshire had known Goldfine ever since the 1940s, when, as speaker of the state House of Representatives, he had encouraged the manufacturer to keep his mills in operation at a time when other textile mills were leaving the area. In early 1954, Goldfine was charged by the FTC with infractions of the government's grade labeling regulations. He reportedly asked Adams to intercede for him, but the latter claimed that all he did was ask FTC chairman Edward F. Howrey, his personal appointee, for a routine report on the nature of the complaint and that he then sent the resulting memorandum to Goldfine. Although the FTC issued a cease and desist order against the textile manufacturer, the following year Goldfine was similarly charged and he asked that Adams obtain an appointment for him with Howrey. In 1956, Goldfine was in trouble with the SEC, which was investigating the failure of his East Boston Company, a realty firm, to file reports on its financing procedures. Adams asked Special White House Counsel Jerry Morgan to look into the question.

Over the years the Adams and Goldfine families had reportedly exchanged gifts, and these became an object of special interest when it was revealed during the subcommittee testimony that Goldfine had claimed his offerings as deductible expenses on his income tax. Public interest in the industrialist's gifts to the Adams family was focused on a vicuña coat, a $2,400 oriental rug, and the fact that Goldfine had on some twenty occasions picked up the tab when the Adams family had stayed in Boston or New York hotels. According to Adams, Goldfine had told him that the hotel accommodations he had occupied were maintained as a convenience for friends and business associates. As for the vicuña coat, "many of the prominent men in public life in New England at that time received such coats and I was one of them. . . . I never had the feeling that there were any strings attached to the gifts on either side. . . ."

The press and public took a different view, partly because of the poor impression that Goldfine made during his blustering appearances before the House investigating committee. Although it seemed to many that Adams had been gulled, and although the President insisted, **"I need him,"** strong pressure built up for his resignation, especially after Republicans were soundly defeated in an early September election in Maine that was felt to reflect public disapproval of the facts revealed. On September 22, 1958, Adams resigned as Assistant to the President under pressure from the party, which feared a debacle at the polls in November. In a nationwide broadcast he insisted on his innocence of all wrongdoing. Much of the pressure for his resignation had been brought to bear by Vice President Richard M. Nixon and by Meade Alcorn, Chairman of the Republican National Committee. President Eisenhower, however, continued to believe in the integrity of Adams and his value to the government.

Administration on Aging Established in the Department of Health, Education, and Welfare under the Older Americans Act of 1965, signed into law by President Lyndon B. Johnson on July 14, 1965. The legislation authorized an initial $13 million for the new agency for matching grants to states undertaking community planning and personnel training in the field; $4.5 million was authorized for experimental projects by public and nonprofit agencies.

Strongly supported by the AFL-CIO, the original bill was sponsored by Sen. Patrick McNamara (D.-Mich.) and Rep. John Fogarty (D.-R.I.).

Advanced Manned Strategic Aircraft (AMSA) Under the AMSA program, work was begun in 1953 to replace the B-52, which many considered obsolete, with a B-70 bomber capable of sweeping in on a target at three times the speed of sound in a high-level attack that would render it immune to fighter interception. Much of the enthusiasm for the B-70 was lost after the 1960 **U-2** incident when the American spy plane piloted by Gary Powers was shot down over Soviet territory by a ground-to-air missile, which apparently proved that no plane could outfly a missile. After two prototype B-70s had been built at a cost of approximately $1.48 billion, the program was definitively scrapped in 1966.

Attention then turned to an aircraft that would fly at supersonic speeds at altitudes too low for them to be detected in time for ground-to-air mis-

sile defense. The result was the **B-1 bomber,** and in mid-1970 North American Rockwell began work on a $1.4 billion contract for three prototypes. There was opposition to the B-1 from the start because of its high cost—a minimum of $87 million per plane by 1976, more than twice the original estimates. President Jimmy Carter killed the program in June 1976, an action that finally won the approval of a reluctant Congress. Attempts to revive the B-1 continued until February 1977, when the House voted to rescind funds appropriated earlier for two additional planes.

Members of the Air Force, impatient with resistance to and criticism of the program, sometimes complained that the AMSA acronym might better have been translated as "America's Most Studied Aircraft."

AEC *See* **Atomic Energy Commission.**

Affirmative Action Originally the phrase referred to the seeking out and preparation of minority groups for better opportunities in business, industry, and education. It has, however, more and more come to mean the establishment of quotas designed to aid previously discriminated against minorities (blacks, women, etc.). As such, it is often attacked by critics as "reverse discrimination."

A well-known example of affirmative action was the **Philadelphia Plan** under which in 1969 the Department of Labor required unions working on federal contracts of $500,000 or more to make good-faith efforts to train black apprentices for full union membership. Though the validity of the plan was upheld in the courts, the Nixon administration failed to follow through on an initiative that was a singular departure from its **Southern Strategy.** Other significant developments were the settlements in the early 1970s under which the American Telephone and Telegraph Company was required to make up millions in back pay and employee benefits for previously discriminated against minorities—including women.

On June 28, 1978, the U.S. Supreme Court upheld the potential constitutionality of flexible, race-based affirmative action programs by its five-to-four ruling in the **Bakke Case.** However, the University of California's plan under which Alan Bakke had originally been denied admission to Davis Medical College in favor of allegedly less qualified minority students was considered extreme in setting a rigid quota of sixteen out of one hundred places for minority students. In a decision that was considered by some ambiguous, the majority opinion noted that while plans to achieve a diverse student body were not in themselves unconstitutional, the establishment of fixed quotas based on race or ethnic origin alone was not permissible.

In a separate opinion, Justice Thurgood Marshall, himself a black, noted that for the last 200 years "the Constitution as interpreted by this court did not prohibit the most ingenious and pervasive forms of discrimination against the Negro. Now, when a state acts to remedy the effects of that legacy of discrimination, I cannot believe that this same Constitution acts as a barrier."

With both proponents and opponents of affirmative action claiming a victory in the Bakke case, its impact on the future of affirmative action is uncertain.

The Affluent Society John Kenneth Galbraith's *The Affluent Society*, an economic analysis of a society that thinks poor and is unwilling to face up to the problems and potential of affluence, was published in 1958. He himself credits its immediate leap to bestsellerdom to the fact that while the book was in production the surprise launching of Russia's **Sputnik** shook up a great deal of "conventional wisdom" about what makes a healthy society.

The author argues wittily and persuasively that the United States, while awash in private opulence, is suffering from a bad case of public malnutrition. Throughout history, people have been concerned with problems of scarcity and the difficulty of meeting basic needs. For the last few decades, however, in many technologically advanced nations "there has been great and quite unprecedented affluence."

In spite of this, the thinking that guides this society is the product of a world in which poverty was the norm. The stress is therefore still on high production and full employment, both of which are dependent on the artificial creation of "needs" through advertising. Public services, considered unproductive, are neglected. As a result "the family which takes its mauve and cerise, air-conditioned, power-steered, and power-braked automobile out for a tour passes through cities that are badly paved, made hideous by litter. . . . They picnic on exquisitely packaged food from a portable icebox by a polluted stream and go on to spend the night at a park which is a menace to public health and morals."

Galbraith urges an end to the poverty of public services and a redistribution of income to provide decent schools, low-income housing, public transportation, and basic research to improve national security and the essential quality of life. He under-

lines the danger of a society increasingly dependent on mounting private debt and urges that employment security be divorced from production by an unemployment compensation system that amounts to a **Guaranteed Annual Wage**. Continued emphasis on luxury consumer production, he stresses, creates a mythical productive power that periodically floods and stalls economic mechanisms and can actually lead to weakening a nation's military security.

He proposes a national sales tax as a means of correcting the problem of imbalance between private and public goods. "The community is affluent in privately produced goods. It is poor in public services. The obvious solution is to tax the former and provide the latter—by making private goods more expensive, public goods are made more abundant."

The way to deal with individual or regional poverty amidst overall affluence, Galbraith argues, is through schools, health programs, and strong social services which will enable people "either to contend more effectively with their environment, or to escape it and take up life elsewhere on more or less equal terms with others." The poor, he warns, have become a demoralized and inarticulate minority whose condition tends to be inherited and self-perpetuating.

Galbraith's analysis is amplified in *The New Industrial State* (1967) and *Economics and the Public Purpose* (1973).

"Africa Is for the Africans" Speaking in Nairobi, Kenya, on February 21, 1961, Assistant State Secretary for African Affairs G. Mennen Williams noted that the new Kennedy administration supported a policy of "Africa is for the Africans." As governor of Michigan, Williams established a reputation as a strong civil rights proponent. His statement caused an immediate furor in London and was strongly objected to by white British settlers in Kenya and elsewhere as unwarranted interference in African affairs. When asked to comment on his assistant secretary's policy pronouncement, President John F. Kennedy ambiguously said, "I don't know who else Africa should be for."

Several days later Williams, who was popularly known as "Soapy" Williams, qualified his original statement by explaining that his use of the word "Africans" was meant to include both whites and blacks. On March 1, President Kennedy clarified his stand by telling reporters that his Africa for the Africans policy defined Africans as "all those who felt that they were Africans, whatever their color might be, whatever their race might be."

President Kennedy seemed to have been more

5

amused than upset by the incident, and later that month he told the bureau chiefs and columnists who made up Washington's Gridiron Club that on receiving a request from Williams that he be allowed to extend his African fact-finding tour, he had wired back: "No, Soapy. Africa is for the Africans."

On his return to this country on March 18, after having visited the Sudan, Ethiopia, Kenya, Tanganyika, Zanzibar, the Congo Republics, Liberia, Ivory Coast, Ghana, and Upper Volta, Assistant Secretary Williams reported that the trip had convinced him that "the people of Africa unquestionably have a great reserve of good will for America."

Agency for International Development (AID) A bill submitted to Congress by President John F. Kennedy on May 26, 1961, called for the formation of a new federal agency under which the foreign aid programs of the United States would be consolidated. Authorization for AID was finally given in the controversial Foreign Assistance Act of 1961, signed by the President on September 4, 1961. The new agency replaced the International Cooperation Administration (ICA) and the Development Loan Fund (DLF). Much to the President's disappointment, AID was dependent on an annual congressional appropriation for long-term development loans because permission for long-time borrowing authority had been rejected. (The President had originally requested that the agency be given authority to borrow up to $7.3 billion from the Treasury over a five-year period.)

The President pointed out:

The fundamental task of our foreign aid program in the 1960s is not negatively to fight communism: its fundamental task is to help make an historical demonstration that in the twentieth century, as in the nineteenth—in the southern half of the globe as in the north—economic growth and political democracy can develop hand in hand.

The performance of AID under the directorship of Fowler Hamilton, a New York lawyer who had originally been considered for the directorship of the CIA, was disappointing to President Kennedy, who, upon resignation in November 1962, replaced him with David Bell, soon recognized as an able administrator. Nevertheless, the annual tussle with Congress over the amounts and kinds of foreign aid that could be made available defeated the President's goals. By the time of his assassination on **November 22, 1963,** funds for foreign aid were actually lower than they had been in 1958. Testifying before the House Foreign Affairs Committee in 1963, Bell

noted that "without economic progress the chances for strengthening democratic processes in the less developed countries would be greatly diminished."

"Agonizing reappraisal" French resistance to ratifying the European Defense Community (EDC) plan (May 1952), which called for a build-up of West German military forces, resulted in blunt warnings from Secretary of State John Foster Dulles when representatives of the **NATO** nations met in Paris late in 1953. Continued delay in the formation of the European Army, meant to be a bulwark against possible Soviet aggression, would cause "an agonizing reappraisal of basic United States policy." Later, he told newsmen that while the United States would honor its NATO commitment to aid any member nation in the event of an attack, "the disposition of our troops would, of course, be a factor in the agonizing reappraisal I spoke about." A "re-study" of ways in which this country's NATO commitment could be maintained would be called for, the secretary noted. This was because congressional impatience with the lack of European unity had resulted in resistance to appropriating funds for military aid.

In August 1954, the French National Assembly rejected the EDC treaty by a 319 to 264 vote. The following October, however, the Western European Union (WEU) was formed. Under WEU, although Western Germany was to provide twelve divisions to the NATO army, it could not remilitarize further without the consent of WEU members.

Agribusiness Generous tax concessions having made it a tax haven for companies with high profits, in the post-World War II era large American corporations began turning their attention to farming. Among the more prominent have been **ITT**, Boeing Aircraft, John Hancock Insurance Company, and Tenneco Oil Corporation. Critics of this trend, such as Sen. Gaylord Nelson (D.-Wis.), have argued that corporate farming will bring about an ultimate power shift in rural America, "a shift in control of the production of food and fiber away from the independent farmers, a shift of control of small town economies away from their citizens."

"Vertical integration," i.e., the control of all stages of production and marketing, has been a particular fear of agribusiness opponents because it eliminates the middleman. (A prime example is said to be the poultry industry.) In addition, because they have enormous purchasing power, the agribusinesses, say critics, can control market prices.

Earl Butz, Secretary of Agriculture under Presidents Richard M. Nixon and Gerald R. Ford, was considered a proponent of agribusiness.

Agricultural Trade and Development Act of 1954 As a result of the high mandatory price supports legislated by the Agricultural Act of 1949, the Eisenhower administration several years later was faced with the problem of mounting farm surpluses in expensively maintained government storage. Under the 1954 legislation, also known as **Public Law 480** (July 10, 1954), the government was authorized to establish a three-year program designed to disperse $1 billion in surplus farm products abroad in exchange for foreign currencies which were to be used for "development of new markets; purchase of strategic and critical materials; procurement of military equipment and facilities; financing of purchases of goods or services to friendly countries; loans to promote multilateral trade and economic development; and financing of international education exchange programs." The President was also authorized to make grants of up to $300 million of surplus stocks to meet famine and urgent relief requirements of friendly nations and to "friendly but needy populations without regard to the friendliness of their government." The new legislation also made surplus commodities available to any United States area declared by the President to be "an acute distress area" if there was no interference with "normal marketing." Under this interpretation, surpluses could be used to provide lunches for school children.

On January 10, 1955, President Eisenhower reported to Congress that $670,800,000 in surplus products had been or were in the process of being disposed of abroad. Of this amount about two-thirds had been paid for in foreign currency; $93 million had been traded for strategic materials; and $125 million had been granted for relief.

Originally scheduled to terminate on June 30, 1957, Public Law 480 was several times extended and is the basis for the revised and expanded **Food for Peace Act of 1966.** Under its Title I provisions, this country can lend foreign nations money to purchase American farm products. In most cases these twenty- to forty-year loans are at 3 percent interest. Under Title II, food products can be donated to foreign governments or turned over for distribution by international relief organizations.

AID *See* **Agency for International Development.**

AIP *See* **American Independent Party.**

Air Force One "When I entered the White House," wrote President Dwight D. Eisenhower, "I traveled in a piston-driven plane, the *Columbine.* But before I left, my Air Force aide . . . had to go to school to learn how to fly a new presidential airplane, a 707 jet."

It was on *Air Force One*, the presidential Boeing 707, that President John F. Kennedy and his wife flew to Texas in November 1963. Vice President and Mrs. Lyndon B. Johnson flew to Dallas on *Air Force Two.* Immediately after the assassination of President Kennedy on **November 22, 1963,** President Johnson was sworn into office aboard *Air Force One,* which returned to Washington with the new President and the body of his slain predecessor. The plane, wrote President Johnson, "is the closest thing to a traveling White House that man can devise. It affords the personnel, the security, and the communications equipment a President must have to do his job." From it, the President could remain in touch not only with the White House and our embassies everywhere in the world but also with a battlefield commander in Vietnam. Its radio crew was required to be adept in multilingual communications with the control towers of airfields on which the huge jet landed on international trips.

President Richard M. Nixon renamed the jet *Spirit of '76* in honor of the nation's approaching bicentennial, and that name was painted on its nose. When President Gerald R. Ford assumed office in 1974, after the resignation of his predecessor, he kept the name on the plane, but it was again referred to as *Air Force One.* After President Jimmy Carter assumed office in January 1977, that name was removed and the plane once more officially became *Air Force One,* a title which it bears only when the President is aboard. Its official call number when it is in use on other occasions is 26000.

Airmobile Authorized in June 1965, the 1st Cavalry Division (Airmobile) was a major American military innovation in the **Vietnam War.** The Division was equipped with 434 aircraft—for the most part helicopters—more than four times the air strength of the conventional infantry division. Later that year, the Airmobile division showed the advantages of its increased mobility in the Ia Drang Valley campaign. As a result of its successes, and those of the later 101st Airborne Division (Airmobile), the Army strove to supply all infantry units with sufficient helicopters to meet operational demands in an attempt to offset enemy initiative and familiarity with the terrain by the fast transfer of ground troops.

In the 1970s the 1st Cavalry was reorganized as a triple capability (TRICAP) unit by the addition of tank battalions and attack helicopters. By this means, Army strategists hope to be able to offset the armored superiority enjoyed by the U.S.S.R. in Europe.

Airstrip Set   The term was invented by newsmen to describe a wealthy group of Texas oilmen. According to one version, a journalist heard Texas Governor John B. Connally, Jr., being invited to "drop by" for a fund-raising party being held for vice presidential candidate Lyndon B. Johnson in 1960. The party was to be held at the host's ranch, and the governor said that he would be pleased to attend if the ranch had an airstrip big enough to handle his DC-3. The ranch did.

Alaskan Pipeline   In 1968, the Atlantic Richfield Company (ARCO) and EXXON Corporation announced the discovery of oil in the Prudhoe Bay area of Alaska's North Slope, and a consortium of oil companies immediately began planning a 789-mile trans-Alaskan pipeline that would carry the oil to the ice-free port of Valez for transportation by tanker to the continental United States. Alarmed environmentalists quickly announced their opposition to the pipeline, pointing out that it would pass through an earthquake zone and interfere with animal migration.

In the initial stages of the struggle, environmentalists successfully fought the project in the courts and, on April 13, 1970, won a temporary federal court injunction against issuing a road permit for the project. However, in an **Earth Day** speech at the University of Alaska, Secretary of the Interior Walter J. Hickel said that he would issue a right-of-way permit for the pipeline, adding that it would be authorized "only after a thorough engineering and decision analysis" and pledging not to approve "any design based on the old and faulty concept of 'build now, repair later.'"

Nevertheless, environmentalist lawsuits successfully blocked the pipeline until November 16, 1973, when President Richard M. Nixon signed the controversial Trans-Alaska Pipeline Authorization Act, which provided that steps necessary for the completion of the pipeline be immediately taken under the National Environmental Policy Act of 1969. The new legislation barred court review of the environmental impact of the project in a provision whose constitutionality could be challanged only within sixty days of the bill's enactment. The President, who had urged passage of the bill in a nationally televised address on the **Energy Crisis,** called the legislation the first step toward making the United States self-sufficient in energy by 1980.

The building and operation of the Alaskan pipeline was the responsibility of Alyeska Pipeline Service Company, a consortium of oil companies including Standard Oil (Ohio), ARCO, EXXON, British Petroleum Co., Ltd., Mobil Oil Corp., Union Oil Company of California, Phillips Petroleum Co., and Amerada Hess Corp. Alyeska estimated the cost of the forty-eight-inch-diameter pipeline at $7.7 billion, but by the time oil started flowing through it on June 20, 1977, costs were closer to $10 billion. (A first estimate in 1974 had been $6 billion, and a 1970 estimate for a pipeline of smaller diameter had been only $900 million.)

In the first month of operation the pipeline suffered five breakdowns, one of which covered fifteen acres of surrounding tundra and its ponds with raw petroleum. Critics charged that in rushing to meet construction deadlines Alyeska had frequently violated state and federal environmental rules to which it had agreed when it signed the pipeline lease in 1974. The result had been violations that led to greater than expected erosion, stream and fish damage, and a large washout of tundra. Government inspectors had charged in May 1977 that there was "no environmental quality control in the area whatsoever. In our opinions, it is beyond belief that the quality-control program is so lax at this late stage of the game." Admitting some violations of environmental regulations, one Alyeska official said: "There are priorities, and we were involved in building a pipeline."

The pipeline's initial flow potential was estimated at 1 million barrels daily.

Alexander v. Holmes County Board of Education   In a unanimous and unsigned decision, the U.S. Supreme Court ruled on October 29, 1969, that school districts must end segregation "at once" and "now and hereafter" operate integrated systems. Although the ruling specifically affected thirty-three Mississippi school districts, its language was considered broad enough for the case to serve as a precedent for pending and future suits involving segregation.

The decision, the first major ruling handed down by the Court since President Richard M. Nixon had appointed Warren E. Burger as Chief Justice, was considered a stinging defeat for the Nixon administration, whose Justice Department had sought to secure delays in instituting desegregation. The Court rejected the request for additional time in which to present desegregation plans, and held that "continued operation of segregated schools under a standard of allowing 'all deliberate speed' for desegregation is no longer constitutionally permissible." Exceptions to an integration plan could henceforth be sought only after the plan had been put into operation.

The Mississippi suits had been brought in behalf of fourteen black children by the NAACP Legal Defense and Educational Fund, Inc. Attorney General John N. Mitchell's favoring delays had been viewed by critics as part of the administration's so-called **Southern Strategy**, by which it hoped to encourage Republican gains in the South during the elections of 1970 and 1972. Delays had been authorized in August 1969 by the U.S. Court of Appeals for the Fifth Circuit, which, under the present ruling, was required to order that all thirty-three school districts involved "may no longer operate a dual school system based on race or color. . . ."

Alianza de los Pueblos Libres *See* **Alliance of Free City-States.**

"Alice Doesn't" At its National Conference held in Philadelphia, October 25-27, 1975, the radical wing of the **National Organization for Women** (NOW) gained control of the organization after an election characterized by bitterness and charges of fraud. The radicals immediately vowed to take NOW "out of the mainstream, into the revolution."

As a result a "general strike against the system" was called for on October 29, the tenth anniversary of the founding of NOW. Women were urged not to work, shop, cook, or carry on any activity capable of giving aid and comfort to their "oppressors." Most NOW chapters ignored the call to strike, although there was a parade of several thousand women in Los Angeles, and in some of the larger cities there were teach-ins, consciousness-raising sessions, and performances of street theater.

The name "Alice Doesn't" was given the strike because of the current popularity of a movie entitled *Alice Doesn't Live Here Anymore*, in which a recently widowed woman decides to create a new and independent life for herself and her son.

Alienation Index Devised by the Harris Poll, it is based on answers by selected samplings of respondents to questions such as: Do you feel the rich get richer and the poor get poorer? That what you think really doesn't count very much? That the people running the country don't really care what happens to you? That the people who have power are out to take advantage of you? That you are left out of things around you?

In 1972, with the turbulent sixties behind us and the **Watergate Scandal** just about to explode, the Index was at 47 percent.

"All in the Family" Although the pilot aired on January 12, 1971, was not particularly successful, this television comedy about life with Archie Bunker, the all-American bigot, had won a regular Saturday night audience of 35 million for CBS by the end of the year. The creation of Norman Lear, who was later to enliven television with "Sanford and Son" and **"Mary Hartman, Mary Hartman"**, the program was inspired by a British television series, "Till Death Us Do Part," which focused on the squabbles between a bigoted conservative father and his liberal son-in-law. Lear picked up the formula, transferred the locale to a lower-middle-class section of Queens, and broke with convention by having the working-class father fill the airwaves with ethnic slurs as he struggles ineffectually to cope with the changing reality of American life in the 1970s.

Some critics protested that the comic and largely sympathetic portrayal of the inevitably defeated Archie (played by Carroll O'Connor) made bigotry "lovable," but the show went on to win four Emmies, including the award for the best new show of the season. It was suggested that the program's popularity was due to the fact that while bigots delighted in Archie's "candor," liberals found consolation in his invincible ignorance, for which they coined the word "Bunkerism."

In addition to Archie, the Bunker family included his browbeaten wife, Edith (Jean Stapleton), his daughter, Gloria (Sally Struthers), and her free-loading husband, Mike (Rob Reiner), a liberal sociology student whose intellectual haziness more than balanced his father-in-law's outrageous stupidities. In the spring of 1978, Gloria and Mike were written out of the show, which was scheduled to continue for at least one more season to the delight of what was by that time an audience of 50 million.

Alliance for Progress At a White House reception for some 250 South American diplomats and members of Congress on March 13, 1961, President John F. Kennedy proposed that the Latin American republics join with this country in an economic and social program designed to raise the living standards for all in this hemisphere. Calling for the transformation of the "American continents into a vast crucible of revolutionary ideas and efforts," the President emphasized that the proposed "alliance for progress" must ensure that political freedom accompanied material improvement. "Therefore, let us express our special friendship to the people of Cuba and the Dominican Republic—and the hope that they will soon rejoin the society of free men, uniting with us in our common effort."

The ten-point program offered by the President included the following:

1. A ten-year plan designed to raise living standards and erase illiteracy

2. That the Inter-American Economic and Social Council begin a "massive planning effort" in which each nation would formulate its development plans, which would provide a basis for the allocation of resources from beyond its borders

3. That Congress be asked to appropriate funds as a first step in fulfilling the Act of Bogotá

4. Support for economic integration as "a genuine step toward larger markets and greater competitive opportunity"

5. Case-by-case examination by the United States of commodity market problems

6. Expansion of this country's emergency **Food-for-Peace** program

7. Increased cooperation on scientific matters and an expansion of training programs for science teachers

8. The expansion of technical training programs, for which the **Peace Corps** would be made available

9. Reaffirmation of the pledge "to come to the defense of any American nation whose independence is endangered"

10. An exchange between this country and Latin American nations of both teachers and students

Meeting in Punta del Este, Uruguay, August 5-17, 1961, delegates to the Inter-American Social and Economic Conference formally drew up and signed the Charter for the Alliance for Progress. Che Guevara, representing Cuba, expressed sympathy for the goals of the Alliance, but denounced it as an instrument of imperialism bound to fail; Cuba abstained from signing the charter to which the delegates of the twenty other nations in the hemisphere put their signatures.

(Meeting in Punta del Este on February 14, 1962, fourteen of the twenty-one nations of the **Organization of American States** [OAS] voted to exclude Cuba from participation in OAS activities because of its communist government; however, since the OAS charter makes no provision for suspension, Cuba remained a member.)

Arthur Schlesinger, Jr., President Kennedy's Special Assistant for Latin American Affairs, pointed out in 1965 that as foreign private investment in Latin America shrank in 1961 and "as Latin America's own private capital continued to flow out of the hemisphere into Swiss banks," Washington was under mounting pressure from American companies doing business in Latin America "to talk less about social reform and more about private investment." The effect was to lead many Latin Americans to view the Alliance as primarily intended to serve the interests of United States business.

On April 15, 1966, the Presidents of the American republics met in Mexico City to discuss ways for strengthening the Alliance for Progress. In a special message to Congress on March 13, 1967, President Lyndon B. Johnson pointed up the success of the Alliance during the previous six years and cited four pillars on which future achievements would rest: elimination of trade barriers and improvements in education, agriculture, and health.

The Presidents of the American republics met again at Punta del Este, April 12-14, 1967, and at the conclusion signed a Declaration of the Presidents of America, the most important feature of which was the proposed creation of a Latin American common market in the 1970s. Writing in 1971, President Johnson noted that although the commitment was still unfulfilled, he remained convinced of its necessity.

By 1969, some $18 billion had been given to Latin American countries in the form of grants and loans; a little more than half of that came from government sources. However, the net U.S. government investment was in actuality considerably smaller, since much of the money received from official U.S. sources was used to service previous public indebtedness in the area. Critics generally agree that the expectations for the Alliance were not met, at least partially, because it was found difficult, if not impossible, to bring about basic social change within a democratic framework. In addition, the **Vietnam War** shifted attention, energy, and finances to other areas of the world.

Alliance of Free City-States Organization whose purpose was to reopen the question of Spanish and Mexican land grants given settlers between 1598 and 1846. Because of the destruction of the original archives, by the twentieth century some four-fifths of old grants were lost to claimants despite guarantees in the Treaty of Guadalupe Hidalgo (1848), which concluded the Mexican War.

The problem began receiving attention again in 1960, when Reies Lopez Tijerina organized the Alianza Federal de Mercedes (Federal Alliance of

Land Grants) in New Mexico, later renamed the Alianza de los Pueblos Libres (Alliance of Free City-States). It attempted in vain to regain land grants lost over the years. In October 1969, Reies Lopez Tijerina resigned because he felt that the organization was focusing on militant nationalism.

Altamont Death Festival Scheduled to give a free rock concert at the Altamont Speedway in Livermore, California, on December 6, 1969, the Rolling Stones hired a motorcycle gang known as **Hells Angels** to maintain order in return for $500 worth of beer. Midway through the concert a scuffle broke out when one member of the audience was said to have kicked the cycle of Ralph "Sonny" Barger, Jr., president of the California group of about 140 Angels and their some 3,000 enthusiasts. Outraged, some fifty Hell's Angels armed with pool cues sailed into the crowd and began flailing about.

At another point, as Mick Jagger, the Stone's lead singer, began a number called "Sympathy for the Devil," an eighteen-year-old black named Meredith Hunter started for the stage, seemingly intent on attack. He was seized by one of the Hell's Angels and stabbed to death.

A film record of the event—the real purpose of the concert seems to have been to shoot an inexpensive **cinéma vérité** documentary of the Rolling Stones' American tour—showed that Hunter had a long-barreled revolver in his left hand. After he had apparently tripped and fallen to the ground, the film showed him being twice stabbed in the back by a member of the motorcycle gang. The victim, however, had five knife wounds in all, and three could not be accounted for, nor was it ever known exactly why Hunter had pulled the gun.

All in all, three died at what *Rolling Stone* magazine in a January 21, 1970, article—highly critical of the security arrangements made by the rock group—baptized the Altamont Death Festival. One member of the audience died of a drug overdose; another was apparently trampled to death in the resulting melée.

Amerasia Case There are various versions of the origins of the *Amerasia* case which captured national headlines in June 1945. According to one version, an analyst of the Office of Strategic Services (OSS) was disturbed to find in the January issue of *Amerasia*, a scholarly magazine founded in 1936, an article which quoted verbatim from a restricted OSS report. As a result, a raid was carried out on the journal's office in March 1945 and a variety of documents and photostats from the files of the State Department, OSS, Office of War Information, Military Intelligence, and Naval Intelligence were discovered and turned over to the FBI. (In another version, the OSS raid came after the British government complained that the text of a report on its Thailand policy had been published in the journal with minor changes.)

As a result of this haul, the FBI established surveillance over the owner and editor of *Amerasia*, Philip J. Jaffe, and his staff. No immediate action was taken—possibly, as some charged, through the intervention of Secretary of the Navy James V. Forrestal; but on June 6, 1945, the new Truman administration apparently reversed this stand, and Jaffe and several of his staff members were arrested and a new document haul was made. Since there was no evidence that any of this material had been passed on to a foreign power, they were charged with possession of "Confidential" documents removed from the files of government offices. Jaffe was fined $2,500 after pleading guilty.

Other arrests included that of a State Department foreign officer, John Stewart Service, and five others on the charge of having stolen government documents; however, a grand jury refused to indict Service on the evidence presented. (The incident was later used by Sen. Joseph R. McCarthy (R.-Wis.) (see **McCarthyism**) as evidence of communist infiltration of the State Department.)

It was generally felt that the documents in the possession of *Amerasia* were innocuous agricultural reports and material that had already been made public in some other form, although according to routine policy they had been stamped "Confidential." Others charged that they included reports on the opposition to the Chiang Kai-shek regime in China.

American Council of Christian Laymen A right-wing organization headed by Verne Kaub which is based in Madison, Wisconsin. It serves as a distribution center for a variety of extremist publications. Typical, perhaps, of the point of view in its pamphlets is the opening paragraph of a booklet entitled "The Fatherhood of God and the Brotherhood of Man," by Ebenezer Myers, a retired Methodist minister: "The doctrine of the Fatherhood of God and the Brotherhood of Man has no foundation for its existence anywhere. It is not taught by the Bible; but on the contrary the Bible condemns it and teaches just the opposite. . . ."

An American Dilemma Originally published in 1944, *An American Dilemma*, Gunnar Myrdal's study of the Negro in the United States, was immediately compared in importance to Alexis de Tocqueville's *Democracy in America*, Frederick Jackson Turner's *The Significance of the Frontier in American History*, and Robert and Helen Lynd's *Middletown*.

The internationally known sociologist and economist had been selected by the project's sponsor, the Carnegie Corporation of New York, not only because of his impressive qualifications, but because it was hoped that as a Swede he could approach his task uninfluenced by traditional attitudes and previous conclusions. The study, in which he was assisted by Arnold Rose and RME. Sterner, lasted from 1938 to 1943.

The "dilemma" as defined by Myrdal results from the conflict between the faith of Americans in the common democratic creed developed in Western civilization and their inability to put this faith into action in all spheres.

When we say that there is a Negro *problem* in America, what we mean is that the Americans are worried about it. It is on their minds and on their consciences.

The Negro problem is not only America's greatest failure but also America's incomparably great opportunity for the future. If America should follow its down deepest convictions, its well-being at home would be increased directly. At the same time, America's prestige and power abroad would rise immensely. The century-old dream of American patriots, that America should give the entire world its own freedoms and faith would come true. America can demonstrate that justice, equality and cooperation are possible between white and colored people. . . . America is free to choose whether the Negro shall remain her liability or become her opportunity.

Myrdal notes and documents the breakdown of American "melting pot" assimilation when it comes to blacks. He concedes racial differences but feels that they probably result from environmental conditions. He urges voluntary birth control as a means to alleviate poverty among the black masses, more touched as a group by "poverty, disease, and family disorganization than is common among the whites in America."

The book dwells at length upon discrimination against blacks economically and in terms of education, housing, public services, and social welfare programs. It underlines the importance of political action by blacks and suggests that their disfranchisement in the South is coming to an end. Writing in 1943 and reviewing the activities of black organizations designed to improve the social and economic condition of the American Negro, Myrdal says that "only when Negroes have collaborated with whites

have organizations been built up which have any strength and which have been able to do something practical."

In a "Postscript" to a 1962 reissue of *An American Dilemma*, Arnold Rose pointed out that the rate of change had been faster than had been foreseen twenty years earlier. He underlined the importance of technological and industrial progress, of new legislation and court decisions, and of groups such as the **Congress of Racial Equality** (CORE), the **Southern Christian Leadership Conference** (SCLC), and the **Student Nonviolent Coordinating Committee** (SNCC). He also somewhat optimistically predicted "the end of all formal segregation and discrimination within a decade, and the decline of informal segregation and discrimination so that it would be a mere shadow in two decades."

One indication of the influence the study had in this country is in the fact that in a footnote to a majority decision in **Brown v. Board of Education of Topeka,** the Supreme Court noted that social scientists such as Myrdal found that to separate children on the basis of race generates a feeling of inferiority as to their status in the community. Segregationists pointed to the footnote as evidence that the Court had substituted personal political and social ideas for "the established law of the land."

American Farm Bureau Federation Along with the National Grange and the Farmers Union, this is one of the largest farm organizations in the country and currently draws its support from the owners of large farms, which are representative of what has come to be called **"agribusiness."** Formed in 1919 on the basis of previously organized local and state bureaus, it worked to strengthen the cooperative movement among farmers and lobbied for government aid in dealing with farm surpluses.

During the administration of President Franklin D. Roosevelt it had a powerful influence on the New Deal agricultural policy, bringing pressure to bear not only on the legislative process but—since it dominated the complex of land grant colleges, the Extension Service, and the county agents—also on the actual administration and enforcement of such legislation through the Agricultural Adjustment Administration (AAA).

Following World War II, the Bureau took an increasingly conservative stance by opposing government interference with agricultural production and distribution. In 1949, under the leadership of Allan B. Kline—who in 1958 was to help organize the right-wing Americans for Constitutional Action

(ACA)—it helped to defeat the **Brannan Plan** by means of which the Truman administration had sought to protect "family-sized" farms in competition with agricultural corporations. President Truman charged that this lobbying effort had cost the bureau well over $500,000.

American Independent Party (AIP) Dissatisfaction with the civil rights stand of the Democratic Party led Alabama's Governor George C. Wallace on February 8, 1968, to announce that he would run for the presidency in the forthcoming election as the candidate of the recently formed American Independent Party. Wallace's decision came after weeks of insisting that he would stay out of the race if either of the major parties nominated a candidate acceptable to him. (It was not until August that the Republicans chose Richard M. Nixon, and the Democrats, Hubert H. Humphrey.)

Meeting in Dallas on September 17, the AIP formally nominated Wallace, who after much hesitation about a running mate—he was said to have been considering civil rights "moderate" A. B. "Happy" Chandler, Kentucky's former Democratic Governor and Senator—announced on October 3 that he would share the AIP ticket with General Curtis LeMay. The new party's plaform was not announced until October 13. It contained no civil rights plank and demanded an end to federal intervention to enforce desegregation in public schools. In addition, it called for increased reliance on police power to maintain law and order, an improved and more militant defense posture, and an end to "minority appeasement." The platform also backed increased Social Security and **Medicare** benefits and called for federal programs that would provide additional public employment and opportunities for job training. The defeat of prosegregationist forces in the courts also led the AIP to propose periodic elections for district judges and mandatory reconfirmation of Supreme Court justices.

No sooner had he been nominated for the Vice-Presidency than General LeMay—who had once suggested bombing North Vietnam "back to the Stone Age"—embarrassed his running mate by announcing that to bring the **Vietnam War** to a successful conclusion he would "use anything that we could dream up—including the nuclear weapons." Although a thoroughgoing "hawk" himself, Wallace had earlier declared that he was against the use of nuclear weapons.

Campaign appearances of the AIP candidate drew large crowds outside the Deep South, where his greatest strength was presumed to lie. However, the enthusiasm Wallace evoked among the discontented when he attacked Washington bureaucrats failed to translate into the strength at the poles predicted by most preelection surveys. Wallace won only forty-five electoral votes—Arkansas (6), Louisiana (10), Mississippi (7), Alabama (10), and Georgia (12). Nevertheless his popular vote was 9,906,141, or 13 percent of the total. (In 1948 **Dixiecrat** Strom Thurmond got 1,169,021 popular and thirty-nine electoral votes; Progressive Henry A. Wallace received 1,157,172 popular and no electoral votes. In 1924, a third-party attempt by Progressive Robert M. La Follette garnered 4,822,856 popular and thirteen electoral votes.)

During the 1968 election campaign, Republicans charged that the Democrats were actively aiding Wallace's drive in areas where it was presumed that he would draw off strength from Richard M. Nixon; in California Democrats were said to have promoted Wallace's drive to obtain the signatures he needed to qualify for the ballot. On the other hand, investigations following the **Watergate Scandal** revealed that among the Republican **"dirty tricks"** carried out by the **Committee to Re-elect the President** (CREEP) in 1972 was the payment of $10,000 to promote a California campaign aimed at inducing AIP registrants to switch their party affiliation to the **American Nazi Party**; AIP registration actually increased by more than 6,000.

Wallace withdrew from the presidential campaign when, in May 1972, he was left half-paralyzed after being gunned down in Laurel, Maryland, by would-be assassin Arthur Bremer.

After 1972, the AIP splintered. In the mid-seventies the main group was controlled by William K. Shearer, Lemon Grove, California; a splinter group known as the American Party was under the direction of Tom Anderson, Pigeon Forge, Tennessee.

American Nazi Party (ANP) An outgrowth of the National Committee to Free America from Jewish Domination, the American Nazi Party (ANP) was founded in March 1959 by businessman Harold N. Arrowsmith, Jr., who was eager to find an outlet for his writings on Jewish influence in American history, and George Lincoln Rockwell, who became its leader.

In July 1960 the ANP attracted national attention following a riot on Washington's National Mall. Rockwell was committed to St. Elizabeth's Hospital for psychiatric observation.

While **Freedom Riders** were trying to desegregate bus terminals in the South in May 1961, the ANP sent a "hate bus" from Washington, D.C., to New Orleans, where the passengers were eventually jailed by local authorities for "unreasonably" alarming the public.

In another publicized incident, "stormtrooper" Roy James attacked Martin Luther King, Jr., during a **Birmingham** protest meeting. For this action he was awarded the ANP's "Adolph Hitler Medal."

On August 25, 1967, Rockwell was fatally shot in Arlington, Virginia, by John Patler, an editor of the ANP's *The Stormtrooper*, who had been expelled from the party several months earlier for creating dissension between dark-haired and blond Nazis.

Matt Koehl assumed leadership of the ANP and changed its name to the National Socialist White People's Party. Its propaganda organ was *White Power*, a bimonthly tabloid.

On July 9, 1978, as the National Socialist Party of America the ANP captured national headlines when a band of some 25 uniformed Nazis held a rally in Marquette Park in Chicago's racially tense Southwest Side. The occasion marked the culmination of a year-long legal battle during which the Nazis, now under the leadership of Frank Collin, contended with the support of the American Civil Liberties Union that they were denied the right of free speech by a Park District regulation requiring that demonstrations attracting more than 75 people be covered by $60,000 insurance. (The rally attracted some 2,000, many of them neighborhood people who were sympathetic to the Nazi goal of keeping blacks out of the white residential area.)

Originally denied a permit for the rally, the Nazis had countered by threatening to hold a march on June 25, 1978, through the predominantly Jewish suburb of Skokie. This march was cancelled on June 20, when a federal judge issued an order allowing the rally in Marquette Park. Though the decision was appealed, on July 7 the United States Supreme Court declined to stay the federal judge's order.

More than 400 helmeted policemen were required to set up a protective barrier around the band of Nazis. Some seventy arrests were made and the police kept many groups of counterdemonstrators from the rally site by closing off streets leading to the park.

As supporters wearing T-shirts marked "White Power" chanted "death to the Jews" and "white power, white power," Mr. Collin, who is himself half-Jewish, told them that "the 1960s were the years of black power. The 1970s are going to be the years of white power and white victory."

"American Revolutionary Army"   The "American Revolutionary Army," a self-proclaimed rightist group, grabbed headlines across the nation on February 20, 1974. Claiming credit for the kidnapping of J. Reginald Murphy, editorial-page editor of the *Atlanta Constitution*, they demanded $700,000 and called for the resignation of the nation's top elected officials. The ransom paid by Murphy's newspaper on February 23 was recovered the next day by police, who arrested the entire "army": Mr. and Mrs. William Williams.

Americans for Democratic Action (ADA)   Meeting in Washington, D.C., on January 4, 1947, some 150 political leaders, union officials, and educators formed the Americans for Democratic Action to formulate liberal domestic and foreign policies, enlist public support of them, and "put them into effect by political action through major political parties." The organizing committee of twenty-five included labor leaders David Dubinsky and Walter Reuther; theologian Reinhold Niebuhr; former Office of War Information director Elmer Rice; Charles Bolte, chairman of the American Veterans Committee (AVC); and Franklin D. Roosevelt, Jr., son of the former president. Eleanor Roosevelt, the late President's wife, also participated in the ADA founding, but asked to be excused from service on the committee.

From the beginning, ADA took a firmly anticommunist stand and was in this unlike the Progressive Citizens of America (PCA), a left-wing amalgamation of political action groups which was to be the driving force behind Henry Wallace's **Progressive Party** in 1948.

An early manifesto stated: "We reject any association with Communists or sympathizers with Communism in the United States as completely as we reject any association with Fascists or their sympathizers." The nonpartisan organization has over the years supported progressive candidates for public office and worked for liberal legislation through public education and the preparation of testimony given before a variety of congressional committees.

The first ADA president was Leon Henderson, who had held several posts as economic adviser to President Franklin D. Roosevelt during the New Deal. In 1978, Sen. George McGovern was the president and Leon Shull the organization's national director. Membership in ADA was between 65,000 and 70,000.

Americans for the Presidency   With pressure mounting for the resignation or impeachment of

President Richard M. Nixon following revelations related to the **Watergate Scandal,** this group of presidential supporters was formed in March 1974 by Donald Kendall, board chairman of PepsiCo and a long-time friend of President Nixon. Its board members included Mrs. Mamie Eisenhower, Bob Hope, Reverend Norman Vincent Peale, former **Housing and Urban Development** (HUD) Secretary George Romney, and former Deputy Secretary of Defense David Packard. The group sponsored full-page ads in newspapers around the country urging continuing support for and confidence in President Nixon.

AMSA *See* **Advanced Manned Strategic Aircraft.**

Amtrak Originally known as Railpax, Amtrak was designed to pump new life into declining intercity passenger railroads by the use of selective subsidies. Heavily promoted by John Volpe, Secretary of the Department of Transportation (DOT) during the Nixon administration, Amtrak won congressional approval in 1970 and began operations in May 1971, in spite of heavy opposition from the highway-oriented oil interests.

Since passenger traffic had declined in the postwar decades, the railroads had tended to let services and equipment deteriorate for lack of new funds. They were, of course, delighted with the Amtrak scheme, which has indeed resulted in better service and increased ridership. However, because railroad deficits require a large annual transfusion of federal funds, there is continuing if cautious congressional interest in decreasing the necessary subsidies by eliminating unprofitable long-haul lines.

Volpe's support of Amtrak probably accounts for his abrupt fall from grace in the Nixon entourage. After the 1972 election he was offered the ambassadorship to Italy as an alternative to quitting the government entirely.

In mid-1978, with Amtrak running increasingly higher deficits, Transportation Secretary Brock Adams suggested the elimination of almost a third of the system's 27,000 miles of track. Service for thirty-six major cities would be assured, but Nashville, Omaha, Dallas, and Salt Lake City would be dropped from Amtrak. This cutback would result in a savings of $118 million in fiscal 1980, the first year in which the proposed change would go into effect.

In the seven years of its operation, Amtrak revenues had grown from $153 million to almost twice that, but revenues cover only 37 percent of operating costs as against 50 percent originally. If costs continued to rise at 9 percent annually, Secretary Adams predicted, Amtrak would require a $1 billion subsidy by 1984.

Andrea Doria In a thick Atlantic fog, the Italian luxury liner *Andrea Doria* sank some forty-five miles south of Nantucket Island after colliding with the Swedish liner *Stockholm* shortly before midnight on July 25, 1956. The final death toll was fifty-one in the worst peacetime maritime disaster since the sinking of the *Titanic* in 1912.

Especially built to break through ice, the bow of the *Stockholm* cut deep into the Italian ship, which had been constructed with eleven watertight compartments to give it stability in the eventuality of such a crash. After listing to a 45° angle—too steep to allow more than a few of its lifeboats to be launched—the *Andrea Doria* sank shortly after ten o'clock the next morning. The majority of its 1,709 Europe-bound passengers and crew had been taken aboard the *Ile de France,* which had rushed to its side within three hours. Others were picked up by the disabled *Stockholm* or by several American vessels that came to the rescue.

Both ships had been radar-equipped, and no suitable explanation for the tragedy was ever announced. The Italian Line and the Swedish American Line launched suits against each another which were dropped by mutual consent on January 28, 1957. Both companies then agreed to work together to handle some 1,200 suits, totalling $100 million, brought by passengers and shippers.

The *Andrea Doria* was named for a sixteenth-century Genoese naval hero. It cost $27 million and was put into transatlantic service in January 1953, after being launched in June 1951.

The largest ship ever built in Sweden at that time, the *Stockholm* was launched in September 1946 and had been making Atlantic crossings since March 1948.

ANP *See* **American Nazi Party.**

Antarctica Treaty To ensure that Antarctica would be used only for peaceful purposes, on May 3, 1958, President Dwight D. Eisenhower invited eleven nations that had territorial claims or had conducted scientific investigations in the area to participate in an international conference to be held at some unspecified time and place. On October 15, 1959, representatives of the U.S.S.R., Argentina, Australia, Belgium, Chile, France, Japan, New Zealand, Norway, South Africa, and the United Kingdom met with their American counterpart in Washington,

D.C., to work out the details of a fourteen-article treaty that was signed the following December first.

In essence, the treaty reserved the continent of Antarctica for scientific work and suspended consideration of all territorial claims for the next thirty-four years. Signatories agreed to ban "the establishment of military maneuvers, as well as the testing of any type of weapons." They also accepted a provision under which they would exchange scientific personnel and information. Disputes about the area that could not be settled by consultation, arbitration, mediation, or conciliation were to be referred to the International Court of Justice. (Conflicting claims to portions of Antarctica have been made by Argentina, Australia, Chile, France, New Zealand, Norway, and the United Kingdom. Neither the United States nor the Soviet Union has made or recognized such claims.)

Writing in 1960, President Eisenhower noted: "The Antarctica Treaty is one small example of what might be accomplished in more populous and significant areas."

Antiballistic Missile System (ABMS) Convinced, after the launching of *Sputnik,* that the Soviet Union had the capacity for intercontinental nuclear missile warfare, Army Chief of Staff Maxwell D. Taylor proposed in November 1957 that an antiballistic missile (ABM) system be developed over the next three years at a cost of almost $7 billion. President Dwight D. Eisenhower sought the advice of the experts on the President's Science Advisory Committee and, as a result, decided against deployment of an ABM system on the grounds of its technical inadequacy. This decision was strongly criticized by the congressional Democratic majority and became a full-blown campaign issue during the 1960 presidential election, when Democratic candidate John F. Kennedy said that the failure to deploy an ABM system had led to a **"missile gap"** between this country and the U.S.S.R.

Once elected, however, President Kennedy was evidently convinced by his scientific advisors that the technology required for an ABM system was still inadequate, and he in turn refused to order its deployment. The ABM system was again an election issue in 1964, but this time the Republicans were charging the Democratic administration with having weakened American defenses by failing to deploy antiballistic missiles.

Nevertheless, after his reelection President Lyndon B. Johnson, who as a Senator had been strongly critical of the Eisenhower administration for rejecting an ABM system, himself turned down a proposal by the Joint Chiefs of Staff for a system oriented against China—which had recently exploded its first nuclear bomb— rather than the U.S.S.R. Although eager to conserve the budget for **Vietnam War** expenses and his **Great Society**, by 1967 Johnson had to retreat from his original position—which had been strongly supported by Defense Secretary Robert S. McNamara—when it became clear that Republican presidential candidate Richard M. Nixon intended to make the ABM system a 1968 campaign issue. Reluctantly, Secretary McNamara announced the administration's decision to go ahead with a "light" ABM system oriented against the Chinese, but warned that pressures would develop to "expand it into a heavy Soviet-oriented system."

In the early days of the Nixon administration, a special Senate subcommittee chaired by Sen. Albert Gore (D.-Tenn.) began hearings in which leading scientists took positions against the system originally proposed by President Johnson, claiming that it would be easily penetrable and that it would merely begin a new arms race with the U.S.S.R.

However, in March 1969, President Nixon endorsed a system he baptized "Safeguard," whose only essential difference from the "Sentinel" system endorsed by the Johnson administration was that it met objections of nervous suburbanites to having "bombs in the backyard" by moving the missile sites away from populated areas.

Testimony given before Senator Gore's subcommittee made it obvious that only pro-ABM information was being made available to it, that the President's Science Advisory Committee had not been consulted by him until three days *after* he had announced for the Safeguard system, and that there had been no outside review of the system by qualified experts. The Senate vote on ABM appropriations was tied, and Vice President Spiro Agnew naturally cast the deciding vote for the administration. President Nixon attacked those who had voted against the ABM as being "new isolationists."

A year later Senator Gore's subcommittee was holding new hearings on the President's request for funds for additional ABM sites. Dr. John Foster, Director of Defense Research and Engineering, presented pro-ABM technical arguments and managed to convey the impression that the members of an ad hoc committee he had headed agreed with his views. However, when, after contrary testimony by two members, the until then secret *O'Neill Report* (Dr. Lawrence O'Neill, Riverside Research Institute, had chaired the committee) was released in July 1970, it showed that the committee had advised that a more cost-effective system than Safeguard could be devised for the defense of the U.S. **Minuteman** strategic bases against surprise attack.

The approval of two additional ABM sites barely managed to get through the Senate in 1970, and opposition to the ABM system was gaining. After the May 1972 **Strategic Arms Limitations Talk** (SALT) agreement had limited ABM bases both here and in the Soviet Union, Defense Secretary Melvin R. Laird claimed that he had accepted the terms because of the administration's inability to get congressional authorization for full national development of the Safeguard system.

ANZUS Word coined from the initials of the members of the Tripartite Security Treaty signed in San Francisco, California, on September 1, 1951, by Australia, New Zealand, and the United States. Article 7 of the treaty set up a council comprising the foreign ministers of the member nations or their deputies. This ANZUS Council, sometimes called the Pacific Council, maintains a consultative relationship with Pacific-area nations or regional organizations such as the later formed and subsequently phased out **Southeast Asia Treaty Organization** (SEATO), with a view toward establishing mutual defense against potential aggression. After the first meeting in Kaneohe, Hawaii, meetings were held annually, most often in Washington, D.C.

Apalachin Conference On November 14, 1957, sixty-three men suspected of being racketeers gathered at the home in Apalachin, New York, of Joseph Barbara, Sr., who had been under police surveillance as a bootlegging suspect. Questioned by the police, they refused to divulge the purpose of the meeting, and on May 13, 1959, a federal grand jury in New York indicted twenty-seven men for conspiracy to obstruct justice. When the FBI proceeded to round them up, six of those indicted were able to elude arrest. Meanwhile, widespread media coverage was given to what appeared a gangland imitation of corporate business methods.

On December 18, 1959, after an eight-week trial, twenty of the men were convicted by a federal jury on charges of having given perjurious or evasive answers about what had been "plotted" at what was by then widely referred to as the Apalachin Conference. In passing sentences ranging from three to five years and imposing fines of $10,000, Judge Irving R. Kaufman (see **Rosenberg Case**) ruled that "when police reasonably believe that a crime might have been committed, those closely connected in time and place to the criminal activity are undoubt-

edly proper subjects for limited police questioning."

On November 28, 1960, the U.S. Court of Appeals unanimously reversed the convictions and ordered the charges dismissed in an opinion that said the defendants had been convicted of "a crime which the government could not prove . . . and on evidence which a jury could not properly assess."

Appalachian Aid Plan *See* **War on Poverty.**

ARA *See* **Area Redevelopment Act.**

Area Redevelopment Act (ARA) Signed into law by President John F. Kennedy on May 1, 1962, it provided $394 million in federal aid to the nation's chronically depressed areas. Under the legislation, "redevelopment areas" were to be defined by the Department of Labor criteria used to designate twenty major and ninety smaller areas having a "substantial and persistent" labor surplus, i.e., high unemployment. The program, which was to be administered by the Department of Commerce, was to terminate on June 30, 1965. President Kennedy appointed William L. Batt, Jr., Pennsylvania's Labor and Industry Secretary, as Area Redevelopment Administrator.

A key and controversial provision of ARA authorized Treasury borrowing to finance three $100 million loan funds. Backed by the Kennedy administration, this provision was denounced as "back-door" spending by conservative critics.

Arica A therapeutic technique originated in Arica, Chile, by Oscar Ichazo, who came to New York and, with the help of forty-two disciples, established the Arica Institute, Inc., in 1971. An eclectic system, it incorporates many Oriental and Mideastern teachings, generating sensory awareness by means of special diet, exercises, interpersonal and group experiences, and meditation. Through these, one reaches "The Permanent 24," a "basic satori" experience that was described in the institute's literature as "a place of inner and outer peace, joy, and harmony."

Disciples believe that the body has three "vital energy centers": (1) the Kath, which is "four fingerwidths below the navel" and grounds the individual on the planet; (2) the Mind Center, or Path, i.e., words; (3) Oth, which is in the heart and is supposed to experience "essential feelings of serenity, humility and equanimity." However, when Kath is asleep, the ego is assumed to take control and reflect its false "passions" of pride, anger, and envy.

Originally, initiation into Arica was based on seven-day-a-week sessions that lasted three months and cost $3,000. Later, a new training technique was offered on the basis of forty days—variations allowed for those who had to show up for work regularly—at an approximate cost of $600. There are at present seventeen other associated Arica institutes in the United States and abroad.

Asia Firstism Phrase used by historian Eric F. Goldman to describe the sentiment of those Americans who felt that the United States had a particular "civilizing" mission in Asia and that therefore in any considerations of foreign policy "they believed in Asia First; some came close to believing in Asia Only."

The fury of this group, whose particular hero was General Douglas MacArthur, was aroused when on January 12, 1950, Secretary of State Dean Acheson spoke of the **"defensive perimeter"** of the United States in the Pacific as running from the Aleutian Islands to Japan, Okinawa, and the Philippines, noting that in other Pacific areas in the event of attack

. . . initial reliance must be on the people attacked to resist it, and then upon the commitments of the entire civilized world—under the Charter of the United Nations, which so far has not proved a weak reed to lean on by any people who are determined to protect their independence against outside aggression.

When, five months later, North Korea invaded South Korea, Secretary Acheson's speech was seen as having incited communist aggression, since Korea had been clearly outside the "defensive perimeter."

Asia-Pacific Triangle Provisions One of the important features of the Immigration and Nationality Amendments to the **McCarran-Walter Act** was the repeal of the so-called Asia-Pacific Triangle provisions designed to keep down the immigration of people from within its borders. Under those provisions, a native of the Triangle area was required to enter this country under the area's immigration quota, even though he or she might be the citizen of a European country. The new legislation phased out the national-origins system, which came to an end on June 30, 1968.

"Ask not what your country can do for you. . . ." President John F. Kennedy's eloquent inaugural address on January 20, 1961, is generally considered one of the finest in the nation's history, and the line "ask not what your country can do for you . . ." has often been quoted and paraphrased in a variety of

contexts. Speaker of the House Sam Rayburn, who had seen service under Presidents Roosevelt, Truman, and Eisenhower, said of the speech afterward that it "was better than Lincoln." Key portions are quoted below:

. . . For I have sworn before you and Almighty God the same solemn oath our forebears prescribed nearly a century and three-quarters ago.

The world is very different now. For man holds in his mortal hands the power to abolish all forms of human poverty and all forms of human life. And yet the same revolutionary beliefs for which our forebears fought are still at issue around the globe—the belief that the rights of man come not from the generosity of the state but from the hand of God.

We dare not forget today that we are the heirs of that first revolution. Let the word go forth from this time and place, to friend and foe alike, that the torch has been passed to a new generation of Americans—born in this century, tempered by war, disciplined by a hard and bitter peace, proud of our ancient heritage—and unwilling to witness or permit the slow undoing of those human rights to which this nation has always been committed, and to which we are committed today at home and around the world.

Let every nation know, whether it wishes us well or ill, that we shall pay any price, bear any burden, meet any hardship, support any friend, oppose any foe to assure the survival and the success of liberty. . . .

So let us begin anew—remembering on both sides that civility is not a sign of weakness, and sincerity is always subject to proof. Let us never negotiate out of fear. But let us never fear to negotiate. . . .

And so, my fellow Americans—ask not what your country can do for you—ask what you can do for your country.

My fellow citizens of the world: ask not what America will do for you, but what together we can do for the freedom of man.

Aswan High Dam Controversy As a cornerstone of his economic development program, Egypt's President Gamal Abdel Nasser announced in 1953 that he would build an Aswan High Dam some four miles south of the old Aswan Dam which had been completed in 1902 and improved in 1933. To finance its construction, in December 1955 he received promises of loans from the United States and Great Britain, and additional offers were made by the World Bank the following February.

The aim of United States policy had been both to steer rising Egyptian nationalism in the direction of a fight against poverty, and to attract that country, a neutral in the **cold war**, into the Western camp. That latter goal was frustrated by President Nasser's recognition of Communist China, his continued hostility toward the **Baghdad Pact,** and his efforts to increase his military arms by dealing with the Soviet Union.

On July 19, 1956, Secretary of State John Foster Dulles abruptly canceled the offer of $56 million in financial aid from the United States. Great Britain soon after canceled its own loan, and the offer from the World Bank faded. In retaliation, on July 26, 1956, President Nasser announced that he would nationalize the Suez Canal and use its $100 million annual income to finance the new dam.

Taking advantage of an Israeli invasion of the Sinai on October 29, 1956, both Great Britain and France landed troops at the northern end of the canal—ostensibly to halt the spread of hostilities. However, when the United States joined the Soviet Union in condemning the action, these forces were withdrawn.

Actual construction of the Aswan High Dam did not begin until 1960, at which time the Russians had stepped into the breach and were supplying both financial and technical aid. In 1976 scientists estimated that the dam, which had submerged many archaeological sites and created a more than 300-mile artificial lake, had so decreased the fertility of the Nile Valley that all the added electrical power it supplied was being absorbed by the need for chemical fertilizer production.

"At this point in time"   One of the most famous of the circumlocutions preferred by H. R. Haldeman, White House Chief of Staff under President Richard M. Nixon. Haldeman's language was adopted and imitated by junior staff members and subsequently came into national prominence in the testimony during the Senate **Watergate Committee** investigations.

The phrase was indicative of a general tendency among "the bright young men" on the Nixon staff to reduce language to a sort of computer symbol, empty of moral content. For example, the 1970 invasion of Cambodia by U.S. troops was referred to as an "incursion" (*see* **Cambodian "Incursion"**); when the White House denied a statement it had previously made, that statement became "inoperative"; a briefing for reporters was an "information opportunity"; and a plan that worked smoothly was said to be a "zero defect system." What the rest of the nation referred to as schedules or deadlines, the White House **Beaver Patrol** called "time frames," and if people got along well together they were said to "track well."

See **Foggy Bottom.**

Atlas Intercontinental Ballistic Missile   When late in 1957 the U.S.S.R. startled the world by successfully launching the earth satellites *Sputnik I* and *II*, it became clear that skeptics had been wrong in doubting the Soviet announcement on August 26, 1957, that it had successfully tested a multistage Intercontinental Ballistic Missile (ICBM). The United States had as yet only developed Intermediate Range Ballistic Missiles (IRBM) and was seriously lagging behind in the vital race to develop high-speed intercontinental missiles that could be armed with atomic warheads.

In July 1957, General Dynamics Corp.'s Convair Astronautics Division had opened a $40 million plant on Kearny Mesa in California and started up production of the Atlas missile. The government had borne half the cost of the original installation and awarded Convair a $145 million Atlas contract, which was later supplemented with a $315 million contract.

On November 28, 1958, the U.S. Air Force fired a 100-ton Atlas ICBM the full range of about 6,325 miles for the first time. Launched from Cape Canaveral, Fla., the missile successfully struck a predesignated target area in the South Atlantic Ocean off the coast of Africa. The eighty-foot, three-stage, liquid-fueled rocket had flown at a speed of 200 miles a minute for thirty minutes. It was the fifteenth Atlas to be tested, but only the second in which an attempt was made to achieve full range. On December 18, 1958, an approximately 8,700-pound Atlas missile was orbited around the earth.

Atomic Energy Act of 1946   *See* **McMahon Act.**

Atomic Energy Commission (AEC)   The **McMahon Bill,** prepared in December 1945 by Connecticut's Senator Brien McMahon, Chairman of the Joint Congressional Committee on Atomic Energy, was the basis for the Atomic Energy Act of 1946 (August 1) under which President Harry S Truman created the Atomic Energy Commission (AEC), a five-man civilian board authorized to develop and control both military and civilian uses of atomic energy. Members were appointed to five-year terms by the President, whose nominations had to be approved by the Senate. It was their function to appoint a general manager, establish production and research policy, and approve contracts with privately controlled businesses and universities. The AEC made annual reports to Congress and was assisted on scientific matters by a General Advisory Committee (GAC) of nine civilians appointed by the President for six-year terms. J. Robert Oppenheimer was the GAC chairman from 1946 to 1952 (see **Oppenheimer Affair).**

Under the Atomic Energy Act, civilian uses of nuclear power were to be given equal emphasis with research and development of military devices which were produced under AEC auspices. As revised in 1954, the law permitted private enterprises to participate in the development of civilian uses of atomic energy. Although the AEC had a monopoly of all fissionable material, it could sell to private companies for use in production covered by AEC contracts and it could also supply small amounts to private laboratories engaged in academic research.

In 1974, the AEC was absorbed by the **Energy Research and Development Administration** (ERDA), which was created under the Energy Reorganization Act of 1974 to consolidate federal activities relating to research and development of various sources of energy—nuclear, fossil, solar, and geothermal.

Atoms for Peace Presented by President Dwight D. Eisenhower in a speech before the United Nations General Assembly on December 8, 1957, the program was widely acclaimed in the West. It was the first proposal for international cooperation in nuclear development since the ill-fated proposal presented at the United Nations in 1946 by Bernard Baruch (see **Baruch Plan).** The present plan bypassed the need for international inspection.

After emphasizing the "awful arithmetic" of the destructive power in the hands of the United States and the Soviet Union, the President proposed to "the governments principally involved, to the extent permitted by elementary prudence, to begin now and continue to make joint contributions from their stockpiles of normal uranium and fissionable materials to an International Atomic Energy Agency" (IAEA) which would be set up under the aegis of the United Nations. The IAEA would be responsible for the storage and protection of the fissionable material and would be charged with devising methods whereby it could be allocated "to serve the peaceful pursuits of mankind"— especially electrical. energy to power-starved areas of the world.

President Eisenhower later noted that his purpose in suggesting the plan was to get the U.S.S.R. working with the United States in a noncontroversial phase of nuclear energy, to gradually expand the cooperation thus obtained into something broader, and to draw to the attention of the smaller nations their stake in the uses to which the world put its limited supply of raw fissionable material.

Before presenting the plan at the United Nations, President Eisenhower met informally in Bermuda with Britain's Prime Minister Winston Churchill and Foreign Secretary Anthony Eden, both of whom approved the proposal. After its presentation, the U.S.S.R. responded with guarded approval, but when months passed without positive action the President threatened to go ahead without Soviet participation. A year after the IAEA was first suggested, the UN General Assembly adopted a resolution advocating the creation of such an agency, and twelve nations, including the U.S.S.R., set to work drafting a statute which was unanimously approved by an eighty-one-nation conference. After the statute had been ratified by twenty-six nations, including the United States, in June 1957, IAEA came into official existence in July 1957.

As part of the Atoms for Peace program, the United States began a cooperative program with the European Atomic Energy Community (EURATOM) in 1958. In 1959, it helped organize the Inter-American Nuclear Energy Commission (IANEC) under the **Organization of the American States** (OAS). In addition, there have been a series of bilateral agreements with foreign nations for furthering peaceful uses of nuclear power.

The original inspiration for the Atoms for Peace proposal was the President's own, but the draft of his speech as presented was prepared by AEC Chairman Lewis Strauss, Special Assistant for National Security Affairs General Robert Cutler, and *Life* publisher C. D. Jackson at Washington breakfast meetings over a period of weeks. Because of this the project originally had the code name "Wheaties."

Attica In what is generally considered the bloodiest prison riot in the history of American penology, on September 9, 1971, inmates of the Attica State Correctional Facility in northern New York State seized control of a portion of the prison compound and threatened to kill some thirty guards and civilian administrators taken hostage unless their demands for prison changes and reforms were met.

Before order was restored on September 13 by 1,500 freely shooting state troopers, sheriff's deputies, and prison guards who stormed the besieged compound, forty-three people were dead: thirty-two inmates and eleven guards and other civilian personnel. Although President Richard M. Nixon called the storming of Attica the only thing the authorities "could possibly do," many felt that this precipitate action by the authorities had caused unnecessary bloodshed. Governor Nelson A. Rockefeller was also severely criticized for rejecting the demand of inmates that he come to Attica and personally negotiate with them.

The origins of the Attica riot will probably always be cloaked in doubt, but the first public sign of inmate protest against the reportedly harsh administration of Attica Superintendent Vincent R. Mancusi goes back to July 1971, when an organization of militant prisoners, calling themselves the Attica Liberation Faction, issued a proclamation asking State Corrections Commissioner Russel G. Oswald to institute reforms. Although Oswald—whose reputation for the reforms he had instituted in the Wisconsin prison system had led to his appointment six months earlier—promised to look into the matter, tension in Attica increased considerably after August 21, when George Jackson (see **Soledad Brothers**) was killed in San Quentin. Sporadic incidents broke out on September 8, and the next day, possibly due to brutal reprisals by prison authorities, some 1,000 of Attica's 2,254 inmates were in full revolt.

Overwhelming the less than 100 guards on duty, they took hostages and seized various prison areas, including the machine shop in which they were able to fashion rudimentary knives and spears. When the rebellious prisoners threatened to execute their hostages, Commissioner Oswald flew to Attica to personally accept their list of demands for reforms. (The original list of fifteen grew to thirty before the four-day siege was over.) The prisoners were also granted their request that a panel of civilian overseers, including members of the press, be admitted to the prison to act as a liaison with authorities.

Commissioner Oswald eventually agreed to twenty-eight of the prisoners' demands, but rejected those calling for total amnesty and the dismissal of Superintendent Mancusi.

On September 13, the commissioner read the rebels an ultimatum demanding the release of all hostages. Soon after, the latter, dressed in prison uniforms, were displayed in all four corners of the besieged compound with makeshift knives being held at their throats. Within an hour the compound was stormed.

A final report by medical authorities revealed that nine of the ten hostages killed during the attack had died of gunshot wounds; the tenth, who had been beaten by the prisoners before they released him, had died in the hospital as a result of the beating. Since only the authorities had guns, it is assumed that their deaths were caused by fire from their would-be rescuers. Despite earlier reports, there was

no sign that the bodies had been mutilated by the prisoners.

The tactics used by police and prison officials in storming the prison were later criticized in a report issued in September 1972 by the nine-member New York State Special Commission on Attica. (Headed by Robert B. McKay, dean of New York University Law School, it was popularly known as the McKay Commission.) A June 1973 report issued by a special Congressional subcommittee, which had conducted extensive public hearing, was also highly critical of the way authorities handled the uprising. Despite charges of what amounted to official murder of prisoners trying to surrender, and despite later accusations that Deputy Attorney General Anthony G. Simonetti had covered up evidence of brutality by state police officials, charges were later brought against prison inmates only.

Critics have noted that, while some 80 percent of the prison population was black or Puerto Rican, all 383 Attica guards were white.

The Autobiography of Malcolm X Written with the assistance of Alex Haley (see **"Roots"**), this account of the life of the prominent **Black Muslim** spokesman appeared in mid-1965—at about the same time as the English translation of Frantz Fanon's influential ***The Wretched of the Earth***. It had an immediate appeal for militant blacks who had been growing more and more disenchanted with the nonviolence advocated by civil rights leader Martin Luther King, Jr.

In the aftermath of the police violence that followed the **Birmingham** demonstrations organized by Dr. King, Malcolm X told a Negro audience in Washington: "You need somebody who is going to fight. You don't need any kneeling in or crawling in." While the book was in preparation, however, Malcolm X somewhat revised his civil rights stand. In March 1964 he left Elijah Muhammad's Nation of Islam and began forming the Muslim Mosque, Inc., and the **Organization for Afro-American Unity**. On February 21, 1965, he was gunned down at a Harlem meeting by two unidentified assassins.

Many young blacks responded enthusiastically to Malcolm X's rejection of Christianity and his advocacy of self-defense in confronting violence. For most readers the *Autobiography* was their first real introduction to the ideas of earlier black leaders such as Marcus Garvey, who advocated black separatism within this country or a mass return to Africa. In addition, the book stimulated general interest in black culture and in the so-called **Third World** liberation movements. The last chapters, in which Malcolm X expressed a new willingness to work with white civil rights groups, were ignored by increasingly militant black radicals.

One of the major twentieth-century American autobiographies, Malcolm X's book is said to have found greater readership among American blacks than any book except the Bible. A paperback edition appeared in 1966 and within four years more than 4 million copies were sold.

Born Malcolm Little in Omaha, Nebraska, on May 19, 1925, Malcolm X was the son of a Baptist minister who was a follower of Marcus Garvey and his "Back to Africa" movement. A school dropout at the age of fifteen, Malcolm began a life of hust-ling, burglary, and pushing drugs. In 1946 he was sentenced to ten years in prison, and it was during this time that he became acquainted with the ideas of Elijah Muhammad, whose Lost-Found Nation of Islam he joined upon his release from jail in 1952. By 1963, his prominence among the Black Muslims was such that many members felt that he posed a threat to the leadership of Elijah Muhammad. After leaving the Black Muslims, Malcolm X made several trips to Europe and Africa, and as a continuing believer in the Islamic religion, he also made a pilgrimage to Mecca. Shortly before his death he changed his name to El-Haji Malik El-Shabazz.

B

Battle of Chicago

Baby Boom In 1940 the population of the United States, as calculated by the official census, was 131,669,275. During the Depression years that preceded World War II, the national birth rate per thousand had fallen from 23.7 in 1920 to a low of 16.6 in 1933, rising again to 21.5 by 1943 in response to the emotional temper of wartime life and increasing economic prosperity.

On the basis of previous trends, social scientists predicted a 1950 population of no more than 145 million and possibly as low as 140 million. In the event, the census figures showed a total population of 150,697,361—an astonishing increase of almost 20 million.

The "baby boom" first became obvious as demobilization went into high gear and births per thousand rose from 19.6 in 1945 to 23.3 the following year and a high of 25.8 the next before beginning a "decline" back to 23.5 by 1950. This was the generation, fathered by GIs returning to civilian and domestic life, that was to be raised according to the relaxed procedures outlined in Dr. Benjamin Spock's *The Common Sense Book of Baby and Child Care* (1946) and to be known by the 1960s as the rebellious **Spock Generation.** Accustomed to postwar affluence, raised by permissive standards, and crowded onto campuses that were intellectually ill-prepared for mass education, these young people sparked the rebellion of the sixties that was to find expression in the **Battle of Berkeley** and the **Siege of Morningside Heights.**

Backgrounder A news technique by which a reporter is briefed, generally by a government official of some status, with the understanding that neither quotes nor a *specific* attribution of source will appear in the final news story. Many in Washington, including those who have often made widest use of it, have deplored the practice. Nevertheless, the "backgrounder" has become a standard way of circulating information, which usually is attributed to "a source close to the White House," "a high government official," etc.

Baghdad Pact *See* **Central Treaty Organization.**

"Bailey" Memorandum At the request of Sen. John F. Kennedy (D.-Mass.), early in 1956 senatorial assistant Theodore C. Sorensen prepared a sixteen-page memorandum analyzing the potential effect on the 1956 Democratic national ticket of a Catholic vice presidential candidate. The material was originally supplied to syndicated columnist Fletcher Knebel, who was preparing a *Look* piece, but copies of it were reprinted or summarized in various magazines.

In essence, the "Bailey" Memorandum sought to allay Democratic fears of an "anti-Catholic vote" by pointing out how this would be more than made up for by capturing a greater share of the conservative Catholic vote that had gone to President Dwight D. Eisenhower in 1952. While no specific Catholic candidates were mentioned in Sorensen's analysis, the growing focus on his religion worried Senator Kennedy, who was uneasy lest it be discovered that the material had been prepared by his own assistant. Arrangements were therefore made for Connecticut Democratic State Chairman John Bailey, a loyal Kennedy supporter, to assume responsibility for the memorandum.

The Democratic vice-presidential nomination went to Sen. Estes Kefauver (D.-Tenn.) in 1956, but in 1960, when Senator Kennedy was the Democratic presidential candidate, a Republican reprinting of the "Bailey" memorandum proved a significant embarrassment. Writing in 1965, Sorensen noted that the memorandum had been "oversimplified, overgeneralized and overextended in its premises in order to reach an impressive conclusion." He pointed out that in-depth postelection analysis had shown that it was Catholic votes which had helped Republican presidential candidate Richard M. Nixon carry Ohio, Wisconsin, New Hampshire, Montana, and California, all of which the memorandum had assigned to Senator Kennedy. Sorensen also noted that Senator Kennedy's Catholicism had been, "other than Republican Party loyalty, the strongest factor against him."

Bobby Baker Affair Robert G. ("Bobby") Baker's rise from Senate page boy to secretary of the Democratic Senate Majority had had the aid and encouragement of Majority Leader Lyndon B. Johnson, who was Vice President when, in October 1963, his protégé resigned under fire after being accused of using his position for personal financial advantage. When in July 1964 a Senate Rules Committee looking into the circumstances surrounding the resignation of the former Capitol Hill aide found him guilty of "many gross improprieties" while in the Senate's employ, the resulting scandal proved a considerable embarrassment to Johnson, who had assumed the presidency after the assassination of President John F. Kennedy on **November 22, 1963.**

Originally, the Senate Rules Committee did not accuse Baker of specific violations of the law, but in its final report in June of the following year it recommended that the Senate take under consideration an indictment for violation of conflict-of-interest laws. It also recommended that the Senate regulate the outside business activities of those in its employ. Dissatisfied with this report, and seeking perhaps to make political capital of Baker's relationship with the President, the committee's Republican minority filed a separate report in which it termed the majority findings "a whitewash" and criticized the manner in which the investigation had been conducted.

In January 1966, Baker was indicted on charges that included grand larceny and tax evasion. Evidence presented in court indicated that he had pocketed about $100,000 in campaign contributions and had failed to report this personal profit on his income tax returns. He was given a one- to three-year sentence, but because of appeals centering on illegal eavesdropping by government agents, he did not actually begin serving his sentence until January 1971. After being paroled in June 1972, he dropped out of the political scene.

Baker v. Carr In a historic six to two decision, the U.S. Supreme Court ruled on March 26, 1962, that federal courts have the jurisdiction to scrutinize legislative apportionments. The decision returned to a three-judge federal court in Nashville the responsibility for deciding whether Tennessee's legislative apportionment violated the constitutional rights of some of its citizens. In 1961, 37 percent of the voters elected 20 of 33 state senators; 40 percent elected 63 of 99 house members.

The majority opinion by Justice William J. Brennan, Jr., was concurred in by Chief Justice Earl Warren and Justices Hugo L. Black, Tom C. Clark, William O. Douglas, and Potter Stewart; Justices John Marshal Harlan and Felix Frankfurter entered vigorous dissents.

The 1962 ruling was seen in some quarters as a reversal of *Colegrove v. Green*, in which the Court split three to one to three in ruling that federal courts had no power to intervene in a dispute over Illinois' apportionment of its congressional districts. In his present dissent, Justice Frankfurter, who had written the *Colegrove* decision, charged that "in effect, today's decision empowers the courts . . . to devise what should constitute the proper composition of the legislatures of the 50 states."

The majority opinion in the *Baker* case denied that the 1946 decision had held that federal courts should not intervene in state redistricting cases. It noted that the majority of justices in *Colegrove* had upheld federal jurisdiction, but had ruled in that

specific case that federal participation was unwise immediately before an election. In *Baker*, the majority decision noted, the plaintiffs had given adequate grounds for federal jurisdiction by basing their argument on the Fourteenth Amendment's provision forbidding a state to "deny any person within its jurisdiction the equal protection of the law." Constitutional experts have felt that if it is illegal to deny the right to vote on the basis of race, sex, or creed, it is just as wrong to dilute a citizen's vote by means of unfair legislative apportionment.

In 1964, the Court handed down decisions in fourteen similar suits in which states failed to meet the requirements of the Equal Protection Clause of the Fourteenth Amendment in the apportionment of both houses of the state legislature. Among the most famous of these reapportionment cases were *Reynolds v. Sims* and *Wesberry v. Sanders.*

Chief Justice Earl Warren considered *Baker v. Carr* one of the most important cases to come before the Court during his tenure. It was, he later noted, the "parent case of the **one man, one vote** doctrine."

Bakke Case Having twice had his application for admission to the University of California's Davis Medical School rejected, Alan Bakke, a 38-year-old white engineer, filed suit in the Yolo County Superior Court (June 1974) charging that an affirmative action program under which sixteen of one hundred openings were set aside for racial minority members was unconstitutional and that he had been passed over in favor of less qualified students. A ruling by Judge F. Leslie Manker (November 25, 1974) ordered the university to reconsider Mr. Bakke's application without reference to his race and stated that the admissions program was invalid.

After both the university and Mr. Bakke had appealed this ruling, the California Supreme Court somewhat exceptionally agreed to hear the case before it had gone to a state appeals court. On September 16, 1976, it ruled that the affirmative action program denied white students equal protection of rights; the court also ordered the university to admit Mr. Bakke in the fall of 1977.

Acting against the advice of many civil rights groups, on December 14, 1977, the university asked for a review of the case by the United States Supreme Court. Two months later such review was granted and later, on October 12, 1977, the Court heard several hours of argument. On October 17, 1977, the Court asked both sides and the federal government—for whom the cases had been argued by Solicitor General Wade McCree as an amicus curiae—to submit new briefs that would focus on the problem of how the case affected that portion of the **Civil Rights Act of 1964** which makes it illegal for institutions aided by federal funds to discriminate against students on the basis of race. (Most state schools receive some federal aid.)

In a five-to-four ruling on June 28, 1978, the Court ordered Mr. Bakke admitted to Davis Medical College. While the Davis affirmative action program was considered extreme because it was inflexibly based on race, the Court ruled that some programs might be admissible. The majority opinion written by Justice Lewis F. Powell, Jr., specifically cited a Harvard special admissions program which was designed to include applicants from various backgrounds.

The somewhat ambiguous nature of the ruling made its future effect, especially on the equal opportunity clauses in Defense Department contracts, difficult to assess.

Ballistic Missile Early Warning System *See* **DEW Line.**

Baltimore Four On October 27, 1967, four members of the Baltimore Interfaith Peace Mission entered the city's Selective Service headquarters and poured a combination of their own blood and duck blood on draft records held there. FBI agents arrested Reverend Philip F. Berrigan, curate of the Roman Catholic St. Peter Claver Church; Reverend James Mengel, a United Church of Christ minister; Thomas Lewis, organizer of Baltimore's Artists Concerned about Vietnam; and David Eberhardt, secretary of the peace mission. They were indicted by a federal grand jury, November 7, 1967, on charges of destroying government property, obstructing draft procedures, and conspiring to violate the law. At a trial ending on April 16, 1968, all four were found guilty and received prison sentences of three to six years on May 24, 1968. In the interval between the end of their trial and their sentencing, Father Berrigan and Mr. Lewis joined with seven other antiwar protesters in burning records taken from Selective Service headquarters in Catonsville, Maryland, a Baltimore suburb.
See **Catonsville Nine.**

Bancroft Strip *See* **Free Speech Movement.**

Baruch Plan Appointed U.S. representative to the UN Atomic Energy Commission on March 16, 1946, financier and presidential advisor Bernard M. Baruch was considered the logical spokesman for the Truman administration's plan for the interna-

tional control of atomic energy because his friendly relations with the Senate might help to neutralize congressional opposition and because of the prestige and influence he had acquired with foreign leaders during his many years as "an elder statesman." The day following his appointment a presidential committee led by Under Secretary of State Dean Acheson and the Tennessee Valley Authority's (TVA) David E. Lilienthal submitted what became known as the *Acheson-Lilienthal Report,* which outlined the basis for proceeding. The report was leaked to the press before Baruch had had a chance to study it thoroughly, and he was disturbed that it might be considered government policy. "Even the superficial and incomplete examination of the subject that I have been able to make in the last few days," he wrote the President on March 26, "convinces me that this report is likely to be the subject of considerable and rather violent differences of opinion." President Truman assured him that it was only "a working paper and not . . . an approved policy document."

Baruch felt that the *Acheson-Lilienthal Report* was weak on provisions for enforcement, and this was his particular contribution to the plan he announced in an address to the UN Atomic Energy Commission on June 14, 1946. His plan called for an international authority with a total monopoly over the production of fissionable materials, a rigid system of international inspection, and sanctions against any nation violating the rules. Only when proper controls had been established would the United States dispose of its A-bomb stockpile. ("My fellow citizens of the world, we are here today to make a choice between the quick and the dead.")

This position was opposed by the U.S.S.R., which insisted upon the destruction of atom bombs prior to agreement on inspection procedures. This would, of course, mean sacrificing the American military advantage should the Soviet Union begin atomic bomb production.

The Baruch Plan was—in spite of objections by Poland and the Soviet Union—essentially endorsed by the UN commission and the General Assembly. When, however, it reached the Security Council, the Soviet veto blocked all further action. In 1949, the U.S.S.R. detonated its first nuclear bomb.
See **Atoms for Peace.**

"Basket Three" *See* **Helsinki Accord.**

Battle of Berkeley Some 2,000 demonstrators battled National Guardsmen near the campus of the

University of California at Berkeley on May 15, 1969. The rioting broke out following Chancellor Roger W. Heyns's attempt to evict "street people" from a university-owned vacant lot they had taken over and established as a "People's Park." More than seventy injuries were reported, and one demonstrator died several days later as the result of birdshot wounds inflicted by the police.

"People's Park" began to bloom on the muddy 445-by-275-foot future site of student housing when on April 20 approximately 500 students, faculty members, and local young people showed up with a rented bulldozer and began laying sod, planting flowers, and installing playground equipment and sculpture. Chancellor Heyns announced that a fence would be set up around the $1 million site "to re-establish the conveniently forgotten fact that the field is indeed the university's and to exclude unauthorized persons from the site." After several hundred policemen evicted groups from the park, work was begun on the fence on May 15. At a rally held at Berkeley's Sproul Hall Plaza, student militants began urging those assembled to "go down and take over the park." The demonstrators were met by Alameda County sheriff's deputies, who fired tear gas and birdshot-loaded riot guns into the crowd. When the young people refused to disperse, Governor Ronald Reagan ordered National Guardsmen to help the police.

Arrests and protests continued during the next three days, and on May 19, about 100 Berkeley faculty members participated in a "protest vigil" to denounce the bloodshed and call for Chancellor Heyns's resignation. The following day 2,000 demonstrators led by more than twenty-five faculty members held a silent "funeral march" for James Rector, a twenty-five-year-old San Jose carpenter who had been fatally wounded during the original May 15 rioting. As some 500 of the mourners advanced on Chancellor Heyns's house shouting "Murderer! Murderer!," they were met by police who attempted to disperse them with tear gas. Soon afterward, a National Guard helicopter began dropping a skin-stinging white powder said to have been used against the Viet Cong in the **Vietnam War**.

On May 22, more than 500 demonstrators were arrested during a march through downtown Berkeley, and the following day the university's academic senate voted to request an investigation by the Justice Department of "police and military lawlessness" on the Berkeley campus; the same group overwhelmingly supported the continuation of "People's Park" in a 642 to 95 vote.

By May 24, most of the National Guardsmen had been withdrawn from Berkeley, and restrictions against student assemblies and marches had been lifted.

Battle of Chicago When plans were announced to hold the 1968 Democratic National Convention in Chicago during the week of August 28, the **National Mobilization to End the War in Vietnam** (Mobe) immediately set about organizing a massive demonstration in that city to protest both the war and the renomination of President Lyndon B. Johnson. After the President announced on March 31, 1968, that he would not be a candidate for renomination, part of the emphasis shifted toward efforts to prevent Vice President Hubert H. Humphrey from receiving the Democratic presidential nomination because of his failure to take a firm antiwar stand.

There is evidence to suggest that Mobe hoped to broaden its organizational base by emphasizing nonviolence, thereby attracting to Chicago some 100,000 demonstrators from all over the nation. Plans originally included peaceful picketing, an "unbirthday" party for President Johnson—born on August 27, 1908—and marching to the site of the convention. However, the political temperature of the nation, and of Chicago in particular, was raised by the riots that followed the assassination of Dr. Martin Luther King, Jr., on April 4, 1968. Although Chicago police had been restrained on April 4, on April 27, under the urgings of Mayor Richard Daley, they brutally broke up a parade of peace marchers. On June 6, 1968, Sen. Robert F. Kennedy (D.-N.Y.), who had taken a firm antiwar stand and on March 16, 1968, had announced that he was a candidate for the Democratic presidential nomination, was assassinated in a Los Angeles hotel.

In addition, it became more and more obvious that Mobe was unable to control the various organizations that had joined the protest coalition. Although small in number, probably the most important of them was the Youth International Party (YIP)—the **Yippies**—formed earlier in the year by Jerry Rubin and Abbie Hoffman. YIP announced a Festival of Life to coincide with the Chicago convention and planned to use the streets of the city as a stage for its "guerrilla theater," in spite of local warnings that Chicago police might react with even greater violence than their New York City colleagues had to earlier, similar demonstrations—notably in Grand Central Station.

The potential for violence was increased by the fact that Chicago authorities had refused to grant permits for the various demonstrations and parades planned by most of the groups cooperating with Mobe. (It was not until August 27, 1968, that Mobe was given permission for a rally at the Grant Park bandshell the following afternoon, at which the turnout, mostly from the Chicago area, was a disappointing 10,000.)

On August 27, the convention tried to push through a postmidnight discussion of a minority antiwar plank, but it was postponed after protests from the delegations of antiwar candidates Sen. Eugene McCarthy (Oreg.) and Sen. George McGovern (S.Dak.). On August 28, as Mobe demonstrators at the Grant Park rally listened on their transistor radios, the majority Vietnam plank was accepted by a three to one vote as antiwar delegations defiantly chanted **"We Shall Overcome"**. Scuffles with the police immediately followed in Grant Park when a demonstrator tried to lower the flag to half-mast. Police charged the demonstrators, many of whom dispersed. By far the larger number, however, gathered to make the march to the convention hall, even though they had been denied a permit. They were quickly surrounded by police and National Guardsmen, but eventually broke out to Michigan Avenue, where they mingled with a "mule train" from the **Poor People's Campaign** which had a permit to march to the Hilton Hotel, headquarters of the convention delegates.

At about 8 P.M., police armed with clubs and Mace charged into demonstrators. As the TV cameras recorded the event, shouts of "Dump the Hump" and "Peace Now" changed to "The Whole World Is Watching." Much of what was going on was shortly afterward seen on videotape broadcasts by convention delegates, some of whom denounced the "gestapo" tactics of the Chicago police.

The events of that week eventually led to the trial of the **Chicago Eight.** They were also the subject of a special investigating commission set up by the National Commission on the Causes and Prevention of Violence (see **Walker Report**).

Battle of Morningside Heights See **Siege of Morningside Heights.**

Bay of Pigs On April 17, 1961, fewer than 1,500 anticommunist Cuban exiles trained and financed by the **CIA** landed on the south coast of Central Cuba at the Bahia de Cachinos (Bay of Pigs) in an attempt to overthrow the government of Fidel Castro. The nationwide uprising the invaders had counted on setting off failed to materialize, and within seventy-two hours more than 1,000 of them

had been taken prisoner and the remainder were dead.

Planning for the Bay of Pigs invasion was started by the CIA during the latter part of the Eisenhower administration when Cuban exiles in this country were recruited and sent to a special camp in Guatemala. The security surrounding the operation seems to have been as amateurish as the intelligence on which it was based, because rumors concerning it were soon rife. The first public indication came from an article printed in October 1960 in Guatemala City's *La Hora* and widely picked up by the South American press. Soon articles began appearing in the *Miami Herald* and *The New York Times.*

President-elect John F. Kennedy was officially briefed on the subject by CIA director Allen Dulles several weeks after his victory at the polls in November 1960. A few days after the President's inauguration a similar briefing was given to Secretary of State Dean Rusk, Secretary of Defense Robert S. McNamara, and Attorney General Robert F. Kennedy by both Dulles and General Lyman Lemnitzer, Chairman of the Joint Chiefs of Staff. The original plan called for a landing at the town of Trinidad, near enough to the mountainous Escambray region for the invaders to "melt" into it should the invasion fail.

President Kennedy was said to be "wary" of an invasion, but he was won over by continual assurances from the military that such an operation had high chances for success. He stipulated, however, that there was to be no direct American participation, specifically air cover. (After the first day, he permitted the use of unmarked Navy planes.)

Arthur M. Schlesinger, Jr., Special Assistant to the President on Latin American Affairs, was officially informed of the project in February 1961 and sent the President a memorandum suggesting that, while the idea sounded plausible as concerned Cuba, arguments against it gained force if the rest of the hemisphere and the world were taken into consideration. It would, he wrote, "be your first dramatic foreign policy initiative. At one stroke you would dissipate all the extraordinary good will which has been rising toward the new Administration through the world. It would fix a malevolent image of the new Administration in the minds of millions."

This point was reinforced in March 1961 when the President received a memorandum from Sen. William Fulbright (D.-Ark.), chairman of the Senate Foreign Relations Committee, who had been alerted by stories appearing in the press with increasing frequency. ("I can't believe what I'm reading," President Kennedy is reported to have said at one time. "Castro doesn't need agents over here. All he has to do is read our papers. It's all laid out for him.") In addition, Under Secretary of State Chester Bowles also sent a memorandum advising against the project to Secretary of State Dean Rusk. The President was never informed of this and it later led to misunderstandings between him and Bowles (*see* **Chet Set**). Otherwise, there seems to have been no opposition within the administration.

The worried President postponed the original invasion date from April 5 to April 10, and finally to April 17. Meanwhile, the landing site had been changed from Trinidad to the Bay of Pigs. The final decision to proceed was made by President Kennedy on April 14 after receiving an enthusiastic report from a veteran Marine colonel who had inspected the Cuban Brigade in Guatemala. ("They say they know their own people and believe that after they have inflicted one serious defeat upon the opposition forces, the latter will melt away from Castro, whom they have no wish to support. . . . I share their confidence.")

The choice of the Bay of Pigs as the invasion site led to a compromise with the President's strictures against direct American participation. Two days before the landing, eight B-26s marked with Cuban insignia and flown by anti-Castro exiles carried out some inconclusive raids on Cuba from bases in Nicaragua. Two of these planes eventually had to make emergency landings in Florida, and one of the pilots told the press that he was a defector from the Cuban air force who had bombed his own base before fleeing.

Unaware that these raids had been undertaken with the consent of the President, Adlai Stevenson, chief U.S. delegate to the United Nations, denied accusations brought by the Cubans and displayed photographs of the insignia as "proof" that the air strikes had indeed been carried out by defectors. Forced to back down by events, Stevenson later claimed that this had been his most "humiliating experience" in years of government service.

The failure of those raids to destroy the Cuban air force condemned the Bay of Pigs invasion, as did the fact that the Cubans showed no inclination to "melt" away from the support of their government. President Kennedy persisted in refusing to rescue the situation by committing American air support.

What could be was salvaged from the situation when President Kennedy assumed full responsibility for the abortive operation and for those taken prisoner when it was crushed. "Victory has a hundred fathers," he noted, "but defeat is an orphan." In December 1962, the Castro government was induced to exchange 1,179 prisoners for $53 million in goods and medical supplies.

The Kennedy administration was criticized for the Bay of Pigs disaster by both the liberals and the conservatives, the former arguing that it should never have been undertaken and the latter that it should have been backed by air cover. Little political capital could be made of it, however, since former President Dwight D. Eisenhower backed the new President and since it was known that when called on for his advice former Vice President Richard M. Nixon had urged President Kennedy to "find a proper legal cover and . . . go in."

Dita Beard Memo *See* **ITT Affair**.

Beat Generation Like its illustrious predecessor, "the lost generation,"which in the wake of World War I exiled itself to Paris to "live" and write, this sometime literary movement of the fifties, though less impressive in its output, was a reaction against the dishonesty the young saw as permeating our society. Repudiating the so-called straight world, they adopted as a model of behavior the hipsters who, in their search for limitless experience, relied on freewheeling sex, drugs, and a rejection of social restraints, becoming in the words of *Time* magazine a "disjointed segment of society acting out of its own neurotic necessity." Taking a more sympathetic view, Norman Mailer saw the "beatnik" as "the torch-bearer of those nearly lost values of freedom, self-expression, and equality which first turned him against the hypocrisies and barren culturelessness of the middle class." A major difference between the beatnik and the hipster is that the former was committed to nonviolence.

The main literary expressions of the mood were Jack Kerouac's **On the Road** (1957), John Clellon Holmes's Go (1952), William S. Burroughs's *Junkie* (1953), and the writings of such "San Francisco poets" as Allen Ginsberg, Gregory Corso, Kenneth Rexroth, and Lawrence Ferlinghetti, proprietor of **The City Lights Bookshop**, which became the West Coast focus of the movement. Following the lead of most bohemian movements, the Beats adopted outlandish modes of dress that were eventually imitated by many of the country's young.

"This Is the Beat Generation" by Holmes appeared in *The New York Times* in 1952 and was one of the first articles in the popular press to focus on the phenomenon. But the expression "beat generation" probably originated with Kerouac, whom

Holmes credited with defining for him the life-style it represented. In 1954, unable to find a publisher for *On the Road*, Kerouac considered changing the title to *The Beat Generation*. According to his biographer, Ann Charters, he told Ginsberg that "beat" could in the context be considered a shortened form of "beatific."

Quickly taken over by the commercial society it despised, the beat movement began to conform in its nonconformism and was to some extent assimilated into the American mainstream.

The word "beatnik" was coined by Herb Caen and used in his *San Francisco Chronicle* column at a time when the Russian **Sputnik** was very much a subject of conversation. Although not intended as a pejorative, it was quickly taken up as such by the public, who resented the denizens of San Francisco's **North Beach** and New York's East Village.

Jack Newfield has noted in *A Prophetic Minority* (1966), a study of the burgeoning **New Left**, that the Beats were neither political nor effective, and, with the exception of Ginsberg and Burroughs, not literarily productive.

They were the children of futility. They withdrew from society into an anti-social subculture, instead of challenging and trying to change the society. But with the traditional voices of dissent mute, the Beat Generation became the only option for those in opposition. The Beats may have been rebels without a cause, but theirs was the only rebellion in town.

Beatnik *See* **Beat Generation.**

Beaver Patrol The name was applied to the younger members of the White House staff during the Nixon administration. Most were candidates of H. R. Haldeman, Chief of Staff, and John D. Erlichman, Assistant to the President for Domestic Affairs, both of whom had been Eagle Scouts in their youth. It was Haldeman who set the busy, scurrying style for these young men, who out of preference or pressure imitated his conservative sartorial and crew-cut tonsorial style. As Dan Rather and Gary Paul Gates put it in *The Palace Guard* (1974), the members of the Beaver Patrol, who were "as indistinguishable as crabs crawling over each other in a bucket," tended to be "physical and temperamental extensions of the man who brought them there."

Haldeman often communicated with his staff by way of memorandums that were laconic to the point of being indecipherable. According to one story, a staff member once got a report back with nothing but "TL²" scribbled in one corner. He later discovered that this meant: "Too little, too late."

"Benign Neglect"

The time may have come when the issue of race could benefit from a period of benign neglect. The subject has been too much taken over by hysterics, paranoids and boodlers on all sides.

We may need a period in which Negro progress continues and racial rhetoric fades. The Administration can help bring this about by paying close attention to such progress—as we are doing—while seeking to avoid situations in which extremists of either race are given opportunities for martyrdom, heroics, histronics or whatever.

When leaked to the press on February 28, 1970, this portion of the memorandum by Daniel P. Moynihan, urban-affairs expert attached to the White House during the early period of the first Nixon administration, caused a furor among liberals. As probably intended by those who leaked it, it was the death sentence of the already moribund **Guaranteed Annual Income** plan inspired by the Kennedy Democrat. (Liberals were already angered by the fact that Moynihan, who in 1968 had campaigned for Democratic presidential candidate Hubert H. Humphrey, had accepted the Nixon appointment as a "right-wing Kenneth Galbraith.")

Moynihan had previously antagonized the black community when, as President Lyndon B. Johnson's Assistant Secretary of Labor, he issued a well-intentioned internal report—also leaked—in which he described the black family as "a tangle of pathology" and "approaching complete breakdown." As a result, the "benign neglect" reference, which in the complete memorandum had been attributed to Lord Durham, the famous Governor General of Canada (1838-1839), brought on a storm. It seems to have often been intentionally misunderstood, as Moynihan's point was to fight the increasing hard-line attitude of the White House caught between the rhetoric of George Wallace and the black militants. It essentially called for perspective on the current civil rights legislation and reaction to it. However, it was widely interpreted as a bid to George Wallace partisans.

When Moynihan eventually resigned as a member of the Nixon staff, he left behind a note for press secretary Ron Ziegler which echoed **Nixon's Last Press Conference**: "Well, you won't have Pat Moynihan to kick around anymore."

The Beautiful People *See* **Jet Set.**

Berlin Airlift By March 1948 relations between the Western and Soviet occupiers of Berlin following World War II had so deteriorated that the U.S.S.R. representatives walked out of the Allied

Control Council. Soon afterward, the Russians began harassing traffic to and from the German capital, which was 100 miles into their occupation zone. After June 23, they sealed off all river, rail, and highway traffic.

Although they cited "technical difficulties" as the cause, it was obvious that their real intention was to head off a Western currency reform that would stanch the flood of inflated currency being printed in the Soviet zone. If they failed to do this, they hoped to score a propaganda victory by forcing the Western powers out of Berlin.

General Lucius D. Clay, the U.S. Military Governor, had made emergency arrangements to have necessary supplies flown into Berlin during the harassment of traffic, and on June 26, President Harry S Truman directed that this "airlift" be expanded to include all planes available in the European Command.

When on July 6, 1948, Secretary of State George Marshall formally protested the blockade, the Soviet authorities first denied that the Western powers had any legal right to be in Berlin, and then said that such rights had been "forfeited."

By July, the airlift—known to the pilots as "Operation Vittles"—was averaging about 2,500 tons of supplies a day using fifty-two C-54s and eighty C-47s, each making two round trips a day. But expansion would be necessary to fly in coal supplies for the winter, and no diplomatic solution was in view. Appeal to Stalin brought answers that promised some flexibility, but when Western negotiators returned to the tables they were faced with an implacable Vyacheslav Molotov, Soviet foreign minister. And so the game continued.

By August, some 3,300 tons of supplies were being flown into Berlin daily, about one-third of them by the British. The city had a twenty-five-day reserve of coal and a thirty-day reserve of food. In September, an average supply day was 4,000 tons, and efforts were being made to allocate additional planes to bring the figure up to 5,000.

The Russian authorities made several offers to lift the blockade—in the United Nations, however, Andrei Vishinsky argued that there was no blockade in terms of traditional international law—but always linked their proposals to the currency question. In replying to a reporter's questionnaire in January 1949, Stalin seemed to drop this demand. The Western powers took their cue and negotiations began in earnest once again. On May 12, 1949, the Berlin blockade ended.

The airlift had by then been going on for more than 300 days, and in April 1949 a daily supply load

of 12,000 tons was being flown in by planes landing every three minutes.

Berlin Crisis (1961)   In November 1958, Soviet Premier Nikita Khrushchev informed the Western powers that unless within six months the four-power city of Berlin was unified under East German control, or Western troops evacuated, the U.S.S.R. would sign a separate peace treaty with the German Democratic Republic and that thereafter the West would have to deal with the GDR (East Germany) for access routes to the former German capital. The West replied with threats of force to enforce its rights, and after inconclusive meetings between Communist and Western representatives in Geneva, the Soviet "ultimatum" was allowed to lapse. (This is sometimes referred to as the Berlin Crisis of 1958-1959.)

However, meeting with President John F. Kennedy in Vienna, June 3-4, 1961, Premier Khrushchev renewed his threats. The reluctance of the Western powers to recognize East Germany, he noted, had caused an intolerable situation in which, sixteen years after the end of World War II, there was still no peace settlement. If the West continued to refuse to conclude such a treaty, the U.S.S.R. would conclude a unilateral settlement with East Germany before the end of the year. The formal conclusion of hostilities would terminate all previous commitments, he noted, including the right of access to Berlin, which would then have to be negotiated with East Germany.

President Kennedy made it clear that he considered that the real intent of the U.S.S.R. was to drive the Western powers out of Berlin. In a sober TV address to the nation on July 25, 1961, he noted that West Berlin had become "the great testing place of Western courage and will," and that the United States would not be driven out of the city either gradually or by force. He called for an extra $3.25 billion in defense spending and an increase in American and **NATO** forces. There was also talk at the time of plans to call up reserve and National Guard units. The Soviets ignored those portions of the speech in which President Kennedy emphasized his determination to reach a peaceful solution of the crisis, and responded with the threat of mobilization.

Meanwhile, as the atmosphere of crisis began to build up, the flow into West Berlin of refugees fleeing the restrictive and economically depressed conditions of life in East Germany increased. Since 1949, more than 3 million had already been processed by West German refugee centers, and the rate of exodus was now said to be one per minute. The flow not only embarrassed the communists but caused a drain of skilled workers that was a contributing factor to East Germany's increasing economic difficulties.

A communique issued by the Communist Warsaw Pact powers made public during the night of August 12–13, 1961, called on East Germany to take "temporary" measures for the "protection and control" of the borders between East and West Berlin, charging that the latter had become a center for espionage and subversion against the Soviet bloc. Within hours the twenty-five-mile border was sealed off by East German police and troops by means of a wooden fence and barbed-wire barricades. Three days later, construction was begun on a concrete barrier that became known as the **Berlin Wall**. (The refugee exodus from East Germany all but ceased, although desperate attempts were made to scale the wall, crash through it, and tunnel under it.)

All the Western powers promptly protested this violation of Soviet pledges to permit free movement within Berlin, but there was no attempt to tear down the wall. President Kennedy, however, warned against any Communist efforts to once more blockade the city. To test the Communist stance, he ordered the 5,000-man U.S. garrison in Berlin to be increased by an additional 1,500 men—"hostages" to our intent to remain. At East German checkpoints along the 110-mile corridors leading to the city no serious attempts were made to stop the armored trucks transporting these reinforcements.

To survey the situation and build up West German morale in this time of crisis, President Kennedy sent Vice President Lyndon B. Johnson to Berlin. Addressing a special session of the West Berlin parliament, Mr. Johnson said: "To the survival and to the creative future of this great city we Americans have pledged, in effect, what our ancestors pledged in forming the United States: 'Our lives, our fortunes, and our sacred honor.'"

Nevertheless, the Berlin Wall remained standing, and for some time American and Soviet tanks faced one another on either side of it. Despite attempts to establish negotiations, the crisis continued until October 17, 1961, when Premier Khrushchev told a congress of the Soviet Communist Party that "the Western powers were showing some understanding of the situation, and were inclined to seek a solution to the German problem and the issue of West Berlin." Under the circumstances, he noted, "we

shall not insist on signing a peace treaty absolutely before December 31, 1961." Following this announcement the tension gradually relaxed, the threat of Soviet intimidation having obviously failed, and in January 1962 both the United States and the Soviet Union withdrew their tanks from the Berlin Wall. On October 10, 1962, however, a congressional resolution reaffirmed the rights of Western nations in Berlin, declaring that this country was determined to prevent any violation of these rights—"by whatever means may be necessary, including the use of arms"—by "either the Soviet Union directly or through others."

Berlin Wall *See* **Berlin Crisis 1961; Mr. Inside and Mr. Outside.**

Bermuda Triangle The area between Bermuda, Puerto Rico, and Norfolk, Virginia, it has achieved a somewhat sinister reputation in recent years because numerous ships, planes, and their crews have disappeared in this corner of the Atlantic Ocean under mysterious circumstances. The Triangle has been the subject of several books and many articles in the popular press. On October 17, 1976, the *Sylvia L. Ossa*, a 590-foot cargo ship sailing under Panamanian registry, disappeared 140 miles due west of Bermuda. There was no trace of its crew of thirty-seven. Discounting fresh speculation about possible supernatural causes for the presumed sinking of the ship, the U.S. Coast Guard stated: "We don't recognize the Triangle as having any special qualities over other areas, but it's in that area where the ship was last heard from." The missing vessel had been bound from Brazil to Philadelphia with a cargo of iron ore.

Legends concerning the area are said to have existed since the mid-nineteenth century. The contemporary incident which gave it its name occurred on December 5, 1945, when five Navy planes disappeared on a routine training mission for which the flight plan was a triangular pattern starting from Fort Lauderdale, Florida, then 160 miles east, 40 miles north, and back to Fort Lauderdale on a southwest course. A Martin Mariner plane participating in search operations also vanished at the time. Since 1945, more than 100 planes flying over the area are said to have vanished without a trace.

Explanations advanced to explain these disappearances range from storms and tidal waves to supernatural phenomena such as sea monsters, time-space warps, and **unidentified flying objects** (UFOs).

Bettercare Presented to Congress in March 1965 by Rep. John W. Byrnes (R.-Wis.), the program was an attempt to provide a conservative alternative to the **Medicare** bill then being considered. Bettercare had the support of Minority Leader Gerald Ford. The plan attempted to incorporate features of the Medicare bill, which opponents stigmatized as "socialized medicine," and **Eldercare,** in which states could apply for federal subsidization of private and voluntary medical insurance. Under Bettercare, a voluntary program was worked out with representatives of the insurance industry. The services offered would have depended on the premium paid.

Better Deal *See* **The Great Society**.

"Bickel Option" *See* **Stennis Plan**.

Big Bang Theory The Belgian astronomer Georges Lemaître suggested in 1927 that at zero-time—some fifteen eons in the past—the matter and energy of the universe were compacted together into a huge mass he called the "cosmic egg." Because that mass was unstable, it exploded and sent fragments, i.e., galaxies, hurtling into space in all directions. The effects of that explosion are still to be observed in the recession of galaxies and clusters of galaxies from one another.

Lemaître's model of the universe was enthusiastically endorsed by the Russian-American astrophysicist George Gamow, who called it the "big bang theory." An opposing cosmogony advanced in 1948 by three astronomers in England—Hermann Bondi, Thomas Gold, and Fred Hoyle—is known as the "steady state theory," and holds that the universe has neither beginning nor end but has always existed and will continue to exist forever.

The Big Enchilada Term used in White House circles during the Nixon administration to describe Attorney General John N. Mitchell and the role he played in the Watergate break-in and subsequent cover-up. It first surfaced in the edited transcripts of the forty-six tapes of conversations between the President and his closest advisors submitted to the House Judiciary Committee and the public on April 30, 1974. In a meeting on March 27, 1973, between the President, White House Chief of Staff H. R. Haldeman, and Assistant to the President for Domestic Affairs John D. Erlichman, the following exchange about the Attorney General is shown to have taken place:

Erlichman: He's the big enchilada.
Haldeman: And he's the one the magazines zeroed in on this weekend. . . . The interesting thing would be to watch Mitchell's face at the time I recommend to Magruder that he go in and ask for immunity and confess.

The term has come to be a synonym for someone thrown to the wolves. For example, in referring to the 1976 suspension of newsman Daniel Schorr by William Paley, head of CBS, William Safire noted in *The New York Times*: "Mr. Paley needs his own Big Enchilada to toss to local affiliate owners who reflect the resentment of what used to be known as the **silent majority**."

"Bigger Bang for a Buck" *See* **Massive Retaliation**.

Bikini Formerly called Escholtz Island, this atoll of the Ralik Chain of the Marshall Islands was selected as the site of the first test of the effectiveness of atomic bombs against warships. Two nuclear devices—one in the air and the other underwater—were exploded there in July 1946; before the program was concluded in 1958 there had been twenty-three tests in all.

The original 167 inhabitants of Bikini were resettled on the Rongerik and Kwajalein atolls before being given Kili Island in the southern Marshalls and an indemnity of $325,000. On September 16, 1969, the **Atomic Energy Commission** (AEC) declared the site once more safe for habitation.

The name of the atoll was picked up by fashion designers in France to designate a woman's bathing suit considered "explosive" because of its abbreviated nature.

Biofeedback An electronic technique for the control of body processes. Some investigators feel that it can be used to correct or control high blood pressure, ulcers, asthma, muscular tension, and migraines.

The basic tool employed is the electroencephalograph (EEG) devised by Dr. Hans Berger in Germany in the 1920s. Because it amplifies electric current, the device makes it possible to measure the minute amounts—perhaps 1/10,000th of a volt—generated by the brain. Dr. Berger called the levels of brain activity alpha, beta, etc.

Originally, this technique was used as a diagnostic tool, but researchers began investigating the possibility of helping patients establish altered brainwave patterns so as to prevent or modify certain reactions. There is some similarity here with autogenics, which used language and thought to achieve similar purposes.

In the biofeedback process, electrodes fixed to the patient's head transmit currents which are transformed into lights, sounds, or a recording on graph paper. It is this "feedback" which is at the basis of learning to control reactions. Mechanisms of individual control are not completely understood and would seem to depend upon personal experimentation by the patient, who attempts to produce the desired readings under supervision.

Biohazards *See* DNA.

Biorhythms Biorhythm enthusiasts suppose the existence in individuals of three cycles: a twenty-three-day physical cycle of physical strength and energy; a twenty-eight-day sensitivity cycle of emotions and the nervous system; and a thirty-three-day intellectual cycle of intelligence and mental capacities. Curves are charted on a special graph having a zero line above which is the "positive" area and below which is the "negative" area in which "recharging" takes place. When the curves of cycles cross the zero line in either direction, a critical period is considered to have begun. This is particularly true where physical and sensitivity cycles are concerned. A "double-critical" day is one on which two curves traverse the zero line.

Proponents of the biorhythm theory believe that awareness of critical days can prevent or reduce accidents. Surgery or critical tests are considered to be particularly dangerous on such days.

The origins of the biorhythm movement can be traced to a number of publications in Germany earlier in the century by Dr. Wilhelm Fliess, a close friend of Sigmund Freud. Fliess developed mystic systems revolving around the numbers 23 and 28, which he felt represented the masculine-physical and the feminine-emotional principle, respectively. The first biorhythm calculator was based on cycles representing the powers of these numbers, but later enthusiasts added a thirty-three-day cycle.

After World War II the biorhythm fad was imported into this country by George Thommen, a Swiss-born industrial consultant who wrote *Is This Your Day?* (1964). By 1978, the fad had become a multimillion dollar business said to be serving more than a million enthusiasts in the United States.

"Bird Dogs and Kennel Dogs" *See* **"What's good for General Motors is good for the country."**

Birmingham Although in 1963 the black community in Birmingham, Alabama, numbered 150,000, or approximately 40 percent of the population, the city remained one of the most rigidly segregated in the South. Writing in *The New York Times* some three years before, Harrison Salisbury had noted that "whites and blacks still walk the same streets. But the streets, the water supply and the sewer system are about the only public facilities they share."

On April 3, 1963, black leader Reverend Fred Lee Shuttlesworth joined with the **Southern Christian Leadership Conference**'s Reverend Martin Luther King, Jr., and Reverend Ralph D. Abernathy, to launch a campaign designed to "peacefully and prayerfully" achieve certain limited goals: the desegregation of lunch counters, rest rooms, and stores; the adoption of nondiscriminatory hiring practices for certain clerical, sales, and secretarial jobs; and the formation of a biracial committee whose job it would be to work out advances in desegregation. The main tools relied on to achieve these demands—which were already being denounced by black militants as humiliating—were **sit-ins** and protest marches.

Black leaders were encouraged by the fact that in November 1962 the segregationist administration of Mayor Arthur G. Hanes and Police Commissioner Eugene "Bull" Connor had been voted out of office in a special election. These men, however, refused to relinquish their posts until their terms of office were completed, and they went to court to argue their case. Meanwhile, they took swift and brutal action against all forms of black protest. Before the week was over, some 150 demonstrators had been arrested, and twenty-four were sentenced to $100 fines and 180-day prison sentences as a result of having been found guilty of breaking city ordinances.

In spite of the fact that the city officials had refused to grant him a permit, Dr. King called for a protest march on April 12, 1963, Good Friday. Such a march was indeed held in the face of injunctions against it, and "Bull" Connor arrested and imprisoned Dr. King, Reverend Abernathy, and Reverend Shuttlesworth as they stood at the head of a hymn-singing column of protesters. (The Supreme Court was eventually to uphold the contempt of court convictions of Dr. King and seven others who were fined $50 and sentenced to five days in prison for defying the injunctions against them. The majority decision—from which Chief Justice Earl Warren and Justices William O. Douglas, Abe Fortas, and William J. Brennan dissented—was based on a 1922 decision that held laws could be tested by disobedience but that court injunctions first must be obeyed and only later tested.)

The weeks that followed were marked by mounting disturbances, arrests, and an increased potential for violence as young blacks—attacked by club-swinging police leading dogs and using high-power hoses to break up demonstrations—became increasingly restive under the restraints of Dr. King's non-violence.

National attention was particularly attracted by a black protest march on May 2, 1963, in which hundreds of children were set upon and arrested by "Bull" Connor's police.

On May 4, 1963, Burke Marshall, Assistant Attorney General in charge of the Justice Department's Civil Rights Division, arrived in Birmingham accompanied by Joseph F. Dolan, Assistant Deputy Attorney General. The brief truce they managed to obtain with the help of Reverend James Bevel, an aide to Dr. King, was broken on May 6, 1963, when about 1,000 blacks—about 40 percent of whom were children—were arrested during an antisegregation march.

Finally, as the result of efforts of Justice Department representatives on the scene, and of phone calls from President John F. Kennedy, Secretary of Defense Robert S. McNamara, Secretary of the Treasury Douglas Dillon, and various industrial leaders who controlled business interests in Birmingham, a nonofficial group of white business and community leaders announced on May 10, 1963, that mediation efforts had been successful and that a limited number of the demands would be met: lunch counters would be desegregated in ninety days; nondiscriminatory hiring and promoting practices would be enforced in certain types of businesses within sixty days; all blacks arrested would be released on bond or personal recognizance; and a biracial committee would be established to create a means of communications between the two races that inhabited Birmingham.

This agreement was immediately denounced by Mayor Hanes and dismissed by Governor George C. Wallace, who was making his first prominent appearance on the national scene.

On May 12, 1963, the home of Dr. King's brother was bombed, as was the A. G. Gaston Motel, which served as headquarters for the black integrationist efforts. Some fifty people were injured. Black patience was at an end, and in the riots that followed, some 2,500 people attacked police and set fire to a number of automobiles and buildings. President Kennedy immediately dispatched troops to ready positions in the area and took steps to federalize the Alabama National Guard, if necessary. Order was restored, but the white community as a whole

eventually rejected the compromise negotiations worked out by their business and community leaders. The protest had essentially failed, but it did focus national attention on civil rights problems and contributed to new civil rights legislation.

See **Civil Rights Act of 1964.**

"Bite the bullet"   In 1968, with inflation spiraling, President Lyndon B. Johnson repeatedly called on Congress for a ten-percent income tax surcharge as a means of controlling prices. But it was an election year and a bad time to ask any congressman to vote a tax increase. In addition, fiscal conservatives such as Wilbur Mills (D.-Ark.), Chairman of the House Ways and Means Committee, were insisting that a tax increase be accompanied by a $6 billion slash in the budget. With the military budget climbing thanks to the **Vietnam War**, liberals feared that the cuts would come in the area of government social services.

Conflicting bills voted in the different branches of Congress were in a Senate-House conference committee that seemed to be in no hurry to act, when on May 3, 1968, President Johnson said in a nationally televised press conference:

I want to make it perfectly clear to the American people that I think we are courting danger by this continued procrastination, this continued delay.... I think the time has come for all members of Congress to be responsible and, even in an election year, to bite the bullet and stand up and do what ought to be done for their country.

President Johnson noted later that his comment "aroused a certain amount of anger on Capitol Hill, but it made headlines all over the country and helped break the logjam." On June 28, he signed the tax bill into law.

The expression comes from the Old West: When surgery was to be performed without anaesthetic, the patient was given a bullet to bite down on, to help him bear the pain and avoid crying out.

Black Advance   *See* **Dirty Tricks.**

The Blackboard Jungle   The title of Evan Hunter's 1954 best-selling novel focusing on violence in the New York public schools quickly entered the language as a term descriptive of the deteriorating situation in American schools generally. Like the author himself, the protagonist of this novel is a Navy veteran who tackles his first teaching assignment in a vocational school with a largely minority student body. As *The New York Times* reported:

It is . . . safe to say that nothing that could conceivably be said about vocational high schools has been left out, from the physical beatings and slashings that teachers now and then take from their underprivileged and occasionally irresponsible charges, to the lengthy musings of philosophically opposed teachers. (There are some who think the students should be sternly suppressed and others who feel they should be understood.)

The events described take place during the course of a single semester during which a teacher, Richard Dadier, manages to win the respect of his initially hostile students.

A movie version of the novel released the following year featured young Sidney Poitier—later turned by Hollywood into a performer representing the epitome of middle-class intellectuality in *Guess Who's Coming to Dinner?* (1973)—in a memorable performance as a troublemaking hoodlum who eventually becomes the teacher's ally.

Black Caucus *See* **Congressional Black Caucus.**

Black Humor An American literary expression of the 1960s—foreshadowed to some extent by the works of English novelist Evelyn Waugh beginning with *Decline and Fall* (1928)—in which tragic personal and social phenomena are treated with humorous incongruity. A major example is Joseph Heller's *Catch-22* (1961), a savage antiwar satire in which the U.S. Air Force in World War II is treated as a bureaucracy gone mad. (A pilot intent on being dismissed from the service behaves in a crazy manner only to find that "there was only one catch and that was Catch-22, which specified that a concern for one's own safety in the face of dangers that were real and immediate was the process of a rational mind.") "I'm not using humor as a goal, but as a means to a goal," noted Heller. "The ultimate effect is not frivolity but bitter pessimism."

Other leading examples of black humor are Bruce Jay Friedman's *Stern* (1962) and *A Mother's Kisses* (1966), Terry Southern's pornographic *Candy* (published abroad in 1955, it did not appear in the United States until 1964), and Philip Roth's ***Portnoy's Complaint*** (1969). In the movies a prime example of the genre was Stanley Kubrick's *Dr. Strangelove or: How I Learned to Stop Worrying and Love the Bomb* (1964). Based on a script by Terry Southern, the movie takes as the object of its satire the ultimate nuclear destruction of civilization.

Black humor is sometimes confused with "sick humor" as exemplified by comedian Lenny Bruce, whose daring use of obscenity ultimately got him into trouble with the law. According to science writer and humor anthologist Isaac Asimov, black humor deals with the tragic, whereas sick humor focuses on "the grotesque and/or disgusting. . . . Naturally, there are no sharp boundaries and sickness grades into blackness. . . ."

Black Manifesto Movement The guiding spirit behind the Black Manifesto Movement was James Forman, who was one of the many black activists invited to participate in the National Black Economic Development Conference (NBEDC) sponsored by the largely white Interreligious Foundation for Community Organization (IFCO) in Detroit, April 25–27, 1969.

The Manifesto was contained in a speech entitled "Total Control as the Only Solution to the Economic Problems of Black People" and was no doubt more than the representatives of the twenty-five participating denominations had bargained for in the way of suggestions for funding projects in ghetto communities. After attacking the United States as racist and capitalist, Forman insisted that whites accept black leadership as the only means of stamping out these evils. He called for revolutionary action designed to cripple state power, and offered the following plan for financing that struggle by blacks:

We are therefore demanding of the white Christian churches and Jewish synagogues, which are part and parcel of the system of capitalism, that they begin to pay reparations to black people in this country. We are demanding $500,000,000 from the Christian white churches and Jewish synagogues. This total comes to fifteen dollars per nigger. This is a low estimate, for we maintain there are probably more than 30,000,000 black people in this country.

Among the projects to which "reparation" funds would be allocated was a Southern land bank that would help blacks organize cooperative farms, an "International Black Appeal" designed to promote cooperative enterprises for blacks both here and in Africa, and a newly created black university.

The first attempt to collect on the reparations demands was made on May 4, 1969, in New York's wealthy Riverside Church. As Dr. Ernest Campbell and most of his startled congregation indignantly headed for the door, Forman read from the chancel steps a list of demands which included the payment of 60 percent of the church's investment income to a permanently established NBEDC in January of each year. On May 6, Forman posted a demand for $50 million on the door of the New York headquarters of the Lutheran Church in America. (The action echoed that of Martin Luther, who in 1517 similarly posted his historic ninety-five theses on the door of the castle church in Wittenberg.)

Although the general public reaction was one of shocked disbelief, there was some recognition of the "moral" justification of the demands, if not of the manner in which they were made and the practical means for carrying them out. Protestant denominations were the most responsive, but confined themselves to investing in black business projects or in raising additional funds for community efforts. What money was received by Forman and his followers was used in setting up a publishing house, Black Star Publications.

Most blacks were cautious in their statements about the Manifesto, but it was denounced by some in both the traditionalist and revolutionary sectors of the black community. Jealous of its prerogatives, the **Republic of New Africa** group led by Milton R. Henry noted that its program already included a reparations demand and that Forman was not truly revolutionary.

Black Muslims The origins of this separatist movement within the United States go back to the 1930s, when Wallace D. Fard, a Detroit peddler of silks from "Mecca," founded the Lost-Found Nation of Islam in the Wilderness of North America. One of his most important disciples was Elijah Poole, son of a Georgia sharecropper who was also a Baptist minister. Upon Fard's unexplained disappearance in 1934, Poole announced that the "Master" had made him "the head of the black man in America." Because there were others in Detroit who claimed that same designation, Poole, who had changed his name to Muhammad, left for Chicago, shortly afterward moving—because of "the enemies, hypocrites, united together to drive me out . . ."—to the East Coast where for seven years he traveled about building the basis for his Nation of Islam.

Elijah Muhammad taught that blacks—"Negro" was rejected as a slave term—were the original creation of Allah and that all whites were subsequent and evil mutations who would eventually destroy themselves in war. "Every white man knows his time is up," he proclaimed, and he urged blacks to prepare themselves for their reign by "waking up, cleaning up, standing up." Christianity was denounced as a slave religion, and Muhammad stressed sobriety, paramilitary obedience, and physical fitness. A judo-trained elite guard known as the Fruit of Islam was formed for "emergencies" and to maintain order at Muslim meetings.

Muhammad first drew the attention of the federal authorities when, after the outbreak of World War II, he openly expressed sympathy for the Japanese and encouraged blacks to avoid the draft. Accused of sedition, he was eventually found guilty of draft evasion and served four years in a federal penitentiary. Upon his return to Chicago in 1946, the mantle of martyrdom conferred on him by his imprisonment made him the undisputed leader of the Nation of Islam, whose membership (Black Muslims) began increasing slowly in the postwar period.

One of the most important converts to the movement was Malcolm Little (*See* ***The Autobiography of Malcolm X***), who as Malcolm X became one of its chief spokesmen after his own release from prison in 1953. A brilliant rhetorician, Malcolm X scornfully rejected the integrationist and nonviolent stand of such civil right leaders as Dr. Martin Luther King, Jr., and he urged blacks to counter violence with violence. Considering the civil rights gains in the United States as mere tokenism, he argued against participation by blacks in elections, which he felt merely sanctioned political immorality. In December 1963, he shocked the nation by characterizing the assassination of President John F. Kennedy as a case of "the chickens coming home to roost."

Such was Malcolm X's meteoric rise in the Nation of Islam that by the early 1960s many Black Muslims saw him as a threat to the leadership of Elijah Muhammad. Tensions arose within the movement, and in March 1964 Malcolm X announced that he was leaving the Nation of Islam to form the Organization of Afro-American Unity, which rejected the racist teaching of the Black Muslims. On February 21, 1965, he was assassinated at a public meeting in Harlem.

The official publication of the movement is *Muhammad Speaks*, a weekly tabloid generally hawked on streetcorners by Black Muslims unable to contribute at least 10 percent of their income to the support of their mosque. It carries the following manifesto:

We believe in the One God Whose Proper Name is Allah. We believe in the holy Qu-ran [Koran] and in the Scriptures of all the prophets of God. We believe in the truth of the Bible, but we believe that it has been tampered with and must be reinterpreted so that mankind will not be snared by the falsehoods that have been added. . . .

Despite the Black Muslim claim of adherence to the Koran, the worldwide Moslem community does not recognize the Nation of Islam.

There are approximately fifty mosques in twenty-seven states throughout the nation holding thrice-weekly meetings. Membership has been variously estimated at from 10,000 to 250,000 members. The Black Muslims own and operate their own business enterprises in major cities such as New York, Chicago, and Washington, D.C. After the death of Elijah Muhammad in 1975, the Nation of Islam became involved in an intense intraorganizational power struggle from which his son, Wallace D. Muhammad, emerged as the new leader. The group changed its name to the World Community of Al-Islam in the West. Members are also known as Bilalians, in honor of Mohammed's first black follower, Bilal.

Wallace Muhammad dropped his father's separatism, opened the ranks to all races, and abolished the Fruit of Islam. Under the new leader's influence Fard is no longer considered divine nor is Elijah Muhammad to be thought of as the "Messenger of God." The emphasis is on orthodox Mohammedanism.

Under Elijah Muhammad the group's most famous convert was heavyweight champion Cassius Clay, who took the name Muhammad Ali. The champion has since broken with Wallace Muhammad and with the black leader's brother Herbert Muhammad, who was Ali's manager.

See **"I am the greatest."**

Black Panther Party (BPP) The Black Panther Party was founded in October 1966 in Oakland, California, by the black militants Huey P. Newton and Bobby Seale, both of whom had been heavily influenced by the teachings of Malcolm X and by the newly translated works of the late Martinique psychiatrist Frantz Fanon, author of **The Wretched of the Earth** (1965). As students at Merritt College, Oakland, California, they had organized a Soul Students' Advisory Council, which became the first group to demand that what became known as a **Black Studies** program be included in the curriculum. They resigned from the Council when it rejected their proposal that the birthday of Malcolm X, who had been assassinated the year before, be marked by bringing onto campus a drilled and armed squad of ghetto youths.

Upon its formation, the BPP issued a ten-point program:

1. We want freedom. We want power to determine the destiny of our Black Community.
2. We want full employment for our people.
3. We want an end to the robbery by the white man of our Black Community. (We are demanding the overdue debt of forty acres and two mules.)
4. We want decent housing, fit for shelter of human beings.

5. We want education for our people that exposes the true nature of this decadent American society. We want education that teaches us our true history in our role in present-day society.
6. We want all black men to be exempt from military service. (We will not fight and kill other people of color in the world who, like black people, are being victimized by the white racist government of America.)
7. We want an immediate end to POLICE BRUTALITY and MURDER of black people.
8. We want freedom for all black men held in federal, state, county and city prisons and jails. (We believe that all black people should be released from the many jails and prisons because they have not received a fair and impartial trial.)
9. We want all black people when brought to trial to be tried in a court by a jury of their peer group or people from their black communities, as defined by the constitution of the United States.
10. We want land, bread, housing, education, clothing, justice and peace. And as our major political objective, a United Nations-supervised plebiscite to be held throughout the black colony in which only black colonial subjects will be allowed to participate, for the purpose of determining the will of the black people as to their national destiny.

The ten points listed above were followed by the Preamble to the Declaration of Independence.

Eldridge Cleaver, author of *Soul on Ice* (1968), joined the BPP in February 1967, taking over its direction later in the year when Seale was arrested after an armed invasion of the Assembly Chamber of the state capital in Sacramento (May 2) and when Newton was jailed on charges of murdering Officer John Frey (October 29) in Oakland. It was Cleaver who helped organize Newton's defense (*see* **Honkies for Huey**). When in 1968 Cleaver was to be jailed for parole violation and prosecuted for assault in a shootout between Panthers and police in Oakland, he fled the country and sought refuge in Cuba. Several months later he opened a Black Panther "embassy" in Algiers, but soon alienated authorities there when he criticized them for refunding to the airlines ransom money obtained by Black Panther skyjackers. Shortly afterward, he settled in Paris. In 1968, in an alliance with the **Peace and Freedom Party** (PFP), the BPP put up candidates in both the California state elections and the national elections; Cleaver was the presidential candidate of the coalition.

The militancy of the BPP and of Cleaver is perhaps best expressed by his statement in November 1970: "A black pig, a white pig, a yellow pig, a pink pig—a dead pig is the best pig of all. We encourage people to kill them."

During his years of exile, Cleaver's views mellowed and diverged from those of the BPP, which went into a decline, partly because of police action that resulted in the scattering and death of many of its members. Interviewed by correspondents from *Newsweek* magazine in Paris in March 1975, he indicated that he had abandoned his Marxist-Leninist orientation, which he found too "static" to be relevant in modern societies. He also modified his pro-Arab stand: "We learned what some of these governments were doing. It's more complicated than we thought it was."

Although he indicated that he would like to investigate police suppression of the BPP, he said that the party and political violence was "a closed chapter." When he voluntarily returned from six years of exile later that year to face charges in both federal and California courts, he was disavowed by the remnants of the BPP. Upon being freed on bail in Oakland (August 1976), he told reporters: "I'm not going out of my way toward reconciliation with the Black Panther Party." He added, however, that he was leaving Alameda County Jail "in a spirit of conciliation." He has since become a "born again" Christian and preaches against revolution.

Huey Newton, against whom charges of murdering Officer Frey were eventually dropped after a court of appeals reversed his original conviction and two trials ended in a hung jury, was once more in trouble with the law in 1974 on charges of pistol-whipping a man and murdering a young prostitute in separate incidents. Scheduled to appear at a pre-trial hearing, he fled to Cuba, but voluntarily returned to face charges in July 1977. He has since maintained that all charges against him were attempts by the government to discredit him and the BPP, over which he apparently kept some control, even during his exile. He is now BPP chairman, having taken over from Elaine Brown, who had filled that position since 1974.

No current figures on BPP membership are available, but in 1970 there were said to be only 1,000 out of a total black population of more than 22 million. Nevertheless, a Louis Harris poll conducted that year reported that 64 percent of those surveyed looked upon the Black Panthers with pride even though they did not rate them very high in effective leadership. Of those under twenty-one, some 43 percent were said to agree with BPP views.

The first use of a black panther as a symbol for black militancy was made by Stokely Carmichael during a spring 1965 voter registration drive in Alabama. The slogan "Power to the People"—an echo of the Bolshevik "Power to the Soviets" during the Russian Revolution of 1917—seems first to have surfaced at a BPP meeting in Oakland on July 19, 1969. It was delivered with a raised clenched fist that recalled a Popular Front gesture during the Spanish Civil War (1936–1939).

Black Power Delivering the baccalaureate address at Howard University on May 29, 1966, Rep. Adam Clayton Powell (D.-N.Y.) noted that while human rights were God-given, civil rights are man-made. "Our life must be purposed to implement human rights. . . . To demand these God-given rights is to seek **black power**—the power to build black institutions of splendid achievement."

The expression was soon afterward popularized as a slogan by the **Student Nonviolent Coordinating Committee**'s (SNCC) leader Stokely Carmichael as he participated in the completion of the Memphis to Jackson March begun on June 5, 1966, by James Meredith (see **Ole Miss**). After that, its popularization was as much the work of the press and TV as of black militants, with whom Dr. Martin Luther King, Jr., pleaded for the slogan to be abandoned. ("Each word, I said, has a denotative meaning—its explicit and recognized sense—and a connotative meaning—its suggestive sense.")

Following Stokely Carmichael's election as SNCC president, the organization issued a position paper which explained its switch in emphasis from civil rights to Black Power. It called for the exclusion of whites from SNCC because of their basic inability to relate to the "black experience." A climate had to be created, it was argued, which would allow blacks to express themselves freely.

The reason that whites must be excluded is not that one is anti-white, but because the effects that one is trying to achieve cannot succeed because whites have an intimidating effect. Oftimes the intimidating effect is in direct proportion to the amount of degradation that black people have suffered at the hands of white people.

Initially, the position paper argued, blacks fell into a "trap" wherein it was thought that their problems revolved "around the right to eat at certain lunch counters or the right to vote, or to organize our communities." The problem was now seen as being deeper. "If we are to proceed toward true liberation, we must cut ourselves off from white people. We must form our own institutions, credit unions, co-ops, political parties, write our own histories."

It was further argued that SNCC

. . . should be black-staffed, black-controlled, and black-financed. We do not want to fall into a similar dilemma that other civil rights organizations have fallen into. If we continue to rely upon white financial support we will find ourselves entwined in the tentacles of the white power complex that controls this country. It is also important that a black organization (devoid of cultism) be projected to our people so that it can be demonstrated that such organizations are viable.

On July 4, 1966, at its national convention in Baltimore, the **Congress of Racial Equality** (CORE), having heard integration denounced as "irrelevant," passed a resolution adopting the concept of Black Power. "As long as the white man has all the power and money, nothing will happen, because we have nothing," said Floyd B. McKissick, CORE's national director. "The only way to achieve meaningful change is to take power."

As president of the **Southern Christian Leadership Conference** (SCLC), Dr. King had been scheduled to address the CORE convention, but he sent word that he was detained in Atlanta by his duties as a pastor. Addressing the convention on July 3, James Farmer, CORE's former national director, noted: "If I am against black power, I would be against myself." He nevertherless expressed concern over the "misinterpretation" of Black Power in the nation's press and stressed that CORE was not "a racist organization."

Although the slogan continued to gain currency among black militants and revolutionaries, its exact meaning was variously defined. Asked to give his definition in August 1968, **Black Panther** leader Huey P. Newton said: "Black Power is really people's power. . . . We have respect for all of humanity and we realize that the people should rule and determine their destiny. . . . We in the black colony in America want to be able to have power over our destiny and that's black power."

As a movement, Black Power advocacy became almost inevitable after 1964 when militant civil rights advocates found themselves increasingly at odds with moderates such as Dr. King and Bayard Rustin. A decisive turning point was the rejection in August of that year of the delegation sent by the **Mississippi Freedom Democratic Party** (MFDP) to the Democratic National Convention in Atlantic City. The MFDP was to compete with an all-white delegation of the regular Mississippi Democratic organization. When the convention refused to seat it, it rejected a compromise under which it would have been granted two delegates at large.

The MFDP had counted on support from President Lyndon B. Johnson, who, however, apparently sent word that he wanted the party regulars seated at the convention. The incident was seen as a breach of faith and contributed to the widening split in the civil rights movement.

In 1966, SNCC noted that "white power has been scaring black people for 400 years. But nobody talks about 'white power' because the society takes it for granted. Why does power become bad when you put the word black in front of it? Because this is a racist society, no matter how many times LBJ sings **'We Shall Overcome.'** *And it will stay that way until there is black power."*

Black Power Conference *See* **National Conference on Black Power.**

Black Studies In 1969, the U.S. Census Bureau reported that the enrollment of blacks in American colleges as of the previous fall was 434,000, or 6 percent of the country's college student population. This represented an increase of 85 percent over 1964.

Not unnaturally, these changes on the campus brought with them a rising demand for changes in curriculum by black students, who wanted to see the contributions of their race represented in academic studies. The problem was complicated, however, by the lack of agreement as to just what constituted black studies, and where trained faculty was to be found. In the summer of 1969, the U.S. Office of Education established a Committee on Ethnic Studies and began collecting data on the different types of black studies programs being offered.

Resistance to black studies programs came not only from conservatives and traditionalists, but from black liberals such as New York University's Roscoe C. Brown, Jr., director of the school's Institute of Afro-American Affairs, who noted that "there is no such thing as black studies per se. When you really get into developing the skills and expertise necessary to change the conditions of the black people, you find that you need the academic tools of disciplines as currently practiced."

Many feared that black studies courses conceived overnight left students unprepared to meet the workaday requirements of the everyday world; others saw these programs as a combination of propaganda and activist training. These fears were heightened by the fact that demands for black studies programs often went hand in hand with demands for student control over curriculum and faculty. To some it seemed particularly ominous that the origins of the movement could, in a sense, be traced to the founding of the Soul Students' Advisory Council organized on the Merritt College campus in

1965 by Huey P. Newton and Bobby Seale, who were to go on to found the **Black Panther Party.**

It was, however, at San Francisco State College that the first black studies program was launched and went from a single course on Black Nationalism in 1966 to a black curriculum including eleven courses in the academic year 1967–1968. Black studies quickly spread to other campuses, most notably Antioch and Yale.

Some of the strongest opposition to the undisciplined mushrooming of black studies came from traditional civil rights leaders such as Bayard Rustin, who, speaking at Cheyney State College in June 1971, noted: "Don't get me wrong. I'm for Afro hairdos, for the study of black literature and art, for soul food—even if it has too much grease. [But] eating soul food will not solve a single problem of housing, employment or education."

In January 1971, speaking of the black studies program at Cornell University, Dr. Alfred E. Kahn, dean of the College of Arts and Science, said: "The Africana center [sic] certainly is one of the most demanding majors in the college—only chemistry might be more demanding." But he went on to note that the programs in most other colleges had "fizzled due either to ineptitude, confusion about what black studies is supposed to be, internal political conflicts or sheer resistance from white administrators and faculty."

In 1969, John Hope Franklin, black chairman of the University of Chicago's history department, had noted:

We have . . . 35 or 40 courses that deal with some aspect of Afro-American life. They were not introduced this morning. But we've never said that this was black studies. I don't like to think of myself as teaching *Negro* history. I teach American history. I teach about all the people, including Negroes.

Black Sunday *See* **Selma-Montgomery March.**

"Blockbusting" In the 1960s, one began to hear charges that this was a common device used to encourage panic selling by homeowners. In practice, the purchase of a house in a previously all-white residential neighborhood is facilitated for limited numbers of a minority group generally discriminated against. Real estate dealers then approach Caucasian residents and convince them that a drop in property values is inevitable. If the dealers are successful, they can then acquire the properties at prices below the real market value and afterward sell them at vastly inflated prices to minority families.

BMEWS *See* **DEW Line.**

Board for International Broadcasting *See* **Voice of America.**

Body Language This 1970 study by Julius Fast popularized the growing "science" of kinesics—nonverbal communication in the form of gestures, facial expressions, eye movements, postures, and the crossing and uncrossing of limbs. (Crossed arms or legs are said to be an announcement of sexual refusal.) Some of the experts in the field, which is closely related to proxemics—the "science" of social distance and spatial relationships—include Erving Goffman and Ray Birdwhistell. It is generally estimated that words convey only about a third of what the individual means to communicate. The rest of the message is unconsciously semaphored by body movements.

B-1 Bomber Planned as the U.S. Air Force's supersonic successor to the B-52, production of which was discontinued in 1962, it was almost from the start challenged on the basis of cost and necessity. In June 1970, North American Rockwell (later called Rockwell International) was awarded a $1.4 billion contract to build three B-1 prototypes. At that time, the Air Force estimated that the fleet of 244 planes it wanted by 1985 would cost about $40 million each. However, by mid-1976, with the three models already in the air, estimates per plane ran from 87 to 100 million dollars per plane, not including the cost of either the weapons themselves or the tank planes that would be required to refuel the fleet. According to Air Force officials, much of this increase was due to inflation.

Unlike the B-70, the program for which was scrapped in 1966 after two prototypes had been built at a cost of $1.48 billion, the B-1 was designed to fly at near supersonic speeds, at altitudes too low for immediate radar detection. The plane has a 150-foot length as compared with 196 feet on the B-70, and its wings can sweep forward and back for maximum maneuverability. It can carry twenty-four short-range attack missiles (SRAMs), which can be released 100 miles from the target before the plane makes a low-level escape.

Two-thirds the size of the B-52, the B-1 requires a runway only half the length and can attain speeds of 1,320 mph. With a crew of four, it can fly 6,100 miles without refueling.

Critics of the bomber not only objected to its cost but argued that American land-based missiles and missile-launching submarines were already available in sufficient quantities to deter a potential enemy. During the 1976 presidential campaign, Democratic candidate Jimmy Carter described the B-1 as "an example of a proposed system which should not be funded and would be wasteful of taxpayers' dollars." On assuming office, President Carter decided against proceeding with B-1 production. As a result, there was a basic shift in the "triad" concept of American strategy—manned bomber, land-based intercontinental missile, and submarine-based intercontinental missile—with bombers seemingly taking on only a complementary role.

Possibly because of the great number of jobs that B-1 production could mean, Congress was still insisting, up until February 22, 1978, on providing funds for the production of two additional B-1s. On that date, after listening to an appeal by Speaker Thomas P. O'Neill (D.-Mass.) "to put the B-1 bomber to rest," the House voted 234 to 182 to rescind the $462 million appropriated for this project nearly two years earlier (see **Cruise Missile**).

Boston Strangler   The name given by the media to the unknown killer of thirteen women in the Boston area during 1962–1964. Arrested in 1964 for armed robbery, assault, and sex offenses against four women, Albert Henry DeSalvo confessed to police that he was responsible for this bizarre series of murders, which had captured national attention. He was committed to the Bridgewater State Hospital for the Criminal Insane while awaiting trial, and on January 16, 1967, he was convicted of armed robbery and nine other counts in Cambridge, Massachusetts. He was given a life sentence on the armed robbery count and a series of three-to-ten-year concurrent sentences on the others.

Among DeSalvo's defense attorneys was the nationally known criminal lawyer F. Lee Bailey, who had unsuccessfully tried to prove that his client was insane by citing the thirteen Boston murders as evidence of schizophrenia. However, since the state had been unable to gather sufficient evidence relating to the murders to which DeSalvo had confessed, they were not in the charge against him and the court therefore refused to hear evidence relating to the stranglings.

Returned to Bridgewater while awaiting an appeal of his trial, DeSalvo and two other inmates briefly escaped from the institution on February 24, 1967. The following September, he was sentenced to an additional seven to ten years.

Bow Amendment   *See* **Girard Case**.

Boynton v. Virginia   On December 5, 1960, in a seven-to-two decision, the U.S. Supreme Court held that racial discrimination in the restaurants of bus terminals forming a part of an interstate network was in violation of the Interstate Commerce Act.

The case concerned Bruce Boynton, a black, who in 1958 was refused service in the Trailways Bus Terminal in Richmond, Virginia, on a trip from Washington, D.C., to Selma, Alabama. Mr. Boynton had been fined $10 when he refused to leave the terminal. The appeal was entered on his behalf by the NAACP.

In their dissent from the majority opinion written by Justice Hugo L. Black, Justices Charles E. Whittaker and Tom C. Clark argued that it was improper for the Interstate Commerce Act to be applied in this instance because it had not been established that either the terminal or the restaurant was controlled by Trailways; however, Justice Black noted that an interstate passenger need not inquire into title in order to determine whether he has a right to service.

"Brainwashing"   The use of intensive propaganda techniques, applied under coercive conditions, to undermine morale, call accepted beliefs into question, and inculcate new beliefs that result in changed behavior patterns.

The term became current in the United States during the **Korean War,** when it was used to indicate the enforced indoctrination by the North Koreans and Chinese of American prisoners of war. What American psychologists called a state of DDD—"debility, dependence, and dread"—was induced by isolating prisoners from their leaders, stimulating guilt by compulsory "confession" and self-criticism, and insistence on political reconditioning in the form of repetitive instruction and highly limited reading material.

Under these stressful conditions, 15 percent of those Americans taken prisoner were said to have cracked, but in July 1953 less than two dozen refused to be repatriated after the ninety-day period of "political persuasion" called for by the terms of the armistice.

Use of the term by Michigan's Governor George Romney in a television interview on September 4, 1967, eliminated him as a potential challenger to Richard M. Nixon for the 1968 Republican presidential nomination. Previously a supporter of the **Vietnam War,** the former president of American Motors now told an interviewer that during his 1965 visit to Vietnam he was given "the greatest brainwashing that anyone can get . . . not only by the generals, but also by the diplomatic corps over there, and they do a very thorough job." The remark caused a storm of protest and although he had previously been considered the leading contender for the Republican nomination, less than two weeks later a presidential preference poll showed him running a poor fourth. Washington wits said he had a "jaw of steel, a heart of gold, and a brain of mush."

Brannan Plan Presented to Congress on April 7, 1949, by Secretary of Agriculture Charles Brannan, this plan became a storm center during the second Truman administration. A radical revision of the traditional notion of parity, it proposed a system of farm price supports that would be determined on the basis of a ten-year average of gross farm income as adjusted for inflation (Income Support Standard). Since farm income had shot up during the years of World War II, high support prices were a certainty in the immediate future. To protect the "family-sized" farms in competition with agricultural corporations, Secretary Brannan proposed that a farmer not receive supports on anything exceeding a limit set at 1,800 units of production, established in relation to corn. At the time, this meant something over $20,000. Small farmers attacked the limit as being too high.

A particulary controversial part of the plan was that for perishables the farmer would receive "production payments." This meant that he would receive "in cash the difference between the support standard for commodities which he produced and the average selling price for those commodities in the market place." The payment would go directly to the farmer.

The purpose was, President Truman explained, to prevent the accumulation of large surpluses in government warehouses when prices fell below the guaranteed level. It was argued that low market prices would advantage the consumer, whose increased purchases would tend to drain surpluses and restore prices.

Attacked as "socialistic," the Brannan Plan was defeated in Congress by the combined opposition of Southern Democrats and Republicans led by the **American Farm Bureau Federation.**

Brewer v. Williams *See Miranda v. Arizona.*

Bricker Amendment Conservative concern over the power of a President to commit the nation without congressional approval—as had been done in the controversial Yalta agreement—led Sen. John W. Bricker (R.-Ohio) to introduce a constitutional amendment that would give Congress power to regulate all executive agreements. As reported out of the Senate Committee on the Judiciary on June 15, 1953, after months of hearings, the Bricker Amendment included the following:

Section 1. A provision of a treaty which conflicts with [the] Constitution shall not be of any force or effect.

Section 2. A treaty shall become effective as internal law in the United States only through legislation which would be valid in the absence of treaty.

Section 3. Congress shall have the power to regulate all Executive and other agreements with any foreign power or international organization. All such agreements shall be subject to the limitations imposed on treaties by this article.

Section 4. The Congress shall have power to enforce this article by appropriate legislation.

The most controversial provision of this proposed amendment was Section 2, the so-called "which clause." As interpreted by President Dwight D. Eisenhower, the clause meant that after a treaty had been ratified, both houses of Congress would be required to act to make it effective as internal law. Failure by Congress to do so would mean that states would not be bound by the treaty as to "domestic" matters. Although Bricker denied this interpretation, the President saw this amendment as giving state legislatures the power to renounce treaties into which this country had entered with other nations. (At one point, in a light mood, he quipped that the Constitution was being dismantled "brick by brick by Bricker.")

As Senator Bricker saw it, his proposed amendment protected the United States from the imposition of "socialism by treaty." He was concerned, for example, that the various agencies of the United Nations were influencing the State Department to use treaties as a means of circumventing the Constitution. In arguing for the need for an amendment, he cited *Missouri v. Holland* (1920), in which the Supreme Court decided that a treaty with Canada regulating the hunting seasons for migratory birds was within the powers of the President and the Senate. In doing so, the Court had rejected arguments that such a treaty was prohibited by the Constitution's Article X, which reserves to the states powers not delegated to the federal government. But Senator Bricker ignored Justice Oliver Wendell Holmes's view in that case that there were other constitutional restraints on executive treaty power.

President Eisenhower later explained his growing

opposition to the Bricker Amendment by referring to a 1783 treaty between the United States and England under which British merchants were to be paid certain debts owed them by colonists, and Loyalists were to be compensated for confiscated property. When many states refused to comply with this treaty made under the Articles of Confederation, the British refused to honor the treaty provisions calling for them to abandon forts on the northern frontier. It was because of this, he felt, that the framers of the Constitution "conferred on the President the authority to conduct the nation's foreign relations" and "described the place and standing of a properly made and approved treaty."

It is more than likely, however, that President Eisenhower's alarm at the Senator's seemingly basic opposition to all treaties stemmed from his attack on the Status of Forces Treaty which, as **NATO** commander, the President had been instrumental in bringing about. Under these agreements, foreign courts were given jurisdiction over American servicemen who had committed offenses that were not in the line of duty (see **Girard Case**).

On July 22, 1953, Senate Majority Leader William F. Knowland (R.-Calif.) introduced a substitute for the Bricker Amendment. Known as the Knowland Amendment, it dropped the controversial "which clause," and basically declared that treaties and executive agreements not in accord with the Constitution should be without legal effect. Although it was designed to correct what Senator Knowland saw as dangerous executive encroachment on legislative powers, it was unacceptable to Senator Bricker without the "which clause." On February 25, 1954, the Bricker Amendment was defeated by a fifty to forty-two Senate vote, which was short of the required two-thirds majority.

The following day a final attempt to curb presidential power was defeated when an amendment introduced by Sen. Walter F. George (D.-Ga.) fell short of the necessary two-thirds majority by a single vote (sixty to thirty-one). Under its provisions, a treaty which conflicted with the Constitution would be invalid. Although it omitted the controversial "which clause," the George Amendment was opposed by the Eisenhower administration. However, it attracted votes from many liberals, including Sen. Lyndon B. Johnson (D.-Tex.). Had it been passed, the **Gulf of Tonkin Resolution**, later forced through by President Johnson, might very well have been found unconstitutional, because it encroached upon the war-making powers invested in Congress, and the effects on the escalating **Vietnam War** might have been significant.

"Bring Us Together" At a whistle-stop campaign talk in Deshler, Ohio, on October 22, 1968, Richard Moore, a member of the campaign staff of Republican presidential candidate Richard M. Nixon, spotted a sign that read "Bring Us Together." Later he drew it to the attention of the candidate, who used it as an ad-lib in his October 31, 1968, speech at Madison Square Garden in New York:

We need the help of every person in this country. . . . It was brought home to me most by the last whistle-stop tour in the State of Ohio . . . it was late in the day. The ninth appearance. The little town of Deshler. We didn't think there would be much of a crowd and five times as many people as lived in the town were there. There were many signs like those I see here. But one sign held by a teenager said, "Bring us together again." My friends, America needs to be brought together. . . .

William Safire, Nixon's speechwriter, has noted that when the phrase did not get picked up by the media at the time, he "tucked it away" for use on another occasion. It made more of a splash when used in the candidate's victory statement after his election on November 5, 1968.

This will be an open administration, open to new ideas, open to men and women of both parties, open to the critics as well as those who support us. We want to bridge the generation gap. We want to bridge the gap between the races. We want to bring America together.

After being fired by President Nixon as Chief of the Civil Rights Section of the Health, Education, and Welfare Department, Leon Panetta employed the phrase in the title of his 1971 book *Bring Us Together: The Nixon Team and the Civil Rights Retreat*. The slogan acquired additional irony in view of the divisiveness in the country following the **Watergate Scandal**.

"Bring the War Home" *See* **Weathermen; Chicago Eight**.

Brinkmanship Applied by opponents of the Eisenhower administration to the concept of statesmanship and diplomacy expressed by Secretary of State John Foster Dulles in an interview that appeared in the January 16, 1956, issue of *Life* magazine. Speaking to James Shepley, chief of the magazine's Washington Bureau, he argued that the United States must take a calculated risk for peace, even if it meant going "to the brink" of war.

The ability to get to the verge without getting into the war is the necessary art. If you cannot master it, you inevitably get into war. If you try to run away from it, if you are scared to go to the brink, you are lost. We've had to look it square in the face—on the question of enlarging the **Korean War**, on the question of getting into the Indo-China war, on the question of Formosa. We walked to the brink and we looked it in the face. We took strong action. It took a lot more courage for the President than for me. His was the ultimate decision.

"Brinkmanship" was seized upon by Democratic and liberal critics—already unhappy with Dulles's concept of **"massive retaliation"**—as an indication of the administration's determination for war. In a quip that echoed the title of Norman Vincent Peale's 1952 bestseller *The Power of Positive Thinking,* Democratic presidential candidate Adlai Stevenson called the Dulles theory "the power of positive brinking."

Broken Treaties Papers   In November 1972, a coalition of militant Indian groups occupied the offices of Washington's Bureau of Indian Affairs (BIA) for seven days. Eventually, a "truce" was arranged by Henry Adams, a Sioux, and the Indians agreed to return home. However, during their occupancy of the BIA they located historical documents which they claimed showed just how the Bureau had consistently betrayed and neglected the Indians it was supposed to protect. They took these documents with them when they left, and FBI attempts to regain them were unsuccessful. The documents were made available to Les Whitten, an associate of columnist Jack Anderson, who used them as a basis for a series of articles. Whitten was arrested and charged with trying to buy stolen documents for his use, but the charges were dismissed by a grand jury.

"Rap Brown Act"   *See* **Chicago Eight**.

Brown v. Board of Education of Topeka   The historic decision of the U.S. Supreme Court on May 17, 1954, unanimously held that separation by race in public schools was in violation of the Fourteenth Amendment since it deprived Negroes of equal protection of the law. The ruling reversed the decision in *Plessy v. Ferguson* (1894), in which an earlier Court had considered racial segregation in railways and held that it did not violate the Constitution, provided that the separate facilities furnished each race were indeed equal. The new decision swept aside questions of the relative merits of the facilities provided and returned to the vigorous dissent of Justice John Marshall Harlan (1833-1911) that segregation was "the badge of slavery."

In writing the decision, Chief Justice Earl Warren noted that education is the principal instrument in awakening children to a nation's cultural values and in providing professional training. It was a right, he emphasized, that must be made available on equal terms.

We come then to the question presented: Does segregation of children in public schools solely on the basis of race, even though the physical facilities and other "tangible" factors may be equal, deprive the children of a minority group of equal educational opportunities? We believe that it does. . . .

To separate them from others of similar age and qualifications solely because of their race generates a feeling of inferiority as to their status in the community that may affect their hearts and minds in a way unlikely ever to be undone. . . .

We conclude that in the field of public education the doctrine of "separate but equal" has no place. Separate educational facilities are inherently unequal. Therefore, we hold that the plaintiffs and others similarly situated for whom the actions have been brought are, by reason of the segregation complained of, deprived of the equal protection of the laws guaranteed by the Fourteenth Amendment.

Southern segregationists objected that in reversing *Plessy v. Ferguson* the justices had substituted political and social ideas for "the established law of the land." However, constitutional experts such as Archibald Cox have defended the decision:

The justices shape, as well as express, our national ideals. *Brown v. Board of Education* restated the spirit of America and lighted a beacon of hope for Negroes at a time when other governmental voices were silent. To make the Court's abstract constitutional declaration a reality has required the support of the legislative branch and will require still more vigorous executive action, but no one can suppose that those would have been forthcoming in the 1960s but for the "nonjudicial power" of the Court.

On May 31, 1955, the Supreme Court instructed federal district courts to order school desegregation "with all deliberate speed." The lower courts were required to see to it that local authorities acted in "good faith" and got off to "a prompt and reasonable start" in undertaking desegregation.

Subsequent rulings of the Court reinforced the *Brown* decision and showed that it was not to be interpreted as being limited merely to schools.
See Southern Manifesto of 1956.

Brown's Ferry Incident   On March 22, 1975, fire broke out in one section of the world's largest nuclear reactor in Brown's Ferry, Alabama, and burned for over seven hours before local firemen brought it under control with water. Officials said that the incident was in no way a nuclear accident, but some opponents of nuclear energy, such as Dr. Henry Kendall, founder of the Union of Concerned Scientists, insist that it was a "very close call."

The fire, which caused $150 million in damages, was started when a workman checked for air leaks by using a candle flame. Only after chemicals failed to extinguish the blaze did plant officials reluctantly allow the use of water, which eventually did the job in fifteen minutes.

Federal investigators found that there had been direct violations of safety regulations at the plant. After the fire, a sprinkler system was installed, and the practice of using a candle flame to check for air leaks was substituted for by a technique employing a feather.

Estimates are that the fire had the potential for causing some 3,000 immediate deaths and that untold thousands might have suffered from radiation effects.

Buckley Amendment Officially known as the Family Education Rights and Privacy Act of 1974, it limits the use schools can make of information in their files concerning students. It also requires the schools to give students access to such files.

The Buckley Amendment—known for its sponsor Rep. James L. Buckley (R.-N.Y.)—created a Privacy Commission to study the effects of the act and make recommendations for changes to the **Department of Health, Education, and Welfare.** Recently, there has been some controversy about whether the Privacy Commission should recommend inclusion, under the provisions of the act, of the Educational Testing Service (ETS), whose examinations are a prerequisite for admission to most colleges and graduate schools. At present, students have no way of knowing what information ETS furnishes the schools, or of challenging it if it is incorrect. The necessity for including it became obvious when, for the 1975-1976 applicant year, ETS acknowledged that it had incorrectly flagged many students who took the Law School Admissions Test as "unacknowledged repeaters."

ETS has also been under pressure from Reverend Jesse L. Jackson's Chicago-based **People United to Save Humanity** (PUSH), which in March 1978 announced that it would lobby in South Carolina for the abandonment of ETS examinations for college seniors who wish to qualify for a teaching career. Reverend Jackson complained that the tests were being used to disfranchise black educators.

"The buck stops here" Weary of the tendency of administrators to pass along the ultimate responsibility for decisions, President Harry S Truman kept prominently displayed on his desk a sign announcing that "the buck stops here." Absent during the succeeding Eisenhower, Kennedy, Johnson, Nixon, and Ford administrations, the sign reappeared in the presidential office when Jimmy Carter assumed the presidency in 1976. Washington wits were soon snickering that while the buck stops here, the yen and mark keep going.

A "buck slip" is traditionally any piece of paper by means of which a problem is passed along to another person or office; hence, the expression "to pass the buck."

President Truman is often credited with having given a political turn to the expression: "If you can't stand the heat, get out of the kitchen."

"Bums, you know, blowing up the campuses. . . ." Following President Richard M. Nixon's announcement of the **Cambodian "Incursion"** on April 30, 1970, protests erupted on the nation's campuses over a move which was seen as widening the unpopular **Vietnam War.** An ROTC office at Hobart College in Geneva, N.Y., was firebombed; the President was burned in effigy at Union College in Schenectady, N.Y.; and even at staid Princeton University students and faculty met in open forum and voted to stage a general strike. Police and students clashed at impromptu antiwar rallies from Philadelphia to Pasadena.

The next morning, May 1, 1970, following a Pentagon briefing on the military situation in Cambodia, President Nixon was reported to have said the following:

You see these bums, you know, blowing up the campuses. Listen, the boys that are on the college campuses today are the luckiest people in the world, . . . and here they are burning up the books, storming around about this issue. You name it. Get rid of the war and there will be another one. Then out there [Indochina] we have kids who are just doing their duty. They stand tall and they are proud. . . .

The President's rambling remarks were carried over the news wires and were to be widely quoted in the weeks to come. They were part of the atmosphere in which the **Kent State Tragedy** took place on May 4, 1970, when four students were killed by National Guardsmen who opened fire on an antiwar demonstration.

Busing Writing in *The New York Times* (October 29, 1972), Reverend Theodore M. Hesburgh, past chairman of the U.S. Commission on Civil Rights, noted that "ever since there have been buses, white parents have been busing their children to where the best education was—as black children were bused only to inferior schools, away from whites. It was only when it looked as if the process might be reversed that the furor began."

In its historic **Brown v. Board of Education of Topeka** decision, the U.S. Supreme Court had ruled that "separate educational facilities are inherently unequal" and therefore a denial of black children's Constitutional rights. However, progress in achieving desegregation of public schools was slow in coming, and in 1966 the **Department of Health, Education, and Welfare** (HEW) established "guidelines to enforce desegregation under the **Civil Rights Act of 1964**. Two years later, HEW guidelines called for "terminal desegregation," and many Southern school districts that were slow in ending de jure segregation were threatened with a loss of federal education funds under the Primary and Secondary Education Act of 1965.

In fighting de facto segregation, HEW issued a directive restricting "freedom of choice" for school children when, in practice, this freedom contributed to the maintenance of segregated educational facilities. HEW planners soon found themselves at loggerheads with the Nixon administration's Justice Department, whose lawyers had backed the efforts of Southern school officials seeking court relief by contending that school districts should be permitted to assign students to neighborhood schools even if this slowed the pace of desegregation.

On April 20, 1971, in **Swann v. Charlotte-Mecklenburg,** the Supreme Court unanimously approved a lower court ruling in upholding a school desegregation plan which required the Charlotte-Mecklenburg County, North Carolina, joint school system to achieve a greater incidence of integration by massive crosstown busing of students. In upholding the decision of U.S. Judge James B. McMillan, the Court said that the Charlotte school district had failed to propose an acceptable alternative plan and that Judge McMillan was forced to draw up his own.

Chief Justice Warren E. Burger, an appointee of President Richard M. Nixon, wrote the decision for the entire Court. "Desegregation plans cannot be limited to the walk-in school," he wrote, noting that busing was a proper means unless "the time or distance is so great as to risk either the health of the children or significantly impinge on the educational process." The decision, which actually dealt with four cases, did not cover de facto segregation resulting from neighborhood housing patterns most frequently found in the North.

Although President Nixon stated that he did not "believe that busing to achieve racial balance is in the interest of better education," he affirmed that whatever he had said that was inconsistent with the Court ruling was "now moot and irrelevant because . . . nobody, including the President . . . is above the law as it is finally determined by the Supreme Court."

On April 21, 1971, the Senate voted down a proposal by Sen. Abraham A. Ribicoff (D.-Conn.) to force the nation's suburban communities to integrate their schools with neighboring inner-city schools within twelve years. This plan had previously been submitted in 1970, but no action had been taken by the Senate.

Busing was to be a major issue in the Democratic presidential primaries of 1972. On March 14, Alabama's Governor George C. Wallace, who had taken a strong antibusing stand, emerged the victor in Florida, where he captured 42 percent of the vote. Florida voters overwhelmingly approved a straw ballot proposing an antibusing amendment to the Constitution.

Three days later, President Nixon proposed to Congress a Student Transportation Moratorium Act and an Equal Opportunities Act. The new legislation would deny courts the power to order busing of elementary school children to achieve racially balanced schools; call a moratorium until July 1, 1973, on all new busing orders; provide a clear congressional mandate on acceptable desegregation methods; and establish a program to concentrate federal aid to education more effectively in underprivileged districts so that "equality of educational opportunity" would be substituted for racial balance as the primary national education goal. In his message and in a nationally televised address the previous evening, the President found that many lower court decisions on busing had "gone far beyond . . . what the Supreme Court said is necessary," and that there had been a "reckless" extension of busing requirements and a tendency toward "extreme remedies."

Complaining that the American voter wanted "action now and not talk," Governor Wallace said that the President did not go far enough in his proposals and that the Justice Department should be instructed to reopen all schools under a freedom-of-choice plan.

Presidential hopeful Sen. George McGovern (D.-S. Dak.) called the President's stand a "frantic effort to capitalize on this emotional issue" in order to distract attention from the problems of taxes, unemployment, and the continuing **Vietnam War.** When in July Senator McGovern became the presidential standard-bearer of the Democratic Party, the platform adopted at the Miami Beach convention called the "transportation of students," i.e., busing, "another tool to accomplish desegregation."

On October 12, 1972, a House-approved bill to limit school busing was shelved after three unsuccessful attempts to end a filibuster against it by Northern liberals. The new legislation had escalated President Nixon's antibusing proposals of March by covering secondary as well as elementary schools and by ruling out long-distance busing under any circumstances. In the final forty-nine to thirty-eight vote against cloture, many previous opponents of filibustering when it was used as a means of fighting civil rights legislation voted against ending the "debate."

Busing continues to be a controversial issue. On January 3, 1978, State Superior Court Judge Paul Egly held that a Los Angeles school integration plan calling for the mandatory busing of 112,000 pupils from the fourth through eighth grades could be put into effect the following September, pending determination of whether it was in keeping with a 1976 California Supreme Court mandate. (Berkeley, California, had in 1968 become the first city with a population of over 100,000 to use busing to achieve a totally desegregated school system.)

See **National Black Political Convention.**

Byrd Amendment In May 1968, the United Nations condemned Rhodesia for white supremacist policies and called for an embargo against that country. As a result, Rhodesian chrome could no longer be imported into the United States.

The move was denounced in some sectors of the industrial community because it made the U.S.S.R. the chief source of supply for chrome, and by mid-1971 the price had risen from 30 to 72 dollars a ton.

Critics put this down to the fact that the U.S.S.R. had cornered the market, and they discounted spiraling international inflation.

As a result, Sen. Harry Byrd, Jr. (Independent, Va.), attached an amendment requiring the President to allow the importation of Rhodesian chrome to a fiscal 1972 military authorization for weapons procurement. After five floor votes, it was passed by the Senate on October 6, 1971, and implemented on January 1, 1972. President Richard M. Nixon opposed the Byrd Amendment, but felt constrained to sign the bill.

The Byrd Amendment was repealed in 1977.

"James F. Byrnes Treaty" During the unfruitful Council of Foreign Ministers meeting in London (September 11–October 2, 1945) following the end of World War II, Secretary of State James F. Byrnes suggested to Soviet Foreign Minister Vyacheslav Molotov a twenty-year treaty among the four major powers to ensure the demilitarization of Germany. He hoped in this way to influence the Soviet attitude toward its neighbors by ensuring Soviet security.

Molotov's response at the time was completely unfavorable, but when Byrnes mentioned the idea to Premier Joseph Stalin when the Council reconvened in Moscow (December 16–26) to discuss Korea, Japan, and the peace treaties, the Soviet dictator was delighted. Byrnes agreed to prepare a draft and circulate it for suggestion.

In the United States, the plan was enthusiastically endorsed by President Harry S Truman, who suggested that it be known as the "James F. Byrnes Treaty," and by Sen. Arthur H. Vandenberg (R.-Mich.), a leading member of the influential Senate Foreign Relations Committee. When it was submitted to the foreign ministers of France and Great Britain, they too were enthusiastic. However, in spite of Stalin's seeming agreement, Molotov hedged and called for "amendments," eventually rejecting the whole idea.

C

Camelot

Calories Don't Count This 1961 bestseller by Dr. Herman Taller touted a weight reduction theory according to which a person could eat as much as he liked and still lose weight, provided he absorbed a minimum daily requirement of safflower oil in the form of CDC capsules. Following the book's publication in September, 1 million copies were sold before the Food and Drug Administration charged fraud and in January 1962 moved to confiscate copies of the book and CDC capsules being sold by Cove Vitamin and Pharmaceutical, Inc., and CDC Pharmaceutical, Inc. All CDC capsules were withdrawn from the market in July 1962.

On March 11, 1964, Dr. Taller and three executives of the firms producing CDC capsules were indicted on forty-five counts of mail fraud, three counts of mislabeling, and one count of conspiracy. The Justice Department contended that the capsules were ineffective in inducing weight loss if used as instructed in Dr. Taller's book. (The CDC diet called for six capsules a day, and the indictment charged that ninety would be necessary.) In addition, it was charged that claims for the capsules as being effective treatment for heartburn, diabetes, complexion deficiencies, cancer, and heightened sexual drive were false.

The three pharmaceutical executives pleaded guilty and were fined $1,000 each in November 1965. Dr. Taller denied complicity and went on trial in April 1967. On May 11, he was found guilty of twelve counts of mail fraud, conspiracy, and violation of federal drug regulations. In his charge to the jury, the judge emphasized that the validity of the dietary theory was not an issue, but that the charges centered on the dosage of CDC capsules recommended.

Cambodian "Incursion" On April 30, 1970, President Richard M. Nixon told a startled and angry nation that several thousand American troops were even then moving from South Vietnam into what was known as the Fishook area of Cambodia, some fifty miles northwest of Saigon. An earlier thrust into the Parrot's Beak area only thirty-three miles from the capital had been announced the day before by the South Vietnam Defense Ministry and confirmed in Washington; it was said to be receiving only logistical and air support from the U.S.

The President insisted that the operation was "not an invasion of Cambodia" since the areas in question were entirely in the hands of North Vietnamese forces, and the only mission of the Americans was to drive them out and destroy enemy supplies. "We take this action not for the purpose of expanding the war into Cambodia, but for the purpose of ending the war in Vietnam" (*see* **Vietnam War).**

Referring to his April 20, 1970, speech announcing his intention to withdraw 150,000 U.S. soldiers from South Vietnam, the President emphasized that in spite of his threat to meet increased communist activity by strong countermeasures, new enemy operations had endangered the security of those troops who would remain, and that Cambodia could therefore "become a vast enemy staging area and a springboard for attacks on South Vietnam" (*see* **Vietnam War).**

The President failed to convince his critics that he had not in effect extended the area of the Indochina conflict. In the days that followed what the Nixon administration preferred to call an "incursion" rather than an invasion, explosive protest meetings were staged all over the nation and especially on the college campuses. Four students at Kent State University, Ohio, died in a tragic confrontation with National Guardsmen on May 4, and a new and even stronger wave of protest was triggered (see **Kent State Tragedy).**

In the Senate, concern over the President's usurpation of congressional authority to wage war resulted in the **Cooper-Church amendment** to a foreign military sales bill on June 30, 1970, the very day the White House announced the completion of the Cambodian operation on June 29, one day before the time the President had promised it would end. In essence, the amendment said that in "concert with the declared objectives of the President of the United States to avoid involvement of the United States in Cambodia after July 1, 1970, and to expedite the withdrawal of American forces from Cambodia" there could be no funds authorized for future military operations there without the express consent of Congress. Although the Cooper-Church amendment was eventually eliminated from the Military Sales Act, a revised version was attached to a foreign aid authorization bill which became law on January 5, 1971.

In announcing the withdrawal of American forces from Cambodia, President Nixon said that they had been successful in destroying communist bases along the South Vietnamese border and that this had enabled "Vietnamization" of the war to proceed as scheduled. Casualty figures released showed that 338 Americans had been killed and 1,529 wounded in the operation. South Vietnamese losses were 866 killed and 3,724 wounded; enemy losses were set at 14,488 killed and 1,427 captured.

Camelot In an article entitled "For President Kennedy: An Epilogue" which appeared in *Life* magazine shortly after the assassination of President John F. Kennedy in Dallas on **November 22, 1963,** Theodore H. White reported the former First Lady as saying:

At night, before we'd go to sleep, Jack liked to play some records; and the song he loved most came at the very end of this record. The lines he loved to hear were:

Don't let it be forgot
That once there was a spot,
For one brief shining moment
That was known as Camelot

The lines were from *Camelot*, a 1970 musical based on T.H. White's *The Once and Future King*, a novel about King Arthur and the Knights of the Round Table.

"There'll be great Presidents again—and the Johnsons are wonderful," said Mrs. Kennedy, "They've been wonderful to me—but there'll never be another Camelot again."

The image caught the imagination of a grief-stricken nation and subsequent articles pouring from the press pictured the Kennedy White House as conveying the atmosphere of a legendary court which in the words of James MacGregor Burns (*Edward Kennedy and the Camelot Legacy*, 1976) was "complete with liegemen, courtiers, and fools."

In later years, as the Kennedy administration came to be reevaluated, the shining Camelot image was often caricatured and extended. When in 1968 former "Kennedy Democrat" Daniel P. Moynihan was appointed to the White House staff by President Richard M. Nixon, critics saw the choice as an attempt by the Republican President, who in 1960 had been defeated by Kennedy, to connect his own administration with the romantic glow of Camelot. Said Garry Wills in *Nixon Agonistes* (1969), "There is something glamorous about being a survivor of Camelot, even if one plays the role, in it, of Mordred." In the legend, Mordred, or Modred, is the treacherous knight who betrays King Arthur. The King is afterward mortally wounded in the battle of Camlan and buried on the island of Avalon.

The Camelot legend, whose advantages and disadvantages are often seen by political commentators as having been inherited by the assassinated President's brother, Sen. Edward Kennedy (D.-Mass.), received a cruel blow when in July 1969 the latter became involved in the accidental death of Mary Jo Kopechne at **Chappaquiddick.**

"Camp" The term was used by novelist and social critic Susan Sontag, writing in *Partisan Review* (December 1964), to describe the tendency of some modern esthetes to revel in the vulgarity of mass culture. Where the nineteenth-century dandy, she explains, was "continually offended or bored, the connoisseur of Camp is continually amused, delighted. The dandy held a perfumed handkerchief to his nostrils and was liable to swoon; the connoisseur of Camp sniffs the stink and prides himself on his strong nerves." Among the examples of Camp are sentimental or semipornographic turn-of-the-century postcards, Tiffany lamps, movies such as *King Kong* (1933), and lurid journalism exemplified by the weekly New York *National Enquirer*. All share in a "love of the unnatural: of artifice and exaggeration." It is passion, naïveté, and pretension that distinguish Camp art from something that is merely bad.

Miss Sontag focused on "a peculiar affinity and overlap" between Camp taste and homosexual taste. Camp is seen as defusing moral indignation by "dethroning the serious." It is "serious about the frivolous, and frivolous about the serious."

Canuck Letter On February 24, 1972, shortly before the New Hampshire presidential primary, the *Manchester Union Leader* printed a letter purporting to come from a man who signed himself Paul Morrison, Deerfield Beach, Florida. It alleged that when Sen. Edward S. Muskie (D.-Maine) was campaigning in Florida for the Democratic presidential nomination, he was asked his opinion of blacks. "We didn't have any in Maine, a man with the senator said. No blacks, but we have 'Cannocks (*sic*).' What did he mean? we asked—Mr. Muskie laughed and said come to New England and see."

The issue containing the Morrison letter featured a front page editorial signed by the paper's right-wing publisher, William Loeb, and entitled "Sen. Muskie Insults Franco-Americans." On the following day, the *Leader* reprinted a *Newsweek* article in which the senator's wife, Jane Muskie, was presented as expressing a fondness for alcohol and dirty jokes.

Answering these charges on February 26, the exhausted senator several times broke into tears. The stories and pictures of his reaction were carried on national television and in most newspapers; they undoubtedly damaged his political stature irreparably.

The "Paul Morrison" letter has been variously ascribed to Kenneth W. Clawson, a former reporter for the *Washington Post*; Patrick J. Buchanan, special consultant to President Nixon; Kenneth L. Khachigian, Buchanan's assistant; and Charles "Chuck" W. Colson, special counsel to the President.

See **Dirty Tricks.**

CAP *See* **Community Action Programs.**

Capehart Amendment Introduced by Sen. Homer Capehart (R.-Ind.), it extended wage, price, rent, and credit controls under the wartime Defense Production Act until June 30, 1952. However, the amendment so weakened these controls that on signing it into law on July 31, 1951, President Harry S Truman called it "the worst I ever had to sign." Critics thought that the amendment was largely responsible for the weakened defenses against inflation during the **Korean War** period, and they pointed to President Truman's prediction that it would result in higher wages and prices, as well as black markets in beef.

Major objections of opponents of the amendment were that it ended the government's right to impose quotas on the slaughtering of livestock and that it barred already scheduled rollbacks in beef prices. It required price ceilings to reflect cost increases between January 1–June 24, 1950, and July 26, 1951, and it allowed both retailers and wholesalers to enjoy the same profit margins they had during May 24–June 24, 1950.

Although rent controls were continued, landlords were authorized increases of no more than 20 percent above June 20, 1947. Payoff time on installment purchases was increased from fifteen to eighteen months, and required down payments were cut from 20 to 15 percent. Import controls on fats and oils competing with American products were extended until mid-1953, and various dairy products were added to the control list.

To stimulate defense production, the measure extended the government's authority to make defense loans or provide other aid. It also established a Small Defense Plants Administration to ensure that small business got a share of defense allocations.

Captive Peoples Resolution On February 20, 1953, little less than a month after Secretary of State John Foster Dulles broadcasted a promise to the "captive peoples" of Soviet-dominated Eastern Europe that they could "count on us," President Dwight D. Eisenhower urged that both houses of Congress join in a resolution proclaiming the hope that these nations would once again enjoy the right of self-determination within a framework that would sus-

tain the peace. The resolution also rejected interpretations of secret World War II agreements that had been "perverted" into bringing about the subjugation of free nations. It charged that the Communist party leaders who controlled the Soviet Union had violated the clear intent of such agreements when the nations concerned were subjected "to the domination of totalitarian imperialism." Such absorption of peoples by the Soviet Union was denounced as a threat against the security of all free people, including Americans.

By carefully avoiding reference to the Yalta and **Potsdam** agreements made under Presidents Roosevelt and Truman, the Eisenhower administration hoped to win Democratic backing for the resolution. Right-wing elements in Congress were disappointed and urged that the wording be strengthened, but speaking before the House Foreign Affairs Committee and the Senate Foreign Relations Committee on February 26, Secretary Dulles declared that he would prefer no resolution to one unacceptable to the Democrats and therefore adopted by a narrow margin.

While the resolution was still being debated, Premier Joseph Stalin died on March 5, 1953, and two days later the resolution was permanently shelved. In spite of the fact that on April 16 the President urged full independence for the nations of East Europe, he declared that there would be no U.S. intervention in the area when in June Soviet troops were used to quell rioting in East Germany.

Carter Energy Program *See* **Energy Crisis.**

Catonsville Nine Entering Selective Service headquarters in Catonsville, Maryland, on May 17, 1968, nine antiwar protesters seized almost 400 individual draft records and burned them in a nearby parking lot. Among those arrested were the Reverend Philip F. Berrigan and Thomas P. Lewis, who were awaiting sentence after having been found guilty as members of the **Baltimore Four,** a group that had destroyed draft records the previous fall in Baltimore by pouring a combination of their own blood and duck blood over them. Others arrested in Catonsville included Father Berrigan's brother, the Reverend Daniel Berrigan; Brother David Darst; John Hogan, a former member of the Maryknoll order; Thomas Melville, a former Maryknoll priest; Mrs. Marjorie B. Melville, his wife and a former Maryknoll nun; George Mische; and Mary Moylan.

At a federal trial in October 1968, they pleaded not guilty to charges of destroying government property and interfering with draft procedures, arguing that the **Vietnam War** itself was both illegal and immoral. They nevertheless were found guilty, the court having refused to allow arguments as to the legality of the war and matters of conscience. In June, they were found guilty of the same charges at a state trial and sentenced to concurrent sentences of two to three and one-half years. There was no jury at the state trial, and the judge's decision was based on transcripts of the federal trial.

Ordered to prison in April 1970, Father Daniel J. Berrigan evaded police and FBI agents until August 11, 1970, when he was captured by FBI agents posing as bird watchers in the area of a secluded house on Block Island, R.I. During his months as a fugitive, Father Berrigan had on several occasions been interviewed by reporters and met regularly with peace groups in the East and Midwest. The Berrigan brothers were denied parole in July 1971, despite Daniel's precarious health. He was finally paroled in February 1972.

The Catonsville Nine episode inspired the Milwaukee Fourteen, in which on September 24, 1968, a group of Roman Catholics, half of whom were ministers, were seized for burning thousands of draft records in a Milwaukee Selective Service office. Twelve of the group were found guilty in a Milwaukee Circuit Court on May 26, 1969. Conducting their own defense, the group used the trial as a forum for attacking both the draft and the Vietnam War.

See **Harrisburg Seven.**

La Causa Cesar Chavez, who cut his teeth on the **Pachucos Movement** of the 1950s, founded the National Farm Workers' Association (NFWA) in 1958 at a time when pressure was building among union, church, and Mexican-American organizations to eliminate *braceros* (literally "arms") labor by seeing to it that Congress did not renew Public Law 78 when it expired on December 31, 1963. Imported by special treaty with Mexico to overcome labor shortages during World War II, the *braceros* were Mexican contract workers who supplied cheap seasonal labor for Texas and California farmers. By 1955, some 300,000 were being legally imported— and thousands more were being smuggled across the border. Ill-paid and badly housed, they were subject to immediate repatriation at the slightest sign of protest.

Chavez' efforts to organize farm labor were painful and slow. "I went from field to field during the day, and in the evening I would drive into the *barrios* or *colonias* and go around. . . . I had some leaflets with me, which had a cutoff section on the bottom, where people could mark if they were interested and mail them." In the early years, less than 1 percent of the California fieldworkers had joined his "union," which had been cautiously named an "association" to quiet fears of repercussions from the farmers.

La Causa ("the cause") was born in 1965 when Filipino workers, who had been established in the area since the 1920s, went on strike in the grape fields of Delano.

Seizing his opportunity, Chavez offered them NFWA support. He organized field kitchens and obtained additional aid from other unions. In 1967 *La Huelga* ("the strike") received national publicity when Chavez organized a nationwide boycott of nonunion grapes.

In February 1968, after a clash between strikers and local police, Chavez, a Roman Catholic who had repeatedly placed emphasis on nonviolence, went on a widely publicized twenty-five-day fast of repentance which ended on March 11, 1968, when Sen. Robert Kennedy (D.-N.Y.) knelt with him in an ecumenical open-air mass, participated in by Protestant ministers, Jewish rabbis, and Catholic priests.

It was not until 1970 that Chavez achieved partial success by signing a contract with twenty-six grape growers of the San Joaquin Valley. His union was at this time known as the United Farm Workers Organizing Committee (UFWOC), having merged with the AFL-CIO Agriculture Workers Organizing Committee (AWOC).

At present, Chavez and the Teamsters unions are struggling for control of farm workers, particularly those in the lettuce fields of the Salinas Valley.

In June 1976, the United Farm Workers gained an east coast organization by merging with the 6,000-member Associacion de Trabajadores Agricoles, an independent Puerto Rican farm workers union founded in 1973 by Juan Irizarry and based in Hartford, Connecticut.

The nationwide boycotts against table grapes, lettuce, and the wines of E & J Gallo Vineyards were ended by Chavez on January 31, 1978. He noted that the boycotts had been instrumental in helping his union win 100 contracts with California growers since 1975 and that there was reason to "look upon 1978 with cautious optimism."

Cedar Falls *See* **Iron Triangle.**

"Cemetery vote" A political adage has it that dead men tell no tales but can be made to vote. When on November 8, 1960, Democratic presidential candidate John F. Kennedy triumphed over the Republican candidate, Richard M. Nixon, by no more than 119,000 votes, it was charged that the "cemetery vote" brought out by Chicago's Mayor Richard Daley had helped put Illinois' twenty-seven electoral votes in the Democratic column.

CENTO *See* **Central Treaty Organization.**

Central High School *See* **Little Rock.**

Central Intelligence Agency (CIA) Established as part of the **National Security Act** of 1947, which united the Army, Navy, and Air Force in the National Military Establishment. The act provided for a National Security Council (NSC) composed of the President and the heads of the Departments of State, Defense, Army, and Navy, as well as of the Munitions Board, the Research and Development Board, and the National Security Resources Board. The CIA was created under the NSC, and its function was to correlate and evaluate intelligence activities and data. Its director is appointed by the President.

The origins of the CIA go back to January 20, 1946, when President Harry S Truman—who on assuming office found that "needed intelligence information was not coordinated at any one place"—issued an Executive Order setting up a Central Intelligence Group (CIG) under the supervision of a National Intelligence Authority made up of the Secretaries of State, War, and the Navy, as well as of his personal representative, Admiral William D. Leahy. The CIG in turn replaced the wartime Office of Strategic Services (OSS), the first United States intelligence agency.

For purposes of secrecy, the CIA was given special powers under the Central Intelligence Act in 1949. From then on its director could, without accounting for them, allot CIA funds at his own discretion. The staff, the size of which is never divulged, is exempt from conventional civil service procedures and may be hired and fired at the sole discretion of the Agency.

In theory, domestic police powers are denied the CIA, which must call upon the FBI for assistance in this area. Under the directorship of Allen W. Dulles (1953-1961), however, the Agency tended to become autonomous, and the investigation into the CIA by the **Rockefeller Commission** (1975) revealed that by 1953 the CIA was illegally opening mail that passed between the U.S.S.R. and the United States. This interference in domestic matters was extended and strengthened when in August 1967, at the request of President Lyndon B. John-

son, the CIA established a Special Operations Group (see **Operation Chaos**) to inquire into the possible influence of foreign powers on American dissidents. According to the Rockefeller Commission, "during six years the operation compiled some 13,000 different files, including files on 7,200 American citizens. The documents in these files and related materials included the names of more than 300,000 persons and organizations which were entered into a computerized index." Under these circumstances, unknown to even many leading members of the CIA itself, the Special Operations Group became a "repository for large quantities of information on the domestic activities of American citizens. This information was derived principally from FBI reports or from overt sources and not from clandestine collection by the CIA, and much of it was not directly related to the question of the existence of foreign connections."

Many Americans were troubled by this disclosure, but the Rockefeller Commission concluded that although "over the 28 years of its history the CIA has engaged in some activities that should be criticized and not permitted to happen again," by and large its domestic activities comply with its statutory authority. It was therefore found that

the evidence within the scope of this inquiry does not indicate that fundamental rewriting of the National Security Act is either necessary or appropriate.

The evidence does demonstrate the need for some statutory and administrative clarification of the role and function of the Agency. . . . Ambiguities have been partially responsible for some, though not all, of the Agency's deviation within the United States from its assigned mission. . . .

Over the years, the CIA has been accused of interference in the domestic affairs of foreign powers. Its involvement in the disastrous **Bay of Pigs** invasion of Cuba led to the resignation of Allen Dulles in 1961. In 1974, it was charged that the CIA had spent more than $8 million to promote the overthrow of Salvador Allende Gossens, Socialist President of Chile, the previous year.

Central Treaty Organization (CENTO) Successor to the Middle East Treaty Organization (METO). The latter was formed, at the urging of the United States, to block the expansion of the U.S.S.R. in the Middle East by establishing a defensive alliance of "northern tier" states closest to the Soviet border. METO had as its basis the 1955 Baghdad Pact, which included Turkey, Pakistan, Iran, Iraq, and Great Britain. To avoid alienating the anticolonial powers of Asia and Africa opposed to the alliance, the United States did not join the Baghdad Pact, but it did send observers to meetings held by the regional organization, and it offered its members both economic and military aid.

To prevent increased Soviet pressure following the 1956 **Suez Crisis,** the United States felt obliged to join with the U.S.S.R. in forcing the withdrawal of Israeli, French, and British forces from Egyptian territory. In November 1956, the Eisenhower administration informed members of the Baghdad Pact that any threat to either their territorial integrity or political independence "would be viewed by the United States with utmost gravity."

To avoid antagonizing Egypt and other Arab states, the United States resisted growing pressure from the Baghdad Pact nations to join METO. However, on January 5, 1957, the President asked Congress for authority to use U.S. troops if it became necessary to protect the Middle East from communist aggression (see **Eisenhower Doctrine**). In addition, this government signed bilateral cooperation agreements with Turkey, Iran, and Pakistan in Ankara on March 5, 1959.

Meanwhile, under the leadership of Abdel Karim Kassim, the government of Iraq was forming ties with the U.S.S.R. On March 24, 1959, having announced the previous month that the Baghdad Pact was now "less than a shadow," Iraq withdrew from METO, and the following May it formally canceled all economic and military agreements with the United States. METO became CENTO, and on March 9, 1959, the headquarters of the nations still adhering to the Baghdad Pact were transferred to Ankara.

On March 12, 1979, Pakistan withdrew from the now almost inactive defense alliance, and Iran seemed likely to follow.

Centralia Mine Disaster On March 25, 1947, an explosion occurred in a four-mile bore of the Centralia Coal Company's Mine Number 5 near Centralia, Illinois, while the 142-man day shift was inside. When rescue operations were terminated four days later, the death toll was set at 111—one of the country's worst mine disasters since 1928, when 195 miners lost their lives in an explosion at Mather, Pennsylvania.

Investigation soon showed that mine inspectors had been reporting dangerous violations of safety codes at Centralia for many years, but little or no action had been taken. Since the federal government was still technically the operator of the mine

as a result of its seizure of all mines in May 1946 following a United Mine Workers (UMW) strike, union president John L. Lewis denounced Secretary of the Interior J. A. Krug as a "murderer" and called the nation's 400,000 bituminous coal miners out on a memorial strike. (The following year the company pled nolo contendere and was fined $1,000 for willful neglect.)

On December 21, 1951, tragedy struck again when 119 miners died in an explosion at West Frankfort, Illinois. Under the impetus provided by these two disasters, Congress was finally persuaded to set federal safety standards for mines in 1952.

The Century of the Common Man Five months after this country's entry into World War II, Vice President Henry A. Wallace delivered an address entitled "The Price of Free World Victory" to the Free World Association in New York on May 8, 1942.

Some have spoken of the "American Century." I say that the century we are now entering—the century which will come out of this war—can and must be the century of the common man. . . .

Those who write the peace must think of the whole world. There can be no privileged peoples. We ourselves in the United States are no more a master race than the Nazis. And we cannot perpetuate economic warfare without planting the seeds of military warfare.

In 1944 Wallace was replaced on the Democratic ticket as vice presidential candidate by Harry S Truman. Wallace accepted an appointment as President Franklin D. Roosevelt's new Secretary of Commerce in 1945, and he continued in this post after Truman succeeded to the presidency upon Roosevelt's death in April 1945. In 1946 Wallace was forced to resign after open disagreement with President Truman's new and tougher policy toward the Soviet Union. It was this basic criticism of U.S. foreign policy that led Wallace to form the **Progressive Party of America** (PPA).

During that campaign "The Century of the Common Man" turned up frequently as a slogan. When Wallace's candidacy was first announced, some political analysts thought that his third party attempt might well equal that of Robert La Follette, who in 1924 drew about 4.8 million votes on the Progressive ticket. However, while the PPA definitely siphoned off enough votes to cost the Democrats New York State, the resemblance of the PPA platform and that of the Communist Party did not escape early Wallace enthusiasts. The final turnout for him was only 1,157,172.

CETA *See* **Comprehensive Employment and Training Act.**

Chappaquiddick On July 18, 1969, a cookout on Chappaquiddick Island in Nantucket Sound was planned by Sen. Edward Kennedy (D.-Mass.) to honor six women who had served the summer before as volunteer workers in the campaign by Sen. Robert F. Kennedy (D.-N.Y.) to win the Democratic nomination for the presidency in 1968. The celebration, apparently a family obligation inherited by Senator Edward Kennedy when his brother Robert was assassinated in Los Angeles by Arab nationalist Sirhan Sirhan in June 1968, ended in tragedy when the car driven by Senator Kennedy plunged off a narrow bridge and the twenty-eight-year-old Mary Jo Kopechne was drowned under suspicious circumstances.

In a statement given the police nine hours after the accident, Senator Kennedy said that shortly after 11 P.M. he had left the cookout party with Miss Kopechne to drive to the two-car ferry that connected Chappaquiddick and Martha's Vineyard. His intention was to drop her at her hotel in Edgartown before going on to his own hotel. "I was unfamiliar with the road and turned onto Dike Road instead of bearing left on Main Street. After proceeding for approximately a half mile on Dike Road I descended a hill and came upon a narrow bridge. The car went off the side of the bridge."

Senator Kennedy told police that he had no recollection of how he himself got out of the car. "I came to the surface and then repeatedly dove down to the car in an attempt to see if the passenger was still in the car. I was unsuccessful in the attempt."

Exhausted and in a state of shock, he reported, he returned to the cottage and eventually asked to be taken back to Edgartown and his hotel. "When I fully realized what happened this morning, I immediately contacted the police."

The press and public opinion responded to the news with shock and suspicion. Questions were asked about what the Senator was doing at this party without his wife, Joan. It also seemed incredible that a man who knew the island and had sailed in the nearby waters could—unless intoxicated—have become disoriented and mistaken a hardtop road for a dirt road. In addition, the Senator could offer no acceptable explanation for having waited nine hours before contacting the police.

Eight days later, Senator Kennedy was given a two-month suspended sentence after pleading guilty to the charge of failing to report the accident. That same day, in an attempt to squelch public rumors about the tragedy and about his relationship to Miss Kopechne, he presented his version of events on television, and asked Massachusetts voters whether they felt he should resign. "I regard as indefensible the fact that I did not report the accident to the police immediately," he said, refusing to accept his doctor's explanation that he had suffered both shock and a cerebral concussion.

Public support in the form of telegrams immediately began pouring in for Senator Kennedy, although many of the nation's news commentators and analysts continued to feel that the delay in reporting the accident to the police represented an attempt at a cover-up. The Senator's television appeal for support was also compared by many to the famous **Checkers Speech** by Richard M. Nixon in 1952. There was particular concern that a man so often mentioned as a strong candidate for the presidency should have shown such confusion and irrationality in a moment of crisis.

A judicial inquest, begun in January 1970, concluded nine months later that Senator Kennedy and Miss Kopechne did not intend to return to Edgartown when they left the cookout and that the car intentionally turned onto Dike Road. Senator Kennedy rejected these conclusions in a public statement.

Books and articles on the Chappaquiddick tragedy continue to appear from time to time; during the events surrounding the **Watergate Scandal** angry Republicans claimed that investigative reporters had shown considerably less zeal in looking into the events and possible cover-up surrounding Miss Kopechne's death. To some extent this may be explained by the fact that in both 1972 and 1976 Senator Kennedy refused to be a candidate for the Democratic presidential nomination.

Chapultepec, Act of During February and March of 1945, as World War II drew to a close, American republics—with the exception of Argentina which still clung to its pro-Axis stance—met at Chapultepec Castle, Mexico City. The result of this Inter-American Conference on Problems of War and Peace was a mutual security agreement signed on March 3, 1945. It committed all the signatories, including the United States, to come to one another's mutual defense in the case of aggression by one state against another. Aggression from both within and without was covered. The door was left open to participation by Argentina, which on March 27, 1945, declared war on the Axis powers.

The provisions of the Act of Chapultepec were binding for the duration of the war; however, on September 2, 1947, the nineteen American states—including Argentina and the United States—implemented them in the Treaty of Rio de Janeiro (see **Rio Pact**). In conformity with Article 51 of the United Nations Charter, under which the right of individual or collective self-defense was recognized, the participants agreed that an armed attack on any one of them was to be considered an attack on all.

Charter of Bogotá *See* **Organization of American States.**

Checkers Speech On September 18, 1952, the New York *Post* headline read: "Secret Rich Man's Trust Fund Keeps Nixon in Style Far Beyond His Salary." The story, datelined Los Angeles and written by Leo Katcher, spoke of the existence of a "millionaires' club" which had established a secret and illegal "slush fund" for the personal benefit of California's Senator Richard M. Nixon, Republican vice-presidential candidate and running mate of General Dwight D. Eisenhower. In the furor that followed as other newspapers and media picked up the story, Senator Nixon's denials were overlooked and soon there were calls from the candidate's own party that he resign.

It seemed to make no difference that the fund differed little from those backing other political candidates—including Democratic presidential candidate Adlai Stevenson—that it was far from secret, carefully audited, used not for Senator Nixon's personal expenses but for various types of campaign expenses, and collected in over two years from seventy-six contributors who had given an average of $240 each. Nor did the candidate himself help matters when he noted in response to a heckler in Sacramento that he had been warned that if he continued "to attack the Communists and crooks in this government they would try to smear me. . . ."

Apparently abandoned by his running mate, General Eisenhower, who neither expressed complete confidence in Senator Nixon nor demanded his resignation—in informal conversation the general insisted that his running mate had to be "as clean as a hound's tooth"—Senator Nixon chose to bring his case before the voters in a $75,000 TV broadcast that was to be paid for by the Republican Party. His fate as a candidate, it was made clear to him, would depend upon whether or not he could win overwhelming public approval.

The result was the famous Checkers Speech (September 23, 1952), in which he gave a full accounting of his assets and made what many considered a humiliatingly personal appeal that ended as follows:

That's what we have and that's what we owe. It isn't very much, but Pat and I have the satisfaction that every dime that we've got is honestly ours. I should say this—that Pat doesn't have a mink coat. But she does have a respectable Republican cloth coat [see **Five Percenters**]. And I always tell her that she'd look good in anything.

One other thing I should probably tell you, because if I don't they'll be saying this about me, too. We did get something, a gift, after the nomination. A man down in Texas heard Pat on the radio mention the fact that our two youngsters would like to have a dog and, believe it or not, the day before we left on this campaign trip we got a message from Union Station in Baltimore, saying they had a package for us. We went down to get it. You know what it was?

It was a little cocker spaniel dog in a crate that he had sent all the way from Texas—black and white, spotted, and our little girl Tricia, the six-year-old, named it Checkers. And you know, the kids, like all kids, love that dog, and I just want to say this, right now, that regardless of what they say about it, we're going to keep it.

Senator Nixon asked that the voters communicate their decision as to whether or not he should withdraw from the election to the Republican National Committee. The outpouring of telegrams, letters, and phone calls in his favor was phenomenal; the nation had been so moved by the somewhat melodramatic television appeal that overnight Senator Nixon was converted from a political liability to an incalculable asset. Nevertheless, speaking in Cleveland, Ohio, immediately after his running mate's successful TV appeal, General Eisenhower still withheld final endorsement, which did not come until Senator Nixon flew to see him in Wheeling, West Virginia, where the general embraced him saying: "You're my boy." (Anguished by the general's apparent indecision during this crisis, Senator Nixon is said to have angrily noted that "there comes a time when you have to piss or get off the pot!")

The success of Mr. Nixon's TV appearance and appeal on this occasion was probably behind his willingness to accept the political risks inherent in the televised **Kennedy-Nixon Debates** of 1960.

Caryl Chessman Affair Convicted in 1948 on seventeen counts of robbery, kidnapping, attempted rape, and sexual abuse, Caryl Whittier Chessman received eight stays of execution before his death in the gas chamber of San Quentin Prison on May 2, 1960. In the intervening twelve years he had written four books—*Cell 2455, Death Row* (1954) sold 500,000 copies in this country and was translated into several languages—which attracted international attention and brought pleas in his favor from the Vatican's *L'Osservatore Romano* and such well-known figures as William Buckley, Jr., Albert Schweitzer, Aldous Huxley, and Pablo Casals. He won the support of thousands of people, both here and abroad, who opposed the death penalty on ethical and philosophical grounds, and his execution provoked anti-American demonstrations in various corners of the world.

Chessman, who studied law on his own, conducted his own defense during his first trial. Later, royalties from his books made it possible for him to hire expert professional counsel.

Chet Set   The name applied to those in the Kennedy administration, the Democratic party generally, and the news media who were partisans of Chester Bowles during his brief incumbency as Undersecretary of State under Dean Rusk.

The first of the nationally known liberals to support the nomination of Sen. John F. Kennedy (D.-Mass.) for the presidency, Bowles had advised the candidate on foreign policy during the 1960 campaign. His star began to decline when on March 31, 1961, he wrote a strong memorandum to Secretary Rusk opposing the planned **Bay of Pigs** operation. The President, who was not told of the memorandum, was said to be irritated at what seemed like an apparent attempt to avoid responsibility for the fiasco when stories of Bowles's opposition began to appear in the press. In addition, he was out of sympathy with Bowles's meditative manner, which did not at all fit in with the tempo at which **New Frontier** decisions were made.

Early in May, President Kennedy complained to Arthur Schlesinger, his Special Assistant for Latin American Affairs, that "Chet is a fine fellow, but he's just not doing the job." However, a premature "leak" to the press of Bowles's impending reassignment is said to have postponed his fate, although it brought glee to the hearts of Foreign Service professionals who had opposed his ambassadorial nominations—particularly that of Edwin Reischauer to Japan.

According to Special Counsel Ted Sorensen, "Bowles himself ignored all hints and opportunities to request reassignment as a matter of service and loyalty to the President." In November 1961, however, President Kennedy reassigned him as special representative and advisor on African, Asian, and Latin American affairs, giving him the rank of ambassador.

Chicago Eight   The events of the **Battle of Chicago** during the 1968 Democratic National Convention led to the indictment of eight antiwar (see **Vietnam War)** demonstrators under the controversial antiriot section tacked on as a rider to the **Civil Rights Act of 1968** and known among civil rights militants as the "Rap Brown Act."

On September 24, 1969, David Dellinger, Rennie Davis, and Tom Hayden, all members of the **National Mobilization to End the War in Vietnam** (Mobe); Abbie Hoffman and Jerry Rubin, members of the Youth International Party (**Yippies**); Lee Weiner, a graduate student of Northwestern University; John Froines, a University of Oregon chemistry instructor; and Bobby Seale, chairman of the **Black Panther Party,** went on trial in Chicago with U.S. District Court Judge Julius J. Hoffman presiding. The atmosphere of the court was tense from the beginning because of the fact that in drawing up the charges against the eight defendants the government had ignored the *Walker Report,* which put much of the responsibility for the convention-week violence on the Chicago police, and because some time before the trial a federal district judge had rejected an American Civil Liberties Union (ACLU) brief challenging the constitutionality of the antiriot statute. In addition, the unconventional dress and behavior in court of the defendants seemed designed to provoke and make a mockery of the legal procedure. Their lawyers themselves—William Kunstler and Leonard Weinglass—were on many occasions admonished by Judge Hoffman both for their own behavior and for their failure to restrain their clients. (A total of 175 contempt citations were handed out by Judge Hoffman.)

Because Bobby Seale's lawyer was recovering from surgery, the Black Panther leader demanded the right to defend himself and to cross-examine witnesses. When Judge Hoffman refused permission, Seale kept interrupting court proceedings and on October 29 the judge took the unusual step of having him bound and gagged while in court. On November 5, 1969, he ordered Seale's case severed from the trial, and the Chicago Eight became the Chicago Seven. Seale was at the time sentenced to four years for contempt of court.

Outside the courtroom militant **Weathermen** of the **Students for a Democratic Society** (SDS) began staging demonstrations and chanting "Bring the War Home." On October 9, 1969, some 2,500 National Guardsmen were called out after a day of rioting. Disturbances continued through October 11, when sixty protesters were arrested.

After forty hours of deliberation, all remaining seven defendants were acquitted on February 18, 1971, of charges of conspiring to incite a riot; however, Dellinger, Davis, Hayden, Hoffman, and Rubin were found guilty of crossing state lines with intent to incite a riot and were sentenced to five years and fined $5,000 each. Judge Hoffman refused to release them on bail pending an appeal, but his ruling was overturned.

Acting on the request of a federal district attorney who felt it would be "inappropriate" to try Seale alone on a conspiracy charge, Judge Hoffman dismissed the riot conspiracy charges against Bobby Seale on October 19, 1970. The contempt sentences were dismissed the following March.

The sentences of the other five men were thrown out almost three years later by a U.S. court of appeals, which found that the trial record showed that Judge Hoffman had assumed a "deprecatory" attitude "from the very beginning," and had behaved antagonistically toward the defendants.

Chicago Seven *See* **Chicago Eight.**

Chicano Term used to designate Mexican-Americans. It most recently came into prominence in 1965 during the strike against California grape growers led by Cesar Chavez (see *La Huelga*).

The word is generally considered an amalgamation coming from the name *Chi*huahua, the city and state in northern Mexico, and Mexi*cano*. It was already common in the 1930s, and was sometimes used in describing the so-called zoot suit riots which took place between young Mexican-American toughs *(pachucos)* and sailors in Los Angeles in June 1943. The Chicano Movement, organized by various civil rights militants in the 1960s to fight for the rights of Mexican-American minorities, is often thought to have its roots in the self-defense groups formed against marauding sailors.

See **Pachuco Movement.**

Chieu Hoi *See* **Open Arms Policy.**

Children's Crusade Expression coined by Washington *Star* reporter Mary McGrory to describe the young enthusiasts who swarmed to aid Sen. Eugene McCarthy (D.-Minn.) in his attempt to win the 1968 Democratic presidential nomination. Senator McCarthy had declared his candidacy in 1967 in order to register his opposition to the **Vietnam War.** To the surprise of most professional politi-

cians, he made a strong showing in the March 12, 1968, New Hampshire primary election, polling 42.2 percent of the Democratic vote to President Lyndon B. Johnson's 49.4 percent, and with the help of 5,511 Republican write-ins he was only narrowly beaten by the President in a final vote of 29,021 to 28,791.

Much of this success was attributed to the hard work of the "ballot children" who were attracted to his cause. *Time* magazine reported: "To escape the hippie image, miniskirted girls went midi, and bearded boys either shaved or stayed in the back rooms, licking envelopes or compiling address lists to the accompaniment of muted Beatle music."

Convening in Chicago in August 1968, as police and antiwar demonstrators clashed (see **Battle of Chicago),** the Democratic National Convention nominated Vice President Hubert H. Humphrey for president and Maine's Senator Edmund S. Muskie for vice president. Addressing his disappointed followers, some of whom were wearing black arm bands and blank campaign buttons, Senator McCarthy said: "I am happy to be here to address the government in exile."

The expression "Children's Crusade" dates from 1212 when Stephen of Cloyes, a French peasant boy, led swarms of children who embarked at Marseilles to fight against the "infidels" in the Holy Land, hoping to succeed where their elders had failed. Many of the children were said to have been sold into slavery by unscrupulous ships' captains.

The same expression was also used by civil rights supporters to refer to a black protest march in Birmingham on May 2, 1963, in which some thousand black children participated (*see* **Birmingham**).

"A Choice—Not an Echo" *See* **Me-too Republicans.**

Church Committee To investigate "the extent, if any, to which illegal, improper or unethical activities were engaged in by any agency or by any persons, acting either individually or in combination with others, in carrying out any intelligence or surveillance activities by or on behalf of any agency of the federal government," the U.S. Senate voted on January 27, 1975, to create an eleven-member, bipartisan subcommittee. Among those eventually appointed to serve were Sen. Frank Church (D.-Idaho)—subsequently named chairman; Sen. Howard H. Baker (R.-Tenn.); Sen. Barry Goldwater (R.-Ariz.); Sen. Gary W. Hart (D.-Colo.); Sen. Philip A. Hart (D.-Mich.); Sen. Walter Huddleston (D.-Ky.); Sen. Charles Mathias (R.-Md.); Sen. Walter F.

Mondale (D.-Minn.); Sen. Robert B. Morgan (D.-N.C.); Sen. Richard Schweiker (R.-Pa.); and Sen. John G. Tower (R.-Tex.). A budget of $750,000 was established, and the committee was ordered to report within nine months.

However, it was not until May 1976—fifteen months and $2.8 million later—that the Church Committee, without the concurrence of Sens. Goldwater and Tower, issued a 110,000-page report covering the testimony of 800 witnesses and making 183 recommendations for protecting the civil rights of American citizens. By then, much of the public indignation about the problem had been dissipated by a series of controversial leaks to the press. Among the revelations was the fact that 75 percent of the covert operations by the **Central Intelligence Agency** (CIA) had never been approved or reviewed outside that agency and that many of its operations were "highly improper." For example, a presidential ban on CIA ties with academia had been sidestepped by the establishment of ties with individual academics who provided intelligence reports and ground out scholarly material supporting the agency's viewpoint.

According to the report, the FBI had used **COINTELPRO** methods in an attempt to discredit civil rights leader Martin Luther King, Jr.; reported to President Dwight D. Eisenhower on the activities of persons such as Eleanor Roosevelt and Supreme Court Justice William O. Douglas; compiled a list of political activists who it felt should be jailed in the event of a national crisis; infiltrated the **Women's Liberation** movement; and spent hundreds of thousands in taxpayers' money in a vain attempt to establish links between the National Association for the Advancement of Colored People (NAACP) and the Communist party. Charges of illegal surveillance and harassment were also brought against the intelligence agencies of the various armed services.

CIA *See* **Central Intelligence Agency.**

Cinéma-Vérité A term that appeared in American film criticism with great regularity after the technique it described found contemporary expression in Jean Rouch's *Chronique d'un été* (1961), a French film made with the help of sociologist Edgar Morin. The term indicates the use of a sound camera—often hand-held—not only to record events in a documentary style but to participate in them by provoking responses. The filmed material is either unscripted or tries to obtain the effect of

being unscripted, thereby conveying the immediacy of an event recorded by television news cameras.

The origins of cinéma-vérité go back to the work of Russian cineast Dziga Vertov and his *Kino-Pravda* (cinema-truth) a filmed magazine of the 1920s. Vertov argued that movies should give up literary outlines, mise-en-scène, professional actors, studios, etc., and simply allow the camera's eye to enregister events as it sees them.

Citizens' Councils *See* **White Citizens' Councils.**

City Lights Bookshop Established in 1953 by Peter D. Martin and poet Lawrence Ferlinghetti, this paperback bookstore at 261 Columbus Avenue, San Francisco, California, soon became the recognized hangout and mailing address for free-floating members of the **Beat Generation.**

City Lights Books, an outgrowth of the shop, sponsored the first publication of some of Ferlinghetti's own poetry as well as the works of Allen Ginsberg and Gregory Corso. The title of the shop and the press refers to Charlie Chaplin's 1931 film, *City Lights.*

Civil Rights Act of 1957 The first such legislation since the Reconstruction Era, its passage on August 29, 1957, was the culmination of a battle begun under former President Harry S Truman to provide legislative means for enforcing civil rights guaranteed by the Constitution. As passed by the Senate, it was reduced from an overall civil rights act to an essentially voting-rights law.

Among its major provisions was the creation of a six-member, bipartisan Commission of Civil Rights to investigate instances in which citizens were deprived of the vote because of race, color, creed, or national origin. The Commission was charged with the study of all aspects of failure to provide equal protection under the Constitution and submit a final report to both Congress and the President within two years, after which time it was to disband. An additional Assistant Attorney General was to be appointed to head a special Civil Rights Division within the Justice Department. Machinery was also set up to "recover damages or to secure equitable or other relief under any act of Congress providing for protection of civil rights, including the right to vote." Under the act, the Attorney General could seek relief from interference with voting rights, even if not specifically asked to do so. Fines and prison terms were established for violation of court orders issued under the provisions of the act; judges could decide cases without a jury if fines did not exceed $300 or jail sentences forty-five days. To protect the rights of blacks to act as jurors, the act established that any twenty-one-year-old citizen who had lived in a judicial district for a year or more could serve if he did not have a criminal record; could speak, read, and write English; and was mentally competent.

A last-minute attempt to prevent passage of the bill was a twenty-four-hour filibuster staged by Sen. Strom Thurmond (D.-S.C.), who insisted that all he was doing was engaging in an "educational debate." No real attempt was made to kill the bill by filibuster, since opponents knew they did not have sufficient votes to defeat cloture and were afraid that the stronger bill originally accepted by the House would pass. Many civil rights leaders opposed the Senate compromise as worse than no bill and vainly urged that it not be signed by President Dwight D. Eisenhower.

On May 6, 1960, the President signed the **Civil Rights Act of 1960,** which authorized federal judges to appoint referees to help register blacks; it also strengthened the 1957 act by establishing new criminal penalties against the use of violence to obstruct a federal court's order.

Critics of both Civil Rights Acts have pointed out that they were largely unsuccessful because the government was slow to take action under its new powers.

Civil Rights Act of 1960 *see* **Civil Rights Act of 1957.**

Civil Rights Act of 1964 Signed by President Lyndon B. Johnson on July 2, 1964, it barred racial discrimination in public accommodations such as theaters, restaurants, and hotels; empowered the Attorney General to bring suits over school segregation and the denial of voting rights; and—under Title VII—prohibited discriminatory employment practices based on color, race, sex, religion, or national origin. It was the most hotly contested piece of legislation since the **Taft-Hartley Act.**

On June 11, 1963, following a confrontation with Governor George C. Wallace over the admission of two blacks to the University of Alabama, President John F. Kennedy had told a national television audience that "if an American, because his skin is dark, cannot enjoy the full and free life that all of us want, then who among us would be content to have the color of his skin changed and stand in his place?" Eight days later he sent Congress the basic legislative proposals on which the 1964 law was to be based.

In his first address to Congress after the assassination of President Kennedy on **November 22, 1963,** President Johnson pledged to translate into action the "dream of equal rights for all Americans, whatever their race or color. . . ."

Basic provisions of the bill as passed were the following:

Voting Rights: Prohibited the unequal application of registration procedures or rejection for minor errors. Tests were to be in writing and a sixth-grade education considered a rebuttable presumption of literacy.

Public Accommodations: Generally barred racial discrimination in restaurants, hotels, theaters. The so-called **Mrs. Murphy clause** specifically exempted owner-occupied rooming houses with five or less rooms for rent.

Public Facilities: Permitted the Justice Department to bring suit against segregated parks, pools, libraries, and playgrounds which were either state or locally owned.

Public Education: The Attorney General was authorized to react to written complaints of segregation by filing desegregation suits; however, the act did not cover steps such as "busing" designed to end unbalanced school populations.

Civil Rights Commission: Extended the commission's life through January 31, 1968, and authorized it to investigate the denial of voting rights.

Federally Assisted Programs: Discrimination under any federally assisted program was barred with certain exemptions.

Employment: Title VII provided for an Equal Employment Opportunity Commission charged with investigating complaints of racial discrimination by either employers or unions with 100 or more employees or members. Over a four-year period this number was to be reduced to twenty-five.

Additional provisions directed the Census Bureau to compile voting and registration statistics requested by the Civil Rights Commission; permitted the Attorney General to intervene in private suits in which it was alleged that equal protection under the Fourteenth Amendment had been denied; established a Community Relations Service in the Department of Commerce to help local communities negotiate disputes involving racial discrimination; and guaranteed jury trials for criminal contempt under the Voting Rights provisions (Title I) with a limit of a six-month prison sentence and a $1,000 fine.

In May 1977, the Supreme Court ruled that the provisions of Title VII do not prohibit the use of "bona fide" seniority systems that perpetuated the effects of discrimination that occurred before the title went into effect on July 2, 1965.

Civil Rights Act of 1965 *See* **Voting Rights Act of 1965.**

Civil Rights Act of 1968 In an atmosphere of urgency created by the riots and disorders following the assassination of black leader Martin Luther King, Jr. (April 4, 1968), the House of Representatives on April 10, 1968, approved a Senate-passed civil rights bill which prohibited racial discrimination in 80 percent of the nation's housing.

In signing the measure into law in the presence of many civil rights leaders the next day, President Lyndon B. Johnson noted that when he had first transmitted his open-housing message to Congress in April 1966 "few in the nation . . . believed that fair housing would in our time become the unchallenged law of this land." He expressed the nation's outrage against both the murder of Dr. King and the "looting and burning that defiles our democracy."

In addition to providing a three-stage reduction of racial barriers in more than 52 million housing units, the act also made it a federal crime to injure civil rights workers, to cross state lines for the purposes of inciting a riot, or to give instruction in firearms or Molotov cocktails to rioters. It also guaranteed American Indians broad rights in their dealings with federal, state, local, judicial, or tribal authorities.

The fate of the bill required Republican support, and though House Republican leader Gerald R. Ford (Mich.) had reversed his earlier opposition, he had asked for a change in the Senate-approved open-housing provision which exempted only single-family homes sold by the owner without the services of a broker. Because of Representative Ford's insistence on an exemption that would permit brokers to discriminate in the sale or rental of single-family houses at the owner's request, the bill was referred to the House Rules Committee on March 14 and not cleared for a House vote until April 9.

Under the antiriot provisions of the act, on March 20, 1969, a Chicago federal grand jury indicted five of the **Chicago Eight** (later the Chicago Seven) for crossing a state line to create disturbances and riots during the August 1968 Democratic National Convention in Chicago.

Clamshell Alliance In the first massive show of civil disobedience as a tactic to block the construction of a nuclear power plant, on April 30, 1977, approxi-

mately 2,000 demonstrators equipped with food and tents occupied the construction site of the controversial $2 billion generating plant at Seabrook, New Hampshire. More than 1,400 demonstrators were arrested when they refused to leave, and two weeks later some 500 who had not bailed themselves out pleaded not guilty to charges of criminal trespass.

The well-thought-out and nonviolent demonstration was organized by a group that called itself the Clamshell Alliance, which had led a similar demonstration at the Seabrook plant in August 1976, when 180 of 1,000 protestors were arrested. The group is made up of various environmental and anti-nuclear power organizations who claim that the Nuclear Regulatory Commission (NRC) has shown a bias in favor of nuclear power plants.

The 2,300-megawatt Seabrook plant and the Clamshell Alliance against it became symbols in the late 1970s of the increasing national debate over the use of nuclear energy as a power source. Construction of the plant was repeatedly halted in 1977 and 1978 as federal regulatory agencies considered arguments against its many licenses. In December 1978, the Public Service Company of New Hampshire, a major investor in the plant, warned that escalating costs and financing troubles might keep the plant from ever being completed.

Regional antinuclear groups sprang up in California, Washington, Louisiana, South Carolina, and Florida, taking such names as Abalone, Crabshell, Oyster Shell, Sunflower, Palmetto, and Conchshell. In Washington, some 300 demonstrators representing an alliance between environmentalists and "ban-the-bombers" were arrested (May 1978) when they attempted to occupy the U.S. Naval Submarine Base at Bangor, Maine, where the Trident nuclear-missile submarines will be stationed. On May 28, 1978, some 10,000 protestors turned out for a Survival Sunday rally at the Hollywood Bowl and were joined by such figures of the anti-**Vietnam War** protest of the 1960s as former Sen. Eugene McCarthy (D.-Minn.), Dr. Daniel Ellsberg (see **Pentagon Papers**), and Father Daniel Berrigan (see **Catonsville Nine**).

The Clan A group of actor-celebrities that became a minor issue in the 1960 presidential campaign of Sen. John F. Kennedy (D.-Mass.) because one of its members, actor Peter Lawford, was married to the Senator's sister Patricia. The acknowledged leader of the informal group was singer Frank Sinatra, and other members included singer Dean Martin, singer Sammy Davis, Jr., and comedian Joey Bishop.

Sinatra helped raise funds for the Kennedy campaign, but became something of an embarrassment to it because of press stories about The Clan and about his own links to the Nevada gambling world. In addition, the group's association with the campaign became a problem in practical politics because of black singer Davis's forthcoming marriage to white actress May Britt.

The Senator's brother Robert, who as Attorney General was to focus on the Nevada mobsters, was said to have been particularly vexed by the association with Sinatra, who he nevertheless realized was a drawing card of importance at popular rallies. As for the presidential candidate, he was quoted by columnist Dorothy Kilgallen as saying of Sinatra: "He's no friend of mine. He's just a friend of Pat and Peter Lawford."

Sinatra helped Lawford plan the president-elect's inaugural ball, but later relations between the singer and the White House were said to have cooled.

"Clean as a Hound's Tooth" *See* **Checkers Speech.**

"Clean" Bomb Controversy On January 31, 1958, the **Atomic Energy Commission** (AEC) disclosed that during recent testing in Nevada silica sands had been added to nuclear bombs in an attempt to imprison **strontium 90** in a soil-insoluble compound that could not be absorbed by plants.

Responding to growing public concern about possible nuclear pollution of the planet, Dr. Edward Teller, the Hungarian-born physicist who had made important contributions to the development of the H-bomb, advised soon afterward that an H-bomb with little fallout was possible. Appearing before a Senate Disarmament Subcommittee on April 16, 1958, he stated that if the United States terminated nuclear tests it might be sacrificing millions of lives in a "dirty" nuclear war at some later date. He argued that the Soviet Union could find "a plethora of methods" to make small nuclear tests undetectable. Although he conceded that thousands of genetic mutations might result from continued testing, he argued that not all mutation was undesirable and that there had been no definite link established between fallout and cancer.

At about this time, Sen. Clinton P. Anderson (D-N. Mex.) charged that the United States military was deliberately stockpiling "dirtier bombs" in spite of the wishes of the State Department.

Appearing before the World Affairs Council of Northern California, the AEC's Dr. Willard F. Libby stated that the bombs scheduled for testing at Eniwetok that July were 96 percent cleaner than the bomb used on Hiroshima during World War II. Nevertheless, their considerably greater force would result in a 100-percent increase in fallout.

Among those who protested the Eniwetok tests were Nobel Prize winner Dr. Linus C. Pauling, who told the press on April 28 that radioactive carbon 14 produced by nuclear devices already exploded would cause millions of genetic defects in years to come (see **Neutron Bomb**).

Clean Water Act of 1972 Supplemented previous water pollution control legislation of 1948, 1956, 1965, 1966, and 1970 by setting quality standards and establishing a national program of pollution abatement. It was passed by Congress on October 18, 1972, over the veto of President Richard M. Nixon, who felt that it "would lead to higher prices and higher taxes."

The bill budgeted $18 billion over three years for local sewage plant construction, with the federal government meeting 75 percent of the cost in each case. (Since funds could be committed in long-term contracts, the annual congressional appropriations fights were eliminated.) An additional $6.4 billion was provided for research to determine the program's impact, and for low-interest pollution loans to small companies.

Under what is formally known as the Federal Water Pollution Control Act Amendments of 1972, private industry was required to install by July 1, 1977, "the best practicable" pollution abatement equipment meeting standards of the **Environmental Protection Agency** (EPA). It had until July 1, 1983, to install "the best available technology economically achievable." Secondary treatment facilities would have to be installed by government sewage plants by July 1977. The best practicable technology would have to be in by July 1, 1983. Although it included no enforcement provisions, the legislation set 1985 as the year by which all pollution discharges were prohibited.

Clean Water Restoration Act of 1966 Signed into law by President Lyndon B. Johnson on November 3, 1966, this act was preceded by the **Water Quality Act of 1965,** under which each state had to set water-quality standards for their interstate waters by July 1, 1967, or have federal standards imposed on it.

Under the new legislation, almost $4 billion in federal money was authorized in fiscal 1967–1971 for water-pollution control programs. Of that sum, $3.55 billion was to be used as grants to communities that had undertaken to construct plants for sewage treatment. Research and development in the area of water-pollution control were to benefit from $308 million in federal grants.

The compromise bill eliminated previous ceilings on government contributions to individual sewage treatment plants, which could now range from 30 percent to 55 percent depending on whether or not they met incentive conditions established by the bill.

Club of Rome Report *See* ***The Limits of Growth.***

COFO *See* **Council of Federated Organizations.**

COINTELPRO It was under the designation COIN-TELPRO that under the orders of J. Edgar Hoover the FBI from 1956 to 1971 conducted a series of counterintelligence operations, some of which, according to a Justice Department report released on November 18, 1974, could "only be considered abhorrent in a free society." Five of the seven operations involved in COINTELPRO were directed against domestic organizations and their leaders, the most prominent being two black civil rights groups: the **Congress of Racial Equality** (CORE) and the **Southern Christian Leadership Conference** (SCLC). In a memorandum dated April 28, 1971, Hoover ordered the immediate termination of these programs.

The first of the COINTELPRO operations was undertaken in 1956 against the Communist Party. In the 1960s, other operations focused on the Socialist Workers Party (1961), White Hate Groups (1964), Black Extremists (1967), and the **New Left** (1968). Operations against foreign intelligence sources and communist organizations came under the headings of Espionage or Soviet Satellite Intelligence (1964) and Special Operations (1967).

According to the Justice Department report released by Attorney General William B. Saxbe and FBI Director Clarence M. Kelley, activities of COINTELPRO included: the distribution of materials designed to create dissension within the organizations under surveillance; informing credit bureaus of members' activities; using religious and civic leaders to disrupt organizations; leaking information from informers to selected media sources; and informing both the families and the business associates of organization members of their activities. Anonymous letters and phone calls were used to arouse the suspicion of organization members against one another.

Between 1958 and 1969, at least three Attorneys General and a number of key White House staff

members were informed of limited aspects of COINTELPRO. In addition to CORE and SCLC, specific organizations against which the program was directed included: the **Student Nonviolent Coordinating Committee** (SNCC), the **Revolutionary Action Movement** (RAM), the **Black Panther Party** (BPP), **Students for a Democratic Society** (SDS), the **Progressive Labor Party** (PLP), the Ku Klux Klan (KKK), the **American Nazi Party** (ANP), and the **Minutemen.**

The first public news of the program came on December 6, 1973, when in response to a suit by Carl Stern (NBC), under the **Freedom of Information Act** (FOIA), the FBI released a May 1968 memorandum in which J. Edgar Hoover ordered a campaign to "expose, disrupt, and otherwise neutralize" the New Left movement.

Cold Launch The name given to a supposedly "secret" technique whereby missiles could be "popped" from their silos previous to the ignition of the booster rockets. Because the launcher tube itself was not subjected to the destructive heat of the rocket engines, it could be reloaded.

Cold War Speaking before the Senate War Investigation Committee on October 24, 1948, financier and presidential advisor Bernard Baruch noted: "Although the war is over, we are in the midst of a cold war which is getting warmer." Baruch had first used the expression in a speech in Columbia, South Carolina, on April 16, 1947: "Let us not be deceived—today we are in the midst of a cold war." Said to have been written into the speech by Herbert Bayard Swope—who had urged its use even earlier—it was at that time considered too strong. The phrase was popularized and became common after Walter Lippmann picked it up and used it in his nationally syndicated column.

The wartime amity that characterized U.S.-U.S.S.R. relations began to deteriorate following the Yalta Conference in February 1945. The trend accelerated after Harry S Truman assumed the Presidency in April 1945. He found that agreements with the Soviet Union "had so far been a one-way street." The President accused the Russians of having, among other things, failed to honor pledges to establish free governments in Hungary, Poland, and Rumania. But former Vice President Henry A. Wallace argued that the "cold war" was the result of efforts by the United States to use its nuclear advantage to force postwar reconstruction solutions on the Soviet Union.

Though debate as to its origins and meanings

continues among historians, the dominant view is that the United States did not initiate the Cold War but was merely responding to Soviet failure to keep its pledges. In "The Origins of the Cold War," published in *Foreign Affairs* (October 1967), Arthur M. Schlesinger, Jr., wrote: "The Cold War in its original form was presumably moral antagonism arising in the wake of the Second World War, between two rigidly hostile blocks, one led by the Soviet Union, the other by the United States." He attacked Wallace's "revisionist" position, but noted the influence on the cold war of the sudden termination of lend-lease aid and the failure of the United States government to grant the Soviet Union the credits it urgently needed for reconstruction. "The Cold War could have been avoided if only the Soviet Union had not been possessed by convictions both of the infallibility of the communist world and the inevitability of a communist world."

See **Containment; Iron Curtain.**

Colegrove v. Green   See Baker v. Carr.

Coleman Report   In passing the Civil Rights Act of 1964, Congress ordered that a study be made of the effects of segregation on education. The survey, carried out under the direction of Professor James S. Coleman, chairman of the Johns Hopkins University sociology department, was released in July 1966 and is historically important because it demonstrated in facts and figures that the only known educational device to have a measurable impact on the disadvantaged black child was integration. It also showed that more than a decade after the U.S. Supreme Court had ordered an end to school segregation in **Brown v. Board of Education of Topeka,** some 80 percent of white first-grade pupils and more than 65 percent of their black contemporaries attended schools which were 90 to 100 percent segregated.

The Coleman Report documented the fact that black students had fewer libraries, laboratories, and other educational facilities available to them and that the teachers assigned in black schools were generally less able than those in schools attended by most white students. Only 4.6 percent of the country's college students were black, and more than half of these attended all-black colleges in the South. The effects of segregation on both whites and blacks were suggested by the fact that by the twelfth grade both white and black students in the South scored below their counterparts in the North. "In addition, Southern Negroes score farther below

Southern whites than Northern Negroes score below Northern whites."

In his education message of March 3, 1970, President Richard M. Nixon referred to the Coleman Report and endorsed the principle that a child's economic and social background have a direct bearing on his learning achievement. Paraphrasing the report, he noted that "quality is what education is all about; desegregation is vital to that quality." Professor Coleman was later quoted as saying that he was gratified by the reference to his work but that he regretted that the President did not follow up his comments with "anything at all about how to make integration work."

Columbine   *See Air Force One.*

"Come Home America"   Addressing the Democratic National Convention in Miami Beach on July 13, 1972, approximately one month following the break-in of Democratic National Committee headquarters in the Capital's Watergate complex, Sen. George McGovern (D.-S. Dak.) urged:

"Come home America, from secrecy and deception in high places. Come home America, to the conviction that we can move our country forward. Come home to the belief that we can seek a newer world. . . ."

The quotation was widely used as a slogan during Senator McGovern's unsuccessful campaign against White House incumbent President Richard M. Nixon. It assumed a special poignancy during the **Watergate Scandal** that ended with the resignation of President Nixon on August 9, 1974.

"Come now, and let us reason together"   This biblical quotation from Isaiah 1:18 was a favorite with President Lyndon B. Johnson. In explaining its origin in a talk given at South Gate, California, October 11, 1964, he told how as a neophyte politician he told off the head of a power company who was opposed to a rural electrification project in his country district in Texas. Afterward, he asked an older politician what he had thought of his statement. The older man pointed out that there was a significant difference between telling a man to go to hell and "making him go." "What you better do," Johnson was told, "is get out the Good Book that your Mama used to read to you and go back to the prophet Isaiah and read what he said."

Committee of One Million   Formed in 1953 by members of the so-called China Lobby, it was originally called the Committee of One Million Against the Admission of Communist China to the United Nations. It hoped to accomplish its object by collecting the signatures of one million people who were in agreement with it. In 1955, in view of "a series of oblique declarations from several major internationally minded American groups hinting at the need to recognize Communist China and to admit that regime to the UN for the sake of 'peace,' " the group reorganized as simply the Committee of One Million.

In a report reviewing its accomplishments during the 1957–1960 period, the group took credit for organizing a postcard campaign that had helped stop proposed Senate hearings on trade with mainland China—a twenty-year embargo was finally lifted in 1971 during the era of **"ping-pong diplomacy"**—for a letter-writing campaign in support of Secretary of State John Foster Dulles's policy during the 1958 **Quemoy and Matsu** crisis, for helping to nullify the effects of the *Conlon Report,* which asked for "de facto recognition" of Red China, and for working in the 1960 elections to defeat "those few candidates who openly supported the admission of Communist China to the UN. . . ."(China was admitted to the UN in October 1971.)

The China Lobby emerged in the period immediately following World War II as an informal confederation of businessmen who had once traded with China and of conservatives opposed to any concessions to communism in Asia. It strongly supported the Nationalist government on Taiwan.

The lobby's unofficial head was Rep. Walter Judd (R.-Minn.). Others active in promoting its policies were Sen. William Knowland (R.-Calif.); Alfred Kohlberg, an importer who headed the American China Policy Association; Frederick C. McKee, an industrialist who headed the China Emergency Committee; and William Loeb, publisher of the *Manchester Union Leader,* which in 1972 was to print the famous **"Canuck Letter"** that was influential in defeating the efforts of Sen. Edward S. Muskie (D.-Maine) to win the Democratic presidential nomination.

Committee for the Preservation of the Democratic Party in California   When in 1962 former Vice President Richard M. Nixon ran for governor of California, H. R. Haldeman was his campaign manager. As part of his strategy, Haldeman set up the above dummy organization, which then sent a "poll" to some 500,000 Democratic voters. This poll presented the state Democratic party as having been taken over by extremists and requested contributions that would be used for party reform. In

1964, a California Superior Court judge ruled the poll a fraud and found that the funds obtained by the mailing had been used for Mr. Nixon's campaign. The "committee," Democrats discovered, was run by a public relations firm.

Although the Democrats named both Mr. Nixon and Mr. Haldeman in their court complaint, they did not cite them as defendants or press for a trial. Of Mr. Haldeman—who under the Nixon administration was to be the President's Chief of Staff and subsequently a key figure in the **Watergate Scandal**—the state Democratic chairman, Roger Kent, noted: "He didn't seem to think that there was anything wrong with it at all."

Committee to Re-elect the President (CREEP, CRP)
Originally known as the Citizens Committee for the Re-election of the President, the Committee to Re-elect the President (CREEP; sometimes CRP) opened its offices at 1701 Pennsylvania Avenue, Washington, D.C., in March 1971. Its purpose was to assure the reelection of President Richard M. Nixon in November 1972. Although Attorney General John N. Mitchell did not resign from the Department of Justice until March 1, 1972, to become director of CREEP, he seems to have been in charge of the committee from the very beginning. After May 1971, Jeb Stuart Magruder, who had served in the White House as Deputy Director of Communications, joined CREEP as its deputy director. On February 15, 1972, Maurice H. Stans resigned his post as Secretary of Commerce to become chairman of the Finance Committee to Reelect the President, beginning a multipronged effort to raise funds for the campaign.

Among other members of CREEP who came into prominence following the break-in of the Democratic National Committee (DNC) headquarters at the Watergate complex on June 17, 1972 (see **Watergate Scandal**), were E. Howard Hunt, Jr., former **CIA** agent and chief operations officer at the **Bay of Pigs,** who served as security chief, and G. Gordon Liddy, a former FBI officer, who was appointed counsel (see also "**Plumbers**").

As investigations continued following the Watergate break-in, strong links were established between it and CREEP, which also played a significant part in the subsequent cover-up. Links were also established between CREEP and such Watergate-related scandals as the **ITT Affair** and the **Vesco Affair.**

Hunt's relation to the Watergate break-in was revealed on June 19, 1972, after his name was found in a memorandum book carried by one of the men arrested. Liddy's connection with CREEP was severed by Mitchell on June 28 when the finance committee counsel refused to answer questions by two FBI agents who had found his name in an address book owned by Eugenio R. Martinez, who had been arrested at the time of the break-in of DNC headquarters. As links between CREEP and Watergate continued to be forged, Mitchell himself resigned as director and withdrew from politics, giving family reasons as having motivated his decision.

Mitchell's resignation was preceded by a series of phone calls from his wife, Martha Mitchell, to Helen Thomas, a reporter for United Press International. In the first call, made on June 22, 1972, from Newport Beach, California, where she had accompanied her husband on a fund-raising expedition, Mrs. Mitchell described herself as a "political prisoner" and barely had time to say "they don't want me to talk," before the phone was pulled out of the wall. The story of that telephone call appeared the next day in most newspapers across the nation. On June 25, Mrs. Mitchell once more managed to telephone the same reporter and complained that she could not stand the life she had been leading since her husband had resigned as Attorney General. She threatened to leave her husband unless he resigned as director of CREEP. (The Mitchells were legally separated in September 1973 and were unreconciled at the time of Mrs. Mitchell's death from cancer on May 31, 1976.)

Common Cause   Organized in October 1970 by John W. Gardner, former head of the Carnegie Corporation and Secretary of **Health, Education, and Welfare** (HEW) under President Lyndon B. Johnson, this national citizens' lobby was designed as a "third force" independent of political parties. Its major goals included ending the **Vietnam War** and bringing about a "drastic change in national priorities" to attack problems relating to poverty, discrimination, consumer fraud, and ecology.

Gardner had previously organized the National Urban Coalition, a national lobbying group made up of businessmen, church leaders, labor leaders, and civil rights activists. Common Cause took over the coalition's separate Action Council of twenty-five, and, although Gardner remained the guiding spirit, he was replaced as the coalition's chairman by Sol M. Linowitz, former chairman of the Xerox Corporation, who served in a part-time capacity while Jack H. Vaughn, former **Peace Corps** director, was made the new group's full-time president. (In 1978, the president was David Cohen.)

Unlike the National Urban Coalition, Common Cause was able to build up mass support. Within a month, it had attracted more than 20,000 members, each of whom paid $15 in annual dues. By the middle of the decade, the new group claimed to have approximately 300,000 members and an annual income of more than $6 million.

Common Cause was deeply engaged in lobbying to end American involvement in Vietnam. When it became apparent that Maurice H. Stans, chairman of the Finance **Committee to Re-elect the President,** had collected some $20 million—much of it in the form of illegal corporate contributions—for President Richard M. Nixon's 1972 presidential campaign before the new campaign finance reporting law went into effect (April 1972), Common Cause brought suit to force disclosure of Stans' biggest secret contributors.

In focusing on the influence of secrecy and money on governmental procedures, Common Cause monitors congressional committee meetings as well as lobbies in state legislatures. In November 1976, its report "Serving Two Masters: A Common Cause Study of Conflicts of Interest in the Executive Branch" pointed out that more than half the top employees of the **Energy Research and Development Administration** previously worked for private enterprise in the energy field. It also focused on the fact that 65 percent of the top employees of the Nuclear Regulatory Commission were working both for the commission and for private enterprises that receive licenses and contracts from it.

By mid-1974 Common Cause was one of the principal lobbyists for new campaign-spending legislation, and it is generally credited with shaping 1976 legislation on public financing of presidential elections. In October 1977, it helped defeat a controversial bill that would have required 9.5 percent of all imported oil to be carried on United States ships when it focused public attention on the fact that more than 200 House members had received almost half a million dollars in campaign contributions from maritime-related unions in 1976.

The Common Sense Book of Baby and Child Care
See **Spock Generation.**

Communications Satellite Corporation   *See* **Comsat.**

Community Action Programs (CAP)   This controversial aspect of the Economic Opportunity Act of 1964 attempted to pass the initiative for the **War on Poverty** from the federal government to local communities by, in the words of President Lyndon

B. Johnson, making it possible to "strike at poverty at its source." Rather than impose antipoverty programs "on hundreds of different situations," the President stated in his congressional message of March 16, 1964, that people in stricken communities were to be encouraged to come up with long-range plans dealing with local circumstances.

By 1967, there were approximately 1,000 community programs operating as nonprofit corporations and drawing on collective funds from federal agencies, local governments, and private foundations. Operated by boards composed of community members and professional social workers, they set up centers offering a variety of services to the poor.

As the militant temper of the 1960s mounted, critics accused these community-directed programs of stirring up unrest. Responding to pressure, Congress began passing legislation that minimized community control by funding programs on a more-or-less take-it-or-leave-it basis.

The basic features of the Community Action Programs had already surfaced in *A Proposal for Reducing Delinquency by Expanding Opportunities*, published in 1961 by the Mobilization for Youth Project set up under the Kennedy administration to combat juvenile crime. Among the more important theorists of this approach to fighting poverty and its effects were Richard Cloward and Lloyd Ohlin, authors of *Delinquency and Opportunity* (1960). Ohlin is among those often credited with incorporating these concepts into the Economic Opportunity Act.

Community Reinvestment Act (CRA) *See* "Redlining."

Compact of Fifth Avenue Frequently in outspoken disagreement with the Eisenhower administration on matters pertaining to defense, foreign policy, and civil rights, New York's Governor Nelson A. Rockefeller met secretly in his Fifth Avenue apartment with Vice President Richard M. Nixon on July 22–23, 1960, to see if they could work out some compromise that would allow them to agree on the principal aims of the Republican platform in the forthcoming presidential election campaign against Democratic candidate John F. Kennedy. On July 26, Governor Rockefeller withdrew his name from consideration for nomination, and urged the ninety-six-man New York delegation to unanimously endorse Nixon, to whom he pledged his complete support. The Vice President was nominated by acclamation on July 27 at the Republican National Convention in Chicago. The platform adopted that

same day was thought to be the compromise worked out in the Compact of Fifth Avenue, which conservative leader Sen. Barry Goldwater (R.-Ariz.) attacked as a "Munich."

At their Fifth Avenue meeting, the Governor and the Vice President had agreed on a fourteen-point statement of essentials for a Republican platform. It called for "inspiring the formation, in all great regions of the free world, of confederations, large enough and strong enough to meet modern problems and challenges. We should promptly lead toward the formation of such confederations in the North Atlantic Community and in the Western Hemisphere." The Nixon-Rockefeller statement also called on the United States to discontinue all nuclear weapons tests in the atmosphere and to discontinue other tests "as detection methods make possible." It demanded a platform that supported the aims of the **sit-in** demonstrations being held by civil rights militants.

Comprehensive Employment and Training Act (CETA) Signed into law by President Richard M. Nixon on December 20, 1973, the Comprehensive Employment and Training Act (CETA) consolidated manpower programs enacted since 1962—the **Manpower Development and Training Act** and the **Economic Opportunity Act**—and authorized needed funding. Under its provisions, training and employment programs are administered by states and by some 400 units of local government exceeding 100,000 in population. These prime sponsors are eligible for federal grants which may be used for classroom and on-the-job training in occupational skills; supportive services such as necessary medical and child care; and testing, placement, and follow-up services. Programs such as the Neighborhood Youth Corps, the **Job Corps,** and Operation Mainstream are funded from CETA grants. Title II of CETA provides for programs of transitional public-service employment in areas with a 6.5 percent or more unemployment rate for at least three consecutive months. The act authorized special assistance for such hard-hit segments of the labor market as youth, Indians, and seasonal farm workers.

By 1978, CETA-funded programs were plagued by charges of mismanagement and fraud. Nevertheless, funding for fiscal 1979 was budgeted at $11 billion and the number of jobs to be filled was set at 660,000. A four-year extension signed by President Jimmy Carter (November 9, 1978) required that the program be more firmly focused on hardcore unemployed rather than on those displaced by economic slowdowns.

Comsat (Communications Satellite Corporation)
One of the more controversial pieces of legislation passed by the Kennedy administration was the Communications Satellite Bill, which was signed into law on August 31, 1962. It established a private corporation to own and operate a satellite communications system and was fought against by liberals who attacked it as a "giveaway." Opponents felt that Comsat would be dominated by the American Telephone and Telegraph Company and that the latter would be in a position to influence foreign policy because, under the terms of the law, Comsat could negotiate with foreign governments in planning and operating the communications system.

Before the Senate could pass the bill on August 18, 1962, the Kennedy forces had to cut off the threat of a continuing filibuster by invoking cloture—limitation of each Senator's debating time to one hour—for the first time since 1927. In signing the bill, President John F. Kennedy tried to reassure its opponents—many of whom were ordinarily his political allies—that it provided "many safeguards to protect the public interest. No single company or group will have the power to dominate the corporation. The general public, the communications industry and the federal government, all will have a voice. . . ." (Arthur M. Schlesinger, Jr., a member of inner White House circles during this period, later noted that the President's decision was "regretted by some of his associates," and that it was one of a number of ways in which the administration had sought to reassure the business community.)

Acting under United Nations auspices, in 1964 nineteen nations formed the International Telecommunications Satellite Consortium (Intelsat) which developed a practical global system. Within six years there were thirteen communications satellites in orbit. The first of these was *Early Bird 1*, also known as **Intelsat 1**, which was put into space on April 6, 1965 (*see* **Syncom**).

At present, there is high interest in the potential of domestic satellites, the first of which, *Westar 1*, was launched April 13, 1974. The U.S.S.R. began developing its own communications satellite system with the launching of *Molniya I* on April 23, 1965.

Comsymps *See* **John Birch Society.**

"Conceptual Overview" Having determined that gradual withdrawal of U.S. troops from the **Vietnam War** would be a cornerstone of the **Nixon Doctrine** first enunciated at Guam on July 25, 1969,

President Richard M. Nixon dispatched Secretary of Defense Melvin R. Laird on March 6 to discuss the matter with General Creighton Abrams, the U.S. Field Commander in Vietnam. Since neither figures nor timetables were mentioned at this time, on his return to Washington on March 10 Secretary Laird was able to report to the President that General Abrams had given his somewhat grudging approval to the plan.

In the weeks that followed, Laird worked with a Pentagon task force headed by Admiral William Lemos to work out a schedule that would determine the time and order in which American troops would be withdrawn from Vietnam. This timetable, known as the "Conceptual Overview," was kept in a locked cabinet in the President's office.

Concorde Developed by British and French interests at a cost of $3 billion, this supersonic passenger plane operates at a speed of 1,350 mph and is said by critics to have an intolerable noise level. Because of this, it was actively fought against by community groups in this country.

After some hesitation, Secretary of Transportation William T. Coleman authorized (February 1976) both Air France and British Airways to make one flight daily to Washington's Dulles International Airport, and two flights daily to New York's Kennedy International Airport on a sixteen-month trial basis. On March 11, 1976, however, the New York Port Authority banned flights into New York pending a study of experience with the Concorde elsewhere. The British and French reacted indignantly and took to the courts to overturn the ban. Pro-Concorde forces argued that the ban violated treaty obligations and that by flouting Secretary Coleman's decision the Port Authority was interfering with Washington's conduct of foreign affairs.

Many of the arguments used against the Concorde are similar to those that caused the demise of the Boeing **Supersonic Transport** (SST) in 1971. For example, it was also feared that supersonic aircraft would emit vapor in quantities sufficient to cause a "greenhouse" effect that would simultaneously screen off the sun and raise the surface temperature of the earth. But some scientists argued that these dangers had been exaggerated, especially since it appeared likely that less than twenty Concordes in all would be produced. Similarly, it was pointed out that the potential destruction of the ozone layer by the nitrogen oxides released in flight is minimal, and is in no way comparable with the effects produced by the supersonic warplanes of the nations of the world.

On May 11, 1977, a federal district court ruled that the Port Authority ban on Concorde landings was in "irreconcilable conflict" with federal prerogatives; an extended legal battle of appeals got underway. The Port Authority extended its ban indefinitely on July 7, 1977, and the court battle continued to rage. On September 29, 1977, the United States Court of Appeals for the Second Circuit upheld a lower court which found the Port Authority ban unreasonable and discriminatory. Plans were made for immediate Concorde landings, and local residents of the Kennedy airport vicinity staged demonstrations in which traffic to and from the airport was blocked. By this time the case was being considered by the U.S. Supreme Court, and on October 7, 1977, Associate Justice Thurgood Marshall reimposed the landing ban until the Court had had time to rule. On October 17, 1977, the Court handed down a procedural decision rejecting a Port Authority request that the Concorde ban remain in effect until a final Supreme Court decision on the overall merits of the Concorde case before it: "The application for a stay presented to Mr. Justice Marshall and by him referred to the Court, is denied."

Regular service began on November 22, 1977.

Conelrad *See* **Emergency Broadcast System.**

Conference on Security and Cooperation in Europe (CSCE) *See* **Helsinki Accord.**

Congressional Black Caucus The origins of this discussion and planning group go back to February 1970 when nine black congressmen requested and were refused a personal meeting with President Richard M. Nixon. By January 1971, the group had increased to thirteen, including Sen. Edward W. Brooke (R.-Mass.), the only black member of the Senate. When, therefore, President Nixon again refused to meet with them, they organized more formally into the Congressional Black Caucus and made Charles C. Diggs (D.-Mich.) the chairman. The White House was informed that all members of the Caucus would boycott the President's State of the Union Message on January 22 and would also refuse to attend the traditional White House breakfast for Congress.

Faced with this new situation, President Nixon reconsidered and met with the Caucus on March 25. He was at that time presented with a list of some sixty black demands, and he appointed a special White House panel to deal with them.

In 1971, with the money obtained from a $100-a-plate fund-raising dinner, the Caucus set up a permanent staff.

Members of the Caucus are particularly active in the House District Committee, which is responsible for the laws and budget for the heavily black District of Columbia.

All twelve black Representatives were included on the master list of political enemies compiled by White House staffers during the Nixon administration.

Congress of Racial Equality (CORE) An offshoot of A. J. Muste's Christian-pacifist Fellowship of Reconciliation (FOR), the Congress of Racial Equality (CORE) was founded at the University of Chicago in June 1942 by an interracial group of six students led by James Farmer. Originally known as the Committee of Racial Equality, it was dedicated to applying the Gandhian principles of nonviolent direct action to the resolution of problems caused by racial and industrial conflict. Early black leaders included Joe Guinn and James R. Robinson—to whom was soon added Bayard Rustin. Among the white founders were George Houser, Homer Jack, and Bernice Fisher, who later noted: "One of our motivations had been the determination that there should be a thoroughly interracial organization . . . not another Negro group with a token membership of whites."

Although it invented the **"sit-in"** in May 1943 at a small restaurant known as Jack Spratt's, CORE did not capture national attention for its civil rights struggle until, under the leadership of Farmer, it challenged segregation in interstate bus terminals by launching the "freedom rides" of May 1961 (see **Freedom Riders**). CORE was afterward to play a major role in the civil rights protests of the 1960s; but with the rise of new leaders such as Floyd McKissick—who succeeded Farmer as national director in 1966—and Roy Innis, its emphasis began shifting away from integration and toward black nationalism as the efficacy of nonviolence came under attack by militants. Justifying "revolution" as a constitutional right, McKissick noted in 1967 that "many good things have occurred for blacks as a result of violence." He charged that **Black Power** was being purposely "misinterpreted to mean violence and fascism," noting that "Black Power is not Black supremacy; it is a unified Black Voice reflecting racial pride in the tradition of our heterogeneous nation."

In the fall of 1968, Innis became national director of CORE, which he said had become "once and for all . . . a Black Nationalist Organization" whose goal was "separation." "When we have control of our own self-destiny, then we can talk about integration" for those who wanted it, he noted.

Cut off from white financial support and alienated from the vast majority of American blacks who did not accept separatism as a goal, the influence and membership of CORE declined in the 1970s—as did rhetoric and confrontation in general. By the middle of the decade, however, CORE was still claiming a membership of 70,000, with chapters in thirty-three states. The organization maintains national headquarters in New York City.

In November 1978 James Farmer and other CORE dissidents requested an audit of the organization's books and asked that the office of national director and national chairman be declared vacant because of Innis's failure to abide by the organization's constitution. In expectation that CORE would be dissolved by the New York courts, on March 4, 1979, Farmer and other former CORE members met and announced that they would soon create a new, racially mixed civil rights organization.

Conlon Report A study commissioned by the Senate Foreign Relations Committee from Conlon Associates, Ltd., a private San Francisco research group. Released on October 31, 1959, it urged a "de facto recognition" of Communist China, toward which it recommended a policy of "exploration and negotiation" rather than a continuation of efforts at "**containment** through isolation."

The *Conlon Report* was the basis for the **"two-Chinas policy,"** which urged the seating of Red China at the United Nations along with Nationalist China. The so-called China Lobby's **Committee of One Million** Against the Admission of Communist China to the United Nations was credited by Roger Hilsman, head of Intelligence in the State Department and then Assistant Secretary of State for the Far East during the Kennedy administration, with having "helped nullify" the effects of this report by working in the 1960 election for the defeat of candidates who openly supported the admission of Red China. The "two-Chinas policy" was to emerge again during the 1971 era of **"ping-pong diplomacy,"** but was defeated when the UN General Assembly rejected an American resolution calling for the seating of Red China on the Security Council and the retention of the Taiwan delegation in the General Assembly. Instead, it overwhelmingly accepted an Albanian resolution calling for the expulsion of the Nationalists.

The *Conlon Report* also urged that American in-

terests in Asia could best be served by increased economic aid to India and Pakistan, support for Japanese and Indian membership on the UN Security Council, and the eventual return of Okinawa to Japan. At the time it was issued, Sen. J. W. Fulbright (D.-Ark.) called it "very provocative," saying that while he was not then in favor of recognition for Red China, he did not believe it was "wise to continue to ignore the over 600 million people on the China mainland in the naive belief that they will somehow go away."

Diplomatic relations between China and the United States were not resumed until January 1, 1979, almost twenty years after the *Conlon Report.*

The Conscience of a Conservative This short political and economic credo by Sen. Barry Goldwater (R.-Ariz.) was a 1960 bestseller. Among the programs advocated by the acknowledged leader of American conservatives was the abolition of the graduated income tax, the prohibition of union engagement "in any kind of political activity," the removal of the federal government from "a whole series of programs that are outside its constitutional mandate—from social welfare programs, education, public power, agriculture, public housing, urban renewal . . . ," preparation for "military operations against vulnerable Communist regimes," and the termination of all farm subsidy programs.

Senator Goldwater's 1964 bid for the presidency on the Republican ticket was defeated by the incumbent, President Lyndon B. Johnson, who carried forty-four states and the District of Columbia, piling up 486 out of 538 electoral votes. The Senator's critics within his own party referred to his backers as "Stone Age Republicans." To emphasize the extreme conservatism of his views, Democrats had sardonically gibed "Goldwater in 1864."

Consensus On assuming office following the assassination of President John F. Kennedy on **November 22, 1963,** President Lyndon B. Johnson saw his primary task as building "a consensus throughout the country, so that we could stop bickering and quarreling and get on with the job at hand."

To the new President's critics the word "consensus" came to be variously interpreted as an effort to find programs whose chief virtue lay in the fact that they were acceptable to the majority, or to bully others into accepting and sharing responsibility for previously determined steps. The President, however, said that consensus meant "first, deciding what needed to be done regardless of the political implications and, second, convincing a majority of the

Congress and the American people of the necessity for doing those things." He believed that the strategy of consensus, which remained a determining principle throughout his term in office, was foreshadowed in a meeting he had with the governors of forty states three days after assuming office. The times, he told them, "demanded that we put away our differences and close ranks in a determined effort to make our system of government function."

In his first month in office, President Johnson made a determined effort "to secure the cooperation of the people who were the natural leaders of the nation" by regular talks with representatives of both political parties. In addition, he called in industrial executives, union leaders, journalists, and government bureaucrats and "I asked them to help me persuade Congress" to pass legislation relating to tax reduction, civil rights, **Medicare,** and minimum wages. "I brought people together who under ordinary circumstances would have fled at the sight of each other." Building consensus, the President argued, was using what Theodore Roosevelt had called the "bully pulpit" of the Presidency to end the divisiveness that had led the nation to the tragedy in Dallas.

There seems little doubt, as was often charged, that the man who as Senate majority leader had won a reputation for legislative arm-twisting did as much bullying as persuading in his effort to win consensus. His favorite Bible quotation was **"Come now, and let us reason together, saith the Lord"** (Isaiah 1:18), but President Johnson admitted that he had no objection to "showing a little garter" in the process.

Consumerism Denotes the contemporary consumer movement which was largely inspired by Ralph Nader's bestselling *Unsafe at Any Speed* (1965), in which the automotive industry was accused of having failed to provide the public with a "safe, nonpolluting and efficient automobile that can be produced economically." In the decade that followed, millions of defective automobiles were routinely recalled; and flourishing consumer groups of various kinds brought pressure on Congress to produce legislation such as the Traffic Safety Act (1966), which established production safety standards included in all automobiles after 1968; the **Fair Packaging and Labeling Act** (1966), covering thousands of food, drug, and cosmetic products; the **Truth-in-Lending Act** (1968), which standardized procedures by which banks and credit-card companies stated their interest charges; and the Consumer Product Safety Act (1972), which created the **Consumer Product Safety Commission.**

Grass-roots consumer-protection groups began springing up everywhere, and in 1968 the Consumer Federation of America was established in Washington, D.C., as an umbrella organization, which by 1978 was representing some 30 million consumers in 225 groups. Nevertheless, consumerism seems to be losing its initial drive, as evidenced by the fact that in February 1978 Congress defeated a bill sponsored by the Carter administration for centralizing the consumer offices scattered throughout the federal government in a new agency that would have been empowered to sue other federal agencies for failing to act in the consumer interest. Business groups lobbying against the legislation had argued that it would produce a massive bureaucracy with unprecedented and unchecked authority to intervene in the private sector.

The failure to obtain what they saw as necessary centralizing legislation was ascribed by consumer leaders to public apathy over what seemed an abstract issue. Rep. Benjamin S. Rosenthal (D.-N.Y.), chairman of the House Consumer Subcommittee, noted that the "consumer movement needs another scandal," and suggested that it would take a botulism panic or a threat such as that posed by thalidomide in the early 1960s to mobilize consumers in their own interests. The Consumer Federation of America, however, urged a return to grass-roots organizing in support of political candidates with known proconsumer views.

Consumer Product Safety Commission Created by the Consumer Product Safety Act of 1972, the Consumer Product Safety Commission was designed to prevent the some 30,000 annual deaths and 20 million injuries ascribed to unsafe products. It has the power to anticipate potential trouble by setting product safety standards which manufacturers would be required to meet, and it was also authorized to inform the public about product safety.

By 1978, such early enthusiasts as consumer advocate Ralph Nader were complaining that what had been meant as a "watchdog" commission had become a bureaucracy entangled in red tape and more responsive to industry pressure than consumer needs. Rep. John E. Moss (D.-Calif.), one of the chief architects of the five-person commission, complained that in the five years since its creation safety standards had been set only for swimming pool slides, architectural glazing, and matchbooks.

See **Consumerism.**

Containment President Harry S Truman's conviction that agreements with the U.S.S.R. had been a "one-way street" rapidly altered postwar relations between the Soviet Union and the United States (see **Truman Doctrine**). The basis for the developing "containment" policy which was this country's response to Soviet aggression and failure to keep promises made at Yalta and **Potsdam** can be found in an anonymous article, "The Sources of Soviet Conduct," which appeared in the influential journal *Foreign Affairs* in July 1947. It soon became generally known that the author was none other than our Moscow chargé d'affaires, George F. Kennan. The article itself was an outgrowth of a five-part cable Kennan sent the State Department on February 22, 1947. It was this cable that no doubt later led Secretary of State George Marshall to appoint Kennan to the department's recently established Policy Planning Staff.

In replying to questions put to him earlier in the month, Kennan's cable analyzed (1) the basic features of postwar Soviet outlook; (2) the background for this position; (3) its "projection" in practical U.S.S.R. policy on an official level; (4) its projection on an unofficial level; and (5) "practical deductions from standpoint of U.S. policy."

In the final section of his cable, Kennan warned:

In summary, we have here a political force committed fanatically to the belief that with U.S. there can be no permanent modus vivendi, that it is desirable and necessary that the internal harmony of our society be disrupted, our traditional way of life be destroyed, the international authority of our state be broken, if Soviet power is to be secure.

Kennan's analysis convinced him that, although the U.S.S.R. was

. . . impervious to logic of reason . . . it is highly sensitive to logic of force. For this reason it can easily withdraw—and usually does—when strong resistance is encountered at any point. Thus, if the adversary has sufficient force and makes clear his readiness to use it, he rarely has to do so.

His concluding recommendations were (1) to recognize unemotionally "the nature of the movement with which we are dealing"; (2) to educate the American public to the realities of the Russian situation by objective information rather than "hysterical anti-Sovietism"; (3) to solve the internal problems of our own society; (4) to "formulate and put forward for other nations a much more positive and constructive picture of sort of world we would like to see than we have put forward in past"; (5) to "have the courage and self-confidence to cling to our own methods and conceptions of human society. After all, the greatest danger that can befall us in coping with this problem of Soviet Communism,

is that we shall allow ourselves to become like those with whom we are coping."

James F. Byrnes was still Secretary of State when this cable was received, and he responded to Republican charges of "appeasement" with a speech on February 28, 1947, that announced a new hard line: "We must make it clear in advance that we do intend to act to prevent aggression, making it clear at the same time . . . we will not use force for any other purpose. . . ."

During the 1952 Presidential campaign, the Republican platform's foreign policy plank, prepared by John Foster Dulles, attacked "containment" as an inadequate response, and, as candidate for the presidency, Dwight D. Eisenhower said:

We can never rest—and we must so inform all the world, including the Kremlin—that until the enslaved nations of the world have in the fullness of freedom the right to choose their own path, that then, and then only, can we say that there is a possible way of living peacefully and permanently with communism in the world.

Democratic presidential nominee Adlai Stevenson attacked the Republican promise of "liberation" as arousing false hopes in the enslaved peoples and endangering the peace. The grip of Soviet tyranny, he argued

. . . cannot be loosened by starting a war which would lead to untold suffering for innocent people everywhere; such a course could liberate only broken, silent, and empty lands. . . . Action for action's sake is the last resort of mentally and morally exhausted men. The free nations . . . must always be ready to sit down at the conference table, insisting only that any agreement must conform to the spirit of our great wartime pledges and the Charter of the United Nations.

"Cool jazz" The term was said to have been coined by black musician Lester Young to describe the development in the 1950s of be-bop, the new jazz that had come into prominence during World War II. Sometimes called "progressive jazz," it retained the harmony, melody, and rhythm techniques of be-bop, but timbres became softer, vibratos slower, and the general effect was more relaxed. Among its chief exponents were Gerry Mulligan, Lennie Tristano, Stan Getz, and Miles Davis, whose album *Birth of the Cool* helped popularize the new style. Dave Brubeck and John Lewis gave cool jazz an intellectual appeal by blending it with elements of classical music.

Cooper-Church Amendment Following the end of the **Cambodian "Incursion"** undertaken by President Richard M. Nixon during the **Vietnam War,**

the Senate voted, on June 30, 1970, the first restrictions ever passed on the wartime powers of the President as Commander in Chief. The amendment proposed by Sens. Frank Church (D.-Idaho) and John Sherman Cooper (R.-Ky.) was attached to a foreign military sales bill. It declared that "in concert" with the President's declared objectives to avoid involvement of the United States in Cambodia after July 1, 1970, and to expedite the withdrawal of our forces from that country

. . . it is hereby provided that unless specifically authorized by law hereafter enacted, no funds authorized or appropriated pursuant to this act or any other law may be expended after July 1, 1970, for the purposes of—

1. Retaining United States forces in Cambodia;
2. Paying the compensation or allowance of, or otherwise supporting, directly or indirectly, any United States personnel in Cambodia who furnish military instruction to Cambodian forces or engage in any combat activity in support of Cambodian forces;
3. Entering into or carrying out any contract or agreement to provide military instruction in Cambodia, or to provide persons to engage in any combat activity in support of Cambodian forces; or
4. Conducting any combat activity in the air above Cambodia in direct support of Cambodian forces.

The amendment was eventually eliminated from the Military Sales Act, but a revised version was part of a foreign aid authorization bill that became law on January 5, 1971.

Cooper v. Aaron The failure of President Dwight D. Eisenhower to place the prestige and moral authority of his office squarely behind school authorities attempting to carry out the Supreme Court's racial desegregation decision in **Brown v. Board of Education of Topeka** (1954) is seen by many critics as having encouraged Southern segregationists to find some "legal" means of circumventing the law. Following the disorders in **Little Rock** when Negro students were admitted to Central High School, on February 20, 1958, the School Board and the Superintendent of Schools filed a petition in district court seeking postponement of their desegregation program in view of extreme public hostility to this move. The board's petition stated that actions by Arkansas's Governor Orval E. Faubus had hardened the core of opposition to the desegregation plan.

The district court granted the relief requested in view of the fact that during the past year Central High School had been marked by conditions of "chaos, bedlam, and turmoil" and that there had been "repeated incidents of more or less serious violence directed against the Negro students and their property." The Negro respondents appealed the district court judgment of June 20, 1958, to the U.S. Court of Appeals for the Eighth Circuit, which on August 18, 1958, reversed the district court. The case then went to the U.S. Supreme Court, which on September 29, 1958, in *Cooper v. Aaron*, upheld the court of appeals, unanimously voiding the two-and-a-half-year suspension order as a violation of the constitutional rights of Negro children. The decision, which firmly announced that there would be no turning back on segregation, noted that "the record before us clearly established that the growth of the Board's difficulties to a magnitude beyond its unaided power to control is the product of state action. These difficulties, as the counsel for the Board forthrightly conceded on the oral argument of this Court, can also be brought under control by state action." Segregation, it found, cannot be continued by "evasive schemes" which attempt to nullify Court decisions.

Cooper was a member of the Little Rock School Board; Aaron was one of the nine black students seeking to be admitted to Central High School.

Coplon Case On March 4, 1949, Judith Coplon, a political analyst in the Justice Department's internal security section, was arrested in New York as she tried to pass to Valentin A. Gubitchev, a Soviet engineer, FBI data and "secret" documents planted with her by government agents. Later that year she was found guilty in Washington of stealing FBI papers and sentenced to from forty months to ten years. In a second trial, on March 9, 1950, she was found guilty of conspiracy to commit espionage and to remove classified documents from government files and pass them to a Russian agent.

An honors graduate of Barnard College in New York City, Miss Coplon had received clearance to handle data on communist espionage in this country. When, however, it was learned that she had been seen with Gubitchev, she was, without her being aware of it, denied access to real material and given FBI-manufactured documents. It was this material, as well as FBI data slips and an explanation of why she had been unable to obtain a desired espionage report, that was found in her purse when she and Gubitchev were arrested.

She claimed to have been in love with the Soviet agent (later deported) and that their furtive meetings were lovers' rendezvous, but the government presented evidence to show that during this same period she had had assignations with another man in hotels and at his apartment.

Although it said that her "guilt is plain," on December 5, 1950, the U.S. Court of Appeals in New York reversed her conviction as a spy on the grounds that since she had been arrested without a warrant the manufactured FBI documents should not have been used at her trial. The court also held that the government had failed to prove that evidence used against her had not been obtained through illegal wire tapping. It also found that the trial judge had been wrong in withholding from the defense certain government documents.

Some of the documents placed in evidence by Attorney General Tom C. Clark proved an embarrassment to the government, as they revealed the names of FBI informants. FBI Director J. Edgar Hoover claimed that his first knowledge that these reports had been produced in evidence was after they had already been presented in court.

Miss Coplon's previous conviction for stealing FBI papers was upheld in 1951, but she was freed on bail pending a hearing on her contention that her phone conversations with her attorney had been tapped. It was not until January 6, 1967, that the Justice Department dropped the espionage charges against her.

CORE *See* **Congress of Racial Equality.**

Corporation for Public Broadcasting (CPB) *See* **Public Broadcasting Act of 1967.**

Cosa Nostra In 1950-1952 the televised hearings of the Senate Special Committee to Investigate Interstate Crime, headed by Sen. Estes Kefauver (D.-Tenn.) focused national attention on racketeering in the United States. These rackets were said to be under the control of the Mafia, a loose association of secret criminal organizations with origins in nineteenth-century Sicily. The Mafia—also known as the Black Hand and the Camorra—again captured the headlines when on November 14, 1957, sixty-three men suspected by the FBI of being racketeers were apprehended by police at a "conference" held in the home of a suspected bootlegger in Apalachin, New York (see **Apalachin Conference**).

Fuller details on the organization of the Mafia in this country were revealed in 1963 when Joseph Valachi, an intimate of underworld figures such as Vito Genovese and Thomas Lucchese, testified before a Senate investigating committee and in televised hearings revealed just how the supposed illegal network functioned. He said that members referred to the combine or "syndicate" as the Cosa Nostra. He claimed that it consisted of independent "families" of Italian origin led by a Capo, or boss, aided by lieutenants who commanded "soldiers." Valachi—whose status with the mob was never confirmed—himself jailed earlier in the year on narcotics charges, told authorities that Cosa Nostra controlled narcotics peddling, illegal gambling, and usurious moneylending—often with the connivance of police and politicians. He also claimed that in recent years its activities had spread into a number of legitimate businesses.

A complete account of Valachi's testimony and the background to it was given in a 1969 bestseller by Peter Maas entitled *The Valachi Papers*.

See **Kefauver Committee.**

Cosmos 954 Launched in September 1977, this Soviet espionage satellite carried ocean-scanning radar and radio circuitry powered by a nuclear reactor including more than 100 pounds of enriched uranium 235. In mid-December, the spy-in-the-sky began to dip from its 150-mile-high orbit and draw closer to the earth with every revolution. To avoid tragedy, the Soviet authorities sent it a radio command which should have caused it to separate into three sections and propelled the nuclear core into an orbit approximately 800 miles high. The Cosmos 954 failed to respond.

As the deadly satellite approached earth, the North American Air Defense Command (NORAD) estimated that the probable reentry point was North America. A diplomatic exchange was opened between American and Soviet authorities, who provided assurances that the uranium carried by Cosmos 954 could not reach critical mass and explode either upon reentry or impact.

The satellite reentered earth's atmosphere on January 24, 1978, near Canada's Great Slave Lake, some 1,000 miles north of the United States border. Two days later, a joint U.S.-Canadian "sniffer" plane reported "an extremely dangerous" radiation level in the area, and on January 28 radioactive debris was reported as having been located. Fragments were recovered on February 3 by teams of Canadian and United States scientists. Soviet offers of help in these operations were rejected, presumably to give Western technicians the opportunity to make the most of a bad situation by taking the opportunity to measure the progress of Russian space engineering.

Council of Economic Advisers *See* **Employment Act of 1946.**

Council of Federated Organizations (COFO) COFO—sometimes CFO—was formed in February 1960 when Mississippi blacks belonging to various professional groups and organizations such as the Elks and Masons met in Clarksdale at the suggestion of Aaron Henry, state president of the NAACP, to formulate strategy for the civil rights struggle. The group requested and was granted a meeting with Governor Ross Barnett to discuss such problems as voter registration, education, unemployment, and welfare in the Mississippi black community. At the end of the meeting, the governor rejected all of their demands and suggestions.

COFO's next meeting did not take place until more than a year later when in the summer of 1961 representatives of the **Student Nonviolent Coordinating Committee** (SNCC), the **Southern Christian Leadership Conference** (SCLC), the **Congress of Racial Equality** (CORE), and Medgar Evers of the NAACP agreed to adopt it as an umbrella organization in which to coordinate the activities of all Mississippi civil rights groups.

Counterattack *See Red Channels.*

Counterculture The term surfaced in the late 1960s and to a large extent reflected the **"generation gap"** which had brought about an ideological struggle between the ripening products of the post-World War II **"baby boom"** and their elders. All-inclusive, it embraced everything from superficial differences in clothing and hair styles to basic revolutions in social thinking, sexual mores, and political conduct. In terms of Charles Reich's popular *The Greening of America* (1970), it represented a switch from the suppressed individuality of Consciousness II, in which change was channeled through established institutions, to the "childlike" Consciousness III, in which emphasis was on personal commitment and development.

The origins of the counterculture are to be found in the **Beat Generation** of the 1950s—in their rejection of increasing American conformity, their interest in drugs, Eastern mysticism, and self-exploration. It found artistic expression in the 1967 musical *Hair,* in the movie *The Graduate* (1967), and in the Woodstock Festival (1969), which saw the ultimate attempt to prove to a nation sunk in the horrors and divisions caused by the **Vietnam War** that love and cooperation were possible—at least on a short-term basis.

In politics the counterculture was represented by all that is generally included in the **New Left,** from the idealism of the **Port Huron Statement** through the tumult of the **Free Speech Movement** to the final anarchy of the **Weathermen.** Its intellectual heroes were the philosopher Herbert Marcuse (see **Marcusean Revolution**), sociologist C. Wright Mills (see *The Power Elite*), and social critic Paul Goodman, who in works such as *Growing Up Absurd* (1960), *Drawing the Line* (1962), and *Compulsory Miseducation* (1962) suggested means by which "the system" they saw as repressive and stultifying could be attacked. In the pantheon of its honored dead were the black political theorist Frantz Fanon and the Cuban revolutionary leader Che Guevara, a poster portrait of whom assumed the status of a totem in many a "pad" or dormitory room. Poet, clown, and resident guru of the counterculture was Allen Ginsberg, the gentle, nonviolent "beatnik."

As the decade wore on, the "hipster," described by novelist Norman Mailer in his influential essay "The White Negro," replaced the "beatnik" as a role model, and the revolt against the institutions of modern American life assumed an increasingly virulent tone. "Make love, not war" was a cherished slogan of the counterculture which found a focus in the protest against the continuing Vietnam War. A "Festival of Life" planned by **Yippie** leaders Jerry Rubin and Abbie Hoffman for the 1968 Democratic National Convention turned into the **Battle of Chicago** due to an almost inevitable clash with Mayor Richard Daley's police force. (For other "historic" moments in the counterculture, see the **Siege of Morningside Heights** and the **Battle of Berkeley**.)

The counterculture was largely inhabited by the children of the affluent middle class. In their revolt against the conformity of their parents' lives, they quickly developed a conformity of their own. Imitation of the clothing styles of the less advantaged economic groups—who paradoxically were often their bitterest critics—became all but obligatory, with the exception that the jeans they favored were often prefaded and prepatched. Eventually, it was no longer enough to "Do your own thing," and the counterculture became increasingly intolerant of other life-styles.

Although it was a revolt against American affluence and technology, the counterculture was dependent on both. Ironically, it was absorbed by the commercial culture it claimed to loathe but which quickly began catering to its own styles of consumption—often more avid than those of their elders, who still had lingering memories of the prewar Depression.

With the end of the Vietnam War and the beginning of the recessions and unemployment that marked the early 1970s, the counterculture began to fade. The children of the middle class docilely returned to their ranks in suburbia, and the counterculture left behind it more relaxed styles in many areas of American life.

Countercyclical Economics In the first Eisenhower administration, the Council of Economic Advisers was headed by Dr. Arthur F. Burns, an economics professor from Columbia University, whose conservative views on the necessity for a balanced budget matched those of the President. In an economy such as ours, Dr. Burns advised, neither the threat of inflation nor of recession can ever be very distant. Upswings and downswings in the nation's economy were cycles that he proposed be handled by measures he explained as "countercyclical."

According to Special Presidential Assistant Sherman Adams, the expression came to be used in White House discussions with increasing frequency. Although intent on keeping the government from interfering with free enterprise, President Dwight D. Eisenhower was ready, if necessary, to take "extraordinary" steps to keep the "recessions" that marked his administration from turning into full-blown depressions. However, he would emphasize that he was not abandoning his basic creed that the best way to combat depression was to spur individuals to greater and freer economic activity.

Asked to advise on government measures that could brake the economic slowdown of 1953, Dr. Burns suggested that the Federal Reserve Board might make credit more abundant and cheaper; that the IRS could start sending out refund checks to taxpayers faster; and that the White House could consult with states on the acceleration of public works.

The expression has found its way into the vocabulary even of those not especially receptive to Dr. Burns's economic theories. For example, in discussing the financial crisis of New York City in December 1976, *The New York Times* said of the possibility of federal aid: "Since immediate direct relief is out of the question, what would be most helpful right now is a psychological boost—a strong commitment from the President and leaders of Congress to move quickly on programs of urban relief, such as stepped-up 'countercyclical' aid. . . ."

Counterinsurgency Program In the final days of the Eisenhower administration, Brigadier General Edward Lansdale, a man experienced in the techniques of guerrilla warfare since the early 1950s when he had helped Ramón Magsaysay defeat the Huk rebellion in the Philippines, returned from an inspection tour of Vietnam. His report was highly critical both of the leadership of Ngo Dinh Diem—whom in earlier days he had helped sponsor—and of the American military presence there. "Our U.S. Team in Vietnam should have a hard core of experienced Americans who know and really like Asians, dedicated people who are willing to risk their lives for the ideals of freedom, and who will try to influence and guide the Vietnamese towards U.S. policy objectives with the warm friendship and affection which our close alliance deserves."

Through the offices of Walt W. Rostow, a deputy for National Security Affairs, this report found its way to President John F. Kennedy, who was said to have been greatly impressed. He asked Rostow to find out what the U.S. Army was doing about counterguerrilla or counterinsurgency training and was informed that the Special Forces (SF) established at Fort Bragg, North Carolina, in 1952 was limited to less than a thousand men. Orders were given for the immediate expansion of this program, which had previously been limited to training cadres for behind-the-lines commando action in case of a third world war. The new emphasis was oriented toward guerrilla warfare in the jungles and mountains of underdeveloped countries. The President insisted that the SF be instructed in the economic and political problems of the area as well as in sanitation, teaching, medical care, etc. "I do not think," said Arthur Schlesinger, Jr., in *A Thousand Days* (1965) "that he ever forgot Mao's warning that guerrilla action must fail 'if its political objectives do not coincide with the aspirations of the people and their sympathy, cooperation and assistance cannot be gained.' "

A counterinsurgency plan for Vietnam was approved by President Kennedy early in 1961. The report containing it proposed a number of extensive military and social reforms and advised that if these were carried out, the war would be over in eighteen months (see **Vietnam War**). In May 1961 an SF mission of 400 men was sent to Vietnam.

Meanwhile, the President's enthusiasm for counterinsurgency was well publicized. He himself was said to be reading the works of Mao Tse-tung, Che Guevara, Lin Piao, etc., and urging all in the government and military to do the same. In October 1961, the White House press corps visited Fort Bragg to watch demonstrations by the SF, who at the insistence of the President were once more allowed to wear the distinctive green berets that had been forbidden after 1956 (*see* **Green Berets**).

In October 1961, Lansdale accompanied Rostow and General Maxwell Taylor to Vietnam on a visit designed to determine how this country might further assist the forces of General Diem (*see* **Taylor-Rostov Mission**). Among the recommendations contained in the report made on their return was one that American support be shifted from advice to limited partnership by furnishing the material and technical aid for a counterinsurgency program. The President, however, took no action on a recommendation that up to 10,000 regular combat troops be sent to Vietnam. Nevertheless, by the time of his assassination (*see* **November 22, 1963**), there were upward of 16,000 Americans in Vietnam and the Military Assistance Advisory Group (MAAG) had become the Military Assistance Command, Vietnam (MACV).

Under the Johnson administration, the limits imposed by counterinsurgency combat gave way to full-scale involvement in the Vietnam War, rising to a maximum of 536,100 troops by the end of 1968.

Cox Commission Following the disturbances at New York's Columbia University (see **Siege of Morningside Heights**) in April 1968, Harvard Law School professor Archibald Cox was appointed on May 5, 1968, to head a five-man commission to look into the causes and handling of the protests which had led to the injury of some 150 students when police were called in by university officials.

On October 5, 1968, following testimony by seventy-nine students, faculty members, administrators, trustees, and community leaders during twenty-one days of hearings, the Cox Commission issued a more than 200-page report entitled *Crisis at Columbia*. Strongly critical of "disruptive tactics" used by student militants, it nevertheless found that the essential causes of the disturbances lay in general student dissatisfaction with a university resistance to change that "too often conveyed an attitude of authoritarianism and invited distrust". Although the spark that ignited the student riots was Columbia's insistence on building a $10 million gym on public parkland leased from the city, the commission faulted Columbia for its general failure to maintain adequate relations and communication with the surrounding black community in Harlem. Recognizing instances of student provocation, the report nevertheless accused the police of "excessive violence" in the performance of its duty. It noted that student behavior was for the most part a consequence of "the brutality of the police."

Criticizing the direct action techniques of student militants, the report appealed to "liberal and reform minded students" to reject disruptive demonstrations and participate in a democratic process by which they "will surely acquire a more sophisticated understanding of the universities' difficulties and complexities and the necessary functions of the faculty and administration, the alumni, and the governing body."

Members of the commission in addition to Cox were: Anthony G. Amsterdam, University of Pennsylvania; Simon H. Rifkind, lawyer; Dana L. Farnsworth, Harvard University; and Hylan G. Lewis, Brooklyn College.

Professor Cox was later to play a leading role in investigations of the cover-up attempts following the Watergate break-in in 1972 (*see* **Watergate Scandal; Saturday Night Massacre**).

CPB *See* **Public Broadcasting Act of 1967.**

CRA *See* **Community Reinvestment Act.**

"Credibility gap" During the administration of President Lyndon B. Johnson, the number of U.S. troops committed in the **Vietnam War** rose dramatically from 16,300 in 1963 to a high of 536,100 by the end of 1968. Although in 1964 he had seemed a "peace candidate" in contrast to Republican Sen. Barry Goldwater (Ariz.), President Johnson had told Henry Cabot Lodge, U.S. Ambassador to South Vietnam: "I am not going to lose Vietnam. I am not going to be the President who saw Southeast Asia go the way China went."

Critics of the war were soon charging that to further his policy the President was not above manipulating and even misinforming the American public. For example, *I.F. Stone's Weekly* (August 24, 1964) noted that the attacks on the U.S.S. *Maddox* and U.S.S. *C. Turner Joy*, which led to the passage of the **Gulf of Tonkin Resolution** on August 7, 1964, were explained in differing versions. One handed out for home consumption, said Stone, explained that in response the United States had "manfully hit back at an unprovoked attack—no paper tiger we. On the other hand, friendly foreign diplomats were told that the South Vietnamese had pulled a raid on the coast and we had been forced to back them up. . . . That our warships may have been providing cover for an escalation in raiding activities never got through to public consciousness at all."

Increasing public suspicion of official optimism and versions of events in the war was reported on in the *New York Herald Tribune* on May 23, 1965, in a story by White House correspondent David Wise headlined "Credibility Gap" in an obvious echo of the 1958 **"missile gap"** controversy. The following June, 23,000 American troops sent to Vietnam as "advisors" were committed in combat in a "search and destroy" operation against Vietnam bands in the area of Dong Xoai, some sixty miles from Saigon. As casualties and troop commitments continued to rise during a year that saw 160,000 additional American combat troops disembark in Vietnam, newsmen recalled President Johnson's 1964 campaign promises of peace. Analyzing the contrast between the President's promises and his actual concrete steps, the *Washington Post* noted on December 5, 1965, that the "problem could be called a credibility gap," and reported "growing doubt and cynicism concerning administration pronouncements. . . ." These doubts were to become open charges of misrepresentation, especially after the communists launched their surprise **Tet Offensive** in January 1968.

In *Lyndon Johnson and the American Dream* (1976), Doris Kearns argues that a leader's authority comes from the public's willingness to suspend its own judgment and accept its leader's because of their trust in him. "By 1968 Johnson had lost this trust."

The phrase "credibility gap" was revived in the course of events following the break-in of Democratic National Headquarters at the Watergate complex in Washington in June 1972. For many Americans, especially after the **Saturday Night Massacre** of 1973, when President Richard M. Nixon fired the Watergate Special Prosecutor Archibald Cox and forced the resignations of both the Attorney General Elliot L. Richardson and Deputy Attorney General William D. Ruckelshaus, the President's public statements about the **Watergate Scandal** had created a "credibility gap."

CREEP *See* **Committee to Re-elect the President.**

"Creeping socialism" Speaking in South Dakota six months after he had assumed office in 1953, President Dwight D. Eisenhower stressed that his new administration had "instituted what amounts to a revolution in the Federal Government as we have known it in our time, trying to make it smaller rather than bigger and finding things it can stop doing instead of seeking new things for it to do." He emphasized that this was an important task because "in the last twenty years creeping socialism has been striking in the United States." At a press conference several days later, he cited the Tennessee Valley Authority (TVA) as an example of what

he had meant by "creeping socialism" (see **Dixon-Yates**).

The phrase was not original with the President and had often been used by Republicans to protest against what they felt was the tendency of government under Presidents Franklin D. Roosevelt and Harry S Truman to "undermine" private enterprise by assuming increased responsibility for the control of the economy and the protection of individual welfare. Such measures were sometimes seen as tending to create a "welfare state" similar to that established in Great Britain following World War II. To archconservatives, even President Eisenhower's mild social measures were suspect. The *Chicago Tribune* denounced his January 1955 State of the Union message—in which he had recommended that Congress raise the minimum wage to ninety cents an hour and extend the coverage of the minimum-wage law to the lowest-paid employees, most of whom were unorganized—as an example of "welfare statism and a tender if meddlesome solicitude for every fancied want of a once self-reliant citizenry. . . ."

Crisis at Columbia *See* **Cox Commission; Siege of Morningside Heights.**

CRP *See* **Committee to Re-elect the President.**

Davy Crockett Craze In November 1954 the Disneyland TV show featured three one-hour episodes focusing on the life of the nineteenth-century Tennessee frontiersman—later congressman—David Crockett. The result was a national craze spearheaded by a merchandising boom on coonskin caps, toys, books, children's clothing, and hundreds of unrelated items such as milk glasses, towels, and the like.

The popularity of the Davy Crockett character played by Fess Parker caught the commercially shrewd Walt Disney by surprise. "Why, by the time the first show finally got on the air, we were already shooting the third one and calmly killing Davy off at the Alamo. It became one of the biggest overnight hits in TV history, and there we were with just three films and a dead hero."

The situation was remedied by splicing the television episodes into a ninety-minute movie featuring "The Ballad of Davy Crockett," written by Tom Blackburn and George Bruns. The film was released in June 1955, and coon tails, which once sold for 25 cents a pound, shot up to almost $5 a pound. (Disney was eventually involved in a number of lawsuits against what he claimed was illegal use of the Davy Crockett trademark.)

The Crockett series was revived on television in fall 1955—*The Legends of Davy Crockett*—and two of the episodes went into a second film entitled *Davy Crockett and the River Pilots,* released in July 1956. Interest in the partly legendary adventures of the frontier hero had already died, however, and the television series was quietly allowed to lapse.

Cruise Missile Powered throughout flight like an unmanned jet aircraft, thanks to a terrain-contour-matching guidance system (Tercom), the airborne cruise missile can hug the land at treetop height and moving along at 550 mph deliver its 200-kiloton nuclear warhead to within 100 feet of targets more than 1,500 miles from its launch platform. It is the technological descendant of the V-1 buzz bomb used by Germany in World War II.

Though it is basically still in the development stage, major emphasis was placed on the cruise missile as a strategic deterrent after President Jimmy Carter killed the **B-1 Bomber** in 1977. According to Department of Defense officials, a single B-52 can be used to bring and launch as many as twenty cruise missiles within target range. (There was serious doubt about the ability of the B-1 to penetrate Soviet defenses of the future.) It is also argued that varieties of the cruise can be used in place of fighters such as the F-4s; as programmed unmanned reconnaissance aircraft; or as backups for **Intercontinental Ballistic Missiles** (ICBMs) launched from either land or sea.

Part of the cruise missile's attraction—especially among American allies in the **North Atlantic Treaty Organization** (NATO) faced with the growing strength of the Warsaw Pact Nations—is its relative cheapness: from $700,000 to $1 million apiece, without the nuclear warhead.

The cruise missile was first tested publicly on June 21, 1978, at White Sands Missile Range, New Mexico. At that time a missile launched from an A-6 aircraft flew at altitudes of from 300 to less than 100 feet and escaped antiaircraft fire. After the tests, Defense Secretary Harold Brown said that they confirmed the Carter administration's decision to emphasize the cruise missile rather than penetration bombers such as the B-1.

CSCE *See* **Helsinki Accord.**

"Cuba and the American Negro" In a report issued on August 27, 1961, by the U.S. Senate Internal

Security Subcommittee chaired by Sen. James O. Eastland (D.-Miss.), it was charged that Cuba's Castro regime had made an unsuccessful attempt to "subvert the American Negro against his own government." Accused of having cooperated with the Cuban government's "nefarious designs" were both the U.S. Communist Party and the **Fair Play for Cuba Committee** (FPCC). Prominence was given in the report to previously unreleased testimony by black boxing champion Joe Louis that the Castro regime still owed his public relations firm $150,000 for ads placed in black-oriented American publications. Urging blacks to spend their vacations in Cuba, the ads stressed that they would receive "first-class treatment as first-class citizens."

Cuban Missile Crisis Shortly after an early July 1962 visit to the U.S.S.R. by Raúl Castro, Cuba's Minister of the Armed Forces, American intelligence agents in Cuba reported to President John F. Kennedy that "something new and different" was taking place in Soviet aid to Cuba: military construction of some unidentified sort was underway, there were some 5,000 Russian "specialists" in the country, and ships with more men and equipment were arriving on a stepped-up schedule.

It was assumed that a defensive build-up involving **surface-to-air missiles** (SAMs) was in progress, and given the **Bay of Pigs** fiasco, the United States was not in a position to object. Nevertheless, the State Department warned Moscow early in September that while there was as yet no evidence of "significant offensive capability either in Cuban hands or under Soviet direction," should such developments become apparent the "gravest issues would arise." Shortly afterward, the U.S.S.R. replied with assurances that the "armaments and military equipment sent to Cuba are designed exclusively for defensive purposes" and accused the United States of "preparing for aggression against Cuba and other peace-loving states. . . ."

Meanwhile, photo-reconnaissance flights over Cuba by U-2 planes were in progress, and on October 14, 1962, hard evidence was brought back that a ballistic missiles launching pad was under construction at San Cristóbal, and that there was even one missile on the ground.

During the next few days, several forms of response were considered in Washington—among them a surprise attack that would wipe out the bases—but President Kennedy chose to make a nationwide television address on October 22, 1962, in which he revealed the situation, condemned the U.S.S.R. for its deception, declared "a strict quarantine" under which all vessels bearing offensive weapons to Cuba would be turned back, and warned that any missile launched from Cuba would be considered a Soviet attack on the United States, requiring full retaliatory response. He called for an immediate convening of the **Organization of American States** (OAS) and an emergency meeting of the UN Security Council to consider this new threat to world peace. Noting that the effort undertaken was both difficult and dangerous, he pointed out that "the greatest danger of all would be to do nothing."

Aerial photographs of Cuban missile bases were exhibited at the United Nations by Adlai Stevenson, and on October 26, President Kennedy received a letter in which Premier Khrushchev said that if the United States would provide assurances that it would not invade Cuba, the Soviet missiles would be withdrawn. However, on the following day, Moscow broadcast a more formal Khrushchev letter saying that the U.S.S.R. would remove the offending missiles in exchange for the removal of American missile bases in Turkey. The President had earlier given instructions to remove these obsolete bases, and their continuing existence now proved a political albatross.

Prepared to respond positively to the first offer, the United States was unsure of how to respond now. In a brilliant maneuver conceived by Attorney General Robert Kennedy, it was decided to respond to the first offer and ignore the existence of the second. (Washington wits later dubbed this the "Trollope Ploy" after a recurrent scene in the works of Victorian novelist Anthony Trollope in which a young lady interprets informal attentions as a marriage proposal.) President Kennedy replied to the Soviet leader, saying he had read his "letter of October 26 with great care and welcomed the statement of [his] desire to seek a prompt solution." This response was delivered to the Soviet Ambassador by Attorney General Kennedy, who added that if no assurances were received in twenty-four hours, the United States was prepared to take military action. On the morning of October 28, Premier Khrushchev replied, saying that the missile sites would be dismantled and the arms "which you described as offensive" would be returned to the U.S.S.R.

UN Secretary General U Thant flew to Cuba to oversee the international inspection of the dismantling, but Premier Fidel Castro refused to permit it (October 30). As a result President Kennedy announced on November 2 that while there was evidence that the sites were being dismantled, the Russian leader's request that **U-2 flights** over Cuba be discontinued could not be honored until UN obser-

vation could be arranged. Because of Cuba's refusal to allow UN inspection, no noninvasion pledge was given.

The missile sites having been dismantled and the missiles themselves recrated and embarked to the U.S.S.R., the President lifted the naval blockade against Cuba on November 20, 1962. Soviet bombers capable of carrying nuclear warheads were also removed from Cuba, and in January 1963 the United Nations received joint U.S.-Soviet assurances that the Cuban missile crisis was over.

While President Kennedy's handling of the crisis was generally approved, critics of his administration have sometimes charged that he merely showed himself a superior cold warrior who was ready to risk nuclear war over what they see as an essentially political issue.

Cultural and Scientific Conference for World Peace
Attended by leftist delegations from all over the world, this series of general meetings and special panels was held in New York's Waldorf-Astoria Hotel, March 25–27, 1949. It was sponsored by the National Council of Arts, Sciences, and Professions, which had been identified by the U.S. State Department as a Communist front organization. The council denounced the **Marshall Plan,** the **Truman Doctrine,** and the **North Atlantic Pact** as destructive of peace. Chairman of the conference was Professor Harlow Shapely, Harvard University astronomer, and the star attraction was probably the Soviet delegation, headed by composer Dmitri Shostakovich and novelist Alexander A. Fadeyeff. Highly visible among the American delegation were playwright Lillian Hellman and screenwriter John Howard Lawson.

The sessions at the three-day meeting were often stormy. Norman Cousins, of the *Saturday Review of Literature,* had originally declined to attend, but reversed his decision on the grounds that it would be a good opportunity to let foreign delegates hear a sampling of noncommunist opinion among intellectuals in this country. His denunciation of the Communist Party as a group which owed its primary allegiance "not to America but to an outside government," was greeted by most of the 2,000 delegates with jeers and boos. But in return, Soviet delegates were challenged from the floor with embarrassing questions about the fate of dissident writers in their country. They declined questions critical of the Soviet Union as not being in the interests of peace.

During most of the conference there seemed to

be as many pickets outside as guests inside. With the endorsement of Governor Thomas E. Dewey, Professors Sidney Hook of New York University and George S. Counts of Columbia Teachers College set up an "Americans for Intellectual Freedom" committee to counteract what they denounced as the communist propaganda emanating from the three-day meeting.

Although delegates from **Iron Curtain** countries were granted visas by American authorities, many from Western Europe and South America were refused permission to enter the country on the ground that they were Communists and that their presence here would not be in the interest of the United States. The State Department also released a report detailing how the Soviet Government had consistently blocked efforts to arrange cultural and scientific exchanges between the two countries.

Cybernetics A science concerned with common factors of control and communications in living organisms, automatic machines, and organizations. It was the outgrowth of work done during World War II by Norbert Wiener and Julian Bigelow on automatic predictors for antiaircraft fire. Suggestions concerning the functioning of the human element in mixed human and mechanical fire-control systems were made by Arturo Rosenblueth.

The word itself was coined by Wiener and comes from the Greek word *kybernētēs*, meaning pilot or governor. It was meant to provide a comprehensive description of phenomena having "a real community of ideas and appropriate methods of study, but belonging to conventionally different disciplines."

In 1948, Wiener published a book entitled *Cybernetics, or Control and Communication in the Animal and the Machine.*

Cyclamates Evidence having been found linking these artificial sweeteners to cancer in animals, on October 18, 1969, the Department of Health, Education, and Welfare (HEW) ordered the removal of all cyclamates from the market by early 1970. In March 1977, the Food and Drug Administration (FDA) said that it would seek to ban saccharin, another artificial sweetener, because government-sponsored Canadian tests on laboratory rats indicated that it was potentially carcinogenic. An outcry against the prohibition of the only artificial sugar substitute now used in foods in this country, caused the FDA to bow to pressure on April 14, 1977, and propose that the over-the-counter sale of saccharin in food stores, restaurants and pharmacies be allowed but that it be banned in the manufacture of foods. Responsibility for demonstrating the safety and effectiveness of saccharin was placed on its manufacturers.

Pressure against the total ban of saccharin, which FDA officials said could cause up to 1,200 deaths from cancer in the United States annually, came from diabetics, diet drink manufacturers, the Calorie Control Council, and the Pharmaceutical Manufacturers Association. Some doctors claimed that the ban on artificial sweeteners could cause a health risk for diabetics and heart disease sufferers far greater than the cancer risk.

D

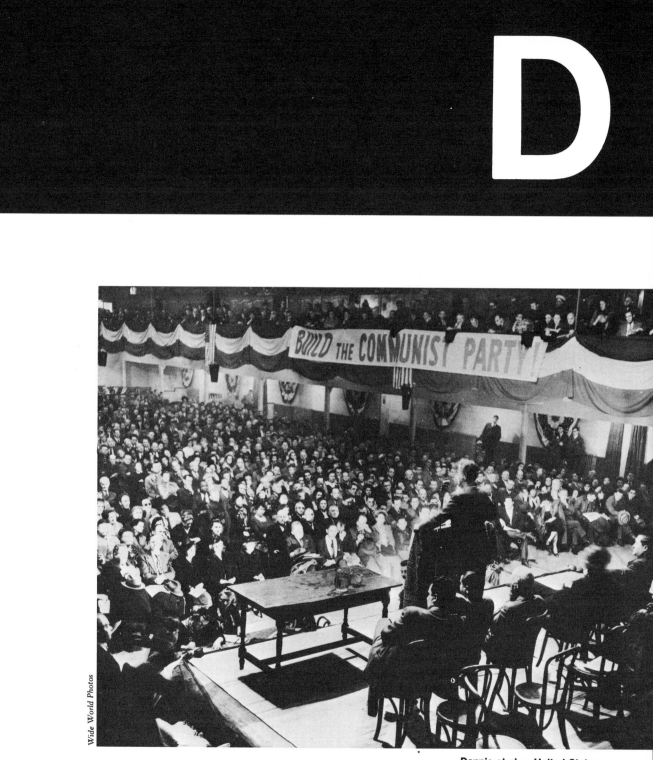

Dennis et al. v. United States

Daisy Girl TV Spot A political commercial used by the Democrats during the 1964 presidential campaign that pitted President Lyndon B. Johnson against Republican challenger Senator Barry Goldwater.

Speaking in Hartford, Connecticut, on October 24, 1963, Senator Goldwater expressed the belief that the American military presence in **NATO** could be reduced by a third if "commanders" were given authorization to use tactical nuclear weapons in a time of crisis. Thereafter, the Democrats skillfully kept him on the defensive on the question of atomic warfare. One particularly dramatic propaganda coup was a television commercial first shown on September 7, 1964. A little girl was shown innocently pulling the petals off a daisy, counting them as they fell. Slowly the picture dissolved into the mushroom cloud that had become familiar to Americans as the symbol of an atomic explosion.

Angela Davis Trial An acknowledged communist, black-militant Angela Davis first came to national attention when in 1969 she was fired from her position as an assistant professor of philosophy on the Los Angeles campus of the University of California. The California and U.S. Supreme Courts having declared that membership in the Communist party did not disqualify a person from teaching in a state university, the board of regents in April 1970 changed the charge against her to incompetence and refused to reinstate her. At this point, a resolution passed by her faculty colleagues urged that she be retained in defiance of the board's decision. Meanwhile, a new turn of events was to complicate the still unresolved issue that kept the campus in a constant turmoil.

Miss Davis was an active member of San Francisco's Soledad Committee, which had been organized to agitate for the release of the so-called Soledad Brothers, who, the committee claimed, were victims of political oppression. The group, including George Jackson, Fleeta Drumgo, and John Cluchette—all blacks—was charged with having killed a white guard at California's Soledad Prison on January 16, 1970. After seeing Jackson during a courtroom hearing in May 1970, Miss Davis began corresponding with him, and it was through this double association that she met his seventeen-year-old brother, Jonathan.

On August 7, 1970, the nation was electrified by the news that in a San Rafael courthouse, only a short distance from San Francisco, Jonathan Jackson had interrupted the trial of James McLain, who was accused of stabbing a San Quentin guard, by brandishing a shotgun at the judge and jury. Ordering McLain and two fellow convicts—Ruchell Magee and Arthur Christmas—to be unshackled, he proceeded to arm them with pistols drawn from a small zipper bag he carried. Then, after taking five hostages, including Superior Court Judge Harold J. Haley and Deputy District Attorney Gary W. Thomas, Jonathan Jackson and the three San Quentin convicts fled the courtroom. McLain, who was now holding the shotgun to the judge's neck called: "We want the Soledad Brothers released by twelve-thirty today!"

Outside the courthouse, a gun battle with police authorities ensued. When it was over, Jonathan Jackson, McLain, Christmas, and Judge Haley were dead. Thomas had been paralyzed by a wound in the spine, and Magee had been wounded in the chest.

Although Angela Davis had not been present at the scene, the weapons were found to have been registered in her name. Shortly after the incident, she vanished after buying a plane ticket at the San Francisco terminal. It was not until the following October 13, 1970, that she was picked up in New York City by FBI agents. The following month, she was indicted under California law, which makes it an act of murder to contribute to a killing, whether or not the person so charged is present at the actual scene of the murder.

Given the charge against her, the judge denied Miss Davis bail. Within days, a "Free Angela Davis" campaign had been launched, and at a news conference in Los Angeles, the Communist party announced "the largest, broadest, most all-encompassing people's movement the country has ever seen to free our comrade, Angela Davis—political prisoner."

Meanwhile, on August 21, 1971, events took another dramatic turn. After receiving a visit from his lawyer, Stephen Mitchell Bingham, George Jackson suddenly produced a small automatic pistol, presumably hidden under an Afro hairdo wig. Before he was gunned down by sharpshooters, Jackson had obtained the release of some twenty prisoners. When it was over, three white guards and two white trustees were dead, and an eighteen-page diary written by Angela Davis was found in Jackson's cell. In it she referred to him as her husband and vowed to free him by whatever means necessary. (Many of Jackson's own letters to her appeared in his book *Soledad Brothers*, which had been published in fall 1970.) After his death, she spoke of "the loss of an irretrievable love."

Angela Davis's own trial on murder, kidnapping, and conspiracy charges began in San Jose on March 27, 1972. During the interval both Drumgo and Cluchette were cleared of the original murder charge which had been at the heart of the Soledad Brothers campaign. In his opening statement the chief prosecutor urged that Miss Davis had been motivated by her "passion" for George Jackson to join in his brother's plot to free him. Acting as one of her own attorneys, she rejected the charge as an example of "male chauvinist" thinking, and described her entire involvement with the Soledad Brothers as having been "within the realm of legality." The weapons registered in her name had been obtained for the defense of the Soledad Committee and, the defense maintained, had no doubt been stolen by Jonathan Jackson without her knowledge.

After 13 weeks of testimony, 95 prosecution witnesses, and 201 exhibits, the jury remained unconvinced that a woman of Miss Davis's intelligence would have involved herself in Jonathan Jackson's reckless scheme to free his brother. She was acquitted on June 4, 1972. Of the famous love letters, one juror later said: "They were just regular love letters. They certainly didn't mean to me that she was going to bust him out of jail."

Asked whether the verdict was a vindication of the American judicial system, Miss Davis replied: "A fair trial would have been no trial at all."

In September 1972, the University of California Board of Regents rejected a recommendation from the philosophy department to reappoint her as acting associate professor for 1973-1974. The vote against her was said to have been "nearly unanimous."

Dawk Used during the **Vietnam War** to indicate a compromise position between a "hawk" and a "dove." Princeton historian Eric Goldman, who formed President Lyndon B. Johnson's **"quiet brain trust,"** has noted that the President disliked the words "hawk," "dove," and especially "dawk." "Nevertheless, his thinking about Vietnam was dawkish in the sense that he was ready to use combat force but in the form of limited war, and he was convinced that his chief problem in doing this would come not from the dove but the hawk sentiment in the country."

Days of Rage *See* **Weathermen.**

James Dean Cult *See Rebel Without a Cause.*

The Death and Life of Great American Cities Published in 1961, Jane Jacobs's attack on current approaches to urban renewal and city planning made an immediate impact. She deplored the tendency to diminish the unique contribution of the city to American culture by destroying the colorful life of the streets and introducing into an urban environment concepts and elements more proper to small town and country living.

Calling for a rethinking of the entire problem of urban decay, she noted that there was a "wistful myth" that given sufficient money we could reverse the decline of "yesterday's and day-before-yesterday's suburbs" and stop the flight of the taxable middle class. She argued that the bulldozer approach to replacing slums with projects that destroyed indigenous neighborhoods had resulted in "worse centers of delinquency, vandalism and general hopelessness." She attacked the creation of cultural centers of such artificiality that they "are unable to support a good bookstore." Among her other targets were standardized commercial centers, promenades that went from noplace to nowhere and consequently had no promenaders, and expressways that cut the heart out of cities. "This is not the rebuilding of cities. This is the sacking of cities."

Mrs. Jacobs currently resides in Toronto.

D.C. Crime Bill Since criminal law enforcement is assigned to local police authorities under most circumstances, the issue of crime had played no significant role in national politics until "law and order" became an important theme in the 1968 campaign of the Republican presidential nominee, Richard M. Nixon. However, once he had assumed office in 1969, President Nixon found that the only immediate anticrime option open to him was, in the words of Associate Deputy Attorney General Donald Santarelli, "to exercise vigorous symbolic leadership" in the District of Columbia, where the federal government did have the responsibility and the necessary machinery for enforcing it.

The result was the Nixon administration's proposed District of Columbia Court Reorganization Act, which was introduced into Congress in July 1969. Among its controversial provisions was a "preventive detention" section which empowered District of Columbia courts—which assumed jurisdiction over local crime cases previously held by the U.S. Court of Appeals of the D.C. Circuit—to jail criminal suspects for sixty days previous to trial. An equally controversial "no-knock" provision allowed Washington police armed with bench warrants to enter private homes without first knocking and identifying themselves. In addition, jury trials for juveniles were eliminated.

A leading opponent of the bill was Sen. Sam Ervin (D.-N.C.), who pointed out that the bill was, in effect, a suspension of constitutional protections and a repeal of the Fourth, Fifth, Sixth, and Eighth Amendments. There is some indication that the Nixon administration had expected the bill to be defeated and that its real purpose was to put the onus for the failure to achieve anticrime legislation on the Democrats. Nevertheless, such was the popular appeal of the law-and-order issue that the bill was finally signed by President Nixon on July 29, 1970. However, constitutional objections continued to mount and on October 28, 1974, President Gerald R. Ford, who had succeeded to the office after the resignation of President Nixon following the **Watergate Scandal,** signed into law a bill repealing the "no-knock" provisions.

Declaration of Conscience Reacting against irresponsible charges of "Communists in government" made by Republican Senator Joseph McCarthy (see **McCarthyism**), in June 1950 Sen. Margaret Chase Smith (R.-Maine) was joined by six other Republican senators—Sen. Charles W. Tobey (N.H.), Sen. George D. Aiken (Vt.), Sen. Wayne L. Morse (Oreg.), Sen. Irving Ives (N.Y.), Sen. Edward Thye (Minn.), and Sen. Robert C. Hendrickson (N.J.), in a "Declaration of Conscience" that deplored the tactics being used by the Wisconsin Senator. Supporting the "Declaration" were Sen. Herbert Lehman (D.-N.Y.), and Sen. Hubert H. Humphrey (D.-Minn.).

In issuing the document, Senator Smith noted that "the record of the present Democratic administration has provided us with sufficient campaign issues without the necessity of resorting to political smears."

The five-point declaration itself noted that (1) both Republicans and Democrats had contributed to the growing confusion, (2) that the Democratic administration had initially created the confusion by its lack of effective leadership and contradictory statements, (3) that "certain elements" of the Republican Party had selfishly exploited the explosive issue for political advantage, (4) that both Republicans and Democrats had unwittingly played into communist hands, and that (5) "it is high time that we stopped thinking politically as Republicans and Democrats about elections and started thinking patriotically as Americans about national security based on individual freedom. . . ."

Although the obvious target of the declaration, Senator McCarthy was not mentioned by name.

Declaration of Goals of Freedom One of three documents issued at the conclusion of the **Manila Conference** in October 1966. In it the leaders of the seven participating nations declared their common goals in the **Vietnam War:**

1. To be free from aggression.
2. To conquer hunger, illiteracy, and disease.
3. To build a region of security, order, and progress.
4. To seek reconciliation and peace throughout Asia and the Pacific.

Declaration of Honolulu After meeting in Honolulu, February 7–8, 1966, to consider problems raised by continued fighting in Vietnam, President Lyndon B. Johnson, Prime Minister Nguyen Cao Ky, and General Nguyen Van Thieu issued a joint statement emphasizing their determination to continue the struggle and to undertake reforms in South Vietnam. In the first part of the declaration, the South Vietnamese leaders made a four-point pledge: the defeat of the Viet Cong "and those illegally fighting with them on our soil"; the eradication of social injustice in their country; the establishment of a stable, viable economy; and the building of "true democracy for our land and our people." They concluded with an appeal to those fighting against them to take advantage of the amnesty offered under the **Open Arms** program and to join them in working "through constitutional democracy to build together that life of dignity, freedom and peace those in the North would deny the people of Vietnam." The American portion of the declaration promised to support the goals set forth in the first part.

Following the Honolulu conference, William J. Porter, Deputy Ambassador to South Vietnam, was given the task of organizing American efforts in "the other war", i.e., economic and political reform in South Vietnam.

Critics of the President's policy in Vietnam were quick to point out that the Honolulu conference had been hastily organized—so hastily, that Australia's Prime Minister Harold Holt, who had mortgaged his political future by committing a contingent of Australian troops in Vietnam, was not invited—to steal newspaper headlines from the sessions of the Foreign Relations Committee being conducted by antiwar foe Sen. J. William Fulbright (D.-Ark.) If so, it failed completely, and Senator Fulbright noted several days later that the conference had put further obstacles to a negotiated settlement in Vietnam by strengthening our commitment to the Saigon government.

Deep-Freeze Scandals *See* **Five Percenters.**

Deep Throat As reported in their 1974 bestseller *All the President's Men,* many of the leads that enabled *Washington Post* reporters Carl Bernstein and Bob Woodward to conduct the investigative journalism that cracked open the **Watergate Scandal** came from an informant in the "Executive Branch." He was Woodward's private contact and had been assured that his identity would never be revealed and that the information he supplied would never be quoted, but only used to confirm data that had been obtained elsewhere. When this arrangement was explained to the *Post*'s managing editor, Howard Simons, the "source" was promptly dubbed "Deep Throat"—a reference to a then popular pornographic movie and to the fact that the information he supplied was known in newspaper terminology as "deep background."

When Woodward wanted to make some inquiry of his informant—who refused to use the telephone lest it be tapped—he would display on his balcony a little red flag of the type used as a warning device by heavy trucks. Deep Throat would signal his desire to meet with Woodward by seeing to it that a marked copy of *The New York Times* was delivered to his door.

It was Deep Throat who advised Woodward that Howard Hunt had been involved in the Watergate break-in and that the operation had been partially paid for by funds controlled by John N. Mitchell, former Attorney General, who was at the time the director of the **Committee to Re-elect the President** (CREEP or CRP).

The identity of Deep Throat has never been revealed, although there was some speculation that he was Robert F. Bennett (son of Sen. Wallace Bennett [R.-Utah]) of the Robert Mullen Company, which was said to be a **CIA** front. That company hired Howard Hunt after he retired from the CIA in 1970. Others have suggested that Deep Throat was W. Mark Felt, Jr., who was deputy associate director of the FBI.

Defense Department Reorganization Act Signed into law by President Dwight D. Eisenhower on August 6, 1958, it made the secretary of each branch of the uniformed services responsible to the Secretary of Defense. It also authorized the President to abolish, merge, or transfer service functions in time of war, but made these latter changes subject to congressional veto in peacetime.

Although the President had noted that the bill met every recommendation he had submitted "except in relatively minor respects," he had at one time objected to the above provisions, as well as to one permitting service chiefs and secretaries to submit recommendations or complaints to Congress "on their own initiative." The President, a former military man, saw the latter provision as encouraging "legalized insubordination."

Under the reorganization, sharper distinctions were made between command authority, centralizing research and engineering within the Department of Defense. Other provisions of the act protected the Marine Corps, National Guard, and naval aviation against weakening or abolition by the President or the Secretary of Defense; provided for centralizing research and development in the Secretary's office under a Director of Research and Engineering; authorized the Secretary to decide which new weapons should be assigned to the different services; gave the Joint Chiefs of Staff chairman a vote in his group's deliberations; expanded the Joint staff from 210 to 400 men.

Defense Early Warning Line *See* **DEW Line.**

Defensive Perimeter In December 1949, Chiang Kai-shek removed the capital of Nationalist China to the island of Formosa. Although it had been Truman administration policy—backed by the support of the Joint Chiefs of Staff—that United States forces would not be used to defend the island, Republican leaders Senators Robert Taft (Ohio) and William Knowland (Calif.) joined with former-President Herbert C. Hoover in publicly advocating its protection by the American navy; the Chinese Communists charged that we were about to occupy Formosa under the pretext that it was part of Japan, with which no peace treaty had yet been signed. On January 5, 1950, President Harry S Truman reaffirmed his determination not to be drawn into the war between Nationalist and Communist Chinas.

In a special White House release he noted:

The United States has no desire to obtain special rights or privileges or to establish military bases on Formosa at this time. Nor does it have any intention of utilizing its armed forces to interfere in the present situation. The United States Government will not pursue a course which will lead to involvement in the civil conflict in China.

On January 12, 1950, Secretary of State Dean Acheson appeared before the National Press Club to explain the basis for the administration's stand in a speech entitled "Crisis in China—An Examination of United States Foreign Policy." As he noted later, the speech was "another effort to get the self-styled formulators of public opinion to think before they wrote, and do more than report as news the emotional or political utterances of political gladiators."

It was the desire of our government, he explained, to help Asians realize their democratic aspirations. He urged a realistic appreciation of what was going on in that area. Four years after having emerged from the war at the head of the greatest military power of any ruler in Chinese history, Chiang Kai-shek had seen his armies melt away until he was a refugee on a small island off the coast of China. This could not be attributed to the lack of support from Western powers but to the emergence of a revolutionary spirit in China, a spirit not created by the communists but seized upon for advantage. The Russians were continuing their long struggle to dominate the area and the United States should not deflect from them to itself the anger and hatred of the Chinese people against their continued exploitation by foreign powers.

Turning from his political examination to "questions of military security," the Secretary of State reiterated the views expressed by General Douglas MacArthur in March 1949, when he had noted that our line of defense "starts from the Philippines and continues through the Ryukyu Archipelago, which includes its main bastion, Okinawa. Then it bends back through Japan and the Aleutian Island chain to Alaska." As Secretary Acheson put it: "This defensive perimeter runs along the Aleutians to Japan and then goes to the Ryukyus. We hold important defense positions in the Ryukyus Islands and these we will continue to hold. . . . The defensive perimeter runs from the Ryukyus to the Philippine Islands."

He later noted that with the authority of the Joint Chiefs of Staff and General MacArthur behind him, it did not occur to him that he would be charged with innovating policy or political heresy. To keep his statement from being "misunderstood or distorted" he went on to say that

. . . so far as the military security of other areas of the Pacific is concerned, it must be clear that no person can guarantee these areas against military attack. . . . Should such an attack occur . . . the initial reliance must be on the people attacked to resist it and then on the commitments of the entire civilized world under the Charter of the United Nations, which so far has not proved a weak reed

to lean on by any people who are determined to protect their independence against outside aggression.

Attacked by Republican leaders, the Secretary's stand on Far Eastern policy was supported by Democratic senators. A week later, however, Republicans and "economy-minded" Southern Democrats joined forces to defeat an administration bill which would have provided appropriation for five hundred U.S. Army officers to serve as technical advisors to the army of South Korea. Nevertheless, when North Korean troops poured over that country's borders in June 1950, Secretary Acheson was accused of having given the green light to this invasion by not including South Korea within the "defensive perimeter." He was to note in his memoirs:

This was specious, for Australia and New Zealand were not included either, and the first of all our mutual defense agreements was made with Korea. If the Russians were watching the United States for signs of our intentions in the Far East, they would have been more impressed by the two years' agitation for withdrawal of our combat forces from Korea . . .

and the defeat in Congress of a minor bill designed to aid that nation.

"Deficit Spending" *See* **Keynesianism.**

Delaney Clause One of a series of 1958 amendments to the Federal Food, Drug and Cosmetic Act (1938), it was introduced by Rep. James J. Delaney (D.-N.Y.), who had been chairman of a Congressional Select Committee to Investigate the Use of Chemicals in Food. The new legislation, similar to proposals introduced and rejected on five previous occasions, says that "no additive shall be deemed to be safe if it is found to induce cancer when ingested by man or animal, or if it is found, after tests which are appropriate for evaluation of the safety of food additives, to induce cancer in man or animal."

The clause had been used by the Food and Drug Administration (FDA) to prohibit the use in foods of Red Dye No. 2 and **cyclamate** sweeteners. In March 1977 it came under attack when the FDA invoked it to prohibit the use of saccharin after tests showed that massive amounts fed to rats caused bladder cancer. Critics contended that any chemical was potentially carcinogenic if fed to test animals in high enough doses. A strong effort to overturn or weaken the clause was made by the manufacturers of the powerful diet food and drinks industry.

Demilitarized Zone *See* **Vietnam War.**

Dennis et al. v. United States Eleven leaders of the Communist Party, arrested in 1948 and charged under the Smith Act (1940) with advocating the violent overthrow of the government, were found guilty by a jury in 1949. An appeal was made to the United States Supreme Court, where a decision (June 4, 1951) upheld the constitutionality of the Smith Act and the convictions obtained under it. In writing the majority opinion, Chief Justice Fred M. Vinson found that whatever "theoretical merit there may be to the argument that there is a 'right' to rebellion against dictatorial governments is without force where the existing structure of the government provides for peaceful and orderly change. We reject any principle of governmental helplessness in the face of preparation for revolution, which principle carried to its logical conclusion, must lead to anarchy. No one could conceive that it is not within the power of Congress to prohibit acts intended to overthrow the Government by force and violence. The question with which we are concerned here is not whether Congress has such *power*, but whether the *means* which it has employed conflict with the First and Fifth Amendments of the Constitution."

Dissenting opinions were entered by Justices Hugo Black and William O. Douglas. The latter wrote that the primary consideration was "the strength and tactical position of petitioners and their converts in this country. . . . If we are to take judicial notice of the threat of Communists within the nation, it should not be difficult to conclude that as a *political party* they are of little consequence. . . . I would doubt that there is a village, let alone a city or county or state, which the Communists could carry. . . . How it can be said that there is a clear and present danger that this advocacy will succeed is, therefore, a mystery. . . . In America [Communists] are miserable merchants of unwanted ideas; their wares remain unsold. The fact that their ideas are abhorrent does not make them powerful."

Department of Energy (DOE) Established by the Department of Energy Organization Act (August 4, 1977), which consolidated the major federal energy functions into a Cabinet-level department, transferring to DOE all the responsibilities of the **Energy Research and Development Administration (ERDA)**, the **Federal Energy Administration,** the Federal Power Commission, and the Alaska, Bonneville, Southeastern, and Southwestern Power Administrations, formerly part of the Department of the Interior. DOE provides a framework for the national energy plan. Programs administered under it include energy research sponsorship, energy technology research, and defense energy research. The first Secretary of Energy was James R. Schlesinger.

Department of Health, Education and Welfare (HEW) During his first six months in office, President Dwight D. Eisenhower, in accordance with the Reorganization Act of 1949, sent Congress ten plans for changes in the organization of the executive branch. Among these was Reorganization Plan Number One (March 12, 1953), which called for the replacement of the old Federal Security Agency by a Department of Health, Education and Welfare, the first new Cabinet department established in forty years. On April 11, 1953, Oveta Culp Hobby, former Federal Security Administrator, became the first HEW Secretary. As such it was her duty to report to the President on health, education, welfare, and income security plans, policies, and programs of the federal government.

The functions of the HEW Secretary are administered through the Office of Human Development Services, the Public Health Service, the Health Care Financing Administration, the Social Security Administration, and the Education Division. In addition, there are specialized units such as the Office for Civil Rights and the Office of Consumer Affairs.

Accountable to Congress and the taxpayers, the Secretary must justify HEW's expenditures by testifying before congressional committees, appearing before national organizations, and preparing special reports that are distributed to the public on request. The HEW Secretary is required by law to submit periodic reports on the department's expenditures and the progress achieved to both the President and Congress.

HEW expenditures for fiscal 1980 are expected to be $199.4 billion, a 10 percent increase over the previous year. At that time the department's share of the national budget will be 37.5 percent.

Department of Housing and Urban Development (HUD) The compromise legislation creating this Cabinet-level department was passed without debate by both houses of Congress and signed into law on September 9, 1965, by President Lyndon B. Johnson, who called it "the first step toward organizing our system for a more rational response to the pressing challenge of urban life." The Secretary authorized by the law was to assume all the functions of the Housing and Home Finance Agency, the Public Housing Administration, the Federal National Mortgage Association, and the Federal

Housing Administration (FHA). The latter, however, was to be retained as a separate entity within HUD and headed by a Federal Housing Commissioner, who would also serve as an assistant secretary.

As the first Secretary of HUD, President Johnson appointed Robert C. Weaver, who was also the first Negro to serve in a presidential Cabinet. (When in 1962 President John F. Kennedy had attempted to establish a Department of Urban Affairs, Weaver had been scheduled for the post of Secretary.)

Writing in 1971, President Johnson noted that "before we could deal with the problems of the cities, we needed to develop the organizational machinery. Three-quarters of a century after the farmers had been given a voice at the Cabinet table, the cities still had none. Our urban programs had grown into a network of separate fiefdoms."

HUD initially put strong emphasis on nondiscrimination in the projects with which it was involved, favoring cities with good records on encouraging integration in both inner-city and suburban developments. However, in May 1971 the U.S. Civil Rights Commission noted: "The harsh facts of housing economics . . . suggest that racial integration cannot be achieved unless economic integration also is achieved. Thus, the change in HUD's 'open communities' policy may not only represent a narrowing of that agency's view of its fair housing responsibilities, but also may mark the beginning of the Federal Government's withdrawal from active participation in the effort to eliminate residential segregation."

During the Nixon administration, HUD Secretary George Romney's enthusiasm for the **Model Cities** program and for integration of the suburbs led to clashes with the President. Romney was replaced by James T. Lynn, who was intrumental in promoting the **Housing and Community Development Act of 1974.** A major revision and extension of urban development programs, it consolidated categorical programs such as Model Cities into block grants for community development. Eligible communities were apportioned funds on the basis of population, degree of overcrowding, and poverty. These grants could be used at the discretion of the community for urban renewal, neighborhood facilities, model cities, water and sewer facilities, and aid to families displaced by building programs.

Depletion Allowances Tax allowances available to owners of exhaustible natural resources such as oil and gas. They were designed to prevent the imposition of a capital levy on the investment in resource property and to encourage the investment of risk capital in the development of untapped resources.

Depletion allowances permitted owners to deduct from income a portion of investment resources as the property is depleted. Under the percentage-depletion method, a fixed percentage of the gross income could be taken off. In 1970, for example, the depletion allowance for oil and gas wells was 22.5 percent of gross income; however, this deduction could not exceed 50 percent of total net income before deduction.

Under Title V of the Tax Reduction Act signed by President Gerald R. Ford on March 29, 1975, percentage-depletion was repealed and deductions were limited to the actual costs of individual projects. Of course, companies can still write off some drilling costs immediately and depreciate other costs during the property's productive life.

Exceptions to Title V were producers of natural gas sold under existing regulated prices. Also exempt were producers who extract less than 2,000 barrels daily of oil or gas equivalents and who have no retailing or refining operations of any significance. However, the limit of exempt production falls by 200 barrels a day annually until 1980.

Executives of the oil industry complained that the same legislation which had cut taxes for individuals and some businesses by $22.8 billion had raised their taxes by approximately $2 billion in 1975.

The impact of Title V on oil and gas production investments was expected to be minimal because, as some tax reformers have pointed out, recent oil price increases have created new investment incentives that easily compensate for the loss of percentage-depletion.

DEW Line (Defense Early Warning Line) In an agreement signed on September 27, 1954, the governments of the United States and Canada proposed to establish a series of radar stations that would provide early warnings of bomber attacks by a potential enemy over the Atlantic and Pacific flanks of the continent or over the North Pole. Stretching across northern Canada from Alaska to Greenland, these new stations were planned to supplement the radar posts of the Pinetree Chain and the Mid-Canada Line completed earlier in the decade. The DEW Line was completed and operating by mid-1957. Later it was reinforced by the even more sensitive Ballistic Missile Early Warning System (BMEWS), construction of which began in 1960.

Diem Cables Two forged State Department cables manufactured some time in 1971 by Charles "Chuck" Colson, special counsel to President Richard M. Nixon, and E. Howard Hunt, Jr., former **CIA** agent serving as consultant to the White House. They were intended to implicate the late President John F. Kennedy in the 1963 assassination of President Ngo Dinh Diem of South Vietnam. Colson presumably reasoned that these forgeries involving a Democratic President in the death of a Catholic leader would help swing Catholic votes to President Nixon in the November 1972 elections.

On September 16, 1971, President Nixon appeared to be referring to these cables when he noted: "I would remind all concerned that the way we got into Vietnam was through overthrowing Diem, and complicity in the murder of Diem." Several days later, Colson made an unsuccessful attempt to "leak" the forgeries to *Life* magazine.

On June 28, 1972, shortly after the break-in of Democratic National Headquarters by men linked to the **Committee to Re-elect the President** (CREEP or CRP), Acting FBI Director L. Patrick Gray was called in by John Dean III, counsel to the President, and John D. Ehrlichman, Assistant to the President for Domestic Affairs, and given two file folders said to contain "political dynamite" that ought "never see the light of day." The folders contained the forged cables—manufactured with the help of a razor and a Xerox machine—and information on Sen. Edward Kennedy (D.-Mass.) collected by Hunt. Gray later testified before the Senate **Watergate Committee** that he had kept these files in his Connecticut home until December 1972, when he had burned them in a trash fire.

See **Vietnam War; Watergate Scandal.**

Diggers Often called the worker-priests of the hippie movement. During the 1967 **Summer of Love** in San Francisco's **Haight-Ashbury** section, they established centers for distributing free lodgings, food, and clothing to the thousands of young people attracted to the city. Diggers would make the rounds of the city, soliciting contributions of money or goods, including tools that might enable hippies to support themselves.

The group, whose leader was Emmett Grogan, took its name from a quickly crushed seventeenth-century English rural movement of revolutionaries who advocated the abolition of money and private property, urging, instead, the establishment of communal farms for the support of all who were willing to work.

Direct-Action Tactics Term often used in the 1960s by civil rights militants engaged in challenging southern segregation laws as applied in education, transportation, and the use of public facilities.

See **Freedom Riders; Sit-Ins.**

Dirksen's Bombers The name applied by Democrats of the Johnson administration during the 1960s to the group of legal assistants working out of the office of Senate Minority Leader Everett M. Dirksen (R.-Ill.) Irritated by the Senator's opposition to their housing and civil rights legislation, Democrats testily insisted that the prime job of his assistants was to discover flaws in proposed legislation.

In 1971, former President Lyndon B. Johnson was to say: "Dirksen could play politics as well as any man. But I knew something else about him. When the nation's interest was at stake, he could climb the heights and take the long view without regard to party."

Dirty Tricks Disclosures subsequent to the **Watergate Scandal** revealed that with the knowledge and acquiescence of members of President Nixon's White House staff a campaign of political sabotage was carried out to block the efforts of Sen. Edmund S. Muskie (D.-Maine) to win the 1972 Democratic presidential nomination. Muskie was the prime target because he was considered the candidate most likely to make the strongest showing against the incumbent. The man most closely associated with this covert operation was Donald H. Segretti, a California lawyer who was a University of Southern Californai classmate of Gordon C. Strachan, assistant to the White House Chief of Staff, H. R. Haldeman, and of Dwight L. Chapin, the President's appointments secretary.

Late in August 1971, with the consent of Haldeman, arrangements were made to have Segretti paid out of a $500,000 secret campaign fund administered by Herbert W. Kalmbach, President Nixon's personal attorney. The operation was originally known as the Black Advance. During the next eight months, Segretti traveled to sixteen states, most of which were having key presidential primaries, and recruited a network of agents. Many of the tricks were sophomoric, i.e., hiring a woman to run naked down the corridor of Senator Muskie's hotel and shout "I love Ed Muskie," but some were of greater political significance. For example, in March 1972, during the Florida primary, Segretti sent a letter written on bogus Citizens for Muskie stationery to supporters of Sen. Henry M. Jackson (D.-Wash.).

The letter read: "We on the Sen. Ed Muskie staff sincerely hope that you have decided upon Senator Muskie as your choice. However, if you have not made your decision you should be aware of several facts." What followed were unsubstantiated charges of sexual misconduct by Senator Jackson, as well as against presidential hopeful Senator Hubert H. Humphrey (D.-Minn.). During the following Wisconsin primary, Segretti saw to it that bumper stickers with sexual slogans aimed at Senator Muskie were widely distributed, and plagued Senator Humphrey's campaign by spreading bogus invitations to a free April Fool's Day lunch through Milwaukee. Bogus invitations were also sent to foreign dignitaries inviting them to a Muskie fund-raising dinner to be held in the nation's capital on April 17, 1972, in preparation for the District of Columbia primary to held on May 2.

A similar "dirty tricks" campaign, codenamed **Sedan Chair,** was set up to harass Democratic presidential contenders by Jeb Stuart Magruder, deputy director, **Committee to Re-elect the President** (CREEP or CRP). In addition, part of the **Gemstone** operation conceived by G. Gordon Liddy and E. Howard Hunt included an operation known as Ruby II in which Thomas J. Gregory, a Brigham Young University history student, infiltrated the campaign headquarters of Senator Muskie and supplied Hunt with typed espionage reports. Murray Chotiner, one of President Nixon's political advisors, had his own version of a "dirty tricks" operation in which writers were hired to pose as reporters and send back potentially valuable information gleaned from following the campaigns of contenders for the Democratic presidential nomination. The reports were codenamed "Mr. Chapman's Friends," a name that derived from the codename used by former New York Governor Thomas E. Dewey when making long-distance calls.

Discoverer Satellites *See* **Project Sentry.**

Displaced Persons Act Designed to admit 205,000 European displaced persons to the United States by temporarily relaxing quotas, the act was signed into law on June 25, 1948, by President Harry S Truman, who denounced it as "flagrantly discriminatory" against Jews and Catholics. This was effected through the "device" of making ineligible all those who entered Germany, Austria, or Italy after December 22, 1945.

The specific provisions of the bill provided for the admission of 200,000 inhabitants of the displaced persons (DP) camps, 2,000 Czechs who left their homeland after the Communist takeover, and 3,000 orphans. Under the breakdown called for, 30 percent of the 200,000 had to be farmers, and 40 percent had to be from eastern Poland or the Baltic countries. The new law also set aside 50 percent of the regular German and Austrian quotas for those of German origin but born in East European nations.

The complicated restrictive provisions kept the number actually admitted to the country during the following two years down to 140,000. In June 1950, the law was amended to admit a total of 415,000 persons without discrimination.

President Truman's concern for the fate of Europe's hundreds of thousands of displaced persons caused him to send Earl G. Harrison, dean of the University of Pennsylvania Law School, abroad in June 1945 to report on the situation of "non-repatriables." In his State of the Union Message of January 7, 1948, President Truman issued one of his many calls that "thousands of displaced persons should be allowed entry into the United States." Shortly after reluctantly signing the discriminatory bill passed by the "do-nothing" Eightieth Congress, in July 1948, Truman accepted the Democratic nomination for president in the forthcoming election. At that time, he announced he would call Congress back into session (see **Turnip Congress**) to pass legislation needed in many areas. Among these items was "adequate and decent laws for displaced persons in place of this anti-Semitic, anti-Catholic law which this Eightieth Congress passed." The 1948 legislation was finally amended in June 1950 to remove discrimination against immigrants from southern and eastern Europe. By 1958 Congress had allowed a million and a half quota immigrants into the United States.

District of Columbia Court Reorganization Act *See* **D.C. Crime Bill.**

Dixiecrats *See* **States' Rights Democrats.**

Dixon-Yates In 1953, the Tennessee Valley Authority (TVA) asked for federal funds with which to build a $100 million steam plant to enable it to provide cheap electricity for the Memphis area in the years ahead. Since the TVA—which had been denounced by President Dwight D. Eisenhower as **"creeping socialism"**—was supplying power to plants of the **Atomic Energy Commission** (AEC) at Oak Ridge, Tennessee, and Paducah, Kentucky, the President, as an alternative, ordered the AEC to contract for a new generating plant near Memphis which would by 1957 be producing 500,000 to 600,000 kilowatts. This power could be made available to the Memphis area, and the TVA would then be free to honor its commitments to the AEC plants without making Memphis suffer because of them.

Upon the recommendation of Budget Director Rowland Hughes, in mid-1954 the AEC negotiated with the executives of two private utility companies—Edgar H. Dixon, president of Middle South Utilities, and Eugene A. Yates, chairman of the Southern Company—for the construction in Arkansas of a plant that would supply power to Memphis. Such a contract was approved and went into effect in November 1954.

Democrats immediately charged that the agreement with Dixon-Yates had been arrived at by means of secret negotiations and that there had been no competitive bidding. They attacked the contracts as "giveaways," and in January 1955 the ten Democrats on the Joint Committee on Atomic Energy voted against the eight Republicans to recommend that the contract be canceled. The Eisenhower administration refused.

In February 1955, it was revealed that Adolphe Wenzell, a retired vice president and director of the First Boston Corporation, an investment banking firm, had been asked to advise the AEC on its negotiations with the Dixon-Yates group. This was embarrassing to the administration because First Boston was planning to invest in the new plant. Administration officials claimed not to have known that Mr. Wenzell was acting in a dual capacity.

In June 1955, the political hornet's nest resolved itself when the city of Memphis announced that it would build its own municipal steam-generating plant, which would be financed by the sale of bonds on the public investment market. President Eisenhower therefore directed the AEC to cancel the Dixon-Yates contract and proceed to a settlement of any costs incurred. On the advice of counsel, however, in November 1955 the AEC informed the Dixon-Yates group that no financial arrangements could be made until the possible conflict-of-interest concerning Wenzell could be adjudicated. The Dixon-Yates group thereupon sued the United States for breach of contract and won a judgment of $1,867,545, but this was struck down by the U.S. Supreme Court on January 9, 1961, on the grounds that Wenzell's dual status in the negotiations made the contract unenforceable.

It was the position of President Eisenhower that the Dixon-Yates group suffered an unjust loss "on a technicality." Presidential Assistant Sherman Ad-

ams insisted that Wenzell did not play a key role in negotiating the Dixon-Yates contract, "although he did take part in some of the conferences on certain financial aspects of the agreement." According to Adams, President Eisenhower's sole motive in sponsoring a privately owned power plant was to check the further growth of the TVA, which he saw as representative of the Truman administration's "whole hog mentality"—the idea that the federal government must undertake major resource development projects on its own, freezing out "the energy and initiative of local government and local people engaged in private enterprise."

In his 1952 campaign against Adlai Stevenson, Eisenhower had decried what he saw as a Democratic policy which tended toward "supergovernment." He denounced "this whole hog mentality which leans toward the creation of a more extensive and stifling monopoly than this country has ever seen," noting that the TVA was a "supergovernment" blueprinted in Washington, D.C., and managed from there.

DMZ (Demilitarized Zone) *See* **Vietnam War.**

DNA (Deoxyribonucleic Acid) Deoxyribonucleic acid, or DNA, is an organic chemical present in chromosomes, where its complex molecular structure encodes genetic data. It was first isolated by biochemists in the nineteenth century, and by 1944 had been shown to be the substance of heredity.

A model of DNA's molecular structure was first devised in 1953 by the American biologist James D. Watson and the British biologist H. C. Crick, who published their findings in the British Magazine *Nature* (April 25, 1953, and May 30, 1953). Their work was based on research by the British biophysicist H. F. Wilkins, and all three men shared the Nobel Prize for it in 1962.

The Watson-Crick model of the molecular structure of DNA is a double helix formed by a two-stranded chain wound around itself to make a spiral ladder whose DNA "rungs" form a genetic code that determines the structure, size, and function of an organism.

DNA was first synthesized in 1956. In recent years there has been considerable concern about the possibility of biohazards unleashed by recombinant DNA research. In the mid-1970s the National Institutes of Health called a moratorium on recombinant research and in the summer of 1976 released controversial guidelines which some scientists feel are inhibiting research in the United States.

In the most common type of recombinant DNA

work, a strand of the helix-like chain is removed from the cell of some organism and implanted in a DNA strand of the bacterial strain *Escherichia coli* (*E. coli*), which lives in the human intestinal system and aids in digestion. Since much is known about the strain, the development of any new variant can be closely followed and well understood.

The hazards of such research can be described as follows: a new, variant strain might turn out to have harmful properties; it might escape from the protective facilities designed for it; and, finally, the fact that the human body is so "used to" *E. coli* could permit a new and possibly harmful strain to slip past our immunological defenses, perhaps causing an epidemic of a new and unknown disease.

DOE *See* **Department of Energy.**

"Dollar gap" and "dollar glut" In the post-World War II period, the demand for U.S. dollars from abroad greatly outran the supply. Rather than allow American currency to rise in relation to foreign currency, the problem of the "dollar gap" was handled by exchange and import controls instituted by nations whose currency was "overvalued" in terms of its real buying power. The situation was also to some extent corrected by American foreign aid programs such as the **Marshall Plan.**

By the end of the 1950s, the situation had reversed itself and the "dollar gap" had turned into a growing "dollar glut." American imports and investments abroad had cut gold stocks in this country from $22.8 billion in 1950 to $18 billion by the end of 1960. Speculation against the dollar increased during the next decade, and on August 15, 1971, President Richard M. Nixon suspended the convertibility of the dollar into gold. As a result of the Smithsonian Agreement (December 18, 1971) with the world's leading industrial nations, the dollar was devaluated in terms of gold from $35 an ounce to $38 an ounce. A second devaluation was announced on February 12, 1973, to $42.22 an ounce.

As the American balance of payments situation worsened in the 1970s, the price of gold on the free market soared to over $200 an ounce. By the end of 1978, the U.S. trade deficit was $28.5 billion, mostly due to oil imports, which ran about $3.7 billion a month. The dollar continued to decline in value as against leading currencies such as the Japanese yen, the Swiss franc, and the German mark.

Domestic Peace Corps Established under the Economic Opportunity Act passed by Congress on August 11, 1964.

See **War on Poverty.**

Dominican Intervention In September 1963, Juan Bosch, who had become president of the Dominican Republic in the first free elections that country had known after more than thirty years under the dictatorship of General Rafael Trujillo, was deposed by a rightist military coup. A conservative civilian triumvirate led by Donald Reid Cabral and supported by the United States came into power. The Reid regime was in turn overthrown by supporters of Bosch in a popular revolution that broke out on April 24, 1965. The rebels appealed to the United States for help in establishing an effective government and were refused.

Fighting against "loyalist" forces led by General Elias Wessin y Wessin continued, and the country was in disorder. With the stated purpose of protecting the lives of American citizens, President Lyndon B. Johnson dispatched 400 Marines to the island on April 28. Three days later there were more than 6,000 American troops in the Dominican Republic, but the Johnson administration still stoutly denied that it was taking sides in the struggle. However, on May 2, 1965, the President told the nation that the Dominican revolution had taken "a tragic turn" and fallen "into the hands of a band of Communist conspirators." Enunciating what is sometimes called the Johnson Doctrine, he noted that "the American nations cannot, must not, and will not permit the establishment of another Communist government in the Western Hemisphere." He explained, on what critics have felt was inadequate evidence, that what had begun as a popular democratic revolution committed to democracy and social justice was now in the hands of "Communist leaders, many of them trained in Cuba. . . .

"We believe that change comes, and we are glad it does, and it should come through peaceful process. But revolution in any country is a matter for that country to deal with. It becomes a matter calling for hemispheric action only—repeat, only—when the object is the establishment of a Communist dictatorship."

On May 6, 1965, the council of the **Organization of American States** (OAS) authorized the creation of an Inter-American Peace Force, and later that month small representative contingents from five South American nations joined the more than 20,000 American troops now in the Dominican Republic for the purposes of maintaining order. Despite a formal truce negotiated on May 5, fighting continued. In August a provisional government was established with American support and the civil war ended. In elections conducted the following March, Joaquin Balaguer, who in 1960 had been General

Trujillo's appointee as premier, was elected president. American troops remained in the country until September 1966.

President Johnson's decision to intervene in the Dominican Republic was widely criticized by American liberals, many of whom were already calling for nonintervention in the continuing **Vietnam War.** Indignant letters flooded the White House. Accounts sympathetic to the pro-Bosch rebels appeared in *The New York Times*, the *New York Herald Tribune*, and the *Washington Post.* In addition, the President's action was roundly condemned by the **Americans for Democratic Action** (ADA).

Domino Effect By 1953 the situation of the French in Indochina, where they had backed the corrupt regime of Emperor Bao Dai against Ho Chi Minh, leader of the Communist Vietminh forces, was becoming increasingly desperate. Appeals for American aid brought a commitment of $385 million from the Eisenhower administration to cover the period up to the end of 1954.

But by March 1954 the decisive battle of Dien Bien Phu had begun, with major French forces besieged in that city. At this point the French appealed for American intervention. Although unwilling to meet this demand, President Dwight D. Eisenhower felt that it was important to keep Indochina from coming under communist domination. On April 7, 1954, he explained his reasons at a press conference: "You have a row of dominoes set up, and you knock over the first one, and what will happen to the last one is the certainty that it will go over very quickly. So you have a beginning of a disintegration that would have the most profound influences."

With the collapse of French power after the fall of Dien Bien Phu on May 7, 1954, following a fifty-six-day siege, a multinational conference in Geneva "temporarily" divided Indochina at the 17th parallel into South and North Vietnam, the latter under communist rule. Free elections to unite the country were to have been held on July 20, 1956. In a switch from his public stance, backed by the President, Secretary of State John Foster Dulles confidentially informed a Cabinet meeting that as a result of this agreement "we have a clean base there, without the taint of colonialism. Dien Bien Phu was a blessing in disguise."

In defending the increased involvement of this country in the **Vietnam War** under the Kennedy administration, Arthur Schlesinger, Jr., wrote: "Whether the domino theory was valid in 1954, it

had acquired validity seven years later, after neighboring governments had staked their own security on the ability of the United States to live up to its pledges to Saigon. Kennedy . . . had no choice but to work within the situation he had inherited."

Referring to a review of their U.S. relations by Thailand and the Philippines after this country's reversals in Cambodia and Vietnam, President Gerald R. Ford, speaking in South Bend, Indiana, on March 17, 1975, noted that recent developments tended "to validate the so-called domino theory."

"Do-Nothing" Eightieth Congress *See* **Turnip Congress.**

Double Eagle II Craft used in the first successful transatlantic balloon crossing. Taking off from Presque Isle, Maine, on August 11, 1978, Max Anderson, Ben Abruzzo, and Larry Newman brought the *Double Eagle II* down in a wheatfield 60 miles west of Paris on August 17 after a flight of 137 hours and 18 minutes. An attempt the previous year by Anderson and Abruzzo had ended in failure when the *Double Eagle I* was ditched off the coast of Iceland.

The black and silver balloon, which cost $150,000 to build, was named in commemoration of Charles A. Lindbergh, Jr.—"the Lone Eagle"—who made the first nonstop flight from New York to Paris in 1927.

Double Helix *See* **DNA.**

Douglas-Kennedy-Ives Act *See* **Welfare and Pension Fund Disclosure Act.**

"Dragnet" A crime-busting television drama based on cases said to have been taken from the files of the Los Angeles Police Department, the program was written by the actor Jack Webb, who starred as the deadpan Detective Sergeant Joe Friday. Reproducing the success it had previously had on radio, the program lasted from 1952 to 1959, during which time Detective Friday's earnest counsel to hysterical witnesses—"All we want is the facts, ma'am"—entered the American language. A decade later the show made a reappearance as "Dragnet 1969."

Dragon Lady Name given in the press to Madame Ngo Dinh Nhu, wife of the influential brother of Ngo Dinh Diem, who, under South Vietnam's 1956 constitution, was twice elected president and who refused to permit the reunification elections called for in the Geneva Accords. The reference was to a serpentine oriental lady in Milt Caniff's popular comic strip "Terry and the Pirates."

In 1963 Madame Nhu and her husband urged the Diem regime's bloody repression of Buddhist demonstrations against the Catholic administration. When between June and October seven monks, or *bonzes*, immolated themselves as an antigovernment protest, she is said to have applauded these "barbecues" and only wished that certain American journalists critical of the Diem government would follow their example. An assault on Buddhist pagodas by Diem troops in late August was described by Madame Nhu as one of the happiest days of her life, but her father, the country's Ambassador to Washington, resigned in protest and publicly denounced his daughter.

Madame Nhu blamed the Kennedy administration for the coup by the military junta that resulted in the assassination of Diem and her husband on November 1, 1963.

She now lives in Italy and is said to be writing her own version of events in South Vietnam.

See **Vietnam War.**

Drug Industry Act Agitation for a new drug control bill was largely sparked by the **thalidomide** scare which caused many people to call for increased consumer safeguards. Signed into law on October 10, 1962, by President John F. Kennedy, who described it as a "strong" one, the bill was largely the work of Sen. Estes Kefauver (D.-Tenn.). In addition to requiring that drugs be proved effective and given government approval before they could be put on the market, the bill called for: the registration of drug manufacturers; labels and advertisements bearing both generic and brand names of all drugs; and batch-by-batch testing of antibiotics destined for use on humans. A requirement that physicians obtain the consent of a patient or his near relatives before dispensing experimental drugs—originally in the House bill passed by 347 to 0—was dropped.

Under the terms of the new legislation, the Secretary of Health, Education, and Welfare was authorized to withdraw from the market any drug that constituted a potential public health hazard. He was also empowered to prohibit the testing of drugs on humans if pre-clinical testing was deemed unsatisfactory.

The fight against the bill was led by Sen. James O. Eastland (D.-Miss.).

"Dump China" Policy The civil war in China was rapidly approaching an end when, on August 5, 1949, the U.S. Department of State issued a "White Paper" officially entitled *United States Relations with China. With Special Reference to the Period 1944-1949.* In this 1,054-page document, preceded by a fourteen-page letter of transmittal from Secretary of State Dean Acheson to President Harry S Truman, the United States formally announced the cessation of military aid to our former World War II ally and conceded that the world's largest nation had fallen into communist hands.

Secretary Acheson, who had succeeded the ailing George C. Marshall, strongly defended American policy and laid the blame for the collapse of resistance to the communist forces under Mao Tse-tung directly at the door of Generalissimo Chiang Kai-shek, whose Kuomintang (KMT) government was seen as corrupt, incompetent, and unresponsive both to the needs of the Chinese people and American insistence on reform. "It has been urged that relatively small amounts of additional aid—military and economic—to the National Government would have enabled it to destroy communism in China. The most trustworthy military, economic, and political information available to our Government does not bear out this view. . . . The only alternative open to the United States was full-scale intervention on behalf of a Government which had lost the confidence of its own troops and its own people."

The White Paper pointed out that since the end of World War II the United States had provided Chiang with over $2 billion in grants and credits, and had by agreement sold his government $1,078 million in nonmilitary supplies for $232 million. Approximately half of the Nationalist war machine was American equipped, and this included thirty-nine Nationalist divisions. However, in the final quarter of 1948, some 80 percent of this equipment had been lost, fully 75 percent being captured intact by the communists.

Still smarting from President Truman's upset victory over Thomas E. Dewey (R.-N.Y.) in November 1948, the Republicans lashed out at what was quickly labeled a "dump China" policy and refused to accept Secretary Acheson's contention that "nothing that this country did or could have done within the reasonable limits of its capabilities" could have prevented the victory of communism in China. "In making Chiang Kai-shek the whipping boy for the Department's own blunders," complained the *New York World-Telegram and Sun,* "Mr. Acheson leaves unanswered the question of most concern to all Americans: What is the Department doing, or planning to do, to protect American interests in the Pacific, not only in China but in the

Philippines, Japan, Hawaii and other threatened areas?" The failure of Democratic policy on China was traced back to the Yalta Pact, which had permitted the Russians to take over from the Japanese in Manchuria and then see to it that captured arms found their way into the hands of Chinese communists.

Meanwhile, the position of the Nationalist forces on the mainland had continued to crumble, and in December 1949, the Kuomintang withdrew to the island of Taiwan. Echoes of the "dump China" charges continued. Although President Truman rejected Republican suggestions that American troops be used to defend Taiwan, he refused to recognize the Communist Chinese government. It was not until 1971 under the Republican administration of President Richard M. Nixon, who had during his career been most vociferous on the need of an American commitment to Nationalist China, that steps were taken to normalize relations between the United States and Red China.

That same year, the United States, which had previously taken the lead in opposition to the seating of Red China at the United Nations, introduced into the General Assembly a resolution that would have allowed the seating of Communist China on the Security Council and the retention of the Nationalist delegation in the General Assembly (see **Two-Chinas Policy; Conlon Report**). It was defeated in favor of an Albanian resolution calling for the ousting of Nationalist China from the United Nations.

Steps toward the normalization of relations with Red China were taken during the administrations of Presidents Nixon and Gerald R. Ford (see **Peking Summit; Pacific Doctrine**). In a nationwide television broadcast on December 15, 1978, President Jimmy Carter announced that diplomatic relations between the two nations would be resumed as of January 1, 1979. "The people of our country," he said, "will maintain our current commercial, cultural, trade and other relations with Taiwan through nongovernmental means."

Dumpling War Incensed because his home in Bavaria had been made uninhabitable by the noise of low-flying jets of the West German Air Force, Hermann Winter built a catapult with which he managed to splatter them with dumplings. On March 1, 1967, the Luftwaffe "capitulated" and agreed to maintain a higher altitude. Two days later, the U.S. Air Force agreed to negotiate when Winter's "flak" managed to hit helicopters flying as low as 150 feet. Received by American authorities with full military honors, Winter was assured that a minimum altitude of 1,600 feet would henceforth be maintained.

"Dump the Hump" *See* **Battle of Chicago.**

"Duty, Honor, Country" On May 12, 1962, General Douglas A. MacArthur, who had graduated from West Point in 1903 and been its superintendent from 1919 to 1922, returned to the U.S. Military Academy for his "final roll call" and to accept the Sylvanus Thayer Award "for outstanding service to the nation." His moving farewell, which has come to be known as the "Duty, Honor, Country Speech," included the following:

Duty, honor, country. Those three hallowed words reverently dictate what you ought to be, what you can be, what you will be. . . . The long, gray line has never failed us. . . .

"You now face a new world—a world of change. The thrust into outer space of the satellite spheres and missiles mark the beginning of another epoch. . . . And through all of this welter of change, your mission remains fixed, determined, inviolable—it is to win our wars. Only the dead have seen the end of war".

General MacArthur died in Washington, D.C., on April 5, 1964.
See **"Old soldiers never die; they just fade away."**

Dynamic Conservatism President Dwight D. Eisenhower's basically conservative tendency was best exemplified by his choice of a Cabinet, which one wit dubbed **"eight millionaires and a plumber."** Chief among the millionaires was Secretary of the Treasury George Humphrey, a former M.A. Hanna Steel Company executive, whose dogmatic views on a balanced budget, tight credit, reduced spending, and lower taxes dominated the first budget.

The result of these policies was the 1954 recession. As the economy slumped, tax revenues declined along with employment and production. In addition, Secretary Humphrey had to agree to a 30-percent increase in foreign aid for 1955. ("Before coming in here, I had no idea of the extent to which our own security was involved in whatever happens in the world.") Nor could the demands for increased expenditures in housing, agriculture, and welfare be any longer ignored.

Responding with a modified form of **"Keynesianism,"** the Eisenhower administration alarmed old-line Republicans who feared a New Deal approach to economic and social problems. It was possibly to allay these fears that the President told the finance committee of the Republican National Committee on February 17, 1955: "I have said we were 'progressive moderates.' Right at the moment I favor the term 'dynamic conservatism.' I believe we should conserve on everything that is basic to our system. We should be dynamic in applying it to the problems of the day so that all our 165,000,000 Americans will profit from it."

E

Earth Day

Eagleton Affair Convening in Miami Beach, Florida, in July 1972, the Democratic National Convention chose Sen. George McGovern (S. Dak.) and Sen. Thomas F. Eagleton (Mo.) as its presidential and vice-presidential candidates in the forthcoming national election. Soon after, rumors began circulating about Senator Eagleton's medical history of mental depression and the McGovern camp found itself in an embarrassing position. Learning that an influential newspaper chain was about to break the story, Senators McGovern and Eagleton called a press conference on July 25, 1972, at Sylvan Lake, South Dakota, during which the vice-presidential candidate revealed that on three separate occasions—1960, 1964, and 1966—he had been hospitalized for nervous exhaustion and that on two of these occasions he had undergone electric shock therapy for depression.

Senator McGovern's immediate impulse was to defend his running mate, and he announced: "I think Tom Eagleton is fully qualified in mind, body and spirit to be Vice President of the United States and, if necessary, to take the presidency at a moment's notice." He went on to say that if he had known every detail that Eagleton now revealed to the press, he would still have chosen him for Vice President.

In the week that followed, however, the presidential candidate came under strong pressure from key Democrats around the country and began to noticeably back away from firm support for Senator Eagleton in a manner that considerably tarnished his reputation for candor and openness. It became obvious that he was making no serious effort to stem the "dump Eagleton" campaign. In addition, stories began to appear in the press indicating that Senator McGovern felt that his running mate was a threat to the success of the Democratic ticket and should therefore withdraw.

To complicate the situation, columnist Jack Anderson announced on July 27, 1972, that he had located photostats of police records indicating that Senator Eagleton had on half a dozen occasions been arrested for drunken driving. The vice-presidential candidate rejected this charge as "a damnable lie." Asked at one point whether he would bring his case before the nation on television, Senator Eagleton said that he would not expose his family in that way, adding, in an obvious reference to President Richard M. Nixon's **Checkers Speech** in 1952: "We have a dog too, called Pumpkin."

Officially, Senator McGovern continued to insist that he was "with Senator Eagleton all the way," but it was obvious that his support was weakening.

However, Senator Eagleton insisted that in the course of a phone conversation the presidential nominee had assured him that "he's 1,000% for me."

Nevertheless on July 31, 1972, at a joint press conference with Senator Eagleton, Senator McGovern announced that his running mate was withdrawing from the race. The following day, columnist Jack Anderson withdrew his drunken driving charges and apologized. On August 8, 1972, the Democratic National Committee nominated Sargent Shriver, former **Peace Corps** head and brother-in-law of the late President John F. Kennedy, for the second spot after Sen. Edmund S. Muskie (D.-Maine) had declined for "family reasons."

Many critics felt that more damage had been done to the Democratic ticket by Senator McGovern's wavering between "1,000%" support for his running mate and undercutting him behind the scenes than had been done by the original disclosure of Senator Eagleton's history of nervous exhaustion.

Early Bird 1 See Intelsat 1

Earth Day In rallies, parades, and demonstrations across the nation on April 22, 1970, millions of Americans called for strong pollution control measures. Suggested by the **Moratorium Days** that helped mobilize public sentiment against the **Vietnam War** in 1969, Earth Day was the idea of Sen. Gaylord Nelson (D.-Wis.), who with Rep. Paul N. McCloskey, Jr. (R.-Calif.), in January 1970 organized an Environmental Teach-in in Washington, D.C., to coordinate activities all over the United States. The group later announced that some form of Earth Day observance was planned in over 2,000 communities and in many colleges, high schools, and elementary schools. Mass rallies in New York, Chicago, and Philadelphia drew an estimated 25,000.

Some critics of the Earth Day observances felt that they were a diversionary action that would only distract from the more important national problems such as peace, civil rights, and poverty. However, speaking in Denver, Colorado, on that day, Senator Nelson emphasized that ecological and environmental problems were being scanted "by the expenditure of $25 billion a year on the war in Vietnam, instead of on our decaying, crowded, congested, polluted urban areas that are inhuman traps for millions of people." Addressing a rally in Philadelphia, Sen. Edmund S. Muskie (D.-Maine) pointed out that an improved ecology would require "hard decisions about our national priorities."

In Massachusetts, the legislature voted unanimously to amend the state constitution to make a pollution-free environment a constitutional right. Bills establishing state environmental departments were signed by the governors of New York and New Jersey, and in Illinois Governor Richard B. Ogilvie recommended a $750 million antipollution bond issue.

Speaking at the University of Alaska, Secretary of the Interior Walter J. Hickel said that he would issue a right-of-way permit for the construction of the 800-mile Alaska oil pipeline (see **Alaskan Pipeline**) opposed by some conservation groups. However, he promised that he would not approve "any design based on the old and faulty concept of 'build now, repair later.'"

President Richard M. Nixon took no part in the observances, but a White House spokesman declared that the President "feels the activities show the concern of people of all walks of life over the dangers to our environment."

Easy Rider In this enormously successful 1969 "road film" directed by Dennis Hopper, two motorcyclists ride across an incredibly scenic nation on their way from California to New Orleans. The movie is in many ways a reverse image of **The Wild One,** the 1953–1954 motorcycle hit, starring Marlon Brando, in which the cyclists represent a threat to the order and essential decency of a small town by their violence and lawlessness. Fifteen years later, the cultural atmosphere in the nation had so changed that it is the violence and basic lawlessness of small-town thinking which eventually destroy two innocent if hop-headed romantics in search of nonconformist freedom.

The movie launched the film career of Jack Nicholson in the role of a lawyer who takes refuge from small-town pressure in alcoholism and cheerful acceptance of his own mediocrity. His articulateness and lively gestures contrast sharply with the stony nonverbalness of the two cyclists (played by Dennis Hopper and Peter Fonda).

Echo I The first of the communications satellites by which radio and TV signals could be flashed to various points on the globe, *Echo I* was launched on August 12, 1960. A "passive" satellite, it was a giant silver balloon inflatable to a diameter of 100 feet once it was placed in orbit of 941 to 1,052 miles high by a Delta rocket. As it passed over the United States, it reflected from the West Coast to the East Coast a taped message by President Dwight D. Eisenhower. Later *Echo I* was used to reflect a series of two-way telephone calls.

A somewhat larger *Echo II* was launched in 1964. It was a similar silver balloon, but it could be inflated to a 135-foot diameter. Its size and high reflectivity made it appear in the night sky as a star.

The importance of the *Echo* satellites was that they demonstrated that the microwave relay technology developed by Bell Laboratories could be applied to international communications if a skyborne microwave repeater could be provided.

Economic Opportunity Act *See* **War on Poverty.**

Economic Research Action Project (ERAP) *See* **Students for a Democratic Society.**

The Edsel Introduced in August 1957 and representing an investment of a quarter of a billion dollars, The Edsel was intended as the Ford Motor Company's answer to the medium-priced General Motors cars that were proving more popular with the public than Ford's own Mercurys. Six years of planning and research—some of it heavily dependent on the Columbia University Bureau of Applied Social Research—had gone into its design, which was a carefully guarded industry secret. Motivational researchers sifted through some 6,000 possibilities—among those consulted was poet Marianne Moore—before it was decided that naming it after the father of the company chairman, Henry Ford II, would convey to the public the vehicle's essential dignity and dependability.

The Edsel featured an interior meant to be the epitome of the push-button era, a flaring gull-wing rear end, and an oval radiator grille that *Time* magazine said "looked like an Oldsmobile sucking a lemon." If it was to show a profit, some 200,000 had to be sold in the first year.

Unfortunately, in the interval between the original motivational research and the time the Edsel went on sale, the stock market broke, the 1957–1958 recession began, and the Russians launched their first **Sputnik.**

As one congressman noted, the time had come to be less concerned about the height of the tail fin on a new car and to be "more prepared to shed blood, sweat, and tears." Automobile dealers were experiencing one of the worst sales seasons in automotive-industry history. In addition, the first Edsels were reported to have a number of operational defects.

In January 1958, the Edsel was merged with Ford's Lincoln-Mercury department. In November

1959 the company announced a halt in Edsel production, citing the fact that retail sales had been "disappointing." (The company had lost $400 million on it.) The word "Edsel" had become a national joke which, like the name "Brooklyn," seemed to automatically evoke laughter. It became a synonym for excessive ambition and disappointing performance.

When during the 1968 presidential campaign the Republican party tried to represent candidate Richard M. Nixon as the "new Nixon," Democrats replied that he was still the same old "Tricky Dick, the human Edsel."

Education Act of 1965 *See* **Elementary and Secondary Education Act.**

Educational Television Facilities Act of 1962 *See* **Public Broadcasting Act of 1967.**

Educational Testing Service (ETS) *See* **Buckley Amendment.**

"Effete corps of impudent snobs" Speaking at a Republican fund-raising dinner in New Orleans on October 19, 1969, Vice President Spiro T. Agnew criticized the recent **Moratorium Day** (October 15) anti-**Vietnam War** protests which he said had been "encouraged by an effete corps of impudent snobs who characterize themselves as intellectuals." Referring to the second Moratorium Day protests planned for November by the New Mobilization Committee to End the War in Vietnam, he warned that "hardcore dissidents and professional anarchists" were planning "wilder, more violent" demonstrations.

A seeming difference within the administration of President Richard M. Nixon about the right to peaceful protest was voiced the following day when Secretary of State William P. Rogers noted in New York that the demonstrators had "wished principally to register dramatic but dignified expression of their deep concern for peace in Vietnam." Although the President himself had declined to comment on the Moratorium Day protest, Secretary Rogers added that "we listened to those voices with respect, because we, too, have a deep concern for peace in Vietnam."

According to a statement by the White House press secretary Ronald L. Ziegler, neither speech had been cleared in advance by the White House, and both men were "expressing personal feeling" in their remarks.

The Vice President's comments on Moratorium Day were attacked by leading Democrats such as Sen. Edmund S. Muskie (Maine), who termed them a "disservice to the country and to the President," and himself characterized the protests as "an outpouring of concerned Americans trying to contribute in a constructive way to the shape of our policy."

See **"Nattering Nabobs of Negativism."**

Egghead Row The stretch of Massachusetts Avenue in Washington, D.C., around which are clustered such prestigious organizations as Resources for the Future, the Brookings Institution, the Carnegie Institution, and a host of lesser known but important research centers.

Eggheads During the Eisenhower administration the expression "egghead" became a popular and stigmatizing reference to intellectuals. It probably first appeared in a syndicated column by Stewart Alsop during the 1952 presidential campaign. Alsop reported that when he told his brother John, who at the time headed the Connecticut Republican Speakers' Bureau, that many intellectuals who had supported the Republican presidential nomination of Dwight D. Eisenhower against Robert A. Taft were now switching their support to the Democratic nominee, Adlai Stevenson, he was told: "Sure, all the eggheads are voting for Stevenson, but how many eggheads are there?"

John Alsop had apparently not meant the word to be pejorative, but it was soon picked up and used as such. Stevenson wittily accepted the challenge and satirically echoing Marx said: "Eggheads unite! You have nothing to use but your yolks."

Typical of the antiegghead view is that of novelist Lewis Bromfield, who complained that "if the egghead will come back into power . . . we will go on the scenic railway of muddled economics, Socialism, Communism, crookedness and psychopathic instability."

"Eight millionaires and a plumber" Upon assuming office in January 1953, President Dwight D. Eisenhower formed a Cabinet that showed his marked tendency to lean more on the nation's business and industrial leaders than on men drawn from the worlds of politics and academia. His unsuccessful Democratic rival, Adlai Stevenson, called the new Eisenhower administration "the Big Deal," and noted that "the New Dealers have all left Washington to make way for the car dealers."

Although in defining his approach to social and economic problems the new President was later (1955) to talk of **"dynamic conservatism,"** his Cabinet was decidedly more conservative than dynamic. For Secretary of State he chose the wealthy corporation lawyer, John Foster Dulles; Charles E. Wilson, head of General Motors, was to head the Department of Defense; George Humphrey, M.A. Hanna Steel Company executive, took over the Department of the Treasury—and immediately hung on his office wall a portrait of millionaire Andrew W. Mellon; conservative farm marketing specialist Ezra Taft Benson, a strong advocate of reduced or eliminated federal aid to farmers, became Secretary of Agriculture; New England industrialist Sinclair Weeks was appointed Secretary of Commerce; and Arthur E. Summerfield, an automobile distributor, was named Postmaster General. Other Cabinet appointments included Oregon's Governor Douglas McKay (Secretary of the Interior) and Herbert Brownell, Jr. (Attorney General). All were wealthy men long associated with the Republican establishment. The only real departure from the type was Martin Durkin, president of the Journeymen Plumbers and Steamfitters' Union, who was given the post of Secretary of Labor. (He shortly resigned, charging that the President had not kept his promise to revise the **Taft-Hartley Act** (1947) so hated by labor.)

Quipped the anonymous TRB (Richard Strout) of the liberal *New Republic:* "Ike's cabinet consists of eight millionaires and a plumber."

An additional millionaire was added to the Cabinet in April 1953, when Mrs. Oveta Culp Hobby, wartime head of the Women's Army Corps (WACs) and the wife of a wealthy Texas publisher, was appointed to the newly created position of Secretary of Health, Education and Welfare (HEW).

Eisenhower Doctrine Continuing tension in the Middle East led President Dwight D. Eisenhower to appear before Congress on January 5, 1957, to ask for authority to use U.S. troops, if necessary, to protect the area from communist aggression. On that same day, Rep. Thomas A. Gordon (R.-Ill.) introduced a resolution to that effect.

Action would result if any Middle Eastern country requested "such aid against overt armed aggression from any nation controlled by international communism." It was to be consonant with U.S. treaty obligations, the United Nations Charter, and recommendations by that international body, all measures to be immediately reported to the Security Council and not to affect either its authority or responsibility. The resolution would authorize the President to use up to $200 million from existing mutual security appropriations without regard to the provisions of other laws or regulations.

Sam Rayburn, Speaker of the House of Representatives and a Democrat, attempted to substitute for the resolution—the features of which had been essentially worked out by Secretary of State John Foster Dulles—a brief declaration which stated that "the United States regards as vital to her interest the preservation of the independence and integrity of the states of the Middle East and, if necessary, will use her armed force to that end." This statement was, however, flatly rejected by the Eisenhower administration. The joint resolution was passed by the House on January 30, 1957, but debate continued in the Senate over what many feared would authorize the President to make an all-out attack on the Soviet Union. After the failure of an attempt to eliminate funds for economic and military assistance, the Eisenhower Doctrine was approved by the Senate on March 7 and signed into law two days later.

Its first invocation came in April of that year when the President sent the U.S. Sixth Fleet to the Eastern Mediterranean following rioting in Jordan when King Hussein—who did not request American aid in this internal affair—asked for the resignation of his premier. On July 15, 1958, President Eisenhower sent the Sixth Fleet and 5,000 marines to Lebanon on the request of President Camille Chamoun, whose government had been overthrown. Disorder spread to neighboring Iraq, and led to the assassination of King Faisal II and Crown Prince Abdul Illad. When the rule of Jordan's King Hussein was threatened, Great Britain dispatched troops. Both American and British forces were withdrawn from the area in October, after order had been restored.

Eisenhower's Farewell Address After half a century in the service of his country during times of both war and peace, President Dwight D. Eisenhower took leave of public office in a farewell address delivered over radio and television on January 18, 1961. His talk, in which he warned against the dangers to this nation of "the military-industrial complex," is considered one of his most important public addresses and ranked by some as perhaps his greatest service to his fellow citizens. It was all the more surprising coming from a man who had spent most of his life in the military and who as President was considered by critics to have been closely allied with the business and industrial community.

Acknowledging that our military establishment was vital to the peace, President Eisenhower noted that until World War II we had no armaments industry, properly speaking. "American makers of plowshares could, with time and as required, make swords as well." At the present time, however, we had "a permanent armaments industry of vast proportions" in which three and a half million people were directly engaged. We were spending more on military security than the combined net income of all United States corporations.

Although recognizing the need for this development, he urged that cognizance be taken of "its grave implications." Our resources and livelihood were involved, as was the very structure of American society.

"In the councils of government, we must guard against the acquisition of unwarranted influence, whether sought or unsought, by the military-industrial complex. The potential for the disastrous rise of misplaced power exists and will persist." Only an alert and informed citizenry, the President emphasized, "can compel the proper meshing of the huge industrial and military machinery of defense with our peaceful methods and goals, so that security and liberty may prosper together."

Allied to the sweeping changes in our industrial-military "posture," he concluded, was the recent technological revolution in which an increasing amount of scientific research is controlled by the federal government. "The prospect of domination of the nation's scholars by federal employment, project allocations, and the power of money is ever present and is gravely to be regarded." While holding scientific research "in respect, as we should, we must also be alert to the equal and opposite danger that public policy could itself become the captive of a scientific-technological elite."

Eldercare In its battle against **Medicare,** in 1965 the American Medical Association (AMA) caused a bill known as Eldercare to be introduced into the House of Representatives. In essence, it was a modification of the Kerr-Mills Act of 1960, which was meant to provide for those people who, though not on welfare, were financially unable to sustain hospital and doctor bills. They were known as the "medically indigent," and a state could apply to the federal government for subsidization of a private and voluntary medical insurance plan to aid them. (In 1965, only half of the states had applied for such subsidies.) Eldercare increased the number of people who would be eligible for such aid and widened the number of services available to them. It was attacked by Medicare proponents as inadequate. Rep. Frank Thompson, Jr. (D.-N.J.)

pointed out that since it was of essentially more use to doctors than their patients, it might more accurately have been called "Doctorcare."

Elementary and Secondary Education Act Signed into law by President Lyndon B. Johnson on April 11, 1965, the act provided $1.3 billion in federal aid to elementary and secondary schools by giving the money directly to the states.

According to President Johnson, previous administrations attempting to provide federal aid to schools had run into three stumbling blocks: opposition to granting federal funds to segregated school systems; fear of federal control of schools; and unwillingness to grant federal funds to parochial schools. The first problem had, however, at the time the bill was introduced in January 1965 been minimized by the **Civil Rights Act of 1964,** which prohibited the use of federal funds for supporting segregated institutions or activities. On the separation of church and state issue, the President felt he had "more flexibility" as a Protestant than had President John F. Kennedy, a Catholic, when his 1961 attempt to secure federal funds for schools was wrecked on that issue because Catholics felt that their needs were ignored. By making the educational grants directly to the states, President Johnson felt that parochial schools would also benefit, and that those who feared federal control over local school boards be reassured.

Federal funds were given individual states on the basis of a formula by which payments would be equal to half the average cost of educating a child in an individual state times the number of school-age children in that state from families on relief or with incomes below $2,000. School districts were also to get federal grants for special services such as shared-time classes and counseling for students in both private and public institutions. In addition, funds were made available for state educational planning, the purchase of books, and the support of supplementary community education centers.

One source of opposition to the bill incorporating the act was from those who pointed out that since the cost of educating a child could vary from state to state by as much as $500 the bill would, in effect, disadvantage the poorer states.

Rep. Edith S. Green (D.-Oreg.), though a supporter of education legislation, offered what became known as the Green Amendment, under which all states would be given a $200-per-child grant. Under her revised distribution formula, the grant to a state such as Mississippi would have risen from $28 million to approximately $46 million; however, in the case of wealthier states such as New York the grant would have been cut from almost $92 million to about $52 million. When her amendment was rejected, she nevertheless supported the bill.

See **Smith Amendment.**

Ellsberg Break-in *See* **Pentagon Papers; "The Plumbers."**

Emergency Broadcast System Instituted in 1964 to replace the obsolete Conelrad (Control of Electromagnetic Radiation) emergency network, which had been initiated in the 1950s to mislead potential enemy bombers and missiles by limiting broadcasting in an area to a single station and confining all broadcasts to two frequencies, the new system was designed to permit emergency broadcasting over 8,000 radio and television stations in less than five minutes. In 1975 the Federal Communications Commission (FCC) began setting up a system which would make portions of the network available for state and local use during emergencies. American radio and television listeners became familiar with the high-pitched, steady-tone test signal that was broadcast weekly.

The Emerging Republican Majority *See* **Southern Strategy.**

Employee Benefit Security Act *See* **Pension Reform Act of 1974; Individual Retirement Account; Keogh Retirement Plan.**

Employment Act of 1946 Nowhere was the inherent American acceptance of the principles of Keynesian economics more obvious than in the full-employment legislation which President Harry S Truman requested of Congress in a twenty-one-point message on September 6, 1945, and signed (February 20, 1946) into law as the Employment Act of 1946. While, as the President was to note, the act "had undergone considerable changes in the process," it made it the responsibility of the federal government to utilize all its potential powers and resources—deficit spending being an implied but unstated principle— to achieve "maximum employment, production and purchasing power."

Cooperation between the executive branch and Congress was to be facilitated by the establishment of a joint congressional committee of seven Senators and seven Representatives to study and report on presidential recommendations regarding full employment. The act also authorized the establishment of a three-man Council of Economic Advisers within the Executive Office to assist the President in formulating policy and in preparing an economic report that was to be submitted to Congress within sixty days after the initiation of each regular session. The first council, appointed in July 1946, was headed by Edwin G. Nourse, vice president of the Brookings Institution, and included Leon Keyserling, general counsel of the National Housing Agency, and Dr. John Davidson Clark, dean of the University of Nebraska's School of Business Administration and a former vice president of the Standard Oil Company of Indiana.

Secretary of the Treasury Fred Vinson prepared for the President's use on signing the legislation a statement which, though unused, remained in the presidential files: "Occasionally, as we pore through the pages of history, we are struck by the fact that some incident, little noted at the time, profoundly affects the whole subsequent course of events. I venture the prediction that history, someday, will so record the enactment of the Employment Act of 1946."

The legislation is sometimes known as the Full-Employment Act of 1946, but in the final version the term "full employment" was sacrificed, as was the specific commitment to spend what might be needed to bring this about. In place of "full employment," the Act uses an accepted definition: "Conditions under which there are employment opportunities, including self-employment, for all who are able, willing and seeking to work."

Encounter Groups A form of psychotherapy designed to provide intense emotional experiences with groups of from ten to fifteen people. The aim of the "group" is to counter feelings of isolation by developing trusting relationships through a variety of verbal and nonverbal techniques. Among the better known is "trust" falling, in which a member of the group is encouraged to fall back into the waiting arms of the group. Bodily awareness, enjoyment, and the expression of feeling is stressed at the expense of intellectual understanding.

Encounter sessions may last anything from a day to an entire weekend. Since the "group" disbands after a relatively short period, critics feel there is little chance of developing lasting feelings of trust and intimacy. In addition, since the sessions are potentially dangerous to those who are seriously disturbed, most psychotherapists of the more conventional schools consider them as—at best—no more than an interesting experience.

The popularity of encounter groups dates back to the founding of the Esalen Institute, Big Sur, California, in the early 1960s by Mike Murphy and Dick Price. By the late 1970s some of their appeal had been taken over by movements such as **est.**

"End-the-War" Amendment *See* **Hatfield-McGovern Amendment.**

Energy Crisis Although it had been building for two decades, ever since the United States ceased being a net petroleum exporter, the energy crisis came to a head in 1973, when domestic demand was running to 17 million barrels daily and domestic production lagged 6 million barrels behind. With reliance on petroleum imports increasing, on April 19, 1973, President Richard M. Nixon warned Congress that "if present trends go unchecked we could face a genuine energy crisis."

His energy policy called for increased production to be stimulated by tax credits to the oil industry for discovering new sources of supply. He also urged more use of coal—our most abundant fuel—and an end to federal regulation of natural gas prices. On May 1, 1973, he discontinued the oil import quota system established fourteen years earlier to protect American producers.

Little more than two months later, President Nixon's tone was charged with considerably more urgency when on June 29 he called for a voluntary conservation drive under which personal oil consumption would be cut 5 percent and the government's consumption by 7 percent in the next year. "America faces a serious energy problem," the President now warned. "While we have 6 percent of the world's population, we consume one-third of the world's energy output." John A. Love was appointed to head a White House Energy Office which would coordinate various energy production and conservation programs. He became the nation's first "energy czar."

The situation became critical when the Arab oil-producing nations meeting in October 1973 declared a ban on oil exports to the United States because of its support of Israel during the Yom Kippur attack launched against that nation by Egypt and Syria on October 6, 1973. Appearing before a nationwide television audience on November 7, 1973, the President outlined a variety of conservation measures. The following day he asked for immediate congressional action on a National Emergency Energy Act. (Congress adjourned on December 22, 1973, without having provided the legislation, chiefly because of a "windfall profits" provision that would have required a rollback in prices in those sectors of the oil industry that could be shown to have profited from the crisis situation.) On November 16, 1973, the President signed into law a bill providing for the controversial **Alaskan Pipeline,** which he called a step toward making this country self-sufficient in energy production by 1980. In the interim, an Emergency Petroleum Allocation Act signed by the President on November 28, 1973, gave the federal government power to set up allocation programs for crude oil and refinery products and thereby prevent discrimination against national regions as well as against independent producers and distributors.

On December 1, 1974, the White House announced the creation of a Federal Energy Administration to be headed by Deputy Secretary of the Treasury William E. Simon. Two days later, in spite of efforts to "keep him on the energy team," John Love resigned his post as head of the White House Energy Office rather than remain in the Capital "twiddling my thumbs" in a now "superfluous" post. At the same time, he confirmed rumors that his ability to win support for gasoline rationing had been hampered by opposition from Secretary of the Treasury George P. Shultz, who wanted to curb consumer demand through higher prices and taxes. On December 4, Simon, who retained his Treasury post, formally became the nation's new "energy czar." He immediately indicated his opposition to rationing, which he said could under no circumstances begin before March 1, 1974. Broad fuel allocation plans to assure "equitable distribution at the wholesale level" were announced as ready to go into effect on December 27. Allocations were based on 1972 consumption. Meanwhile, on December 23 the Organization of Petroleum Exporting Countries (OPEC) announced that the price of Persian Gulf crude oil would be doubled. A month later major American oil producers reported record profits in 1973, mostly from overseas earnings.

Increased taxation of the foreign profits of oil companies and the elimination of the 22-percent **depletion allowance** for foreign crude oil production were proposed by President Nixon on January 23, 1974. Emphasizing production rather than conservation of energy, he recommended the faster licensing and building of nuclear power plants, and he urged wider exploration of the oil and gas sources of the outer continental shelf.

Meeting in Vienna on March 18, 1974, the majority of the OPEC nations ended the five-month oil embargo against the United States. The following day, President Nixon announced that some energy-consumption restrictions—such as the ban on Sunday gasoline sales—would be lifted and that gasoline rationing was no longer being considered.

The return to abundant gasoline supplies during the incumbency of President Gerald R. Ford fed voter apathy concerning an energy program, and no effective action was taken by Congress. However, in the winter of 1976-1977 a shortage of natural gas caused the temporary closing of hundreds of industrial firms in the Middle West. On April 20, 1977, three months after assuming office, President Jimmy Carter outlined to a joint session of Congress an energy program which would keep demand growth to under 2 percent annually, cut imports by 50 percent, establish a 1 billion-barrel reserve oil supply, reduce gasoline consumption by 10 percent, and raise coal production by two-thirds. To prevent a "national catastrophe," he proposed a complete change—based on higher taxes and prices and a program of incentives—in our approach to energy consumption. While the Carter Energy Program called for additional atomic plants, there was to be no immediate action on a possible breeder-reactor program. The President asked for the decontrol of gasoline prices and an adjustment of utility rates to reflect production costs. By allowing homeowners tax credits for installing storm windows and doors as well as solar energy systems, he hoped to have such energy saving devices installed in 2.5 million homes by 1985.

One year after the President had described the struggle for energy conservation as "the moral equivalent of war," most of his energy plan, which included 113 separate initiatives, was still stalled in Congress. OPEC imports were down 9 percent and critics of the plan were predicting an oil and natural gas "glut" that made—at least temporarily—the Carter Energy Program unnecessary.

However, in 1978 oil imports were higher than ever, and finally, a year and a half after he had first requested it, on October 15, 1978, Congress gave the President a much modified version of his energy package, having lopped off the tax he wanted on domestic crude oil, a standby tax on gasoline, and a tax on industrial and utility use of oil and natural gas. Somewhat unconvincingly, the President announced that "we have declared to ourselves and the world our intent to control our use of energy, and thereby to control our own destiny as a nation."

Early in 1979, a "second energy crisis" was created when, after four months of unrest during which oil exports were cut from 5.5 million barrels daily to zero, the Shah of Iran was ousted. The price of oil was expected to rise to $20 a barrel.

Energy Research and Development Administration (ERDA) *See* **Atomic Energy Commission; Department of Energy.**

Engel v. Vitale The U.S. Supreme Court found on June 25, 1962, that the reading of a nondenominational prayer in New York public schools was in violation of the First Amendment to the Constitution in that it was a breach in the wall separating Church and State.

"Under the Amendment's prohibition against government establishment of religion, as reinforced by the provisions of the Fourteenth Amendment [which extended most of the provisions of the 'Bill of Rights' to the states], government of this country, be it state or federal, is without power to prescribe by law any particular form of prayer which is to be used as an official prayer in carrying on any program of governmentally sponsored religious activity."

In his dissenting opinion, Justice Potter Stewart said: "With all respect, I think the Court has misapplied a great constitutional principle. I cannot see how an 'official religion' is established by letting those who want to say a prayer say it."

Major post-World War II cases relating to religion and the public school system include: *Everson v. Board of Education* (1947), *McCollum v. Board of Education* (1948), and *Zorach v. Clauson* (1952).

See **"Released time."**

Enola Gay The B-29 used to drop an atomic bomb (the first of two to be used against Japan in a three-day period) on Hiroshima, August 6, 1945, in the final days of World War II. The Superfortress was the flagship of Colonel Paul W. Tibbets, Jr., commanding officer of the 509th Composite Group, to which the mission had been assigned; it had long before been named for his mother.

Enterprise *See* **National Aeronautics and Space Administration.**

Environmental Protection Agency (EPA) On July 9, 1970, calling for a major reorganization of the federal government's environmentally related activities, which had "grown up piecemeal over the years," President Richard M. Nixon proposed that the majority of federal pollution-control functions be unified in a new independent agency. In the same message to Congress, he also proposed "a unified approach to the problems of the oceans and atmosphere" by the creation of a **National Atmospheric Administration** (NOAA).

Both plans were offered under the President's executive reorganization authority and, in the absence of congressional opposition, went into effect ninety days later. The EPA, which was to employ 5,600 and have a 1971 budget of $1.4 billion, was to oversee clean air and water activities, radiation monitoring programs, and pesticide control. The President proposed no new powers for the agency, which inherited responsibilities carried out under the **Department of Health, Education, and Welfare** (HEW) by the National Air Pollution Control Administration, the Bureau of Solid Waste Management, the Bureau of Water Hygiene, the Air Quality Advisory Board, the Bureau of Radiological Health, and the Federal Drug Administration's (FDA) pesticide control section. The EPA also took over from the Department of the Interior functions carried out by the Federal Water Quality Administration, the Gulf Breeze (Florida) Biological Laboratory of the Bureau of Commercial Fisheries, the Water Pollution Control Advisory Board, and the Fish and Wildlife Service's pesticide investigations. Ecological systems studies were also inherited from the Council on Environmental Quality created in 1969, and the pesticides registration program was transferred to the EPA from the Department of Agriculture's Agricultural Research Service. In addition, the new agency, legally established on October 2, 1970, completely absorbed the Federal Radiation Council.

Opposition to the EPA came from HEW Secretary Robert Finch and Secretary of the Interior Walter J. Hickel, who had wanted environmental protection programs united under his department, which would then have been renamed the Department of the Environment. Both Finch and Hickel were soon forced from the Nixon Cabinet.

Environmental Science Services Administration (ESSA) *See* **Tiros.**

EPA *See* **Environmental Protection Agency.**

Equal Pay Act The elimination of pay differentials based exclusively on sex was covered in legislation signed into law by President John F. Kennedy on June 10, 1963. Effective June 11, 1964, it was unlaw-

ful for an employer to pay women wages "at a rate less than the rate at which he pays wages to employees of the opposite sex in such establishment for equal work on jobs the performance of which requires equal skill, effort, and responsibility, and which are performed under similar working conditions. . . ." The law excluded supervisory workers, professionals, and administrative personnel. Men could continue to outearn women on the same job on the basis of seniority, merit, and other reasons.

The Equal Pay Act took the form of an amendment to Section 6 of the Fair Labor Standards Act of 1938. It incorporated the "Equal Pay for Equal Work" principle established during World War II by the National War Labor Board (NWLB). For example, on June 19, 1943, the NWLB ruled in a dispute brought before it that "the same rates of pay shall apply on all operations which were formerly performed by men and are now being performed by women employees unless there have been changes in job content whereby these operations require servicing by men employees, which were not required prior to such changes."

Equal Rights Amendment (ERA) As approved by Congress on March 22, 1972, the proposed 27th Amendment to the Constitution reads as follows:

Section 1. Equality of rights under the law shall not be denied or abridged by the United States or by any State on account of sex.

Section 2. The Congress shall have the power to enforce, by appropriate legislation, the provisions of this article.

Section 3. This amendment shall take effect two years after the date of ratification.

The measure, as passed, is essentially similar to that first introduced in Congress in 1923 by Sen. Charles Curtis (R.-Kan.) and Rep. Daniel Anthony (R.-Kan.). For almost half a century it remained bottled up in various committees, and the language of the crucial Section 1 was revised to its present form by the Senate Judiciary Committee in 1943. In both 1950 and 1953 it was actually approved by the Senate, but each time with a rider (the so-called Hayden Amendment) introduced by Sen. Carl Hayden (D.-Ariz.) stating that the amendment "shall not be construed to impair any rights, benefits or exemptions now or hereafter conferred by law upon members of the female sex." As a result of this rider, the House failed to act, and the amendment was never submitted to the states for the required ratification by three-forths of their legislations, a total of thirty-eight. The amendment in its present form originally had until March 22, 1979, to obtain such ratification, but in 1978 Congress extended the deadline until June 30, 1982.

Support for the amendment as passed began to build during the 1960s, especially after the foundation by Betty Friedan of the **National Organization for Women** (NOW) in 1966. The House Judiciary Committe, chaired by Rep. Emanuel Celler (D.-N.Y.), had managed to keep it bottled up for two decades, but on July 20, 1970, it was voted out of committee and brought to the floor for debate, largely through the efforts of Rep. Martha W. Griffiths (D.-Mich.), who had the support of Rep. Gerald R. Ford (R.-Mich.). On August 10, 1970, it was approved by the House (350 to 15).

In the Senate, opposition to ERA was led by Sen. Sam Ervin (D.-N.C.). As a result of his efforts the amendment was referred back to the House in a revised form that made it no longer acceptable.

In 1971 the House Judiciary Committee voted to add to ERA the so-called Wiggins Amendment (offered by California Democrat Charles Wiggins), which read: "This article shall not impair the validity of any law of the United States which exempts a person from compulsory military service or any other law of the United States or of any State which reasonably promotes the health and safety of the people." Again through the efforts of Representative Griffiths the revision was rejected and the measure as it originally stood was voted by the House on October 12, 1971. In the Senate again, several attempts were made to defeat the bill by adding to it language similar to that of the Hayden and Wiggins amendments. Nevertheless, on February 29, 1972, the Senate Judiciary Committee approved ERA in its original form (fifteen to one), with Senator Ervin casting the only dissenting vote. When it was finally approved (eighty-four to eight) by the Senate less than a month later, Senator Ervin, who is said to have feared that his colleagues were about to "repeal the handiwork of God," prayed on the Senate floor: "Father, forgive them for they know not what they do."

At present, probably the most vocal and best known opponent of ERA is Illinois conservative Phyllis Schlafly, founder of STOP ERA. By the end of 1978 thirty-five states had ratified the amendment.

ERA *See* **Equal Rights Amendment.**

ERAP *See* **Economic Research Action Project.**

ERDA *See* **Energy Research and Development Administration; Department of Energy.**

Erhard Seminars Training *See* **est.**

Ervin Committee *See* **Select Committee on Presidential Campaign Activities.**

Esalen Institute *See* **Encounter Groups.**

ESSA *See* **Environmental Science Services Administration.**

est An acronym for Erhard Seminars Training, est is a therapy system founded in San Francisco in 1971 by Werner Erhard. Partaking of elements of Zen, transcendental meditation, and scientology, among many other systems, it stresses the idea that emotional and energy-draining problems arise because people tend to live by belief systems, constructing their ideas of reality to corroborate preconceived notions rather than what they know from experience.

The basic format of the "experience" involves two intensive weekends of training during which some 250 people who have committed themselves to a total of about sixty hours of "sharing," go through "processes" (exercises of guided meditations) designed to enable them "to get in touch with themselves." est stresses total responsibility for individual life experience during these marathon sessions that may last from 9 A.M. of one day until 2:30 A.M. of the following day. In the highly disciplined situation, participants are forbidden to talk, take notes, wear watches, sit next to a friend, or make use of tranquilizers, alcoholic beverages, or any mood-changing substance.

Werner Erhard stresses the fact that the insights provided by est cannot be "explained" but rather must be "experienced." "In the training, you 'get it' by experiencing it." est literature stresses that "the training" is *not* like group therapy or **encounter group** therapy since virtually all the interchange is between the trainer and those in the training.

The growth of est has been phenomenal. By the middle of the decade it had spread from the West Coast to most large cities, and in 1975 was reported to have grossed $9,000,000. In addition to the general "training" sessions, there are also "trainings" designed for the clergy, for convicts, for teenagers, and for children from ages six to eleven. Graduate seminars are offered on specific topics such as communicating, money, and sex.

Not surprisingly, many of the traditional therapies have shown themselves hostile to est, whose somewhat Spartan methods—long sessions infrequently broken by opportunities to eat or go to the bathroom—have led to charges of "fascism." Former participants in the "training," are generally enthusiastic, however, and tend to volunteer time and effort to spread the gospel. A somewhat worshipful attitude often develops toward Erhard, who is generally referred to as "Werner." An offshoot of est is Erhard's "Hunger Project" in which over 200,000 people have enrolled and "taken responsibility" for eliminating hunger everywhere in the world by 1997.

"Ethnic purity"   In an interview with Sam Roberts of the New York *Daily News,* Jimmy Carter (former Democratic Governor of Georgia and then an active campaigner for the 1976 Democratic presidential nomination) was asked on April 2, 1976, what he thought of low-income scatter-site housing as a means of achieving racial integration of neighborhoods. Mr. Carter replied that he thought the housing emphasis should be on the downtown areas of deteriorating cities. "I see nothing wrong with ethnic purity being maintained. I would not force a racial integration of a neighborhood by government action. But I would not permit discrimination against a family moving into the neighborhood."

Mr. Carter's use of the phrase "ethnic purity" went unnoticed when the story was published, but several days later CBS correspondent Ed Rabel, acting on instructions from his home office, asked him to explain what he had meant. Once more using the phrase, the candidate went on to note that he didn't "think the government ought to . . . try to break down deliberately an ethnically oriented neighborhood by artificially injecting into it someone from another ethnic group just to create some sort of integration."

This time the phrase, with its unfortunate associations, caught the attention of the various media and consequently of the nation. Mr. Carter expressed his resentment at attempts to twist his remarks out of context and give them racist overtones. However, at this point even such staunch black supporters as Rep. Andrew Young (D.-Ga.) were calling the remarks "a disaster . . . . He shouldn't have answered in those terms. I don't think he understood the loaded connotations of the words. They summoned up memories of Hitler and Nazi Germany. I can't defend him on this."

While in retrospect it would seem that the candidates's explanations were made in good faith, the incident did demonstrate the insensitivity of Mr. Carter and his staff to big-city politics. Said campaign aide Hamilton Jordan: "It was just an unfortunate remark, but it took me several days to realize how serious a problem it was. . . . We just tried to plow through. We figured the best way to show it didn't hurt us was to put Jimmy in situations with black groups where he could explain his own feelings. . . ."

ETS   *See* **Educational Testing Service.**

Eurodollars   These are United States dollars on deposit in private banks abroad. In the 1950s a pool was organized by British bankers who realized that by taking advantage of the billions of dollars already overseas—and being increased by continuing annual deficits in the U.S. balance of payments—they could lend them out at a substantial profit. By the beginning of the 1970s, the global Eurodollar market involved more than 500 banks in some forty countries.

The pool has been a resource for speculators eager to convert into hard currencies such as the German mark. Rates of 10 percent for three-month loans of from $100,000 are not uncommon. Because interest rates on their domestic currencies were sometimes lower, European investors would often borrow money on their home markets and convert the loans into dollars which could be lent out at the higher rate.

A parallel growth was the Eurobond market, which began in July 1963, when the United States imposed an interest equalization tax in an effort to stop the export of American capital via investment in foreign bond issues. A Eurobond is one underwritten by an international syndicate and marketed in countries other than that of the denominating currency. In the first three months of 1977, approximately $285 billion had been issued, and between 60 and 70 percent of these were dollar denominated, with the German mark accounting for much of the rest. In April 1977, the European Investment Bank made its first public offering of a yen-dominated Eurobond issue.

By the end of the year, as the American balance of payments situation continued to worsen, Arab and Swiss international money managers began a boycott of U.S.-dollar-denominated securities in the Eurodollar market. A flight from the dollar began, and U.S. corporations began finding it hard to raise capital overseas. The dollar continued to decline against Swiss francs, German marks, and Japanese yen. As one expert put it: "The message is very clear in London. Bail out of Eurodollar bonds, go short into bank deposits, and switch into hard currency paper."

European Recovery Plan *See* **Marshall Plan.**

EVA *See* **Spacewalks.**

Everson v. Board of Education (1947) *See* "**Released time.**"

Executive Privilege *See* **Watergate Scandal.**

"**Expletive deleted**" *See* "**Stonewalling.**"

Explorer I Stung by the blow to American scientific prestige delivered by the launching of *Sputnik I* in October 1957, the United States began to close the space gap when, on January 31, 1958, an Army Jupiter-C rocket carried into earth orbit *Explorer I,* a six-foot, thirty-one-pound cylindrical satellite packed with miniaturized instruments capable of transmitting space information back to Earth. Among the important results of this achievement is the discovery that the Earth is circled by a dense zone of radiation, which was named the Van Allen Belt after Dr. James A. Van Allen, who devised many of the instruments carried on *Explorer I.* For a time, scientists feared that the Van Allen Belt might prevent man's exploration of space.

Extravehicular Activity (EVA) *See* **Spacewalks.**

"**Extremism in defense of liberty**" Meeting in San Francisco on July 13, 1964, the Republican National Convention selected Sen. Barry Goldwater (Ariz.) as its candidate in the forthcoming presidential election. The convention had been dominated by the right wing of the party, and although the platform adopted had pledged enforcement of the **Civil Rights Act of 1964,** against which the militantly conservative Senator Goldwater had voted, it rejected a proposal repudiating the support of the extremist **John Birch Society.**

In his acceptance speech, Senator Goldwater noted:

"Anyone who joins us in all sincerity we welcome. Those, who do not care for our cause, we don't expect to enter our ranks in any case. And let our Republicanism so focused and so dedicated not be made fuzzy and futile by unthinking and stupid labels.

"I would remind you that extremism in the defense of liberty is no vice.

"And let me remind you also that moderation in the pursuit of justice is no virtue!"

Shortly after, the senator's Democratic rival, President Lyndon B. Johnson, noted that "extremism in the pursuit of the Presidency is an unpardonable vice."

F

Freedom Riders

"Facts Forum" From 1951 to 1955 this right-wing radio program sponsored by Texas millionaire H. L. Hunt was aired weekly from Dallas. Its "moderator" was Dan Smoot, who, though he prided himself on presenting "both sides" of controversial issues, insisted on making the entire presentation himself. Since Mr. Smoot made no secret of the fact that he felt that most of what the federal government had done or was attempting to do was "unconstitutional," he generally had no trouble establishing which side in a controversy was "right." After leaving the program, he established the *Dan Smoot Report*, which had the approbation of the **John Birch Society.**

Fair Campaign Practices Act *See* **Federal Election Campaign Act.**

Fair Deal Six months after succeeding to the presidency following the death of President Franklin D. Roosevelt on April 12, 1945, President Harry S Truman on September 6, 1945, sent Congress a twenty-one-point domestic legislation program which, he later noted, "marked the beginning of the 'Fair Deal'," and symbolized for him his assumption of the office in his own right. In it, he first spelled out "the details of the program of liberalism and progressivism," which was to be the foundation of his administration.

Actually, the President did not use the phrase "Fair Deal" until his State of the Union message of January 5, 1949, following his triumphant and unexpected—by anybody but himself—victory over Republican contender Thomas E. Dewey. It was, as he himself later explained, "an extension of the New Deal; fundamentally, both mean greater economic opportunity for the mass of the people. There are differences, not of principle but of pace and personnel; the New Deal in the beginning, because of the times and its very newness, was marked by a tempo at times almost frenetic. Now there is a steady pace, without the gyrations of certain early New Dealers."

In the all-important field of civil rights, the Fair Deal called for the elimination of discrimination against blacks in the matters of voting rights, jobs, and access to education and public facilities. It recommended the permanent establishment of the wartime Fair Employment Practices Commission (FEPC), a Civil Rights Commission, and a Civil Rights Division within the Department of Justice.

The program expressed the President's continuing opposition to the **Taft-Hartley Act,** called for

federal loans to finance new housing, advocated a comprehensive program of national health insurance, recommended federal aid to education, and in the so-called **Brannan Plan** insisted on a radical revision of the traditional notion of farm parity. It also emphasized the need for wage, price, and credit controls to fight inflation, and a reform of tax laws that would put a more equitable burden on big corporations.

A coalition of Republicans and conservative Democrats were to defeat new civil rights legislation, the attempted repeal of the Taft-Hartley Act, national health insurance, and federal aid for secondary education. Some gains were made in the fields of housing, slum clearance, and expanded social security coverage.

Fair Debt Collection Practices Act Passed by a reluctant Congress, the act went into effect on March 20, 1978, and focuses almost completely on third-party collection agencies. It prohibits telephone harassment of various kinds—calls at unconventional hours, calls at work that may cause friction with employers, improperly identified calls, and the like—and requires a collector to deal only with a consumer's lawyer in cases where the debt has been disputed and legal counsel retained. Collectors attempting to locate debtors are required to identify themselves to those being questioned, but may not disclose the reasons for their inquiries. Among the unfair practices proscribed are the use of bogus telegrams threatening legal action.

The Federal Trade Commission has prime responsibility for enforcing the legislation, and complaints should be directed to its Bureau of Consumer Protection, Pennsylvania Avenue and Sixth Street, N.W., Washington, D.C. 20580.

Fair Packaging and Labeling Act *See* **Truth-in-Packaging Law.**

Fair Play for Cuba Committee (FPCC) Formed early in 1960 by pro-Castro enthusiasts as relations between the United States and Cuba continued to deteriorate, the Fair Play for Cuba Committee (FPCC) numbered among its more prominent members sociologist C. Wright Mills, novelists James Baldwin and Norman Mailer, and physicist Linus Pauling. It sponsored pamphlets and newspaper ads that urged American acceptance of the revolutionary government established by Fidel Castor after the overthrow of the Fulgencio Batista dictatorship in January 1959.

In the days following the disastrous **Bay of Pigs** invasion of Cuba by anti-Castro exiles who had received American support, the FPCC staged a number of demonstrations on the nation's campuses, picketed the White House, and organized protest meetings in San Francisco and New York, where it had its headquarters. Testifying before the U.S. Senate Internal Security Subcommittee in Washington, D.C., May 16, 1961, Richard Gibson, acting FPCC secretary, said that his group kept no membership records and only minimal financial records. He did, however, furnish the subcommittee with a list of FPCC chapters in twenty-three cities and at thirty-seven colleges. Gibson, a former CBS news writer who was at the time the United Nations correspondent for the Cuban newspaper *Revolución*, had on April 25, 1961, invoked the First and Fifth Amendments in refusing to say if the FPCC had received money from the Castro government. He denied any link between his group and the U.S. Communist Party.

When Lee Harvey Oswald was arrested for the assassination of President John F. Kennedy, **November 22, 1963,** he described himself as the secretary of the New Orleans FPCC chapter. This assertion hastened the demise of the FPCC, which disbanded on December 27, 1963.

"The Family"   On August 8, 1969, intruders entered the Hollywood Hills, Los Angeles, home of pregnant movie actress Sharon Tate, wife of director Roman Polanski, stabbed her to death, and killed four others. The following day, in an apparently unconnected tragedy, Leno LaBianca and his wife, Rosemary, were murdered in their Los Angeles home.

The crimes shocked the nation, and local detectives are said to have spent more than 8,000 man-hours investigating it without results. The first break came in December when Susan Atkins, arrested on unrelated charges, began telling her Los Angeles cellmate an incredible story that led to the arrest of Charles Manson and several young women who were members of what he called "The Frigate Family" and what the rest of the nation soon knew as "The Family."

As pieced together from the stories of Miss Atkins and Linda Kasabian—state's witness of the murders in which she had participated—the thirty-five-year-old Manson, who had spent the greater part of his life in jail on a variety of charges, was the leader of a hippie commune characterized by drugs, sadism, and sex. He was said to have had authoritarian and hypnotic control over members of his "family." ("He mesmerized me," said Miss Atkins.)

The Sharon Tate murders were carried out at his instigation, but without his participation, by "Family" members said to have been high on **LSD.** The victims were apparently selected at random by Manson, who had an abiding hatred of rich "pigs." The next day he led his followers to the home of the affluent LaBiancas and, after seeing to it that they were bound, left, giving orders for their murder.

The eventual trials concluded in February 1971 with the conviction of Manson and the "Manson girls"—Patricia Krenwinkel, 23; Leslie Van Houten, 21; and Susan Atkins, 22—for the Tate and LaBianca murders. At one time during the thirty-two-week trial, proceedings were cast in doubt when President Richard M. Nixon publicly expressed his conviction that Manson was guilty.

In December 1975, Lynette Alice ("Squeaky") Fromme was given a life sentence for her attempted assassination of President Gerald R. Ford on September 5, 1975. A former "Family" member, Miss Fromme had previously expressed her feelings that President Nixon was responsible for Manson's conviction. She blamed President Ford for a continuation of Nixon's policies. "I can't believe the stories they're telling about us," she once said. "Charlie is such a warm and wonderful person. . . . We had a very clean life [in the commune]."

Family Assistance Plan (FAP)   In a nationally televised speech on August 8, 1969, President Richard M. Nixon proposed to replace the tangled welfare system that had developed over the years with the Family Assistance Plan (FAP), under which outright grants of money would be made on the basis of income. Calling the program "workfare," he emphasized FAP provisions that would penalize those who did not work and would require all unemployed heads of families—except for the disabled or the mothers of preschool children—to take job training.

FAP had originally been conceived of as Guaranteed Annual Income (GAI), but had been rebaptized to avoid phraseology potentially inflammatory to conservatives. Now, although the plan he proposed did, in fact, call for a minimum income level of $1,600 annually for a family of four in which there was no wage earner, the President insisted that it was not a "guaranteed income." To discourage a "system which makes it more profitable for a man not to work than to work," the plan announced would make graduated grants until a family income of $3,920 annually was reached. Anyone making less than $60 a month would be entitled to full welfare payments.

Attacked from both the left and right as either inadequate or too expensive, the essentials of the original FAP were nevertheless approved by the House on April 16, 1970, thanks in large measure to Rep. Wilbur Mills (D.-Ark.), the chairman of the House Ways and Means Committee. In the Senate, however, the bill ran afoul of flak from both liberals and conservatives and remained lodged in the Finance Committee. When the Ninety-second Congress adjourned in 1972 without taking action on it, there was some hope that after his reelection the President might return to what he had once called "a crusade for reform." However, FAP was formally dropped in March 1973. Explained Health, Education and Welfare Secretary Caspar Weinberger: "Many people in this administration were never really comfortable with the idea."

The chief architect of FAP was Daniel P. Moynihan, a Harvard professor and Democrat who had served in both the Kennedy and Johnson administrations and was somewhat surprisingly appointed by President Nixon as an adviser on urban affairs. Moynihan's original plan was modified by Secretary of Labor George Shultz, who introduced the notion of incentives and provisions calling for adult and healthy members of welfare families to accept available work or take vocational training leading to work. ("What the country needs is not more welfare but more *work*fare.")

President Nixon's growing disenchantment with the liberal policies advocated by Moynihan, whom he had once told that "Tory men and liberal policies are what have changed the world," led the latter to resign from the White House staff in 1971. He left behind him a saucy note echoing the ill-considered concession statement made by Nixon after his unsuccessful fight in the 1962 California gubernatorial election. Said Mr. Moynihan: "Well, you won't have Pat Moynihan to kick around anymore." (See **Nixon's Last Press Conference.**)

In spite of his differences with the Nixon administration, Moynihan attributed the defeat of FAP to the fact that liberals were unwilling to accept their own program from the hands of a Republican President.

Family Education Rights and Privacy Act of 1974
See **Buckley Amendment.**

FAP *See* **Family Assistance Plan.**

Far Eastern Commission *See* **Supreme Commander for Allied Powers.**

"Farmgate" Squadrons Codename given to the special U.S. Air Force squadrons secretly assigned by President John F. Kennedy for use in small-scale guerilla warfare in Vietnam. They consisted of relatively slow, propeller-driven B-26s and T-28s.

The "Farmgate" squadrons had been recommended to the President in the report filed at the end of the **Taylor-Rostow mission** which he had sent to Vietnam in October 1961. General Maxwell Taylor had felt that these squadrons would give the South Vietnamese participating in guerilla actions an edge in firepower that would match the advantage in mobility offered by the use of helicopters (see **Counterinsurgency Program**).

In one important action on January 21, 1962, they took part in an operation against Binh Hoa, close to the Cambodian border. Roger Hilsman, Assistant Secretary of State for the Far East, reported that they were to have been used to attack a cluster of huts in which intelligence reports said there were some 300 Viet Cong, but due to an error in map reading they, in fact, attacked a Cambodian village across the border, killing and wounding many of the inhabitants.

Fascinating Womanhood (FW) One of the various countercurrents to the **Women's Liberation** movement, Fascinating Womanhood (FW) is an eight-week self-help seminar in which women are urged to accept their husbands rather than try to change or challenge them. Any modification necessary is seen as the duty of the wife, who should attempt to give up criticism, i.e., "nagging," and become "Angela Human, the Ideal Woman."

Such as they are, the ideas first appeared in Helen Andelin's self-published *Fascinating Womanhood* (1965), and are said to be based on pamphlets issued in the 1920s. Feminists have claimed that the popularity of the FW seminars that sprang up all over the country in the mid-1970s is right-wing inspired and due mostly to women who would rather abandon their own personalities than face the threat of divorce.

"Teachers" of FW seminars are trained at the Fascinating Womanhood Center run in Santa Barbara, California, by Mrs. Andelin and her husband, Aubrey, a retired dentist, who with somewhat less success, is the author of *Man of Steel and Velvet*.

(*Fascinating Womanhood* was picked up by a paperback publisher in 1974 and in two years sold 700,000 copies.)

Although supposedly nonpolitical, FW aligned itself with the forces against the **Equal Rights Amendment** (ERA), and some seminar leaders petitioned the Girl Scouts of America to remove feminist Betty Friedan and "others of a like persuasion" from its board of directors.

See **Total Woman.**

Federal Election Campaign Act   Sometimes known as the Fair Campaign Practices Act, it was signed into law on February 7, 1972, by President Richard M. Nixon, who had vetoed similar legislation in October 1970. Under its provisions, candidates for federal offices were limited to campaign spending of no more than ten cents per constituent, and of that total only 60 percent could be spent in a single medium—press, TV, etc. Presidential candidates and their running mates were permitted to spend a maximum of $8.4 million in post-convention campaigns. In addition, candidates for the Presidency or Vice Presidency could spend no more than $50,000 of their own money. (Senate and House candidates were limited to $35,000 and $25,000, respectively.)

The act—the first comprehensive revision of campaign finance legislation since the Corrupt Practices Act of 1925—also required candidates and committees receiving more than $1,000 to report contributions and expenditures of more than $100. Following the revelation of campaign expenditure irregularities that came to light during the **Watergate Scandal** inquiries, critics charged that the President had purposely delayed signing the legislation until ten days after he had received it from Congress. As a result, the act's provisions did not go into effect until April 7, 1972, thus giving Republican fund raisers and the **Committee to Re-elect the President** (CREEP; CRP) additional time to push for anonymous contributions (*see* **Milk Fund**).

Additional campaign funding legislation was signed by President Gerald R. Ford on October 15, 1974. Effective the following year, it was designed to eliminate undue influence of special-interest groups and large contributors by providing public financing of presidential primaries and elections. It also set ceilings on contributions and spending in House, Senate, and presidential campaigns, but did not extend public financing to congressional elections.

In urging the bill, Rep. Wayne L. Hayes (D.-Ohio) pointed out that had it been adopted two years ago, "Watergate would never have happened."

See **Watergate Scandal.**

Federal Energy Administration   *See* **Energy Crisis.**

The Feminine Mystique   Considered the catalytic work of the women's movement, this 1963 bestseller by Betty Friedan, who in 1966 was to be the founder and first president of **National Organization for Women** (NOW), argued that there was something "very wrong with the way American women are trying to live their lives today." Drawing on her own experience as a wife and mother of three small children, she notes that almost in spite of herself she felt guilty about using her abilities and education in work that took her away from home. "There was a strange discrepancy between the reality of our lives as women and the image to which we were trying to conform, the image that I came to call the feminine mystique. I wondered if other women faced this schizophrenic split and what it meant."

Having herself "said no to that feminine mystique," Ms. Friedan touched the concerns of thousands of women who resented the pressure to sacrifice the diverse aspects of their talents and personalities to their roles as housewives and mothers. Having analyzed the problem, she avoided nostrums which at the time she could not see as applying either to her personal life or to women in general. Instead she concluded with a series of questions:

"Who knows what women can be when they are finally free to become themselves? Who knows what women's intelligence will contribute when it can be nourished without denying love? Who knows of the possibilities of love when men and women share not only children, home, and garden, not only the fulfillment of their biological roles, but the responsibilities and passions of the work that creates the human future and the full human knowledge of who they are? It has barely begun, the search of women for themselves. But the time is at hand when the voices of the feminine mystique can no longer drown out the inner voice that is driving women to become complete."

Although many women were outraged by the charge that they were attempting to live through their husbands instead of seeking their individual identities, the book was also greeted by an outpouring of letters from women who were relieved to find that their half-guilty and sometimes carefully concealed feelings of resentment were shared by others.

In 1964, Ms. Friedan was hired by the *Ladies' Home Journal* to turn that bastion of the feminine mystique around by putting out a special June issue entitled "Women: The Fourth Dimension." Although promised a free hand, many of her suggestions for altering traditional departments—"no real ordinary women could be shown modeling clothes," she later reported—were rejected by the male editors, as was "*all* the fiction, with its deeper personal truth."

"Disillusioned at the possibility of really turning the existing women's magazines around, I tried to interest five or six publishers in starting a new mass women's magazine aimed at that market. It was about six years too soon. It wasn't until after 1970 that they saw the commercial possibility of *Ms.*" That magazine quickly established itself as a leading feminist publication.

In *It Changed My Life* (1976), a collection of her writings on the women's movement, Ms. Friedan acknowledges the influence on her of *The Second Sex* (1949) by the French existentialist writer Simone de Beauvoir. "It . . . introduced me to that approach to reality and political responsibility— that, in effect, freed me from the rubrics of authoritative ideology and led me to whatever original analysis of women's existence I have been able to contribute."

51st State Statehood for New York City, an idea which had originated in 1861 with Mayor Fernando Wood, became a temporary political issue again in 1971 with the formation by Rep. Bella S. Abzug (D.) of a "Committee to Make New York City a State." The idea received dramatic support when the office of Mayor John V. Lindsay issued a staff memorandum in which it was estimated that the city, which has a greater population than forty-three of the states, "lost" $1 billion annually in taxes it forwarded to the state government in Albany. "New York City can no longer depend on a body of upstate legislators, who are out of touch with urban problems, to respond to the city's crucial needs. . . . Statehood is not an unrealistic possibility; indeed, it may well be the only sensible approach to governing New York City."

Representative Abzug attempted to collect 45,000 signatures on a petition calling for a referendum on secession from the state.

The campaign was essentially meant to focus attention on the city's worsening financial condition and to highlight the need for federal and state aid to urban centers. Critics of statehood pointed out that the cost of duplicating state services would more than wipe out any possible gains on taxes "saved."

Finlandization Term often used in international political analyses to describe the potential Soviet takeover of a Western nation without exterior signs of control.

Finletter Commission Convinced that the United States would maintain its atomic monopoly for some time to come, and eager to be rid of an outsized military expenditures appropriation that ate up as much as a fourth of the federal budget, there were those in the government who argued in 1947 that the United States could abandon the "balance of force" concept and place increasing reliance on the Air Force as a strategic deterrent. On January 1, 1948, the President's Air Policy Commission (chaired by Secretary of the Air Force Thomas Finletter) issued a report which argued that the Soviet Union would not have its own atomic bomb before 1953. (The first atomic device was detonated by the U.S.S.R. in 1949. Red China detonated its first atomic bomb in October 1964.)

During this period, known as Phase I, it was considered unlikely that any "aggression-minded nation" would take action against this country. Since, however, in the following Phase II it would not be possible to "support in peace a force capable of dominating the enemy's mainland," the report emphasized the need for "a reasonably strong defensive establishment" and for concentrating on "a counteroffensive air force . . . which will be so powerful that if an aggressor does attack, we will be able to retaliate with the utmost violence and seize and hold the advanced positions from which we can divert the destruction from our homeland to his."

The Fire Next Time One of the most articulate spokesmen of the black civil rights movement of the 1960s, novelist James Baldwin warned in this influential 1963 bestseller that Negro patience with white intransigence was at an end. The short book consists of two "letters": "My Dungeon Shook: Letter to My Nephew on the One Hundreth Anniversary of the Emancipation" and the considerably longer "Down at the Cross: Letter from a Region of My Mind." In the latter, Baldwin uses the occasion of a meeting with Elijah Muhammad, leader of the **Black Muslim** movement, to assess his stand in response to being asked where his sympathies lay. Although accepting as true the history of oppression that led to the foundation of this black separatist movement, he finds the response politically inadequate and morally wrong since it is based on hatred and must necessarily cut blacks off from their American past.

Instead, Baldwin urges: "If we—and now I mean the relatively conscious whites, and the relatively conscious blacks, who must, like lovers, insist on, or create, the consciousness of the others—do not falter in our duty now, we may be able, handful that we are, to end the racial nightmare, and achieve our country, and change the history of the world. If we do not now dare everything, the fulfillment of that prophecy, recreated from the Bible in song by a slave, is upon us: *God gave Noah the rainbow sign, No more water, the fire next time!*"

"Firestorm" *See* **Saturday Night Massacre.**

First Strike Capability The possession of strategic offensive weapons of sufficient number, power, and target accuracy to deliver a preemptive attack, using either aircraft or missiles, that would destroy a major part of the enemy's offensive weapons before launch, thereby reducing the possibility of retaliatory damage to a level considered "acceptable."

First Women's Bank Opened in New York City on October 16, 1975, it was the first full-service bank directed primarily by women; women stockholders owned more than 80 percent of the bank's shares. Madeline McWhinney, who was formerly an officer of the Federal Reserve Bank, headed a staff of twenty-five, only four of whom were men.

Fiscal Drag Theory *See* **Manpower Drag Theory.**

Five Percenters As chairman of the Senate's Special Committee Investigating the National Defense Program, on January 15, 1942, Sen. Harry S Truman (D.-Mo.) made a report which, among other things, condemned lobbyists whose attempts to buy and sell influence were undermining public confidence in government officials. Businesspeople, he noted, had become the dupes of peddlers of influence who claimed close connections in Washington from whom they could obtain government contracts if they were given five or ten percent commission.

The so-called five percenters were to haunt the Truman administration when, on August 8, 1949, a Senate Investigations Subcommittee chaired by Sen. Clyde R. Hoey (D.-N.C.) began hearings on the charges of "influence peddling" in Washington. Among the more famous incidents the committee

turned up was evidence that Major General Harry Hawkins Vaughan, the President's military aide and personal friend, had in 1948 interceded with Federal Housing Expediter Tighe E. Woods to obtain scarce construction materials for the repair of a racetrack in San Bruno, California. Vaughan and others were also accused of having accepted $520 deep-freeze units as gifts from Albert Verley Company, a Chicago perfume manufacturer eager to expedite the importation of European oils.

In testimony given the committee by Paul D. Grindle, a Massachusetts furniture manufacturer, James V. Hunt, a former army colonel and employee of the War Assets Administration, was accused of having offered to obtain government contracts for him provided that he be paid a retainer and a 5-percent commission. According to Grindle's testimony, Hunt told him: "I have only one thing to sell and that is influence." Among the friends in high quarters claimed by Hunt were Vaughan, former War Assets Administrator Major General Alden H. Waitt, and Major General Herman Feldman, Army Quartermaster General. A name that constantly cropped up during committee investigations was that of John Maragon, who apparently had numerous government and industry connections and had been employed by the Albert Verley Company at the time the deep-freeze units were given to Vaughan and others.

President Truman staunchly defended Vaughan, who denied interceding for the racetrack and claimed that the deep-freezes had been represented to him as experimental models and factory rejects. Nevertheless, the subcommittee report issued on January 18, 1950, reprimanded him for aiding Maragon, "an outright fixer," and accepting gifts from the perfume manufacturer. Waitt, who was Chief of the Army Chemical Corps, retired as a result of the investigations, but Feldman was retained by the army in spite of his "bad judgment."

Deep-freezes were shortly afterward joined by mink coats as the national symbols for corruption when Sen. J. William Fulbright's (D.-Ark.) subcommittee of the Senate Banking and Currency Committee began investigating the Reconstruction Finance Corporation (RFC) and found that the American Lithofold Company, several times turned down for a loan, received $565,000 after it had retained William Boyle, Jr., chairman of the Democratic National Committee, as its lawyer. In addition, it was revealed that the wife of a former RFC loan examiner received a $9,540 mink coat with the financial help of an attorney who had represented a company applying for a $150,000 RFC loan. There were quips about the "Mink Dynasty," but before the Republicans could take political advantage of the situation, it was found that Guy Gabrielson, Republican National Committee chairman, had intervened to obtain an extension on a loan to a company of which he was president.

"Flexible and Limited Response" *See* **Massive Retaliation.**

"Float like a butterfly, sting like a bee" *See* **"I am the greatest."**

Flying Bedstead Nickname given to an early lunar module designed for moon landing in Project Apollo. Awkward to handle, it was equipped with two engines: one for continuous thrust equaling five-sixths of the modules's total weight, the other, gimbaled, which allowed for steering during the actual moon landing.

"Flying saucers" *See* **Unidentified Flying Objects.**

Foggy Bottom Often used—especially during the 1950s—as a synonym for the Department of State, whose new offices were built in a Washington area so named because in earlier days it was a section of swamps and flats. During the Eisenhower administration liberal and Democratic critics liked to suggest that the old miasmatic influence had survived to cloak the operation of the Department in secrecy and confusion and to blur its prose to the point of incomprehensibility. Writing in *The Reporter* in 1954 about the controversial R. W. Scott McLeod, who through the influence of Sen. Joseph McCarthy (R.-Wis.) had been appointed the State Department's powerful security chief, William Harlan Hale called his article " 'Big Brother' in Foggy Bottom."

In "A Note on Language," in his *A Thousand Days* (1965), Arthur Schlesinger, Jr., points out that "the men from State would talk in a bureaucratic patois borrowed in large part from the Department of Defense. We would be exhorted to 'zero in' on 'the purpose of the drill' . . . to 'crank in' this and 'phase out' that and 'gin up' something else, to 'pinpoint' a 'viable' policy and behind it, a 'fall-back position' . . . Thus one never..said 'at this point' but always **'at this point in time.' "**

The last expression was to gain national prominence when it was frequently used by members of President Richard M. Nixon's White House Staff during hearings of the **Select Committee on Presidential Campaign Activities** in the summer of 1973.

See **Watergate Scandal.**

FOIA *See* **Freedom of Information Act.**

F-111 Bomber *See* **TFX Controversy.**

Food for Peace Beginning with the **Agricultural Trade and Development Act of 1954** (Public Law 480), by early 1977 the United States had spent more than $30 billion on a program which sent food to 130 countries. According to Orville Freeman, Secretary of Agriculture during both the Kennedy and the Johnson administrations, "No similar effort in history . . . has done so much for so many people—both to those who give and those who receive."

Originally conceived during the Eisenhower administration as a means of disposing of the nation's agricultural surpluses by means of a three-year program, it was continuously extended, and was completely revised and expanded in the Food for Peace Act signed into law by President Lyndon B. Johnson on November 11, 1966. At that time the federal government was meeting the Food for Peace program by buying commodities on the open market. Although the program was being increasingly attacked by critics, President Johnson, in special signing ceremonies at his Texas ranch, called it "the beginning of one of the most important tasks of our time."

During the lifetime of Public Law 480, most of the food had been sent to ten countries: Turkey, Israel, South Korea, South Vietnam, Pakistan, Egypt, India, Yugoslavia, Brazil, and Indonesia. Critics charged that in some cases the program seemed to be used not so much for humanitarian purposes as to allow friendly nations to use the proceeds from sales for investment in arms. In 1976, one government report concluded that "it was difficult to say that the . . . programs were helping the poor."

Shipments under the Food for Peace program reached an all-time high of 18 million tons in 1966, but during the Nixon administration levels rapidly declined. In 1974 they were at somewhat more than 3 million tons. However, the program began to be increasingly used to bypass congressional restrictions on military assistance programs. In fiscal 1974, for example, 70 percent of all Food for Peace shipments went to South Vietnam and Cambodia.

Officials of the Department of Agriculture and the **Agency for International Development** (AID) who administer the program have found it increasingly difficult to balance humanitarian and military interests, as well as those of the American farmer. The world food crisis of 1973–1974, for example, found them unprepared. Food shipments were said to be badly timed and often arrived after the need had passed. As a result, some nations, newspapers reported, went from famine to glut conditions.

In December 1974 Congress reacted to mounting criticism of the program by passing legislation requiring that 75 percent of all shipments under Public Law's Title I—which authorizes loans to countries for the purchase of American farm products—be restricted to nations in which the average individual income was less than $300 annually. Largely responsible for this change was Sen. Hubert H. Humphrey (D.-Minn.), whose 1957 congressional hearings on the program had shaped its development as both a humanitarian and a political tool. (Assistant Secretary of Agriculture Earl Butz argued at the time that the Food for Peace program should not be allowed to become a permanent feature of the American agricultural scene.)

The Food for Peace program was due to expire at the end of 1977, but in spite of increasing criticism was extended (September 29, 1977) for an additional four years.

Current estimates are that the United States spends over $1 billion annually on food aid, most of it under the Food for Peace program.

Ford Foundation established in 1936 by Henry Ford, founder of the Ford Motor Company, and his son Edsel, this private nonprofit corporation was originally concerned with philanthropic activities in the Michigan area. In the 1950s, after receiving the bulk of the estates of various members of the Ford family, its philanthropies—possibly responding to provisions of the Internal Revenue Act of 1950, which barred the accumulation of unreasonable foundation surpluses—became nationwide. Because of the large sums at its disposal, the foundation was sometimes described as "a large body of money surrounded by people who want some."

In 1952 the Foundation established the controversial **Fund for the Republic** as an autonomous subsidiary whose goal it was to eliminate restrictions on freedom of thought, inquiry, and expression in the United States. (According to Robert M. Hutchins, president of the fund after 1954, it was "officially disowned" by Ford trustees with a $15 million grant.) Other independent subsidiaries established by foundation trustees include the Fund for the Advancement of Education (1951).

Engaging in neither teaching, research, nor other direct operations, the Ford Foundation works toward its goal of identifying problems in American society and underwriting attempts at their solution by making grants to other nonprofit organizations. By the 1960s, its multibillion dollar endowment made it the world's largest philanthropic trust. It has financed studies in education, science, the various arts, urban and regional development, the problems of aging, economic and business administration, educational television, and international affairs. Emphasis has often been on the initial attack on the analysis of problems.

In 1957 the foundation established the first national arts program in the United States, and through fiscal 1976, grants totaled $283 million, principally for music, theater, dance, and the visual arts. From 1951 through 1976, grants to public television totaled 285 million, early funds going to support the establishment of noncommercial broadcast facilities in local communities and at colleges and universities. Since 1967, almost $46 million has been given to community development corporations to spur the growth of jobs, business opportunities, and housing in impoverished urban and rural areas.

Through mid-1977, the Ford Foundation had expended more than $5 billion, including grants to 7,200 institutions and organizations in the United States and in ninety-six foreign countries. In addition, grants have been made to more than 100,000 individuals for research, training, and other activities related to the foundation's program interests.

"Ford to City: Drop Dead" In the now-famous headline of its October 30, 1975 issue, the New York *Daily News* succinctly summed up the import of a forty-minute talk given by President Gerald R. Ford before the National Press Club in Washington, D.C., the day before. As the largest city in the nation faced the greatest financial crisis in its history, the President vowed "to veto any bill that has as its purpose a federal bailout of New York City to prevent default." This seemed to leave the city facing certain default in mid-November, when it had to come up with $150 million to meet payrolls and pay off due securities. If it survived this date without bankruptcy, New York seemed certain to go under in early December, when it was due to redeem $437.8 million in short-term notes.

In what appeared to many critics a deliberate attempt to upstage the right-wing tactics of his rival for the 1976 Republican presidential nomination, former movie star and California Governor Ronald Reagan, President Ford castigated the management and tactics of New York City and state officials. Pollsters were indicating that national sentiment was more than four to one against federal aid to the Big Apple. There was little understanding of the fact that, as Vice President Nelson Rockefeller had recently warned, default by New York would be a "catastrophe. "Although President Ford had implied that the city's more than $12 billion in notes and securities were held by banks, estimates were that probably at least half of them were held by private citizens across the nation. The Vice President's brother, David Rockefeller, chairman of New York's Chase Manhattan Bank, had testified before the Senate Banking Committee that default by New York might badly damage the world economy because of a domino effect it would set up.

President Ford decried such "scare talk" and implied that federal funds would become available to the city after default. He gave assurance that "the Federal Government will work with the court to assure that police, fire, and other essential services for the protection of life and property in New York are maintained." It was not, however, made clear if this cooperation with the federal court would take the form of financial aid.

Despite the threat of a presidential veto, on October 30, 1975, the Senate Banking Committee approved by an eight to five vote legislation that would provide a $4 billion loan guarantee to prevent default by New York. On November 3, 1975, the House Banking Committee approved by a twenty-three to sixteen vote legislation to authorize a $7 billion loan guarantee to New York City before or after default.

On the advice of his economic aides, President Ford softened his stand on aid to New York, and on November 26, 1975, he called for $2.3 billion in short-term seasonal loans that would enable the city to avoid default.

On December 15, 1978, Cleveland, Ohio, became the first American city to default since 1933, when Detroit bit the dust.

Formosa Resolution   At the request of President Dwight D. Eisenhower, on January 28, 1955, both houses of Congress passed the Formosa Resolution, which authorized him "to employ the Armed Forces of the United States as he deems necessary for the specific purpose of securing and protecting Formosa and the Pescadores against armed attack, this authority to include the securing and protection of such related positions and territories of that area now in friendly hands and the taking of such other measures as he judges to be required or appropriate in assuring the defense of Formosa and the Pescadores." The language of the resolution was specifically left vague regarding the Matsu and Quemoy islands, which had been under Red Chinese bombardment since September 3, 1954, so that Nationalist China could not claim an American commitment to defend them, and Communist China would remain unsure as to whether or not the U.S. government would risk war if they attempted to invade these offshore islands.

The crisis leading to the Formosa Resolution had been building up for some time. In his 1954 Easter message, Nationalist China's Generalissimo Chiang Kai-shek had called for a "holy war" against the Communists, and in August Red China's Premier, Chou En-lai, had announced that Formosa had to be liquidated. In addition, South Korea's President Syngman Rhee had appeared before a joint session of Congress to propose that the United States join South Korea and Nationalist China in attacking the communist mainland.

Relations between the United States and Nationalist China were clarified by a mutual security pact—signed December 1, 1954, and ratified by the Senate on February 9, 1955—in which the United States guaranteed the defense of Formosa and the Pescadores from communist attack; no assurances were made regarding the **Quemoy and Matsu** islands. The Tachen islands had been under communist air bombardment since November 1954, and in February 1955 the U.S. Seventh Fleet helped evacuate more than 40,000 Nationalist troops and civilians; the communists made no attempt to interfere with this operation.

Contributing to the atmosphere that led to the Formosa Resolution was the announcement by Peking Radio in November 1954 that a communist court had condemned thirteen Americans, eleven of whom were airmen in uniform, to prison terms of four years to life for espionage. Pressure was immediately brought on the Eisenhower administration by Sen. William Knowland (R.-Calif.) to establish a naval blockade of the China mainland, with or without United Nations approval. Senator Knowland's insistence on calling for such a blockade in spite of the rejection of such a policy by both the President and Secretary of State John Foster Dulles led to a public rebuke by the President, who pointed out that while he and the Senator were in agreement in principle, the distinction in their methods might mean the difference between war and peace. (On August 1, 1955, the communists released the eleven uniformed airmen.)

The Formosa Resolution was either sufficiently strong or sufficiently vague to discourage attempts by Red China to invade Formosa after first taking the Quemoy and Matsu islands off the mainland. Secretary Dulles considered that the day had been saved by the resolution, though he acknowledged it had brought the United States to the brink of war (see **"Brinkmanship"**). When bombing of Quemoy and Matsu was renewed in August 1958, President Eisenhower sent the Seventh Fleet to the Formosa Strait area. This show of force was considered by some to have once again prevented an invasion of the offshore islands as a stepping stone to Formosa.

The Formosa Resolution established a precedent that is thought by many critics to have led Congress to the easy abandonment of its war-making powers in the **Gulf of Tonkin Resolution** of 1964.

Four-Power Council *See* **Supreme Commander for Allied Powers.**

FPCC *See* **Fair Play for Cuba Committee.**

"Free at Last!" An old Negro spiritual, the words of which provided a stirring close to Dr. Martin Luther King, Jr.'s, famous **"I Have a Dream"** speech during the 1963 **March on Washington.**

Freedom Democratic Party *See* **Mississippi Freedom Democratic Party.**

Freedom March *See* **March on Washington.**

Freedom of Information Act (FOIA) Designed to provide freer public access to government data, it was originally passed in July 1966, after a decade of efforts by Rep. John E. Moss (D.-Calif.) of the Foreign Operations and Government Information Subcommittee of the House Committee on Government Operations. The act was, however, widely flouted by officials who delayed meeting requests for compliance and charged excessive "search" fees for often illegible material.

With the help of Sen. Edward Kennedy (D.-Mass.), chairman of the Administrative Practice and Procedure Subcommittee of the Senate Judiciary Committee, Moss led the fight to improve the law by the addition of seventeen amendments. Accepted by both houses of Congress in October

1974, these amendments strengthened FOIA by providing procedures and penalties when data were withheld "arbitrarily or capriciously"; permitting the recovery of legal fees by successful petitioners; calling for the publication of agency decisions; and permitting access to "reasonably" described data.

Although President Gerald R. Ford, on assuming office after the resignation in August 1974 of President Richard M. Nixon following the **Watergate Scandal,** had announced his support for the new legislation, on October 14 he vetoed the bill as "unconstitutional and unworkable." He particularly objected to the authority it gave the courts to declassify documents, and to the provision that an agency's files could be made public on request unless that agency could prove that the disclosure would harm the national interest. His veto was overridden by Congress in November 1974, and the amended law went into effect on February 19, 1975.

Under the present FOIA, a government agency has ten working days to respond to a formal request, and there is a twenty-day limit for rulings on appeals. Federal employees found to have arbitrarily withheld documents are subject to disciplinary action by the Civil Service Commission.

Information on how to use the FOIA is contained in the *Attorney General's Memorandum on the 1974 Amendments to the Freedom of Information Act,* U.S. Government Printing Office, Washington, D.C., 20402.

Freedom of Thought Foundation *See* **Unification Church.**

Freedom Riders The Freedom Rides of the summer of 1961 were essentially the inspiration of James Farmer, who was at the time the national director of the **Congress of Racial Equality** (CORE). In 1947, Farmer had been among those who tested to see the extent to which a 1946 U.S. Supreme Court ban on discrimination in trains engaged in interstate travel was being honored in the upper southern states.

CORE's decision to conduct Freedom Rides to challenge segregation in interstate bus terminals was announced on March 13, 1961 (see also **Boynton v. Virginia**), and on May 4 two buses loaded with both black and white passengers left Washington, D.C., and started for New Orleans. Although there were minor scuffles with segregationists and law enforcement authorities in Virginia, North Carolina, South Carolina, and Georgia, the situation was relatively uneventful until the Freedom

Riders arrived in Anniston, Alabama, where a bus was set on fire when an incendiary bomb was tossed through a window; twelve of the passengers had to be hospitalized. Several of those on the second bus were also beaten before it left for Birmingham, where, in spite of the advance warnings of violence, no police were on hand to control the mob which attacked it on May 14. The bus drivers refused to continue on to Montgomery the following day, and the original Freedom Riders, many of whom were suffering from the effects of the bloody attacks, flew to New Orleans, where on May 17 they met and decided to disband.

At this point the Nashville Student Movement entered the struggle, as did the **Student Nonviolent Coordinating Committee** (SNCC), the **Southern Christian Leadership Conference** (SCLC), and individual religious, academic, and professional leaders. Denied bus service from Birmingham, one group spent eighteen hours in the terminal before being taken to Montgomery on May 20, where again, in spite of FBI warnings to authorities, no police were on hand to control the full-scale riot that ensued. Among those injured were John Seigenthaler, President John F. Kennedy's personal envoy to Alabama's Governor John Patterson.

After various unsuccessful attempts to reach the governor by phone, Attorney General Robert F. Kennedy dispatched 500 federal marshals to Montgomery under the direction of Deputy Attorney Byron R. White. At this point Governor Patterson was suddenly heard from with a protest that blithely ignored the assaults on the Freedom Riders, and insisted that Alabama did not need help from the federal government to maintain order. The **American Nazi Party** (ANP) added to the confusion by sending a "hate bus" from Washington, D.C., which reached Montgomery on May 23 and continued on to New Orleans.

Additional antisegregationist protesters began arriving in Montgomery from both the North and South. In spite of the fact that he received no cooperation from Governor Patterson, Alabama Public Safety Director Floyd Mann made a valiant attempt to maintain order and was praised by black leaders. When on May 21 Martin Luther King, Jr., flew from Chicago to Montgomery to preach nonviolence to 1,500 blacks who jammed the First Baptist Church, a violent mob that had formed outside was eventually dispersed by federal marshals and state police.

On May 23, James Farmer and other black leaders announced their determination to continue the Freedom Rides at whatever the cost, the next stop being Jackson, Mississippi. The next day, under an escort of National Guardsmen, two busloads of Freedom Riders were taken to the state border after some had triumphantly breakfasted at the Montgomery bus terminal lunch counter. Upon their arrival in Jackson, James Farmer and twenty-six other were arrested when they sought to use the terminal's all-white lunchroom and rest room facilities. Many of them spent close to two months in the Hinds County jail and in the Parchman Penitentiary.

Meanwhile, Freedom Riders continued to pour into Montgomery. On May 27, representatives of CORE, SNCC, SCLC, and the Nashville Student Movement formed a Freedom Riders' Coordinating Committee to arrange for the subsequent rides that continued throughout the summer. Black leaders rejected a plea for a "cooling off" period from Attorney General Kennedy: blacks in America had been cooling off for over a century, they replied.

On May 29, the Attorney General asked that the Interstate Commerce Commission (ICC) ban segregation in interstate bus terminals, but this was not done until September 22 and did not become effective until the following November. Although most of the South complied with these orders, on November 29 five black students were beaten in McComb, Mississippi, when they tried to obtain service at the bus terminal.

Some 1,000 people are thought to have participated in twelve Freedom Rides, and an estimated $300,000 was spent on their legal defense by the NAACP Legal Defense and Educational Fund, a separate organization from the NAACP, which did not participate in the Freedom Riders' Coordinating Committee. Some critics have felt that the Freedom Rides were primarily of a symbolic nature, and they have pointed out that several weeks before the Freedom Riders arrived, the Greyhound station in Montgomery had already been integrated by a small group of blacks from elsewhere in the state. They felt that the terminals in the South could have been effectively integrated if the job had been done without advance publicity.

Freedom Schools In the summer of 1964, the civil rights movement in the South reached a new height of intensity when hundreds of students from northern universities and colleges arrived to participate in voter-registration campaigns and to help in the creation of parallel political and educational institutions free of racial bias. Among the more influential of the latter were the Mississippi Freedom Schools. Staughton Lynd, who was in charge of the project, noted after the Freedom School Convention held in Meridian, Mississippi, August 7–9, 1964, that few who planned the curriculum and administrative structure of these schools had had any experience in similar institutions already existing in northern urban centers. Their approach to curriculum "was to have no curriculum and our approach to administrative structure was not to have any. . . ." He advised that the best way to start a Freedom School was to begin with a Freedom School Convention and let the curriculum evolve from it.

He noted that originally two residential schools for high school students recommended by the **Council of Federated Organizations** (COFO) had been planned as centers into which a network of some twenty day schools would feed. Local resistance and lack of money made this impossible, and leaders of the movement eventually decided that this was all for the best. "It meant that teachers would live within Negro communities rather than on sequestered campuses. It meant that we would have to ask ministers for the use of church basements as schools. In short, it meant we would run a school system without buildings, equipment or money. . . ."

As potential teachers arrived for orientation in Oxford, Ohio, they were informed that they were on their own, that when "they were referred to an old lady of the local church for help in finding lodging, and to a youngster hanging around the COFO office for help in finding students—as they did these things, they would be building their school, their teaching would have begun." In spite of, or perhaps because of, this informal approach, the schools met with an enthusiastic response. For example, although the Freedom School in Jackson was expected to attract, at best, 1,000 students, approximately 1,500 were "enrolled."

See **Mississippi Summer Project.**

Freedoms Foundations, Inc. Established in June 1949 by advertising man Don Belding and oil company executive Kenneth P. Wells to make a series of annual awards for achievements in "defending and extending the freedom philosophy of Americanism." Critics charged that winners tended to exemplify an exclusively conservative approach to American political and social philosophy. Among the recipients over the next twenty years were General Dwight D. Eisenhower, Secretary of State John Foster Dulles, former President Herbert C. Hoover (honored twice), cartoonist and movie-maker Walt Disney, rocket specialist Wernher von Braun, comic-strip artists Harold Gray ("Little Orphan Annie")

and Al Capp ("Li'l Abner"), *Chicago Tribune* publisher Colonel Robert R. McCormick, and singer Anita Bryant.

Freedom Summer *See* **Mississippi Summer Project; Freedom Schools.**

"Free Huey!" A slogan used nationally by activist groups to focus attention on the court trials of **Black Panther** leader Huey P. Newton for the murder of Officer John Frey in Oakland, California, in October 1967. The slogan had an element of intimidation in it, for black radicals were quoted as saying that if Newton was imprisoned "the sky's the limit." He was, however, found guilty and served two years. No major incidents were reported.

See **Honkies for Huey.**

Free Speech Movement (FSM) When on September 14, 1964, officials of the University of California ruled that the Bancroft Strip, a twenty-six- by sixty-foot area just inside the Berkeley campus' principal pedestrian entrance, could no longer be used to recruit support for off-campus political and social demonstrations, philosophy student Mario Savio and others formed the FSM. Savio had previously taken part in civil rights demonstrations in the South, but the student FSM temporarily cut across all political and social alignments as undergraduates of all persuasions united against the summary action by the university in a series of demonstrations and classroom boycotts.

In November, the university rescinded its order and decided to allow political recruitment in the Bancroft Strip and in additional areas never before used for such purposes. However, FSM leaders objected to the new ruling, which specified that only "lawful" off-campus activities could be planned in these so-called Hyde Park areas. It was argued with some force that the determination of an activity as "unlawful" could only be made by the courts. Campus unity evaporated to a large extent as militants attacked the sprawling university as a "multiversity" that had become a bureaucracy fronting for the "power structure."

This charge was angrily rejected by University of California president Clark Kerr, who in 1960 had resisted demands to suspend or expel Berkeley students arrested for disrupting a San Francisco hearing of the **House Committee on Un-American Activities** (HUAC), and had taken a similar stand when earlier in 1964 undergraduates had been arrested during a civil rights sit-in at the Sheraton-Palace Hotel. ("It just would not have been in character for us to say that the only place students could fight for Negro rights was in Mississippi.")

Student political agitation reached a climax in December 1964 when thousands of undergraduates occupied Sproul Hall, the campus administration building. They were eventually ejected by police and some 800 were arrested, including Savio, who shouted as he was dragged from the building: "This is wonderful—wonderful. We'll bring the university to our terms." The faculty supported the student protest by eight to one, and President Kerr acknowledged: "We fumbled, we floundered, and the worst thing is I still don't know how we should have handled it."

Kerr, who had been absent from the campus when the decision to close the Bancroft Strip had been made, later noted that the decision was a mistake. In 1959, foreseeing that the Strip could become a source of conflict, he had attempted to turn it over to the city for use as a public plaza, but, although the Board of Regents had agreed, no action was ever taken.

The student demonstrations sparked by FSM at Berkeley were to transform the American campus during the late 1960s and make it a focus of intense political conflict as students demanded a greater share in university decisions and rejected the claim of university authorities to act *in loco parentis* (in the place of a parent). Student protests were to culminate in 1968 with the **Siege of Morningside Heights** on the Columbia University campus in New York City.

See **Battle of Berkeley.**

French Connection Notorious narcotics traffic route from Marseilles to New York City in the 1960s. In 1962 an almost 400-pound shipment was intercepted by New York police. The incident provided the basis for an enormously popular movie, *The French Connection* (1971), starring Gene Hackman as a maverick narcotics detective. (The film was based on a 1969 novel by Robin Moore, who four years earlier had written a bestseller about the **Green Berets,** a special forces group that played an important part in the **counterinsurgency program** in the **Vietnam War.**)

The heroin involved in the case was kept in the property office of the New York City Police Department and disappeared from there in 1972 under circumstances that have never been explained. Vincent C. Papa, who had been linked to the drug theft, was stabbed to death in July 1977 while an inmate in the federal penitentiary in Atlanta. The following April, Dominique Orsini, a Corsican who

was said to have been a major link in the French Connection and who in 1976 had been sentenced to ten years, was found slashed to death in the same prison.

"French Polio" *See* **Swine Flu.**

Friendship 7 Name given to the 2,400-pound bell-shaped Mercury space capsule in which, on February 20, 1962, Lieutenant Colonel John H. Glenn, Jr., circled the earth three times and became the first American to go into orbit. Glenn had been preceded into space by the Russian "Cosmonauts" Major Yuri A. Gagarin and Major Gherman S. Titov in 1961, and in lauding the American astronaut's achievement, President John F. Kennedy noted that "we started late. But this is the new ocean, and I believe the United States must sail on it and be in a position second to none."

Friendship 7 was launched from Cape Canaveral, Florida, in the nose of an Atlas rocket booster at 9:47 A.M., and it splashed down near the Grand Turk Island in the Bahamas at 2:43 P.M. Traveling at a top speed of 17,545 mph, the space capsule established an orbit that had an apogee of 162 miles and a perigee of 99 miles.

Originally scheduled for launching on December 20, 1961, the flight of the *Friendship 7* was successfully completed only after ten delays caused by weather or mechanical flaws.

See **Project Mercury.**

Fulbright Act Sponsored by Sen. J. William Fulbright (D.-Ark.) and signed into law by President Harry S Truman on August 1, 1946, the Fulbright Act authorized the use of foreign currencies obtained from the sale of surplus U.S. Army property in Allied countries after World War II to finance educational exchanges.

. . . the Secretary of State is hereby authorized to enter into an executive agreement or agreements with any foreign government for the use of currencies, or credits for currencies of such government acquired as a result of such surplus property disposals, for the purpose of providing by the formation of foundations or otherwise, for (A) financing studies, research, instruction, and other educational activities of or for American citizens in schools and institutions of higher learning located in such foreign country, or of the citizens of such foreign country in American schools and institutions of higher learning located outside the continental United States, Hawaii, Alaska (including the Aleutian Islands), Puerto Rico, and the Virgin Islands, including payment for transportation, tuition, maintenance, and other expenses incident to scholastic activities;

or (B) furnishing transportation for citizens of such foreign country who desire to attend American schools and institutions of higher learning in the continental United States, Hawaii, Alaska (including the Aleutian Islands), Puerto Rico, and the Virgin Islands, and whose attendance will not deprive citizens of the United States of an opportunity to attend such schools and institutions . . . .

Selection is influenced by scholastic and personal qualifications as well as by the potential value of the project, with preference going to veterans. All grants for "Fulbright Scholarships" must be approved by a board appointed by the President, and are usually for one year.

Full Employment Act *See* **Employment Act of 1946.**

Fun City The term was said to have first been used in the mid-1960s by New York's Mayor John V. Lindsay in a light-hearted attempt to promote his city as a convention and tourist center. As the troubles of "the Big Apple" in crime, corruption, budget management, etc., grew, it was often sardonically used by reporters and television commentators in news stories covering these events. Dick Schaap is credited with having publicized the term in his New York *World-Journal-Tribune* column "What's New In Fun City."

Fund for the Republic A 1949 report to the Ford Foundation recommended as a major goal: "The elimination of restrictions on freedom of thought, inquiry and expression in the United States, and the development of policies and procedures best adapted to protect these rights in the face of persistent international tensions." Spurred by the growing threat to traditional American liberties posed by Sen. Joseph R. McCarthy's (R.-Wis.) reckless charges of subversion in government—as well as by provisions of the Internal Revenue Act of 1950, which barred foundations from accumulating unreasonable surpluses—the trustees of the Ford Foundation established the independent Fund for the Republic on December 12, 1952, with a $15 million grant.

Under its first president, Clifford Case, the Fund undertook as a precondition to future activities in the field of civil liberties a $500,000 study on communism in American life. When Case, a liberal Republican, was elected to the Senate from New Jersey, the presidency of the Fund was taken over by Robert M. Hutchins, formerly the president of the University of Chicago and then an associate director of the Ford Foundation. Under Hutchins the

Fund began a more active defense of threatened civil liberties. A controversial study of fifty government employee security cases (August 1955) found that "the evidence offered to show that a man is a danger to American institutions has often been farcically remote," Hutchins noted in his first report as Fund president.

In 1956, the Fund came under attack from the **House Committee on Un-American Activities** (HUAC) following the publication of a two-volume *Report on Blacklisting* written by John Cogley, a former executive editor of *Commonweal*, a liberal Catholic magazine. The report charged that blacklisting had become an institution in movies, radio, and television and that hundreds of people with supposed communist associations were being arbitrarily denied employment by industry leaders who were meekly accepting the "guidance" of publications such as **Red Channels,** which listed entertainers and media people with "dubious" political associations.

During the same period, the Fund's failure to support research projects of the "cold-war liberals" of groups such as the American Committee for Cultural Freedom also brought it under attack from the "left," and many combined efforts were made to revoke its tax-exempt status.

In defense of the Fund's various controversial stands, Hutchins noted: "We are trying to save the Republic. We can expect few cheers from those we are trying to save it from. . . . This is the first time an organization dedicated to civil liberties has had any money. That fact alone, as soon as it appeared that the organization meant business, would account for the clamor we hear."

Furman v. Georgia On June 29, 1972, the U.S. Supreme Court ruled in a five to four decision that the death penalty, as generally enforced in this country, was a violation of the Constitution's Eighth Amendment, which prohibited the infliction of "cruel and unusual punishments." However, three of the five who filed separate majority opinions—Justices Potter Stewart, Byron R. White, and William O. Douglas—indicated that they might approve of new capital punishment laws which precluded discretion by judges and juries in imposing death sentences. The dissenting judges, all recent appointees of President Richard M. Nixon, filed separate opinions in which they expressed disapproval of capital punishment but saw the majority decision as a violation of the separation of powers and federalism as expressed in two 1971 rulings by the Court. Chief Justice Warren E. Burger was joined by Justices Harry A. Blackman, William H. Rehnquist, and Lewis F. Powell, Jr., in expressing the opinion that the federal and state legislatures might meet majority objections by "more narrowly defining the crimes for which the penalty is to be imposed."

The case before the Court involved Henry Furman, Lucius Jackson, and Elmer Branch, three black men convicted of rape. In his opinion, Justice Douglas pointed out that because the law permitted judges and juries to exercise discretion in imposing the death penalty, it was too often "selectively applied, feeding prejudices against the accused if he is poor and despised, poor and lacking political clout, or if he is a member of a suspect or unpopular minority, and saving those who by social position may be in a more protected position."

The three convicted men were represented by lawyers of the NAACP Legal Defense and Educational Fund, whose national drive against the death penalty had blocked executions since June 1967. At the time of the Court ruling, 600 men and women were awaiting execution. Of this number, 329 were blacks.

Future Shock In an article written for *Horizon* magazine, Alvin Toffler, a former associate editor of *Fortune* magazine, coined the expression "future shock" to describe the stress and disorientation that can be induced by too much change in too short a period of time. He then spent the next five years doing research on this concept and interviewing "Nobel prize winners, hippies, psychiatrists, physicians, businessmen, professional futurists, philosophers, and educators" on their "anxieties about adaptation." The result was *Future Shock* (1970), a vastly influential bestseller both in the United States and abroad.

The book stressed the fact that future shock was no longer a distant and potential hazard, but a current psychobiological condition, a disease of change that could be described in medical and psychiatric terms. Stressing our inadequate knowledge in the field, it underlined the fact that the "*rate* of change has implications quite apart from, and sometimes more important than, the *directions* of change," arguing that any attempt to understand human adaptability and to define the "content" of change must take into account the fact that pace itself is a part of that content. Future shock was seen as a result of the growing lag between the rate of environmental change and the "limited pace of human response."

The author argued that, whereas men had previously studied the past for insights into the present, the current rate of change made it imperative to have "a coherent image of the future" as a guide to how we live now. One of goals of his book was to increase the "future-consciousness" of its readers.

In studying the social and psychological implications of the technological revolution we are currently undergoing, Toffler employed not only statistical analysis and operational research, but the insights of social scientists and artists. He concluded that the most pressing need in building a "humane future is to halt the runaway acceleration that is subjecting multitudes to the threat of future shock while, at the same moment, intensifying all the problems they must deal with—war, ecological incursions, racism, the obscene contrast between rich and poor, the revolt of the young, and the rise of a potentially deadly mass irrationalism." Among the "suggested palliatives for the change-pressed individual" are new social services, the regulation of technology, and a "future-facing" education system.

FW *See* **Fascinating Womanhood.**

G

L.B.J. Library

The Great Society

GAI *See* **Guaranteed Annual Income.**

Gaither Report In the spring of 1957 President Dwight D. Eisenhower appointed a group of private citizens to what was officially known as "The Security Resources Panel of the Office of Defense Mobilization Science Advisory Committee." Led by H. Rowan Gaither, Jr., board chairman of the **Ford Foundation,** this group was to investigate and evaluate the state of defense readiness by working with the cooperation and guidance of the National Security Council.

The Gaither Report was completed and submitted to the President on November 7, 1957, and rumors of its contents soon began appearing in the press. Some of them were so alarming that Sen. Lyndon B. Johnson (D.-Tex.) asked the President to make the report public, but Eisenhower took the position that its contents were purely an executive matter, noting "I consider it improper and unwise for me to violate the confidence of the advisory relationship that has existed between me and these Panels or to make public the highly secret facts contained in their reports."

But news of it kept appearing in the press and the indication was that the report predicted that the U.S.S.R., given its increasing military budget, would, by the end of 1959, have the potential of a strike against this country with 100 **Intercontinental Ballistic Missiles** (ICBMs) armed with megaton nuclear warheads. The report also contained recommendations for a massive fallout shelter program, which, according to a *Washington Post* news story of December 20, 1957, "would come at a fortuitous moment in the American economy . . . with benefit both to the economy and national defense."

According to a later account by Presidential Assistant Sherman Adams, Eisenhower's reluctance to release the report was not based on an unwillingness to "face the realities of the security situation," but on a conviction that although its estimated American casualties from a surprise Soviet attack were hypothetical, they would nevertheless be deeply shocking. It is also known that he felt that following the recommendations for the fallout shelter program would mean "writing off our friends in Europe," who were financially unable to undertake such a burden.

The complete Gaither Report, the contents of which had largely become known through newspaper leaks, was not declassified and made public until January 1973, when this action was undertaken by the Interagency Classification Review Committee

headed by John S. D. Eisenhower, son of the former President.

Game Plan "The Game Plan would be the tool used to tackle major objectives and plan them on a consistent long-term basis. The Game Plan would only be used for major Administration goals, i.e., Vietnam, the Welfare Program, the Haynsworth Situation," recalled Jeb Stuart Magruder, White House aide and later deputy director of the **Committee to Re-elect the President** (CREEP) during the Nixon administration.

The phrase was coined by football coach Vince Lombardi in the 1950s and was a favorite with President Richard M. Nixon and his Chief of Staff, H. R. Haldeman. Journalist William Safire, a member of the Nixon inner circle, has said that Haldeman insisted on "game plans" from Magruder on everything from publicizing a speech to putting together a book of press clippings.

Musing on the fate of the Nixon administration following the **Watergate Scandal,** Elliot Richardson, who had resigned as Attorney General during the **Saturday Night Massacre,** said later of President Nixon: "His use of football analogies was so revealing—anything was ok except what the referee sees and blows the whistle on."

Games People Play *See* **Transactional Analysis.**

GAO *See* **General Accounting Office.**

Garner et al. v. Louisiana In its first decision resulting from the **"sit-ins"** staged in the South by civil rights militants, the U.S. Supreme Court on December 11, 1961, in *Garner et al. v. Louisiana,* reversed the breach-of-peace convictions of sixteen black students who were arrested March 28–29, 1960, after they sought service at "white" lunch counters in a drug store, a department store, and a bus terminal in Baton Rouge, Louisiana.

Chief Justice Earl Warren said in the majority opinion handed down that there was "no evidence to support a finding that petitioners disturbed the peace, either by outwardly boisterous conduct or by passive conduct likely to cause a public disturbance."

Separate but concurring opinions were filed by Justices John Marshall Harlan and William O. Douglas, the latter noting that the Constitutional ban against segregation applied to privately owned restaurants.

Garwin Report *See* **Supersonic Transport.**

Gatt *See* **General Agreement on Tariffs and Trade.**

In re Gault A major decision regarding the rights of children was handed down by the U.S. Supreme Court on May 15, 1967, when it ruled that those involved in juvenile court proceedings were entitled to the procedural guarantees and protections afforded adults under the U.S. Constitution's Bill of Rights. Among these were the right to be represented by counsel, the right to timely and adequate notification of charges, the right to confront and cross-examine both witnesses and plaintiffs, and the right to be warned that he or she could remain silent to avoid self-incrimination. In the majority decision following the eight to one ruling—with only Justice Potter Stewart dissenting and Justice Hugo L. Black filing a separate but concurring opinion—Justice Abe Fortas wrote: "Under our Constitution, the condition of being a boy does not justify a kangaroo court."

The ruling came about as the result of an appeal by Paul and Marjorie Gault, Globe, Arizona, whose fifteen-year-old son, Gerald, was sentenced to six months in a reformatory for allegedly making obscene phone calls to a woman neighbor.

Gemstone Overall code name assigned to the plan conceived by G. Gordon Liddy and E. Howard Hunt for the breaking in and electronic bugging of the headquarters of the Democratic National Committee at the Watergate in Washington, D.C. (see **Watergate Scandal**). When the plan was first presented to former Attorney General John N. Mitchell, who was at the time (January 1971) the director of the **Committee to Re-elect the President** (CREEP; CRP), Liddy used six color charts, each of which was codenamed for a different intelligence activity: Diamond, Ruby, Sapphire, Opal, Crystal, etc. Later, tapes of the buggings were transcribed on special stationery headed "Gemstone."

The original plan included not only the electronic surveillance, wiretapping, and breaking in of the Democratic headquarters but the use of call girls to compromise Democratic leaders at the 1972 Democratic National Convention in Miami Beach, Florida, and the employment of special squads to kidnap radicals such as *Yippie* leaders Jerry Rubin and Abbie Hoffman to prevent them from demonstrating at the Republican National Convention to be held in San Diego, California. In addition, squads of toughs were to be used to prevent hostile demonstrations at the convention.

General Accounting Office (GAO) Established in 1921, this little known office functions as the "watchdog" or "auditing arm" of Congress. In 1976, it released over 1,000 reports covering various topics ranging from investigations of the fertilizer situation to the Ford administration's response to the *Mayaguez* **Incident,** which involved a U.S. cargoship. It was because of this last report, undertaken at the request of a subcommittee of the House International Relations Committee, that this nonpartisan agency was thrust into national prominence.

Originally classified as secret, the report was made public in October 1976, some six months after its completion, as a result of pressure from the subcommittee's Democratic majority. Its criticism of the Ford administration's response to the *Mayaguez* crisis was given wide coverage in the various media, since the presidential elections were only a month away.

Commented Phillip Hughes, an assistant comptroller: "There is a general problem the GAO has in its relations with Congress of avoiding being used improperly. I guess I would say we were used in this set of circumstances." The report was one of many recent investigations by the GAO into governmental responses to crises.

General Agreement on Tariffs and Trade *See* **Kennedy Round.**

General Services Administration (GSA) In conformity with recommendations of the **Hoover Commission,** the General Services Administration (GSA) was established on July 1, 1949, to systematize government civilian purchasing. Working through ten regional offices throughout the nation, it "establishes policy and provides for the government an economical and efficient system for the management of its property and records, including construction and operation of buildings, procurement and distribution of supplies, utilization and disposal of property . . . and management of government-wide automatic data processing programs" (*Government Manual*, 1977–1978).

A series of articles in the *Washington Post* in September 1978 focused on alleged fraud, bribery, and kickbacks in GSA purchases. Testifying before a Senate subcommittee on federal spending practices, GSA head Jay Solomon said on September 19, 1978, that "the fraud, the corruption, the thievery, the mismanagement and downright abuse of the public trust that have been exposed to this date are only the beginning." To correct the situation,

Solomon said he had instituted a program to train GSA officials in procurement methods; established an overall procurement policy; centralized GSA budgeting; and set ceilings on the values of contracts an official could award without seeking prior approvement from those higher up in the hierarchy.

On September 29, 1978, eighteen GSA officials were indicted by a federal grand jury in Baltimore on charges of corruption. They were immediately suspended from the GSA without pay, and methods were being investigated by which companies charged with defrauding the GSA could be barred from doing business with the government.

"Generation Gap" The traditional clash of the generations was emphasized in the 1960s by the fact that the overall American population was rapidly approaching a point at which half of it would be under twenty-five. A war generation with memories of the Depression having parented the **"baby boom"** of the mid-1940s, which provided a **"Spock generation"** raised on affluence and parental laissez faire, the birth of a **"counterculture"** that caused a "generation gap" was probably inevitable.

Put in terms of Charles A. Reich's 1970 bestseller, *The Greening of America,* the generation gap was caused by a clash between Consciousness II, which glorified "power, success, rewards, competence," and the newly emerging Consciousness III, which rejected—at least temporarily—all the above and called for a transformation of American society by means of personal development and a commitment to comradeship, honesty, and simplicity.

The rejection by the young of the values of their parents took place on a number of levels: sartorial (jeans, beads, boots, and a general imitation of working-class dress style), tonsorial ("hair down to there"), musical (rock), sexual (relaxed, uni-, bi-), linguistic (an emphasis on words and images often designed to provoke), and political (a rapidly increasing impatience with the democratic process in favor of the "selective tolerance" of the **New Left** and the **Marcusean Revolution).** An essentially good-humored expression was to be found in the popular rock musical *Hair* (1967). Although in the words of one critic it was meant to underscore "the deep chasm between the love generation and the adult phonies who miss the point even when they try to be understanding," those same adults smothered it with love and made it a commercial success first in New York and then all over the world. They did the same for *The Graduate,* a 1967 movie in which, to a Simon and Garfunkel score, a young

man fresh from the halls of academe rejects the establishment values of the older generation by winning as his bride a young girl whose mother had been his mistress.

By and large, the older generation was less enthusiastic about the clash of values demonstrated in the revolt on American campuses that climaxed at Columbia University with the **Siege of Morningside Heights** (1968) when students took "direct action" against university policy.

Blossoming almost simultaneously with the "generation gap," and like it linguistically echoing the controversial **"missile gap"** of 1958, was the **"credibility gap"** of the Johnson administration which promoted the disenchantment of both young and old with the **Vietnam War.**

Generation of Peace When President Richard M. Nixon assumed office in 1969, an attempt was made to find a slogan or phrase which would catch the essence of his administration as the **New Frontier** had for the Kennedy administration. Generation of Peace, New Federalism, and the New American Revolution were tried, but failed to attract the attention of either the public or the press.

Geneva Accords of 1954 *See* **Vietnam War.**

George Amendment *See* **Bricker Amendment.**

Gideon v. Wainwright On March 18, 1963, the U.S. Supreme Court ruled that defendants in criminal cases were entitled to legal counsel and that in the case of indigents it was the responsibility of the state to supply an attorney. The Court also found that paupers were entitled to free transcripts of trial records even if the judge and the court-appointed attorney felt that an appeal was useless; in addition, the Court ruled that convicted persons were entitled to legal advice in helping them file an appeal.

The case involved Clarence Gideon, an indigent electrician, who was convicted of burglary in Panama City, Florida, after a trial in which he defended himself without the aid of an attorney. Sentenced to Florida's Raiford Penitentiary, Gideon filed a hand-printed appeal in which he charged that Louis Wainwright, director of the Florida prison system, was not his proper keeper. The Court concurred and ruled that since Gideon had been denied proper legal defense, he had been improperly imprisoned. At his retrial, Gideon was acquitted.

As a result of the above decision, within a year 1,118 prisoners left the Florida penitentiary. Of this number 321 were retried, 232 received shorter sentences; 77 had their original sentences confirmed; and 12 received longer sentences. Of those who had been set free, 48 committed new crimes. Many critics found that these statistics suggested that society did not require protection against many who were then serving jail sentences.

Gideon v. Wainwright overturned *Betts v. Brady* (1942), in which the Court found that free legal aid for paupers was incumbent on a state only when deprival of the same was "shocking to the universal sense of justice." In effect, the Court held at that time the conviction of a man who had not been provided with proper defense was shocking only in a capital case. (Smith Betts, an unemployed Maryland farmhand convicted of burglary, had been denied free legal aid because that state made it available only to those charged with murder or rape.)

In 1972, the *Gideon* decision was extended by *Argersinger v. Hamlin*, in which the Court ruled that all those accused of offenses potentially punishable by prison sentences were entitled to free legal aid if necessary.

Ginzburg Obscenity Case *See Roth v. United States.*

Girard Case As commander of **NATO** forces in Europe in 1951, General Dwight D. Eisenhower had been instrumental in drawing up the terms of the so-called **Status of Forces** treaty, under which foreign govenments had jurisdiction in the cases of legal action against American servicemen or women for offenses committed overseas, unless such offense occurred in the line of the defendant's military duty. This treaty embodied a policy of the Defense Department, which Eisenhower strongly supported in the face of considerable opposition.

On January 30, 1957, Specialist Third Class William S. Girard, who was serving in Japan, fired an empty mortar shell at a group of Japanese women who were searching for brass casings on a firing range near Tokyo, killing one of them. After an investigation by a commission which concluded that Girard could not be considered as being on official duty at the time of the incident, he was turned over to Japanese authorities for prosecution.

As President, Eisenhower was pressured by Sen. William F. Knowland (R.-Calif.) to see to it that Girard was given a trial by American authorities. When Eisenhower refused to interfere, Girard was tried by a Japanese court, found guilty, and sentenced to three years in prison. Because the court found dereliction but no malice, the sentence was immediately suspended.

However, while the controversy was still capturing national headlines, Rep. Frank Bow (R.-Ohio) introduced a resolution which became known as the Bow Amendment. It called on the United States to withdraw from all Status of Forces treaties with those nations in which U.S. troops were stationed. According to Presidential Assistant Sherman Adams, to the embarrassment of the Republican administration this amendment was favored by the Democrats. However, the President warned that its passage would almost inevitably mean that many foreign powers would refuse to allow American forces within their borders on an extraterritorial basis. The amendment failed.

GI Riots *See* **Wanna-Go-Home Riots.**

"Give-away" Program Republican charges of **"creeping socialism"** under President Franklin D. Roosevelt's New Deal and President Harry S Truman's **Fair Deal** were met by Democratic countercharges that when President Dwight D. Eisenhower assumed office in 1953 the federal government embarked on a "give-away" program under which public resources were turned over to private investors.

A major instance of this struggle was the defeat under the Eisenhower administration of a proposal to build a high, multipurpose dam at Hell's Canyon—the deepest gorge on the North American continent—on the Snake River at the Idaho-Oregon boundary. This federal project had been offered to block an alternative proposal by the Idaho Power Company to build three smaller dams—the Oxbow, Brownlee, and Hell's Canyon—with private funds.

On April 24, 1953, Secretary of the Interior Douglas McKay announced that his department was withdrawing the Truman administration's objections to the Federal Power Commission's licensing the Idaho Power Company to build the Oxbow Dam. Then, after two years of hearings on the three-dam project, the commission issued the license on August 4, 1955.

In defending this and similar licensing decisions, President Eisenhower was to say that such licenses were not "hunting permits for private predators," since investor-owned utilities paid taxes and were regulated by the Federal Power Commission and often by state commissions. Moreover, of the 5 million kilowatts of private power licensed during his administration, he pointed out, more than 80 percent went to "local *public* organizations, of a sort which, being subject to the control of local people who elect their board of directors—and often subject to state regulation as well—are far more directly responsive to the will of the people served than are the Bureau of Reclamation, the Corps of Engineers, or the TVA."

See **Dixon-Yates; Tidelands Oil Controversy.**

"Give 'em hell, Harry" The origin of this cry of encouragement yelled out by enthusiasts of President Harry S Truman as he attacked his Republican opponents at political rallies is variously given. However, in the course of recorded interviews made in 1963-1964 the President himself gave this version: "Well, I was in Albuquerque, New Mexico, making a speech on this campaign, and, some big voice, bull voice, burst way up in the corner of that 7,000 people auditorium said, 'Give 'em hell, Harry.' Well, I never gave them hell. I just told the truth on these fellows and they thought it was hell. That's all there was to it" (*see* **Whistle-Stop Campaign**).

The cry became a popular one that often greeted the appearance of President Truman, who was also known to speak bluntly on matters other than politics. When in December 1950 his daughter, Margaret, made her professional debut as a singer in the Capital's Constitution Hall, *Washington Post* music critic Paul Hume wrote that she "cannot sing very well," and was "flat a good deal of the time." The day after the review appeared, Hume received a letter from the White House: "I have just read your lousy review of Margaret's concert. . . . It seems to me that you are a frustrated old man. . . . Some day I hope to meet you. When that happens you'll need a new nose, a lot of beefsteak for black eyes, and perhaps a supporter below."

The sensation was worldwide, and the President later commented that "sometimes the frailties of the human get the better of me."

Glassboro Conference In June 1967 Premier Aleksei N. Kosygin headed a special delegation to the United Nations following the disastrous Arab defeat in the Six Day War with Israel. Although the primary function of his visit seemed to be to boost Arab morale and sagging Soviet prestige, he made it clear that he would welcome a chance to meet with President Lyndon B. Johnson. The Premier was accordingly invited to the White House, but indicated that he preferred not to be an official guest in the nation's capital at this time of tension. Alternative sites for the meeting were suggested, and both Camp David and New Jersey's Maguire Air Force Base were rejected in turn, the one as being too close to Washington and the other because the Pre-

mier thought that an attempt might be made to impress him with American military might. President Johnson refused to come to New York because he could "visualize a sea of pickets and protesters around any site we picked."

At the suggestion of New Jersey's Governor Richard J. Hughes (D.) both leaders agreed to meet in Glassboro, New Jersey, a small college town about midway between Washington and New York.

The first meeting was held on June 23, 1967, at "Hollybush," the residence of Dr. Thomas E. Robinson, president of Glassboro State College. It lasted more than five hours, during which time the Soviet leader conveyed without comment an offer by Hanoi, North Vietnam, to begin peace talks to end the **Vietnam War** if the American bombing of the North were halted. He seemed reluctant to discuss strategic arms control, however, and as the President later noted, "each time I mentioned missiles, Kosygin talked about Arabs and Israelis."

The two men met again on June 25, and although there were no concrete results from their talks, the Premier was impressed by the friendliness of Glassboro and the seeming relaxation of tension it created. Although disappointed by the failure to solve "any major problem," President Johnson voiced his belief that the meetings "had made the world a little smaller and also a little less dangerous."

The Godfather This 1969 bestselling novel by Mario Puzo presented a not unsympathetic portrait of a Mafia patriarch, Don Vito Corleone, who watches sometimes benevolently, sometimes cruelly, over the destinies of his relatives and friends, as well as of his underworld employees. Not unwilling to proceed to violence and murder when necessary, Don Corleone sagely argues that "a lawyer with his briefcase can steal more than a hundred men with guns."

In 1972, this compelling story of the Mafia or **Cosa Nostra** subculture was made into an epic film starring Marlon Brando and Al Pacino, and directed by Francis Ford Coppola, who also directed *Godfather II* (1974), which starred Al Pacino and Robert de Niro. It was from the first movie that the menacing "I'm going to make you an offer you can't refuse" entered the popular language as a jocular threat.

"God Is Dead" Controversy In the mid-1960s, the rallying cry of the nineteenth-century German philosopher Friedrich Wilhelm Nietzsche received unexpected endorsement from a group of Protestant ministers who argued for the secularization of Christianity since it was no longer possible for men to conceive of a transcendent Being who guides human history and destiny. Leaders of what is sometimes called the God Is Dead Movement were theologians Paul van Buren, Temple University; Gabriel Vahanian, Syracuse University; William Hamilton, Colgate–Rochester Divinity School, and Thomas J. J. Altizer, Emory University. The concept was perhaps given its most succinct form by Altizer, who stated in 1965: "We must recognize that the death of God is a historical event: God has died in our time, in our history, in our existence."

For attempting to redefine Christian tenets without reference to a God, whose death, they insisted, imposed on men a reemphasized need to accept Jesus Christ as an exemplar of conduct, these radical theologians were accused of reducing Christianity to a mere humanistic morality. Hamilton, for example, noted: "In the time of the death of God, we have a place to be. It is not before an altar, it is in the world, in the city, with both the needy neighbor and the enemy." Aligning himself with the black civil rights struggle of the 1960s, he said that the "place" of Christ was in that fight, as well as in the effort to establish the new forms of society, art, and science.

Summing up the seeming contradictions in the ideas of men such as Vahanian, who argued that only God, if there is one, could have a concept of God, Daniel Day Williams of the Union Theological Seminary concluded: "There is no God, and Jesus is his only begotten son."

Among the basic works of the movement were Altizer's *The Gospel of Christian Atheism* (1966) and Hamilton's *The New Essence of Christianity* (1961).

Golden Rule   To protest the atomic tests scheduled by the **Atomic Energy Commission** (AEC) for spring 1958, four pacifists led by Quaker architect Albert Smith Bigelow announced in a letter to President Dwight D. Eisenhower in January 1958 that they would sail the ketch *Golden Rule* 6,500 miles from San Pedro, California, to the Marshall Islands proving grounds. On May 1, 1958, their ship was seized by the U.S. Coast Guard when they attempted to sail from Honolulu to Eniwetok. Ignoring a court injunction, the four made another attempt in June and were again intercepted. This time they were given sixty-day prison sentences by a federal judge in Honolulu.

A combat naval commander in World War II, Bigelow had become a Quaker and pacifist in 1955 after he and his wife had been hosts to several Hiroshima victims who had been sent to this country for plastic surgery. In August 1957, he and ten others were given a suspended jail sentence after they entered into the restricted zone of Camp Mercury, Nevada, during a nuclear-test period.

Gonzo Journalism   *See* **New Journalism.**

Gray Board   *See* **Oppenheimer Affair.**

Gray Panthers   A nondenominational group of senior citizens founded in Philadelphia in 1970 with the financing of the United Presbyterian Church and the United Church of Christ. Under the leadership of Margaret "Maggie" Kuhn, it has fought against nursing home abuse and organized to apply pressure on Congress to raise the mandatory retirement age, improve social security benefits, and increase the amount and quality of health care available to the elderly.

It has chapters in several major cities, and in October 1977 held a four-day convention at which some 300 delegates from all over the nation gathered in Chevy Chase, Maryland, a suburb of the nation's Capital.

Great Books Program   Introduced in 1946 by the University of Chicago's President Robert M. Hutchins (see **Ford Foundation; Fund for the Republic**) and author-educator Mortimer J. Adler, the Great Books program was a plan whereby adult discussion groups had biweekly, two-hour meetings in which books basic to Western civilization were analyzed under guidance. The plan was widely adopted by colleges and universities, but the best-known program was the one given at the University of Chicago.

Hutchins and Adler, whom Hutchins had invited to teach at Chicago in 1930, had in 1943 conceived the idea of reprinting a selection of classics based on courses they had taught. In cooperation with the *Encyclopaedia Britannica*, the university began work on a series of fifty-four volumes containing 443 works by seventy-four authors. Publication of *Great Books of the Western World* was completed in 1952 and included Adler's *Syntopicon*, a two-volume "synthesis of topics" covering highpoints of Western thought.

The Great Books program was to some extent inspired by courses given earlier at Columbia University by author John Erskine, who had among his pupils Adler, Mark Van Doren, Clifton Fadiman (later instrumental in founding the Book of the Month Club), and Rexford Guy Tugwell. Adler later taught similar courses in Chicago and at St.

John's College, Annapolis, where he was a visiting lecturer in 1937. In them, he expressed his rejection of the philosophic pragmatism of John Dewey—who had taught at Columbia from 1904 to 1930—and affirmed his belief in the existence of absolute truths and values.

In 1952, Adler left the University of Chicago to found San Francisco's Institute for Philosophical Research, the purpose of which was to take stock of "great ideas" in Western history. Among the first results of the staff's research was the two-volume *The Idea of Freedom*, published by Adler in 1958 and 1961, before he returned to the University of Chicago in 1964. Among Adler's more popular works was the 1940 bestseller *How to Read a Book*.

The Great Debate Reacting to President Harry S Truman's decision to send four additional U.S. divisions to Europe (September 9, 1950), on November 10, 1950, Sen. Robert A. Taft (R.-Ohio) proposed a "re-examination" of the nation's foreign and military policies and raised the question of whether or not the defense of Western Europe was essential to American security. A long-time isolationist, Senator Taft was perhaps inspired to take this new stand by a victory at the polls that had only days before returned a strong Republican congress and made this three-time Republican presidential candidate one of the most influential men in the country.

In an obvious reply to Senator Taft, Secretary of State Dean Acheson charged on November 17, 1950, that those who were demanding a reexamination of the nation's foreign programs wanted to tear up the roots of policies on which the future of the free world was dependent. Such "re-examinationists," he noted, were in reality isolationists incapable of "constancy of purpose."

The next major round of what came to be known as the Great Debate was on December 20, 1950, when in a radio address former President Herbert C. Hoover noted that "the prime obligation of defense of Western Contintental Europe rests upon the nations of Europe . . . . To warrant our further aid they should show they have spiritual strength and unity to avail themselves of their own resources. But it must be far more than pacts, conferences, paper promises, and declarations. Today it must express itself in organized and equipped combat divisions of such huge numbers as would erect a sure dam against the red flood. And that before we land another man or another dollar on their shores. Otherwise we shall be inviting another Korea."

On January 5, 1951, Senator Taft opened congressional debate on the Truman administration's foreign policy by charging that President Truman had violated the Constitution in sending U.S. troops to Korea without advance congressional approval. He suggested that the containment of communism on the continents of Europe and Asia called for the creation of a superior air and naval power rather than an expanded army. Two days later, Senator Taft called for the pullout of American forces in Korea and the establishment of a line of defense based on Japan and Formosa. On January 9, 1951, he offered to join with President Truman in preparing a policy based on the unleashing of Nationalist Chinese forces on Formosa against Red China.

Senator Taft, who had urged that it might be necessary to "bring about the dissolution of the United Nations and the formation of a new organization which could be an effective weapon for peace," somewhat softened his position when on February 1, 1951, General Dwight D. Eisenhower reported to Congress on his recent tour of **NATO** capitals and urged that American troops in Europe be increased. Senator Taft then took the position that he "would not object to a few more divisions, simply to show the Europeans that we are interested and will participate in the more difficult job of land warfare while we carry out also our larger obligations."

Meanwhile, the debate raged in Congress, where on January 8, 1951, Senate Minority Leader Kenneth S. Wherry (D.-Neb) had introduced a resolution urging that "pending the adoption of a policy with respect thereto by the Congress," no American ground forces be sent to Europe. However, as a result of General Eisenhower's testimony and testimony by General George C. Marshall (February 15, 1951) to the Senate Armed Services and Foreign Relations Committees, on April 4, 1951, the Senate approved a "fair share" contribution of American ground forces to NATO; although the resolution called for Senate approval before more than four divisions could be dispatched to Europe, it was hailed by President Truman as a "clear endorsement" of his troop policies.

The Senate's failure to push its claim for prior endorsement before American troops could be committed abroad opened the way for United States involvement in the **Vietnam War.**

The Great Fear Term applied by some liberal historians to the 1949–1954 period when fear of a communist take-over in the United States drove many Americans to commit what were seen as politically irrational acts. Similar in some ways to the Red Scare of 1919 which followed the conclusion of

World War I, it more or less subsided when Sen. Joseph R. McCarthy (R.-Wis.) was censured by the U.S. Senate in 1954 after he had brought unfounded charges of "communism" in the federal government and the army.

The term has its historical antecedent in *La Grande Peur*, which in 1789 seized French peasants who went on a rampage of burning and looting attacks against those suspected of being unsympathetic to the Revolution.

The Great Society In a televised interview on March 15, 1964, President Lyndon B. Johnson was reminded of Roosevelt's New Deal, Truman's **Fair Deal,** and Kennedy's **New Frontier,** and he was asked if he had a slogan by which to identify his domestic affairs program. "I have had a lot of things to deal with the first hundred days," said the new President, "and I haven't thought of any slogan, but I suppose all of us want a Better Deal, don't we?"

In the days that followed, President Johnson used the expression Better Deal on a number of occasions, but it failed to ignite the imagination of either the public or the press. He therefore recalled a speech originally written for him by Richard Goodwin on the occasion of the White House presentation to Judge Anna M. Kross of the first Eleanor Roosevelt Memorial Award (March 4, 1964). Shelved in favor of an address on the role of women in modern American life, the speech had urged the nation to accept the challenge posed by poverty and build a society that would not merely be prosperous and powerful but also a "great society," in which the very quality of American life would be improved.

The "great society" reference was actually used for the first time on April 23, 1964, at a Democratic fund-raising dinner in Chicago when President Johnson told his listeners: "We have been called upon—are you listening?—to build a great society of the highest order, a society not just for today or tomorrow, but for three or four generations to come."

In the month that followed, the phrase was frequently used by the President, most notably when he told graduates at the University of Michigan on May 22, 1964, that "we have the opportunity to move not only toward the rich society and the powerful society, but upward to the Great Society." (The capitalization significantly appeared in the advance texts. Conservative critics later charged that the slogan had been lifted from Graham Wallas's *The Great Society* [1914], an exposition of socialist doctrine.)

The Great Society, the President went on to explain, rested on abundance and liberty for all, and it demanded an end to poverty and racial injustice. It "is a place where every child can find knowledge to enrich his mind and to enlarge his talents. It is a place where leisure is a welcome change to build and reflect, not a feared cause of boredom and restlessness. It is a place where the city of man serves not only the needs of the body and the demands of commerce but the desire for beauty and the hunger for community."

The legislation needed to achieve the President's goals was outlined by him in his State of the Union message of January 4, 1965. However, the Great Society, in which the **War on Poverty** was to play a major role, was soon being pointed to by some as a victim of the **Vietnam War.** In 1966, Sen. Wayne Morse (D.-Oreg.) angered the President by announcing that "the Great Society is dead."

Writing in 1971, President Johnson defended the Great Society achievements of his administration when he noted that during his five years in office annual investments in programs for health had increased from 4.1 billion to 13.9 billion dollars; for education from 2.3 billion to 10.8 billion dollars; and for the poor from 12.5 billion to 24.6 billion dollars. "I was never convinced that Congress would have voted appreciably more funds for domestic programs if there had been no struggle in Southeast Asia. If we had succeeded in stilling the guns in Vietnam, as we tried desperately to do, I believe that many Congressmen would have demanded tax reductions rather than providing increased funds for the beleaguered cities."

Green Amendment *See* **Elementary and Secondary Education Act.**

Green Berets Special Forces group established at Fort Bragg, North Carolina, in 1952 to cope with the problems of guerrilla warfare. Ideally, members were multilingual and highly trained in such specialties as communications and demolition. Following the lead of British commandos in World War II, members of this elite group sported distinctive green berets, but in 1956 these were forbidden as being "too foreign."

Little was heard about the group until 1962, when some 600 were serving as special advisors participating in a **counterinsurgency program** in the **Vietnam War.** At that time, President John F. Kennedy reinstated the green beret and noted that it was becoming "a symbol of excellence, a badge of courage, a mark of distinction in the fight for freedom."

By 1969 there were 3,000 Green Berets in South Vietnam, where, in addition to being assigned to tasks such as border surveillance and the disruption of enemy supply routes, they spearheaded groups of anticommunist irregulars trained in some seventy camps. Rumors circulated about their execution of prisoners and the use of poison and torture.

On August 3, 1969, Colonel Robert B. Rheault and seven Green Berets under his command—the Fifth Special Forces Group (Airborne) at Nah-trang—were arrested by the Army and charged with the killing of Thai Khac Chuyen, an alleged communist double agent who had infiltrated an Intelligence unit. They were scheduled to be court-martialed, and criminal lawyer F. Lee Bailey was among those retained for their defense. However, late in September the charges were dropped, presumably because the **CIA** refused to allow its agents to testify in any trial which it deemed would not be "in the national interest." Some observers felt that given the conditions of warfare in Vietnam the charges were ridiculous and basically the result of interservice rivalry.

A romanticized and idealized portrait of the Special Forces was given in Robin Moore's 1965 bestseller *The Green Berets.*

The Greening of America In this bestselling analysis of American society published in 1970, Yale University law professor Charles A. Reich foresees the growth of a new "consciousness" which will ultimately and peaceably transform—"green"—what he sees as present-day life-suppressing institutions. The heart of the book traces the evolution of the American spirit and breaks it down into three stages.

Consciousness I: Associated with the early days of the republic, it is freedom-loving, democratic, expansive, and egalitarian. The growth of competition encourages a decline of this spirit and an increase in the repression of the human spirit. Political institutions become a mere parody of true democracy, and well-meaning attempts at reform, i.e., the New Deal, only worsen the situation by introducing more rules and regulations. The post-World War II technological revolution completes the process.

Consciousness II: A grim and colorless stage in which individuality is suppressed and all attempts at amelioration are channeled through the closely allied institutions of the Corporate State: Industry and Government. Those in this stage of consciousness reject "awe, mystery, helplessness, magic," and glorify "power, success, rewards, competence."

Consciousness III: An early representative of this spirit was the nineteenth-century American writer Henry David Thoreau. Those who have entered this stage—their number increased rapidly during the 1960s—are concerned with transforming American society by means of their personal commitment to comradeship, honesty, and simplicity. They reject all violence, and they work to make human institutions increasingly responsive to human needs. Consciousness III people have "rediscovered a childlike quality that [they] supremely treasure," giving to it the "ultimate sign of reverence, vulnerability and innocence, 'Oh Wow!' "

Reich's course on "Individualism in America" was described in the *Yale Course Guide* as "the finest and most flexible course in Yale College. . . . Perhaps the most cogent remark to be made about [it] is that he thinks kids are neat and what can be bad about someone telling you how the system and the older generation have warped and destroyed things for us?"

Griswold et al. v. Connecticut Held unconstitutional an 1879 Connecticut statute making it a crime for anyone, even if married, to use contraceptives. Mrs. Estelle T. Griswold, executive director of a New Haven birth control clinic, was arrested along with the clinic's medical director and fined $100 for giving birth control information and advice to married couples. The case came before the U.S. Supreme Court after the convictions and fines were upheld by an intermediate appellate court and the state's highest court. Among the amici curiae briefs entered in urging reversal of the convictions was one by the Catholic Council on Civil Liberties which complained against the "profane interference" with the closest expression of feelings between a man and a woman.

Grunts Name often given to American soldiers who fought in the **Vietnam War.** It never obtained the popular currency of "GIs" during World War II, or "doughboys" during World War I.

GSA *See* **General Services Administration.**

Guam Doctrine *See* **Nixon Doctrine.**

Guantanamo Incident In reprisal for the seizure by the U.S. Coast Guard, on February 2, 1966, of four Cuban fishing boats and their thirty-eight crewmen, the Cuban Communist government cut off the water supply (February 6) normally piped to the U.S.

naval base at Guantanamo Bay on the southeastern coast of the island. Premier Fidel Castro said that the base would henceforth receive water only one hour a day, since he considered it immoral to "deny water, even to the enemy." He protested against the "unjustified" seizure of the boats and claimed that American authorities had been informed in advance that the vessels would be operating off the Dry Tortugas, a small group of islands some sixty miles from Key West, Florida.

In answer to a protest filed with the United Nations Security Council by the Cuban foreign minister, UN Ambassador Adlai Stevenson noted that two of the captains of the ships concerned admitted that "they were knowingly fishing in U.S. waters."

Spurning the communist offer of water during one hour each day, the commander of Guantanamo ordered the pipes leading into the base to be cut. Beginning on February 9, American tankers brought water in from Jamaica and Florida. On February 10, the U.S. Defense Department announced plans to build a $5 million permanent salt water conversion plant at the base.

In a related move, President Lyndon B. Johnson (February 7) ordered that any of the base's 2,500 Cuban national employees who refused to spend their dollar earnings at Guantanamo be discharged. This denied the Castro government approximately $5 million in hard American currency annually.

During the Spanish-American War (1898) American troops landed in Cuba at Guantanamo Bay. In 1901, the site was leased to the United States for ninety-nine years under the terms of the Platt Amendment.

Guaranteed Annual Income (GAI) *See* **Family Assistance Plan.**

Guaranteed Annual Wage Under a true guaranteed annual wage plan, to ensure a year-round stable labor force employers agree that workers are to be paid each week of the year whether or not work is available. On June 6, 1955, the Ford Motor Company and the CIO United Auto Workers (UAW) agreed on a precedent-setting three-year contract which incorporated a modified guaranteed wage in the form of Supplemental Unemployment Benefits (SUB). "For the first time, " said John S. Bugas, Ford's vice president for industrial relations, "a major corporation has devised a sound workable plan to provide supplements to state unemployment compensation benefits for its employees during pe-

riods of layoff." In what the company called "a significant departure from the historical pattern of labor management agreements," Ford would make contributions at the rate of five cents an hour per employee to funds from which beginning in June 1956 laid-off workers would get payments of $2 to $25, depending on their wage rates and length of employment. When unemployment compensation was taken into account, this meant that for the first four weeks a laid-off worker would get 65 percent of his normal take-home pay and 60 percent for the next twenty-two weeks.

True to UAW President Walter P. Reuther's prediction that there was "a Ford in General Motors' future," on June 13, 1955, a similar contract was signed by GM. Before the end of the year American Motors and Studebaker-Packard Corp. had made SUB plans. By the beginning of the 1970s, other major companies having employer-financed SUB plans included: American Can Company, Continental Can Company, Goodyear Tire and Rubber Company, U.S. Steel Corp., and Pittsburgh Plate Glass Company.

Guillain-Barré Syndrome *See* **Swine Flu.**

Gulf of Tonkin Resolution On August 2, 1964, the U.S.S. *Maddox*, a destroyer assigned to intelligence operations in the Gulf of Tonkin, bordered by North Vietnam, China, and the Chinese island of Hainan, was attacked by three North Vietnamese PT boats while it was reported to be in international waters thirty miles off the North Vietnamese coast. Since there had been some South Vietnamese raider activity in the area, President Lyndon B. Johnson considered it possible that the *Maddox* had been mistaken as part of that operation. "Though we had decided to treat the first North Vietnamese strike against our destroyer as a possible error, we drafted a stiff note to the Hanoi regime."

The protest was broadcast over the **Voice of America** (VOA) radio and released to the press. When on August 4 Washington was informed that there had been a second attack, this time on the *Maddox* and the U.S.S. *C. Turner Joy*, President Johnson authorized a single retaliatory attack on North Vietnamese torpedo boats, their bases, and an oil depot. In a nationwide television broadcast, he told the American people: "Aggression by terror against the peaceful villages of South Vietnam has now been joined by open aggression on the high seas against the United States of America. . . . Yet our response, for the present, will be limited and fitting. We Americans know, although others appear to forget, the risks of spreading conflict. We still seek no wider war."

But the incident was to be the turning point in American participation in the **Vietnam War.** Since it was an election year, President Johnson sought for and obtained bipartisan approval of what he had done. In the explosion of outraged patriotism that followed, on August 7, 1964, Congress gave near unanimous approval—the only negative votes were cast by Sen. Ernest Gruening (D.-Alaska) and Sen. Wayne Morse (R.-Oreg.)—to the Gulf of Tonkin Resolution which not only endorsed the retaliatory raid but gave the President advance approval to "take all necessary steps, including the use of armed force, to assist any member or protocol state of the Southeast Asia Collective Defense Treaty requesting assistance in defense of its freedom."

The resolution was similar to those passed at the requests of Presidents Eisenhower and Kennedy to meet threatening situations in Formosa (1955) (see **Formosa Resolution**), the Middle East (1957) (see **Eisenhower Doctrine**), and Cuba (1962) (see **Cuban Missile Crisis**). Senator Morse was quick to point out that like its predecessors it unconstitutionally gave the President permission to wage war without congressional consent. Since it was to remain in force until the President felt it was not needed, or until it was repealed by a majority of both houses, for the moment President Johnson had a free hand in developing policy and tactics in the growing American entanglement in Vietnam.

Once the atmosphere had cooled somewhat,

Congress began to take a closer look at what it had done. The Johnson administration version of the Gulf of Tonkin incident was challenged: had the *Maddox* indeed been in international waters? Had the Pentagon known from the very beginning that the original attack on the destroyer was based on the assumption that it had been part of the South Vietnamese raiding party? And had there really been a second attack on the *Maddox* and the *C. Turner Joy?* Finally, had President Johnson been misled by the Pentagon, or had he engineered the situation to "entrap" Congress?

(The publication of the so-called **Pentagon Papers** beginning in June 1971 indicated that President Johnson had had the resolution drafted several months before the attack on the *Maddox.*)

In the growing disenchantment with the escalating war in Vietnam, a somewhat embarrassed Congress voted unanimously on November 16, 1967, to require future congressional approval for sending American troops abroad except to repel an attack on this country or to defend its citizens; the resolution did not cover the Vietnam War. Feeling that President Johnson may have "overreacted" to the Gulf of Tonkin incident resulted, on January 30, 1968, in a decision by the Foreign Relations Committee to reexamine the incident.

In December 1970, Congress repealed the Gulf of Tonkin Resolution in a foreign military sales bill signed into law on January 13 by President Richard M. Nixon, who did not view it as necessary to justify further United States involvement in Vietnam.

The Gutenberg Galaxy *See Understanding Media.*

H

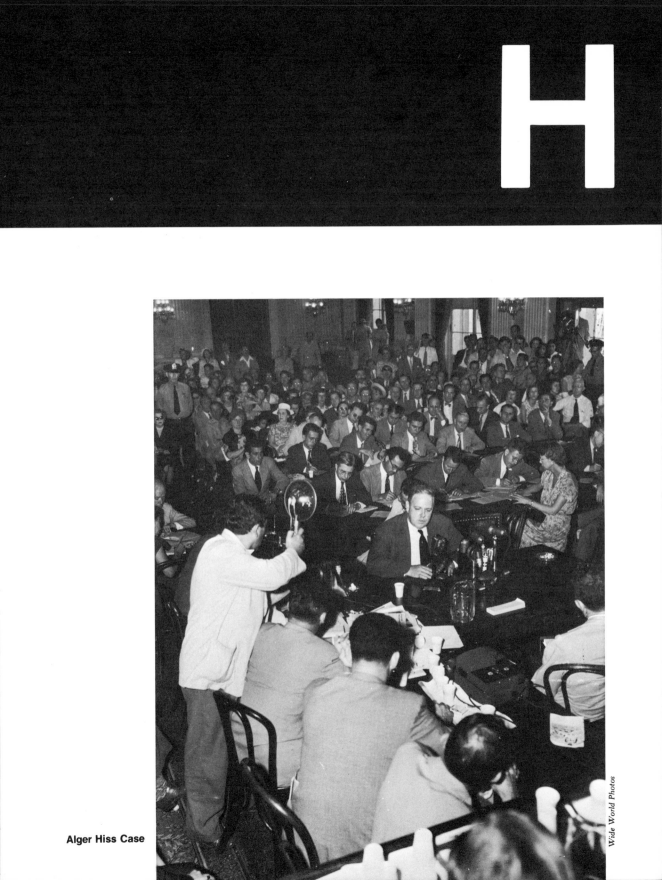

Alger Hiss Case

"Had Enough?" The enormous popularity that President Harry S Truman had enjoyed on assuming office in April 1945 had declined alarmingly as the end of World War II decreased the pressure for American unity, and the President made a number of unpopular moves that lost him support in traditionally Democratic voting sectors (see **"To err is Truman"**). During the 1946 congressional campaigns, the Democrats were on the defensive and Republicans cleverly played on national discontents by making wide use of the above slogan devised for them by Boston's Harry M. Frost Advertising Company. Democrats defiantly replied with: "Had Enough? Vote Republican and You'll Never Have Enough." The voters had—temporarily at least—had enough, and the Republicans regained control of both houses of Congress.

Haight-Ashbury During the 1960s, the area of San Francisco formed by the intersection of Haight and Ashbury Streets became a magnet which attracted "hippies" and "flower children" from all over the nation.

In the 1950s the district was home to white blue-collar families and later to black families forced to relocate by urban redevelopment projects. In the beginning of the next decade, low rents began to attract **"beatniks"** and artists unable to find accommodations in the **North Beach** district, and by 1965 a bohemian culture not unlike that of New York City's East Village was solidly established. Because of widespread drug usage the area was often referred to as "Hashbury."

Originally, the new people attracted to the district got along reasonably well with the older inhabitants, but the character of the area began to change radically when in January 1967 some 20,000 young people were attracted to San Francisco by the "World's First Human Be-In," at which **LSD** enthusiast Timothy Leary and poet Allen Ginsberg were among the star attractions. With the attention of the press and TV now trained on Haight-Ashbury, plans were made for the **"Summer of Love"** which increased the flow into San Francisco of the disaffected and alienated. The "pads" into which they crowded began to be feared as potential epidemic contagion centers. In addition, the community attracted dope pushers and petty criminals of various sorts who preyed on the pacifically oriented flower children. That fall the latter held a symbolic funeral for "Hippie, devoted son of Mass Media," and the age of innocence in Haight-Ashbury came to an end.

Nevertheless, the area's population continued to zoom, as did the crime rate. On February 18, 1968, the first of several serious riots broke out when a tourist driving down Haight Street ran over a dog. By midsummer the section had developed such a bad reputation that the flood of middle-class tourists who had made the area a commercial success began to thin out. Most of the hippies who had given the neighborhood its colorful character had long since left—too frightened to walk the streets.

Hair The ultimate expression of some of the more innocent aspects of the **counterculture,** this musical with a book and lyrics by Gerome Ragni and James Rado, and music by Galt MacDermot, opened off-Broadway in Joseph Papp's New York Public Theater on October 29, 1967. A paean to "long, beautiful, shining, gleaming, steaming, flaxen, waxen, long, straight, curly, fuzzy, snaggy, shaggy, ratty, matty, oily, greasy, fleecy, down-to-there hair," it was an immediate success and quickly transferred to Broadway in a souped-up version. Soon there were road companies in Chicago, Los Angeles, and San Francisco, followed by productions in Germany, France, England, Italy, Japan, the Netherlands, Australia, Israel, and Finland.

Vaguely concerned with the loves of dropout Berger, poster-maker Sheila, and draftee Claude in various combinations, this "American Tribal Love-Rock Musical" was weak on plot and was essentially a celebration of a variety of moods and ritual events. The hit songs included "Good Morning Starshine," **"Hare Krishna,"** and "Aquarius," the rock beat of the music and the noncomformist attitudes and language of the book and lyrics underscoring the **"generation gap"** between the beaded, bangled, and sometimes nude "love generation" and the conformist Establishment. ("Also take note," read the eventual printed text, "of the ever-present threat of the outside world on The Tribe, as expressed through the presence of the large police puppets, the projections on the walls of FBI, **CIA,** dark mysterious men, and Mom and Dad at times.")

As so often happens in America, the "squares" took this demonstration of revolt to their hearts. Gushed the staid *New York Times:* "*Hair* is a celebration, not a story. It celebrates the human body, marijuana, love and sex . . . . Beside [it] the plays of Tennessee Williams seem like exercises in voyeurism."

A Broadway revival in 1977 proved considerably less successful: much that had seemed titillatingly shocking a decade ago seemed dated and even quaint. A movie version opened in 1979.

Halloween Massacre In a move so sudden that it echoed the **Thanksgiving Massacre** of the Kennedy administration and the **Saturday Night Massacre** of the Nixon administration, on November 2, 1975, President Gerald R. Ford dismissed Secretary of Defense James R. Schlesinger and **CIA** Director William E. Colby. At the same time, Secretary of State Henry A. Kissinger was asked to relinquish his post as National Security Adviser in the White House, a position from which for almost five years he helped determine the nation's foreign policy during the Nixon administration before being appointed (September 1973) to replace William P. Rogers as Secretary of State.

Mr. Kissinger was asked to and agreed to stay on as Secretary of State, although he had previously let it be known that he would consider any attempt to make him give up his role as National Security Adviser a vote of no confidence that would require his resignation from the Ford administration. Washington observers suggested that the price he exacted for agreeing to carry on at a time when critical **Strategic Arms Limitations Talks** (SALT) negotiations were underway was the resignation of Mr. Schlesinger, with whom he had had increasing friction over his policy of détente.

The move was interpreted in some administration quarters as an attempt to stave off mounting attacks on President Ford from the Republican party's conservative wing, whose major spokesman was former Governor Ronald Reagan of California. If so, its effectiveness was dubious, since Mr. Reagan's comment on the major reshuffling of the administration's top national security posts was that "if it shakes down as a victory for Henry, it's not going to help Ford very much. A lot of people in the party and the country think Henry has too much power already. A lot have thought of Schlesinger as a ballast against Kissinger in the nuclear arms talks, and there would be more doubt now about whatever is negotiated." (The *New York Times* commented that "the fact remained that Mr. Kissinger was the survivor and that two of his main rivals within the administration were gone.")

The post of Secretary of Defense went to Donald H. Rumsfeld, who on many occasions had taken issue with Mr. Kissinger and had often noted that "Henry is now a political liability to the President." In the months that followed, President Ford dropped the word "détente" from his vocabulary and in 1976 he agreed to a Republican party plat-

form that seemed to downgrade Mr. Kissinger's foreign policy achievements.

George Bush was appointed CIA Director to replace Mr. Colby. The son of Sen. Prescott Bush (R.-Conn.), Mr. Bush had formerly been the chief U.S. representative at the United Nations, chairman of the Republican National Committee, and U.S. representative in China.

Secretary Kissinger's national security post went to Lt. General Brent Scowcroft, who was known to share many of his views on foreign policy.

Hamburger Hill Site of a combined U.S.-South Vietnamese assault on May 10, 1969, against Apbia Mountain during the **Vietnam War.** The 3,000-foot summit was stormed eleven times before it was finally captured on May 20. Allied losses were said to have been fifty-five, and the communist dead were figured at ten times that amount.

Critics such as Sen. Edward Kennedy (D.-Mass.) protested that the strategic value of the hill did not justify the battle, which GIs dubbed Hamburger Hill because it was one of the bloodiest in that unpopular war. The U.S. Army claimed that the capture of the site had prevented North Vietnamese from massing for an attack on Hue.

"Hang Tough" An expression that was originally popular during the early 1960s, when it was used in California centers for narcotics treatment to encourage those going through a situation of stress, such as a period of withdrawal from drugs. During the Nixon administration it became popular with White House staffers such as H. R. Haldeman, Chief of Staff, who came from the West Coast. William Safire (at the time, one of Nixon's speech writers; now a columnist for the *New York Times*) reports that ". . . throughout Nixon's first term, every weekday morning at eight-fifteen the senior staff would gather in the Roosevelt Room with Haldeman at the head of the table. In times of crisis or when it was otherwise important to present a united front, about thirty people were packed in to hear the President and then Haldeman or [Secretary of State Henry] Kissinger exhort us to hang tough."

Happening A participational art form in which planned and unplanned "theatrical" events take place in environments formed of traditional artistic materials as well as nonconventional materials drawn from other aspects of the culture. Both planned and random sounds may be part of the overall composition.

The name was suggested by *18 Happenings in 6*

Parts, by Allan Kaprow, which was performed in October 1959 at New York's Reuben Gallery. Among those in this country who were associated with this art form in its earliest days were Jim Dine, Claes Oldenburg, Red Grooms, Al Hansen, and Robert Whitman. Because of the kinesthetic nature of the form in which prepared effects were combined with unprogrammed plastic, aural, and mobile effects, "happenings" soon moved out of the art gallery and into gymnasiums, parking lots, stores, lofts, and the city streets in general.

Writing in *Art News* in October 1967, Allan Kaprow complained that the term had become so widespread to indicate exciting events and people—"Bobby Kennedy Is a Happening," announced one magazine cover—that most artists "including myself, have tried to get rid of the word 'Happening,' but this seems futile by now."

He noted six "prevalent" directions in which the "happening" seemed to be developing.

1. *Night Club, Cock Fight,* or *Pocket Drama.* Takes place in a confined area in which spectators press close to performers and are sometimes drawn into the action, which may be anything from shredding paper to cooking dinner to the accompaniment of music, sounds, lights, stable or mobile props, free or choreographed movements.

2. *Extravaganza.* An extension of the above, it resembles "three-ring circuses and vaudeville reviews" as developed by Dada and Surrealist antecedents. "Watered-down, it has emerged as the stock-in-trade of the discotheque and psychedelic scene."

3. *Event.* Audience seated in a theater watches a brief, single, and repeated occurrence which may also make use of audio effects; i.e., "a trumpet sounding while a balloon emerges from its bell until it bursts."

4. *Guided Tour* or *Pied Piper.* Selected group is led through a selected country or urban environment.

5. *Idea Art.* It may be acted out or simply retained in the mind as an idea; i.e., "Red light on Brooklyn Bridge."

6. *Activity.* "Selects and combines situations to be participated-in, rather than watched or just thought-about." It takes place in the everyday world and is more active than meditative; i.e., "ceremonies, fairs, mountain climbing. . . ."

Hard-hat Demonstrations   On May 6, 1970, a group of students from New York's Whitehall Medical Center held an anti-**Vietnam War** rally in Battery Park during the course of which a flag flying over a recently completed construction job was ripped down. Two days later, some 200 construction workers wearing yellow hard hats and chanting their support of the Nixon administration and its conduct of the war in Vietnam and Cambodia charged a Wall Street antiwar rally, breaking through virtually unresisting police lines and seriously beating some forty to sixty peace demonstrators. Then chanting "All the way U.S.A.," the hard-hats surged up Broadway to City Hall, where they forced officials to raise the flag which, on Mayor John V. Lindsay's orders, was flying at half-mast in deference to the victims of the **Kent State Tragedy.** They also broke into nearby Pace College, where students had hung out an antiwar banner.

Critics charged that the police had had ample warning of the fact that the hard-hats were planning the May 8 riot but failed to take precautions. In addition, it was said that the rioters were encouraged and directed by a representative of the New York *Graphic,* a small right-wing newspaper. Only six arrests were made.

On May 11, hard-hats once more surged through the Wall Street area, but this time the police prevented major violence. Then on May 20 some 100,000 hard-hats and their sympathizers paraded through New York in support of the Vietnam War and in denunciation of Mayor Lindsay. There were similar sporadic outbreaks by hard-hats across the nation.

President Richard M. Nixon seemed to be encouraging these outbursts of patriotic fury when on May 26 he received the representatives of construction worker unions and accepted a hard hat on which was lettered "Commander-in-Chief."

As a result of these incidents "hard hat" came to mean not only a headgear but a political attitude. However, toward the end of the **Watergate Scandal** investigations, polls showed that even the hard-hats had turned on the President.

Hare Krishna Sect   The International Society for Krishna Consciousness was founded in New York City sometime after the arrival there from India of His Divine Grace A. C. Bhaktivedanta Srila Prabhupad in 1965. Establishing a "temple" in the East Village, he soon attracted disciples from among the local hippies and flower children. They became a familiar sight on the busy city streets, where—clothed in saffron-colored robes and to the accompaniment of tinkling bells—they chanted "Hare Krishna" in homage to the Hindu god Krishna.

The sect, which regards itself as the most orthodox exponent of Hinduism, is said to have attracted tens of thousands of "Krishna people" in the United States alone. It distinguishes itself from other mystical sects by emphasizing that "Krishna consciousness" demands a life style from which gambling, smoking, drinking, drugs, the eating of meat, fish, or eggs, and indulgence in sex for any purpose other than procreation are rigorously excluded.

By the late 1970s, the society was said to have some thirty temples in the United States—including a fourteen-story temple-hostel in New York City—and many more than that in parts of Western Europe. By combining American resourcefulness with Indian spiritual wisdom, Swami Prabhupad would often say, the sect progressed much as a lame man and a blind man moving together. The movement claimed some 10,000 full-time monks in various parts of the world by the time of the swami's death in 1977. It was said to have an annual income of $16 million from its various properties and from the sale of books interpreting the ancient Vedic scriptures. In January 1978, the society, still dominated by American converts, opened a $2-million temple in Juhu, India.

Harlem Riots On July 16, 1964, James Powell, a fifteen-year-old black, was shot by Lt. Thomas Gilligan, a New York City police lieutenant, who claimed that the boy had drawn a knife on him. Negro witnesses disputed the officer's version of events and claimed that the killing was unprovoked.

Two days later a crowd gathered in Harlem at 125th Street and Seventh Avenue at a **Congress of Racial Equality** (CORE) meeting. The meeting was originally planned to protest anti-civil rights events in the South, but the black community had been seething with resentment over young Powell's death, and the talk rapidly turned to that. When the rally officially broke at about 8:30 in the evening, the crowd began moving toward the 28th Precinct Station House. Gathering outside, protesters called for the ouster of the city's police commissioner. Soon they began pelting the station house with garbage and bottles, and two squads of the Tactical Patrol Force were called in to disperse the demonstration. By midnight a full-fledged riot was raging in the streets of Harlem and there was widespread looting. Peace was not restored until the early hours of the morning.

In September, a New York county grand jury, after taking testimony from forty-five witnesses, found that Lt. Gilligan's version of how the boy's death came about was essentially correct. The tragedy stemmed from an incident in which the superintendent of a building on East 76th Street opposite Robert F. Wagner Junior High School turned a hose on a group of youngsters taking summer school courses. The boys and girls responded by pelting the superintendent and chasing him into the building. Powell then attempted to go after him with a knife, and Lt. Gilligan, who was off-duty at the time, came along, identified himself by holding out his badge, and tried to arrest the youth, who lunged at him with the knife. After firing a warning shot, the police officer fired into the youth's chest and abdomen.

The testimony offered the twenty-three-man grand jury—which included two blacks—was highly contradictory, and at least one witness withdrew charges that Gilligan had fired into the fallen body. Negro leaders expressed outrage at the findings, and NAACP Executive Secretary Roy Wilkins pointed out that "an experienced officer should be able to arrest a 15-year-old boy without killing him."

Within a month of the Harlem riots, similar disturbances broke out in Brooklyn; Rochester, New York; Jersey City, New Jersey; Paterson, New Jersey; and Elizabeth, New Jersey. In Jersey City, three nights of rioting followed the spread of rumors that a black woman arrested for drunkenness had been beaten by the police. At least two people were shot and forty-six were injured—twenty-two of them police. Property damage was set at $100,000.

Approximately a week later, rioting broke out in Paterson when a gang of ghetto youths began pelting police cars. Mayor Frank X. Graves, Jr., noted: "Ever since the Harlem riots, we've been on pins and needles." The rioting continued for three nights.

In Elizabeth, the trouble began when a gang of hoodlums boarded a public bus and terrorized passengers.

Harrisburg Seven On November 27, 1970, FBI director J. Edgar Hoover revealed an "incipient plot on the part of an anarchist group" to raid draft boards, bomb the heating tunnels in the Capital's federal buildings, and kidnap presidential adviser Henry Kissinger. The information, as it turned out, had been supplied by a paid FBI informer who had been serving a term in Lewisburg Federal prison with anti-**Vietnam War** protester Father Philip Berrigan (see **Catonsville Nine**). In April 1970 this informer, who was on a study-release program, had approached Father Berrigan and offered to become the courier for an illegal correspondence between him and Sister Elizabeth McAlister. He thereafter supplied copies of this exchange of letters to the FBI, and it was largely on the basis of these that

Father Berrigan, Sister Elizabeth, and five others were brought to trial in Harrisburg, Pennsylvania, in February 1972, on an indictment obtained by Guy L. Goodwin, chief of the Special Litigation Section of the Justice Department's Internal Security Division and the special nemesis of the **New Left.**

In a joint statement with his brother, Father Daniel Berrigan, Father Berrigan had on January 13, 1971, denounced the charges against him, stating that "the Government has embarked on a tragic and outrageous course—to stigmatize millions of morally dedicated opponents of our military involvement in Indochina as violent and deranged people." Nevertheless, in the letters read in court Sister Elizabeth outlined a plan "to kidnap—in our terminology make a citizen's arrest of—someone like Henry Kissinger," and in his reply Father Berrigan had said: "Why not coordinate it with the one against capital utilities? . . . To disrupt them, and then grab the Brain Child—This would be escalation enough."

The trial lasted fifty-six days and is said to have cost the government over $1 million. It ended on April 5, 1972, with a mistrial of all defendants on the conspiracy charges and the conviction of Father Berrigan and Sister Elizabeth on the charges of smuggling letters. Father Berrigan was sentenced to four concurrent two-year terms and Sister Elizabeth to one year and one day. (On June 27, 1973, a federal appeals court overturned six of the seven counts, finding that, although the law under which they were tried stipulates that letters cannot be sent into a prison without the consent of the warden or supervisor, since six of the letters involved were transmitted by an inmate informer, the law did not apply.)

"Hashbury" *See* **Haight-Ashbury.**

Hatfield-McGovern Amendment Sometimes known as the "end-the-war amendment," its rejection by a Senate coalition of Republicans and Southern Democrats on September 1, 1970, came shortly before that body approved a long-debated $19.2 billion military procurement bill by an eighty-four to five vote. As proposed by Sen. Mark O. Hatfield (R.-Oreg.) and Sen. George S. McGovern (D.-S. Dak.), the amendment provided for the withdrawal of all American troops from South Vietnam by the end of 1971. Although its rejection was interpreted as a victory for the Nixon administration's policy in Indochina, some who opposed the unpopular **Vietnam War** voted against the amendment in the be-

lief that it would hamper current negotiations to bring the war to an end.

In urging passage of the amendment, cosponsor McGovern noted that "every Senator in this chamber is partly responsible for sending 50,000 young Americans to an early grave . . . for the human wreckage . . . all across the land—young boys without legs, without arms, or genitals, or faces, or hopes. If we don't end this damnable war, those young men will some day curse us for our pitiful willingness to let the Executive carry that burden that the Constitution places on us."

To gain support for the Hatfield-McGovern amendment, the sponsoring Senators organized Project Pursestrings, which on May 12, 1970, made a televised appeal for moral and financial support. Listeners contributed $480,000, mostly in small sums, which was used to pay for the cost of the program and for additional spot announcements and newspaper ads.

"Have you no sense of decency, sir?" *See* **McCarthyism.**

Hayden Amendment *See* **Equal Rights Amendment.**

Head Start Originally begun as a summer "project" to prepare 561,000 preschool children from disadvantaged backgrounds for registration in public schools that fall, the Head Start program was launched at a special White House ceremony by President Lyndon B. Johnson on June 30, 1965. It was created by the **Office of Economic Opportunity** (OEO) as part of the Johnson administration's **War on Poverty,** and on August 31, 1965, the President announced that "Operation" Head Start would become a permanent year-round effort.

Head Start is currently administered by the Department of Health, Education and Welfare, and by mid-1977 more than 6 million children had benefited from the program. There are some 8,000 centers run by 1,200 community centers in the nation, including special programs for the children of migrant workers and programs set up on Indian reservations by tribal councils. In August 1977, there were more than 300,000 children enrolled in Head Start programs on a year-round basis (at a cost of $1,505 per child) and some 46,000 in summer programs (at a cost of $175 per child). Ever since 1972, Congress has required that some of those enrolled be handicapped children. Average enrollment is for one year, but some children stay on for an additional year.

According to James Robinson, 1977 director of the program, studies have shown the Head Start pupils have been able to achieve consistently better academic results than those of their peers who have not benefited from this preschool training. "People in the community see it as their program," Robinson explained, "and support from Congress was its salvation in recent years." (The 1977 budget for Head Start was $475 million, up from the initial annual cost of $96.4 million.) "We try to explain to the family that they are the most important teachers. When we recruit children, we make it clear that the family must co-operate or our program won't work. Parents also sit with the staff on policy-making bodies, even are involved in hiring teachers."

Health Care Financing Administration (HCFA) *See* **Medicaid** and **Medicare.**

"Hear It Now" *See* **"See It Now."**

Patty Hearst Kidnapping On February 4, 1974, nineteen-year-old Patricia Hearst, the granddaughter of William Randolph Hearst, founder of the Hearst publishing empire, was dragged screaming from her Berkeley, California, apartment by two armed black men and a white woman. Responsibility for the kidnapping was claimed by a group which identified itself as the Symbionese Liberation Army (SLA), headed by a man who called himself "Field Marshal" Cinque. The SLA contacted the girl's father, Randolph A. Hearst, publisher of the *San Francisco Examiner*, and demanded that $230 million in free food be distributed to the city's poor in return for her release. Rejecting this as impossible, the publisher countered with an offer to distribute $2 million and then $6 million—the majority of funds coming from the Hearst Corporation—and a food distribution program began in the East Oakland area.

A taped message from Miss Hearst (March 9) bitterly complained that not enough was being done to obtain her release, and the SLA demanded that food of better quality be distributed. The distribution program ran out of funds on March 26.

A new recorded message from Miss Hearst (April 3) announced that she had rejected an SLA offer of freedom and decided to join the group in its struggle for "the freedom of oppressed people." She was later identified as one of an armed group who robbed the Hibernia Bank, San Francisco, on April 15, 1974. In another tape, she announced her *nom de guerre* as "Tanya" and denied that she had been coerced into participating in the robbery.

On May 16, following her participation in the holdup of a sporting goods store, the FBI classified Miss Hearst as "an armed and dangerous fugitive," and the following day Los Angeles police besieged a suspected SLA hideout. In the shootout that followed, six SLA members were killed, including their leader Cinque, alias Donald D. Defreeze.

Miss Hearst was not apprehended by the authorities until September 18, 1975, when she was arrested in San Francisco along with Wendy Yoshimura, who was also wanted by the police. After a trial in which she was defended by the famous criminal lawyer F. Lee Bailey, on March 20, 1976, Miss Hearst was found guilty on charges of having voluntarily taken part in the Hibernia Bank robbery, in spite of the fact that she now contended she had been coerced. She was released (November 19, 1976) on $1 million bail pending an appeal. In a brief notice on April 24, 1978, the U.S. Supreme Court announced that it had denied an appeal for review and left standing her original conviction. In San Francisco on November 7, 1978, a federal district judge refused to set aside Miss Hearst's bank robbery conviction or to modify her sentence. (Her father had claimed that her trial had been "a sham because of ineffective assistance to counsel.") Miss Hearst was released from prison on February 1, 1979, after serving twenty-two months of a seven-year sentence, under an executive clemency order signed by President Carter.

Heartbreak Ridge One of the major battles of the **Korean War,** it was fought for more than three weeks in the razorback eastern mountains of the peninsula, and ended on October 12, 1951, when American, French, and Dutch infantrymen captured for the third time what had come to be called Heartbreak Ridge. (When the position had originally been taken by a small American force on September 23, only to be lost to a North Korean counterattack the very next day, a wounded soldier was reported in the press to have said, "It's a heartbreak, it's a heartbreak.")

Preliminary truce talks designed to end the war had begun at Kaesong in July 1951, but been broken off by the North Koreans on August 22 because of an alleged UN air attack on the negotiations site. During the fighting that followed, Heartbreak Ridge was considered part of the main line of communist resistance because it commanded a major supply route. Kaesong itself came within the grasp of battling UN troops, and the North Koreans, who had previously rejected any proposed shift of the negotiations site, changed tactics and on October 8, 1951, proposed moving the truce teams to the village of Panmunjom. Formal negotiations were resumed on October 25.

Heart of Atlanta Motel v. United States In two simultaneous rulings on December 14, 1964, the U.S. Supreme Court upheld the constitutionality of the public accommodations section of the **Civil Rights Act of 1964,** and held that it also barred a state from prosecuting demonstrators who had used peaceful means to bring about desegregation of such accommodations. At the time of the rulings there were said to be some 3,000 **sit-in** demonstration prosecutions awaiting action; some of the cases went back four years.

The Court ruling on the accommodations section upheld a federal district court decision that enjoined an Atlanta motel from discriminating against blacks; the Court also reversed another federal district court decision that had held the public accommodations section unconstitutional in a case involving a Birmingham restaurant.

The majority decisions of the Supreme Court were written by Justice Tom C. Clark, who emphasized that the power of Congress in the field of interstate commerce is broad and sweeping. "Where it keeps within its sphere and violates no express constitutional limitation it has been the rule of this Court, going back almost to the founding days of the Republic, not to interfere. The Civil Rights Act of 1964, as here applied, we find to be plainly appropriate in the resolution of what the Congress found to be a national commercial problem of the first magnitude. We find it in no violation of any express limitations of the Constitution and therefore declare it valid."

The ruling on the accommodations section was unanimous, but the one covering the prosecution of peaceful demonstrators was five to four. In a dissenting opinion Justice Hugo L. Black expressed opposition to the concept that the law could aid those who "took the law into their own hands."

"Hell, no, we won't go!" *See* **National Conference on Black Power.**

Hell's Angels One of the more famous motorcycle gangs that flourished in the sunshine of attention from the various media during the 1960s. It has since faded from public view, but not from existence. Although California's attorney general identified them in 1957 as a public menace, the gang had a brief flirtation with the hippie culture and radical left; when they weren't hitting people on the head, they sometimes served as a "people's police

force," and could often be found maintaining their own brand of order at West Coast rock concerts in exchange for a few kegs of beer. In December 1969, they were hired in this capacity by the English rock group, the Rolling Stones; the result was the disastrous **Altamont Death Festival.**

National attention was first focused on the motorcycle gangs in the successful 1953 movie *The Wild One,* starring Marlon Brando as the leader of a group of marauding cyclists who terrorize a small town. In September 1964, Hell's Angels made the headlines when several teenage girls claimed to have been raped during a gang celebration near Monterey. The gang was back in the news in October 1965 when they attacked demonstrators participating in the Oakland **Moratorium Day** parade and announced plans to do more of the same to those taking part in a second demonstration planned for November. At the last minute they called off these plans to avoid arousing sympathy for "this mob of traitors" and in a telegram sent to President Lyndon B. Johnson volunteered to serve as "a crack group of trained gorillas" behind the lines in Vietnam.

Under increased police surveillance after the Rolling Stones concert, the gang seemed to some extent to have grown fat on the profits of such lurid movies about them as *Devil's Angels* (1967), in which cyclists were shown breaking up an outlaw sanctuary.

Hell's Canyon Dam *See* **"Give-away"** Program.

Helsinki Accord Document signed at the conclusion of the third and last meeting of the Conference on Security and Cooperation in Europe (CSCE), held in Helsinki, Finland, July 30–August 1, 1975. (The CSCE had met in Helsinki in 1972 and in Geneva in 1973.) Although nonbinding and of no legal status as a treaty, the accord expressed recognition of Europe's postwar boundaries—a provision pressed for by the U.S.S.R., particularly in view of the partition of Germany and the incorporation of Estonia, Latvia, and Lithuania into the Soviet Union—and established principles for assuring peace and both cultural and economic cooperation between the signatories.

The Helsinki Accord was signed by the leaders of the thirty-five nations—including the United States and Canada—participating in the CSCE. At the insistence of the Western Powers, it included the so-called basket-three section, which called for the right of citizens to cross borders on family visits, the reunification of families, the right of marriage between citizens of different nations, and the facilitation of working conditions for foreign journalists.

President Gerald R. Ford's participation in the CSCE was highly criticized by some who felt that the Helsinki Accord was a retreat from this country's previous insistence on the principle of self-determination for the Baltic and Eastern European states, whose current status seemed to have thereby obtained de facto recognition. Defending his position, President Ford stated on July 26, 1975, that "our official policy of nonrecognition is not affected by this conference." Stressing the fact that the accord had no legal status, he noted: "We are not committing ourselves to anything beyond what we are already committed to by our own legal and moral standards."

Among the President's most outspoken critics was former California Governor Ronald Reagan, who was disputing with him for the 1976 Republican presidential nomination, and the exiled Soviet writer Aleksandr I. Solzhenitsyn, who said that American participation in the CSCE was "a betrayal of Eastern Europe."

Although the Helsinki Accord expressed support for the freer movement between nations, many have felt that the U.S.S.R. has ignored the spirit if not the letter of the agreement. Particular focus has been placed on the fact that Soviet Jews are still by and large prevented from emigrating to join their families in Israel and elsewhere, that many political dissidents are still in prison, and that Soviet citizens are still barred ready access to Western sources of information.

With the exception of Albania, all the nations of Europe—including Spain, Vatican City, East Germany, and West Germany—signed the Helsinki Accord.

Herter Commission In 1947, House Speaker Joseph W. Martin, Jr. (R.-Mass.) named Rep. Charles A. Eaton (R.-N.J.) to head a 19-member group to investigate conditions in postwar Europe and to make foreign policy recommendations. When the group eventually went overseas on August 27, 1947, it was headed by Rep. Christian Herter (R.-Mass.).

In November of that year Representative Herter raised demands in Congress that in return for aid the United States be granted Western Hemisphere bases and strategic materials such as uranium. Although supporting Secretary of State George C. Marshall's interim aid program, he informed Congress that the French had at least $2 billion in gold and dollars within its borders and another $500 mil-

lion in the United States. Herter's Select Committee on Foreign Aid warned that the **Marshall Plan** would eventually cause shortages in steel, gasoline, and fuel oil in this country. He personally warned that this country should not promise more than it could deliver, making special reference to wheat promised Italy.

The Hidden Persuaders Vance Packard's 1957 bestseller was a popular presentation of the use and abuse of sociopsychological research in selling the American public anything from products to politicians. Special emphasis was put on the use of "motivational research" (MR), and the book is filled with specific examples of how the buying public's wants and opinions are manipulated by the unscrupulous application of psychologically developed techniques to advertising.

Although most critics agreed that the book made for exciting reading, the absence of professional evaluation of the techniques and the lack of necessary reference data made it all but impossible to judge the actual effectiveness claimed for MR.

"Higby" Within White House circles during the Nixon administration, "a higby" was the designation for the perfect staff man. The word derived from the name of Chief of Staff H. R. Haldeman's right-hand man, Lawrence M. Higby. One of the top graduates of UCLA in 1967, Higby had been recruited for the J. Walter Thompson advertising agency by Haldeman and then in 1968 asked to join Richard M. Nixon's staff for the coming presidential campaign. When Haldeman accompanied the victorious President Nixon to the White House, Higby accompanied Haldeman. Newsman Theodore H. White noted that "Haldeman spoke for the President on the highest level; Higby spoke for Haldeman on an operational level; and whether it was an affair of state or a spurt of annoyance with the press, the machinery moved to respond." Higby's zeal was such that he became "Haldeman's Haldeman."

Higher Education Act of 1965 Given top priority by the Johnson administration, the act provided the first federal scholarships to college undergraduates, authorized a Teacher Corps to serve in schools in low-income areas, provided for insurance of student loans, and established aid for small colleges. Passed by the House and the Senate on October 20, 1965, it was signed into law by President Lyndon B. Johnson at special ceremonies on November 8, 1965, at his alma mater, Southwest Texas State College in

San Marcos. The act authorized $803,350,000 for fiscal 1966 and an additional $42 million in interest subsidies.

During his term in office, President Johnson signed sixty different education bills. "All of them," he later noted, "contributed to advances across the whole spectrum of our society. When I left office, millions of young boys and girls were receiving better grade school education than they once could have acquired. A million and a half students were in college who otherwise could not have afforded it."

On signing the 1965 bill, President Johnson noted that the federal government had neither the desire nor the power to dictate education; its intention was to be "a partner and not a boss."

In establishing a National Teacher Corps, the act authorized over $36 million in fiscal 1966 and almost $65 million in fiscal 1967 to provide specially trained experienced and intern teachers, who at the request of local school agencies could be assigned to schools in poverty areas. Other provisions authorized $70 million in fiscal 1966-1968 to provide scholarships of from $200 to $800 to needy first-year undergraduates, the awards being made by the colleges. Funds were also made available for the extension of such scholarships for three more academic years. In addition, the act authorized both states and nonprofit organizations to establish student loan-insurance programs. The federal government was to insure these loans and pay interest on them while the student was attending school; afterward, the federal government would pay half of the 6-percent interest on the unpaid principal for those from families with an adjusted income not exceeding $15,000.

On June 29, 1967, President Johnson signed additional legislation extending the Teacher Corps by authorizing $135 million in fiscal 1968-1970. The same bill eliminated the National from the title and shifted control of the corps from the federal government to local school systems. Recruitment and selection of volunteers was placed under the control of local agencies and colleges working under contracts with the U.S. Office of Education. Corps members sent into local school districts had to have the approval of the state's education agency. At least 10 percent of their salaries were to be paid by local school districts.

Attempts to eliminate the Teacher Corps from the new legislation had been twice made in the House. Rep. Edward J. Gurney (R.-Fla.), who led the fight against the corps, charged that it was "a federally-oriented elite group of teachers financed by federal money." It was due to the efforts of Rep.

Edith Green (D.-Oreg.) that control of the corps was shifted from federal to local control.

Highway Beautification Act *See* **Lady Bird Bill.**

Alger Hiss Case Appearing before the **House Committee on Un-American Activities** (HUAC) on August 3, 1948, Whittaker Chambers, a self-confessed Soviet agent, who had now become a senior editor of *Time* magazine, accused Alger Hiss of having been a secret communist between 1934 and 1938. Hiss, who had had a brilliant career in the State Department after serving as special attorney of the Nye Committee on Munitions (1934-1935), was now the president of the Carnegie Endowment for International Peace. The charge was unsubstantiated and rested on the value of Chambers' word.

Denying that he had ever even known Chambers, Hiss telegraphed HUAC and demanded to be called to testify against the charge under oath. His "cooperative" appearance before the committee on August 5, 1948, made an excellent impression on all its members except Rep. Richard M. Nixon (R.-Calif.), who asked for a face-to-face confrontation between Hiss and Chambers.

At the next HUAC session, however, only Chambers was called, and he then presented testimony offering a wealth of detailed personal information to support his statement that he had known Hiss (who was excluded, as was the public, from this session). The most exotic item was that Hiss was a devoted bird watcher, a fact established by the committee, when Hiss was later recalled, by asking him a much publicized question about the nesting habits of the prothonotary warbler in the Washington area.

Hiss continued to maintain that he did not know or recognize Chambers on the basis of the news photographs he had seen, but he said that he might have known him in 1935 as George Crosley—a name which Chambers denied ever using. When the two men met at a HUAC session at the Commodore Hotel, New York, on August 25, Hiss stated that he was now certain that Chambers and Crosley were one. He challenged Chambers to repeat his accusation in public so that he might be sued for libel.

On September 2, at another HUAC session, this time in Washington, Hiss was confronted with Chambers' statement that he (Chambers) had been given the Hiss family's 1929 Ford for Communist Party use. Hiss stated that to the best of his recollection he had given such a car to "Crosley." He was unable to produce witnesses to the fact that he had known Chambers as Crosley. Vehicle records established Chambers' possession of the car some ten years earlier.

On September 4, Chambers appeared on the radio program *Meet the Press* and stated that Hiss had been a Communist "and may be one now." For several weeks, Hiss took no action, but on September 27, 1948, he brought a $75,000 defamation suit.

Required to prove his case, Chambers now extended his accusation to include espionage, charging that in 1937 and 1938 Hiss had given him classified government documents and both handwritten or typed summaries of others. At a pretrial hearing he produced a selection of such material, which he said had been kept for him by his wife's nephew since 1938, when Chambers had broken with the Communist Party. Then on December 2, Chambers led HUAC investigators to his Maryland farm, where from a hollowed-out pumpkin he produced several microfilm rolls of documents he said had been given him by Hiss. The contents of those documents released seemed unimportant, but since they had been transmitted in the State Department's secret Code D cipher they gained added significance. As for the handwritten summaries, Hiss said they had been prepared for his chief, Francis B. Sayre—who, however, denied that there was such a department procedure. (The typed summaries had been copied on a machine that Hiss claimed to have disposed of before the date of the documents.)

President Harry S Truman, whose administration was considerably embarrassed by the melodramatic revelation of the "pumpkin papers," said that the HUAC investigations were a "red herring" designed to draw public attention away from the inability or unwillingness of the Republican-controlled "do nothing" Eightieth Congress to deal with more pressing national problems. However, when challenged by HUAC to "authorize publication of all the documentary evidence the committee had," he did not reply.

On December 15, Hiss was indicted on two charges of perjury; he was being brought to trial on May 31, 1949. The presiding judge was Samuel Kaufman, who was accused of being "pro-Hiss." Such was the bitterness at the trial that when it ended with a hung jury, Representative Nixon declared that Judge Kaufman's "prejudice for the defense and against the prosecution was so obvious . . . that the jury's 8-4 vote for conviction came frankly as a surprise to me." Nixon demanded an investigation of Judge Kaufman, and he said of the

Hiss trial that "the average American wants all technicalities waived in this case."

A second perjury trial began on November 17, 1949, and ended with Hiss's conviction on January 21, 1950. Still protesting his innocence, he was sentenced to five years; he was released after serving forty-four months. In June 1975, Chambers having died in 1961, Hiss announced that he was suing the federal government under the newly amended **Freedom of Information Act** to obtain documents and film which he said would discredit the "pumpkin papers" as forgeries and clear him of his perjury conviction a quarter of a century earlier. At a press conference on March 18, 1976, he pointed out that three of the five microfilms had never been produced at his trial. One now turned out to be blank and the other two contained unimportant technical documents, many of which, he said, the FBI knew at the time were available on the open shelves of the Bureau of Standards library.

Although a day after they were first found the "pumpkin papers" were exhibited in public as an imposing three-foot pile of letter-sized reproductions, few of the details about them were actually released. Writing in the *New York Times*, April 1, 1976, I. F. Stone in an article entitled "The 'Flimflam' of the Pumpkin Papers" said that "it is a pity now that Truman did not accept the dare" to publicize the contents of these documents. Nevertheless, the controversy over Hiss remains unresolved.

Hobby-Brownell Plan On January 14, 1955, Secretary of Health Oveta Culp Hobby and Federal Commissioner of Education Samuel Brownell presented President Dwight D. Eisenhower and his Cabinet with a plan that called for the federal government to give limited financial help to a state school authority: a public corporate device for the financing of school construction through public bond issues and other borrowing plans without burdening the state government or school districts with the direct responsibility for the debt structure. Under the Hobby-Brownell Plan the federal government was to purchase bonds from these state authorities when the latter were unable to sell them on the market at reasonable rates.

Republicans estimated that the long-term cost of the program would be only about $15 million. To get new school construction started, $100 million would be advanced to the state authorities, but this money would have to be returned over a three-year period.

Critics argued that the plan would lead to charges that the federal government was competing in the bond market. In addition, a school-aid program that did not call for major federal expenditures aroused no enthusiasm among the country's major educators, none of whom endorsed the plan.

Ho Chi Minh Trail *See* **Vietnam War.**

Hollywood Ten A probe into possible communist infiltration in Hollywood captured the national headlines in October 1947 when the **House Committee on Un-American Activities** (HUAC), chaired by Rep. J. Parnell Thomas (R.-N.J.), turned its attention to the film colony. The proceedings were among the first congressional investigations to be televised, and millions watched as beginning on October 20, producers Louis B. Mayer, Jack L. Warner, and Sam Wood testified that many in Hollywood, principally writers, held views favorable to communism. The following day actor Adolphe Menjou told HUAC investigators that Hollywood was "one of the main centers of Communist activity in the United States," and, testifying on October 22, actor Robert Taylor called for the outlawing of the Communist Party in this country.

Meanwhile Representative Thomas, using a technique that foreshadowed that of Sen. Joseph R. McCarthy three years later (see **McCarthyism**), announced that his committee had uncovered evidence linking seventy-nine Hollywood personalities with subversive activities. "We are going," he announced, "to continue to expose, and if you will just sit around here every day this week you will see more exposure and more spotlighting of Communists than you have ever seen before."

The "Hollywood Ten" were subpoenaed by HUAC as "unfriendly" witnesses. They included Alvah Bessie, Herbert Biberman, Lester Cole, Edward Dmytryk, Ring Lardner, Jr., John Howard Lawson, Albert Maltz, Samuel Ornitz, Adrian Scott, and Dalton Trumbo. All decided that their rights under the First Amendment entitled them not to answer when questioned as to whether or not they were members of the Communist Party. (A group of celebrities, including Humphrey Bogart, Lauren Bacall, William Wyler, and John Huston had reportedly urged the "Ten" to testify freely, and later flew to Washington to publicly condemn the HUAC hearings.)

Cited for contempt because of their defiance of HUAC, all of the "Hollywood Ten" were eventually (1950) given prison sentences of up to a year and fines of $1,000. In addition, they found themselves blacklisted in Hollywood, though many of them continued to write scripts under pseudonyms.

In 1957 the Academy of Motion Picture Arts and Sciences made anyone who had refused before a legislative committee to reply to a question concerning membership in the Communist Party ineligible for an Academy Award. Although Dalton Trumbo's *The Brave One* won an Oscar that year, he was unable to claim it since he had written the film under the name Robert Rich. The Academy rule was revoked in January 1959.

Honkies for Huey When Huey P. Newton was jailed for the murder of Officer John Frey in Oakland, California, in October 1967, the leadership of the Panthers was taken over by Eldridge Cleaver. Once the latter had set about organizing a **"Free Huey!"** campaign, he began to realize that Newton's attacks on black cultural leaders had so antagonized the traditional spokesmen of the black community that though a movement was formed quickly enough it just as quickly collapsed.

Cleaver had no better luck in retaining competent black lawyers for Newton's defense, and so he turned to sympathetic white groups. As a result, Charles Garry, a white lawyer who had represented many radicals who had come into conflict with the law, was hired to take on Newton's defense. At about the same time, a committee of black activist writers which had been formed proved unable to agree on adequate means of publicizing the trial. The task was soon taken over by white radicals who took the provocative name "Honkies for Huey." An alliance was formed with the predominantly white **Peace and Freedom Party.**

At his trial (July 15–September 8, 1968) Newton insisted on his innocence and maintained that he had been framed. He was nevertheless found guilty of voluntary manslaughter in 1968 and served a term in state prison before a California appeals court reversed his conviction. In 1969 and 1971, trials on the same charge ended in hung juries, and the charges were eventually dropped.

In 1974, the man who with Bobby Seale had founded the Black Panther Party (BPP) in 1966 was once more in trouble with the law on charges of murdering a young prostitute who had allegedly insulted him and of pistol-whipping a man in a separate incident. Scheduled to appear at a pretrial hearing, he fled to Cuba, where he remained until his voluntary return to this country in July 1977. He has since steadfastly maintained that he is not guilty of any of these charges and is a victim of government plots to discredit him and other Black Panthers.

Tried and acquitted on the pistol-whipping

charge, as a former convict he was given two years for weapon possession. The murder charge heard in March 1979 resulted in a hung jury.

Hoover Commission Officially known as the Commission on the Organization of the Executive Branch of the United States Government, the Hoover Commission was created on July 7, 1947, to investigate flaws in the setup of the executive branch and to make recommendations for reforms. Under the chairmanship of former President Herbert C. Hoover, the commission provided the basis for the Reorganization Act of 1949, which gave the President some authority to reorganize the executive branch subject to congressional approval, and established new salary levels for the President, Vice President, and Speaker of the House.

Members of the commission were appointed by the President, the Speaker of the House, and the President *pro tempore* of the Senate.

President Harry S Truman appointed Dean Acheson as vice chairman and gave him the task of making sure that no attempt was made to use the Hoover Commission to influence the presidential election campaign of 1948. A major disagreement arose as to whether the commission was to concern itself with considerations of organization that would enable the executive branch to administer the law as it then stood, or if it should be concerned with changing laws considered unwise. Under Acheson's urging, the commission agreed on the former stance.

Among its important recommendations was the organization of the Joint Chiefs of Staff as it now exists: a committee of service chiefs, each with a vote, presided over by a chairman who has no vote. One controversial recommendation was that the personnel in the permanent State Department establishment in Washington and the personnel of the Foreign Service above certain levels be amalgamated over a period of years into a single foreign affairs service obligated to serve at home or overseas and constituting a safeguarded career group administered separately from the General Civil Service.

In an additional attempt to have this recommendation adopted, when Dean Acheson became Secretary of State he appointed the **Rowe-Ramspeck-Decourcy Committee** in December 1949. Although some progress was made, it was not until the **Wriston Committee** was appointed by Secretary John Foster Dulles in 1954, during the Eisenhower administration, that the reform was carried out.

A Second Hoover Commission sat in 1953–1955 and many of its recommendations were carried into law.

The emphasis of both commissions was upon the elimination of overlapping services and the reduction of expenditures. Hoover himself felt that they had saved the government $10 billion annually.

J. Edgar Hoover Foundation Incorporated on June 10, 1965, on its application to the Internal Revenue Service for a tax-exempt status the J. Edgar Hoover Foundation listed its purpose as: "to safeguard the heritage and freedom of the United States of America, to promote good citizenship through an appreciation of its form of government and to perpetuate the ideals and purposes" to which Mr. Hoover, as director of the FBI, had devoted himself. An additional purpose was to combat "communism or any other ideology or doctrine" opposed to the principles set forth in the United States Constitution. Louis B. Nichols, former assistant to Mr. Hoover, was made director of the foundation.

Funds for the foundation were largely in the form of gifts of Schenley Distillers stock and were conferred on it by the Dorothy H. and Lewis S. Rosenstiel Foundation, set up by the Schenley chairman. The existence of the Hoover Foundation was not known until 1968, when it received two separate gifts of more than $700,000 in Schenley stock.

Horsemeat Harry On July 1, 1946, the authority on which the Office of Price Administration (OPA) had been established in April 1941 to control spiraling prices was to expire. President Harry S Truman had pleaded with Congress for extension of the OPA, but the amended price-control legislation offered him was in his opinion so weak that he vetoed it on June 29 as offering nothing but a choice between inflation with a statute and inflation without one. He specifically objected to a price-raising amendment for manufacturers introduced by Sen. Robert A. Taft (R.-Ohio), charging that in conjunction with a revised price-raising amendment for distributors introduced by Sen. Kenneth Wherry (R.-Neb.) it amounted to a mere pretense of protection and was actually "a sure formula for inflation."

On July 25, he reluctantly signed into law a new act offered by Congress. While removing some of his objections, it did not, he felt, give the government the necessary machinery to assure price stability.

Weak as it was, it was strongly objected to by cattle raisers who withheld their product from the market. Meat vanished from the stores and soon

Republicans were jeeringly referring to "Horsemeat Harry."

Hot Line Popular name for the emergency teletype system linking the White House with the Kremlin after September 1, 1963. The agreement on the system had been signed at the last session of the 1963 Geneva disarmament conference on June 20, after technical details had been worked out by Brigadier General George P. Sampson, deputy director of the Defense Department Defense Communications System, and Ivan Kokov, Soviet communications minister.

A 4,883-mile duplex cable permitting simultaneous transmission in both directions between Washington and Moscow via London, Copenhagen, Stockholm, and Helsinki—but, as Theodore Sorensen pointed out, "with no kibitzers"—was the system's primary circuit. It was to be open twenty-four hours a day for the transmission of coded messages. A radio circuit by way of Tangier, Morocco, was to serve as a stand-by system.

Similar systems to ensure emergency communications between the two capitals in the event of a crisis had been proposed in previous years. The deciding factor that led to agreement was, however, the communications failure during the 1962 **Cuban Missile Crisis** that forced President John F. Kennedy and Premier Nikita Khrushchev to broadcast several proposals for agreement over the public radio in order to avoid the four-hour delay made inevitable by conventional transmission and routine diplomatic presentation. "A future crisis—which could be caused not only by some actual conflict but by an accidental missile firing or some misleading indication of attack—might not permit either four hours or a public broadcast," Sorensen later noted.

In spite of the rapidity of the system, President Kennedy noted: "If he [Khrushchev] fires his missiles at me, it is not going to do any good for me to have a telephone at the Kremlin . . . and ask him whether it is really true." He therefore emphasized that agreement on communication was not as important as what was to be communicated.

The "hot line" was originally labeled the "purple telephone."

House Committee on Un-American Activities (HUAC)

The origins of the House Committee on Un-American Activities (HUAC) go back to May 26, 1938, when by a 191 to 41 vote the House authorized the appointment of a seven-member committee

. . . for the purpose of conducting an investigation of (1) the extent, character, and object of un-American propaganda activities in the United States, (2) the diffusion within the United States of subversive and un-American propaganda that is instigated from foreign countries or of a domestic origin and attacks the principle of the form of government as guaranteed by the Constitution, and (3) all other questions in relation thereto that would aid Congress in any necessary remedial legislation.

Expected by one of its chief supporters (Rep. Samuel Dickstein (D.-N.Y.)) to concentrate on agents of Nazi Germany and the Soviet Union active in prewar United States, under Rep. Martin Die, Jr. (D.-Tex.)—chairman from 1938 to 1944—it turned its attention increasingly to liberals active in labor, government, and the arts. Rep. Maury Maverick (D.-Tex.), who had led the fight against the establishment of a committee with "blanket powers to investigate, humiliate, meddle with anything and everything . . . from the German Saengerfest to B'nai B'rith," angrily defined "un-American" as "something that somebody else does not agree to."

HUAC was given permanent status on January 3, 1945. In the postwar era, under the chairmanship of Rep. J. Parnell Thomas (R.-N.J.), it turned its attention to communist infiltration in Hollywood, beginning with a hearing on October 20, 1947, during which Jack L. Warner testified that many writers—including Clifford Odets and Irwin Shaw—were Communists. As hundreds of reporters, supported by photographers and newsreel cameramen, recorded the scene, Americans were treated in the days that followed to a Hollywood spectacular with an unprecedented cast: Adolphe Menjou, Gary Cooper (whose notions of communism were limited to "from what I hear, I don't like it because it isn't on the level"), Robert Montgomery, George Murphy, and Ronald Reagan—all of whom appeared as friendly witnesses. The second week of hearings was given over to the testimony of nineteen unfriendly witnesses—including Bertolt Brecht—ten of whom decided to stand on their Constitutional rights under the First Amendment and refused to reply when asked if they were members of the Communist Party (see **Hollywood Ten**).

The following year HUAC was back in the headlines when at a hearing on August 3, 1948, Whittaker Chambers, a self-confessed Soviet agent, accused Alger Hiss, a former member of the State Department, of having been a communist (see **Alger Hiss Case**). It was by his close questioning of Hiss that HUAC member Rep. Richard M. Nixon (R.-Calif.) established his national reputation.

In the 1950s the meteoric rise of Sen. Joseph R. McCarthy (R.-Wis.) as the nation's chief communist-hunter upstaged HUAC's activities (see **McCarthyism**). Nevertheless, its spokesmen pressed some twenty-nine contempt citations against witnesses who had appeared before it in 1953 and 1954 and who pleaded the Fifth Amendment or challenged HUAC's right to inquire into their political activities and associations. In 1955, his own career having gone into a decline, Senator McCarthy supported efforts by Representative Dies to regain a role in HUAC. ("The leadership of the Democratic Party said, 'We won't put you on that Committee,' because they knew that Martin Dies wouldn't trifle with Communists.")

Meanwhile HUAC appropriations continued to climb. In 1959, the year former President Harry S Truman called it the "most un-American thing in the country today," they were up to $327,000. Rep. James Roosevelt (D.-Calif.) suggested without success on April 25, 1960, that HUAC be abolished, pointing out that it was getting and spending substantially more money than important bodies such as the Ways and Means Committee and the Judiciary Committee.

When in May 1960 a HUAC subcommittee went to San Francisco to hear testimony on supposed operations of the Communist Party of northern California, the hearings were disrupted by protests of more than 5,000 anti-HUAC demonstrators, many of whom could be seen on television being hosed down by police or dragged along the marble steps of San Francisco's City Hall. FBI Director J. Edgar Hoover charged that the demonstrations were communist-inspired (see **Operation Abolition**).

During the 1960s HUAC ran into an increasing number of rebuffs from the courts. In an era concerned with growing civil rights and anti-**Vietnam War** protests, HUAC's April 1967 hearings on Soviet espionage went largely unnoticed. When that same year the committee appeared eager to investigate the civil rights movement, it was forced to back off: the then chairman, Rep. Edwin E. Willis (D.-La.), reluctantly announced that HUAC had "no jurisdiction in such matters and it has no intention of trying to inject itself into them." (In the early 1940s, Chairman Dies had deplored "the fact that throughout the South today subversive elements are attempting to convince the Negro that he should be placed on social equality with white people, that now is the time for him to assert his rights.")

Renamed the Internal Security Committee in 1969, HUAC struggled along fitfully until it was finally abolished by the House in January 1975.

Housing and Community Development Act of 1974 Promoted under the Nixon administration by **Department of Housing and Urban Development** (HUD) Secretary James T. Lynn, this $11.1 billion legislation signed by President Gerald R. Ford on August 22, 1974, consolidated many of the programs that had mushroomed since the Housing Act of 1949 by authorizing block grants to local governments. Arrived at through a ratio based on population, degree of overcrowding, and poverty—which was given double weight in the formula—these locally administered grants for community development were to substitute for categorical-aid plans such as **Model Cities.** Of the sum voted, $8.6 billion was to be spent during the first three years, no community receiving less than the total amount previously available under the categorical programs. The block grants were to be used at the discretion of the community to meet its development needs: **urban renewal,** planning, aid to displaced families, housing-code enforcement, water and sewer facilities, etc.

A separate provision of the legislation established a $1.23 billion rent-subsidy program for low-income families, with tenants paying from 15 to 25 percent of their gross income toward local fair-market rentals.

Under the new legislation, emphasis shifted from centralized control of housing programs to local initiative. Although cities were expected to survey their needs accurately and avoid overconcentrations of low-income housing, they were freer than ever before to decide just how federal urban redevelopment funds would be used.

Howard Hughes Hoax On February 11, 1972, the McGraw-Hill Book Company, Inc., announced that it was canceling plans for the publication of what had been represented to it as the memoirs of billionaire-recluse Howard R. Hughes. The book had been contracted for through the agency of the author, Clifford Irving, who said that it was based on a series of tape-recorded interviews he had held with Hughes. To support his claim, Irving, a McGraw-Hill author for over a decade, supplied a series of letters which had been checked by experts and authenticated as being in the handwriting of Hughes. The publisher had given Irving a $750,000 advance in the form of checks made out to "H. R. Hughes." It had also accepted from *Life* magazine $250,000 for three 10,000-word installments from the "memoirs" that were to appear in advance of the book's publication on March 22, 1972.

Doubts as to the authenticity of the manuscript began to surface immediately after its publication was first announced in December 1971. Then on January 7, 1972, from his retreat in the Bahamas, Mr. Hughes held a more than two-hour telephone press conference with seven journalists in Los Angeles who were familiar with his voice and history. He branded the book a fraud and denied that he had ever endorsed the checks, which had been deposited in a Swiss bank account by a German-speaking woman who said she was Helga R. Hughes.

Investigators soon discovered that "Helga R. Hughes" was none other than Edith Irving, the author's wife. Although Mr. Irving admitted this, he claimed that she was acting under Howard Hughes's direction. However, his story about the tape recordings was discredited soon afterwards, when an entertainer named Nina Van Pallandt revealed that during the time the taped interviews were supposed to have been made, Mr. Irving had been with her almost constantly as they traveled across Mexico. In addition, it was learned that the supposed memoirs were based, in part, upon an unpublished manuscript by Stanley Meyer, a former assistant to Mr. Hughes.

Eventually, it was determined that the manuscript furnished McGraw-Hill was a concoction by Mr. Irving and Richard Suskind, who was to receive 25 percent of the illegal profits. The Irvings and Suskind were sentenced to brief prison terms. McGraw-Hill was able to recover most of its advance and repaid *Life* in full.

As the result of irregularities turned up during the scandal, authorities in the Bahamas caused Mr. Hughes to remove his headquarters to Nicaragua before his death in 1976.

HUAC *See* **House Committee on Un-American Activities.**

The Hucksters Frederic Wakeman's 1946 novel caused a stir by focusing on the advertising industry at a time when radio was king. The plot concerns an advertising agency man, Victor Norman, who lands as one of his major "accounts" the Beautee Soap company, which is run by a more than vaguely monstrous genius named Evan Llewelyn Evans.

In addition to telling a rattling good story, Wakeman was generally credited with having presented an accurate picture of incredible people unrestrained by conventional morality in an industry devoted to marketing commonplace necessities by creating a fantasy world for the buying public. Many of the scenes devoted to showing the naked use of absolute power in the interplay between agency, client, and the various types of "talent" for hire seemed to be stretching the truth somewhat, but are, in essence, no more unbelievable than what to this day clutters the airwaves at a time when the emphasis is on television (*see* **TV Wasteland**).

A popular movie version the following year starred Clark Gable as the agency man and Sidney Greenstreet as the despotic soap tycoon.

HUD *See* **Department of Housing and Urban Development.**

La Huelga The word literally means "the strike" in Spanish. It gained some prominence when in 1965 workers in the California grape fields of Delano went on strike and **La Causa** was born with the support of Cesar Chavez's National Farm Workers' Association.

In Kern County an attempt was made to outlaw the use of *huelga* because it was not an American word. Chavez saw the opportunity to attract national publicity by defying this overbearing attempt to abridge freedom of speech. On October 20, 1965, more than forty strikers chanted the word in unison as they picketed and newsmen watched. They were arrested on the charge of unlawful assembly. By the following day a protesting crowd had gathered before the Kern County courthouse chanting *huelga*. No additional arrests were made. The courts found the prohibition against the chant unconstitutional.

Hula-Hoop Craze In May 1958 the Wham-O Manufacturing Co., in San Gabriel, California, began marketing three-foot polyethylene rings as toys which children could cause to gyrate about their hips in various configurations, depending on their skill. They caught on immediately, and soon children all over the world were joined by adults using them for calisthenic purposes—in spite of the fact that medical associations here and abroad warned that they were potentially dangerous to those unused to strenuous exercise. Within six months, however, the Wham-O Company had some forty imitators, and approximately 30 million hoops had been sold to enthusiasts who staged local and national contests.

Human Sexual Response and **Human Sexual Inadequacy** *See* **Masters and Johnson Institute.**

Humphrey-Hawkins Full Employment Bill Urgently supported by organized labor and minority groups, as originally introduced in 1976 by its sponsors, Sen. Hubert H. Humphrey (D.-Minn.) and Rep. Augustus F. Hawkins (D.-Calif.), this legislation was seen as an expression of national commitment to the goal of full employment. As eventually passed by the 95th Congress on October 15, 1978, in the final hours before adjournment, the bill was in the words of an AFL-CIO publication "more symbol than substance." Gone was the provision which committed the government to being the employer of "last resort" for those unable to find jobs in private industry. The legislation signed into law by President Jimmy Carter on November 9, 1978, set as a goal the reduction of unemployment to 4 percent by 1983 and the reduction of the inflation rate to 3 percent in that same year and zero percent five years later. (In early 1979, the U.S. inflation rate was over 10 percent.) However, it instituted no programs to achieve these goals, which were now presumably the responsibility of the President. To many, the legislation seemed a less than satisfactory memorial to Senator Humphrey, who had died of cancer on January 13, 1978.

Hunger Project *See* **est.**

Hurricane Agnes After hitting Florida on June 19, 1972, Hurricane Agnes went on a ten-day rampage of the eastern seaboard, taking an estimated 134 lives and causing property damage of from 2 to 3 billion dollars along a 250-mile swath. According to an announcement by the **National Oceanic and Atmospheric Administration** (NOAA), the storm caused the most extensive flooding in the nation's history.

As it swept in from Cuba and the Gulf of Mexico, it was originally downgraded to a tropical storm, but it picked up in intensity as it moved from Florida to Georgia, the Carolinas, and Virginia. President Richard M. Nixon declared those portions of New York, Virginia, Florida, Maryland, and Pennsylvania where flash flooding had occurred eligible for federal relief and recovery aid. Following a tour of the five-state disaster area, he ordered the Office of Emergency Preparedness to provide $92 million in federal assistance. He also asked Congress for an additional $100 million in relief aid.

Hurricane Audrey *See* **Hurricane Camille.**

Hurricane Camille Struck the Gulf Coast area on August 17, 1969, and for five days raged through Mississippi, Louisiana, Tennessee, West Virginia, and Virginia, leaving more than 300 dead and property damage estimated at $1 billion. The National Hurricane Center in Miami called it "the greatest storm of any kind that has ever affected this nation by any yardstick you want to measure with." The barometer dropped to 26.61 inches and winds of more than 200 mph were recorded. It was the greatest killer since Hurricane Audrey (June 26–28, 1957), which struck Louisiana and Texas, leaving 500 dead in its wake and property damage of $150 million.

Beginning in 1953, the National Weather Service has used female names to identify tropical storms in the Atlantic, the Caribbean, and the Gulf of Mexico. An alphabetical list of ten sets of names was established in 1971 for the annual hurricane season which goes from the beginning of June to the end of November.

The Hustle Dance craze which swept the nation in 1975. Said to have originated in New York's black and Puerto Rican circles years before, it became a national vogue on the strength of the popularity of a series of successful dance recordings which emphasized rhythm, blues, and a strong "Latin" beat. Foremost of these recordings was Van McCoy's *The Hustle* and Consumer Rapport's *Ease on Down the Road*, which came from the successful Broadway musical *The Wiz*.

Unlike such dances as the Frug, Monkey, and Boogaloo, it reintroduced bodily contact into dancing and had a definite basic step which consisted of variations on a tap, 1-2-3, 4-5-6 pattern. The Hustle was prominently featured in the popular 1978 movie *Saturday Night Fever*, starring John Travolta, and became the mainstay of discotheques such as New York's Studio-54.

Huston Plan In June 1970, Tom Charles Huston, a junior member of the White House staff of President Richard M. Nixon, submitted a plan for the "coordination" of intelligence activities by the FBI, the **CIA,** the White House, and various government agencies of both a military and civilian character. The plan envisaged illegal entry, wire tapping, the use of student informers, and "mail coverage," i.e., opening mail.

Huston was well aware that it called upon members of the government to commit felonies: "Use of this technique is clearly illegal; it amounts to burglary. It is also highly risky and could result in great embarrassment if exposed. However, it is also the most fruitful tool and can produce the type of intelligence which cannot be obtained in any other fashion." In spite of these negative factors, the "decision memo" embodying the plan of the young Indiana lawyer was endorsed by President Nixon on July 23, 1970. According to William Safire, a member of the White House inner circle, it was actually in effect for five days. It was killed upon objections from FBI director J. Edgar Hoover, who won the support of Attorney General John Mitchell in con-

vincing the President to shelve the plan. Huston resigned shortly afterward and returned to Indianapolis and his law practice.

Subsequently, it was disclosed that many of the illegal activities proposed in the Huston Plan were already being carried out by the FBI and the National Security Agency. In addition, even though the plan itself was withdrawn, an interagency group was created and lasted for three years. The significance of the plan was that it obtained presidential approval for clearly unconstitutional acts.

Wide World Photos

"I Am the Greatest"

IAEA *See* **Atoms for Peace.**

"I am not a crook" *See* **Operation Candor.**

"I am the greatest" When black boxer Cassius Marcellus Clay, Jr., challenged the title of heavyweight champion Sonny Liston in 1964, sportswriters and other experts were convinced that this twenty-two-year-old, 210-pounder would present no problem to the "man-monster" who had knocked out Floyd Patterson in 1962 and again in 1963. The confident challenger, whose strategy was to **"float like a butterfly, sting like a bee,"** mockingly taunted: "I am the greatest. I am the prettiest. I am so pretty that I can hardly stand to look at myself. . . . Next to me, Liston will look like a dump truck." On February 24, 1964, Clay KOd Liston in the seventh round. (In 1965, he repeated his triumph in one minute flat.)

Shortly after the Liston match, Clay announced his membership in the **Black Muslims,** changing his name first to Cassius X and later to Muhammad Ali. In 1966 he condemned the **Vietnam War** and refused to be inducted into the army. The Illinois Boxing Commission suspended his boxing license and the World Boxing Association stripped him of his championship. For more than three years, Ali remained professionally inactive, but he began a "comeback" when in 1970 the courts ruled that the suspension of his license had been "arbitrary and unreasonable." (Ali also successfully appealed a $10,000 fine and a five-year prison sentence for draft evasion imposed by a federal judge in Houston.)

Although defeated in a championship bid against Joe Frazier (March 8, 1971), he later regained the crown after knocking out George Foreman on October 30, 1974. (In the interval he had been triumphant in a rematch with Frazier on January 28, 1974.) He remained champion until his defeat on February 15, 1978, by young Leon Spinks in a fight that was compared for its emotional content to the Clay-Liston match of 1964. In a return match with Spinks on September 15, 1978, Ali regained the championship. Both fights with Spinks went the full fifteen rounds.

IANEC *See* **Atoms for Peace.**

ICBMs *See* **Intercontinental Ballistic Missiles.**

"Ich bin ein Berliner" ("I am a Berliner") During the course of a triumphal tour of West Germany, Ireland, and England, President John F. Kennedy visited the Berlin Wall (see **Berlin Crisis of 1961**) on June 24, 1963. Obviously shocked and appalled, he later told an impassioned crowd before the city hall: "Two thousand years ago, the proudest boast was 'Civis Romanus sum.' Today in the world of freedom, the proudest boast is 'Ich bin ein Berliner!'" As the crowd roared, the President noted that there were many people who did not really understand the great issue between the free world and the communist world. If so, "Let them come to Berlin." Freedom has many difficulties, he emphasized, and democracy is not perfect, but it has never resorted to a wall to keep its people in. "All free men, wherever they may live," he concluded, "are citizens of Berlin, and, therefore, as a free man, I take pride in the words 'Ich bin ein Berliner.'"

The President is said to have rapidly passed from exhilaration to anxiety at the response he evoked by these words. Upon his return home he noted that if he had told the crowd to march to the wall and tear it down, he was sure they would have done so.

IDA *See* **Siege of Morningside Heights.**

"Identity crisis" Term used by psychologist Erik H. Erikson—most importantly in *Identity, Youth and Crisis* (1968)—to describe a confused stage in adolescent development experienced by those unable to adopt the ideological perspectives of their culture and unable to find a place in the prevalent technology. Extreme self-doubts arising from an inability to test one's worth are manifested in an inability to concentrate, concentration on insignificant details, and a wavering between overconfidence and feelings of extreme worthlessness. Erikson found that factors in preadolescent history—for example, status-conscious parents who express their love in a desperate and intrusive manner—often create a personality system whose needs do not correspond to the demands of the social system.

I. F. Stone's Weekly The first issue appeared in January 1953, and for the next two decades it provided one of the country's most incisive journalists with an independent organ which he used to question and challenge various aspects of American foreign and domestic policy.

I. F. Stone had first come to prominence when his columns appeared in the late 1940s in *P.M.,* a daily New York newspaper that tried the doomed experiment of attempting to survive without the income—or the pressures—of advertising revenue. After the demise of that paper, his columns were carried in such of its reincarnations as the *New York*

Star and the *Daily Compass* until they in turn folded.

Stone established his weekly at a time when **McCarthyism** was at its worst and no other newspaper would have him. Each issue, usually four pages, was written almost entirely by himself. Although his targets generally lay in the country's conservative sectors, he sometimes managed to sting liberals, as for example in an early 1953 piece called "Challenge to the Left: Back Ike for Peace" in which he suggested that President Dwight D. Eisenhower's **Korean War** truce moves be accepted by the Left as a rallying point for public support of a broader settlement. Braving the public piety after the tragic assassination of President John F. Kennedy in Dallas on **November 22, 1963,** and re-examining his own announced enthusiasm for the young president, he concluded that "Kennedy, when the tinsel was stripped away, was a conventional leader, no more than an enlightened conservative, cautious as an old man for all his youth, with a basic distrust of the people and an astringent view of the evangelical as a tool of leadership." Although he supported the foundation and preservation of Israel as a state, he was highly critical of many aspects of that nation's domestic and foreign stance.

In 1968, because Stone found the drain on his energy too much, the journal began to appear bi-weekly. By the time it ceased publication altogether in December 1971, its circulation was 70,000. I. F. Stone is at present a contributing editor of the *New York Review of Books*.

IGY *See* **International Geophysical Year.**

"I have a dream" The phrase was first used when more than 200,000 blacks and their white sympathizers participated in a **March on Washington** (August 28, 1963) intended to focus national attention on the demands by blacks for immediate equality in employment and civil rights. Ten of the marchers' leaders were received by President John F. Kennedy and then returned to address the crowd waiting at the Lincoln Memorial. Among the speakers was Reverend Dr. Martin Luther King, Jr., president of the **Southern Christian Leadership Conference** (SCLC), whose speech was perhaps the most moving of the day.

I say to you today, my friends, that in spite of the difficulties and frustrations of the moment I still have a dream. It is a dream deeply rooted in the American dream.

I have a dream that one day this nation will rise up and live out the true meaning of its creed: "We hold these truths to be self-evident; that all men are created equal."

I have a dream that one day on the red hills of Georgia the sons of former slaves and the sons of former slave-owners will be able to sit down together at the table of brotherhood.

I have a dream that one day even the state of Mississippi, a desert state sweltering with the heat of injustice and oppression, will be transformed into an oasis of freedom and justice. . . .

I have a dream that one day every valley shall be exalted, every hill and mountain shall be made low, the rough places will be made plain, and the crooked places will be made straight, and the glory of the Lord shall be revealed, and all flesh shall see it together. . . .

"When we let freedom ring, when we let it ring from every village and every hamlet, from every state and every city, black men and white men, Jews and Gentiles, Protestants and Catholics, will be able to join hands and sing in the words of the old Negro spiritual, "**Free at last!** Free at last! Thank God Almighty, we are free at last!"

On April 4, 1968, while in Memphis, Tennessee, where he had gone to march with striking sanitation workers, Reverend King was assassinated by James Earl Ray.

Illinois ex re McCollum v. Board of Education On March 8, 1948, the U.S. Supreme Court ruled that the use of public school buildings for the purposes of religious instruction was unconstitutional. The case examined related to one such program set up in Champaign, Illinois, under which pupils whose parents had signed "request cards" were given "released time" from their regular studies to attend religious-instruction classes taught in the school building by outside teachers chosen by an interfaith religious council. Although the teachers were not paid from public funds, attendance records were reported to school authorities.

In its ruling the Court found that since tax-supported property was used for religious instruction with the cooperation of the school authorities, the operation of the state's compulsory education system thus was integrated with the program of religious instruction carried on by separate religious sects. "Pupils compelled by law to go to school for secular education are released in part from their legal duty upon the condition that they attend the religious classes. This is beyond all question a utilization of the tax-established and tax-supported public school system to aid religious groups to spread their faith."

See **"released time."**

I'm OK—You're OK *See* **Transactional Analysis.**

"Impeach Earl Warren" *See* **Warren Court.**

Inchon Landing To cut the communications lines of the North Korean forces in South Korea during the **Korean War,** on September 15, 1950, a combined force of U.S. and South Korean Marines landed at Inchon, the port city of Seoul. This maneuver placed them some 150 miles behind the main body of the North Korean Army on the fighting front. Simultaneous landings were also made at the west coast city of Kunsan and near the east coast city of Pohang.

The success of this operation caused the North Korean forces to retreat behind the **38th parallel,** where on the recommendation of the UN General Assembly they were followed by the UN forces fighting in Korea.

Individual Retirement Account (IRA) Part of the pension reform legislation contained in the **Employee Benefit Security Act** (September 2, 1974) permits persons not covered by corporate pension or profit-sharing plans to reduce their currently taxable income by putting 15 percent of their annual "compensation"—up to a total of $1,500—into special IRA accounts which accumulate interest on a tax-deferred basis. The principal and interest become taxable only after retirement—between the ages of 59½ and 70½—when income is generally less and therefore taxable at a reduced rate, if at all.

IRA savings can take the form of bank accounts, insurance company retirement annuities, or investments under the custodianship of a bank. Although compensation is construed as being limited to annual wages, salaries, and professional fees, a special "rollover" provision of the law makes it possible for individuals to place unlimited sums in IRA accounts if a pension plan under which they have been working comes to a halt or if they withdraw accumulated pension funds on leaving employment.

Within a year after the legislation was passed, more than 500,000 IRAs had been established. The "rollover" provision is said to have made it possible for some executives who had been laid off to put as much as $400,000 into tax-deferrable IRA accounts.

"I need him." *See* **Adams-Goldfine Scandal; Washington Merry-Go-Round.**

"Instant Analysis" In the first of many speeches in which he was to take the nation's news media to task for their increasingly critical attitude toward the Nixon administration, Vice President Spiro Ag-new, speaking in Des Moines, Iowa, on November 13, 1969, specifically directed his fire at the treatment given President Richard M. Nixon's recently televised speech on the continuing **Vietnam War.** Complaining that though the President had "spent weeks" preparing what was to be the most important address of the decade, he had no sooner finished speaking than "his words and policies were subjected to instant analysis and querulous criticism. The audience of seventy million Americans—gathered to hear the President of the United States—was inherited by a small band of network commentators and self-appointed analysts. . . ."

A month earlier, the Vice President had denounced the **Moratorium Day** anti-Vietnam War protests as having been "encouraged by an **effete corps of impudent snobs** who characterize themselves as intellectuals," and almost a year later, as the war lingered on, he denounced critics as the **"nattering nabobs of negativism."**

The "instant analysis" phrase, which may have been a contribution from speech writer Patrick Buchanan, was picked up and popularized by the news media it was meant to castigate. It seemed a natural in what poet e.e. cummings had once mockingly described as the "land above all of Just Add Hot Water And Serve."

Institute for Defense Analysis (IDA) *See* **Siege of Morningside Heights.**

Intelsat 1 Developed and built by the Hughes Aircraft Company for Communications Satellite Corp. (Comsat), the world's first commercial satellite was launched from Cape Kennedy on April 6, 1965. Its mission was to provide a commercial telephone, telegraph, and television link between North America and Europe after assuming a synchronous circular orbit 22,300 miles above the Atlantic at the equator. The first test signals were exchanged between the United States and stations in Great Britain, France, and West Germany on April 12.

The eighty-five-pound satellite—often called *Early Bird 1*—was the first in a global network for which forty-six nations had signed agreements with Comsat. Shot into preliminary orbit by a Thrust-Augmented Delta (TAD) booster rocket, it was switched from an elliptical orbit with a perigee of 900 miles and an apogee of 23,000 miles into a circular orbit at almost maximum altitude when on April 9 a small solid-propellant rocket aboard the satellite was fired from earth by means of a radio signal. Comsat paid **NASA** $3.3 million for putting up the man-made satellite, which could handle 240 telephone connections between this country and Europe. It was followed by *Intelsat 2, 3,* and *4.* In 1977, there were three *Intelsat 4*'s—each having a life expectancy of about seven years—handling international voice and TV communications.

Inter-American Conference on Problems of War and Peace *See* **Act of Chapultepec.**

Inter-American Nuclear Energy Commission (IANEC) *See* **Atoms for Peace.**

Intercontinental Ballistic Missiles (ICBMs) Ballistic missiles with ranges of up to 8,000 statute miles. According to data released by London's International Institute for Strategic Services, as of mid-1976 the United States had deployed 1,054 land-based ICBMs. These included fifty-four Titan 2s, liquid-fueled missiles which are stored in underground silos and have an estimated warhead yield of five to ten megatons; 450 Minuteman 2s, solid-fueled missiles which are stored in underground silos and have an estimated warhead of one to two megatons; and 550 Minuteman 3s, solid-fueled missiles which are stored in underground silos and have an estimated warhead yield of 3 to 170 kilotons. The Minuteman 3s carry **Multiple Individually Targetable Reentry Vehicles** (MIRVs), separate warheads which are on a single booster and can be delivered against individual targets. A Minuteman Defense Program calling for five underground ICBM launch sites in the Western states went into operation in December 1962, but was not considered complete until June 1965.

A proposed replacement of the Minuteman 3s by giant and mobile 100-ton MX (mobile experimental) missiles that would move along tunnels ten to twenty miles long was a center of controversy beginning in late 1977. The cost of the system, which would be deployed in the Western United States, was variously estimated at between $40 and $100 billion.

(In August 1978 General David C. Jones, Chairman of the Joint Chiefs of Staff, said that he considered that the mobiles were "authorized." The rationale for deploying mobile missiles is that ICBMs are increasingly vulnerable because they require silos that are a potential prey of new and improved Soviet missiles. Estimates are that a force of 200 to 300 MX missiles could only be destroyed by a comparable force of 4,000 to 6,000 Soviet missiles.)

The first successful American ICBM test was carried out on February 1, 1961, when a range of 4,200 miles was achieved. Speeds of from 6,000 to 15,000 miles per hour are possible.

Ballistic missiles with a maximum 200-mile range were first used in German V-2s during World War II. Rocket propelled because they travel at altitudes where the thin air will not support any other kind of engine, they continue toward the target along a ballistic trajectory after the fuel supply has been either exhausted or cut off by guidance equipment.

Other ballistic missiles include Intermediate Range Ballistic Missiles (IRBMs), with ranges of up to 2,000 miles; "tactical ballistic missiles," with ranges of up to 200 miles; and the Submarine-Launched Ballistic Missiles (SLBMs), with ranges of up to 2,800 miles. The SLBMs include—as of 1978—160 Polaris A-3s carrying three warheads not individually targetable. Succeeding the Polaris A-1 and A-2, which carried single warheads with an approximately one-megaton yield, the Polaris A-3 is carried aboard a nuclear-powered submarine of the *Polaris* class. The first underwater launching of Polaris missiles took place on July 20, 1960.

The Poseidon SLBM, successor to the Polaris submarine program, which it began to replace in 1965, carries a warhead yield of ten 50-kiloton MIRVs. In mid-1978, 496 Poseidons were deployed. At that time the Soviet Union was said to have deployed 2,090 land-based ICBMs of various kinds, and 1319 SLBMs.

See **Poseidon Submarines.**

Intermediate Range Ballistic Missiles (IRBMs) *See* **Intercontinental Ballistic Missiles.**

Internal Security Act *See* **McCarran Act.**

International Atomic Energy Agency (IAEA) *See* **Atoms for Peace.**

International Geophysical Year (IGY) In the eighteen months between July 1, 1957, and December 31, 1958, some 30,000 scientists and technicians from seventy countries cooperated in a series of intensive experiments and studies dealing with space as well as the earth's weather, oceans, and polar regions. The IGY is usually considered to include the extension to December 31, 1959, officially known as the International Geophysical Cooperation (IGC).

A congressional appropriation of $39 million to the **National Science Foundation** (NSF) permitted the participation of American scientists. Although important advances were made in man's understanding of sun-spot activity and weather mechanisms, the charting of ocean bottoms, and the discovery of counter-currents in the equatorial tide and the Gulf Stream, the most sensational activity of the IGY was probably the launching of *Sputnik I,* the first artificial satellite, by the U.S.S.R. on October 4, 1957. On January 31, 1958, the United States launched its own earth satellite, *Explorer I,* which confirmed the existence of the Van Allen Belts of radiation surrounding the earth. In addition, observations made in the polar regions during the IGY gave rise to a new theory for magnetic phenomena based on the existence of an outer nucleus surrounding the radioactive central nucleus of the earth.

As preparation for participation in the IGY, in 1955 the United States established Operation Deep Freeze for the study of Antarctica. Although Admiral Richard E. Byrd was the "officer in charge," the project was actually directed by Rear Admiral George J. Dufek, whom Congress had especially promoted from the rank of lieutenant commander. Consisting of 1,800 men and seven ships, that expedition arrived at McMurdo Bay on December 17, 1955, and began work on the world's first international airport in Antarctica, at which eight planes that had flown directly from New Zealand landed three days later.

The origins of the IGY date back to the first International Polar Year (1882-1883), participated in by the United States and ten other nations. At the time, it was decided that similar projects should be organized every fifty years. The second polar year, in which thirty-four nations participated, took place in 1932-1933. In 1952, however, the International Council of Scientific Societies decided to cut the interval between international years—the next should theoretically have been 1982-1983—and set up a special committee to plan the IGY beginning in 1957, a year that coincided with the opening of a period of intense solar activity.

The success of the IGY caused the establishment of a number of international cooperative research programs such as the International Year of the Quiet Sun (1964-1965) and the International Hydrological Decade (1965-1975).

International Tribunal on War Crimes Organized by British philosopher Bertrand Russell, this unofficial tribunal of opponents of United States policy in Vietnam met in the convention hall of the Swedish Social Democratic Party in Stockholm, May 2-7, 1967, to hear charges of atrocities committed by the American armed forces in pursuance of the **Vietnam War.**

Originally, the "court" was to meet near Paris, but in a letter to its executive president, novelist-philosopher Jean-Paul Sartre, President Charles de Gaulle explained that he could not permit the meeting to be held on French soil because he felt it his obligation to ensure that a nation traditionally friendly to France "shall not be the object of proceedings that are beyond the bounds of justice and international practices." He noted that he took this action in spite of the fact that France was opposed to the American stance in Vietnam.

Cochairmen of the tribunal were British historian Isaac Deutscher—who did not arrive until a day before the hearings ended—Yugoslav author Vladimir Dedijer, and French mathematician Laurent Schwartz. Russell, who was ninety-four at the time, was represented by his American secretary, Ralph Schoenman. The United States government rejected an invitation to send a representative to Stockholm.

Among the charges made was that the United States had made use of fragmentation bombs that were ineffective against military targets but caused heavy civilian casualties. Particular attention was focused on the Cluster Bomb Unit (CBU), which, according to testimony by Dr. Jean-Pierre Vigier of the University of Paris, consisted of a principal explosive which from a height of five-eighths of a mile scattered 640 secondary bombs—or "guavas." (The U.S. Defense Department denied these charges, but conceded that up to 10 percent "scattershot" fragmentation bombs—"usually around 5 percent"—were used on raids.)

At an additional hearing held in Tokyo, August 28-30, 1967, under the sponsorship of the leftist Japan Committee for Investigation of U.S. Crimes in Vietnam, it was charged that the Japanese government was guilty of aiding American Vietnam War efforts.

Reconvening in Roskilde, Denmark, November 20-December 1, 1967, the "tribunal" found the United States guilty of charges of genocide, of mistreating and causing the death of prisoners of war, and of employing forbidden weapons. The decision also held that with the aid of Japan, Thailand, and the Philippines, the United States was guilty of aggression against Laos and Cambodia.

The Invisible Man Ralph Ellison's 1952 novel of a black man's search for identity won the National Book Award and immediately established him as one of the country's leading writers.

I am an invisible man. No, I am not a spook like those who haunted Edgar Allan Poe; nor am I one of your Hollywood-movie ectoplasms. I am a man of substance, of flesh and bone, fiber and liquids—and I might even be said to possess a mind. I am invisible, understand, simply because people refuse to see me. Like the bodiless heads you see sometimes in circus sideshows, it is as though I have been surrounded by mirrors of hard, distorting glass. When they approach me they see only my surroundings, themselves, or figments of their imagination—indeed, everything and anything except me.

The unidentified protagonist's odyssey is traced from the time of his expulsion from an all-black southern college after an encounter with a white trustee to a nightmarish climax in which the tensions of Harlem explode into a bloody race riot. In a prologue and epilogue we learn that he has literally withdrawn from the world and is living underground in a basement hole illuminated by "exactly 1,369 lights."

Criticized by some for the free intermingling in his novel of realistic and surrealistic elements, Ellison has replied: "I didn't select the surrealism, the distortion, the intensity, as an experimental technique but because reality is surreal." It is interesting to compare the book with Richard Wright's novella *The Man Who Lived Underground* (1942, revised 1944).

"In your heart, you know he's right" This slogan was widely used in the 1964 campaign of Republican presidential candidate Sen. Barry Goldwater (Ariz.) against the Democratic incumbent, President Lyndon B. Johnson. It was meant to appeal to voters by suggesting that the Senator's conservative economic views—as outlined, for example, in *The Conscience of a Conservative* (1960)—were much more in line with traditional American free enterprise and individual responsibility than with the ambitious social and economic schemes of President Franklin D. Roosevelt's New Deal, President Harry S Truman's **Fair Deal,** President John F. Kennedy's **New Frontier,** or President Johnson's **Great Society.**

But Senator Goldwater had also taken a strongly hawkish view on the **Vietnam War** and had recommended the use of American troops and aircraft to aid South Vietnam, whereas President Johnson, in an appeal to the peace vote, had noted (September 28, 1964): "I have not thought we were ready for American boys to do the fighting for Asian boys." In addition, Senator Goldwater had aroused widespread fears by suggesting that nuclear weapons might be placed at the disposal of **NATO** "com-

manders" or used to "defoliate" the **Ho Chi Minh Trail,** which supplied communist forces fighting in South Vietnam. Democrats therefore slyly turned the slogan around into "In your heart, you know he might!" (see **Daisy Girl TV Spot**).

A popular bumper sticker during the Goldwater campaign advocated "Au H_2O in 1964," using the chemical symbols for "gold" and "water."

IRA *See* **Individual Retirement Account.**

IRBMs *See* **Intercontinental Ballistic Missiles.**

Iron Curtain With President Harry S Truman in the audience, Great Britain's wartime prime minister, Winston Churchill, fired what many considered the opening gun of the **Cold War** in an address at Fulton, Missouri, on March 5, 1946.

A shadow has fallen upon the scenes so lately lighted by the Allied victory. Nobody knows what Soviet Russia and its Communist international organization intends to do in the immediate future, or what are the limits, if any, to their expansive and proselytizing tendencies . . .

From Stettin in the Baltic to Triest in the Adriatic, an iron curtain has descended across the Continent. Behind that line lie all the capitals of the ancient states of central and eastern Europe. Warsaw, Berlin, Prague, Vienna, Budapest, Belgrade, Bucharest, and Sofia, all these famous cities and the populations around them lie in the Soviet sphere and all are subject in one form or another, not only to Soviet influence but to a very high and increasing measure of control from Moscow. Athens alone, with its immortal glories, is free to decide its future at an election under British, American, and French observation. The Russian-dominated Polish government has been encouraged to make enormous and wrongful inroads upon Germany, and mass expulsions of millions of Germans on a scale grievous and undreamed of are now taking place.

President Truman claimed that he had not known in advance what the former prime minister intended to say. However, as long before as June 4, 1945, Churchill had noted in a telegram to the President: "I view with profound misgivings the retreat of the American Army to our line of occupation in the Central Sector, thus bringing Soviet power into the heart of Western Europe and the descent of an iron curtain between us and everything to the eastward."

At the **Potsdam Conference,** July 1945, Churchill had objected to Stalin that an "iron fence" was being built in Eastern Europe, to which the Russian dictator replied: "All fairy tales." However, reports of Soviet repression continued to flood the U.S. State Department.

The expression was also used by Nazi Propaganda Minister Joseph Goebbels in *Volkischer Beobachter*, March 29, 1945.

Iron Triangle Used to describe the area twenty miles northwest of Saigon during the **Vietnam War.** Beginning on January 8, 1967, it was the scene of Operation Cedar Falls, one of the most important American offensives of the war. Throwing in 16,000 infantrymen (30,000 troops were to be used in **Operation Junction City** the following March), the United States initiated a scorched earth policy that was designed to make the area permanently uninhabitable to Viet Cong troops. The civilian populations of the area were transplanted, and houses, plantations, and tropical thickets were razed. Tunnels used by the Viet Cong were cleared by first pumping them through with nausea gas and then blasting.

On the triangle's western flank, a vast network of tunnels under the Ho Bo woods was discovered. The network had reportedly been the headquarters of the Viet Cong's Fourth Military Region, an area which included Saigon.

Once the Iron Triangle was cleared, some three weeks later, it became a "free bombing zone" in which anyone in the area was automatically fired on as a Viet Cong.

"I shall go to Korea" Talks aimed at a negotiated peace for the **Korean War** had begun in Kaesong in July 1952, but were deadlocked on the question of prisoner-of-war repatriation. The Republicans realized that they had a major issue in this unpopular war, and speaking in Detroit on October 24, 1952, presidential candidate Dwight D. Eisenhower made effective use of it.

The first task of a new administration will be to review and reexamine every course of action open to us with one goal in view—to bring the Korean War to an early and honorable end. That is my pledge to the American people. . . .

That job requires a personal trip to Korea. I shall make that trip. Only in that way could I learn how best to serve the American people and the cause of peace.

I shall go to Korea.

On November 29, 1952, the victorious president-elect kept that campaign promise and began a three-day visit which remained secret until after he had left the danger area. It was not, however, until the following July that an armistice was signed and hostilities ceased.

The speech was written for candidate Eisenhower by Emmet J. Hughes.

"It'll play in Peoria" The phrase is particularly associated with John D. Ehrlichman, Assistant to the President for Domestic Affairs during the Nixon administration and a leading figure in the **Watergate Scandal** that brought about its downfall. It was used by Ehrlichman and others to indicate that a given policy decided upon would appeal to the so-called **Silent Majority.** Peoria, Illinois, had been one of the few big cities that had voted for Nixon in the 1968 presidential campaign.

ITT Affair In 1969 the Antitrust Division of the Justice Department filed suits against International Telephone and Telegraph (ITT) to make the giant corporation—the nation's twelfth largest—divest itself of the recently acquired Canteen Corporation, the Grinnell Corporation, and the Hartford Fire Insurance Company. President Richard M. Nixon, who on many occasions expressed his opposition to suits of this nature, attempted to interfere with Justice Department procedure in April 1971 when he made a direct phone call to Deputy Attorney General Richard G. Kleindienst, who was supervising the suits, demanding that word be passed on to Richard McLaren, head of the department's Antitrust Division, that unless the suits were dropped he would be forced out. ("I want something clearly understood, and, if it is not understood, McLaren's ass is to be out within one hour. The ITT thing—stay the hell out of it. Is that clear? That's an order.")

However, on the advice of Attorney General John N. Mitchell—who had removed himself from the case because his former law firm had represented an ITT subsidiary—President Nixon backed down. On July 31, 1971, the Justice Department announced a settlement under which ITT would retain the Hartford Insurance company—the fourth largest of its kind—if it divested itself of the Grinnell and Canteen corporations and two other subsidiaries.

Public attention first began to focus on attempts to squash the Justice Department actions against ITT when, on December 9, 1970, syndicated columnist Jack Anderson charged that after first vetoing the ITT-Hartford merger, Connecticut insurance commissioner William Cotter had reversed his position following a series of meetings with ITT executives. It was said that part of the pressure brought to bear on him was an ITT promise to open a new office and build a new hotel in downtown Hartford.

Then on February 29, 1972, four months before the **Watergate Scandal** broke on the front pages of the nation's newspapers, Anderson printed a memorandum written by ITT lobbyist Dita Beard and signed June 25, 1971, in which she indicated that the compromise between the Justice Department and ITT had been reached after ITT agreed to contribute $400,000 to the Republican National Convention, which was scheduled to be held in San Diego, California, in 1972. "I am convinced," Mrs. Beard wrote William Merriam, head of ITT's Washington headquarters, ". . . that our noble commitment has gone a long way towards our negotiations on the mergers. . . . Certainly the President has told Mitchell to see that things are worked out fairly."

Shortly after the Anderson column appeared, Mrs. Beard was taken ill on a flight to West Yellowstone, Montana, where she was to vacation, and admitted to Denver's Rocky Mountain Osteopathic Hospital, where she was said to be suffering from "coronary artery disease with angina pectoris." She was visited there in March by White House consultant E. Howard Hunt, who obtained from her a firm denial that she had written the memorandum.

In spite of subsequent disclosures following the Senate Watergate hearings, the settlement between the Justice Department and ITT remained unchallenged and there were no prosecutions arising from it. ITT continued to maintain that its proposed contribution was not political in nature because it was to have been made to the San Diego County Tourist and Convention Bureau.

In his columns, Jack Anderson also charged that those ITT officials who had known in advance that the ITT-Hartford merger would receive government approval had been able to take illegal advantage of their knowledge to make windfall profits in trading company stock. The Securities and Exchange Commission (SEC) investigated these charges, but no action was taken.

After the ITT affair broke, Lawrence F. O'Brien, as national Democratic chairman, naturally tried to use it to discredit the Republicans in the 1972 elections. According to H. R. Haldeman, President Nixon's Chief of Staff, this made the President particularly eager to obtain evidence that would indicate that O'Brien had been on a $180,000 annual retainer from millionaire Howard Hughes and serving as his lobbyist. It was an attempt to obtain such "proof" that indirectly led to the Watergate break-in, said Haldeman.

J

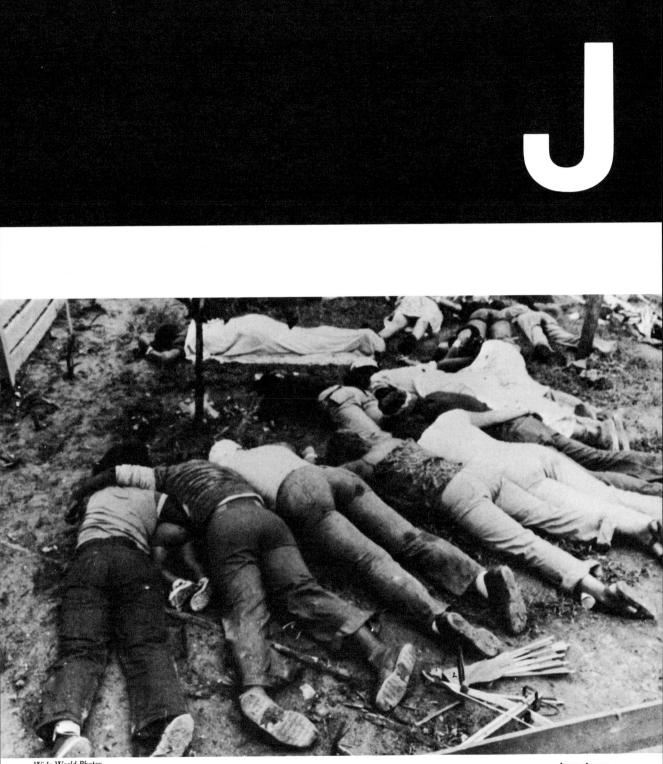

Jonestown

Jackson State Tragedy Two blacks were killed and eleven wounded when on May 14, 1970, state highway police opened fire on students following disorder at the all-black Jackson State College, Jackson, Mississippi. The dead were Philip L. Gibbs and Earl Green.

The origins of the violence are unclear but were reported to have begun after white motorists were harassed by students on a street adjacent to the school. When the police were called in, students were demonstrating in front of the women's dormitory. Witnesses claimed that about forty police officers lined up facing the building and riddled the crowd with bullets from a distance of some fifty feet.

President Richard M. Nixon expressed his regret over the shootings and noted that "in the shadow of these past troubled days, this tragedy makes it urgent that every American personally undertake greater efforts toward understanding, restraint and compassion." He sent Attorney General John N. Mitchell and Leonard Garment, Special Presidential Assistant, to confer with Jackson officials. Later, the Attorney General declared himself satisfied that the discussion had been helpful "not only in connection with the circumstances here in Jackson but in connection with similar potential problems in the country. . . ." But Dr. John A. Peoples, Jr., president of Jackson State, restricted his comments to the fact that the Justice Department had assured him that it was "deeply concerned about this tragedy." On May 22, Vice President Spiro Agnew dismissed accusations that he and the President had contributed to the violence on campuses by inflammatory statements about student militants.

The Jackson State Tragedy did not have nearly the effect of national shock generated by the **Kent State Tragedy** two weeks earlier, and with considerable justification black leaders ascribed the difference in response to racism.

The nine-member President's Commission on Campus Unrest headed by William W. Scranton, former governor of Pennsylvania, accused local police of "unreasonable, unjustified overreaction," and said that the police had lied about the circumstances surrounding the tragedy.

Jaybirds In *Terry v. Adams* (1953) the U.S. Supreme Court outlawed a Texas organization known as the Jaybird Association or Party, a Fort Bend County political association that excluded blacks. An opinion written by Justice Hugo Black noted that it was the function of the Jaybird Association to choose nominees for the Democratic primary, and that since these nominees invariably won that primary, it was evident that the basic purpose of the Jaybird elections was to circumvent the Fifteenth Amendment and exclude blacks from the vote.

In his written opinion, Justice Black noted that membership in the Jaybirds—whose origins went back to 1889—was then and had always been limited to whites, who were automatically elected to it if their names appeared on the official list of county voters. As in regular political parties, candidates for county offices submitted their names to the Jaybird Committee in accordance with the usual practices of political parties all over the United States. With few exceptions, Jaybird candidates "have run and won without opposition in the Democratic primaries and the general elections that followed. Thus the party has been the dominant political group in the county since organization, having endorsed every county-wide official elected since 1889."

JDL *See* **Jewish Defense League.**

Jensenism In 1969, Professor Arthur Jensen, a psychologist at the University of California, Berkeley, reported on studies which he said indicated that genetic heritage was the reason blacks scored lower on IQ tests than did whites. He emphasized data that showed blacks scoring low on abstract material and indicated that such performance was therefore not explainable as "cultural deprivation." He also noted a pattern in which the IQs of black children seemed to decline as they grew older.

Professor Jensen's data were attacked by responsible members of the scientific community, and his appearances on campuses and elsewhere were generally the cause of hostile student demonstrations. It was pointed out that initial poor performance on abstract test material was common to immigrant groups entering the American cultural mainstream as evidenced by tests made at Ellis Island in 1917 by psychologist H. H. Goddard. Additional tests made on children of white immigrants indicated that the continuing impact of an early situation often resulted in an IQ pattern that declined as they grew older.

When in 1977 Professor Jensen was elected a fellow of the American Association for the Advancement of Science (AAAS), the association became embroiled in bitter dissension. The anthropologist Margaret Mead denounced his work as "unspeakable," and other members of the group saw his election as "an endorsement of racism." William D. Wallace, director of Harvard University's health-career programs, resigned from the AAAS in protest. The controversy over "Jensenism" has led to an increasing challenge to the worth of IQ tests in general.

Jet Set "The moment you had jet airplanes and people who flew on them," noted Charlotte Curtis, who assiduously and somewhat acidly reported on the comings and goings of the rich and famous for the *New York Times*, "you began to have a Jet Set. It really didn't get its name until the early Sixties, when people began to forsake travel by ocean liner and go almost exclusively by jet. Flit about the world: this season in London and this season in Paris, this season in Rome, New York, California."

Fame, talent—or at least "exquisite" taste—fortune, and peripatetic habits were enough to qualify one for identification with the group, which unlike "Society" of earlier days did not insist on "family." Princess Lee Radziwill, sister of Jacqueline Kennedy Onassis, seemed, however, to combine all the above qualifications and was often considered representative.

The **Vietnam War** and the economic recession of the 1970s put a damper on some of the "elegant hell" raised by jet setters during the prosperous 1960s. "They're slightly quieter now," observed Ms. Curtis in 1973. "They're in hiding, waiting in part for the next renaissance."

Vogue magazine—chronicler of the doings of the Richard Burtons, the William Paleys, the Winston Guests, the Carter Burdens, and the Wyatt Coopers—decided that "the Beautiful People" was perhaps a more apt description of a group whose activities were the constant focus of attention by the news media.

Jewish Defense League (JDL) Established in New York City in June 1968 as the Jewish Defense Corps, the Jewish Defense League (JDL) was renamed, according to founder Rabbi Meir Kahane, out of consideration for "present Jewish knee-jerk fear of anything sounding militant." Its angry rhetoric and threats, which matched the potential for violence often displayed by various **Black Power** groups that were on the rise during the 1960s, quickly alienated traditional leaders of the Jewish community such as Rabbi Maurice N. Eisendrath, President of the Union of American Hebrew Congregations, who labeled JDL militants "goon squads." Because of its vigilante approach to combatting antisemitism, the JDL was also strongly condemned by the American Jewish Committee, the American Jewish Congress, and the Anti-Defamation League.

Soviet unwillingness to permit free Jewish emigration, and the death sentences passed on two Jewish "subversives" in Leningrad on December 24, 1970, brought as countermeasures a JDL campaign to harass Soviet officials in this country and to kill "two Russians for every Jew." (On December 28, 1970, Soviet authorities commuted the sentences of the two members of the so-called Leningrad Twelve.)

A rash of bombings of Soviet offices in the United States were laid to the JDL. When on January 8, 1971, a bomb went off in Washington's Soviet cultural offices, various news agencies received calls stating: "This is a sample of things to come. Let our people go. Never Again!" (The "Never Again" slogan adopted by the JDL referred to the Nazi World War II holocaust during which 6 million Jews died.)

The JDL philosophy can best be summed up by an advertisement that appeared in the *New York Times* on July 24, 1969. Over a picture of a group of young men wielding lengths of pipe was the question: "Is this any way for a nice Jewish boy to behave?" According to the text below: "Maybe some people and organizations are *too* nice. Maybe in times of crisis Jewish boys should not be that nice. Maybe—just maybe—nice people build their own road to Auschwitz."

On September 12, 1971, Rabbi Kahane emigrated to Israel, violating the terms of a five-year probation sentence imposed by the courts in July of that year. A month after his return to this country in January 1975, he was sentenced to one year in prison.

Job Corps To many, this attempt under the **Economic Opportunity Act** of 1964 to provide training and work experience for young people from poverty backgrounds had echoes of the Civilian Conservation Corps (CCC) legislated by the Roosevelt administration during the Depression of the 1930s. President Lyndon B. Johnson credited an appeal to conservationists, who were assured that at least 40 percent of the Job Corps workers would be used on conservation projects, with rallying "as many as twenty key votes" in support of the bill incorporating it.

As set up by Sargent Shriver, director of the **Office of Economic Opportunity** (OEO), the Job Corps provided residential training centers for men and women between the ages of sixteen and twenty-one. Some centers were administered by private industrial firms and others by state agencies, universities, the Department of Agriculture, and the Department of the Interior. It was felt that the removal of the young from their poverty-stricken environments was as important as the technical and educational training they received.

By 1967 there were more than 100 Job Corps centers throughout the country with a total enrollment of 42,000, mostly men. Many were school dropouts who had been unable to find employment and whose education and physical condition was such that about half had been refused by the Armed Forces in spite of the enlistment needs caused by the **Vietnam War.**

According to President Johnson, some of the congressional resistance to the Economic Opportunity bill was inspired by segregationist fears that the Job Corps would be used as a tool for enforced integration. When Rep. Howard Smith (D.-Va.), chairman of the House Rules Committee, warned the bill's sponsor, Rep. Phillip Landrum (D.-Ga.), that "white boys in your state or mine have a very deep feeling about living with Negroes," he was told that racial integration was a matter of law and that, in any case, enrollment was entirely voluntary.

Plagued by high turnover and discipline problems, Job Corps centers were under constant conservative attack, and many were closed during the Nixon administration. Under the 1973 **Comprehensive Employment and Training Act** (CETA), the Job Corps program was consolidated under the Department of Labor. Enrollees spend a maximum of two years in the program.

Job Opportunities in the Business Sector (JOBS) In a special message to Congress on January 23, 1968, President Lyndon B. Johnson asked for additional funds with which to attack the problem of hardcore unemployment. The target he proposed was to find 100,000 jobs in the next eighteen months and 500,000 by mid-1971.

A special focus of the program was a pilot project to provide direct subsidies to private employers undertaking to train and hire the chronically unemployed. Cooperating employers signing federal contracts with JOBS would be reimbursed for the "extra costs" entailed, including productivity losses or the salary costs of promotions necessary to make jobs available.

To promote the program, a National Alliance of Businessmen (NAB) was formed on March 16, 1968, under the leadership of Henry Ford II, chairman of the Ford Motor Company, and Leo Beebe, that company's vice president.

In *The Vantage Point* (1971), former President Johnson noted that by 1969 the NAB revised goal

of 100,000 new jobs in the first year of JOBS had been met without difficulty. "I think this program—improved, I hope, with time and experience—should become a continuing government-industry effort." If it persists, he noted somewhat overoptimistically, the term hardcore unemployed "will encompass those who cannot work or will not, but never again will it include men and women who were not given the fullest opportunity."

JOBS *See* **Job Opportunities in the Business Sector.**

Jobs or Income Now (JOIN) *See* **Students for a Democratic Society.**

John Birch Society A rightwing organization founded by Robert Welsh, a Massachusetts candy manufacturer and former vice president of the **National Association of Manufacturers** (NAM), in December 1958 during a two-day meeting in Indianapolis, Indiana, with eleven friends and business associates from various states. Welch took the name of his group from John Birch, a Georgia Baptist preacher serving with the U.S. Intelligence Service, who shortly after V-J Day ended World War II was killed in a quarrel with the leader of a Chinese Communist patrol near Succhow. (Birch's commanding officer was later to note: "In the confusing situation my instructions were to act with diplomacy. Birch made the Communist lieutenant lose face before his own men. Militarily, John Birch brought about his own death.")

Although militantly anticommunist, the John Birch Society imitated the Communist Party in that it was semisecret, relied on a cell structure of "from 10 to 20 dedicated patriots" in each group, and advocated the extensive use of front organizations. (Among those later formed were the Patrick Henry Society, the Minutemen, the Sons of the American Revolution, and the Movement to Restore Decency—an anti-sex-education group.) The principles of "The Founder," as later recorded in the society's *Blue Book*, called for the organization of chapters in various parts of the country to carry on recruitment, distribute rightwing literature, book rightwing speakers before civic groups, and make extensive use of "the powerful letter-writing weapon" to exert pressure on community groups and various levels of government. Among the goals to be achieved were the abolition of the graduated income tax, withdrawal from the United Nations, an end to the Federal Reserve System, the repeal of social-security legislation, and the removal from office of high government officials such as Chief Justice Earl Warren (see **Warren Court**).

By the early 1960s there were said to be some 100,000 "Birchers" organized in chapters in more than thirty states. Welch and his society first came to national attention when in mid-1960 the *Chicago Daily News* disclosed that he was the author of a privately printed book called *The Politician*, in which he charged President Dwight D. Eisenhower with being a "dedicated, conscious agent of the Communist conspiracy" and said that his brother, Milton Eisenhower, the distinguished American educator, had for thirty years been "an outright Communist." Others identified as being members of the Communist conspiracy in this country were the late George C. Marshall, World War II hero and Secretary of State under President Harry S Truman, Secretary of State John Foster Dulles, and the latter's brother, Allen Dulles, director of the Central Intelligence Agency.

At the end of 1963, the John Birch Society was spending $2 million annually to spread its "message" to the American voter. Although originally conceived of as a nonpolitical organization, it had begun to move into the political arena. The conservative forces of the 1964 Republican National Convention which nominated Sen. Barry Goldwater (R.-Ariz.) as its presidential candidate voted down attempts to reject the support of the John Birch Society, and in his acceptance speech Senator Goldwater noted: "**Extremism in defense of liberty** is no vice. . . ." The platform of the Democratic Party, however, specifically condemned "the extreme tactics of such organizations as the Communist party, the Ku Klux Klan, and the John Birch Society."

The society "enriched" the American language with the word "Comsymp," invented by Welch to stand for "Communist sympathizer." (After 1970 some conservatives used that word interchangeably with "radic-lib," a neologism invented by Vice President Spiro Agnew to designate leftist critics of the Nixon administration.) To agree with Welch, wrote William F. Buckley, Jr., publisher of the conservative *National Review*, was to accept his contention that the United States Government was "under the operational control of the Communist Party."

Johnson Crime Commission In 1965, President Lyndon B. Johnson assembled a blue-ribbon panel of police chiefs, judges, and lawyers headed by Attorney General Nicholas Katzenbach to make a detailed study both of crime and the system of criminal justice in the United States. The report given the President in early 1967 centered on three vital points requiring urgent correction: (1) most American police organizations were outmoded and inefficient and in need of new equipment and better training; (2) the whole court system needed overhauling to cope with delays in meting out justice; (3) the fact that most criminals were repeaters suggested that a drastic overhauling of the correction system was in order.

The commission recommended that the federal government be authorized to contribute financial assistance to the individual states to help stimulate reforms. This was the basic principle behind the Safe Streets legislation shortly introduced by the President, but it was to be sixteen months before, on June 19, 1968, he was able to sign the Omnibus Crime Control and Safe Streets Act, which he said "responds to one of the most urgent problems in America today—the problem of fighting crime in the local neighborhood and on the city street." It established the Law Enforcement Assistance Administration (LEAA) as part of the Justice Department. Working with $100 million authorized by Congress for fiscal 1969—three times that amount in the following year—LEAA administered grants to the states for use in improving both law-enforcement and criminal-justice operations.

Although the bill restricted the sale of handguns, the President expressed regret that this provision was "only a halfway step," and he urged legislative action on proposals to extend controls to rifles, shotguns, and ammunition. He also objected to provisions sanctioning electronic eavesdropping and wiretapping by federal, state, and local officials "in an almost unlimited variety of situations," and he asked for their repeal. (The law banned all wiretapping and electronic eavesdropping by private individuals and banned the sale of such equipment in interstate commerce.) The President also expressed disapproval of provisions attempting to overturn rules of evidence as established by recent Supreme Court decisions such as **Miranda v. Arizona** (June 1966).

Johnson Doctrine *See* **Dominican Intervention**.

Johnson Grass Technically known as *Sorghum malepense*, this extremely high-growing weed covered vast areas in Vietnam. During American operations there (see **Vietnam War**) it was reported to have created a tactical problem by providing cover for attacking communist forces. Its popular name probably derived from an American agriculturist, but when GIs used it they no doubt had President Lyndon B. Johnson in mind.

JOIN *See* **Students for a Democratic Society.**

Jonestown On November 18, 1978, more than 900 members of a colony established in Guyana by Jim (James Warren) Jones, founder of a California cult known as the People's Temple, shocked the world by participating in a mass suicide ritual instigated by their leader. The tragedy followed swiftly on the heels of the gunning down at a nearby airstrip of Rep. Leo J. Ryan (D.-Calif.) and four others. Ryan had come to Guyana three days earlier with a party of seventeen staffers and newsmen to investigate reports of the abuse of human rights in the Jonestown colony. He had apparently angered Jones when he agreed to take some twenty disaffected colonists back to the United States with him.

Born in Indiana, where he was ordained as a minister of the Disciples of Christ, Jim Jones had originally attracted attention by his apparently deep and true interest in social causes. In the 1970s, he moved to California and established the People's Temple cult in San Francisco and Los Angeles. His work among the poor led to his being appointed in 1976 to the San Francisco Housing Authority by Democratic Mayor George Moscone. Then in August 1977 *New West* magazine published the first exposure of activities within the People's Temple, which under Jones's charismatic leadership was said to have grown to 20,000 members. There were accusations of beatings, death threats, and extortion practices under which cult members had been forced to sign over financial assets estimated in the millions. Affidavits filed by former members indicated that Jones's socialist fervor had turned to messianic madness recalling that of Charles Manson's **The Family.** Jones resigned his post in the housing authority and moved to establish his cult on a 900-acre area in Guyana, having obtained permission from Guyanese authorities three years earlier. (Among the many letters of recommendation

written for Jones in 1974 and later was one from Mrs. Rosalynn Carter.) He is said to have been convinced that the **Central Intelligence Agency** (CIA) and other government agencies were determined to destroy him and that the United States was doomed to an apocalyptic race war.

Under extraordinary conditions work went ahead on clearing a rain-forest area for the People's Temple colony, which he named Jonestown. California relatives of colonists were soon making accusations that Jones considered any form of criticism as treason. There were charges of beatings, the denial of free egress from the colony, and humiliating sexual practices.

It was because of these continuing accusations that Representative Ryan decided—against forceful efforts to dissuade him—to investigate the situation personally.

Within hours after Ryan's murder, Jones had begun organizing the mass suicide with which he is said to have often threatened authorities if any effort was made to interfere in Jonestown. As Jones exhorted his followers over loudspeakers, they either voluntarily or under coercion partook of a mixture of Kool-Aid and cyanide prepared in a large barrel. The victims included some 180 children. Jones himself was found at the site with a bullet in his head.

The bodies of the victims were transferred at U.S. government expense to Dover Air Force Base in Delaware, from which point they could be claimed by relatives. Investigations are now underway to determine exactly what happened in Jonestown, why accusations of abuses in the People's Temple cult were not investigated sooner, and what has happened to the vast sums of currency and gold said to have been accumulated by cult leaders.

Journey for Peace *See* **Peking Summit.**

Junction City *See* **Operation Junction City.**

"Junketeering Gumshoes" *See* **McCarthyism.**

K

Kent State Tragedy

Kefauver Committee Officially known as the Senate's Special Committee to Investigate Organized Crime in Interstate Commerce, the Kefauver Committee began hearings under the chairmanship of Sen. Estes Kefauver (D.-Tenn.) in May 1950. Moving from city to city (in several of the larger urban centers the hearings were televised), the committee's work attracted little attention until March 12, 1951, when sessions began in New York City's Foley Square Courthouse.

Arrangements had been made for routine broadcasting of the hearings as a public service by WPIX-TV, which was to feed stations across the nation. Soon men suspected of operating a major crime syndicate began parading across the small screen. By the time underworld figure Frank Costello was being questioned by committee counsel Rudolph Halley about his connections with Roosevelt Raceway—which for four years had paid him $15,000 annually for doing what Costello himself described as "practically nothing"—an estimated 30 million Americans were tuned into the hearings. At the insistence of his lawyer, when the camera turned to Costello it was permitted to photograph only his increasingly agitated hands. When indications of perjury were brought out by testimony, Costello temporarily walked out on the hearings. (He later served eighteen months in prison for contempt.)

Highlights of the committee's eight-day session in New York included testimony by Mrs. Virginia Hauser, who was questioned about her possible role as a gangsters' bank courier. (Mink-draped and angry, she later denounced overeager photographers: "You bastards, I hope a goddamn atom bomb falls on every goddamn one of you.") Former New York mayor William O'Dwyer conceded under cross-questioning that large-scale gambling in the city could not have gone on during his administration without police protection. Asked why he had named a protégé of Costello to a judgeship, he noted that there were "things that you have to do politically if you want to get cooperation."

The committee filed their findings on May 1, 1951. In the report, they stated that in large cities across the nation gangs were "firmly entrenched" in bookmaking, narcotics, and prostitution. Gambling profits were spotlighted as the "principal support of racketeering and gangsterism." The existence of major crime syndicates in New York and Chicago was reported, and the committee noted that thanks to bribery "leading hoodlums in the country remain, for the most part, immune from prosecution and punishment." Organized crime was seen as infiltrating legitimate businesses such as sports, liquor, and news transmission.

Of former Mayor O'Dwyer, then serving as ambassador to Mexico, the report said that "neither he nor his appointees took any effective action against the top echelons of the gambling, narcotics, waterfront, murder or bookmaking rackets." His behavior was seen as having "contributed to the growth of organized crime, racketeering and gangsterism in New York City."

The televised hearings of his committee made Senator Kefauver a national figure and a contender for the presidency. In 1956 he was the running mate of Democratic presidential contender Adlai Stevenson.

Kennedy-Nixon Debates In July 1960 Republican Vice President Richard M. Nixon and his Democratic challenger Sen. John F. Kennedy (Mass.) accepted a proposal from officials of the three major networks—CBS, NBC, and ABC—to participate in a series of televised debates focusing on the issues in the upcoming presidential election. The way was formally cleared for what are sometimes referred to as "The Great Debates" when on August 24, 1960, the House of Representatives approved a Senate Joint Resolution suspending the so-called equal opportunities section of the Communications Act of 1927, under which the networks would otherwise have been required to provide free television time for the candidates of the minor parties. A basic format for the debates was agreed to in a series of meetings that fall: a panel of newsmen, chosen according to a lottery system, who would formulate and ask questions as directed by a moderator.

The first—and possibly the most influential—of the debates took place on September 26. Broadcast from Chicago, it was devoted to domestic issues and included a short opening statement by both candidates, answers to questions from the press, and short closing statements. Senator Kennedy's opening statement charged that "the issue before the American people is: Are we doing as much as we can do . . . ? If we fail, then freedom fails. . . . I am not satisfied as an American, with the progress that we are making. . . . I think it's time America started moving again."

Vice President Nixon's opening statement was surprisingly mild—possibly because of an earlier phone call from his running mate Henry Cabot Lodge, who is said to have advised that he attempt to erase the "assassin image" often associated with him. Assuming an "elder statesman's" good humor he noted: "The things that Senator Kennedy has said, many of us can agree with. . . . I subscribe completely to the spirit that Senator Kennedy has expressed tonight. . . . I know Senator Kennedy feels as deeply about these problems as I do, but our disagreement is not about the goals for America but only about the means to reach those goals." As a result, it was generally agreed that the Vice President sounded weak and defensive, whereas his young rival appeared vigorous and aggressive. In addition, Nixon's problems were complicated by a bad makeup job—subsequently corrected—that made the television cameras project an unflattering image of him as heavy-jowled, sweating, and needing a shave. (He was often later to joke that a powder puff had stood between him and the White House.)

Nixon, who may have accepted the challenge to debate because of the success of his remarkable **"Checkers Speech"** on TV in 1952, later noted that Kennedy had the debating advantage because he was free to attack the record of the Eisenhower administration, whereas as Vice President he, Nixon, was required to defend it.

During the second debate, broadcast from Washington, D.C., on October 7, the format consisted of questions from the news panel followed by answers and rebuttals. Nixon managed to get his opponent on the defensive by attacking what he termed Kennedy's contention that **Quemoy and Matsu,** islands off the mainland of Red China still in the hands of the Nationalist forces of the Taiwan government, would have to be surrendered. The Vice President continued the attack during the third debate, which followed the format of the second and was broadcast on October 13 with Kennedy in New York and Nixon in Los Angeles. Most critics felt that Nixon was at his strongest in this debate and some ascribed it to the fact that he was more at ease because the two men were separated by some 3,000 miles.

Questioned on former President Harry S Truman's use of strong language during the campaign, Kennedy noted that he doubted if there was anything he could do to get President Truman to change his particular manner. ("Perhaps Mrs. Truman can, but I don't think I can.") Nixon strongly disapproved of President Truman's language and expressed the hope that should he become President he would maintain the high personal standards expected of the office.

The fourth and final debate was broadcast from New York on October 21 and followed the format of the first debate. It focused on foreign policy and covered many of the topics already debated, with the rivals more or less repeating their stances. In the national interest, Nixon was said to have dropped whatever advantage he may have enjoyed on the Quemoy and Matsu issue.

Shortly before the election from which he was to emerge the victor, Senator Kennedy noted that "the network television debates between Mr. Nixon and myself have been a great service by the television industry to the American people. More than 60 million Americans have had some opportunity through each of these debates to hear extensive discussions of major issues. . . . I place the highest value on television in any campaign, whether for the Presidency or for a county or city."

There is no general agreement about the effect of the debates on the final vote. Nixon noted in May 1961 that "what we now need is a close and careful estimate of their precise effect on the election returns and, on this basis, a sober judgment of their worth and future status." However, in his classic study of the campaign, *The Making of the President 1960* (1961), Theodore H. White concluded: "When [the debates] began, Nixon was generally viewed as being the probable winner of the election contest and Kennedy as fighting an uphill battle; when they were over, the positions of the two contestants were reversed."

Kennedy Round After four years of negotiations conducted under the auspices of the General Agreement on Tariffs and Trade (GATT, Geneva, October 30, 1947), on May 15, 1967, fifty-three nations reached provisional agreement on tariff reductions affecting about 60,000 items involved in $40 billion in world trade annually. In a departure from previous negotiations, what had come to be called the Kennedy Round was conducted on an across-the-board rather than an item-by-item basis. Although the agreement fell short of the 50-percent cut in industrial tariffs that had been hoped for, it did achieve reductions of up to 40 percent which were to be carried out by stages in the five-year period beginning January 1, 1968. The agreement included a significant liberalization of agricultural trade, established a food-aid program under which underdeveloped nations were to receive 4.5 million metric tons of grain annually, and included an antidumping code that would guard against discriminately low export prices. Agreement between the United States and Common Market nations over chemical cuts, steel, and grains had proved a dangerous stumbling block to the pact, which had been supported in this country by agricultural leaders but strongly criticized by the textile, steel, and chemical industries.

American participation in the Kennedy Round was under the **Trade Expansion Act** (October 11, 1962) which authorized the President to reduce tariffs up to 50 percent in exchange for reciprocal benefits. (Congress had never specifically authorized or officially recognized United States membership in GATT, to which this country was able to adhere by virtue of presidential authority to negotiate reciprocal trade agreements.) Since these powers expired July 1, 1967, our chief negotiator, Christian A. Herter—selected as presidential representative for trade negotiations by President John F. Kennedy, he was retained by President Lyndon B. Johnson—was under pressure to complete the agreements within that period.

As President Johnson wrote in 1971: "I knew that if we could demonstrate our ability to move ahead in economic partnership, especially with the Common Market, we would greatly improve the chances for a healthy **NATO** and for increased international monetary cooperation. If we failed, Europe might become more insular and more anti-American. Strong protectionist and isolationist groups in the United States might react in the same way."

Final agreement on the pact was not hammered out in detail until June 30, 1967, only hours before the Trade Expansion Act expired.

"Kennedy's Children" Name originally applied in some corners of the world to volunteers of the **Peace Corps** organized by President John F. Kennedy. The term later came to be used for those men and women who came of age during the brief Kennedy administration and whose lives were marked by the dramatic events of an era of hope and crisis that concluded with President Kennedy's assassination on **November 22, 1963.**

Kent State Tragedy When President Richard M. Nixon announced on April 30, 1970, that United States troops involved in the **Vietnam War** were invading Cambodia (see **Cambodian "Incursion"**), where North Vietnamese forces were said to have taken sanctuary, protests spread across the country, taking place particularly on the nation's campuses. On May 4, students who had gathered on the commons of Ohio's Kent State University were ordered to disperse by National Guardsmen. The students refused, taunted the troopers, and started tossing rocks. The Guardsmen replied by firing tear gas canisters, some of which were picked up by students who ineffectually tried to toss them back into the

line of soldiers. The latter retreated to some high ground and once there suddenly knelt and fired their rifles into the laughing, jeering crowd of young people, thirteen of whom were hit, four of them fatally.

The Guardsmen later claimed that they had been the target of sniper fire and feared for their lives, but FBI investigators of the incident reported: "We have some reason to believe that the claim by the National Guard that their lives were endangered by the students was fabricated subsequent to the event." The antiwar protest had begun as a peaceful demonstration, and the students had begun to throw rocks only when an attempt was made to disperse them by force.

The original trouble on campus in the four days beginning on May 1, 1970, had been nonpolitical in nature. But on May 2, militants organized a rally attended by less than 4 percent of the student population of 20,000. It nevertheless quickly got out of hand and the Kent State ROTC building was burned down. At the request of Kent's Mayor LeRoy Satrom—who acted without consulting university authorities—Governor James Rhodes transferred to the campus National Guardsmen who had been on riot duty in the Cleveland-Akron area, where on April 29 violence had erupted during a wildcat teamsters' strike. These exhausted and inexperienced troops patrolled the Kent campus Sunday and Monday. Arriving on the Kent campus on May 3, Governor Rhodes changed the Guardsmen's assignment from protecting property and lives to breaking up student assemblies.

As Ohio's Senator Stephen Young has pointed out, on the day of the tragedy there had been no rioting on the campus. Not one of the students killed or wounded was a radical. Not one participated in any disorder or rioted in Kent on the preceding Saturday or Sunday nights. Classes were being held throughout Monday right up to the time officers and Guardsmen fired sixty-one shots at the students with intent to wound or kill. None of the Guardsmen had sustained serious injury.

In a special report on the Kent State Tragedy issued on October 4 by the President's Commission on Campus Unrest **(Scranton Commission),** it was noted that no evidence was found of a sniper attack on the Guardsmen. The commission condemned the fact that the National Guard had been issued live ammunition for this campus assignment.

In October 1970, a special Ohio state grand jury indicted twenty-five people—none of them Guardsmen—in connection with the incident and lay the major responsibility for the outbreak of violence upon the "permissiveness" of university authorities. The members of the jury were never presented with the FBI report cited earlier. It was not until March 29, 1974, that eight of the Guardsmen were indicted for the deaths of the four students. On November 8, all were acquitted.

Kent v. Dulles *See* **Loyalty Probes.**

Keogh Retirement Plan The rules governing tax-sheltered pension plans for the self-employed were originally established under the Keogh Act (1962) sponsored by Rep. Eugene J. Keogh (D.-N.Y.). They made it possible to place 10 percent of earned income—up to a maximum of $2,500 annually—into tax-deferred custodial and trust bank accounts, insurance annuities, investment funds, or special United States retirement-plan bonds. The principal and accumulated interest in Keogh Plans became taxable only after retirement—between the ages of 59½ and 70½—when income is generally less and therefore taxable at a reduced rate. Distributions from the plan could be made earlier if an individual became disabled. The legislation made it mandatory for an individual setting up a plan for himself to include full-time employees who had worked for him for three or more years.

Participation in Keogh Plans was slow getting started but increased significantly as a result of pension reform legislation requested by President Richard M. Nixon in 1973 and signed into law by President Gerald R. Ford on September 2, 1974 **(Employee Benefit Security Act).** Under the new provisions, self-employed persons were permitted to skim off 15 percent, or a maximum of $7,500, from annual earned income.

Kerner Commission *See* **National Advisory Commission on Civil Disorders.**

Keynesianism The direct influence of British economist John Maynard Keynes on American economic practice dates from 1934, when through the good offices of Felix Frankfurter, then a member of the Harvard Law School, a meeting was arranged between him and President Franklin D. Roosevelt.

A staunch defender of capitalism, Keynes (pronounced Kanes) nevertheless departed sufficiently from the concepts of classical economics to point out that the government had a right and a duty to control the economy for the good of all by making use of its powers of taxation and spending. For example, during periods of economic depression the

fluctuations of private industry could be compensated for by massive deficit spending on the part of the government to stimulate the economy. Tax rates could be lowered or raised, Keynes pointed out, to increase or dry up the flow of money as desired. In addition, income could be redistributed by draining the superfluous savings of the rich through the introduction of progressive taxes and lower interest rates.

To some extent Keynesianism came after the fact where New Dealers were concerned, and provided an academic and theoretical backing for a program that had already been put into effect by President Roosevelt and his advisers. Yet in future years, its basic theories—as outlined in *Treatise on Money* (1930) and especially in *The General Theory of Employment, Interest and Money* (1936)—were to have a profound effect through disciples such as economists Alvin Hansen and Seymour E. Harris of Harvard University.

Arthur M. Schlesinger, Jr., has observed of President John F. Kennedy that "his experience as a young Congressman watching the fluctuation of the economy in the late forties confirmed him in an incipient Keynesianism." Keynes had considered President Roosevelt an economic "illiterate," but Professor Harris, an old friend and part-time adviser of President Kennedy, thought him "by far the most knowledgeable President of all time in the general area of economics."

As chairman of the **Council of Economic Advisers** during the Kennedy administration, Professor Walter Heller of the University of Minnesota helped expand the principles of Keynesianism by applying them not only to combat recession but also to aid an expanding economy. This new emphasis came to be known as the New Economics.

Gardner Ackley, who was the chairman of the Council of Economic Advisers under the Johnson administration, said in 1965: "The New Economics is based on Keynes. The fiscal revolution stems from him." Toward the end of the Johnson administration, Ackley was succeeded as Chief Economic Adviser by Arthur M. Okun, a Yale University economist, who had first expounded the "growth gap" theory to President Kennedy.

A most unlikely convert to Keynesianism was President Richard M. Nixon, who during the greater part of his political career had spurned and belittled Keynesian theory, as had other orthodox Republicans such as Sen. Barry Goldwater (Ariz.). (University of Chicago economist Milton Friedman, who was Senator Goldwater's economics adviser during the 1964 presidential campaign, was to say later: "We are all Keynesians now.") In a nationally televised interview on January 4, 1971, President Nixon announced: "I am now a Keynesian in economics." In other words, in the now classical Keynesian manner recession was to be fought by means of high government spending and increased budget deficits.

Keynes had noted thirty-five years earlier that the ideas of economists and political philosophers, whether they were right or wrong, were more powerful than was generally understood. "Practical men, who believe themselves to be quite exempt from any intellectual influences, are usually the slaves of some defunct economist."

Kinesics *See* **Body Language.**

Kinsey Report Popular name for *Sexual Behavior in the Human Male* published in 1948 by Alfred C. Kinsey and his associates at Indiana University's Institute for Sex Research. Based on data collected from interviews with 5,300 white American males, this controversial study revealed a wide discrepancy between the nation's professed standard of sexual conduct and actual sexual behavior which could in theory have left 95 percent of the country's entire male population open to legal prosecution of some sort.

Among the more startling statistics turned up by Dr. Kinsey's ten-year investigation was the fact that a total of 85 percent of all American males have premarital intercourse and 30 to 45 percent have extramarital intercourse. Relations with prostitutes were shown to have been experienced by 70 percent of the male population, and oral-genital contact by 59 percent. Statistical projections showed that 37 percent—more than one out of every three men—have had some form of homosexual experience at least once in their lives.

The men interviewed by Kinsey researchers came from all walks of life, including inmates of prisons. On a volunteer basis they submitted to interviews that lasted from one to six hours and included anywhere from 300 to 500 questions designed to expose attempts to mislead or misinform the researcher. The data obtained were then broken down by marital status, age, education, geographical origin, religion, occupation, etc. Such a breakdown revealed contrasting sexual attitudes between the different economic and sociological groups. For example, lower level groups showed prejudices against nudity, oral-genital contact, and unconventional sexual postures that were not shared by upper level groups. Extramarital intercourse declined with age among the lower socioeconomic groups and increased in the upper groups, which tended to begin marriage with a strong preference for monogamy. Masturbation was found to be twice as frequent among single, college-educated males as it was among single men with only a grade school education.

A storm of criticism greeted the publication of the *Kinsey Report.* Many critics objected to the sampling as being insufficiently representative of America as a whole—most of those interviewed came from the northeastern quarter of the country. There were charges that the percentages of professional and college-educated people were too high and the percentages of men over thirty were too low. In addition, critics felt that there was too much emphasis on the mechanics of sex and not enough on the emotional content of sexual experience. Nevertheless, it could not be denied that the statistics indicated a lag between biological maturity—sexual arousal was shown to be highest between the ages of fifteen and seventeen—and the economic maturity that made marriage possible.

A biologist by training, Dr. Kinsey began his investigations into sexual activity in about 1938. He was eventually joined in the project—which was supported both by Indiana University and the Rockefeller Foundation's Division of Medical Sciences—by Wardell B. Pomeroy, a clinical psychologist, and Clyde E. Martin, a statistician. Several other reports were issued by the Kinsey group, among them *Sexual Behavior in the Human Female* (1953).

"Kissing" Case International attention was drawn to the absurd lengths Southern segregationists would sometimes go, when in October 1958 two North Carolina blacks were arrested and charged with rape: they were David Simpson, seven, and Hanover Thompson, nine.

The boys had been playing "house" with some white children and one of the girls had perched on little Hanover Thompson's lap and kissed him on the cheek.

Informed of what had happened, the girl's mother called the police and the two boys were placed in the county jail, where they were held without the knowledge of their parents for several days. At a speedy hearing, a local judge sentenced them to fourteen years in reform school. The scandal caused by this case prompted President Dwight D. Eisenhower to intervene, and the boys were released after a few months.

Kitchen Debate In a story datelined Moscow, July 24, 1959, the *New York Times* said: "Vice President Richard M. Nixon and Premier Nikita S. Khrushchev debated in public today the merits of washing machines, capitalism, free exchange of ideas, summit meetings, rockets and ultimatums." The occasion for this unusual "diplomatic" exchange was the opening of the American National Exhibition in the Soviet capital's Sokolniki Park. The United States exhibit was the counterpart of the Soviet Exhibition of Science, Technology and Culture which had opened in New York on June 28, 1959.

The apparently unplanned Kitchen Debate or Conference (sometimes known as the Sokolniki Summit) made international headlines. As both leaders toured the exhibit they seemed very aware of the reporters who swarmed about them in a situation in which security arrangements had broken down. Premier Khrushchev, sensitive to the eager interest of the ordinary Russian in the consumer paradise on display, began by announcing early in the exchange that "in another seven years we will be on the same level as America."

The high-point of the "debate" took place in the kitchen of the six-room model ranch house to which the Americans had given a great deal of advance publicity. Although for days the Soviet press had been suggesting that the house could not be considered a typical worker's dwelling, Vice President Nixon made a point of explaining that the model house, said to cost $14,000, was in fact within the means of many.

Nixon: Let me give you an example you can appreciate. Our steel workers, as you know, are now on strike. But any steel worker could buy this house. They earn $3 an hour. This house costs about $100 a month to buy on a contract running twenty-five to thirty years.

Noting that the house was filled with interesting but useless gadgets, Premier Khrushchev said somewhat defensively that Americans had hoped to astonish Soviet citizens but that "the fact is that all our new houses have this kind of equipment." Then ignoring the well-known and continuing Russian housing shortage he noted: "In Russia all you have to do to get a house is to be born in the Soviet Union. . . . In America, if you don't have a dollar you have the right to choose between sleeping in a house or on the pavement. Yet you say that we are the slaves of communism."

As the talk turned to washing machines—and the cameras ground away—the following exchange took place:

Nixon: Is it not far better to be talking about washing machines than machines of war, like rockets? Isn't this the kind of competition you want?

Khrushchev: Yes, this is the kind of competition we want. But your generals say they are so powerful they can destroy us. We can also show you something so that you will know the Russian spirit.

Nixon: You are strong and we are strong. In some ways you are stronger, but in other ways we might be stronger. We are both so strong, not only in weapons but also in will and spirit, that neither should ever put the other in a position where he faces in effect an ultimatum.

Speaking to reporters and referring to implied Soviet threats about Berlin, Mr. Nixon said that he hoped the Premier had understood all the implications of what had been said.

Knowland Amendment *See* **Bricker Amendment.**

Korea "GI Bill of Rights" Signed into law by President Harry S Truman on July 16, 1952, the bill provided for **Korean War** veterans benefits that paralleled those of the 1944 bill for World War II veterans. Those who had served in the armed forces for at least ninety days since June 27, 1950, were entitled to educational benefits, government loan guarantees, mustering-out pay, and $26-a-week unemployment payments for up to twenty-six weeks. The provisions of the 1952 legislation were considerably less generous than those of the 1944 legislation. For example, World War II veterans were entitled to fifty-two weeks of $20 unemployment payments, hence the jocular reference to unemployed veterans as members of the 52-20 Club.

Korean War At the conclusion of World War II, Soviet troops occupied Korea north of the 38th parallel, and U.S. troops took over everything south of that line. At the **Potsdam Conference,** Premier Stalin had endorsed a free and independent Korea, and it was expected that the division of that country would be temporary.

However, by autumn of 1947, President Harry S Truman concluded that direct negotiations with the Soviets about Korea would be futile and he therefore instructed Secretary of State George C. Marshall to place the issue before the General Assembly of the United Nations. The result was the UN Temporary Commission on Korea, whose job it was to supervise national elections for a constituent assembly. The commission met in Seoul on January 12, 1948, but the Soviets not only barred access to the area above the **38th parallel** but refused to accept communications from the commission. On UN orders, therefore, elections were held in May 1948 only in the American zone. The National Assembly, once elected, met at the end of that month and, choosing Syngman Rhee as a chairman, wrote the constitution for the Republic of Korea (ROK), of which Rhee was elected president in July. In September, the U.S.S.R. occupation authorities countered by establishing the Democratic People's Republic of Korea and soon after informed Washington that its forces would be withdrawn by the end of the year.

Although aware of the Soviet-sponsored "People's Army" built up in the north, President Truman, advised by his Joint Chiefs of Staff—including General Douglas MacArthur—that with American aid the ROK's "prospects for survival may be considered favorable," agreed to a withdrawal of U.S. occupation forces.

On June 24, 1950, the communist People's Army invaded South Korea. When a UN Security Council call for a cessation of hostilities and a withdrawal to the 38th parallel was ignored, the Council—which had been boycotted by the U.S.S.R. after the UN refusal to seat Communist China—called on all UN members to render assistance in repelling the invasion.

On June 27, President Truman ordered the U.S. Air Force and Navy to Korea, and three days later he authorized the use of American ground forces to prevent the take-over of South Korea, whose capital, Seoul, had already fallen. The intervention was hesitatingly endorsed by Republican leaders. "I feel," said Sen. Robert Taft (R.-Ohio), "that we must back up our troops, where they have been sent by the President, with unstinted support." The Senator, however, called for the resignation of Secretary of State Dean Acheson, whose view of Far Eastern policy as expressed in a speech on January 12, 1950, was felt by some to have encouraged communist aggression in Korea (see **Defensive Perimeter**).

The offer of 30,000 troops by Nationalist China leader Chiang Kai-shek was rejected by Washington; General MacArthur, Far Eastern commander of U.S. forces and UN commander in Korea, was dispatched to Formosa to explain American fears that such a step might bring Communist China into the war. At the end of that meeting, MacArthur issued the first of his communiqués that indicated his split with the Truman administration on political and military policy. His announcement that arrangements had been made to coordinate U.S. and Nationalist forces in the event of an attack on Formosa caused President Truman to send W. Averell Harriman to brief him on this country's position. But in August 1950, General MacArthur's projected message to the Veterans of Foreign Wars showed that he had not accepted administration policy on Formosa. ("In view of misconceptions currently being voiced concerning the relationship of Formosa to our strategic potential in the Pacific, I believe it in the public interest to avail myself of this opportunity to state my views thereon to you, all of whom, having fought overseas, understand broad strategic concepts.") On President Truman's orders the message was withdrawn, but it had already been released to the press.

The landing of U.S. Marines at Inchon Harbor in September 1950 forced the North Korean forces to retreat behind the 38th parallel, where the UN forces followed on October 7, after a UN General Assembly recommendation that "all appropriate steps be taken to ensure conditions of stability throughout Korea" (see **Inchon Landing**).

In view of threats from Red China that it would enter the war, President Truman flew to Wake Island to confer with General MacArthur in mid-October. Unknown to both men, a stenographic record of their exchange was made by the secretary to Ambassador Philip Jessup; it did not become public until the hearings following the general's relief from command in April 1951:

The President: What are the chances for Chinese or Soviet interference?

General MacArthur: Very little. . . . We are no longer fearful of their intervention.

However, by the end of October, UN troops were taking Chinese prisoners, and on November 4, General MacArthur felt that there was a "distinct possibility" of a major Chinese intervention. A later communiqué announced that "we face an entirely new war." President Truman gave his reluctant permission for a bombing raid against the Yalu River bridges between Korea and Manchuria; the bombing of dams, power plants, and other targets on the Yalu was, however, specifically forbidden. General MacArthur complained that the present restrictions imposed on his area of operation provided a complete sanctuary for hostile aircraft immediately upon their crossing the Manchuria-North Korean border. "The effect of this abnormal condition upon the moral and combat efficiency of both air and ground troops is major."

Nevertheless, President Truman continued to

avoid any action that might extend the fighting in Korea into a general war, which he and the Joint Chiefs of Staff felt was a "gigantic booby trap," inevitably leading to World War III.

On November 24, General MacArthur had launched what he announced as a general offensive to end the war and bring the troops home by Christmas. On November 26, Chinese "volunteers" poured across the frozen Yalu (see **Yalu River Offensive**). Later President Truman wrote: "Now, no one is blaming General MacArthur, and certainly I never did, for the failure of the November offensive. . . . I do blame General MacArthur for the manner in which he tried to excuse his failure." The general, said the President, "publicized" his view that the failure lay in orders from Washington to limit hostilities to Korea. An exchange of letters between General MacArthur and House Republican Leader Joseph W. Martin, Jr. (Mass.), in March 1951 was particularly important in this respect.

On April 10, 1951, President Truman relieved General MacArthur of his command, which was turned over to General Matthew Ridgway. In a radio address to the nation the following day, President Truman explained that because of the general's reluctance to accept administration policy "I have, therefore considered it essential to relieve General MacArthur so that there would be no doubt or confusion as to the real purpose and aim of our policy. . . . World peace is more important than any individual."

U.S. troops, which after the failure of the November offensive had retreated south of Seoul, were back at the 38th parallel at this time. Efforts were being made to secure a negotiated peace. Talks with communist military leaders began in July at Kaesong and moved to Panmunjom in October, but the fighting continued. Deadlocked on the question of prisoner-of-war repatriation—the communists insisted on the mandatory return of even those Chinese and North Koreans who wished to remain in the south—negotiations were recessed indefinitely in October 1952.

On October 24, 1952, presidential candidate Dwight D. Eisenhower promised that if elected he would go to Korea to negotiate a final truce (see **"I shall go to Korea"**). He made his Korean trip on November 29, 1952, but it was not until July 27, 1953, that an armistice was signed and hostilities in "the forgotten war" actually ceased.

The armistice set up a two-and-a-half-mile demilitarized zone (DMZ) between North and South Korea. Prisoners who did not wish to be repatriated were to be released as civilians after a ninety-day period of political persuasion.

Sixteen members of the United Nations had sent troops to South Korea, but the United States supplied the major forces. Some 110,000 U.S., UN, and South Korean soldiers were killed or died during hostilities, and about a half a million South Korean civilians were casualties or died of starvation and disease. Estimates of communist losses are over 1.5 million, not including the hundreds of thousands who were victims of war-associated deaths.

Attempts at Korean unification still continue in the United Nations. A call by North Korea in March 1974 to initiate talks designed to replace the July 1953 armistice was rejected by both Washington and Seoul. In 1977, the United States announced a gradual withdrawal of ground forces from the DMZ over the next five years. North Korea has denounced this as too slow and called for direct talks with the United States after working-level talks with South Korea on reunification broke down in 1978.

See **"Old soldiers never die"; Pueblo Incident; Heartbreak Ridge; Pork Chop Hill.**

Krebiozen Banned from interstate distribution by the Food and Drug Administration (FDA) in July 1963, Krebiozen, an "anticancer" drug, was discovered and manufactured by Dr. Steven Durovic, who claimed that it was a serum extracted from horses that had been infected with a specific bacterium. It had been in use since 1950, but the FDA had refused it official approval for commercial marketing, asserting that its effectiveness was yet to be proved.

In June 1963, Dr. Durovic filed with the FDA for permission to use the drug in experiments on humans, but he withdrew his application after complaints that there was insufficient information about the drug's exact chemical composition and the facilities used in its manufacture. The following month he filed a harassment suit against the FDA, which then made public documents contending that Krebiozen, said to cost $170,000 a gram to produce, was in reality creatine, a common amino acid produced by the body and available commercially for thirty cents a gram. Some 5,000 cancer victims were said to have paid close to a hundred dollars a dose—as a "donation"—for what could be manufactured at eight cents a dose.

The similarity of Krebiozen to creatine was discovered by Ruth Kessler, a University of Pennsylvania student, in the course of experiments in which infrared spectrograms of Krebiozen and creatine were compared. In May 1963, patients who felt they owed their lives to the "miracle" drug flocked to Washington, and in July Sen. Paul H. Douglas (D.-Ill.) introduced a Senate resolution which urged that the drug be made available to those already under treatment with it.

Krebiozen was denounced as ineffective against cancerous tumors by both the National Cancer Institute and the American Medical Association.

L

Wide World Photos

Little Rock

Labor-Management Relations Act of 1947 *See* **Taft-Hartley Act.**

Labor-Management Reporting and Disclosure Act of 1959 *See* **Landrum-Griffin Act.**

Labor Rackets Committee *See* **McClellan Committee.**

Lady Bird Bill Popular name for the Highway Beautification Act strongly urged by Lady Bird Johnson and signed by her husband, President Lyndon B. Johnson, in a special White House ceremony on October 22, 1965. Opponents such as Rep. William C. Cramer (R.-Fla.) had accused the administration of using "armtwisting" to keep the House in session the night of October 7–8 so that news of its passage could be made as a gift to the first lady at the "Salute to Congress" reception that evening. House passage actually came shortly before 1 A.M. on October 8 and the Senate gave its approval by a voice vote on October 13.

The bill authorized the use of federal funds to help individual states control the glut of billboards and junkyards along noncommercial sections of interstate and primary highways. The Secretary of Commerce and the states concerned were to collaborate in determining outdoor advertising standards of unzoned areas. The states were given until July 1, 1970, to remove billboards within 660 feet of the highway; junkyards within 1,000 feet were to be similarly removed. To compensate billboard and junkyard owners for as much as 75 percent of the removal and landscaping costs involved, $80 million in federal funds was to be made available over a two-year period. In the same period another $240 million was made available for landscaping and roadside development of areas along federally aided roads. States that did not comply with the provisions by January 1, 1968, would lose 10 percent of their federal highway funds.

In signing the bill, President Johnson noted that it was only a first step and that it did not contain all he had hoped for or "all the national interest requires." By 1979, almost a third of the 296,006 offending billboards had been removed, but only 1,413 out of 12,953 roadside junkyards had been dealt with. President Jimmy Carter made no allowance for the program in his budget for fiscal 1980.

Lady Bird Special During President Lyndon B. Johnson's 1964 campaign for office, Lady Bird Johnson suggested to her husband that she undertake a solo whistle-stop campaign through areas of the South opposed to his candidacy. On October 6,

1964, the sixteen-car Lady Bird Special pulled out of Alexandria, Virginia, and for five days the first lady traveled through eight southern states and made more than forty speeches. On board were experts experienced in Southern political ways, "hostesses" drawn from among the wives of Southern members of the White House staff, and at times the President's daughters, Luci and Lynda.

The first lady courageously defied Southern tradition by taking a low-keyed but clear-cut stand on civil rights. Her train was visited by the governors of every state through which it passed; the only exception was Alabama's George C. Wallace, who nevertheless took the precaution of sending an outsize bouquet.

Commentators were quick to note that complicated notions of Southern chivalry beyond the comprehension of most Yankees made it possible for those who opposed the President for his strong civil rights stand to nevertheless offer him some degree of support after the Lady Bird Special had visited their region.

Laetrile Publicized as an anticancer drug, this commercial preparation of an extract from apricot pits is said to be taken by 75,000 Americans annually in spite of the fact that it has been condemned as worthless by the Food and Drug Administration (FDA), the American Cancer Society, and the National Cancer Institute. When it was banned from importation and interstate commerce by the federal government, amygdalin—as it is known in pharmacology—became second only to marijuana as a contraband substance smuggled across the Mexican border. As the result of a grass-roots revolt similar to the reaction to the FDA ban on saccharin (*see* **Cyclamates**), it has been legalized in more than a dozen states in spite of FDA opposition. On July 10, 1978, a U.S. court of appeals in Denver ruled that terminally-ill cancer patients were legally entitled to it since the federal law questioning its safety and effectiveness could have no meaning in their case.

Laetrile (pronounced *lay*-uh-trill) was first developed in 1926 in California by Ernst Krebs, Sr., who was investigating the use of enzymes in cancer treatment. He tested it on mice but was unable to produce a safe product because it seemed to kill as many mice as it apparently helped. In the 1940s, his son, Ernst Krebs, Jr., managed to produce a purified extract into a product that was apparently harmless to humans. It was patented as a possible anticancer drug in 1949. Three years later it was labeled Laetrile B17 in an attempt to link it to the growing movement of those who feel that vitamins can be effectively used in the eradication of both physical and psychological illnesses. One of the foremost proponents of this movement is Linus C. Pauling, a two-time Nobel Prize winner.

See **"Clean" Bomb Controversy.**

Landrum-Griffin Act Appearing on national television on August 6, 1959, President Dwight D. Eisenhower urged a reform law "to protect the American people from gangsters, racketeers and other corrupt elements who have invaded the labor-management field," and he announced his support of a measure by Rep. Phil M. Landrum (D.-Ga.) and Rep. Robert P. Griffin (R.-Mich.). Similar measures were already being considered by Congress, and the Landrum-Griffin Act, signed by the President on September 14, 1959, drew on a Senate bill offered by Sen. John F. Kennedy (D.-Mass.) and Sen. Sam J. Ervin, Jr. (D.-N.C.), as well as on an amendment to the **Taft-Hartley Act** proposed by Sen. John L. McClellan (D.-Ark.) and a so-called Bill of Rights offered by Sen. Thomas H. Kuchel (R.-Calif.) to protect union members against unfair union practices.

Senator Kennedy was the chairman of the conference committee which hammered out a compromise version of the Landrum-Griffin bills passed by the Senate and the House, and he had urged its passage as less harsh to unions than the House bill and the best that could be realistically expected.

Among its provisions were reform measures that protected the democratic rights of union members against arbitrary actions by unions; guaranteed a secret ballot in union elections; limited the terms of international officers to five years and of local officers to three years; barred convicted felons and ex-communists from serving as union officials for five years after completing their sentences or leaving the party; and made it mandatory for unions to make periodic and detailed financial reports. (Employers were required to report on sums spent in attempts to influence unions.)

President Eisenhower had complained in his TV address that under existing law states had practically no authority over labor cases. Under the Landrum-Griffin Act state agencies and courts had jurisdiction under state law of cases which the National Labor Relations Board (NLRB) had refused to accept—the so-called no-man's-land cases rejected as having little effect on interstate commerce, but in which states had been powerless to interfere because of a 1957 Supreme Court decision.

The new legislation also prohibited "hot cargo"

clauses in collective bargaining agreements, under the provisions of which employers were prevented from doing business with a firm in dispute with the union. In addition, it prohibited picketing for the purposes of recognition where another union had recognition, where an NLRB election had been held within the previous year, and where picketing had been conducted for "a reasonable period not exceeding 30 days" and no request for an election had been made by the union.

The Landrum-Griffin Act was attacked by AFL-CIO president George Meany as the "most damaging anti-labor bill since the Taft-Hartley Act." He called it part of a big-business effort to restrict union activities in the name of labor reform. All those who voted for the bill received a letter from James B. Carey, president of the AFL-CIO International Union of Electrical Workers, saying that "we shall do all in our power to prove to the working men and women in your district that you have cast your lot against them and they should therefore take appropriate action at the ballot box."

The only Senators to vote against the bill were Sen. Wayne Morse (D.-Oreg.) and Sen. William Langer (R.-N.Dak.). In the House 138 Republicans and 214 Democrats voted for it.

"Landslide Lyndon" Ironic nickname applied to Lyndon B. Johnson after his 1948 campaign to win the senatorial nomination in the Democratic primary in Texas. He won by only eighty-seven votes, but went on to become the minority leader (1953–1955) and finally the majority leader (1955–1960) before going on to share the Democratic presidential ticket with Sen. John F. Kennedy (Mass.) in 1960. After the assassination of President Kennedy in Dallas on **November 22, 1963,** he succeeded to the Presidency.

Owen Lattimore Affair *See* **McCarthyism; Tydings Committee.**

"Laugh-In" From 1967 to 1973 this free-wheeling hour of comedy hosted by Dan Rowan and Dick Martin was a Monday night NBC hit. A combination of stand-up comedy routines, blackout sketches, madcap dances and songs, and material that took full technical advantage of the potential of the television camera, the program made stars of Lily Tomlin, Goldie Hawn, JoAnne Worley, and Arte Johnson. Many of the catchphrases used without fail week after week caught the national fancy and passed into the language—"sock it to me," "is that a chicken joke?" "here come the judge," "look that up in your Funk and Wagnall's," and "verrry interrresting, but dumb!"

League for Nonviolent Civil Disobedience Against Military Segregation Formed in June 1948 by A. Philip Randolph, founder and leader of the Brotherhood of Sleeping Car Porters, the league urged blacks to resist induction into the Armed Services unless that branch were desegregated. In that same year, President Harry S Truman ordered a review of the segregation policy, and his Committee on Equality of Treatment and Opportunity in the Armed Forces recommended swift and total integration. Most military units were desegregated by 1954, but the process was not completed until 1960.

League of Spiritual Discovery *See* **LSD.**

Legionnaire's Disease A mysterious ailment that broke out among the men and women attending the American Legion convention in Philadelphia, July 21–24, 1976. It captured national headlines when 182 people became ill and twenty-nine died.

Investigation of the causes of the disease was undertaken by the Center for Disease Control, a federal agency in Atlanta, which on January 18, 1977, announced that they had been traced to an unnamed bacterium capable of causing atypical pneumonia. The following March it was announced that some success had been achieved by treating the disease with antibiotics such as erythromycin and tetracycline. A never-explained outbreak of pneumonia at St. Elizabeth's Hospital, Washington, D.C., in 1965, and of the so-called Pontiac fever which gripped Pontiac, Michigan, in 1969, have been linked to the Legionnaire's Disease by some researchers.

Legislative Reorganization Act Signed into law by President Harry S Truman on August 2, 1946, it included provisions requiring congressional lobbyists to register as such and furnish records disclosing both their expenditures and sources of income. This legislation had been sought by the President, who though he felt that "in some instances the representatives of special-interest groups can be useful around Capitol Hill," was convinced that lobbyists had played "an important role in hampering" his administration's efforts to keep prices from "skyrocketing" during the immediate post-World War II period.

Other provisions of the law cut House and Senate standing committees from, respectively, forty-eight

to nineteen, and thirty-five to fifteen; provided congressmen with a $2,500-a-year tax-free expense account for which no accounting was necessary; made members of Congress eligible for federal pensions; and allowed each Senator a $10,000-a-year assistant.

Additional legislation in October 1970 liberalized the procedures of congressional committees.

"Let's get this country moving again!" Slogan coined by Walt W. Rostow, professor of economic history at the Massachusetts Institute of Technology, for the 1960 presidential campaign of Democratic candidate John F. Kennedy. Rostow had originally been slated for the State Department after President Kennedy's election, but because of objections to him by Secretary of State Dean Rusk, he was appointed to the White House staff as deputy to McGeorge Bundy, Special Assistant for National Security Affairs. Later he did go over to the State Department as counselor and chief of the Policy Planning Council.

"Let us continue" Addressing Congress for the first time after the assassination of President John F. Kennedy in Dallas on **November 22, 1963,** President Lyndon B. Johnson pledged himself to continue his predecessor's programs in international relations, the war on poverty, and

. . . above all, the dream of equal rights for all Americans, whatever their race or color. . . .
On the 20th day of January, in 1961, John F. Kennedy told his countrymen that our national work would not be finished "in the first thousand days, nor in the life of this administration, nor even perhaps in our lifetime on this planet. But"—he said—"let us begin." Today in this moment of new resolve, I would say to my fellow Americans, let us continue.

"Let us never negotiate out of fear. But let us never fear to negotiate." *See* **"Ask not what your country can do for you. . . ."**

The Limits of Growth Published in 1972, this report on a computer analysis of growth limits in population, agricultural production, industrial production, natural resources, and pollution was attacked for the Malthusian pessimism with which it predicted that if the present trends continued, within a hundred years or less the results would be mass starvation and death due to pollution. The report also foresaw an absolute and widening gap between the rich and poor nations of the world if growth continued unchecked.

The report was commissioned in 1970 from Massachusetts Institute of Technology professor Dennis H. Meadows and his associates by the Club of Rome, a group of some 100 scholars, industrial leaders, and government leaders organized by Dr. Aurelio Peccei to meet periodically for discussions and research on world problems. The Meadows group was instructed to develop a global model of growth which could aid an ongoing project on "The Predicament of Mankind."

The Meadows, or Club of Rome Report, as it is often called, saw faint hope only if global equilibrium could be achieved by making industry and population constant in size and by establishing growth and death or depletion rates that cancelled each other out. Its global model, based on a more complex systems model described by Jay W. Forrester in *World Dynamics* (1971), was, however, criticized for excluding adjustment mechanisms which had always previously come to the aid of mankind, and because it did not admit the possibility of technological breakthroughs that would solve the problems of depleting resources and growing pollution, and might even—optimists insisted—result in an overabundance of food products and raw materials such as oil.

An interesting aspect of the report was its emphasis on the fact that growth rates of a society reflect its social values. Social equality, for example, was seen as capable of being increased or decreased by changing the balance established between population and available resources. A society based on equality and justice, the report found, was better able to achieve a state of global equilibrium that could control the problems of growth and release the energies of mankind to tackle the other difficulties besetting it.

The group later softened some of its harsher predictions.

Lindley Rule   Named after journalist Ernest K. Lindley, the Lindley Rule is an agreement between a reporter and his news source—usually a high-ranking administration official—that the information imparted will be used without attribution. It first began to be heard of during the first Truman administration, and its function was to allow members of the government to discuss matters of importance without having to worry about the embarrassment of later having to eat their words. Since neither quotations nor attributions of any kind are admissible under a strict interpretation of the rule, information passed along under this agreement often appears in print as a personal insight of the reporter's.

See **Backgrounder.**

Little Rock   In compliance with the U.S. Supreme Court's 1954 decision in ***Brown v. Board of Education of Topeka*** that "separate educational facilities were inherently unequal," Central High School in Little Rock, Arkansas, prepared to admit a limited number of black children on September 3, 1957. The evening before, however, Governor Orval Faubus, having previously attempted to block integration by pleading that it would lead to violence, announced that he was placing the National Guard around Central High to prevent just such an eventuality. The next morning, none of the nine black youngsters who had been scheduled to be enrolled appeared—on the advice of the school board.

Governor Faubus had previously been considered a moderate on race relations and his anti-integration stand took many by surprise. But commentators were quick to point out that he was involved in an uncertain fight for a new term and was trying to build a new political base. (He was reelected by a massive plurality in 1958 and retained the governorship until his retirement in 1967.)

On September 4, having been told by a federal district judge that the National Guardsmen were to be considered as "neutral," the nine incredibly brave black children surrounded by a screaming and threatening mob attempted to enter Central High but were turned away by the Guardsmen. After a variety of legal steps had been taken, an injunction was granted against the governor, and on September 23 the children again attempted to enter the school. The Guardsmen had been withdrawn, but a crowd worked up to fever pitch forced the children to leave the school after only a few hours. While the black students were in Central High, white students exited en masse, chanting "Two, four, six, eight, we ain't gonna integrate."

This blatant interference with the law was denounced by President Dwight D. Eisenhower, who, however, refrained from making any personal gesture—urged by many—such as himself leading the children up the steps of the school. Instead, he federalized the Arkansas National Guard, and on September 25 the black students were back in the school. The mob dispersed, and eventually attendance by white students slowly increased. The tension remained, however, and in June 1958, Federal Judge Harry J. Lemley granted a Central High school board petition to suspend its integration plan for two and a half years. The case was brought to the U.S. Supreme Court ***(Cooper v. Aaron)***, which on September 29, 1958, unanimously voided the suspension order as a violation of the constitutional rights of the black children.

At this point Governor Faubus ordered all Little Rock high schools closed, once more basing his stand on a desire to avoid the very violence he had provoked. However, he bowed to a federal judge's order to reopen the schools, and on August 12, 1959, three black children were admitted to Central High. Once more the mob appeared, but this time local police maintained order.

Little Switch On February 22, 1953, during a suspension in the talks at Panmunjom designed to end the **Korean War,** General Mark Clark, commander of the United Nations forces, wrote a routine letter to the high command of the North Korean forces suggesting the repatriation of seriously sick and wounded prisoners of war in accordance with the Geneva Convention. Somewhat to his surprise, the communists, who had previously ignored similar requests, expressed both a willingness to exchange prisoners and to resume truce negotiations. The immediate result was "Little Switch," a dramatic operation in which 6,670 captured communists were exchanged for 684 United Nations personnel held by the North Koreans.

Joan Little Trial Sentenced to up to ten years for breaking and entering, Joan Little, a twenty-year-old black woman, fled the Beaufort County Jail, North Carolina, on August 27, 1974, after murdering a white jailer, Clarence T. Alligood, with an ice pick. Miss Little later pleaded self-defense and contended that the dead man—who had been found with his pants off and sperm on his thighs—had forced her into sexual intercourse. The state claimed that she had enticed Mr. Alligood into her cell, and charging first-degree murder, Chief Prosecutor William Griffin asked for the death penalty.

Miss Little's case attracted the attention of civil rights militants, feminists, prison reformers, and those opposed to the death penalty. Wide publicity attended the pretrial proceedings, and a $350,000 legal defense fund was raised on her behalf. A battery of defense attorneys was assembled, with Jerry Paul named chief defense counsel.

A change of venue having been asked for by the defense to assure a fair trial, the six weeks of testimony began on July 14, 1975, in Raleigh, North Carolina (Wayne County). Before the case went to the carefully selected jury of six whites and six blacks, Judge Hamilton Hobgood dismissed the first-degree murder charge for lack of evidence. On August 15, 1975, after deliberating less than an hour and twenty minutes, the jury acquitted Miss Little of second-degree murder. Chief Defense Counsel

Paul was sentenced to fourteen days in jail for contempt of court charges stemming from derogatory remarks he made about Judge Hobgood early in the trial.

On October 15, 1977, Miss Little escaped from a North Carolina minimum security prison in which she was serving the remainder of her original sentence. Apprehended in New York City the following December 7, she was returned to North Carolina after the U.S. Supreme Court refused without comment (June 5, 1978) to block her extradition. She was later sentenced to an additional six months to two years.

Living Theatre Founded in New York after World War II by Julian Beck and his wife, Judith Malina, this experimental theatrical company was to develop a pacifist-anarchist orientation which eventually brought it into conflict with the authorities. Its initial productions were avant-garde poetic dramas by playwrights such as Kenneth Rexroth, William Carlos Williams, W.H. Auden, and T.S. Eliot, "or plays in which the language was that kind of prose which makes the unconscious telegraphic leaps that poets are master of."

In 1959 the Living Theatre began experimenting with a realism that seemed improvised but was actually strictly controlled. It presented Jack Gelber's *The Connection*, in which the fiction is maintained that the audience is present at a moment when a group of drug addicts are waiting for a "fix." The next important production of the group was Kenneth H. Brown's *The Brig* (1963), a terrifyingly "realistic" presentation of a day in a Marine prison camp. The production showed the influence on the group of Antonin Artaud's Theatre of Cruelty. Writing in 1964, Mr. Beck called it "the distillation of the direction of The Living Theatre's history. You cannot shut off from it, as from a dream. It is there, real, in the pit of your stomach. Defy the audience. Tell them you don't want to involve them. Don't run into the aisle to embrace them. Put up a barricade of barbed wire. Separate until the pain of separation is felt, until they want to tear it down, to be united. Storm the barricades."

It was at about this time that the Internal Revenue Service took the Becks to court for nonpayment of taxes. Their theater was closed and they served brief jail sentences before taking their troupe to Europe, where for the next four years it lived as a commune and gave a series of productions that stressed its increasingly political orientation.

The most controversial of these was *Paradise Now*, an amorphous series of radical declarations in which this time the actors did indeed run down the aisle to embrace the audience and urge it to join them in their choreographed protest against all forms of repression—including clothing. During its American tour, federal authorities on several occasions closed the theaters the group was appearing in, and by the end of the year members of the cast had been arrested fifteen times.

Aggressively urging the importance of love, the cast appealed to audiences to stop the **Vietnam War** and empty the prisons. Although the reactions of those witnessing the performances were invariably made part of the presentation, they were allowed no influence on its intention.

Critics such as Robert Brustein, who had formerly encouraged the Living Theatre, now condemned it for having become "a self-generating and self-perpetuating organism whose existence was more important than any work it performed; and it was infused with a sense of mission that was less theatrical or even political than religious and evangelical." He noted that the company had taken on "the very authoritarian qualities it had once denounced; the very repressiveness that had driven it from the country four years before."

The troupe returned to Europe in 1970 and shortly afterward disbanded.

The Lonely Crowd This 1950 study of "the changing American character" by sociologist David Riesman and his associates, Nathan Glazer and Reuel Denney, postulates that where our society was once dominated by the "inner-directed" person of a highly individualistic bent, the current dominant type is the "other-directed" person whose values and behavior are chiefly determined by imitation of his peers.

The inner-directed person is seen as having early in life "incorporated a psychic gyroscope which is set going by his parents and can receive signals later on from other authorities who resemble his parents." This person goes through life "obeying this internal piloting."

In contrast, the other-directed person is seen as responding to signals "from a far wider circle than is constituted by his parents." That person therefore lacks the "inner-directed person's capacity to go it alone."

The study contrasts the reactions of these two types in relation to social status, politics, child-rearing practices, popular culture, and sexual habits. It points out that in other-directed persons distinctions between work and leisure time tend to be blurred, the work day becoming varnished with sociability and leisure time contaminated with the anxieties of work. As a result, the entertainment fields, for example, "serve the audience today less and less as an escape from daily life, more and more as a continuous sugar-coated lecture on how to get along with the 'others.' " Pressure is put on children to be "well-adjusted," i.e. "gregarious," and it becomes "inconceivable to some supervising adults that a child might prefer his own company or that of just another child."

The years of research that went into *The Lonely Crowd* were sponsored by the Yale University Committee on National Policy. Additional aspects of the study were later published in *Faces in the Crowd* (1952).

Love Canal Citing an unusual number of miscarriages and defective births in the Love Canal area of Niagara Falls, New York, State Health Commissioner Robert P. Whalen recommended on August 2, 1978, that pregnant women and children under two leave the residential district immediately. The danger stemmed from the fact that beginning in the early 1940s and until 1953 when it sold the sixteen-acre site to the Niagara Falls Board of Education for $1, the Hooker Chemical & Plastics Corp. had been dumping chemical wastes into the unused canal.

The first signs of trouble appeared in 1976 when unusually heavy rains caused pollutants sunk in the soil to bubble to the surface and seep into cellars. Soon some eighty toxic chemicals could be identified.

Federal funds for evacuating the area become available when on August 7, 1978, President Jimmy Carter declared the Love Canal a disaster area. Governor Hugh Carey announced at the same time that the state would join with the federal government in paying for the clean-up on "a fifty-fifty basis" and Hooker, which disclaimed all responsibility for the situation, offered to finance a ditch to drain the dump.

Officials of the **Environmental Protection Agency** (EPA) have estimated that there are some 1,000 similar chemical dumping grounds throughout the nation and that in years to come they can be expected to cause an ever-increasing problem.

Loving v. Virginia In a ruling interpreted as sufficiently broad to void the antimiscegenation laws of fifteen other states as well, on June 12, 1967, the U.S. Supreme Court, by a vote of nine to zero, declared Virginia's "racial integrity law" unconstitutional.

The specific case under consideration dealt with Richard P. Loving, a white, and Mildred Loving, his part-Indian, part-Negro wife, whom he had married in Washington, D.C., in 1958. Natives of Virginia, the Lovings returned to their home state after their marriage and were prosecuted under the 1924 law which had been upheld by the Virginia Supreme Court of Appeals.

In writing the decision, Chief Justice Earl Warren noted: "We have consistently denied the constitutionality of measures which restrict the rights of citizens on account of race. . . . There can be no doubt that restricting the freedom to marry solely because of racial classifications violates the central meaning of the [Constitution's] equal protection clause."

Loyalty Probes   Worsening post-World War II relations with the U.S.S.R., the *Amerasia Case* in which confidential government documents were found in the files of a leftist magazine, and a report by a Canadian investigatory commission on the operation of espionage rings in that country were among the contributing factors that led President Harry S Truman on March 22, 1947, to issue Executive Order 9835 inaugurating a loyalty check of all federal employees by the Civil Service Commission and the FBI. In a procedure recommended by the President's Temporary Commission on Employee Loyalty created the previous November, persons accused of belonging to a subversive organization—a list of which had been compiled by the Attorney General—were given a hearing before a loyalty board. They were allowed to have counsel, were given a résumé of the charges—with the exception of what was considered secret—and were confronted by their accusers—but only when the latter agreed to appear.

The loyalty board's findings were passed on to the head of a given government agency, who could either accept or reject them. If they were permanent civil servants, the accused had the right of appeal to a presidentially appointed Loyalty Review Board, and to a regional board if their status was temporary. Those found guilty after these appeals were exhausted were dismissed. (In 1949, Congress began including in various appropriation bills riders giving department heads the power to discharge employees on security grounds without any right of appeal.)

While critics of the loyalty probes brought charges of "witch hunting" and "guilt by association," conservatives in Congress countercharged that the Truman administration was taking inadequate measures to purge communists from the federal payrolls and from positions of trust. Among these was Rep. J. Parnell Thomas (R.-N.J.), who as chairman of the **House Committee on Un-American Activities** (HUAC), kept the issue of communist infiltration in government alive by reckless charges that captured the nation's headlines in a manner that anticipated the **"McCarthyism"** of the next decade.

In November 1949, Representative Thomas was found guilty of padding the federal payroll and accepting "kickbacks," and there was some hope of a more judicious handling of the loyalty issue. However, fuel had been added to the fire by the **Coplon Case,** which involved a young woman employed by the Justice Department and who, in June 1949, was found guilty of passing secret documents to a Soviet agent. In addition, the nation became alarmed by the **Alger Hiss Case,** in which a former Department of State employee was accused of espionage by a self-confessed Soviet agent.

Abuses of the loyalty probe program were widespread. Confidential reports of the Civil Service Commission and the FBI containing uninvestigated and unevaluated charges found their way into the press, and even if people had been cleared of charges by a loyalty board or by the Loyalty Review Board, these charges remained part of their files and might be brought up again upon their transfer to another department.

The loyalty probes ended early in 1951 after some 3 million employees had been cleared and the FBI had made approximately 14,000 investigations of "doubtful" cases. All in all, about 200 persons were dismissed, and another 2,000 chose to resign during this period.

In *Kent v. Dulles* (1958) the U.S. Supreme Court sidestepped the issue of whether a federal employee might be dismissed on the basis of evidence of a secret informer by ruling that the case in issue had been improperly appealed to the Loyalty Review Board, which had therefore lacked the authority to issue a dismissal order.

LSD (lysergic acid diethylamide)   A hallucinogenic drug discovered in 1938 by the Swiss chemist Albert Hofmann, who was originally unaware of its effect on the mind. In doses of from seventy-five micrograms and more, it can produce changes in color, space, time, and emotional perception that can last upward of six hours. Such changes can be a pleasant experience (a "good trip"), or they can be terrifying losses of reality (a "bad trip"). In addition, in some people there can be "flashbacks" which are capable of reinducing the LSD state months after taking the drug.

During the 1960s, use of this drug by students and young people increased rapidly, many "acidheads" taking it once or twice a week.

In April 1966, the Swiss firm Sandoz Pharmaceuticals, the sole legal distributors of the drug in the United States, withdrew all supplies because it felt that black-market supplies manufactured in "basement labs" were giving the company a bad reputation. At the time, it estimated its total output at no more than a few pounds since it developed the drug in 1943.

In May 1966, the federal government barred the distribution of LSD ingredients except for restricted use in authorized research.

In the early 1960s, Harvard psychologists Dr. Timothy Leary and Dr. Richard Alpert conducted experiments with LSD, using volunteers as subjects. Both men were dismissed by the university in 1963. In September 1966, they founded the "League of Spiritual Discovery" which planned the use of LSD and other drugs in "sacramental" rites. Members of the league were supposed to use LSD once a week in "mind expanding" experiments.

The popularity of the growing drug culture on the campus and in bohemian centers such as New York's East Village and San Francisco's **Haight-Ashbury** section, was exemplified by songs such as the Beatles' "Yellow Submarine," "Strawberry Field," and **"Lucy in the Sky with Diamonds."** On Easter Sunday, March 26, 1967, the spring of the disillusioning **"Summer of Love,"** Dr. Leary advised some 15,000 cheering young people in San Francisco: "Turn on to the scene, tune in to what's happening, and drop out—of high school, college, grade school . . . follow me, the hard way."

Writing in the "Bulletin of the Atomic Scientists" (1968), Daniel X. Freeman noted that

. . . the chief abuse of LSD is irresponsible, alluring, and provocative advertising by the bored mass media. Couched in the language of drugs, an ideology has been insinuated into youth culture by a band of articulate writers and vagrant professionals. These have replaced the old medicine show with an updated campus version complete with readings and tempting arguments, if not pills, to sell: "Tune in, turn on, drop out."

He warned that the cost of "sustained euphoria" is yet to be assessed. "We do not know whether or not there are individuals with sufficient strength to take these drugs for growth or pleasure within the social order without increased and credulous alienation from it."

Luci's Little Monks On June 28, 1966, President Lyndon B. Johnson gave permission for air strikes against North Vietnamese oil storage facilities at Haiphong (see **Vietnam War**). According to a story leaked to the press the following May, the President so feared that he might have launched a new World War that he could not sleep that night. He confided his fears to his daughter Luci ("Your daddy may go down in history as having started World War III. You may not wake up tomorrow."), who suggested that they pray together in the capital's St. Dominic's church, which was run by an order she referred to as her "Little Monks." The President is said to have agreed.

"Lucy in the Sky with Diamonds" This 1968 Beatles song hit was thought by some to be an underground celebration of the joys and pleasures of the drug scene. It was pointed out that the initial letters of each noun in the title formed the acronym **LSD.**

Lunar Orbiters I–V The first of the series of unmanned spacecraft designed to orbit the moon and send back photos that could be used in selecting a landing site for **Project Apollo** was launched from Cape Kennedy on August 10, 1966, and—from altitudes as low as twenty-eight miles—photographed about 2 million square miles of the lunar surface. The craft (developed by the Boeing Company under the direction of Langley Aeronautical Laboratory) took ninety-two hours to reach orbit. In addition to cameras, it carried instruments capable of studying the shape and gravitational field of the moon and of making meteoroid and radiation measurements.

Lunar Orbiter II (November 6, 1966) provided wide-angle and telephoto coverage of an additional 1.5 million square miles not previously covered. Boeing received a more than $1 million "incentive" award for *Lunar Orbiter III* (February 4, 1967), which made it possible for the **National Aeronautics and Space Administration** (NASA) to announce the selection of eight possible sites for a manned Apollo landing on the surface of the moon. Some 99 percent of the moon's front surface was photographed by *Lunar Orbiter IV* (May 4, 1967), and the improved resolution of the telephoto lenses made for "a hundredfold increase in discernible detail." Earth-directed engine ignitions on June 5 and 8, 1967, made it possible to lower the apolune of the craft's orbit from 3,850 to 2,450 miles; the perilune was dropped from 1,625 to forty-eight miles, and the period decreased from five hours to forty-four minutes.

The final mission of the series, *Lunar Orbiter V* (August 1, 1967), rephotographed five potential moon-landing sites, obtained views of the remaining 40 percent of the hidden side of the moon, and provided scientists with glimpses of the "hot spots" of the Aristarchus Crater. It also made additional measurements of the moon's shape and gravitational field and provided more instrumental data on radiation.

The first manmade craft to orbit the moon was the U.S.S.R.'s *Luna X*, which was launched in April 1966.

Lyndonology Popular during the administration of President Lyndon B. Johnson (November 1963 to January 1969), the term Lyndonology was applied in Washington circles to the art, science, technique, or what have you connected with foreseeing what the President's reaction might be to any given situation. It was an obviously satirical echo of "Kremlinology," the supposed expertise in projecting policy or reaction by officials of Moscow's Kremlin, the political and administrative center of the Soviet Union.

M

McCarthyism

MAAG *See* **Military Assistance Advisory Group.**

M-Day *See* **Moratorium Day.**

MacBird Echoing Shakespeare's *Macbeth*, this blank verse political satire by Barbara Garson enjoyed a certain vogue among younger opponents of the Johnson administration in 1966. By turns biting and tasteless, it implied the involvement of President Lyndon B. Johnson in the assassination of his predecessor in office, President John F. Kennedy **(November 22, 1963).** Among those caricatured were President Johnson and his wife, Lady Bird (MacBird and Lady MacBird), former President Kennedy and his brothers Robert and Edward (Ken O'Dunc, Robert O'Dunc, and Teddy O'Dunc), Adlai Stevenson (The Egg of Head), Chief Justice Earl Warren (The Earl of Warren), and Defense Secretary Robert MacNamara (Lord MacNamara).

In retrospect, only the bitter feeling aroused by opposition to the **Vietnam War** can explain or excuse the enthusiasm aroused by this satire in critics who might have been presumed to know better. In rejecting the Johnson administration's Vietnam policy, the playwright also cast scorn on some of the President's nobler aspirations. Thus his moving **Great Society** speech of May 22, 1964, is parodied as follows:

"We have an opportunity to move/Not only toward the rich society,/But upwards toward the Smooth Society."

"Mack the Knife" This hit tune which swept the United States in the 1950s was originally introduced in Berlin (August 1928) as part of *Die Dreigroschenoper*, written by Kurt Weill and Bertolt Brecht. Called *Moritat*—from the German words *mord* (murder) and *tat* (dead)—it was modeled after the songs sung at German streetfairs to recount the deeds of arch criminals.

As "The Ballad of Mack the Knife," sung by Gerald Price, it became the hit song of Marc Blitzstein's *The Threepenny Opera*, a 1954 off-Broadway adaptation of the Weill-Brecht work which ran for over six years. The song was recorded in more than twenty different versions, among the more famous of which were those by Louis Armstrong (1957), Bobby Darin (1959), and Ella Fitzgerald (1960).

The ballad recounts the crimes of Macheath, a criminal in the London slums who is compared to a pearly-toothed shark. Unlike the latter, he keeps his weapon, a jackknife, well out of sight.

McCarran Act In an atmosphere of increasing legislative and public turmoil brought on by the **Alger Hiss Case,** the **Judith Coplon Case,** the **Amerasia Case,** and the arrest for espionage in Great Britain of Klaus Fuchs, who had contributed to the A-bomb project at Los Alamos, New Mexico, Congress passed on September 23, 1950, over President Harry S Truman's veto, an Internal Security Act sponsored by Senator Pat McCarran (D.-Nev.). Incorporating elements of a rival bill by Harley Kilgore (D.-W.Va.), the act required the registration of communist organizations and "front" groups with the Attorney General, forbade entry into the United States of anyone who belonged or had belonged to a totalitarian organization, and provided for the internment of such people in the event of national emergencies. Such was the atmosphere that even liberal Senator Paul Douglas (D.-Ill.) said: "I had pictured myself as defending civil liberties, and yet there is a Communist danger in this country."

While membership in a communist organization as such was not made illegal, it was criminal to contribute to the establishment of totalitarianism in the United States. Communists were denied passports and the right to work in establishments contributing to national defense.

In vetoing the bill, President Truman specifically objected to the following:

1. It would aid potential enemies by requiring the publication of a complete list of vital defense plants, laboratories, and other installations.

2. It would require the Department of Justice and its Federal Bureau of Investigation to waste immense amounts of time and energy attempting to carry out its unworkable registration provisions.

3. It would deprive us of the great assistance of many aliens in intelligence matters.

4. It would antagonize friendly governments.

5. It would put the government of the United States in the thought-control business.

6. It would make it easier for subversive aliens to become naturalized as United States citizens.

7. It would give government officials vast powers to harass all of our citizens in the exercise of their right of free speech.

He stressed that though the danger of subversion was present, "we already have on the books strong laws which give us most of the protection we need from the real dangers of treason, espionage, sabotage, and actions looking to the overthrow of our government by force and violence." Most of the McCarran Act provisions had no relation to these dangers, said the President.

The Internal Security Act of 1950 was amended on March 28, 1951, to make it possible for those who had joined totalitarian organizations to protect their livelihood, or those who had been coerced into such organizations when under sixteen, to enter this country.

The original McCarran Act incorporated elements of the Mundt-Nixon Bill on subversive activities which had been introduced by Rep. Richard M. Nixon (R.-Calif.) in 1948 but had failed to pass Congress.

McCarran-Walter Immigration and Nationality Act
Like the **McCarran Act,** this legislation was passed by Congress (June 1952) over President Harry S Truman's veto. Under it, although Asiatic nations were now granted an annual quota of 100 (previously, all immigration from these countries had been forbidden), existing legislation was codified on the basis of the 1924 quota system, which reflected the 1920 census. In addition, the Attorney General was empowered to deport aliens and naturalized citizens who engaged in what was vaguely described as activities "prejudicial to the public interest."

In his veto message to Congress, President Truman pointed out the inequities of a quota system which, in effect, said "that Americans with English or Irish names were better people and better citizens than Americans with Italian or Greek or Polish names." He noted the political insanity of entering into a **North Atlantic Treaty Alliance** (NATO) with Italy, Greece, and Turkey while at the same time discouraging immigration from those shores as undesirable. He argued that it was both unnecessary and inhumane to be "protecting ourselves, as we were in 1924, against being flooded by immigrants from Eastern Europe" at a time when communist repression in those nations had seen to it that "no one passes their borders but at the risk of his life." In commenting on the security provisions, he said that they would "restrict or eliminate judicial review of unlawful administrative action."

In 1965, the Immigration and Nationalization Act in effect eliminated the national-origins quota system.

McCarthyism In the years 1950 to 1955 the American political scene seemed dominated by Sen. Joseph R. McCarthy (R.-Wis.), whose reckless charges of subversion in government succeeded in creating an anticommunist hysteria that paralyzed government procedures, threatened traditional civil liberties, and, paradoxically, made it increasingly

difficult to deal realistically with the growing Soviet challenge to western democracy.

On February 6, 1950, the Republican National Committee proclaimed that the major domestic issue of that year's congressional elections would be "Liberty Against Socialism." "We advocate a strong policy against the spread of communism or fascism at home and abroad, and we insist that America's efforts toward this end be directed by those who have no sympathy either with communism or fascism." Three days later, speaking in Wheeling, West Virginia, Senator McCarthy launched the era that was to bear his name. (The term is said to have been originated by *Washington Post* cartoonist Herbert Block, who later drew a reluctant GOP elephant being pushed by Sen. Robert A. Taft (R.-Ohio) and other Republican leaders toward a large barrel of tar labeled "McCarthyism.")

McCarthy's talk—based at least in part on remarks delivered in the House (January 26, 1950) by Rep. Richard M. Nixon (R.-Calif.)—has been variously reported. According to some present, its most famous passage was as follows:

> While I cannot take the time to name all the men in the State Department who have been named as members of the Communist Party and members of a spy ring, I have here in my hand a list of 205 that were known to the Secretary of State [Dean Acheson] as being members of the Communist Party and are still working and shaping the policy of the State Department.

Senator McCarthy—who could not subsequently find the "list"—later said he had spoken not of communists but of "bad security risks." As read in the Senate on February 20, the Wheeling speech on "Communists in Government"—which had been followed up by a telegram asking President Harry S Truman to furnish Congress with a list of all State Department employees considered security risks—was as follows: "I have in my hand fifty-seven cases of individuals who would appear to be either card-carrying members or certainly loyal to the Communist Party, but who nevertheless are still helping to shape our foreign policy." The number was subsequently altered to eighty-one.

Hearings by a subcommittee of the Senate Committee on Foreign Relations (see **Tydings Committee**) were begun on March 8, 1950, to investigate the charges of the senator, who proved unable to come up with the name of a single member of the State Department who was a communist. Dr. Owen Lattimore, director of the Johns Hopkins School of International Relations and a sometime State Department consultant, was cleared by the committee after McCarthy had charged that he was "the top Russian espionage agent" in the United States. A majority report—issued by the Tydings Committee in July 1950 and denounced in advance by McCarthy—called the charges against the State Department part of "the most nefarious campaign of half-truths and untruth in the history of the Republic."

Nevertheless, McCarthyism attracted support from conservative elements at a time when the country was shaken by the revelations of espionage in the **Coplon Case** and the **Rosenberg Case,** and by the perjury conviction earlier in 1950 of Alger Hiss (*see* **Alger Hiss Case**). The following year, Senator Tydings's clash with McCarthy was to cost him a Senate seat he had held since 1927.

In his no-holds-barred attack on the Truman administration, McCarthy had attracted support from Republican leaders such as Guy Gabrielson, chairman of the Republican National Committee, and Senators Robert A. Taft, Kenneth Wherry, and Styles Bridges. However, his irresponsible charges were deplored by Maine's Senator Margaret Chase Smith, who in June 1950 joined with six other Republican Senators in issuing a **"Declaration of Conscience"** which condemned McCarthy tactics without mentioning McCarthy by name.

On June 14, 1951, McCarthy denounced World War II hero General George C. Marshall, former Secretary of State and architect of the **Marshall Plan** and the Truman administration's Far East policy, as having taken part in a conspiracy directed "to the end that we shall be contained, frustrated, and finally fall victim to Soviet intrigue from within and Russian military might from without." In a nationwide radio and television broadcast (October 27, 1952) he tried to link Democratic presidential candidate Adlai Stevenson with Alger Hiss when he referred to the former as "Alger—I mean Adlai."

The congressional reorganization following the Republican victory at the polls that swept President Dwight D. Eisenhower into office in November 1952 made McCarthy chairman of the Senate Permanent Investigating Subcommittee of the Government Operations Committee. From this vantage point he continued his reckless "investigation" of communism, ruthlessly savaging the reputations of persons connected with the State Department and the **Voice of America** (VOA). Serving on the subcommittee as chief counsel and an unpaid consultant were, respectively, McCarthy's protégé Roy Cohn and the latter's friend, G. David Schine. In April 1953 they made an eighteen-day whirlwind

tour of American information centers in Western Europe, and subcommittee hearings on subversive literature in American libraries abroad soon followed. On State Department orders there was a purge of "all books and other material by Communists, fellow travelers, *et cetera*" from these centers. Not content with merely removing "suspect" books, many librarians burned them. When news of this reached President Eisenhower, he denounced the "book burners" in a speech at Dartmouth College (June 14, 1953). On July 29, 1953, Robert F. Kennedy, who for seven months had served as assistant counsel for the McCarthy subcommittee, resigned in what he later said was a protest against the investigatory methods of Cohn and Schine, who were described by critics as "junketeering gumshoes." ("I thought Senator McCarthy made a mistake in allowing the committee to operate in such a fashion, told him so and resigned.")

Beginning in December 1953, McCarthy turned his attention to the Department of the Army and, in January 1954, focused attention on the case of Major Irving Peress, who received both a promotion and an honorable discharge although he had refused to testify before the subcommittee on the grounds of possible self-incrimination. Called before the subcommittee to explain why Major Peress had not instead received a dishonorable discharge, Brigadier General Ralph Zwicker was denounced by McCarthy as "a disgrace to the uniform" and accused of "shielding Communist conspirators."

On February 4, 1954, speaking in Charleston, West Virginia, McCarthy described the years of Democratic administration under Presidents Roosevelt and Truman as "twenty years of treason." Probably the most famous broadcast of Edward R. Murrow's popular **"See It Now"** television program was the one on March 9, 1954, which spotlighted the threat to civil liberties posed by McCarthy and his subcommittee. It is often seen as a turning point in the senator's increasingly reckless career, which had begun to strain relations even with his own party.

From April 22 to June 17, 1954, McCarthy himself was the subject of investigations by his own subcommittee—whose chairman pro-tem was Sen. Karl E. Mundt (R.-S.Dak.)—when charges were brought by Secretary of the Army Robert T. Stevens that McCarthy had tried to obtain preferential treatment for his former consultant, G. David Schine, who had in the interval been inducted into the army. McCarthy, in turn, charged that the Army was holding Schine as a "hostage" to force him into calling off an investigation of Signal Corps operations at Fort Monmouth, New Jersey.

The thirty-six days of televised hearings exposed McCarthy's investigatory techniques to the nation as the senator was subjected to skillful questioning by Special Army Counsel Joseph N. Welch. When the angered senator struck back by trying to ruin the reputation and career of Frederick G. Fisher, Jr., a youthful member of the Boston law firm to which Welch belonged, the nation was shocked. (In a famous and emotional reply, Welch said: "Have you no sense of decency, sir, at last?") McCarthy added a catch-phrase to the language when he constantly kept interrupting the proceedings for what he called "a point of order." Although the majority report of the subcommittee exonerated McCarthy from charges of having personally exercised improper influence on Schine's behalf, it noted his failure to exercise "more vigorous" discipline over his staff. After the hearings, Roy Cohn resigned as counsel and Francis Carr as staff director of the subcommittee. (McCarthy lost his chairmanship after the 1954 elections caused a reorganization of Congress.)

The tide had definitively turned against McCarthyism. On May 31, 1954, President Eisenhower had spoken out against "demagogues thirsty for personal power and public notice." Early in August charges against McCarthy for abuse of power were brought before the Senate by Sen. Wayne Morse (Independent-Oreg.), Sen. J. William Fulbright (D.-Ark.), and Sen. Ralph E. Flanders (R.-Vt.). These charges resulted in public but nontelevised hearings (August 31 to September 13, 1954) by a six-man committee chaired by Sen. Arthur R. Watkins (R.-Utah). The Watkins Committee—referred to by McCarthy as a "lynch committee"—recommended formal "censure" of McCarthy. On December 2, 1954, the Senate voted (sixty-seven to twenty-two) to "condemn" its Wisconsin colleague on a variety of counts, including contempt toward a Senate Subcommittee on Privileges and Elections investigating his campaign finances and tactics. The vote marked an end to McCarthyism, and the senator himself died on May 2, 1957, at the age of forty-eight.

McClellan Committee Following the disclosure of corrupt labor practices by the Permanent Investigations Subcommittee then chaired by Sen. John L. McClellan (D.-Ark.), the Senate established a special investigating committee on labor rackets. It drew on the McClellan subcommittee and the Senate Labor Committee. Senator McClellan served as chairman and Robert F. Kennedy as chief counsel; Sen. John F. Kennedy (D.-Mass.), chairman of the Senate Labor Committee's Subcommittee on Labor Legislation, was asked to join.

The focus of what is sometimes called the Labor-Rackets Committee was the International Brotherhood of Teamsters, which was led by David Beck and was undoubtedly the nation's most powerful labor aggregation. Testimony revealed the blatant misuse of union funds, extortion, rigged union elections, the widespread use of violence and terror, association with racketeers, and the connivance of union officials with management to set up fake unions, phony welfare funds, and so-called sweetheart contracts designed "to keep wages low and unions out."

On May 2, 1957, Beck was indicted for income tax evasion; shortly afterward he was removed from executive positions within the AFL-CIO when it was found that he had made use of union funds for personal profit. Convicted of embezzlement in December of that year, he was succeeded by his lieutenant, James R. Hoffa. Because of its domination by corrupt leaders—Hoffa was also to be charged with misappropriation of funds and close underworld connections—the Teamsters Union was expelled from the AFL-CIO.

The McClellan Committee hearings were to lead to the **Welfare and Pension Fund Disclosure Act** (1958), requiring detailed disclosure of all employee welfare and pension plans, and the **Landrum-Griffin Act** (1959), which placed new restrictions upon labor's power by broadening aspects of the **Taft-Hartley Act** (1947).

McCollum v. Board of Education *See* "Released time."

McCone Report *See* **Watts Riots.**

McKay Commission *See* **Attica.**

McMahon Act President Harry S Truman felt strongly that atomic energy should be under civilian control and that "the government should have a monopoly of materials, facilities, and processes." On December 20, 1945, Sen. Brien McMahon (D.-Conn.) introduced into Congress S. 1717, which contained this approach and on August 1, 1946, became the Atomic Energy Act of 1946. Under its provisions full control over nuclear fission materials, production, research, and information was transferred from the War Department to a five-man civilian Atomic Energy Commission (AEC) which was to be appointed by the President with the approval and confirmation of the Senate. On November 1, 1946, David E. Lilienthal was sworn in as the first AEC chairman.

See **Atomic Energy Commission.**

McNamara's War As Secretary of Defense during the Kennedy administration, Robert S. McNamara's enthusiasm for a vigorous prosecution of the **Vietnam War** was such that it became fashionable in Washington circles to refer to it as "McNamara's War." Although he was sometimes described as a man who was "frequently in error but never in doubt," McNamara evidently had second thoughts about American involvement in Indochina. It was his desire to know how this country had been trapped—or trapped itself—in an untenable situation that led him, shortly before he left office during the Johnson administration, to order the research that led to the **Pentagon Papers.**

McNamara-Taylor Mission Deteriorating relations with the government of South Vietnam's President Ngo Din Diem, growing disunity in the non-Communist camp in Saigon, and the need for a new appraisal in the progress being made in the **Vietnam War** caused President John F. Kennedy to dispatch Defense Secretary Robert S. McNamara to that area late in September 1963. He was accompanied by the President's military advisor, General Maxwell Taylor.

A statement on the nonclassified sections of their report was made public by the White House on October 2, 1963. It noted that the United States would adhere to its policy of working with the "people and Government" of South Vietnam, whose security was a "major interest of the United States and other free nations." The military program was seen as making progress "and sound in principle, though improvements are being energetically sought."

"Secretary McNamara and General Taylor reported their judgment that the major part of the U.S. military task can be completed by the end of 1965" and that by the end of 1963 the United States program for training South Vietnamese "should have" progressed to the point where 1,000 American military personnel could be withdrawn from Vietnam. (According to Department of Defense figures, the number of U.S. troops in Vietnam went from 11,300 in 1962 to 16,300 by December 31, 1963. The following year it jumped to 23,300 and by the end of 1968 it had reached 536,100.)

The earlier **Taylor-Rostow Mission** had called for the institution of democratic and political reforms by the Diem government, but now, two years later, the new report noted that the political situation remained deeply serious and that our government had "made clear its continuing opposition to any repressive actions" in South Vietnam. "While such actions have not yet significantly affected the military effort, they could do so in the future."

In November 1963 the Diem government was overthrown by a military coup. President Diem and his brother Ngo Dinh Nhu were assassinated. Within the next year and a half there were ten successive governments in South Vietnam.

Magnet Schools An attempt made in some Northern cities to achieve racial integration in the school system by creating special programs that would attract students to schools located in black enclaves. The program originated in Detroit in 1971 with eight "magnets" for grades five through eight. In 1975 the president of the city's school board charged that these schools had become "white havens," and that their success was mostly due to the fact that white pupils had largely abandoned schools in other areas of Detroit to take advantage of the smaller classes and more stimulating curriculum offered. Despite this initial result, the board included in its recommendations to the federal court charged with the desegregation of Detroit schools a proposal to continue and expand the experiment.

In many cities, strict racial quotas are enforced. For example, in the twenty-two magnet schools scheduled to open in Boston in the fall of 1975, the breakdown was to be 52 percent white, 36 percent black, and 12 percent other minorities, figures that were said to reflect the city's total public school enrollment.

MANIAC Acronym for the Mathematical Analyzer, Numerical Integrator and Computer developed by Los Alamos scientist John von Neumann, MANIAC was instrumental in the perfection of the H-bomb tested in the Marshall Islands on November 1, 1952. Capable of completing within twenty-four hours computations that would otherwise have required three months, MANIAC accelerated the search for what Neumann thought of as "the hell weapon." The new computer could retain 40,000 data entries—unusual at the time. It was not until the device had been patented and gone into use that its inventor realized that the initial letters in its name combined unfortunately.

Manila Conference On the joint invitation of President Ferdinand Marcos of the Philippines, President Chung Hee Park of South Korea, and Prime Minister Thanom Kittikachorn of Thailand, the heads of those nations that had troops fighting against the communists in the **Vietnam War** met in Manila on October 24–25, 1966. The "guests" included General Nguyen Van Thieu and Prime Minister Nguyen Cao Ky of South Vietnam, Prime Minister Harold Holt of Australia, Prime Minister Keith Holyoake of New Zealand, and President Lyndon B. Johnson.

As a result of this conference, three statements were issued. The first, **Declaration of Goals of Freedom,** declared that the purpose of the seven nations meeting in Manila was to unite in seeking "the goals of freedom in Vietnam and in the Asian and Pacific areas." These goals were defined as freedom from aggression; the conquest of hunger, illiteracy, and disease; the building of regional order, security, and progress; and the search for reconciliation and peace throughout Asia and the Pacific.

The second document, which took the form of a communiqué from the South Vietnamese government, called on that country's allies to withdraw as soon as peace had been restored, and these nations promised to do so "after close consultation, as the other side withdraws its forces to the North, ceases infiltration, and the level of violence thus subsides."

The third document was a Declaration of Peace and Progress in Asia and the Pacific. It emphasized that the seven signatories were united not only in fighting aggression but in establishing programs that would deal with poverty, illiteracy, and disease and seek an "environment in which reconciliation becomes possible. . . ."

In reviewing the current war situation, General William C. Westmoreland, Commander of U.S. Forces in Vietnam, who had accompanied President Johnson to Manila, noted that despite the fact that there were 370,000 U.S. and allied troops supporting them, "the major burden of the war is still being borne" by South Vietnamese troops, of whom more than 114,000 had been killed or were missing in battle since the beginning of the year. Allied losses were set at 4,000. He emphasized that allied "successes" were being hampered by a "war of assassination and terror" in which government officials were killed or kidnapped.

Manila Pact *See* **Southeast Asia Treaty Organization.**

The Man in the Gray Flannel Suit The title of this 1955 best-selling novel by Sloan Wilson became a descriptive term for the American businessman at midcentury. The hero is an up-and-coming corporate executive who rejects the pressures of that life for the comforts of family and life in the suburbs.

Wilson reports that while working for *Time* he was advised to buy himself a gray flannel suit at Brooks Brothers—"charcoal gray . . . little things like that are important around here." When he complained that he could not afford one, he was told to go the boys' department: "They have clothes for boys of all sizes."

Wilson originally intended to call the book *A Candle at Midnight*, but the final title was urged on him by his wife and enthusiastically endorsed by his publisher, who reported that on a commuter train from Bronxville to Manhattan he had counted eighty men in gray flannel suits one morning. "It's a uniform for a certain kind of man. . . ."

Twenty years after the publication of his novel, Sloan Wilson wrote: "The men in the gray flannel suits, now in their fifties, still look pretty good when you see them on the commuting trains. Some of them will stand up to give a lady a seat, and they will open doors for ladies when they are walking from one car to another. When called a male chauvinist pig, a man in gray flannel looks confused. He is supporting a wife, a former wife, maybe a mistress and three daughters in college. On weekends he also does the dinner dishes. What more do women expect of him?"

Manpower Development and Training Act (MDTA) Of the fifty-four major Kennedy administration recommendations for legislation in 1962, forty were enacted into law. Among these was the Manpower Development and Training Act (MDTA) (March 15, 1962), which like the **Area Redevelopment Act** (ARA) that had preceded it the year before, stressed programs aimed at the training or retraining of the unemployed to give them marketable skills. Under the new legislation the Department of Labor was directed to study the effects of technological changes such as automation on manpower requirements and then to recommend ways of training young people and adults in required skills. The act provided in-school and on-the-job training programs administered by the Office of Education.

Further attempts to deal with the problem of hard-core unemployment were made with the passage under the Johnson administration of the Economic Opportunity Act of 1964, which established the **Job Corps** to provide training and work experience for young people from poverty backgrounds. A major expansion of manpower training took place in 1968 when President Lyndon B. Johnson asked Congress to provide increased funds for job training for the chronically unemployed. The result was the creation of **Job Opportunities in the Business Sector** (JOBS), under which cooperating employers in the private sector received direct federal subsidies to defray the "extra costs" involved.

See **Comprehensive Employment and Training Act.**

Manpower Drag Theory By the beginning of 1961, the first year of President John F. Kennedy's administration, unemployment in the United States had reached 8.1 percent of the labor force. Economists attempting to analyze and ameliorate the situation divided roughly into those who preferred either structural or fiscal approaches to the problem.

Among those belonging to the structural school were Professor Charles Killingsworth of Michigan State University and Sweden's Gunnar Myrdal (see **An American Dilemma**). They argued that part of this unemployment was due to structural changes in the economy, i.e., automation, which created a lag in the availability of skilled labor which might be in surplus in some areas of the country and in short supply in others. It was felt that this "manpower drag" could be handled only through education, better labor exchanges, area redevelopment, and the retraining of part of the labor force.

Opposed to this view were economists of the fiscal school, who located the source of growing unemployment in insufficient aggregate demand. Representative of this approach was the "fiscal drag theory" of economist Walter Heller of the University of Minnesota. In this view the loss of purchasing power caused by high tax rates could be made up for by government monetary and fiscal policies. They were, as Arthur Schlesinger, Jr., pointed out, similar to the Keynesian economists of the Second New Deal (see **Keynesianism**), who proposed to end the Depression through deficit spending. The structuralists, on the other hand, resembled those "institutionalists" of the early days of the New Deal, who urged that the economy could be restored only through a reorganization of the nation's social structure.

Manson Family *See* "The Family."

"Mantra" *See* **Transcendental Meditation.**

Mapp v. Ohio Overturning a 1949 decision in *Wolf v. Colorado*, the U.S. Supreme Court ruled on June 19, 1961, that "all evidence obtained by searches and seizures in violation of the Constitution is, by that same authority, inadmissible in a state court."

The case before the Court dealt with the 1957 conviction of Dollree Mapp, a Cleveland boarding house owner, who had been convicted under Ohio law for the possession of obscene literature. Looking for gambling equipment, the police had raided the Mapp house without a search warrant, but had instead found pornographic materials.

In the five to four majority decision written by Justice Tom C. Clark, the Court held that the admission of illegal evidence—at the time permitted by twenty-four states—was an "ignoble shortcut to conviction" that encouraged disobedience to the Constitution. Justice Potter Stewart did not deal with the same constitutional issue that was the basis of the majority decision, but he agreed with the reversal of the conviction—which had been upheld by the Ohio Supreme Court—by finding that the Ohio obscenity law under which it was obtained was itself unconstitutional.

March on Washington To dramatize black demands for jobs and civil rights, more than 200,000 Negroes and an estimated 60,000 white sympathizers came from all over the country and assembled in the nation's capital on August 28, 1963. The demonstrators, who included about 200 Protestant, Catholic, and Jewish religious leaders, gathered at the Washington Monument, and as they waited for the march to begin they were entertained by some of the nation's leading celebrities, including folk singer Joan Baez, singer Harry Belafonte, actor Marlon Brando, singer Odetta, former baseball player Jackie Robinson, and actor Paul Newman. Meanwhile, a thirteen-man delegation called on leading congressional figures to present their case.

The march itself moved in orderly fashion along both Constitution Avenue and Independence Avenue to the Lincoln Memorial, where the demonstrators waited while a delegation called on President John F. Kennedy. Those received by the President included A. Philip Randolph, director of the march and president of the Brotherhood of Sleeping Car Porters; Reverend Martin Luther King, Jr., president of the **Southern Christian Leadership Conference** (SCLC); Roy Wilkins, executive secretary of the NAACP; Whitney M. Young, Jr., executive director of the National Urban League; Walter P. Reuther, president of the United Automobile Workers; Reverend Eugene Carson Blake, of the United Presbyterian Church; Rabbi Joachim Prinz, chairman of the American Jewish Congress; John Lewis, chairman of the **Student Nonviolent Coordinating Committee** (SNCC); Matthew Ahmann, executive director of the National Catholic Conference for Interracial Justice; and Floyd B. McKissick, national chairman of the **Congress of Racial Equality** (CORE), standing in for the organization's president, James Farmer, who was jailed in Louisiana as the result of a civil rights demonstration.

Following the meeting with the President, the delegation returned to the Lincoln Memorial and members addressed the waiting crowd.

It was on this occasion that Dr. King made his moving **"I have a dream"** speech ending with the stirring **"Free at last"** vision. Once the speeches were over, the crowd dispersed with a speed and order that emphasized the stressed nonviolent nature of the demonstration. There were no clashes with law enforcement authorities by marchers; the only arrests made involved four men who attempted to interfere with the demonstration.

President Kennedy later said that "the cause of 20 million Negroes has been advanced by the program conducted so appropriately before the nation's shrine to the Great Emancipator," and he praised the dignified and peaceful comportment of those involved.

Marcusean Revolution "Marcuse is one of those utopian madmen," complained anthropologist Konrad Lorenz, "who believe that it's possible to build from the ground up. He believes that if everything is destroyed, everything automatically regrows. It's a terrifying error. Marcuse does not really understand the mechanisms by which evolution and culture work in tandem and complement one another—nor did Karl Marx and Engels understand these mechanisms."

Along with Mao Tse-tung and Karl Marx, German-born philosopher Herbert Marcuse formed the intellectual trinity of the **New Left,** and his *One Dimensional Man* (1965) was a campus favorite both here and abroad during the turbulent 1960s. The focus of his criticism was the United States, in which he saw the material comfort of life militating against qualitative change. Modern industrial civilization, he argued, had depersonalized life so that "people recognize themselves in their commodities; they find their soul in their automobile, hi-fi set, split-level home, kitchen equipment." The traditional channels of protest are therefore blocked by

a "state of anesthesia" that prevents us from becoming aware of what we could be. Even the so-called sexual and pornographic revolution, he felt, prevented essential change by "desublimating" tensions that lead to protest. By absorbing opposition, the United States dissipates resistance and conditions us to be "one dimensional"—unable to reason dialectically and therefore content to be less than we might or could be. "The goods and services that the individuals buy, control their needs and petrify their faculties. They have innumerable gadgets that keep them occupied and divert their attention from the real issue—which is the awareness that they could both work less and determine their own needs and satisfactions."

As long as people can be controlled by "a non-terroristic economic-technological coordination which operates through the manipulation of needs by vested interests," they cannot be trusted to know their own minds. As a result, the workers who were the traditional opposition to the capitalist state are not only unrevolutionary but antirevolutionary—and indeed both workers and owner-managers are reduced to tools in the hands of a technology run riot. Given this situation, Marcuse argued, violent revolution is the sole way in which man can rid himself of an oppressive structure and discover the potentialities of freedom.

Critics saw in his distrust of an individual's ability to evaluate his own situation the seeds of the elitism that marked radical groups in the 1960s; Marcuse's emphasis on "selective tolerance" was viewed as mere intolerance of other points of view.

Of a somewhat less pessimistic hue is his *An Essay on Liberation* (1968), which conceded the possibility of change in those who turned their backs on the mainstream of American culture, abandoning "plastic cleanliness," allowing their hatred to burst "into laughter and song, mixing the barricades and the dance floor, love play and heroism."

Marcuse teaches on the San Diego campus of the University of California, where one of his students and disciples was Angela Davis (see **Angela Davis Trial**).

Marigold Code name assigned to secret negotiations in 1966 designed to bring the **Vietnam War** to an end.

U.S. Ambassador Henry Cabot Lodge had been approached in the summer of that year by Janusz Lewandowski, the Polish member of the International Control Commission, after Lewandowski returned to Saigon from a visit to Hanoi. On the basis of their talks, the Polish diplomat drafted ten points covering the American position on peace talks. This draft—which indicated President Lyndon B. Johnson's willingness to stop all bombing *after* agreement on de-escalation had been reached—was supposedly conveyed to Hanoi, and arrangements were then to be made for exchanges between the American and North Vietnamese representatives. However, the North Vietnamese failed to show up for a Warsaw meeting set for December 6, 1966. The excuse given by the Poles was that the United States had bombed targets near Hanoi only two days before.

After six months of secret exchanges through Lewandowski, President Johnson decided that "this channel was a dry creek." The assumption was that Marigold had been planned by the Poles in an effort to draw up a peace plan acceptable to this country and then try to get the North Vietnamese to agree to it as a basis for negotiations.

Mariner Space Probes Hailed as "a technological feat of the first magnitude," the launching of *Mariner 2* on August 22, 1962, provided American scientists with basic information about Venus's temperature and cloud cover when on December 14—after 109 days—the space probe passed within 21,600 miles of that planet and transmitted data for forty-two minutes. After having been launched from earth and then from a "parking" orbit around earth, the *Mariner 2* was placed in a solar orbit on the ninth day, when it had already traveled 1.5 million miles. It was able to recover its proper orientation with respect to the sun and earth even after being struck by an object in space.

Mariner 4 was launched from Cape Kennedy toward Mars on November 28, 1964, and when on July 15, 1965, it passed from 7,000 to 10,500 miles above the planet it relayed twenty-one photos to earth. *Mariner 5*, launched on June 14, 1967, passed behind Venus on October 19, 1967, and transmitted data to earth. *Mariners 6* and *7* were launched in February and March of 1967; each carried a TV camera which on July 31 and August 5, respectively, transmitted "close-ups" (from about 2,130 miles) of the surface of Mars. *Mariner 9*, launched on May 30, 1971, went into orbit around Mars on November 13, 1971.

Marshall Plan "We had sent food to Europe, but millions there still did not have enough to eat. We had made loans to the countries of Europe, but the war had so disrupted the patterns of trade and industry there that the amounts we loaned were far less effective than we had hoped. . . ."

It was with these words that President Harry S Truman later introduced a discussion of the events that led to the European Recovery Plan, popularly known as the Marshall Plan.

Reporting to the President in April 1947, on the Moscow conference of foreign ministers, Secretary of State George C. Marshall argued that the Soviet Union was determined to exploit Europe's postwar economic collapse. Western Europe's economic problems, he emphasized, had to be tackled as a whole if American aid was to encourage recovery. The President also believed in a unified and cooperative approach, and the result was a plan first enunciated by Under Secretary of State Dean Acheson in Cleveland, Mississippi, on May 8, 1947. American security, Acheson argued, was linked to the reconstruction of Europe, which could not be dealt with on a piecemeal basis.

As finally worked out, the European Recovery Plan was first announced by Secretary Marshall in a speech at Harvard University on June 5, 1947. It was logical, he noted, that this country should do what it could to bring about a return to normal economic health in the world, as without it there could be neither political stability nor peace.

It is already evident that, before the United States Government can proceed much further in its efforts to alleviate the situation and help start the European world on its way to recovery, there must be some agreement among the countries of Europe as to the requirement of the situation and the part those countries themselves will take in order to give proper effect to whatever action might be undertaken by the government. It would be neither fitting nor efficacious for this government to undertake to draw up unilaterally a program designed to place Europe on its feet economically. This is the business of Europeans. The initiative, I think, must come from Europe. The role of this country should consist of friendly aid in the drafting of a European program and of later support of such a program so far as it may be practical for us to do so.

To organize procedures for receiving and allocating American aid, Great Britain and France invited twenty-two nations to meet in Paris, but only sixteen western countries eventually participated. The Soviet bloc, including an anguished Czechoslovakia, soon withdrew.

The resulting Marshall Plan Conference (July 12) set up a Committee of European Economic Cooperation which eventually called for up to $22 billion in U.S. aid. In December, President Truman asked Congress for $17 billion, and Congress responded in April 1948 with an immediate $5.3 billion. By 1961 foreign aid had totaled $80 billion.

Soviet critics such as Foreign Minister Vyacheslav Molotov and UN representative Andrei Vishinsky denounced that plan as an attempt to interfere with the internal affairs of European countries and a smoke screen behind which American "capitalist monopolies" could protect and advance their interests. American conservatives denounced the plan as placing a heavy burden on the U.S. taxpayer and as supporting European socialist governments. In addition, European critics chafing under what they saw as the insufficiencies, restrictions, and limitations of the Marshall Plan took to referring to the United States as "Uncle Shylock." American critics of the plan on the left and right dubbed it the "Martial Plan" or the "Share-the-American-Wealth Plan."

Martha Movement Founded in May 1976, by Mrs. Jinx Melia, its basic purpose is to give a "voice" to the estimated 60 million American women whose prime self-identification is as housewives or homemakers. Its headquarters is in Arlington, Virginia, the Melias' home; and it is said to include 6,500 members organized into seventy-five chapters spread through all fifty states.

The movement takes its name from the biblical Martha, who in Luke 10 invites Jesus into the home she shares with her sister, Mary. While Martha attends to the household chores, Mary sits at the feet of Jesus and listens to his teachings and philosophy. When Martha complains of this and asks for Mary's help in completing the household tasks, Jesus suggests that Mary has chosen the better role.

"Martha Matters" is the organization's motto, and one of its leaflets argues that "we feel that most of today's attention is to the Marys, with Martha continuing unrecognized."

The Martha Movement is not antifeminist—it considers the feminist movement as the most significant social movement of the 1970s—but it has been hotly criticized for failing to take a position on both abortion and the **Equal Rights Amendment** (ERA). "Mary's out in the world, Martha's at home," insists Mrs. Melia.

"Mary Hartman, Mary Hartman" (M²H²) Although viewers were never sure whether this syndicated program was soap opera or a spoof of soap opera, "Mary Hartman, Mary Hartman" (M²H²) was successfully featured on some 100 stations around the country during 1976. Written and produced by Norman Lear, who had made the nation laugh at bigots and bigotry in the initially controversial **"All in the Family,"** M²H² dealt with such daring sex-oriented situations as impotence, adultery, homosexuality, and "flashing" in a lower middle-class community. The program made a star of Louise Lasser, who played the title role, but the series ended in summer 1977 because the strain of five one-hour shows a week was too great on all concerned.

"The Mary Tyler Moore Show" Television comedy which was the cornerstone of the CBS Saturday night lineup from 1970 to 1977. Miss Moore starred as an unmarried young woman trying to build a career as a member of a small Minneapolis television station. Scenes focusing on her social life largely took place in her apartment, which was constantly being visited by neighbors such as Rhoda and Phyllis (Valerie Harper and Cloris Leachman), who were eventually starred in spin-off programs of their own.

Masscult and Midcult The terms were popularized by critic and social observer Dwight Macdonald, who used them as the title of an essay which appeared in *Partisan Review* in 1960. He noted that ever since the Industrial Revolution there have been two kinds of culture: the traditional variety—which he called High Culture—and "a novel kind that is manufactured for the market." Labeling the latter Masscult, he noted that in essence it was a parody of High Culture. Examples in literature were the works of Edna Ferber, Fannie Hurst, Eugene Burdick, Alan Drury, James Michener, and Leon Uris. As a prime example in art, he chose the late Norman Rockwell, whose works were said to echo earlier academics such as Rosa Bonheur and Adolph William Bourguereau; as an example in thought he pointed to Norman Vincent Peale, the popular Protestant minister and author of the 1952 bestseller, *The Power of Positive Thinking.*

According to MacDonald, the productions of Masscult in literature, art, and "philosophy" were not merely bad but without any innate possibility of ever having been good.

Midcult was seen as essentially middlebrow culture which used the techniques of High Culture and had pretentions to its standards. As examples in literature, MacDonald cited Ernest Hemingway's novel *The Old Man and the Sea*, Archibald MacLeish's verse drama *J.B.*, Thornton Wilder's play *Our Town*, and Stephen Vincent Benét's epic poem *John Brown's Body*. Midcult, noted MacDonald, was in many ways more insidious than Masscult.

A prime target of MacDonald and those who adopted his terms was President Lyndon B. Johnson, whose admiration for television programs such as *Gunsmoke* and whose rejection of Peter Hurd's portrait of him seemed to infuriate the intellectual establishment.

Massive Resistance Among the leaders of Southern defiance of the 1954 U.S. Supreme Court school desegregation decision in **Brown v. Board of Education of Topeka** was Virginia's Democratic Senator Harry Flood Byrd. There seems little doubt that his stance influenced Governor Thomas B. Stanley, who reversed an originally mild response to the desegregation ruling and announced that he would use "every legal means" to combat it.

An amendment proposed by Governor Stanley to the Virginia constitution would have permitted state tuition grants to children in private schools. In essence, this meant that it would become more economically feasible for white parents to withdraw their children from desegregated public schools. This "moderate" program—approved by Virginia voters in 1956—seemed a completely inadequate response to Senator Byrd, who led a demand for "massive resistance" in the form of laws that would mandate the automatic closing of any desegregated school.

Massive Retaliation Speaking in January 1954, Secretary of State John Foster Dulles noted that "Local defense will always be important. But there is no local defense which alone will contain the mighty land power of the Communist world. Local defenses must be reinforced by the further deterrent of massive retaliatory power. A potential aggressor must know that he cannot always prescribe battle conditions that suit him."

President Dwight D. Eisenhower felt strongly that the United States could not long survive the expense of trying to meet communist threats around the globe if it had to maintain both large conventional forces and nuclear deterrents. From a budgetary point of view, he considered it a more sensible approach to concentrate on building a stockpile of nuclear weapons, the existence of which alone would be sufficient to discourage potential Soviet aggression. In this approach to fiscal responsibility, even though it held the threat of nuclear holocaust, he was probably supported by Secretary of the Treasury George Humphrey, who was concerned with the necessity of a balanced budget.

The strategy behind "massive retaliation" was worked out by Admiral Arthur W. Radford, who

succeeded General Omar Bradley as chairman of the Joint Chiefs of Staff. It was Admiral Radford who referred to a reduction of conventional forces and an increased reliance on nuclear weapons as the **"New Look"** in our military posture. Because of it, $2.3 billion in expenditures and about $5.3 billion in defense-spending authority was trimmed from the Truman administration proposals for the fiscal year 1954. In popular parlance, this was known as getting "a bigger bang for a buck."

But there were many—among them Sen. John F. Kennedy (D.-Mass.)—who felt that our conventional military forces should be kept equal to our commitments so that we could reply to a Soviet threat without the risk of turning a minor confrontation into a nuclear war. Defeated Democratic presidential candidate Adlai Stevenson charged that the new Republican administration was putting dollars before defense and threatening the unity of the Western world, especially since an over-reliance on massive retaliation made our **NATO** allies fear that the American contribution to the alliance's ground forces would be cut.

In 1957, Henry A. Kissinger, who was the director of Harvard's Defense Studies Program (later Secretary of State in the administration of Richard M. Nixon), published *Nuclear Weapons and Foreign Policy*, in which he argued that nuclear diplomacy limited the alternatives open to American policy. Pointing to the need for a graded deterrent, he urged the development of tactical nuclear weapons and seemed to believe for a time in the possibility of limited nuclear war. By then, Secretary Dulles himself had backed away from the original concept of massive retaliation and favored tactical nuclear weapons, but critics argued that limited nuclear war would inevitably escalate into a full-scale nuclear holocaust.

Some historians have argued that in practice Secretary Dulles's policies were considerably more cautious than his language. In any case, no attempt was made to use "massive retaliation" in dealing with the growing crisis in Indochina (see **Vietnam War**).

By the time President John F. Kennedy assumed office in 1961, "massive retaliation" was a dead issue and was replaced by a policy directed toward "flexible and limited response."

Masters and Johnson Institute Popular name for the Reproductive Biology Research Foundation supported by the Washington University School of Medicine, St. Louis, Missouri, and established by Dr. William H. Masters and Virginia E. Johnson in the late 1950s. They originated the concept of sex clinics and demonstrated that "sexual dysfunction"—a condition they say afflicts 50 percent of the population at some time in their lives—is often a fear of failure and rejection.

Masters and Johnson themselves trained pairs of man-woman therapist teams who later established reputable clinics of their own, but the success and publicity attending the sex clinics led to many imitations of what in 1973 Dr. Masters complained were "street-corner clinics" which frequently have no trained personnel and operate "at low professional standards or no standards at all. They are, in fact, more business ventures than therapy centers."

The results of some of the Masters and Johnson laboratory research—often dependent on what some critics felt was overly elaborate technical equipment for measuring and recording sexual behavior—were published in such highly technical works as their *Human Sexual Response* (1966) and *Human Sexual Inadequacy* (1970). *The Pleasure Bond* (1976) was directed at the general reader.

The Maximum Leader In White House circles the name was sometimes applied to President Lyndon B. Johnson during his administration. Richard H. Nelson, a member of the Johnson team when the latter was still Vice President, is credited with this ironic sobriquet that has obvious overtones of El Lider Maximo, the official designation of Cuba's Fidel Castro.

***Mayaguez* Incident** Bound from Hong Kong to the Thai port of Sattahip, the U.S. cargo ship *Mayaguez* was fired on by a Cambodian Naval vessel on May 12, 1975. In Washington that afternoon, the White House announced that the ship had been seized in what President Gerald R. Ford considered "an act of piracy" and forced to the port of Kompong Som.

Within twelve hours diplomatic notes requesting the release of the ship and its crew of thirty-nine were delivered to the Cambodian Embassy in Peking and to the Chinese government; they were returned without response. Meanwhile, the United States had alerted B-52 bombers and ordered them onto the runways at Guam for possible retaliatory raids on Cambodia. (The B-52s were not used in the subsequent action.)

On May 14, the same afternoon on which President Ford had requested the intercession of UN General Secretary Kurt Waldheim, the President ordered a company of marines protected by fighters from the carrier *Coral Sea* to retake the *Mayaguez*, which was found to be not in Kompong Som but

moored off Tang Island, a rocky inlet some thirty miles away. The captured crew was retrieved from Sihanoukville and after a thirty-mile voyage in a small boat found safety aboard the destroyer *Wilson*. Casualties resulting from the raid were announced as one dead and a number of missing and wounded. Three Cambodian gunboats were sunk. Meanwhile air strikes—presumably designed to protect the marines—were in progress against an airfield near Sihanoukville even as the *Mayaguez* crew was being ferried to safety. The approximately 200 marine raiders were evacuated by helicopter, presumably under the cover of these bombings.

A nation still smarting from the outcome of the **Vietnam War** greeted the government's response to Cambodian provocation with enthusiasm, and President Ford's decision to order the rescue raid was widely applauded by both Republicans and Democrats. However, some critics charged that the President had violated both the law and the constitutional limitations on his power. The specific issue was the War Powers Act of 1973, which had been passed over President Richard M. Nixon's veto. Enthusiasm continued to wane in some quarters as casualty figures began to mount. On May 18 it was announced that three marines and two airmen had died, sixteen were listed as missing, and seventy to eighty as wounded. By May 21 the figures had been revised to fifteen dead, three missing, and fifty wounded. The final figure was forty-one Americans killed, presumed dead, or listed as missing. There were charges that the casualty figures had been deliberately delayed or falsified to maintain the exhileration that followed the rescue operation.

On June 23, 1975, a subcommittee of the House International Relations Committee, headed by Rep. Dante B. Fascell (D.-Fla.), asked the **General Accounting Office** (GAO) to investigate the incident. Released in October 1976, only one month before the forthcoming presidential election, the GAO report—originally sent to the subcommittee on May 11 but classified as secret at the direction of the National Security Council—concluded that the Ford administration had not exhausted all diplomatic channels for action before launching the marine raid and retaliatory bombings of the Cambodian mainland. President Ford defended his actions and expressed disappointment in the fact that the report's release "interjected political partisan politics at the present time." In 1979, the now 35-year-old vessel was scheduled to be scrapped.

Mayday Tribe A radical faction of the People's Coalition for Peace and Justice, an umbrella organization of pacifist organizations such as the American Friends Service Committee, the War Resisters League, and the Fellowship of Reconciliation. Mayday scheduled an anti-**Vietnam War** protest in Washington, D.C., beginning on May 1, 1971, the day following the conclusion of the so-called **People's Lobby** in the nation's capital.

According to a "tactical manual" read to demonstrators, the aim of Mayday actions was "to raise the social cost of the war to a level unacceptable to America's rulers. To do this we seek to create the specter of social chaos while maintaining the support or at least toleration of the broad masses of American people." Nonviolence was the selected tactic recommended to bring activity in the capital to a temporary halt.

Violence erupted when at dawn on May 2, 1971, some 750 helmeted police raided West Potomac Park in the Lincoln Memorial area where thousands of young people had gathered for a rock concert. Demonstrators had originally been granted a permit to use the park, but this was revoked by Police Chief Jerry V. Wilson—on orders from President Richard M. Nixon and Attorney General John Mitchell, critics charged—because of "numerous and flagrant" violations, including the use of drugs.

Acting under Presidential orders to keep the Capital "open for business," Washington police started a series of mass arrests which in the next four days amounted to more than 12,000. The jails overflowed and many demonstrators—as well as passersby who had been swept into the dragnet—were detained in Robert F. Kennedy Memorial Stadium, where to the tune of the Beatles' *Yellow Submarine* they chanted: "We all live in a con-cen-tra-tion camp." Arrest procedures had been illegally abbreviated by the police and the courts eventually threw out the charges, though police were allowed to retain the fingerprints and photographs of those detained.

Mayday leader Rennie Davis of the **National Mobilization Committee to End the War in Vietnam** (Mobe) admitted that the action had "failed . . . to stop the U.S. government," but called it "almost the most major nonviolent demonstration" in the nation's history.

On May 5, 1971, demonstrators were addressed by Rep. Bella Abzug (D.-N.Y.), Rep. Warren Mitchell (D.-Md.), Rep. Charles B. Rangel (D.-N.Y.), and Rep. Ronald V. Dellums (D.-Calif.), who welcomed them to the Capital as their "guests." On that same day, in a speech in New Rochelle, New York, Sen. Edward Kennedy (D.-Mass.) charged that the Nixon administration had "undermined the Constitution" by forcing Washington police to adopt illegal mass arrest procedures. Referring to Attorney General Mitchell's boast the previous day that "traffic is flowing," he noted: "Of course the city may have been safe for cars at the time, but it was a very unsafe place for citizens." President Nixon, who had been in San Clemente during the demonstrations, later compared the demonstrators to Nazi Brownshirts and congratulated Police Chief Wilson on doing "a magnificent job."

The name Mayday was taken from the internationally recognized distress signal traditionally sent out in cases of extreme emergency.

MDAA *See* **Mutual Defense Assistance Act.**

MDS *See* **Movement for a Democratic Society.**

MDTA *See* **Manpower Development and Training Act.**

Medicaid Established in Section 1901 of Title XIX of the Social Security Act amendments of July 30, 1965, Medicaid expanded upon and replaced the former Medical Assistance to the Aged (MAA) program. Effective January 1, 1966, a combination of federal funds and state and local tax money was made available to pay medical bills for persons requiring public assistance. To be eligible for federal funds a state must have had its medical assistance program approved by the **Department of Health, Education, and Welfare** (HEW). Many such programs also cover the "medically indigent"; i.e., those whose incomes are sufficient unless medical expenses are incurred. As of the mid-1970s, all states except Arizona participated in the Medicaid program and approximately half of them made provision for the "medically indigent."

Federal contributions to state programs are based principally on per-capita income in the state and range from 50 percent to as high as 83 percent. Total Medicaid expenditures rose from $372 million in 1966 to $9.366 billion in fiscal 1973, with the federal government paying somewhat more than half. Two-thirds of the program went to pay hospital, nursing home, and intermediate institutional care, with the remainder going for noninstitutional costs such as physicians' services and medication. In 1972 the original legislation was modified to require that state programs covering the "medically indigent" include a nominal premium for Medicaid enrollment.

In the mid-1970s, there were widespread charges of "ripoffs" in Medicaid programs in Illinois and New York, where on March 11, 1976, a nursing home operator pleaded guilty to charges of defrauding the program of $1.2 million. Investigation of "Medicaid mills"—private clinics in underprivileged neighborhoods—revealed abuses such as "ping-ponging," in which a patient is briefly and unnecessarily examined by several doctors who submit individual bills, and "family ganging," in which authorities in a clinic insist on examining each child in a family in which only one child is ill.

At the insistence of HEW's Medicaid Division, states began installing automated claims-processing techniques with the federal government paying most of the costs. "Profiles" fed into computers spot check for possible investigation excessive medication costs and physicians who are charging for an unusually high number of visits.

After March 8, 1977, Medicaid and **Medicare** were placed under the Health Care Financing Administration (HCFA), which was created as a principal operating component of HEW.

Medicare Incorporated in a bill designed to increase Social Security benefits and to expand health and welfare programs, the Medicare program signed into law by President Lyndon B. Johnson on July 30, 1965, provided medical aid to the aged through Social Security.

The program included both a basic and a supplementary plan to provide health insurance for most persons over sixty-five. Under the basic plan, patients would be entitled to sixty days of hospital care for each period of illness and be responsible for only the first $40 of costs; an additional thirty days of care could be had for $10 a day. In addition, patients could have twenty days of nursing home care per illness and an additional eighty days at $5 a day. For diagnostic services provided by a hospital, a patient would be liable for $20 per test and 20 percent of costs above that figure.

Upon payment of a $3 monthly premium—matched by the federal government—enrollees were entitled to a supplementary plan that would include coverage of the services of physicians, radiologists, anesthesiologists, pathologists, and psychiatrists, as well as ambulance services, prosthetic devices, and surgical bandaging. They would also—even if not previously hospitalized—be entitled to 100 annual home nursing visits. Patients would be

responsible for only $50 and 20 percent of all costs above that figure.

The first attempts to provide federal health insurance under Social Security were made by President Harry S Truman in 1945, but were defeated by strong opposition from the medical profession and its American Medical Association lobby. To honor the former President's pioneering effort, President Johnson arranged to sign the Medicare bill in the presence of the former President and his wife at the Harry S Truman Memorial Library, Independence, Missouri. On that occasion, President Johnson, who had included Medicare among his 1964 campaign promises, noted that he marveled "not simply at the passage of this bill, but that it took so many years to pass it."

The Health Care Financing Administration (HCFA) created on March 8, 1977, as a principal operating component of the **Department of Health, Education, and Welfare** (HEW) now oversees both Medicare and Medicaid.

"The medium is the message" *See Understanding Media.*

Merci Train Conceived and organized by a French citizens' committee in the afterglow of World War II, this train consisted of forty-nine boxcars containing gifts to the people of each state and of the District of Columbia. It traveled across the nation February 2-22, 1949.

Meredith March for Freedom *See Ole Miss.*

The Mess in Washington The expression was first used by Republicans in the 1952 presidential campaign to draw attention to charges of corruption and "influence peddling" in the Truman administration (see **Five Percenters**). These charges were largely aimed at Major General Harry Hawkins Vaughan, the President's military aide and personal friend.

In June 1958 it was ironically revived by Democrats when President Dwight D. Eisenhower's personal friend, Sherman Adams, who served as Chief Presidential Assistant, was accused of having accepted a vicuña coat and other gifts from Boston industrialist Bernard Goldfine in exchange for intercession with the Federal Trade Commission and the Securities and Exchange Commission. Adams was eventually cleared of these charges, but the scandal forced his resignation in September 1958. *See* **Adams-Goldfine Scandal.**

Metabolic Clock An expression popularized by jet travel, which often leaves voyagers feeling tired and disoriented for twenty-four to forty-eight hours because of the switches in time zones. The jet age has been characterized by some as a time in which one could have breakfast in Paris, lunch in New York, dinner in Los Angeles, and baggage in Bangkok. But on a more serious level, John Brooks pointed out in *The Great Leap: The Past Twenty-five Years in America* (1966): "Who knows what meetings of foreign ministers, businessmen, scientists, or scholars may have resulted in blank failures of understanding because someone's metabolic clock was out of whack—or may in the future?"

Me-too Republicans The Republican-controlled "Turnip Congress" called into session by President Harry S Truman in July 1948 to pass legislation in the realm of inflation-control, national health, civil rights, Social Security, and housing disbanded without taking any concrete action. Since an endorsement of such legislation—in some form or another—was contained in the Republican platform to which his 1948 presidential challenger, Governor Thomas E. Dewey of New York, was pledged, speaking in Pittsburgh on October 23, 1948, President Truman noted: "The candidate says, 'me, too.' But the Republican record still says, 'We're against it.' These two phrases, 'me, too,' and 'we're against it,' sum up the whole Republican campaign."

Governor Dewey had already been condemned as a "'me-too' candidate who conducted a 'me-too' campaign" by the conservative *Chicago Tribune*, whose publisher, Colonel Robert R. McCormick, had walked out of the Philadelphia convention hall on June 24, 1948, rather than cast his vote for the winning candidate. During the 1940 presidential campaign, the nominally Republican *New York Daily News* had similarly castigated liberal Republican candidate Wendell L. Willkie as "Me-too Willkie."

Defending himself against the charge of "me-tooism," Governor Dewey was later to say that he saw no reason "to be against the Ten Commandments just because the Democrats say they are for them." In 1952, Democratic presidential candidate Adlai Stevenson said that his Republican rival, General Dwight D. Eisenhower, was "a 'me-too' candidate running on a 'yes but' platform, advised by a 'has-been staff.'"

To emphasize the difference between his program and that of President Lyndon B. Johnson, conservative Arizona Republican Barry Goldwater campaigned in 1964 on the slogan: "A Choice—Not an Echo." Ironically enough, after his victory at the polls, President Johnson, whom many had considered a "peace candidate," adopted some of the aspects of the **Vietnam War** stand that had made his Republican challenger anathema to antiwar liberals.

Metroamericans A term used by historian Eric Goldman (*see* **Quiet Brain Trust**) in 1969 to identify under-forty, college-educated, and urban-dwelling business and professional people of liberal persuasion. Their opposite numbers are, perhaps, members of the **Silent Majority,** to which the Nixon administration was to appeal.

The Johnson administration men, Goldman felt, "overlooked the millions of Metroamericans, strategically located across the nation and rapidly expanding in influence.... They had little feel for the union executive, the accountant and his wife in the suburbs of New York, Chicago, or San Francisco, both deriving a sense of status from reading Saul Bellow's *Herzog,* John Kenneth Galbraith's *The Affluent Society* and David Riesman's *The Lonely Crowd,* tending sincerely to react to public figures and public issues in a way similar to these intellectuals, caring about political leaders who cared about men like Bellow, Galbraith and Riesman."

Metroamericans, naturally enough, lived in Metroamerica.

MFDP *See* **Mississippi Freedom Democratic Party.**

Midas Satellites *See* **Project Sentry.**

Middle America The term was invented by syndicated columnist Joseph Kraft in an article on June 23, 1968, to describe what he later called "the great mass of some 40 million persons who have recently moved from just above the poverty line to just below the level of affluence." He noted that as a group they have been "the chief beneficiaries of the past decade of unbroken prosperity," and having "switched from renting to owning their homes, from public to private transportation, from beer to whisky," they have also switched their emphasis from economic security to "ease of life."

Time magazine took up Kraft's term in the cover story of its January 5, 1970 issue: "Man and Woman of the Year: The Middle Americans." Noting that Middle Americans tend to be grouped in the nation's heartland rather than on its coasts, the article called Middle America "a state of mind, a morality, a construct of values and prejudices and a complex of fears." Its ranks were described as including few blacks or intellectuals and to offer "no haven to the **New Left.**" Middle America is said to have drawn comfort from Vice President Spiro Agnew's attack on anti-**Vietnam War** dissenters as an **"effete corps of impudent snobs,"** and from the success of **Project** *Apollo.* "The astronauts themselves were paragons of Middle American aspiration."

There is some reason to assume that it was largely to Middle America that President Richard M. Nixon was addressing himself when on November 3, 1969, he appealed to the **"silent majority"** to support his policy on the Vietnam War.

The Midi Early in 1969, *Women's Wear Daily,* John Burr Fairchild's powerful and influential New York-based fashion journal, announced the demise of the popular mini-length hemline and decreed that 1970 would be the year of the midi—originally described as the "longuette"—or mid-calf-length skirt or dress. Heralded as a much-needed shot in the arm for the ailing New York garment industry, the somewhat arrogant and mishandled midi campaign was actually to cause the financial ruin of some manufacturers who went all out on the new length.

By fall of 1970, it was evident that the midi was a debacle, and stores that had heavily invested in it were rumored to be bringing unfair pressure to bear on saleswomen to help launch the fashion by adopting it themselves. Among the organizations that sprang up to fight the midi were Preservation of Our Femininity and Finances (POOFF) and Society of Males Who Appreciate Cute Knees (SMACK). Many women reacted by retreating into pants, which showed a 50-percent increase in sales.

With less fanfare, however, the fashion industry succeeded in inexorably lowering the hemline in the years that followed.

Military Assistance Advisory Group (MAAG) *See* **Vietnam War.**

Military-Industrial Complex *See* **Eisenhower's Farewell Address.**

Milk Fund Early in 1969, a representative of the nation's largest milk cooperative, Associated Milk Producers, Inc. (AMPI), approached Herbert W. Kalmbach, President Nixon's personal attorney, to see what could be done about obtaining administration backing for milk price supports at 90 percent

of parity. Given to understand that "contributions" might be helpful, on August 2, 1969, he delivered to Kalmbach $100,000 in cash which later became part of a $500,000 secret fund, some of which was eventually used to finance the **"dirty tricks"** by which Donald H. Segretti attempted to sabotage the 1972 Democratic presidential campaign.

The initial contribution did little to further the AMPI cause, and to convince the Nixon administration of its good faith and underlying support the dairy organization pledged $2 million to the President's 1972 campaign. In September 1970, AMPI was urging the limiting of imports on a variety of milk products. Late in December, two weeks after receiving a letter from an AMPI legal representative who stressed the importance of import quotas and drew attention to AMPI political contributions and pledges, President Nixon did establish quotas that were gratifying if nowhere as low as the domestic industry would have liked.

On March 12, 1971, Secretary of Agriculture Clifford M. Hardin announced that milk price supports would be maintained at 79 percent of parity, and two weeks later seventeen dairy industry representatives met with President Nixon to protest that decision. In the interval, the President had discussed the matter with Secretary of the Treasury John B. Connally, who had various connections with AMPI and was a good friend of one of its legal representatives, Jake Jacobson, an Austin lawyer who had served as a special assistant to President Lyndon B. Johnson. Connally, a former Democrat, urged the President to accept demands for a minimum 85-percent parity.

Soon after, AMPI representatives met with Kalmbach and affirmed the $2 million pledge for President Nixon's 1972 campaign.

Pleading a "reconsideration" of the evidence, on March 25, the Secretary of Agriculture announced an "upward adjustment" of milk support parity to approximately 85 percent.

By taking advantage of a number of loopholes in the **Federal Election Campaign Act** of 1972, contributions from the milk trusts were variously disguised. Nevertheless, when the facts came to light following the many revelations attendant on the **Watergate Scandal,** a number of indictments involving bribery and illegal campaign contributions were handed down. Secretary Connally was eventually acquitted of charges, but Harold S. Nelson and David L. Parr, organizers of AMPI, were fined $10,000 each and sentenced to three years in prison, all but four months of those sentences being suspended.

On January 8, 1974, President Nixon acknowledged having taken "traditional political considerations" into account when he had decided to increase milk price supports, but he denied that that decision had been a direct result of the pledged $2 million contribution to his campaign.

During investigations into the milk fund, it was revealed that over the years Senator Hubert H. Humphrey (D.-Minn.) had also received AMPI contributions and that those made during his 1968 presidential campaign were illegal because they had been made from corporate funds. While freely acknowledging the contributions, Senator Humphrey said he knew of no illegal donations. In June 1975, Jack L. Chestnut, who had been the senator's campaign manager in 1970 and 1972, was fined $5,000 and sentenced to four months in prison for accepting a $12,000 illegal AMPI contribution.

Miller v. California In decisions in five obscenity cases (one of them *Miller v. California*) all decided by a five-to-four vote, on June 21, 1973, the U.S. Supreme Court reversed a fifteen-year trend toward the relaxation of controls against pornography. In each case Chief Justice Warren E. Burger was joined by the four other appointees of President Richard M. Nixon—Justices Harry A. Blackmun, Byron R. White, William H. Rehnquist, and Lewis F. Powell, Jr.—in a majority opinion which set aside the former standards for pornography handed down by the Court in 1957 and 1966. Previously, obscene material was guaranteed the protection of the First Amendment unless taken as a whole the work was "utterly without redeeming social value," appealed to prurient interest, and exceeded current standards of candor in representing matters relating to sexual intercourse. Under the Court's new guidelines, a book, play, magazine, or movie could be found obscene if the "average person, applying contemporary community standards, would find that the work, taken as a whole, appeals to prurient interest; the work depicts or describes, in a patently offensive way, sexual conduct specifically defined by applicable state law, and the work, taken as a whole, lacks serious literary, artistic, political or scientific value."

The majority decision made it clear that juries ruling on cases involving pornography would be free to decide prurience on the basis of local standards. "It is neither realistic nor constitutionally sound to read the First Amendment as requiring that the people of Maine or Mississippi accept public depiction of conduct found tolerable in Las Vegas or New York City," said Chief Justice Burger. The majority opinion also gave states the right to assume, in the absence of clear proof, that there was a causal connection between pornographic material and antisocial behavior.

The four dissenting judges—Justices William J. Brennan, Jr., Potter Stewart, Thurgood Marshall, and William O. Douglas—criticized the new guidelines as vague and an impingement upon the right of free speech and a free press. Justice Douglas objected to the "ominous gloss" the ruling put on the First Amendment, and Justice Brennan noted that if a state desiring to create a particular moral tone could prescribe what material its citizens could have access to, it followed that "a state could decree that its citizens must read certain books or must view certain films."

Miltown Trade name for meprobamate, the first of the tranquilizers, it was marketed by Wallace Pharmaceuticals beginning in 1955. Its most advantageous feature was that it suppressed overactivity in the brain's emotive tissue without causing a corresponding loss of activity in the cerebral cortex. Excessive use could, however, cause drowsiness.

Extensively advertised, Miltown was often too freely and incautiously prescribed by physicians for therapeutic use. The name entered the language and became a popular subject for humor and cocktail party chatter. (S.J. Perelman named his 1957 collection of humorous essays *The Road to Miltown* and TV comedian Milton Berle quipped that he was thinking of changing his name to Miltown Berle.) It soon became apparent, however, that meprobamate—which was also marketed by Wyeth Laboratories as Equanil—was addictive and could cause severe withdrawal symptoms. In September 1965, it was dropped from the *U.S. Pharmacopeia*. The antianxiety agents most widely used now are Valium and Librium, which were introduced by Roche Laboratories in the early 1960s. Although the manufacturer warns that they should be used with caution, they are said to be only minimally addictive.

Milwaukee Fourteen *See* **Catonsville Nine.**

Mink Coat Scandal *See* **Five Percenters.**

Minnesota Strip The area in Manhattan that extends along Eighth Avenue between 42d and 52d Streets. The *New York Times* has described it as the city's "sleaziest vice supermarket for prostitutes, pimps, massage parlors, pornography stores, topless bars and assorted criminals." Its nickname is said to derive from the fact that many of the teenage prostitutes who walk the avenue were attracted to the city from the Midwest.

Minuteman Defense Program *See* **Intercontinental Ballistic Missiles.**

Minutemen *See* **John Birch Society.**

Miranda v. Arizona In a controversial five-to-four decision, the U.S. Supreme Court ruled on June 13, 1966, that the Fifth Amendment's protection against self-incrimination restricted police interrogation of a suspect under arrest. Among the points made in the majority decision written by Chief Justice Earl Warren were:

To summarize, we hold that when an individual is taken into custody, or otherwise deprived of his freedom . . . and subjected to questioning, the privilege against self-incrimination is jeopardized . . . . He must be warned prior to any questioning that he has a right to remain silent, that anything he says can be used against him in a court of law, that he has a right to the presence of an attorney and that if he cannot afford an attorney one will be appointed for him. . . .

After such warning having been given and such opportunity afforded him, the individual may knowingly and intelligently waive these rights. . . . But unless and until such warnings and waiver are demonstrated by the prosecution at the trial, no evidence obtained as a result of interrogation can be used against him.

Prolonged interrogation was construed by the Court as the absence of such a waiver, and a suspect could reclaim the right to silence even after having granted such a waiver.

The case before the Court involved Ernesto A. Miranda, a mentally retarded twenty-three-year-old who was convicted of rape and kidnapping in Arizona. Although he confessed after being identified, the Court held that he had not been adequately warned of his right to counsel or that his statements could be used against him in a subsequent trial.

The decision also reversed the convictions of three other prisoners convicted on charges ranging from robbery to murder. Dissents were entered by Justices Tom C. Clark, John M. Harlan, Potter Stewart, and Byron R. White in three of the four cases. In one case, in which Roy Allen Stewart was convicted of murder in Los Angeles, Justice Clark joined the majority because he felt that a confession had been involuntarily obtained. He nevertheless dissented from the curbs on interrogation in all the cases before the Court.

The Court subsequently ruled that the new restrictions on interrogation were not to be considered retroactive.

Many law enforcement agencies throughout the nation attacked the ruling as giving "a green light to criminals," and a popular slogan urged "Handcuff Crooks, Not Cops." On March 23, 1977, in a five-to-four decision (*Brewer v. Williams*), the Court declined a request by twenty-two states that the Miranda decision be overturned. In an emotional dissent from the bench in open court, Chief Justice Warren E. Burger attacked the 1977 decision as "weird" and in "error."

MIRV *See* **Multiple Individually Targetable Vehicle.**

Missile Gap References to the "missile gap" began showing up in the speeches of Sen. John F. Kennedy (D.-Mass.) in about 1958 and may have been inspired by a projection of **intercontinental ballistic missiles** (ICBMs) that was published by newspaper columnist Joseph Alsop. "The deterrent ration during 1960–1964 will in all likelihood be weighted against us," warned the Senator.

As a result of the U-2 aerial reconnaissance flights over Soviet territory since 1956, President Dwight D. Eisenhower, the object of these attacks, knew that this was not true and that there was no evidence of the deployment of Soviet ICBMs, but he could not use this information to reply to a political attack (see **U-2 flights**).

Similar charges were being made by Sen. Stuart Symington (D.-Mo.), who on August 29, 1958, wrote the President a long letter charging that the United States was unjustifiably lagging behind the U.S.S.R. in missiles, and "giving as his authority," President Eisenhower later noted, "his own intelligence sources."

These attacks were due in part to the fact that the President, on the advice of his technical experts, had rejected a Pentagon proposal for an **antiballistic missile system** (ABMS).

The "missile gap" charges began showing up with greater frequency as the 1960 presidential election campaign got underway. Speaking to an American Legion audience in October, Senator Kennedy, now the Democratic presidential candidate, again denounced the Eisenhower administration for having allowed a "missile gap" to develop and for having failed to deploy an ABM system.

It was not until he had actually assumed office that President Kennedy learned just how wrong his campaign charges had been. To begin with, on the advice of his technical experts, he too rejected an

ABM system as being technologically unachievable. In addition, according to Jerome B. Wiesner, his chief science adviser, "soon after President Kennedy took office, we learned that the Soviet missile force was substantially smaller than earlier estimates which provided the basis for the so-called missile gap. We learned, in fact, that the United States probably had more missiles than the Soviet Union, a somewhat surprising and reassuring fact."

In *A Thousand Days* (1965), Arthur M. Schlesinger, Jr., a member of the Kennedy administration inner circle, notes that the "missile gap" was first publicly suggested by President Eisenhower's second Secretary of Defense, Neil McElroy, in 1959 when he claimed that the U.S.S.R. would have a three-to-one superiority by the 1960s.

Mississippi Freedom Democratic Party (MFDP) At a statewide meeting on April 26, 1964, Mississippi civil rights militants met to map future programs. Activists of the **Student Nonviolent Coordinating Committee** (SNCC; Snick) urged the creation of a parallel Democratic party set up in accordance with the Mississippi state constitution but free of the racist taint with which the regular state party was charged. The resulting Mississippi Freedom Democratic Party (MFDP—sometimes FDP) failed a crucial test when it sent a delegation to the Democratic National Convention in Atlantic City in August. Its members had counted on backing from President Lyndon B. Johnson, or at least a neutral stand, but the White House wanted the party regulars seated, and this was done when conservative civil rights spokesmen joined the forces against the MFDP. The MFDP was ousted from the convention and the result was a widening split between liberal and radical forces in the civil rights movement.

Mississippi Freedom Schools *See* **Freedom Schools.**

Mississippi Summer Project After the **Birmingham** demonstrations in April–May 1963, black militants began turning more and more to direct action. The necessity for this was made all the more obvious by the spectacle of Southern Senators who in the early summer of 1964 carried on a marathon filibuster against the **Civil Rights Bill of 1964.**

The Mississippi Summer Project, sometimes known as Freedom Summer, was organized by the **Student Nonviolent Coordinating Committee** (SNCC; Snick) under the sponsorship of the **Council of Federated Organizations** (COFO), an um-

brella group that included the NAACP, the **Southern Christian Leadership Conference** (SCLC), the **Congress of Racial Equality** (CORE), and the National Council of Churches. Assembling in Oxford, Ohio, approximately a thousand white and black volunteers moved down into Mississippi, where they were joined by local SNCC groups in an effort to register black voters and set up **Freedom Schools** under the direction of Staughton Lynd.

Aware that they could expect no protection from local law-enforcement officials, they requested President Lyndon B. Johnson to send federal marshals into the area. At a public hearing held in Washington, D.C., Mississippi blacks told of police brutality, and many constitutional lawyers pointed to the government's obligation to provide militants with adequate protection. Transcripts of the hearing failed to evoke a response from either the President or Attorney General Robert F. Kennedy, who told NAACP representatives that preventive police action by the federal government was impractical and no doubt unconstitutional.

On June 20, 1964, only one day after the first group of volunteers had reached Jackson, James Chaney, a black, and Michael Schwerner and Andrew Goodman, both white, disappeared after being detained in the Philadelphia, Mississippi, jail. In spite of calls by Governor Paul B. Johnson, Jr., for public assistance in locating them, no clues to their whereabouts were discovered until two men responded to an approximately $30,000 reward offered by the FBI. On August 4, the bodies of the three civil rights volunteers were discovered buried in a nearby earthen dam.

It was not until December 4 that the FBI arrested twenty-one men, and a federal grand jury later indicted eighteen of them for violating an 1870 statute by conspiring to violate the constitutional rights of the murdered civil rights workers. In October 1967, seven men were found guilty by a federal jury of white Mississippians; eight men were acquitted, and the jury could not reach a decision about the other three.

Mr. Bad News During the Nixon administration this was one of several names (*see* **Big Enchilada**) by which Attorney General John N. Mitchell was known in White House circles. It was he who was often given the task of carrying out what was generally considered an unpleasant duty. For example, it was Mitchell who attempted to get Secretary of the Interior Walter Hickel to resign quietly, and who with no more success informed George Romney that he would be better off resigning his **Depart-**

ment of **Housing and Urban Development** (HUD) post after he had irritated President Richard M. Nixon by aggressive policies such as support for the **Model Cities** program begun under the Johnson administration.

Mr. Chapman's Friends *See* **Dirty Tricks.**

Mr. Inside and Mr. Outside Those familiar with the White House staff during the Nixon administration (1969–August 1974) would often use these names to refer to presidential aides H. R. Haldeman and John D. Ehrlichman.

Haldeman, a former advertising executive with J. Walter Thompson, quickly developed the reputation for being inaccessible after he became President Richard M. Nixon's Chief of Staff. When the groundwork had to be prepared for eliminating from the White House circle men for whom the President's enthusiasm had waned—George Romney, Arthur Burns, Daniel P. Moynihan, and others—he was given the job and is said to have performed it with a certain cold relish. "Every President needs an S.O.B.," he is quoted as saying. "I'm Nixon's."

Ehrlichman, a former Seattle lawyer and a classmate of Haldeman's at UCLA, presented a somewhat more relaxed image and, as Assistant to the President for Domestic Affairs, was generally accessible to cabinet members, newspapermen, and other legitimate petitioners. It was therefore the more surprising when at the Senate hearings following the **Watergate Scandal,** he was the more aggressive and hostile witness of the two.

The duo were sometimes also known as the "Knights of the Woeful Countenance," an ironic sobriquet borrowed by Victor Gold from Cervantes' *Don Quixote;* Gold was Vice President Spiro Agnew's press secretary. Most of the other names applied to them were German oriented: Hans and Fritz, the Berlin Wall, the Teutonic Trio (when Secretary of State Henry Kissinger was lumped with them), the Katzenjammer Kids, and All the King's Krauts. The Palace Guard—later the title of an account of the Nixon inner circle by newsmen Dan Rather and Gary Paul Gates—was another "in" name for the men who so effectively isolated President Nixon not only from the members of his own cabinet and staff, but from all official Washington.

Mr. Republican Because of his devotion to the cause of American conservatism, Sen. Robert A. Taft (R.-Ohio) was given this sobriquet by admirers. A staunch opponent of President Franklin D.

Roosevelt's New Deal and President Harry S Truman's **Fair Deal,** he was the coauthor of the **Taft-Hartley Act** (1947), which was bitterly resented by labor; because of this, the Congress of Industrial Organizations (CIO) tried to make political capital by drawing attention to his initials: R.A.T.

A perennial candidate for the Republican presidential nomination, Senator Taft never received this honor in spite of the fact that he was for many years a leading spokesman of his party's conservative wing. In 1952, he supported the candidacy of Dwight D. Eisenhower, who adopted many aspects of his conservative program. In 1953, the year of his death, having served in the Senate since 1938, he became Senate Majority Leader.

Despite the vast differences in their political and economic points of view, Sen. John F. Kennedy (D.-Mass.) included Senator Taft among the eight Senate leaders on whom he focused in his bestselling *Profiles in Courage* (1956).

Mr. Television Because of the immense popularity of his Texaco Star Theatre featured on NBC from June 1948 to June 1956, comedian Milton Berle, the first major personality of the infant television industry, became nationally known as Mr. Television. In homes throughout the country, Tuesday night was reserved as "Milton Berle Night," and viewers expectantly awaited the appearance of "Uncle Miltie," who might appear as anything from Howdy Doody to an enormous pie. In 1951, NBC signed Berle to a thirty-year contract, paying him $100,000 in addition to his regular fees to keep him from appearing on opposition networks. The contract was renegotiated in 1965, and later Berle returned on ABC in "The Milton Berle Show," which duplicated the previously successful formula of vaudeville humor and a galaxy of celebrity guest stars.

"Mrs. Murphy" Clause *See* **Civil Rights Act of 1964.**

MLF *See* **Multilateral Force.**

Mobe *See* **National Mobilization Committee to End the War in Vietnam.**

Model Cities The Demonstration Cities and Metropolitan Area Redevelopment Act, incorporating the Model Cities program of his administration, was signed into law by President Lyndon B. Johnson on November 3, 1966. It had been proposed early in the year and passed by Congress in September after stormy debate. Aimed at the decentralization of urban planning and the establishment of a means for diverting a more equitable share of a city's resources to neglected inner-city residents, the program was designed to meet community needs by adding additional federal funds to those available from already existing federal aid programs. It blended physical reconstruction with social programs and called for participation by neighborhood residents, municipal officials, and local business people. One part of the program provided land-development mortgage insurance for developers of "new towns." Any city in the nation could submit an application for funds under the program to the **Department of Housing and Urban Development** (HUD); however, an approved target area had to contain 10 percent of the city's population or 15,000, whichever was greater.

A task force assembled by the President to plan the Model Cities program had originally thought to select disadvantaged neighborhoods in six or seven cities for a massive infusion of federal funds into projects that would then become "models" for other communities. However, the bill presented to Congress was targeted for seventy-five cities, and the legislators raised this to 150 cities—half to be chosen in late 1967 and the rest in 1968.

Many critics felt that the Model Cities program was symbolic of the ambitious and essentially unplanned quality of the Johnson administration's **Great Society**. It had been assumed that Model Cities would die a quick death when President Richard M. Nixon assumed office in 1969; however, a team of urban experts chosen by the new President described the program as "a long step in the right direction."

Former President Johnson was to describe the program "as one of the major breakthroughs of the 1960s" because it forced cities "to develop the actual renewal plans and to devise their own visions for the future." He also felt that the legislation "provided a graphic test of the federal government's ability to work in harmony with other levels of government."

In June 1974, after an expenditure of some $2 billion, the Model Cities program ceased to exist as a separate federal program, though many of its aims continued to be carried out with money from other federal programs. To many observers it was not a victim of overambition and underplanning but of the continuing financial drain of the **Vietnam War.** Robert C. Wood, who was part of the original Model Cities task force, has noted that the program

"was predicated on a budget surplus of $12 billion a year. Vietnam wiped that out."

Molly Brown *See* **Project Gemini.**

Montgomery Bus Strike It was this protest against segregation that first propelled the Reverend Martin Luther King, Jr., into national prominence.

Although almost half of Montgomery, Alabama (population: 125,000), was black, segregation on public transportation was "accepted" and unquestioned—by whites. However, on December 1, 1955, Mrs. Rosa Parks, who was black, boarded a bus to ride home after a long day working as a seamstress. Because her feet hurt, she took a seat just behind the front section customarily reserved for whites. The bus filled up and she was told by the driver to surrender her seat to a white man. When she refused, she was arrested and ordered to stand trial on December 5 on the charge of violating segregation laws.

On December 2, however, black community leaders met in the Dexter Avenue Baptist Church of Reverend King—who was then twenty-seven—and decided to organize a bus boycott as a protest. The organization they formed was named the Montgomery Improvement Association—at the suggestion of another minister, Ralph D. Abernathy—and Dr. King was elected president. The "strike" was originally aimed at a compromise solution by which blacks would be seated from the back forward but not required to give up seats as the bus became crowded. However, its goal soon became full desegregation.

When the boycott began on December 5, the buses had 10 percent of their usual black fares. The company counted on the enormous hardship worked on the black community—whites were considerably less dependent on public transportation—to end the strike soon; but blacks organized efficient car pools or walked to work. As the bus company's income dropped to less than half, it resorted to raising fares and cutting schedules. It also took to the courts, and on February 22, 1956, some 100 black community leaders, including Dr. King, were charged with conspiracy to conduct an "illegal" boycott. The following day, 2,000 blacks crowded in and around Reverend Abernathy's First Baptist Church to hear addresses from those under indictment. Announcing the themes of nonviolence that were afterward to characterize his integrationist campaigns, Dr. King said: "We must use the weapon of love. We must have compassion and understanding for those who hate us."

On March 22, Rev. King was fined $500 and ordered to pay another $500 in court costs for having led the boycott; prosecution of the others under indictment was delayed until Dr. King could appeal his sentence. Faced with a year in jail, he eventually agreed to pay $500 in all.

The bus boycott continued, however, and blacks added legal protest to their efforts. A federal suit challenging segregation on intrastate buses was filed, and while legal steps were still being taken, on April 23, 1956, the U.S. Supreme Court ruled in favor of a Miss Sarah Mae Flemming, whose suit against the bus company in Columbia, South Carolina, had been dismissed without trial. This Supreme Court ruling was widely understood to have declared segregation on intrastate buses unconstitutional.

By the time it was realized that the Court had merely indicated that Miss Flemming had a right to have her case heard in the federal court, the bus companies in many southern cities, including Montgomery, had desegregated their facilities. On learning the Court's real intent, the Montgomery company reversed its action and announced that it would continue to enforce segregation.

Meanwhile, the original challenge to intrastate segregation was still in effect, and on June 3 a federal district court found that bus segregation was unconstitutional. The decision was challenged but upheld by the Supreme Court on November 13, 1956. It was not, however, until December 21, 1956, that Montgomery bus facilities were again desegregated and the boycott ended. During the weeks that followed, a black woman on a bus was wounded by a sniper, and the homes and churches of black and white ministers who had taken an antisegregation stand were bombed.

The nonviolence and passive resistance that characterized Dr. King's antisegregation campaigns after Montgomery have often been said to be a translation of Gandhi's philosophy of passive resistance into Alabaman terms. It should be pointed out, however, that the Indian leader himself took his inspiration from Henry David Thoreau's essay on "Civil Disobedience," which dates from 1849.

See **Southern Christian Leadership Conference.**

"Moonies" *See* **Unification Church.**

Moral Re-Armament Founded in England during the 1920s by the American Lutheran evangelist Frank Buchman, who preached "world-changing through life-changing"; the organization was originally known as the Oxford Group Movement. The emphasis was on shared personal confession during informal meetings of groups gathered at educational and religious institutions or in private homes. Buchman stressed four "absolutes": honesty, love, purity, and unselfishness.

A "Moral Re-Armament" campaign begun in 1938 spread to more than fifty countries, and in 1958 there was a world assembly. In centers at Mackinac Island, Michigan, and Caux, Switzerland, political and industrial leaders from all over the world were brought together in an effort to solve problems on the basis of Christian fellowship. Buchman died in 1961.

Moratorium Day On October 15, 1969, Americans all over the nation participated in massive demonstrations against the continuance of the **Vietnam War.** In a peaceful challenge to government policy unprecedented anywhere in the world, hundreds of thousands of people of all ages and in all walks of life attended rallies, paraded, and went to special religious services.

In Washington, D.C., members of Congress participated in the demonstrations, and the widow of Martin Luther King, Jr., the slain civil rights leader, led a candlelight procession of over 40,000 people from the Washington monument to the White House, before which they silently passed for over two hours.

Backing the charge by Nguyen Van Thieu, president of South Vietnam, that M-Day gave aid and comfort to the enemy, many supporters of the Nixon administration's stand attended smaller counter-rallies, drove their automobiles with headlights on during daylight hours, and flew the flag at full mast. In New York's Central Park, parachutists landed in the midst of a peace demonstration and planted a flag.

At a second Moratorium Day, November 15, 1969, more than 200,000 people gathered in the nation's capital and similar rallies were held in most large cities.

The M-Day demonstrations were ignored by President Nixon, who had already announced: "Under no circumstances will I be affected whatever by it." His attitude was scored by Sen. Edward S. Muskie (D.-Maine), the Democratic candidate for Vice President in 1968: "I regret that the President has not seen this day as an opportunity to unite rather than divide the country. His participation, in a forum of his choosing, could have added a constructive dimension to this national dialogue."

According to reports, the President spent the second M-Day stonily watching a football game on television while 40,000 demonstrators, each bearing a card with the name of an American war casualty, marched past the White House.

Although the law-abiding deportment of the demonstrators received general praise, Attorney General John N. Mitchell, seizing upon minor incidents of violence caused by **Yippie** and **Students for a Democratic Society** (SDS) groups bent on provocation, noted "extensive physical injury, property damage, and street confrontations" and refused to recognize the overall peaceful nature of the occasion.

Morgenthau Plan Sponsored by the Secretary of the Treasury, Henry Morgenthau, Jr., this plan for the postwar treatment of a defeated Germany was first introduced in September 1944 at the Second Quebec Conference at which President Franklin D. Roosevelt and England's Prime Minister Winston Churchill met to consider possible strategy once the Axis powers involved in World War II had been defeated. It called for the elimination of Germany's industrial and military potential by converting that nation into an essentially agricultural one. Although tentatively approved at that time, it was rejected by President Roosevelt a few weeks later.

When President Harry S Truman was preparing to go to **Potsdam** in July 1945, Secretary Morgenthau asked to be made a member of his party. He was refused and thereupon offered his resignation. President Truman, who had opposed the plan while he was still a Senator, accepted the resignation then and there. "I thought it proper to disarm Germany, and to put her under an over-all Allied control until we could restore the peace. But I did not approve of reducing Germany to an agrarian state. Such a program could starve Germany to death. That would have been an act of revenge, and too many peace treaties had been based on that spirit."

Moscow Declaration of Principles At the conclusion of President Richard M. Nixon's visit to Moscow, May 22–29, 1972, the U.S. and the U.S.S.R. released a joint communiqué announcing their "desire to strengthen peaceful relations with each other and to place these relations on the firmest possible basis. . . ." What followed was a set of twelve principles in which both nations agreed:

1. [to] proceed from the common determination that in the nuclear age there is no alternative to conducting their mutual relations on the basis of peaceful coexistence

2. to avoid military confrontations

3. to promote conditions in which all countries will live in peace and security and will not be subject to outside interference in their internal affairs

4. to widen the juridical basis of their mutual relations

5. to continue the practice of exchanging views on problems of mutual interest

6. to make special efforts to limit strategic armaments

7. [to strengthen] commercial and economic ties as an important and necessary element in the strengthening of their bilateral relations

8. to develop mutual contacts and cooperation in the fields of science and technology

9. to deepen cultural ties with one another

10. [to] establish in all fields where this is feasible joint commissions or other joint bodies

11. [to] recognize the sovereign equality of all states

The twelfth and final principle noted that all the previous items "do not affect any obligations with respect to other countries earlier assumed by the U.S.A. and the U.S.S.R."

As a result of the so-called Moscow Summit, the first President to visit the Soviet Union returned with an agreement (May 26) of "unlimited duration" limiting **antiballistic missile systems** (ABMS) to one "centered on the party nation's capital" and another to be located elsewhere in the country. "National technical means," i.e., spy satellites, were to check on violations. As a result of this agreement Defense Secretary Melvin R. Laird ordered the Army to halt construction of a Safeguard antimissile base in Montana and to drop plans for other projected sites. In an "interim" executive agreement limited to five years, both nations agreed "not to start construction" of additional land-based **intercontinental ballistic missile** (ICBM) launchers after July 1, 1972.

Other agreements covered the establishment of a joint commission to resolve economic differences; cooperation in science and technology and the exploration of outer space; the prevention of incidents between the naval vessels and aircraft of the two nations; and cooperation in both health research and environmental protection.

Mt. Clemens Pottery Case *See* **Portal-to-Portal Pay.**

The Movement *See* **New Left.**

Movement for a Democratic Society (MDS) Formed in New York City in 1968 as an organization for radicals who were no longer part of the student population, its function was to maintain liaison between "young adults" and various aspects of the national **New Left** by providing an organizational base from which to establish radical analyses of events and to create "counter-institutions." The organization also functioned as an employment agency, with its focus on the college-educated "working class."

A working paper prepared by Bob Gottlieb, MDS leader, and Marge Piercy, poet and novelist, for the Vocations for Radicals Conference in Boston in March 1968 gives the most complete account of MDS goals. It notes that the MDS chapters

. . . are beginning to have to immediate constituencies. The first is Movement graduates—old **SDS** people who have drifted away, or who feel the Movement has stayed on campus and thus shoved them out. Our second constituency is all the discontented, alienated, radical, or potentially radical people who can be brought into the Movement.

These were defined as those who took part in the first stages of the civil rights movement of the early 1960s, or who arrived at opposition to the "system" because of their opposition to the **Vietnam War.** "Others are fed up because they are sickened by what it means to try to be a good teacher in a coercive school in a rotten city, or a good case worker monitoring the sex lives of poor black women on ADC [Aid to Dependent children] dole."

Moynihan Doctrine As Assistant Secretary of Labor under President Lyndon B. Johnson, Daniel Patrick Moynihan was in on the conception of the **Office of Economic Opportunity** (OEO) legislation that was at the heart of the **War on Poverty.** Although sharply critical of the OEO in his *Maximum Feasible Misunderstanding* (published in 1969, it was written earlier), when he was somewhat surprisingly appointed by President Richard M. Nixon to be Executive Secretary of the Urban Affairs Council he was eager to ensure that the new President did not proceed to a wholesale dismantling of President Johnson's **Great Society** and War on Poverty. He attempted to persuade President Nixon that a conservative administration cannot undo the basic legislation of a preceding liberal administration without creating serious national divisions. It was under his influence that in February 1969 the President proposed the renewal of OEO legislation, and instead of killing the **Job Corps** only transferred its operations to the Department of Labor.

Moynihan's influence in the Nixon administration was short-lived and he soon resigned.

Moynihan Report In November 1965, while he was a member of the Department of Labor's Policy Planning and Research office, Daniel Patrick Moynihan issued a closely reasoned analysis entitled "The Negro Family." In it he argued that the only realistic way to attack problems within the black community was to face up to some of the legacy left by slavery. Three centuries of "sometimes unimaginable mistreatment," he pointed out, have taken their toll on blacks, and "in terms of ability to win out in the competitions of American life, they are not equal to most of those groups with which they will be competing."

Focusing on "the deterioration of the Negro family," the so-called *Moynihan Report* pointed out that nearly a quarter of urban Negro marriages end in divorce or separation and that in New York City ("the urban frontier") the proportion of absent husbands was 30.2 percent in 1960, *not* including divorce.

While both white and black illegitimate births had been increasing in the last two decades, Moynihan noted, from 1940 to 1963 the rate in the black community had gone from 16.8 percent to 23.6 percent as against 2 percent and 3.07 percent among whites.

"As a direct result of this high rate of divorce, separation, and desertion, a very large percentage of Negro families are headed by females"—almost one-fourth, the report pointed out, and estimated that "only a minority of Negro children" of eighteen have spent all their lives with both parents. In addition, an extrapolation of data from the **Department of Health, Education, and Welfare** showed that 56 percent of nonwhite children received public assistance under the Aid to Dependent Children Program at some time in their lives, as against 8 percent of white children.

Moynihan felt that an important index of failure among black youth is their "consistently poor performance on the mental tests that are a standard means of measuring ability and performance in the present generation." He eliminated the possibility of genetic differential: "Intelligence potential is distributed among Negro infants in the same proportion and pattern as among Icelanders or Chinese or any other group. American society, however, impairs the Negro potential."

The report did not offer any solutions but confined itself to analyzing a problem; however, it did reject the notion that "this problem may in fact be out of control."

In spite of Moynihan's apparent sympathy with the black community, the spotlight on the facts presented in his report offended many militants, who branded him a "racist."

M²H² *See "Mary Hartman, Mary Hartman."*

Multilateral Force (MLF) By the final days of the Eisenhower administration, considerable pressure had been built up by this country's **NATO** allies for greater participation in nuclear decisions and an end to the American nuclear monopoly. Eager to avoid nuclear proliferation by the creation of independent deterrent forces, in 1960 the State Department asked Robert Bowie, former head of the Policy Planning Council, to search for a formula which would give our NATO allies a greater role in the control of nuclear weapons meant for their defense without encouraging nuclear proliferation and without making such weapons available for individual national use. The plan he eventually devised called for a seaborne force which would be "mixed-manned"—consisting of crews drawn from different nations. As a result, the outgoing Eisenhower administration in December 1960 suggested to a NATO ministerial meeting in Paris the possibility that the United States would make available to NATO five ballistic missile submarines and eighty **Polaris** missiles. This would be done before 1963, provided a system of multilateral control could be agreed upon.

After John F. Kennedy had assumed the presidency in 1961, the "flexible and limited response" policy formulated by General Maxwell Taylor replaced the **"massive retaliation"** global strategy relied on by the previous administration. It was in this new context that in May 1961, speaking in Ottawa, Canada, President Kennedy said that the United States was ready to assign to NATO five or more Polaris atomic missile submarines, this commitment being subject to "any agreed NATO guidelines on their control and use, and responsive to the needs of all members but still credible in an emergency." He also spoke of the future possibility of a seaborne NATO force that would be truly multilateral in ownership and control "once NATO's non-nuclear goals have been achieved." In line with the flexible response strategy, he considered the strengthening of conventional NATO forces a "matter of the highest priority."

Building a conventional force, however, had little appeal to America's NATO allies because such a force was expensive, politically unpopular, and suggested the possibility that Europe might become a battleground for a struggle between the United States and the Soviet Union, with these two superpowers remaining relatively free from the possibility of nuclear attack. The only positive response came from West Germany in 1962, when that country proposed—making no mention of meeting NATO's conventional force requirements—the creation of a missile-equipped fleet of mixed-manned surface vessels.

The MLF concept was urged by the United States throughout the Kennedy administration and during the early part of President Lyndon B. Johnson's term in office. An alternative plan, which like MLF would have required American consent before nuclear bombs or missiles could be used—was Great Britain's Atlantic Nuclear Force (ANF), which would have brought under a unified command bombers and other means of delivering nuclear weapons.

President Johnson later noted that the **Cuban Missile Crisis** had demonstrated that "nuclear blackmail" was not an effective instrument of national policy if the threatened nation was "strong and determined." He noted that "as anxiety lessened, allied diplomats and military leaders concluded that a joint nuclear force was not essential to the vitality of NATO, and that trying to work out details of such a force might be more divisive than unifying."

Multiple Independently Targetable Reentry Vehicle (MIRV) A system that carries several separate warheads on a single missile or booster. A guidance system makes it possible for each of the warheads to be delivered against a different target. MIRVs are incorporated into Minuteman 3 and Poseidon **Intercontinental Ballistic Missiles.**

Mundt-Nixon Bill *See* **McCarran Act.**

Mutual Defense Assistance Act (MDAA) Members of the **North Atlantic Treaty Organization (NATO)** are obliged by Article 5 of the pact—ratified by the U.S. Senate in July 1949—to consider an armed attack against one or more of them as an attack on all of them. To help them meet such a potential obligation, the NATO nations appealed to the United States for military assistance. As a result, the Truman administration presented Congress with a military assistance plan that called for $1.45 billion in fiscal 1950, of which $1.13 billion would go to the NATO nations. After acrimonious debate, on September 28, 1949, spurred by the announcement five days earlier that the U.S.S.R. had exploded its first atomic bomb, Congress authorized the appropriation of $1.314 billion, of which $1 billion was earmarked for our NATO allies. The Mutual Defense Assistance Act was signed by President Harry S Truman on October 6, 1949, and two weeks later Congress appropriated the full amount asked for by the President.

In 1950 President Truman invoked this legislation when he began stepping up aid to the French forces battling against the Communist Vietminh in Indochina. This was done by interpreting the act as making it necessary to maintain France as a viable NATO ally.

See **Vietnam War.**

My Lai Massacre One of the most savage incidents of the **Vietnam War** occurred on March 16, 1968. A unit of C Company, 1st Battalion, 20th Infantry of the 11th Infantry Brigade of the American Division was responsible for the slaughter of an estimated 109 to 567 unarmed men, women, and children in My Lai (also known as Song My), a hamlet in the Quang Ngai province. Led by Lieutenant William L. Calley, the unit had been instructed by company commander Captain Ernest Medina to clean out the village, which was said to be in the hands of the 48th Battalion of the Viet Cong.

Delivered to the My Lai area by helicopter, the approximately ninety men under Lt. Calley's command entered the hamlet, in which according to their own later testimony they found no Viet Cong and met with no armed resistance. Under Lt. Calley's orders, they nevertheless proceeded to round up and slaughter all My Lai inhabitants, regardless of age or sex. Only a few of the men under Lt. Calley's command refused to participate in the massacre, and the official records describing the operation merely noted that it had been "well-planned, well-executed, and successful." The cover-up engineered within the American Division commanded by Major General Samuel Koster was initially successful, but a year later twenty-three members of the government—including President Richard M. Nixon—received an account of the My Lai massacre from a member of C Company who, although he had not been present, had learned of the incident from his comrades. Shortly afterward, the army opened a full-scale inquiry into events at My Lai, and on September 5, 1969, only one day before he was scheduled to be discharged, Lt. Calley was arrested and charged with the murder of 109 Vietnamese civilians.

Denounced in a White House statement as "abhorrent to the conscience of all the American people," the My Lai massacre appalled a nation shocked by both its mindless savagery and the fact that it had been carried out by men who in the words of *Time* magazine were "depressingly normal." It was advanced by way of explanation that the men in C Company were under great nervous strain and that in the little more than three months preceding the massacre they had lost more than half of the company's 190 men to sniper fire, guerrilla action, and booby traps.

Court martial proceedings against Lt. Calley began at Fort Benning, Georgia, on November 12, 1970, and ended on March 31, 1971, with a life sentence for the murder of at least twenty-two unarmed civilians in My Lai.

To the surprise of many, a wave of protest swept the nation. In addition to those who proclaimed that Lt. Calley had only been doing his duty as a soldier in time of war, there was another group of protesters who felt that he was being used as a "scapegoat" for the crimes of more highly placed military and civilian leaders. Resolutions urging clemency for Lt. Calley were passed in the legislatures of Arkansas, Kansas, Tennessee, and Texas, and the White House was reported to have been inundated with mail denouncing the court martial verdict and sentence.

In the midst of this clamor, President Nixon ordered Lt. Calley released from the Fort Benning stockade and placed under house arrest until such time as he, the President, could review the case. Critics denounced the move as an attempt to wring political advantage from a tragic situation. Special attention was focused on an indignant letter written to the President by the prosecutor at the trial, Captain Aubrey Daniel III, who wrote: "Your intervention has damaged the military judicial system and lessened any respect it may have gained . . . . What took place [at My Lai] has to be considered a tragic day in the history of our nation. But the greatest tragedy of all will be if political expediency dictates the compromise of such a fundamental moral principle as the inherent unlawfulness of the murder of innocent persons." Later the President seemed to back off.

The most complete account of the My Lai massacre is contained in the *Peers Report*, the result of two years of investigation by Lt. General W. R. Peers and a team of researchers. It was not until four years after its completion that this report was declassified and released in November 1974. It listed thirty individuals whom it recommended for general courts-martial. Of those named, six were tried and only Lt. Cally was convicted; his life sentence was reduced by appeal to ten years and he was paroled after completing one-third of his sentence.

M-X Missile *See* **Intercontinental Ballistic Missiles.**

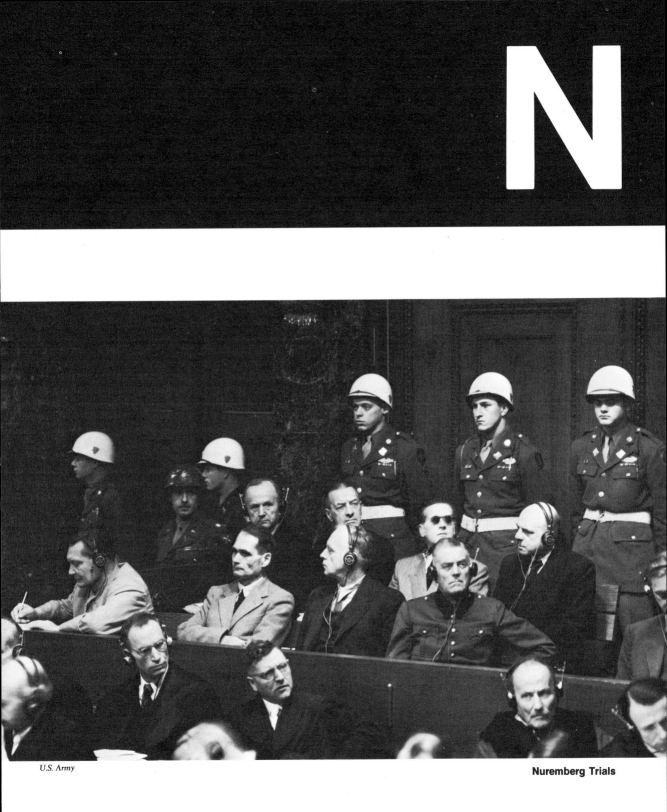

N

U.S. Army

Nuremberg Trials

NAACP v. Alabama In an attempt to frustrate desegregation efforts, southern legislators passed a series of laws requiring the NAACP to disclose its membership lists, records, and finances. On July 25, 1956, the NAACP was fined $10,000 in Montgomery, Alabama, for contempt of court when it refused to produce its records during an injunction case against it. Arguing that such disclosure would make it possible to bring economic pressure to bear on its members, the NAACP persisted in its refusal and the fine was automatically increased to $100,000. However, on June 30, 1958, the U.S. Supreme Court unanimously reversed the fine and ruled (*NAACP v. Alabama*) that past experience had shown revelation of such lists had exposed members "to economic reprisal, loss of employment, threat of physical coercion and other manifestations of public hostility." Laws requiring such disclosure were therefore held a violation of the constitutional right of freedom of association.

Nader's Raiders *See* **Unsafe at Any Speed.**

NAM *See* **National Association of Manufacturers.**

NASA *See* **National Aeronautics and Space Administration.**

National Advisory Commission on Civil Disorders The **Watts Riots** of August 1965, in which thirty-four died, 1,032 were injured, and property damage was estimated at over $40 million, were followed by "the long hot summer" of 1967. In July 1967, charges of police brutality led to widespread disorder in the black ghettos of Newark, New Jersey, where twenty-six died before order was restored. Later that same month similar charges resulted in riots in Detroit; order was restored with the aid of federal troops only after forty-three persons were killed.

"This was the context in which I created the National Advisory Commission on Civil Disorders, headed by Governor Otto Kerner of Illinois and Mayor John V. Lindsay of New York," wrote President Lyndon B. Johnson. The Kerner Commission, as it is sometimes referred to, was instructed to find out "What happened, why did it happen, and what can be done to prevent it from happening again and again?" On February 29, 1968, the commission issued a 1,400-page report which attributed Negro unrest to white racism, and it recommended more than 150 steps to remedy the situation. Among the most important of these was the creation of 2-million new jobs in the next three years;

additional low and moderate income housing; federal income supplements based on need; and decentralized city governments capable of greater responsiveness to community needs.

As President Johnson later wrote:

At the moment I received the report, I was having one of the toughest fights of my life, trying to persuade Congress to pass the 10 percent tax surcharge without imposing deep cuts in our most critical **Great Society** programs. I will never understand how the commission expected me to get this same Congress to turn 180 degrees overnight and appropriate an additional $30 billion for the same programs that it was demanding I cut by $6 billion. This would have required a miracle.

In its controversial analysis of the reasons for the riots, the Commission saw white racism as essentially responsible for the explosive mixture made up of "pervasive discrimination and segregation," "black migration and white exodus" to and from major cities, and "black ghettos" in which "segregation and poverty have intersected to destroy opportunity and hope and to enforce failure."

Noting that almost invariably routine arrests by police precipitated the outbreak of violence as in Watts, Newark, and Detroit, the report emphasized:

. . . to many Negroes police have come to symbolize white power, white racism and white repression. And the fact is that many police do reflect and express these white attitudes. The atmosphere of hostility and cynicism is reinforced by a widespread perception among Negroes of the existence of police brutality and corruption, and of a "double standard" of justice and protection—one for Negroes and one for whites.

In a *Newsweek* interview (March 6, 1978) former Mayor Lindsay complained that the report by the Commission failed to prompt significant government action.

National Aeronautics and Space Administration (NASA) In April of 1958, President Dwight D. Eisenhower asked Congress to create a civilian "agency" charged with the scientific exploration of space. No doubt still smarting from the blow to American scientific prestige delivered by the successful Soviet **Sputnik** launchings of 1957, Congress had the National Aeronautics and Space Act of 1958 ready for the President's signature on July 29, 1958. The act created NASA to replace the National Advisory Committee for Aeronautics (NACA) established forty-three years earlier. The final legislation called for an "administration."

Governed by a nine-man council headed by the

Vice President, NASA is administrated by a presidential appointee—President Eisenhower chose T. Keith Glennan, president of Case Institute, who had previously been a member of the **Atomic Energy Commission** (AEC). The first NASA Deputy Administrator was Dr. Hugh L. Dryden, who had previously headed NACA.

NASA is concerned with all aspects of manned or unmanned flight both within and beyond the Earth's atmosphere. Its primary purpose is to develop techniques for the peaceful exploration of space, but its activities mesh with goals and projects of the Department of Defense. In July 1960 it took over the operations of the Army Ballistic Missile Agency at Redstone Arsenal, Huntsville, Alabama. German-born rocket scientist Wernher von Braun, who had been director of the Huntsville missile facility which was largely responsible for the successful *Explorer I* launching in January 1958, remained on as director of the rebaptized George C. Marshall Space Flight Center at Huntsville.

In September 1959, NASA launched its first satellite, *Vanguard III*, which provided additional data on the Van Allen radiation belts, whose existence had been confirmed by *Explorer I.* Project Mercury had been established in 1958 and by 1963 Mercury astronauts had made four orbital missions.

A moon-landing plan devised by NASA in 1960 received the backing of President John F. Kennedy, who the following year set a national goal "of landing a man on the moon and returning him safely to earth" before the end of the decade: the program was christened **Project Apollo**.

By 1965 NASA employed some 36,000 people in its Washington headquarters, four development centers, five research centers, and various other installations. Its annual budget for that year was $5.25 billion. After the achievement of a lunar landing with the July 1969 launching of *Apollo 11*, public interest and congressional support for space exploration as it concerned the moon began to wane. Faced with cuts in personnel and budget—in recent years its budget has tended to hover around $3.5 billion—in 1973 NASA nevertheless established **Project Skylab,** to develop a manned orbital space station. In an unusual example of international cooperation, the program led in July 1975 to a linkup in space between *Apollo 18* and the U.S.S.R.'s *Soyuz XIX*.

In September 1976, the NASA/Rockwell International facility, Palmdale, California, completed work on the *Enterprise*, a space shuttle orbiter which will be used in a Space Transportation System planned for the future. During 1977, this craft successfully completed a number of approach and landing flight tests. Flights of the space shuttle are expected to be operational in the next decade and NASA has already selected a number of astronaut candidates.

National Alliance of Businessmen *See* **Job Opportunities in the Business Sector.**

National Association of Manufacturers (NAM) A voluntary association of some 20,000 companies and corporations engaged in manufacturing and related fields. It was formed in Cincinnati, Ohio, in 1895 "to foster trade, business and financial interests, to reform abuses therein, to secure freedom from unlawful and unjust exactions, to diffuse accurate and reliable information . . . for the mutual benefit of its members." To achieve these ends the association lobbies for and against legislation in Washington—in the immediate post-World War II period it led the fight against consumer price controls and the Office of Price Administration (OPA)—and publicizes the domestic and international policies which it helps industry formulate.

The NAM, which maintains divisional and regional offices across the nation, sustains itself by dues which are supposed to be proportional to the member-company's net worth.

National Black Political Convention (NBPC) Meeting in Gary, Indiana, March 10-12, 1972, some 3,000 voting delegates—including elected black office holders, delegates chosen at local conventions, and representatives of civil rights organizations from the militant **Black Panther Party** to the traditionalist National Association for the Advancement of Colored People (NAACP)—voted to establish a 427-member National Black Assembly chosen from the District of Columbia and the 43 states represented at the convention.

Divisions among the delegates surfaced immediately, and the Gary convention was unable to resolve strategy differences between those who favored working within the nation's two-party structure and those who insisted on separatist action. In addition, many delegates walked out of the convention when it went on record as opposing busing, which it labeled "racist" and "suicidal," to achieve racial integration in public schools.

In the last minutes of the convention, Imamu Amiri Baraka (formerly the poet and playwright LeRoi Jones) successfully introduced a resolution calling for the "dismantling" of Israel. (It was retained in a somewhat modified form in the "black agenda" issued by the NBPC the following May 19.) Later, the NAACP withdrew from the NBPC because of "ideological" differences, most of which centered on the resolutions dealing with busing and Israel.

Although it initially refused to back any candidate for the Democratic presidential nomination at the forthcoming Democratic National Convention in Miami, on June 26, 1972, the NBPC endorsed South Dakota's Senator George McGovern.

In October 1972, some 300 delegates set up the National Black Assembly as a permanent organization structure with Rep. Charles Diggs (D.-Mich.) as president. Richard Hatcher, mayor of Gary, was named chairman of a fifty-four-member political council, and Baraka was made secretary general of both the assembly and the council.

National Commission on the Causes and Prevention of Violence *See Walker Report.*

National Conference on Black Power Some 1,000 delegates representing 197 Negro organizations of all political hues met in Newark, New Jersey, on July 20, 1967, for a four-day conference designed "to concentrate in an introspective way on the means of empowering a largely benighted and hopeless community to stand on its own and to add its unused potential for the enrichment of the lives of all." Among the groups represented were the National Association for the Advancement of Colored People (NAACP), the **Organization for Afro-American Unity,** the National Urban League, the **Southern Christian Leadership Conference** (SCLC), the **Congress of Racial Equality** (CORE), and the **Student Nonviolent Coordinating Committee and** (SNCC; Snick). Whites were excluded from all meetings and workshops, but white reporters were permitted to attend press briefings.

The conference was chaired by Floyd B. McKissick, national director of CORE, and Rep. Charles C. Diggs (D.-Mich.) It had been conceived of by Adam Clayton Powell, who did not attend but was named an honorary cochairman, and organized by Dr. Nathan Wright, Jr., executive director of the Department of Urban Work of the Episcopal Diocese of Newark. Because it occurred shortly after six days of racial rioting in Newark during which twenty-six people died, it was strongly objected to by New Jersey's Governor Richard J. Hughes. (The conference issued a report condemning the riots as "the inevitable results of the criminal behavior of a society which dehumanizes people and drives men to utter distraction.")

Delegates also passed a unanimous resolution demanding that full restitution and reparation be made to blacks for losses sustained during the Newark riots, and that "all of our black brothers and sisters be released from jail without bail immediately." The Newark police were charged with indiscriminately murdering, beating, and arresting black people, and with wanton destruction of black property.

Among the more than 100 resolutions adopted before the conference disbanded on July 23 was a call for the establishment of Negro housing and building cooperatives; a condemnation of the **Vietnam War** and an exhortation to black youths to respond to the draft with "Hell, no, we won't go!"; the endorsement of "selective patronage" programs; the call for a guaranteed annual income; the establishment of black universities to train "professional black revolutionaries"; the institution of paramilitary training for young black people; the setting up of black financial institutions able to provide housing and business loans to community credit unions; and the rejection of birth control programs as a covert means of "exterminating" the Negro.

National Defense Education Act (NDEA) Signed into law by President Dwight D. Eisenhower on September 2, 1958, the National Defense Education Act (NDEA) was to some degree inspired by a 1957 U.S. Office of Education report on Education in the U.S.S.R. The act provided almost $300 million for low-interest loans to college students, with special inducements for those who entered elementary or secondary school teaching for at least five years following the completion of their education. The legislation also established a fund of an approximately equivalent amount to be used as matching grants for states establishing facilities in languages, mathematics, and the sciences. Additional sums were also provided for the development of a variety of audiovisual aids, including movies, radio, and educational television.

NDEA was part of the nation's startled response to the Soviet Union's successful *Sputnik* satellite launchings of late 1957. As Vannevar Bush, wartime director of the Office of Scientific Research and Development, told a congressional subcommittee on November 25, 1957: "The *Sputnik* was one of the finest things that Russia ever did for us. It has waked this country up."

National Foundation on the Arts and Humanities In his **"Great Society"** message to Congress on January 4, 1965, President Lyndon B. Johnson noted: "We must also recognize and encourage those who can be pathfinders for the Nation's imagination and understanding. To help promote and honor creative achievement, I will propose a national foundation of the arts."

Created on September 29, 1965, as part of the executive branch, the National Foundation on the Arts and Humanities consists of a National Endowment for the Arts, a National Endowment for Humanities, and a Federal Council on the Arts and the Humanities. The endowments have separate councils composed of a leader and twenty-six members appointed by the President to advise on applications for financial support. Both heads are part of the fourteen-member federal council whose job it is to coordinate the activities of the endowments and related programs of other federal agencies.

The purpose of the Arts Endowment is to encourage the arts and make them more generally available by awarding grants to individuals and to nonprofit, tax-exempt organizations representing the nation's best in literature, theater, the public media, dance, architecture, music, and painting. Similar goals are established by the Humanities Endowment in the fields of language, literature, archaeology, history, philosophy, etc. Most grants to organizations are on a matching basis, as, for example, the $1 million grant to New York City's Metropolitan Opera in 1974.

In the mid-1970s, appropriations for the foundation were well over $80 million annually.

National Liberation Front (NLF) Formed in December 1960 by communist insurgents against the government established in South Vietnam by Ngo Dinh Diem after he refused to permit the reunification elections which—according to the 1954 Geneva Accords that put an end to the French-Indochina War—were to take place no later than July 1956. The Viet Cong were the guerrilla forces of the NLF.

See **Vietnam War.**

National Merit Scholarship Corporation (NMSC) Established in 1955 by grants from the **Ford Foundation** and the Carnegie Corporation of New York as an independent, nonprofit organization, the National Merit Scholarship Corporation (NMSC) administers the Merit Scholarship Program and—since 1964—the National Achievement Scholarship Program for outstanding black students. Under the former, students achieving top scores in the Prelimi-

nary Scholastic Aptitude Test (PSAT)/National Merit Scholarship Qualifying Test (NMSQT) may be considered for one-time National Merit $1,000 Scholarships and for four-year Sponsored Merit Scholarships. Every year some 15,000 students are designated as Merit Program Semifinalists on the basis of the PSAT/NMSQT, and another 40,000 are given Letters of Commendation.

Most semifinalists who substantiate their previous test scores on the Scholastic Aptitude Test (SAT) of the College Entrance Examination Board are accepted as finalists after being endorsed by their schools and supplying NMSC with biographical information—including family financial data, which are used only in determining the annual stipend if the student wins a four-year sponsored scholarship of from $100 to $1,500 annually.

The selection procedure governing the naming of Negro Achievement Semifinalists and winners of National Achievement $1,000 Scholarships is based on the number of blacks in the population of six geographic regions. Under the Achievement program, qualifying students are eligible for some 225 one-time $1,000 scholarships and about 100 four-year sponsored scholarships. Black students taking the qualifying PSAT/NMSQT may register for consideration in either the Merit or Achievement programs, but not in both.

National Mobilization Committee to End the War in Vietnam (Mobe) Soon after some 100,000 people marched in New York on April 15, 1967, to protest the continuing **Vietnam War, Students for a Democratic Society** (SDS) pacifist David Dellinger, one of its organizers, established the National Mobilization Committee to End the War in Vietnam (Mobe) and began planning for a similar protest march, which eventually took place in Washington, D.C., on October 21, 1967. Other prominent Mobe members were Rennie Davis and Tom Hayden, who along with Dellinger were to figure in the trial of the **Chicago Eight** which began on September 24, 1969.

When in October 1967 it was announced that the Democratic National Convention would be held in Chicago in August 1968, Mobe immediately began making plans for a massive demonstration that would protest both the war and the renomination of President Lyndon B. Johnson. Tentative plans were made at a meeting of Mobe's Administration Committee in December 1967, and the following February Tom Hayden, SDS member and author of the **Port Huron Statement,** was named the group's Chicago coordinator.

Although early Mobe statements appeared to indicate that nonviolence would be the favored tactic, it soon became apparent that Mobe lacked control and discipline over many of the groups that planned to participate in the Chicago protest. Chief among these were the **Yippies** (Youth International Party), founded in 1968 by Jerry Rubin and Abbie Hoffman, who planned a Festival of Life to coincide with the national convention. Their apparent eagerness for a confrontation with the Chicago police worried both Davis and Hayden, who feared that Yippie antics would frighten off many potential antiwar demonstrators. Mobe had hoped to attract 100,000 supporters to Chicago, but in the event probably no more than 10,000 participated, most of these coming from the Chicago area.

These factors—coupled with police intransigence in refusing to issue permits for parades, rallies, and the nighttime use of Lincoln Park—led to the **Battle of Chicago.**

The original organization having been discredited by violence, a New Mobilization Committee to End the War in Vietnam (New Mobe) was formed by Sidney Peck, chairman of the Cleveland Area Peace Action Committee. Both the SDS and the Yippies were excluded, but the organization's base was considerably expanded by the inclusion of groups such as the United Methodist Church, the Episcopal Peace Fellowship, and the American Friends Service Committee. New Mobe played an important role in planning the October 1969 **Moratorium Day.**

National Oceanic and Atmospheric Administration (NOAA)

Citing the need for "a unified approach to the problems of oceans and atmosphere" given the increasing importance of oceanic food and minerals in meeting rising world demand, President Richard M. Nixon proposed the National Oceanic and Atmospheric Administration (NOAA) to Congress on July 9, 1970, in a message which also proposed the **Environmental Protection Agency** (EPA). Assigned some of the functions formally carried out by the Department of the Interior's Bureau of Commercial Fisheries and the Fish and Wildlife Service, NOAA also took over from the Department of Defense the Great Lakes Survey and from the Department of the Navy the National Oceanographic Data Center and the National Oceanographic Intrumentation Center. Additional functions were also inherited from the Coast Guard, the Department of Transportation, the Department of Commerce, and the **National Science Foundation.** The

initial proposed budget for NOAA was $250 million.

In all, NOAA consists of six major offices—the National Ocean Survey, the National Weather Service, the National Marine Fisheries Service, the National Environmental Satellite Service, the Environmental Data Service, and the Environmental Research Laboratories—whose combined duty it is to chart and explore the ocean's potential resources, to predict weather changes, to provide ample warning of environmental hazards, and to establish means by which the impact of natural destructive events can be mitigated. The administration monitors the condition of both U.S. coastal waters and ocean bodies in other areas by means of a system of buoys.

See **Tiros.**

National Organization for Non-Parents (NON)

A tax-exempt, nonprofit educational organization founded in 1972 "to make the childfree life-style a realistic and socially accepted and respected option." NON's headquarters in Baltimore, Maryland, maintains liaison with forty-eight local groups in the United States and abroad and has a watchdog committee designed to assure that those who have rejected "pronatalism"—defined as an "attitude that exalts motherhood and assumes or encourages parenthood for all"—receive social encouragement and equitable treatment before the law.

National Organization for Women (NOW)

As a result of the President's Commission on the Status of Women established in 1961 by President John F. Kennedy—and chaired by Eleanor Roosevelt—fifty similar commissions were established at a state level. Representatives of these groups met in Washington, D.C., in June 1966, for the Third National Conference of Commissions on the Status of Women, and it was here on June 30 that the National Organization for Women (NOW) was born.

The refusal of conference officials to bring to the floor a resolution urging the Equal Employment Opportunity Commission (EEOC) to make sure that Title VII of the **Civil Rights Act of 1964,** i.e., the provision against sex discrimination, be enforced on a par with the race provision led directly to NOW, which was conceived of as a civil rights organization for women. Most active in NOW's formation was Betty Friedan, author of **The Feminine Mystique** (1963), in whose hotel room a small group of women who had been for the resolution met. By the end of the day, Ms. Friedan had invented the organization's name and signed up twenty-eight members. An organizing conference held the following October signed up more than 300 charter members.

A *Statement of Purpose* issued by NOW noted that "the time has come for a new movement toward true equality for all women in America, and toward a fully equal partnership of the sexes, as part of a world-wide revolution of human rights now taking place within and beyond our national borders." It went on to urge the rejection of "the token appointment of a few women to high-level positions in government and industry as a substitute for a serious continuing effort to recruit and advance women according to their individual abilities." It rejected "the current assumptions that a man must carry the sole burden of supporting himself, his wife, and family, and that a woman is automatically entitled to lifelong support by a man upon her marriage, or that marriage, home and family are primarily woman's world and responsibility—hers, to dominate, his, to support." Women were urged to exercise their political rights to avoid segregation into "separate-and-not-equal ladies' auxiliaries in political parties. . . ." Declaring itself independent of any political party, NOW committed itself to work toward changing "the false image of women now prevalent in the mass media, and in the texts, ceremonies, laws, and practices of our major social institutions."

NOW chapters were rapidly established all over the country, and the organization was the driving force behind the **Women's Strike for Equality** (August 26, 1970) and for formation of the **National Women's Political Caucus** (NWPL) (July 10, 1971).

At NOW's National Conference held in Philadelphia, October 25-27, 1975, a "Majority Caucus" of radicals seized control of the organization after three days and nights of voting characterized by charges of fraud and the appearance of the American Arbitration Association, which was called to the scene to police the election. The new leaders vowed to take NOW "out of the mainstream, into the revolution." On November 9, 1976, a dissident group of thirteen, led by Betty Friedan, met at a New Orleans, Louisiana, motel to deal with the crisis in the movement and form their own "network."

NOW has more than 700 chapters and approximately 60,000 members throughout the country. At its annual meeting on October 8, 1978, in Washington, D.C., members voted to concentrate the organization's resources on passage of the **Equal Rights Amendment** (ERA) to the exclusion of other feminist causes.

National Purpose Controversy Beginning with its May 23, 1960, issue, *Life* magazine launched a five-part series in which leading Americans were asked to explore what the phrase "the national purpose" has meant to the United States in the past "and what it means—or should mean—today."

The series seems to have been planned as a response to those social critics who, like columnist Walter Lippmann, charged that

. . . the critical weakness of our society is that for the time being our people do not have great purposes which they are united in wanting to achieve. The public mood of the country is defensive, to hold on and to conserve, not to push forward and to create. We talk about ourselves these days as if we were a completed society, one which has achieved its purposes, and has no further great business to transact.

To provide a "framework" for the articles to come, John K. Jessup, *Life*'s chief editorial writer, wrote the introductory installment, which examined national purpose as expressed in the Declaration of Independence, the Constitution, the Monroe Doctrine, and similar historic documents, as well as by such spokesmen as Washington, Jefferson, Andrew Jackson, Lincoln, Theodore Roosevelt, Woodrow Wilson, and Franklin D. Roosevelt. In the four succeeding issues the theme was continued by former Democratic presidential candidate Adlai Stevenson, poet and playwright Archibald MacLeish, evangelist Billy Graham, RCA chairman David Sarnoff, Carnegie Corporation of New York president John Gardner, Rand Corporation national defense specialist Albert Wohlstetter, constitutional expert Clinton Rossiter, and political commentator Walter Lippmann.

"That something has gone wrong in America most of us know," wrote MacLeish. "We are richer than any nation before us. We have more Things in our garages and kitchens and cellars than Louis Quatorze had in the whole of Versailles." But in spite of material prosperity and technological progress, he argued, "We feel that we've lost our way in the woods, that we don't know where we are going—if anywhere." He urged a rededication to the goals of the American Revolution.

Adlai Stevenson, noting the same affluence in American society, pointed up the "contrast between private opulence and public squalor." No nation with the supermarket as its temple and the singing commercial as its litany, he argued, is likely to fire the world with an irresistible vision of its exalted purposes and inspiring way of life. The gap between the world's rich and poor, he emphasized, was as great "a threat to peace as the arms race." He urged the nation to accept the cost in money and sacrifice of recovering "the public image of a great America. . . . No preordained destiny decrees that America shall have all the breaks and soft options. Neither greatness nor even freedom lies that way . . . ."

Evangelist Billy Graham wrote: "I am convinced that regardless of the outward appearance of prosperity within the corporate life of America today there is present a form of moral and spiritual cancer which can ultimately lead to the country's destruction unless the disease is treated promptly and the trend reversed." Like most of the panelists participating in the series, he urged a return to the principles of freedom, justice, and equality on which the republic was originally founded.

"Can a nation that has fulfilled the mission of its youth expect to find a second mission in its later years?" asked Clinton Rossiter. "And can a nation that has known the material success of ours shake loose from the clutch of self-indulgence?" Once a lean and hungry people, he noted, "we are [now] fat and complacent, a people that 'has it made,' and we find it hard to rouse to the trumpet of sacrifice—even if anyone in authority were to blow it."

Pointing up—as most of the panelists did—the enormous challenge to freedom represented by the Soviet Union, Walter Lippmann drew attention to the fact that in the fifteen years since the end of World War II, "the condition of mankind has changed more rapidly and more deeply than in any other period within the experience of the American people." As a consequence, he argued,

. . . the formulations of national purpose which were made in the first half of this century are now inadequate. In part we have fulfilled them. In part we have outlived them. In part they have become irrelevant because of the unexpected changes in the conditions of things. In part they are out of focus. All in all, they do not now mobilize our energies.

Necessity would be the mother of invention and help us form new goals, Lippmann felt. For

. . . all the danger and trouble and worry it causes us, the Soviet challenge may yet prove to have been a blessing in disguise. For without it, what would become of us if we felt that we were invulnerable, if our influence in the world were undisputed, if we had no need to prove that we can rise above a tranquil self-satisfaction?

In August 1960, *Life* extended the National Purpose series with articles by Sen. John F. Kennedy (D.-Mass.) and Vice President Richard M. Nixon, the Democratic and Republican presidential candidates in the forthcoming national election. Senator Kennedy noted that if Americans are to recharge their sense of national purpose, they should "accept no invitations to relax on a patent mattress stuffed with wooly illusions labeled peace, prosperity and normalcy. We should congratulate ourselves not for our country's past glories and present accumulations but for our opportunities for further toil and risk. Rather than take satisfaction in goals already reached, we should be contrite about the goals unreached. . . ."

In the final article of the series, Vice President Nixon wrote of his belief that "it is America's national purpose to extend the goals of the preamble of our Constitution to our relations with all men." He summarized these as the formation of a more perfect union, the establishment of justice, the insurance of domestic tranquility, provision for the common defense, promotion of the general welfare, and the assurance of the blessings of liberty for ourselves and posterity. The appeal of communism, he noted, is based on the fact that it purports to offer mankind "four of these six goals. . . . In place of two of them, justice and liberty, they demand a social discipline enforced by tyrannical state power." He concluded by emphasizing that the six goals were inseparable and that this "inseparability applies not to ourselves alone but to all mankind."

National Science Foundation (NSF) Founded in 1950, it is the responsibility of this governmental agency to "promote the progress of science; to advance the national health, prosperity and welfare; to secure the national defense." The NSF does this by sponsoring research in the various sciences, by providing a central source for information about scientists and technicians, and by facilitating an exchange of information.

The NSF can trace its origins back to the government's experience with the Office of Scientific Research and Development (OSRD) during World War II. Continuation of federal subsidies to basic research was urged in *Science—The Endless Frontier*, a report made to President Harry S Truman in 1945, and similar recommendations were made as the result of congressional hearings chaired by Sen. Harley M. Kilgore (D.-W.Va.). A legislative stumbling block, however, was the manner in which federal funds were to be distributed, the disposal of patents developed as a result of government-sponsored research, and the amount of autonomy any such agency should enjoy. Because the original legislation passed failed to give the President control of the agency's governing board, President Truman vetoed the bill in 1947. It was not until 1950 that compromise legislation was approved and the NSF was established with a modest budget of $3 million. By the early 1970s that budget had grown to well over $500 million.

The NSF governing board is made up of twenty-five people appointed by the President. In spite of its enormous influence and increasing budget, the NSF probably controls no more than 10 percent of the *total* amount of government-sponsored research. According to one NSF report, in the 1960s federal funds were being used to support approximately 90 percent of all research being done in aviation and aeronautics, 65 percent of the work being done in electricity and electronics, and almost 25 percent of basic automotive research.

In the early 1970s, in keeping with the basic attitude of the Nixon administration, there was some shift from pure to practical research, and in 1970 the NSF implemented the Interdisciplinary Research Relevant to the Problems of Our Society (IRRPOS) program.

National Security Act President Harry S Truman wrote that one of the strongest convictions he brought to the office of President was that "the antiquated defense setup of the United States had to be reorganized quickly as a step toward insuring our future safety and preserving world peace." As a former member of the Appropriations and Military Affairs Committees of the Senate and as chairman of the Special Committee to Investigate the National Defense Program, he had become convinced that unless the activities of the Army and the Navy could be coordinated "we would finally end up with two departments of defense and eventually three when the Air Force succeeded in obtaining its special committee in the House and Senate."

In February 1947 President Truman sent a bill to Congress that was designed to regroup the armed forces into a National Military Establishment under a Secretary of Defense with Cabinet status. As finally signed by him on July 26, 1947, the bill was not as strong as he had wished, because it "included concessions on both sides for the sake of bringing together the Army and the Navy."

Under the act, executive departments of the Army, Navy, and Air Force were established with Secretaries for each. These Secretaries did not hold Cabinet rank but could submit recommendations and reports to the President or the Budget Director.

The Air Force was created from the Army Air Corps, but the Navy retained its air arm, as well as the Marine Corps. The Secretary of Defense—the first appointee was former Secretary of the Navy James V. Forrestal—had no authority over the civilian personnel of the three branches.

The act provided for a National Security Council (NSC) as the chief policy-making body. The NSC was to be presided over by the President or his appointee and was to include the Secretaries of State, Defense, Army, Navy, Air Force, and the heads of a Munitions Board, a National Security Resources Board, and a Research and Development Board—all created by the act—and others designated by the President. Under the NSC and responsible to it was a **Central Intelligence Agency** (CIA) created to collect and evaluate information relating to national security; however, the CIA was to have no domestic security functions.

Secretary Forrestal was soon beset by weaknesses in the act, which provided for no single Chief of Staff and allowed the subsidiary secretaries too much autonomy. Rivalry between the services is said to have broken his health and led to his resignation in March 1949 and his shocking suicide two months later.

As a result, Congress was inspired to pass new legislation, and on August 10, 1949, President Truman signed into law the National Security Act Amendments of 1949, which he considered one of the outstanding achievements of his administration. These amendments reorganized the National Military Establishment as the Department of Defense and increased the authority of its secretary—now Louis A. Johnson—over the three branches of the armed forces. In addition, it provided for a nonvoting chairman of the Joint Chiefs of Staff. The first to be appointed to this position was General Omar Bradley.

After 1949, the NSC was to be composed of the President, the Vice-President, the Secretaries of State and Defense, the chairman of the National Security Resources Board, and such other executive department heads as the President may appoint.

National Student Association (NSA) Activists returning from the founding congress of the International Union of Students (IUS) held in Prague (1946) called for a national meeting in Chicago later that year at which some 500 student delegates discussed the desirability of creating a national student union in the United States. The result was a founding convention in September 1947 at the University of Wisconsin, Madison. At this meeting approximately 800 representatives from 351 colleges and universities and various national organizations drafted a Student Bill of Rights and established the U.S. National Student Association (NSA).

Although dominated by a liberal coalition, NSA ran the political gamut from a small group of communists on the left to a well-organized anticommunist Catholic group on the right. A significant conservative influence was also exerted by a nominally "liberal" Southern regional caucus which called for a "moderate" position on race relations.

Although by the end of the 1950s NSA had established a strong civil rights position, it was never prominent in the activist civil rights protests of the 1960s.

NSA received a crippling blow when on February 13, 1967, its president, Wayne Eugene Groves, revealed that since 1952 it had received more than $3 million from foundations serving as conduits for the **Central Intelligence Agency** (CIA). These funds were used for "broad programs of international affairs which worked with other unions of students," especially in developing nations. The money was said to have been used to send representatives to student congresses to maintain a "democratic and progressive" presence abroad as an alternative to front organizations financed by the U.S.S.R. Because of the influence of **McCarthyism,** it had become impossible to obtain congressional approval of funds for liberal-oriented, anticommunist organizations.

NSA president Phil Sherburne had tried to end the CIA connection in 1966 by appealing to Vice President Hubert H. Humphrey for other sources of revenue. When he revealed the CIA funding to Michael Wood, NSA development director, the later sent a fifty-page memorandum to the radical magazine *Ramparts*, which was preparing to publish the full story in its March 1967 issue. It was to anticipate that publication that the new president, Groves, released information on the CIA funding. He noted that no CIA money would be accepted for the 1967–1968 NSA budget.

On February 23, 1967, a three-member commission appointed by President Lyndon B. Johnson to investigate CIA funding of overseas programs reported that the CIA had acted in accord with policies established by the National Security Council.

National Teacher Corps   *See* **Higher Education Act of 1965.**

National Urban Coalition   *See* **Common Cause.**

National Wilderness Preservation System   *See* **Wilderness Areas Act.**

National Women's Conference   Meeting in Houston, Texas, November 19–21, 1977, delegates to the Government-sponsored National Women's Conference approved twenty-five proposals which were later (March 28, 1978) submitted to President Jimmy Carter as a guide to federal legislation. The 1,442 delegates elected at fifty-six regional meetings formed what was probably the most significant political concentration of women since the 1848 Seneca Falls Convention held under the leadership of Elizabeth Cady Stanton and Lucretia Mott.

Among the more controversial proposals were those urging freedom of abortion, homosexual rights, and passage of the **Equal Rights Amendment** (ERA). The original platform drafted by a forty-six-member presidentially appointed commission headed by Bella S. Abzug, former New York Democratic Representative, included a proposal to create a Cabinet-level department of women's affairs. It was rejected when some members complained that it would separate and "ghettoize" women's concerns.

Other proposals approved by the delegates included recommendations for improved child-care centers, federal programs for battered wives and abused children, expanded women's studies in public schools, and an effort to fill more elective and appointive offices with women.

Opposition to the endorsement of ERA and the right to abortion was centered around some 300 "pro-life" and "pro-family" delegates whose leader was Phyllis Schlafly, head of StopERA. Representing some 20 percent of the total number of delegates, they claimed they were seldom or never given a chance to speak or to amend resolutions. Singing "God Bless America," they strode from the convention hall in the final moments of the meeting.

National Women's Political Caucus (NWPC)   Meeting in Washington, D.C., July 10–11, 1971, more than 200 women formed the National Women's Political Caucus (NWPC) and established its goal as the achievement of equal representation for women at all levels of the nation's political system. A twenty-one-member steering committee was elected, and it set up a program for rallying voter support to women candidates, registering new women voters, and pressuring political parties into accepting women in decision-making roles.

NWPC declared that it would support candidates of both sexes who would join in the struggle against "sexism, racism, violence and poverty." At the opening session, Rep. Bella Abzug (D.-N.Y.) noted that once organized for political power, women could play "a very significant role in the national political party conventions, in the formulation of platforms and in the choice of candidates." Betty Friedan, author of **The Feminine Mystique** (1963) and founder of the **National Organization for Women** (NOW) emphasized that since men make up "98 or 99 percent of the House, Senate, the State Assembly, City Hall, women are outside the body politic."

Ms. Friedan was later to consider NWPC "an abortive attempt to introduce a new kind of political power onto the American scene. . . . At best [it] galvanized a lot of women into running for office in 1972 and afterwards who had not thought of running before, and introduced some new issues, relevant to women, on the political agenda. At worst, it prematurely siphoned off the political power implicit in the women's movement, to be too easily controlled and manipulated by a few ambitious women who served—inadvertently perhaps—the interest of those who didn't want women to control their own new power themselves."

NATO *See* **North Atlantic Treaty Organization.**

"Nattering Nabobs of Negativism" During his first year in office, Vice President Spiro Agnew had built up a reputation as a speaker capable of attracting the attention of the news media—largely by ignoring President Richard M. Nixon's 1969 inaugural plea that Americans "stop shouting at one another." ("If, in challenging, we polarize the American people, I say it is time for a positive polarization.") In the 1970 off-year elections, he was to campaign for the Republican party in thirty-two states and concentrate on attacking critics of the administration's record on the **Vietnam War,** inflation, and unemployment. His speeches—many of them written or polished by presidential aides Pat Buchanan and William Safire—had as their trademark a somewhat baroque use of language and an emphasis on the rhetorical device of alliteration: e.g., "vicars of vacillation," "pampered prodigies," "pusillanimous pussyfooters."

During a speech in San Diego on September 11, 1970, he said: "In the United States today, we have more than our share of nattering nabobs of negativism. They have formed their own 4-H Club—the 'hopeless, hysterical hypochondriacs of history.' "

The line had been written for him by William Safire, who evidently expected the Vice President to choose one of the two alliterative series.

A 1970 Gallop poll ranked the Vice President as third among the nation's most respected men, the first two being President Nixon and evangelist preacher Billy Graham. On October 10, 1973, Agnew became the first Vice President to resign from office. That same day he pled nolo contendere to charges of income tax evasion, after charges of bribery and conspiracy had been dropped. He was fined $10,000 and placed on probation for three years.

Natural Gas Bill Scandal of 1956 The U.S. Supreme Court having ruled in 1954 that under existing law the federal government was required to regulate the price that independent gas producers could charge for gas piped into another state, the Eisenhower administration sought "corrective legislation" because of the President's belief that the rights and responsibilities of the states were being curbed. Legislation exempting independent producers from control by the Federal Power Commission was approved by Congress in February 1956, but its passage was surrounded by rumors of bribery and corruption connected with lobbying for the bill.

On February 3, 1956, Sen. Francis Case (R.-S.Dak.) announced in the Senate that he was voting against the bill, whose goal he was inclined to approve, because he had been offered a $2,500 bribe under the guise of campaign expenses. Similar incidents were brought to the President's attention privately.

As a result, on February 17, 1956, President Dwight D. Eisenhower vetoed the bill, with which he was in basic accord, giving as his reason the fact that "a body of evidence has accumulated indicating that private persons, apparently representing only a very small segment of a great and vital industry, have been seeking to further their own interests by highly questionable activities. These include efforts that I deem to be so arrogant and so much in defiance of acceptable standards of propriety as to risk creating doubt among the American people concerning the integrity of governmental processes." He asked for new legislation that "in addition to furthering the long-term interest of consumers in plentiful supplies of gas, should include specific language protecting consumers in their right to fair prices."

On April 7, a Senate Select Committee investigating the matter concluded that though "there was neither a bribe nor an intent to bribe . . . this is a case of irresponsibility run riot" and that the "gift" to Senator Case had indeed been intended to influence his vote. The following July 24, the Justice Department indicted lawyers John M. Neff and Elmer Patman, as well as the Superior Oil Company they represented, on charges of conspiracy. After pleading guilty of failing to register as lobbyists, both men were fined $2,500 each and given one-year suspended jail sentences. The oil company was fined $5,000 for "aiding and abetting" these men in their failure to register.

Proponents of the bill had argued that federal regulation would discourage the search for new gas sources and "force" producers to confine sales to their own state.

NBEDC *See* **National Black Economic Development Conference.**

NBPC *See* **National Black Political Convention.**

NDEA *See* **National Defense Education Act.**

Negative Income Tax First proposed in the United States by conservative economist Milton Friedman in *Capitalism and Freedom* (1962), it is a modification of the "reverse income tax" proposals made in Great Britain during the 1930s. Under the negative-tax plan, an individual or family whose annual income fails to reach a designated level would not only be excused from taxes but would receive a supplement from federal tax funds. Congress would be required to establish the income level below which "negative" payments would be forthcoming. Congress would also determine the percentage of the gap between actual income and the established minimum that would be made up.

Unlike the **Family Assistance Plan** (FAP) proposed by President Richard M. Nixon in August 1969, the negative tax would not be limited to families with children; eligibility would be based on income level alone. In addition, there would be no payment "in kind," i.e., food stamps and public housing—factors that some economists feel hinder the operation of the free market. Because of this reduced expenditure, it has attracted support from conservatives, who also see it as a means of doing away with a fragmented welfare bureaucracy that has continued to increase in size and cost. Liberals have been attracted to the plan because it promises a more equitable distribution of income.

Opposition to negative income tax proposals has largely been based on fears that it could signifi-cantly weaken work incentives. As part of a wide-spread planning program, in the late 1960s the federal government sponsored negative income tax experiments among low-income groups whose reactions were checked with control groups in the same economic bracket. The focus was on changes in the labor supply due to a loss of incentive; in addition, data were gathered on the ways in which the additional income or leisure gained under the program was spent, and whether or not the changes induced enhanced a family's overall employability.

All in all, close to 9,000 families in six areas of the country took part in the experiment. An analysis released late in 1976 showed that the negative income tax aid received by 1,400 families in the New Jersey area did not change the employment rates of working husbands, but did result in a 5- to 9-percent drop in hours worked, to some extent because overtime was cut. There was also a significant upward shift in the number of adolescents completing a high school education. In addition, families tended to make greater use of medical services, to purchase more basic appliances, and to improve their housing situation.

These results checked out with a preliminary analysis of an experiment in Gary, Indiana, with approximately 1,800 families, approximately 60 percent of which were headed by women, most of whom were receiving assistance under Aid For Dependent Children (AFDC). Because AFDC provided less aid, researchers had expected a decline in productivity under the negative income tax experiment. However, the only statistically significant declines were found to be among female-headed families who had not been benefiting from AFDC. In families headed by men, the work output decline compared with the 5 to 9 percent found in the New Jersey program. There was no decline in employment, but family heads who had been unemployed at the beginning of the experiment tended to remain jobless.

Data obtained from the various experiments have been incorporated into a "response model" which is being used to determine the national costs and effects of a variety of negative income tax proposals.

"Nervous Nellies" In a speech delivered at a Democratic Party fund-raising dinner in Chicago, May 17, 1966, President Lyndon B. Johnson defended his administration's policy of escalation in the continuing and increasingly unpopular **Vietnam War.** He outlined the failure of recent American peace initiatives and noted that the "time had not arrived" when the North Vietnamese were willing "to reason these problems out." Concluding that American arguments needed to be "more persuasive" and "compelling" than they had been previously, he announced that "the road ahead is going to be difficult."

"There will be some Nervous Nellies and some who will become frustrated and bothered and break ranks under the strain. And some will turn on their leaders and on their country and on our own fighting men. There will be times of trial and tensions in the days ahead that will exact the best that is in all of us."

Several weeks later American planes began bombing oil storage facilities in the Hanoi-Haiphong area of North Vietnam. By the end of 1966 the U.S. troop levels in Vietnam had risen dramatically from 184,300 the previous year to 385,300.

Neutron Bomb The 1978 fiscal budget of the **Energy Research and Development Administration** (ERDA) released in mid-1977 carried a brief reference to a "W70 Mod 3 Lance Enhanced Radiation Warhead." Translated into everyday English, this meant an intensely radioactive device that would be potentially more dangerous to life than to property. The neutron bomb—actually a warhead for eight-inch artillery shells and the Lance ground-to-ground missiles deployed in Europe—was spotted in the ERDA budget by alert journalists and promptly dubbed the "Doomsday shell." Amidst heated controversy and after semisecret debate, Congress nevertheless approved funds for its development.

Present *nuclear* weapons are said to release 50 percent of their energy as blast, 35 percent as heat, 5 percent as "prompt" radiation, and 10 percent as "lasting" radiation. A *neutron* warhead would change these proportions to 35 percent blast, 25 percent heat, and 40 percent "prompt" radiation. In practical terms, this would mean less physical damage to battlefields; in addition, the lower level of "lasting" radiation—approximately 1 percent—would mean that territory that had been subjected to neutron bombing could be more quickly occupied by advancing troops.

In April 1978, President Jimmy Carter announced his decision to "defer" immediate production of neutron weapons.

New Economics *See* **Keynesianism.**

New Federalism *See* **New Federalist Paper #1.**

New Federalist Paper #1 President Richard M. Nixon's congressional message of October 13, 1969, in which he announced an unexpected wide-ranging program of reform, was attacked by conservative Republicans as a betrayal of their party's principles of states' rights. Originally, he planned to reply to critics in a speech setting forth a New Federalism as the ideological basis for his program, but he contented himself instead with having his senior speechwriter, William Safire, prepare for distribution to the White House staff and selected journalists a paper entitled as above. Both the name given it and the signature "Publius" were meant to recall the *Federalist Papers* of Alexander Hamilton, James Madison, and John Jay in the early days of the Republic.

The document noted a "sea-change" in the approach to the limitation of centralized power, and that the "new" aspect of New Federalism was that " '*States' rights' have now become rights of first refusal.* Local authority will now regain the right to meet local needs itself, and gain an additional right to Federal financial help; but it will not regain the right it once held to neglect the needs of its citizens." In a process described as "national localism," States' rights were redefined as States' duties, and this change was seen as removing the "great fault" of federalism "without undermining its essential local-first character." It was seen as providing the New Federalists "with two of their prime causes: the cause of regaining control, and the cause of fairness."

It was generally unknown that the President himself had contributed to formulating this ideological rationale, as had John D. Erhlichman, Assistant to the President for Domestic Affairs. As a result, White House staffer Tom Charles Huston—who in 1970 was to be the author of the **Huston Plan** for the "coordination" of intelligence activities by the White House, the **CIA,** and the FBI—issued a rebuttal entitled *Federalism: Old and New—Or, the Pretentions of New Publius Exposed by Cato.* In it, Huston argued that the right of first refusal implied "the right to say No and make it stick; it includes the right of a state to decide for itself whether a 'problem exists.' "

Apparently taking this into account, on March 19, 1970, administration spokesman Secretary of Labor George Shultz said in a speech at the University of Chicago Graduate School of Business that in essence "the New Federalism calls upon us to act as one nation in setting the standards of fairness, and then to act as a congeries of communities in carrying out those standards. We are nationalizing equity as we localize control, while retaining a continued federal stewardship to insure that national standards are attained."

See **Revenue Sharing.**

New Foundation It was not until after two years in office that President Jimmy Carter introduced the theme of his administration in his State of the Union speech on January 23, 1979. "The challenge to us is to build a new and firmer foundation for the future—for a sound economy, for a more effective government, for more political trust, and for a stable peace," the President stressed. Observers noted that the slogan—said to have been the brainchild of presidential speechwriter Rick Herzberg—was evocative of President John F. Kennedy's **New Frontier** and that it reached back into history to remind voters of President Franklin D. Roosevelt's New Deal and President Woodrow Wilson's New Freedom.

In the week that followed his address to the joint session of Congress, the President used the phrase "New Foundation" often enough to leave no doubt that he wanted it to be established in the mind of the public as describing the main thrust of his administration. At a press conference he explained that many of the decisions made since he first took office "do not pay off in immediate political benefits. But it's an investment at the present time for future dividends for America." Asked if he thought the slogan would survive, he said he doubted that it would. Originally it had found little favor with the President's staff but was eventually settled on as the best way to describe the difficult problems the Carter administration faced in developing long-term solutions.

New Frontier The first important use of this phrase was made by Sen. John F. Kennedy (D.-Mass.) on July 15, 1960, in a speech accepting the presidential nomination of the Democratic National Convention meeting in Los Angeles. Noting that the old pioneers gave up their safety, their comfort, and sometimes their lives to build a new world in the West, he emphasized that

. . . we stand today on the edge of a new frontier—the frontier of the 1960s, a frontier of unknown opportunities and paths, a frontier of unfulfilled hopes and threats . . . .

The new frontier of which I speak is not a set of promises—it is a set of challenges. It sums up not what I intend to *offer* the American people but what I intend to *ask* of them. . . . It holds out the promise of more sacrifice instead of more security. . . . Beyond that frontier are uncharted areas of science and space, unsolved problems of peace and war, unconquered pockets of ignorance and prejudice, unanswered questions of poverty and surplus.

In the subsequent presidential campaign, the words "new frontier" were used on many occasions and became a slogan implying an effort at reform that would parallel the New Deal of President Franklin D. Roosevelt in presenting a sustained approach to problems of national welfare and peace. After President Kennedy's election, the New Frontier came to stand for his administration's ambitious programs in the fields of civil rights, space exploration, education, medical care for the aged, and farm legislation. Those who participated in the youthful administration came to be popularly known as New Frontiersmen. Whereas 42 percent of President Dwight D. Eisenhower's appointees came from business backgrounds, in the Kennedy administration there was a heavy preponderance of men drawn from government and the universities, and only 6 percent of the first 200 top appointments came from the business world.

Much of the new President's domestic program was slowed down by congressional opposition and the various international crises he faced in Cuba (*see* **Bay of Pigs** and **Cuban Missile Crisis**) and Germany (*see* **Berlin Crisis**). Defending his administration's achievements against comparisons with those of the New Deal, the President said: "Everyone says that Roosevelt did this and that, why don't I? Franklin Roosevelt faced the task of passing a domestic program over and against violent opposition. The great issue today is in the field of foreign policy."

After the assassination of President Kennedy on **November 22, 1963,** many of the domestic goals of the New Frontier found a place in President Lyndon B. Johnson's plans for the **Great Society.**

New Journalism When in 1963 Clay Felker was appointed editor of *New York*, the Sunday supplement of the *New York World Journal Tribune* (*NYWJT*), he began featuring journalism of a highly personal and expressionistic kind by such writers as Jimmy Breslin, Tom Wolfe, and Dick Schaap. The material, for which he himself is said to have coined the name "New Journalism," aimed at the expression of an essential truth—sometimes, according to critics, with the effect of a personalized distortion of what traditional journalists considered the overall picture. Its technical presentation depended heavily on the experimental techniques of fiction, creating an air of drama and involvement by unusual juxtapositions, colorful uses of language, bizarre punctuation, and a somewhat muckrakerish tone.

The trend was continued and escalated when Felker established *New York* as an independent publication after the demise of the *NYWJT* in 1967: *New York* magazine. It was later reflected in the *Village Voice*, Felker's New York weekly "newspaper." New Journalism—variations of which became known as "Gonzo journalism," "consumer journalism," or "advocate journalism,"—was featured elsewhere in the nation in publications such as *Cervi's Rocky Mountain Journal*, the *San Francisco Bay Guardian*, and the *Maine Times*. In 1973, George A. Hirsch, who had formerly been associated with *New York*, founded the nationally distributed *New Times*, which successfully exploited the technique until it folded in 1978.

Writers who have at various times also been associated with New Journalism include Nicholas von Hoffman, Nora Sayre, Gail Sheehy, Gay Talese, Jack Newfield, Pete Hamill, and James F. Ridgeway. A prime example of the technique is *Fear and Loathing: On the Campaign Trail '72* (1973) by Hunter S. Thompson—"the Prince of Gonzo"—which provides an interesting contrast with the more traditional account of the 1972 struggle for the presidency as presented in Theodore White's *The Making of the President 1972* (1973). New Journalism techniques are at the heart of Norman Mailer's account of the anti-**Vietnam War** protests in *The Armies of the Night: History as a Novel, The Novel as History* (1968) and of the 1968 Republican and Democratic conventions in *Miami and the Siege of Chicago* (1968). They were effectively used by Truman Capote to create a "nonfiction novel" in his *In Cold Blood* (1965), a retelling of the savage murder of a Kansas family in 1959.

New Left Writing in 1970, former **Students for a Democratic Society** (SDS) president Tom Hayden noted that "the New Leftists of the early sixties, and many of the black radicals as well, were preoccupied not with the danger of fascist repression but with liberal co-optation. We saw a power structure with such vast wealth and weaponry that it seemed beyond defeat. More than that, it seemed capable of preventing even the emergence of a real political challenge. . . . We accepted Mills [*see* **The Power Elite**] and the early Marcuse [*see* the **Marcusean Revolution**] as prophets of a new social order that had managed to stabilize all its major contradictions."

A mixture of anarchism, pacifism, Maoism, existentialism, black separatism, humanism, and social-ism, the New Left born in the early 1960s is variously considered to include such disparate tightly organized groups as the **Student Nonviolent Coordinating Committee** (SNCC; Snick), the **Black Panthers Party** (BPP), the SDS—and its **Weathermen** offshoot—the **Republic of New Africa** (RNA), the Berkeley **Free Speech Movement** (FSM), and the **Symbionese Liberation Army** (SLA), as well as many of the more amorphous bohemian movements generally lumped under the heading of the **Beat Generation.** Its prophets were C. Wright Mills, Albert Camus, Herbert Marcuse, Frantz Fanon, Eldridge Cleaver, Jack Kerouac, Allen Ginsberg, Paul Goodman, and Timothy Leary; its adherents were very often young ("Never trust anyone over thirty!"), and the children of affluent white middle-class parents; its enemies were racial injustice, the **Vietnam War,** social injustice, **the affluent society,** the **Great Society,** Puritan morality, and a technology that seemed to have run riot.

"The Movement"—a vague and affectionate term used by various factions of the New Left to describe themselves—traced its roots back to the **sit-ins** of the early 1960s and drew inspiration from the pacifist and socialist British New Left as exemplified by the publication *New Left Review.* One of its basic documents is the 1962 **Port Huron Statement** of the SDS, which sponsored the massive antiwar demonstration in Washington D.C., on April 17, 1965, that focused the attention of the news media on this new political phenomenon. In that same year, Herbert Marcuse published his *One Dimensional Man*, which soon became the philosophical bible of the movement and continued the revival of Hegelianism begun in 1940 with his *Reason and Revolution.*

Borrowing from Marcuse the idea of "selective tolerance," the New Left rapidly developed an elitist impatience with other points of view. Even as sympathetic a critic as Michael Harrington (*see* **The Other America**) complained in 1966 that though its enthusiasts were "courageous, dedicated, and existential in a way that sometimes borders on the anti-intellectual," they were also "rather weak on social and political theory, and they have dismissed most of the veterans . . . of the American movements for social changes as irrelevant failures." When the need shifted from the courage and determination shown in the civil rights and antiwar demonstrations "to the complicated interrelationships of jobs, education, housing, the need for national planning, the way in which a truly effective poverty program could be developed, etc., political thought and strategy were desperately needed and sadly lacking."

By the end of the decade the increasing arrogance of the New Left, which tended to demand "amnesty" even as it ignored "establishment" law, had alienated all but a hard core of sympathizers by increasing emphasis on violence and on acceptance by others of "nonnegotiable demands." Early in 1970 a group calling itself Revolutionary Force 9 bombed the New York offices of IBM, Mobil Oil, and General Telephone and Electronics.

On March 6, 1970, a townhouse in Greenwich Village was completely demolished when Weatherwoman Cathlyn Platt Wilkerson turned her home into an SDS bomb factory during the absence of her millionaire father. Among the dead were Diana Oughton, a Bryn Mawr graduate and the daughter of a wealthy Illinois conservative, and Ted Gold, who had been an active member of Columbia University's SDS chapter. Weatherwomen Wilkerson and Kathy Boudin, the daughter of Leonard B. Boudin, a lawyer prominent in radical causes, fled the building and disappeared. Both had been under indictment for participating in the October 1969 Days of Rage in Chicago, where the **Chicago Eight** were on trial for disturbances during the 1968 Democratic National Convention.

New Look　During World War II, Government Regulation L-85 limited the amount of material that could be used in manufacturing women's dresses and skirts. In the fall of 1945, French designer Christian Dior startled and delighted the fashion world by dramatically decreeing that skirts were to descend to a mere twelve inches from the ground. The garment industry enthusiastically backed the campaign, which exploded from the women's fashion pages onto the front page in 1946. With shortages still afflicting most of the world, the New Look was attacked as "immoral," and women's groups launched Little Below the Knee campaigns in opposition, but by 1947 Dior and the fashion industry had won out. It is interesting to compare this victory with the bungled **"Midi"** campaign of 1970.

The term New Look was afterward applied in a variety of contexts, most notably when Admiral Arthur Radford, chairman of the Joint Chiefs of Staff, used it in 1954 to describe a new approach to defense in which Army manpower was reduced in favor of reliance on **"massive retaliation."**

New Mandarins　Term critically applied to many of the intellectuals who participated in the Kennedy administration. In *American Power and the New Mandarins* (1969) Noam Chomsky emphasized the dual role of American intellectuals, who represent a society with incomparable wealth and power, and who at the same time participate in the application of that power. He paralleled the increasing power of intellectuals in this country with the rise of Bolshevism in Russia.

Analyzing the support of many of these intellectuals for the **Vietnam War,** he recalls social critic Randolph Bourne's comments that World War I had revealed a younger intelligentsia "ready for the executive ordering of events, pitifully unprepared for the intellectual interpretation or the idealistic focusing of ends. . . . They have absorbed the secret of scientific method as applied to political administration. . . . What is significant is that the technical side of the war appeals to them, not the interpretative or political side."

New Mobe　*See* **National Mobilization Committee to End the War in Vietnam.**

"New Nixon"　During the course of his political career, Richard M. Nixon had been a vigorously partisan figure who was often accused by critics of engaging in ruthless or unfair tactics. For example, in 1946, campaigning in California against Democratic Representative Horace Jeremiah ("Jerry") Voorhis, he consistently accused the latter of being a puppet of the communist-dominated Political Action Committee (PAC) of the CIO and of having accepted their support in spite of the fact that Voorhis himself had denounced the communist influence in CIO-PAC. Later, in his 1948 campaign against Helen Gahagan Douglas, he unfairly stigmatized the actress-turned-congresswoman as "The Pink Lady," presenting her vote record in the House to make it seem as though she was in political agreement with East Harlem's radical Representative Vito Marcantonio. In his unsuccessful 1962 campaign against California's Governor Edmund G. ("Pat") Brown, the focus of his oratory had been that Governor Brown was "not capable of dealing with the Communist threat within our borders," and that he had not introduced "a single item of antisubversive legislation in four years."

Part of his strategy in his 1968 campaign for the presidency against Democratic candidate Hubert H. Humphrey seemed to be to take advantage of the image of a more relaxed, confident, and open to ideas "new Nixon," which the press had started to report beginning in about 1964. Less harsh in his rhetoric, the "new Nixon" tended to favor "law and justice" rather than "law and order." At a time when Nixon's political rival was saddled with the **Vietnam War** record of Democratic President Lyndon B. Johnson, veteran columnist Walter Lippmann wrote that there were compelling reasons for believing in a " 'new Nixon,' a maturer and mellower man who is no longer clawing his way to the top, and it is, I think, fair to hope that his dominating ambition will be to become a two-term President. He is bright enough to know that this will be impossible if he remains sunk in the Vietnam quagmire." (The candidate's mother, however, was quoted as saying: "Oh, no. There's no such thing as a new Richard. He has always been exactly the same; even as a boy I never knew a person to change so little.")

After Nixon became President in 1969, the closest thing to the "old Nixon" seemed to be Vice President Spiro Agnew, who in multisyllabic speeches harshly questioned the loyalty of those protesting the Nixon administration's shifting policies on civil rights and the continuing Vietnam War (see **"Effete corps of impudent snobs"** and **"Nattering nabobs of negativism."**) As late as January 25, 1971, *Newsweek* magazine could say of the President that "true to his own precepts, he seems to have begun weighing the wisdom of his past two years' purposes and examining the strength of his resources—and the result may well be yet another new Nixon, softer-voiced, more charitable and as pragmatic as ever, settling into stride for the long run-up to the 1972 elections."

For many, the "old Nixon" seemed to emerge abruptly when the offices of the Democratic National Committee were broken into on June 17, 1972, by men who were subsequently shown to be connected with the **Committee to Re-elect the President** (CREEP; CRP) (see **Watergate Scandal**).

Dr. David Abrahamsen notes in *Nixon vs. Nixon: An Emotional Tragedy* (1977): "The 'old' Nixon was the real one, his shield against a hostile world, a protection for his inner world."

New York Dock Probe Testimony at New York State Crime Commission hearings held in New York, December 3-19, 1952, revealed that ship and stevedoring corporations had been forced by officials of the International Longshoremen's Association (ILA) to pay thousands of dollars in order to avoid labor troubles on the Port of New York waterfronts. As part of the "deal," exconvicts were often hired as pier bosses.

In addition, officials of stevedoring and terminal operating firms testified that they often had to pay off top executives of steamship companies as well as union officials. On the first day of testimony the president of one of the world's largest stevedoring firms, Jarka Corporation, revealed that his company had made almost $500,000 in such payments during the period between 1947 and 1951. A list of illegal payments compiled by the commission on December 15 showed that ninety-nine ILA officials had received money from ship, stevedoring, and dock companies.

Among the sensational charges made during hearings was that former New York City Mayor William O'Dwyer had, as Kings County District Attorney, in 1941 refused to take action after receiving testimony identifying the murderers of Peter Panto, an insurgent longshoreman.

The Night the Lights Went Out A gigantic power failure affecting 25 million people in New York, all of New England except Maine, parts of New Jersey and Pennsylvania, and the Canadian provinces of Ontario and Quebec struck on November 9, 1965, beginning at 5:16 P.M. Full service was not restored until 8:30 A.M. the following morning.

The power drain was first discovered in Ontario, and in fifteen minutes had spread to an 80,000-square-mile area. At 5:27 P.M. New York was blacked out when Consolidated Edison Company of New York spotted a flow reverse which had originated in Canada and cut the city away from an interchange system; the outflow from the city's nine generating stations was moving upstate and was automatically cut off to prevent equipment damage.

Most dramatically hit by the technical failure was New York City itself, in which an estimated 800,000 people were stranded in stalled subways, many of them until midnight and later. In addition, thousands were trapped in elevators, some for up to seven hours.

In the blacked-out metropolis, to which more than 5,000 National Guardsmen had been dispatched by Governor Nelson A. Rockefeller, there were no major incidents of vandalism and the crime rate for the period was actually reported as having been lower than normal. Service in Manhattan was not restored until 6:58 A.M. on November 10.

In spite of the potential for disaster, most New Yorkers remembered the blackout as a time of friendliness and mutual aid that broke through the usual big-city anonymity. *Life* magazine reported that "perhaps the best thing about such an event is that it gives all of us a story to tell. . . . We will be listening to versions of The Night the Lights Went Out long after a federal commission discovers that it all started when a little boy in upstate New York dropped his electric toothbrush in the toilet."

Consolidated Edison Company claimed that it had taken precautions to ensure against a similar power failure, but twelve years later, on July 13, 1977, at 9:34 P.M. the five boroughs of New York City were blacked out again and full service was not restored until more than twenty-four hours later. The cause of the failure was said to have been an electrical storm which caused the short-circuiting of major power transmission lines in the vicinity of Consolidated Edison's Indian Point Nuclear Power Plant 3.

This time the blackout was marked by widespread arson, vandalism, and looting in low-income sections of the city; more than 3,000 were arrested.

Nimbus I Also known as *Nimbus-A*, it was an 830-pound advanced meteorological satellite launched into space by means of a Thor-Agena-B carrier rocket fired from Vandenburg Air Force Base in California on August 28, 1964. *Nimbus I* had been planned for a 575-mile-high circular orbit, but trouble with the rocket's second stage caused it to go into an elliptical orbit with an apogee of 578 miles and a perigee of 262 miles. Because of this, it could check on weather conditions on only 70 percent of the earth's surface.

Nimbus I circled the earth fourteen times daily and ceased operation after a month. It was an improvement of the earlier **Tiros** satellites in that it was always pointed toward the earth by a hexagonal attitude control system. Its high-resolution infrared radiometer system gave meteorologists the first high-resolution night cloud-cover pictures and cloud-top temperature readings to be taken from a satellite. An automatic picture-transmission system previously tested by *Tiros 7* (December 1963) made it possible to transmit weather photos to ground stations anywhere the satellite passed.

By mid-1975 five other improved *Nimbus* satellites had been launched. Plans called for launching an advanced model—*Nimbus G*, a General Electric satellite that would monitor pollution—in September 1978. However, technical difficulties caused a postponement until October 24, 1978.

Nixon Doctrine The basic features of an Asian policy distinguished by a somewhat lower United States profile in that area were outlined by President Richard M. Nixon on July 25, 1969, at an informal news conference on the island of Guam, a stopover point on a tour that was to include the Philippines, Indonesia, Thailand, India, Pakistan, Rumania, and Great Britain. No direct quotations from the President's talk were permitted, but the Nixon Doctrine, as it came to be known, indicated that the United States would reduce its military commitments throughout Asia, and that while it would honor its treaty commitments and keep an eye on developments in the area, it would not become involved in wars such as the one continuing in Vietnam (see **Vietnam War**). The President suggested that new forms of economic aid were under consideration to replace reduced military assistance from this country. He indicated that, except for a nuclear threat from a major power, the nations of Asia would have to deal with defense problems on their own, predicting that the economic progress of Asian nations would make them less vulnerable to communism.

The Nixon Doctrine—sometimes known as the Guam Doctrine—was to evolve into the **Pacific Doctrine** enunciated by President Gerald R. Ford in December 1975.

Nixonomics Neologism coined by Professor Walter Heller, University of Minnesota, who had served as chairman of the Council of Economic Advisors during the Kennedy and Johnson administrations. Nixonomics describes a situation in which inflation and recession attack the economy simultaneously. Other indicators are a depressed stock market at a time when interest rates are rising.

The expression was first used in an off-the-record talk in San Francisco on July 6, 1969. It surfaced and gained currency after a talk by Professor Heller to the National American Wholesale Grocers Executive Conference held in Honolulu on September 27, 1969.

Nixon's Last Press Conference The political career of Richard M. Nixon was destined to be studded with farewells, but none was more dramatic than the press conference with which he terminated the 1962 California gubernatorial campaign in which he was defeated by Governor Edmund G. ("Pat") Brown. The former Vice President had delayed conceding defeat until the early hours of the morning, when his press secretary, Herb Klein, was sent to give a concession statement to the press. As Klein was speaking, Nixon himself, looking haggard and angry, appeared and pushed his way to the microphones to give a quarter-hour meandering and bad-tempered speech that most political observers felt precluded the possibility of any political comeback.

In this notorious "concession" statement, he alternately patronized and lashed out at Governor Brown and at President John F. Kennedy, who had defeated Mr. Nixon in 1960. He indirectly also criticized the 100,000 volunteers who had aided his campaign when he noted that although they had done a "magnificent job" he wished "they could have gotten out a few more votes in the key precincts, but because they didn't Mr. Brown has won and I have lost . . . ."

But the bitterest words of the "last" press conference were saved for the press itself:

And as I leave the press, all I can say is this: For sixteen years, ever since the **Hiss case,** you've had a lot of fun—a lot of fun—that you've had an opportunity to attack me and I think I've given as good as I've taken. . . . Before I leave you I want you to know just how much you're going to be missing.

You won't have Nixon to kick around anymore, because, gentlemen, this is my last press conference.

"A man ought to be a good loser," said former President Harry S Truman, commenting on Mr. Nixon's performance, and by and large the nation seemed to agree with him. But after the assassination of President Kennedy on **November 22, 1963,** Richard Nixon decided on a political comeback, and in 1968 he was elected to his first term as President.

A pixieish echo of the California concession statement was provided by the Kennedy Democrat Daniel Patrick Moynihan, who somewhat confusingly found himself on President Nixon's White House staff. When he finally realized that he could not function effectively as a member of the Nixon administration, Moynihan resigned and reportedly left for press secretary Ron Ziegler a note which read: "Well, you won't have Pat Moynihan to kick around anymore."

"Nixon's NEP" *See* **Phase One.**

Nixon's Nixon When in 1969 Vice President Spiro Agnew made a series of slashing public attacks on the communications media, critics responded by saying he tended to use many of the polemic techniques associated with Richard M. Nixon in the California campaigns against Jerry Voorhis and Helen Gahagan Douglas in the 1940s. The "old Nixon" was said to have resurfaced in the Vice President's speeches when, for example, he said that Sen. Hubert H. Humphrey (D.-Minn.) was "squishy soft" on communism.

"Nixon's the One" Slogan used by partisans of former Vice President Richard M. Nixon as part of the campaign to obtain the Republican presidential nomination for him in 1968. At the Republican National Convention in Miami Beach, in August 1968, the slogan was effectively used against Mr. Nixon by political prankster and consultant Richard Tuck, who hired several obviously pregnant women to carry signs on which it was boldly emblazoned.

Following the **Watergate Scandal** during President Nixon's second term in office, the slogan surfaced again. This time it was the intention of hostile critics to indicate the President's guilt in the original break-in and the subsequent cover-up. After Vice President Spiro Agnew's resignation from office in October 1973 following charges of "kickbacks" and income tax evasion, critics of the Nixon administration coined a new slogan: "Nixon's the One—Not Agnew."

Nixon Tapes Testifying on July 16, 1973, before the Senate **Select Committee on Presidential Campaign Activities** chaired by Senator Sam J. Ervin, Jr. (D.-N.C.) (see **Senator Sam**), Alexander P. Butterfield, a former presidential aide, revealed the existence of a secret White House recording system which automatically taped meetings and telephone conversations in the White House offices of President Nixon and in the adjacent Executive Office Building (*see* **Watergate Scandal**).

The existence of the secret recordings was first revealed to staff members of the Select Committee on July 13, 1973, when during routine questioning Butterfield was asked "out of the blue" about testimony by Chief White House Counsel to the President John Dean III on June 25 that he suspected the President of making a recording of one of their meetings together. At this point Butterfield somewhat reluctantly revealed that he and Secret Service agents had indeed set up such a voice-activated system at the President's request.

On July 23, 1973, Watergate Special Prosecutor Archibald Cox subpoenaed recordings of nine presidential conversations, but two days later President Nixon refused to turn over these tapes, taking his stand on the grounds of executive privilege. When on August 29, 1973, Judge John J. Sirica, chief judge of the U.S. District Court, Washington, D.C., ruled that the President must turn over the subpoenaed tapes, the White House announced that it would appeal the decision. On October 12, 1973, the U.S. Court of Appeals upheld Judge Sirica's ruling that the tapes must be surrendered, and the following

October 23 Charles Alan Wright, special White House legal consultant on Watergate, announced that the tapes would indeed be turned over.

Meanwhile, Leon Jaworski had succeeded Archibald Cox as Watergate Special Prosecutor as a result of the **"Saturday Night Massacre"** (October 20, 1973) in which President Nixon fired Cox, Attorney General Elliot L. Richardson, and Deputy Attorney General William D. Ruckelshaus. On October 31, it was disclosed that two of the subpoenaed tapes were not in existence, and on the following November 12, J. Fred Buzhardt, Jr., special counsel to President Nixon, testified in Judge Sirica's court about the missing tapes. On November 21, 1973, White House attorneys told Judge Sirica about an 18½-minute gap in another of the tapes.

The House Judiciary Committee subpoenaed forty-two tapes on April 11, 1974, and one week later, after weeks of fruitless negotiations with the White House, Special Prosecutor Jaworski subpoenaed an additional sixty-four tapes.

President Nixon appeared on national television on April 29, 1974, and announced that he would supply the Judiciary Committee with edited transcripts of the subpoenaed tapes and that these transcripts would be made public. The following day 1,254 pages of transcript were released by James D. St. Clair, special counsel to the president, who said that President Nixon would not turn over tapes and documents sought by Special Prosecutor Jaworski. However, on July 24, 1974, the U.S. Supreme Court ruled eight to zero that the President must turn over the tapes requested by the Special Prosecutor. Among these was the tape of June 23, 1972, the so-called smoking pistol tape, on which the President and H. R. Haldeman, the President's Chief of Staff, are heard discussing plans to have the **CIA** impede an FBI investigation into the break-in of Democratic National Headquarters at the Watergate a few days earlier. Transcripts of three taped conversations dealing with the White House "cover-up" of the Watergate break-in were released on August 8, 1974, and on August 9, 1974, Richard M. Nixon became the first man in United States history to resign from the Presidency. He was immediately succeeded in office by Gerald R. Ford, whom President Nixon had nominated for Vice President following the resignation of Vice President Spiro Agnew on October 10, 1973.

The origin of the recording system was discussed by President Nixon in a by-lined story by James J. Kilpatrick which appeared in the *Washington Star* on May 14, 1974:

They were made, curiously enough, in a very offhand decision. We had no tapes, as you know, up until 1971. I think one day Haldeman walked in and said, "The library believes it is essential that we have tapes," and I said, why? He said, well, Johnson had tapes—they're in his library at Austin, and these are invaluable records. Kennedy also had tapes. . . . I said all right. I must say that after the system was put in, as the transcribed conversations clearly indicated, I wasn't talking with the knowledge or with the feeling that the tapes were there. Otherwise I might have talked very differently. My own view is that the taping of conversations for historical purposes was a bad decision on the part of all the Presidents. I don't think Kennedy should have done it. I don't think Johnson should have done it, and I don't think *we* should have done it.

In 1977 the U.S. Supreme Court upheld by a seven to two decision a 1974 law giving the government rather than the former President control of the tape recordings and Presidential papers. The decision was not expected to set a precedent that would affect future Presidents.

Nixopedia Theodore C. Sorensen reported that during the 1960 campaign, Myer Feldman, who headed a staff of researchers working for Democratic nominee John F. Kennedy, compiled a miscellaneous collection of everything Republican candidate Richard M. Nixon had said on major issues and exactly the stand he had taken on legislation as both a senator and Vice President. The collection was continuously supplemented and updated during the campaign, and political capital was made out of contrasting "glaring inconsistencies between his past and present, or North and South, speeches."

NLF *See* **National Liberation Front.**

NMSC *See* **National Merit Scholarship Corporation.**

NOAA *See* **National Oceanic and Atmospheric Administration.**

"No-knock" entry *See* **D.C. Crime Bill.**

NON *See* **National Organization for Non-Parents.**

North Atlantic Treaty Organization (NATO) "To maintain and develop their individual and collective capacity to resist armed attack," on April 4, 1949, the United States, Great Britain, France, Canada, Norway, Denmark, Iceland, Belgium, Holland, Luxembourg, Portugal, and Italy formed

NATO. The treaty specified that an armed attack against one or more of the signatories was to be considered an attack against all.

The NATO pact was ratified by the United States Senate on July 21, 1949, in spite of opposition on the right led by Sen. Robert A. Taft (R.-Ohio), who argued that the pact carried with it an obligation to assist in arming, at our expense, the nations of western Europe. That obligation, he stressed, would "promote war in the world rather than peace, and I think that with the arms plan it is wholly contrary to the spirit of the obligations we assumed in the United Nations Charter." He feared the Russian reaction to seeing "itself ringed about gradually by so-called defensive arms, from Norway and Denmark to Turkey and Greece. . . ."

Critics on the left, such as the 1948 presidential candidate of the Progressive Party, Henry A. Wallace, argued that the pact "substitutes the divided nations for the United Nations. . . . Stripped of legal verbiage, the North Atlantic military pact gives the United States Army military bases up to the very borders of the Soviet Union."

Dean Acheson, Secretary of State in the new Truman administration, defended the pact in a speech on March 18, 1949:

Successful resistance to aggression in the modern world requires modern arms and trained military forces. As a result of the recent war, the European countries joining in the pact are generally deficient in both requirements. The treaty does not bind the United States to any arms program. But we all know that the United States is now the only democratic nation with the resources and productive capacity to help the free nations of Europe to recover their military strength.

Three years after it was formed, NATO was joined by Greece and Turkey; in 1955, reversing their policy of opposition to German rearmament, the NATO nations admitted the Federal Republic of Germany.

NATO maintains an international secretariat, originally in Paris, which is directed by a Secretary General; Washington, D.C., is the seat of its Military Committee composed of the chiefs of staff of member nations. Within this Committee is a Standing Group composed of the chairman and the chiefs of staff of the United States, France, and the United Kingdom. It is the job of these men to guide the activities of the three NATO commands: Supreme Allied Commander Europe (SACEUR), whose headquarters, also originally outside of Paris, is the Supreme Headquarters of the Allied Powers in Europe (SHAPE); Supreme Allied Commander Atlantic Ocean (SACLANT); and Commander in Chief English Channel. There is also a Canada-United States Regional Planning Group under the direction of the Standing Group.

In 1963 France, then under President Charles de Gaulle, rejected a multilateral NATO nuclear force and withdrew its naval units from NATO's command. In 1966, France withdrew all its forces from NATO command and demanded the removal of the secretariat and SHAPE from French soil. New headquarters were set up in Brussels.

The continuing importance of NATO in American policy is indicated by President Jimmy Carter's talk in Brussels on January 6, 1978.

We know that the path to lasting peace depends on human understandings, negotiated agreements, acts of good will . . . . But we are united in believing that our defense must always be strong enough to deter any thoughts of aggression—that we must be prepared for combat we always hope to avoid. . . . Together, we are setting the NATO Alliance on a course that will reaffirm our shared commitment to peace, to a strong and vital Alliance, and to meeting any challenge to our strength and cohesion in the years ahead.

See **Mutual Defense Assistance Act.**

North Beach Area in San Francisco where, beginning in about 1953, bohemians of what was to become known as the **Beat Generation** tended to congregate. By the 1960s, many who were unable to find accommodations in the North Beach section were attracted to **Haight-Ashbury,** a district largely inhabited by white blue-collar workers and blacks who too often found that urban renewal meant in practice "Negro removal."

San Francisco's North Beach and Haight-Ashbury districts, like Los Angeles' Venice West, developed a "hippie" and "beatnik" subculture similar to that of the East Village in New York.

November 22, 1963 On the second day of a fence-mending speaking tour of Texas, President John F. Kennedy and his party—Mrs. Jacqueline Kennedy, Vice President Lyndon B. Johnson, and Mrs. Lady Bird Johnson—arrived at the Dallas airport after triumphant receptions in San Antonio, Houston, and Fort Worth, and proceeded by motorcade to a luncheon meeting at which the President was to speak. President Kennedy, the first lady, Texas Governor John Connally, and Mrs. Connally were seated together in an open car, when suddenly three shots were heard. The President slumped forward, wounded in the throat and head. Governor Connally had been hit in the shoulder. Both men were rushed to Parkland Memorial Hospital, but within half an hour the President was dead.

The shots had come from the sixth-floor window of the Texas Book Depository, where the police found the sniper's abandoned carbine. Within a matter of hours Lee Harvey Oswald, who worked at the depository as a stockman, was arrested for the crime, but not before he apparently murdered J. D. Tippit, a Dallas policeman who had attempted to question him.

A former Marine who had received an "Undesirable" discharge, Oswald had had a troubled history. He had lived for more than two years in the Soviet Union, where he married a Russian girl, and on his return to the United States had been active in pro-Castro agitation in New Orleans, Louisiana. He described himself as the secretary of the local chapter of the **Fair Play for Cuba Committee** (FPCC).

On *Air Force One,* the plane that was to bear the dead President's body back to Washington, Lyndon B. Johnson was sworn in as the 36th President of the United States.

In the days that followed, a shocked and anguished nation remained glued to its television sets, which they offered little news but seemed to satisfy a need to somehow join together in mourning. Two days later, on November 24, horrified viewers watched as Oswald himself, shown while being transferred from one jail to another, was in turn assassinated by night-club owner Jack Ruby. The following day, in a funeral procession followed by the representatives of ninety-two nations, President John F. Kennedy's body was brought to Arlington National Cemetery for burial.

See **Warren Report.**

NOW *See* **National Organization for Women.**

"No-win Policy" Although it has been broadly applied to the efforts of later Presidents to achieve peaceful coexistence with the U.S.S.R. and Communist China as an alternative to nuclear war, the term was first applied by critics to President Harry S Truman's insistence on limited goals during the **Korean War.**

In his April 11, 1951, broadcast explaining his controversial dismissal of General Douglas MacArthur—around whom much of the militancy centered—President Truman noted that he had taken such action because "a number of events" had demonstrated that the general was in basic disagreement with government policy and that his dismissal had been dictated by the necessity of removing "doubt or confusion" about the aims of the United States

in Korea. (Indeed, in justifying his conduct before a joint session of Congress on April 19, 1951, General MacArthur later expressed his conviction that "in war . . . there can be no substitute for victory.")

One of the strongest critics of President Truman's Korean policy was Sen. Richard M. Nixon (R.-Calif.). However, when he was himself later President, the derogatory "No-win Policy" was seldom or never applied to his friendly overtures to both the U.S.S.R. and Communist China.

NSA *See* **National Student Association.**

NSF *See* **National Science Foundation.**

Nuclear Test Ban Treaty Signed in Moscow by representatives of the United States, Great Britain, and the Soviet Union on August 5, 1963, the treaty was approved by the Senate on September 24 and became effective on October 10, 1963. Under its provisions the three nations agreed

. . . to prohibit, to prevent, and not to carry out any nuclear weapon test explosion, or any other nuclear explosion at any place under its jurisdiction or control: (*a*) in the atmosphere, beyond its limits, including territorial water or high seas; or (*b*) in any other environment if such explosion causes radioactive debris to be present outside the territorial limits of the state under whose jurisdiction or control such explosion is conducted.

The ban did not apply to underground tests. In addition, it contained an escape clause which permitted a nation to withdraw from the treaty "if it decides that extraordinary events related to the subject matter of this treaty have jeopardized the supreme interests of its country."

Eventually more than 100 nations endorsed the treaty. Among those who abstained were France and Communist China.

Because of the hazards of radioactive fallout, pressure to ban nuclear tests began building up in the early 1950s. In May 1955, the U.S.S.R. proposed a test ban linked to general disarmament. It was rejected because of the refusal of the U.S.S.R. to allow for adequate on-site inspection procedures. However, in October 1958, this country joined with Great Britain and the Soviet Union in an unwritten moratorium on nuclear testing. This was abruptly terminated in the summer of 1961 when the U.S.S.R. began a two-month series of tests in the atmosphere, including the explosion of a fifty-megaton bomb said to have 2,500 times the force of the bomb that had destroyed Hiroshima in World War II. In April 1962, further attempts to secure a test ban having failed, the United States launched a new series of tests, which was followed by more Soviet tests.

Speaking at American University, Washington, D.C., on June 10, 1963, President John F. Kennedy launched a new initiative. Proposing a **"strategy of peace,"** he said that this country would refrain from further testing in the atmosphere as long as other nations did, and he announced that representatives of the three major nuclear powers would soon meet in Moscow to resume negotiations for a test ban. The talks began on July 15, 1963, with Averell Harriman as the United States representative. This time efforts were crowned with success because the development of reconnaissance satellites had to a large extent eliminated the need for on-site inspection. In addition, the continuing deterioration of Sino-Soviet relations had convinced the U.S.S.R. of the necessity for such a ban. At about the time the treaty went into effect, President Kennedy authorized the sale of $250 million in wheat to the U.S.S.R., which had experienced a disastrous harvest that year.

Nuremberg Trials In August 1945 the United States joined with France, Great Britain, and the U.S.S.R. in establishing a four-man International Military Tribunal to act "in the interests of all the United Nations" by trying military and civilian leaders of Nazi Germany for war crimes during World War II. Charges against twenty-four leading Nazi officials were heard in Nuremberg beginning on November 21, 1945. The indictment included crimes against the peace such as the planning and waging of aggressive war; violation of the codes of conduct under which warfare has been traditionally conducted; and crimes against humanity: "murder, extermination, enslavement, deportation, and other inhumane acts committed against any civilian population . . . or persecution on political, racial, or religious grounds."

The trials ended on October 1, 1946, with the sentence to hanging of twelve—including Hermann Goering, who cheated the hangman by swallowing poison, and Martin Bormann, who was tried *in absentia* but was presumed dead. Seven were given prison sentences, and of these only Rudolf Hess, who had preceded Bormann as Deputy Fuehrer, was still imprisoned in 1979; three were acquitted over the dissent of the Soviet member of the tribunal. Of the others included under the original indictment, Robert Ley committed suicide while in custody, and Gustav Krupp von Bohlen und Halbach was adjudged too ill to appear for trial and proceedings against him were suspended indefinitely.

During the ten months the trials lasted, the world had watched in horror as evidence of mass murder, enslavement, looting, and disregard for all forms of human decency mounted during the voluminous testimony heard. By and large, the sentences were greeted with approval in this country, but Sen. Robert A. Taft (R.-Ohio) severely critized them as a violation of "the fundamental principle of American law that a man cannot be tried under an *ex post facto* statute." Attacked by both Republicans and Democrats for his "defense of the Nazi murderers," Senator Taft ignored public opinion to support what he considered traditional concepts of law and justice.

NWPC *See* **National Women's Political Caucus.**

O

"Old Soldiers Never Die; They Just Fade Away"

OAS *See* **Organization of American States.**

OBC *See* **One Big Computer.**

OECD *See* **Organization for Economic Cooperation and Development.**

OEO *See* **Office of Economic Opportunity.**

Office of Economic Opportunity (OEO) Umbrella agency created by the Economic Opportunity Act of 1964 to coordinate activities in President Lyndon B. Johnson's **War on Poverty.** Although it was located in a separate office building—scornfully referred to by critics as "The Poverty Palace"—the OEO functioned as part of the Executive Office of the President. Its first director was Sargent Shriver, who had helped set up the **Peace Corps.**

Among the programs controlled by OEO were the **Job Corps, Job Opportunities in the Business Sector** (JOBS), **Volunteers in Service to America** (VISTA)—also known as the Domestic Peace Corps—**Community Action Programs** (CAP), **Head Start, Upward Bound**, and the Neighborhood Youth Corps.

Criticism of OEO began to mount rapidly, with the special targets being the Job Corps and CAP. In his 1967 State of the Union message, President Johnson said he would propose "certain administrative changes suggested by Congress as well as some that we have learned from our own trial and error." But conservatives seemed intent on dismantling both the War on Poverty in general and the OEO in particular and substituting for it what they called an Opportunity Crusade. The Johnson administration, however, was successful in getting an extension of its poverty bill passed by the House on November 15, 1967. "OEO would live to see another day," President Johnson was to write, "and to fight other and even more difficult battles."

When President Richard M. Nixon assumed office in 1969, he made it clear that he intended to transfer many OEO programs to other agencies. He signed bills extending OEO in 1969 and 1972, but his 1974 budget provided no funds for it even though its extension had been approved through that fiscal year. OEO staggered on for another year and was finally terminated on January 4, 1975. Some of its programs were rescued, however, and transferred to the Community Services Administration and the **Department of Health, Education, and Welfare** (HEW).

Office of Management and Budget (OMB) Established by Executive order under President Richard

M. Nixon's Reorganization Plan 2 (July 1, 1970), the Office of Management and Budget (OMB) absorbed the former Bureau of the Budget. Although its basic function is to assist the Chief Executive in the preparation and administration of the national budget presented to Congress every January, it also advises him on legislative programs, develops statistical data, recruits and evaluates personnel, checks on the functioning and efficiency of federal agencies, and coordinates legislative requests by the latter. To help it carry out some of these duties, President Nixon created a Domestic Council and appointed John D. Ehrlichman, Assistant to the President for Domestic Affairs, as executive director.

OMB is concerned with administration goals as well as with fiscal policy. Working with the **Council of Economic Advisors** and the Department of the Treasury, it evaluates and advises on the appropriation requests of federal agencies within all Cabinet departments.

Offshore Oil Controversy *See* **Tidelands Oil Controversy.**

Oh! Calcutta! Billed as "the most controversial musical show in history," this nude entertainment featuring both male and female performers, opened with great fanfare in New York on June 17, 1969. Devised by British drama critic Kenneth Tynan, it included unattributed dialogue and sketch ideas by such well-known writers as Samuel Beckett, Jules Feiffer, Dan Greenburg, John Lennon (of the Beatles), Leonard Melfi, and Sam Shepard. The music and lyrics were by Peter Schickele ("P.D.Q. Bach"), Stanley Walden, and Robert Dennis.

If the producer had hoped to shock, he was disappointed, because the general view of the critics smacked more of condescension than outrage. "There is no more innocent show in town—and certainly none more witless," concluded the *New York Times.* Less difficult to please, the public enthusiastically chose this relatively painless way to join the avant-garde. The success of the loosely woven series of skits was such that it opened the following year in London, where once more critics concluded that it was unlikely to deprave and was embarrassing to watch only because it lacked humor.

The title of the show, which has nothing to do with the city of the same name in India, is taken from that of a painting by the French artist Clovis Trouille showing the somewhat fulsome charms of a young lady with a tatoo on her buttocks. In a rather overcomplicated manner, the title conceals the French pun on the words: "Oh! Quel cul t'as!"

In 1977 the show was revived on Broadway and this time barely caused a ripple, though it continued into 1979 as a tourist attraction and a prime example of what visitors liked to think of as big-city wickedness.

OIC *See* **Opportunities Industrialization Center.**

"Old soldiers never die; they just fade away" Disagreements between the Truman administration and General MacArthur over Formosa policy and the conduct of the war in Korea (see **Korean War**) led President Harry S Truman to relieve the popular general of his various Far Eastern commands on April 10, 1951. The following evening, the President made a nationwide radio broadcast in which he explained the reasons for this controversial action.

I believe that we must try to limit the war to Korea for these vital reasons: to make sure that the precious lives of our fighting men are not wasted, to see that the security of our country and the free world is not needlessly jeopardized, and to prevent a third world war.

A number of events have made it evident that General MacArthur did not agree with that policy. I have, therefore, considered it essential to relieve General MacArthur so that there would be no doubt or confusion as to the real purpose and aim of our policy.

Far from returning in disgrace for having ignored the orders of his Commander in Chief, General MacArthur found a hero's welcome on his return. (A Gallup Poll showed that 69 percent of the public backed him.) Invited to address a joint session of Congress on April 19, 1951, he attempted to justify his conduct and urged military action against China. "War's very object is victory—not prolonged indecision. In war, indeed, there can be no substitute for victory."

In closing, the general quoted the refrain of a popular West Point ballad of his youth: "Old soldiers never die; they just fade away."

Like the old soldier of the ballad, concluded General MacArthur, "I now close my military career and just fade away. . . ."

Beginning on May 3, 1951, two Senate committees (the Armed Services and the Foreign Relations) held an "Inquiry into the Military Situation in the Far East and the Facts Surrounding the Relief of General of the Army Douglas MacArthur from His Assignments in that Area." The general himself was the first witness. Hearings lasted until June 25, and two days later the two committees

adopted a "declaration of faith" which affirmed American unity and warned against communist aggression. The issue had been successfully defused.

General MacArthur continued to speak out in public, but his audiences quickly shrank in size. Social commentator H. L. Mencken was later to comment that the general was "fading satisfactorily." During the height of the furor, however, Sen. Richard M. Nixon (R.-Calif.) had called upon the Senate to censure President Truman and restore General MacArthur to his command.

Writing in 1969, former Secretary of State Dean Acheson noted: "Such detached opinion as there was concluded that the hero had been a troublesome one and the harassed President had done about what he had to do."

Ole Miss

I am an American-Mississippi-Negro citizen. With all the occurring events regarding changes in our educational system taking place in our country in this new age, I feel certain that this application does not come as a surprise to you. I certainly hope that this matter will be handled in a manner that will be complimentary to the University and to the state of Mississippi.

This note accompanied an application for admission to the University of Mississippi, Oxford, made in January 1961 by James H. Meredith, a transfer student from the all-black Jackson State College, Jackson, Mississippi, who needed three more semesters to complete a degree in political science. The U.S. Air Force veteran's application was turned down twice on the grounds that it was not accompanied by letters of recommendation from alumni of the all-white university. In June 1961, lawyers for the NAACP filed suit in federal court charging that racial bias had been the grounds for Meredith's rejection, and a complex legal battle of court orders, reversals, and reversals of reversals ensued. The U.S. Justice Department entered the case on Meredith's behalf and on January 12, 1962, the U.S. Court of Appeals for the Fifth Circuit ruled that Ole Miss's requirement concerning letters of recommendation from alumni was unconstitutional, and in June it held that Meredith had been rejected solely because he was a Negro. After further legal battles, U.S. Supreme Court Justice Hugo L. Black ordered on September 10 that Meredith be admitted to the university.

The black veteran's first admission attempt on September 20, 1962, was blocked by Governor Ross Barnett, who invoked a 1956 state resolution of the interposition of state sovereignty between the federal government and the citizens of Mississippi and proclaimed that all public schools and institutions of higher learning were henceforth under state supervision. He had himself appointed "Special Registrar" to handle Meredith's application, which he proceeded to deny. On September 25, the circuit court enjoined the governor from blocking Meredith's admission, and the latter made a second attempt on September 25, only to again be blocked by Governor Barnett. After a secret agreement between Attorney General Robert F. Kennedy and the governor, Meredith made a third attempt on September 26, but the governor broke his word, and a fourth unsuccessful attempt was made on September 27. On the following day the circuit court found Governor Barnett guilty of civil contempt and ordered that he purge himself by September 30, 1962, or face a $10,000-a-day fine and arrest. At this point, the governor ordered an end to resistance and told the university to admit Meredith.

Under the protection of United States marshals, Meredith took up residence on the university campus on the last day of September, and a few hours later rioting that resulted in two deaths broke out and continued even as President John F. Kennedy made a televised appeal for peaceful compliance with the law of the land.

Active in leading the pro-segregationist forces was former Major General Edwin A. Walker, who in 1957 had commanded federal troops used to quell the riots in the **Little Rock**, Arkansas, desegregation crisis. Order was finally restored the following day by 3,000 federal troops, 400 marshals, and National Guardsmen federalized by the President. State troopers were reported to have made no attempt to interfere with rioters.

Meredith attended classes that day and the next without major incident, but on October 3 a relatively small group of white students demonstrated before his campus residence before being dispersed by federal troops.

Writing in the *Saturday Evening Post* later that year, Meredith said: "It hasn't been all bad. Many students have spoken to me pleasantly. They have stopped banging doors and throwing bottles into my dormitory now."

On January 30, 1963, in spite of predictions that he would not stick it out, Meredith, accompanied by NAACP state secretary Medgar Evers, appeared to register for the spring term. (Evers was shot down the following June and Byron de la Beckwith, Greenwood, Mississippi, was charged with the murder, but two successive juries failed to convict him.)

James Meredith was in the national news again in June 1966, when he began a March from Memphis,

Tennessee, to Jackson, Mississippi, 225 miles away, to prove that blacks were unafraid. He was shot and wounded on the way and the Meredith March for Freedom was continued from the spot at which he had fallen by Martin Luther King, Jr., **Southern Christian Leadership Conference** (SCLC); Floyd B. McKissick, **Congress of Racial Equality** (CORE); Stokely Carmichael, **Student Nonviolent Coordinating Committee** (SNCC; Snick); and comedian Dick Gregory.

OMB *See* **Office of Management and Budget.**

One Big Computer (OBC) One of the many criticisms of the New York and American Stock exchanges is that they are anachronisms that have failed to take full advantage of the potential of twentieth-century technology. Critics have long advocated a fully automated market in which the entire country would be linked by electronic equipment to facilitate the purchase of stocks and bonds. At present, the very existence of the New York exchanges is being questioned because the Securities and Exchange Commission (SEC) is under a mandate to investigate a national market for trading securities.

Such a system has, of course, been fought against if for no other reason than it would weaken the necessity for the Wall Street securities industry to remain in New York City and would cause technological unemployment among the more than 2,000 people employed by the major exchanges alone. OBC proponents, sometimes called "black boxers," have pointed out that such sensitivity to personnel is rare when it is a question of the introduction of automated devices in industry as a whole.

O'Neill Report *See* **Antiballistic Missile System.**

One Man, One Vote *See* **Baker v. Carr; Reynolds v. Sims.**

"One small step for man, one giant step for mankind." *See* **Project Apollo.**

On the Road Published in 1957, this novel by Jack Kerouac immediately became a bestseller and the bible of the "**beat generation.**" It recounts in somewhat mythic form the cross-country adventures of Sal Paradise and Dean Moriarty as they search for a life style that breaks with middle-class values and conformity. In Kerouac's frequently quoted words:

. . .the only people for me are the mad ones, the ones who are mad to live, mad to talk, mad to be saved, desirous of everything at the same time, the ones who never yawn or say a commonplace thing, but burn, burn, burn like fabulous yellow roman candles exploding like spiders across the stars and in the middle you see the blue centerlight pop and everybody goes "Aww!"

The book made something of a legend of Kerouac's friend and sometime lover Neal Cassady, with whom he had made a similar trip in the late 1940s. The author himself appears as Paradise, and other "beat" writers such as Allen Ginsberg ("Carlo Marx"), John Clellon Holmes ("Tom Saybrook"), and William S. Burroughs ("Old Bull Lee") are represented in the narrative.

The first draft of the novel was written in three weeks in 1951, but publication had to wait for six years. Its vision of a freedom unshackled by conventional restraints appealed to young people, but hostile critics attacked Kerouac as a "Hippie Homer." Even those who found it "a stunning achievement" were disturbed by its lack of conventional character development. Writing in the *New York Times*, David Dempsey cautioned: "But it is a road, as far as the characters are concerned, that leads nowhere—and which the novelist cannot afford to travel more than once." Kerouac's later books failed to find serious critical acceptance.

Op Art The roots of this movement, which uses modern scientific and technical processes to effect an alteration of a viewer's physiological perception of a work of art, are to be found in the Constructivist works of Naum Gabo and Antoine Pevsner, and in such geometric canvases as Josef Albers' *Hommage to the Square: Broad Call* (1933) and Piet Mondrian's *Broadway Boogie Woogie* (1942-1943).

Op Art, or Optical Art, which appears to have gone into a decline, emerged in the 1960s and was popularized by "The Responsive Eye" exhibit mounted at New York's Museum of Modern Art in 1965 by William G. Seitz. Although some works were in black and white, typical paintings used high-keyed colors combined with graphs, screens, facets, and the like, to produce optical illusions such as pulsing or vibrating. Often, kinetic effects were produced by the use of superimposed transluscent plastic or by slats mounted so that a composition altered when viewed from a changed or changing position. In some instances actual moving parts—many of them of an industrial nature—constantly altered the physical composition of the work.

Open Arms Policy The Open Arms (Chieu Hoi) policy instituted by the South Vietnamese authorities during the **Vietnam War** was designed to encourage Viet Cong guerrillas to defect from the communists ranks. Offers of amnesty and job training were spread by dropping leaflets, broadcasting over the radio, and using loudspeakers. "Returnees," or Hoi Chanhs, were taken into special camps, where they were fed, reoutfitted, interrogated, and given both political indoctrination and vocational training. Those who brought heavy machine guns with them were given $42.50; a submachine gun was worth $17, and a rifle $10. (The program was financed by the United States and in 1967 was budgeted at $11 million.)

According to original reports, the program was successful, with some 20,000 defectors in 1966 and an estimated 1,200 a week reported early in 1967. However, by 1968 the Open Arms policy seemed to be in trouble, in spite of a $9 million U.S. budget. Part of the problem was apparently in keeping South Vietnamese from treating Hoi Chanhs as enemy prisoners, in spite of guarantees in appeals to "rally" to the noncommunist cause. In addition, reoriented former members of the Viet Cong found that they were afterward eligible for a draft into the South Vietnamese fighting forces.

By late summer 1968, American officials in Vietnam were admitting that defection from the communist ranks was down 73 percent from the previous year. The Chieu Hoi Center at Binh Dinh, near Qui Nhon, for example, had been set up to process between 700 and 1,000 defectors every month, but was handling little more than 50.

Open Marriage This 1972 bestseller by a husband and wife team of anthropologists, Nena and George O'Neill, urged in essence that a marriage bond be loose or nonpossessive enough to allow both partners to develop their individual identities and pursue their personal interests. This was done by giving each other "space," and by avoiding inflexible "roles": i.e., domestic chores and child rearing completely the responsibility of the wife; sole responsibility for keeping the family afloat financially that of the husband. Perhaps the most controversial part of the book was the section dealing with the right of each of the partners to open sex outside the marriage. "Outside sexual relationships when they are in the context of meaningful relationships may be rewarding and beneficial to an Open Marriage."

When in 1977 Nena O'Neill published *The Marriage Premise* she revised her views on open sex. Reporting on follow-up interviews with couples whose views on the matter were presented in *Open*

Marriage, she noted that very few who were open about extramarital affairs were able to maintain marriages for even as long as two years. It is now felt that since the options for premarital sex are so much greater than in the past, there is more reason to adhere to vows of fidelity. Current marriage was seen as tending toward "serial monogamy," in which sexual partners marry after first living together for some time, are more or less faithful during the term of the relationship or marriage, and eventually divorce and remarry.

Open Skies When Western and Soviet leaders met in Geneva for a summit conference on disarmament and German reunification in July 1955, President Dwight D. Eisenhower proposed—as a counterplan to the U.S.S.R. suggestion that disarmament be based on the establishment of a fixed number of inspection points—that the United States and the Soviet Union grant one another the right of aerial inspection of each other's territory.

There had been previous suggestions of a similar nature within the Eisenhower Cabinet, but up until the time of the "Open Skies" program no such plan had been thoroughly explored. The proposal as now presented by the President had been worked out by Nelson A. Rockefeller with the aid of his **Quantico Panel.** The idea was based on the assurance from military experts that given the advanced state of photographic technology any significant armament buildup could be detected by aerial inspection. However, Secretary of State John Foster Dulles viewed the prospects for disarmament and specifically Soviet acceptance of the Open Skies proposal with skepticism.

As outlined by President Eisenhower on July 21 the plan was essentially the following:

To give to each other a complete blueprint of our military establishments, from beginning to end, from one end of our countries to the other; lay out the establishments and provide the blueprints to each other.

Next, to provide within our countries facilities for aerial photography to the other country—we to provide you the facilities within our country, ample facilities for aerial reconnaissance, where you can make all the pictures you choose and take them to your own country to study, you to provide exactly the same facilities to us and we to make these examinations, and by this step to convince the world that we are providing as between ourselves against the possibility of great surprise attack, thus lessening danger and relaxing tension . . . what I propose, I assure you, would be but a beginning.

Britain's Prime Minister Sir Anthony Eden and France's Premier Edgar Faure immediately approved the plan and declared that their countries were ready to participate in such an agreement. N. A. Bulganin, chairman of the Soviet Council of Ministers, spoke encouragingly of it and said that his country would give it sympathic consideration. But during the informal session that followed his talk, President Eisenhower found himself in conversation with Nikita S. Khrushchev, who attended the conference as a member of the Presidium of the U.S.S.R. He obviously disapproved of the Open Skies proposal, which he said was merely a bald espionage plot against the Soviet Union. His tone, though bantering, was one of complete authority and rejection. "I saw clearly then, for the first time," President Eisenhower wrote afterward, "the identity of the real boss of the Soviet delegation."

The plan was eventually rejected by the Russians. President Eisenhower put this down to Khrushchev's determination *"at all costs to keep the U.S.S.R. a closed society."* He was also aware that even without Open Skies the Soviet government had available to it "a vast volume of information about us which was constantly being accumulated at little or no cost from United States newspapers, road maps, aerial photographs, magazines, journals, and government reports—some of it of types that could not be obtained even from aerial reconnaissance."

Operation Abolition Following the demonstrations against hearings by a subcommittee of the **House Committee on Un-American Activities** (HUAC) in San Francisco in May 1960, this forty-five minute movie was put together from subpoenaed television newsreel films. Narrated by rightist news analyst Fulton Lewis, Jr., the film was said by many to have distorted events by presenting them out of sequence. In spite of protests from critics, it was widely shown before conservative groups throughout the country and circulated as an official HUAC document.

The Northern California Civil Liberties Union attempted to counterbalance the influence of *Operation Abolition*—the title comes from a 1957 report on the Emergency Civil Liberties Committee—by using some of the same film footage to show how untruths and distortions had been introduced. Unfortunately, *Operation Correction* received only limited exposure and publicity.

Several of the people connected with *Operation Abolition* later put out a film entitled *While Brave Men Die*, which dealt with the 1967 demonstrations against the **Vietnam War.**

Operation Big Lift In order to demonstrate the speed with which the United States could increase its ground forces in Europe should emergency need arise, the Second Armored Division was airlifted from Texas to West Germany on October 24, 1963. Scheduled to take seventy-two hours, Operation Big Lift was completed in only sixty-three.

Operation Big Switch The mutual voluntary repatriation of prisoners under the terms of the July 1953 armistice concluding the **Korean War.** When the switch was completed early in September 1953, approximately 22,500 North Koreans and Chinese prisoners in American hands refused to return to their homelands. During a ninety-day period of political explanation provided for in the armistice, 333 of these prisoners were persuaded by the communists to accept repatriation.

In all, some 350 members of the United Nations forces—including twenty-two Americans, many of whom later changed their minds—elected to stay under communist rule.

See **Little Switch.**

Operation Bootstrap Name generally given to the plan for the economic and industrial expansion of Puerto Rico initiated in about 1940 by Luis Muñoz Marín, leader of the Popular Democratic Party. In 1941, Marín became Speaker of the Puerto Rican Senate while the island was still a U.S. Territory, and he had the support and cooperation of Rexford G. Tugwell, who was appointed governor in 1941. After 1944, new businesses were allowed ten years of tax exemption, and a governmental development corporation encouraged investment by United States entrepreneurs. In 1963 tax exemption was extended for up to seventeen years. As a result, San Juan became a center for plants producing clothing, pharmaceuticals, chemicals, plastics, electrical goods, cement, and metal products. There was also an increase in the processing of agricultural products such as tobacco and sugar.

Muñoz Marín became the first elected governor of Puerto Rico in 1948, and was reelected three successive times before choosing to run for the Puerto Rican Senate in 1964. After 1952, Puerto Rico became an Estado Libre Asociado, or Commonwealth, linked to the United States in a voluntary association.

As a result of Operation Bootstrap, gross capital investment in Puerto Rico was $1.69 billion in 1976; per capita income for the same year was $1,989 as compared to $1,078 in 1965. Puerto Rico's largest income is now from manufacturing—more than three times that from agriculture. Among the major industries are textiles, leather, electronic components, and, increasingly, petrochemicals.

Operation Breadbasket Developing and expanding a **Selective Patronage Program** first conceived by civil rights leaders in Philadelphia, this job-seeking campaign by the **Southern Christian Leadership Conference** (SCLC) first attracted national attention when its possibilities were explored in Chicago in 1966 under the direction of Reverend Jesse L. Jackson. Pressure was brought to bear on companies operating within Negro neighborhoods to increase the number of blacks in their employ, make use of black service companies, stock products made by black manufacturers, and deposit some portion of their profits in Negro-owned banks. If these demands were resisted, negotiations were instituted in an attempt to broaden understanding of Negro problems, sometimes by getting company executives to visit ghetto areas. "We want them to think of profit in terms of flesh and blood, not only dimes and dollars," said Reverend Jackson.

When negotiations failed, the ministers of black churches organized boycotts—known as "selective buying" campaigns—in the community, backing them up by picketing and demonstrations.

Within a year, fourteen major Chicago companies had signed Operation Breadbasket agreements, and deposits in banks owned by blacks had risen from 5 million to 22 million dollars. The greatest success in opening jobs came after the Great Atlantic & Pacific Tea Company (A&P) bowed to boycott pressure and agreed to hire 900 blacks.

Success in Chicago induced the SCLC to expand the campaign nationally. In Cleveland, for example, after a month-long boycott against its products, the Sealtest Division of National Dairy Products agreed in August 1967 to open up a minimum of fifty new and upgraded jobs to blacks, to make use of black-owned service companies, manufacturers, and banks, and to establish a recruitment program in the black community. The Operation Breadbasket organization was also influential, that same year, in getting out the vote in behalf of Cleveland's black mayor, Carl Stokes.

Reverend Jackson remained the director of the campaign until 1972, when after a dispute with SCLC he left to form Operation PUSH (**People United to Save Humanity**), which has its headquarters in Chicago.

Operation Breakthrough When George Romney joined the Nixon administration in 1969 as Secretary of **Housing and Urban Development** (HUD), he tried to introduce the assembly line techniques he had been familiar with as president of American Motors (1954-1962) to the solution of the urgent housing problem. Operation Breakthrough was essentially a research and development program designed to bring about inexpensive and mass produced housing through the use of prefabricated modular components. It was tested with mixed results in various cities—probably no more than 3,000 units in all were built—before Secretary Romney resigned in 1973 and was succeeded by James T. Lynn.

Secretary Romney's charge that President Richard M. Nixon gave little attention to housing and urban development problems seems borne out by the President's proposal in 1971 that HUD be merged into a larger entity to be known as the Department of Community Development. In 1973, all housing subsidy programs were stopped, and in 1974 Romney's charge was repeated by Floyd Hyde, who resigned as HUD Under Secretary because he felt that the Nixon administration was letting the **Model Cities** program, of which he had been the director, die.

Of Operation Breakthrough, social analyst Michael Harrington has noted that although there was a great deal of talk about technical innovation, "it produced little beyond the press releases, while the reality of Section 235 of the Housing Code subsidized private speculators to sell shoddy homes to the poor."

Operation Candor Faced with growing pressure to resign from office or face impeachment as a result of the disclosures attendant upon the **Watergate Scandal**, in November 1973 President Richard M. Nixon launched a vigorous counterattack which the news media soon dubbed "Operation Candor." In a nationwide TV address on November 6 he noted that he had "no intention whatever of walking away from the job I was elected to do."

In the days that followed, the President held an unprecedented series of meetings with most Republican members of Congress, as well as with some Democrats, in which he made a personal appeal for their support. On November 15, President Nixon assured some 4,000 members of the National Association of Realtors that "the President has not violated his trust and he isn't going to violate his trust now." During a five-day trip through the South, he made himself available for a series of questions from those attending the annual meeting of the Associated Press Managing Editors Association held at Disney World. Questions from regular White House correspondents were forbidden, and those questions that were asked by others tended to be highly deferential. It was on this occasion that President Nixon made the later much-quoted disclaimer: "People have the right to know whether or not their President is a crook. Well, I am not a crook."

On November 20, at a Memphis, Tennessee, meeting with nineteen Republican governors, he assured Oregon's Governor Tom McCall that there would be no more bombshell disclosures relating to Watergate. However, the following day the President's special counsel, J. Fred Buzhardt, Jr., revealed that there was an 18½-minute gap on the tape of a crucial conversation (see **Nixon Tapes**) between the President and H. R. Haldeman, his former Chief of Staff.

In an effort to answer the growing number of questions about his personal finances, on December 8, 1973, President Nixon released a massive financial statement that included his tax returns. However, instead of laying to rest some of the charges being brought against him, this step led to demands for further information.

Given the obvious failure of Operation Candor to overcome the **credibility gap** that had been widening in the last year and a half, late in December President Nixon reversed a promise made early in November to release detailed summaries of those tapes already in the hands of the courts.

Operation Cedar Falls *See* **Iron Triangle**.

Operation Chaos Name later given to the **CIA** Special Operations Group established in 1967 on orders from President Lyndon B. Johnson to "collect, coordinate, evaluate and report on the extent of foreign influence on domestic dissidence." Details on Operation Chaos were made public in the **Rockefeller Commission** report published in June 1975.

In spite of the fact that the group's assignment had been limited to establishing whether or not American dissidents had foreign contacts, in the six years the operation lasted, some 13,000 files were collected, more than half of them on U.S. citizens. In addition, the names of 300,000 people and organizations figuring in these files were entered into the CIA computer. According to the Rockefeller Commission, Operation Chaos prepared some 3,500 memorandums for CIA use and another 3,000 for distribution to the FBI; thirty-seven memorandums were distributed to the White House and top government officials.

Said to have been "steadily enlarged in response to repeated presidential requests for more information," the Operation Chaos staff reached a maximum of fifty-two during the first term in office of President Richard M. Nixon. Proper "cover" was sometimes obtained by recruiting agents from the dissident groups themselves.

The Rockefeller Commission found that "some domestic activities of Operation Chaos exceeded the CIA's statutory authority . . . . More significantly the operation became a repository for large quantities of information on the domestic activities of American citizens . . . and much of it was not directly related to the question of the existence of foreign connections."

Supervisory responsibility for Operation Chaos was the job of Richard Helms, who directed the CIA from 1966 to 1973. According to testimony before the Rockefeller Commission, the operation was so isolated from the regular CIA chain of command that even the head of the counterintelligence section was unaware that it existed.

Operation Deep Freeze *See* **International Geophysical Year.**

Operation Head Start *See* **Head Start.**

Operation Junction City In the largest assault of the **Vietnam War** to date, beginning on March 19, 1967, the United States command sent 30,000 troops under Lt. General Jonathan O. Seaman into a 1,000-square-mile swampy pocket some seventy-five miles northwest of Saigon and bulging into Cambodia. The area had long been thought to contain a major concentration of Viet Cong troops, but as the scorched earth operation proceeded, very little defense was put up and it was assumed that communist troops had vanished across the border into Cambodia—although Prince Norodom Sihanouk denied that his country was being used as a Viet Cong sanctuary.

Operation Junction City was named for Junction City, Kansas, where General Seaman's family lived.

Operation Phoenix Some of the success of the January 1968 **Tet Offensive** of the communist forces during the **Vietnam War** was ascribed to the fact that the **National Liberation Front** (NLF) had received fifth-column help. As a result, the South Vietnamese authorities undertook an American-endorsed program designed to weed out secret NLF supporters and possible agents. Critics maintained,

however, that Operation Phoenix merely gave the regime of General Nguyen Van Thieu a legalized method of murdering or imprisoning some 40,000 political opponents.

Operation PUSH *See* **People United to Save Humanity.**

Operation Rolling Thunder The continuous bombing of North Vietnam was begun on March 2, 1965, with an attack by 160 U.S. and South Vietnamese planes that was described as one of the heaviest in the Vietnam war up to that time. The bombings followed closely upon the release of a white paper on February 27 in which the U.S. State Department charged that "massive evidence"—gathered by South Vietnam and "jointly analyzed by South Vietnamese and American experts"—indicated that "beyond question . . . North Vietnam is carrying out a carefully conceived plan of aggression against" South Vietnam. The raids into North Vietnamese territory were defended as necessary since "clearly the restraint of the past was not providing adequately for the defense of South Vietnam against Hanoi's open aggression." The raids were to continue until "Hanoi decided to halt its intervention in the South or until effective steps are taken to maintain peace and security in the area."

The effectiveness of the raids was, according to some critics, limited by the fact that there was too much emphasis on merely building up large sortie totals. In addition, losses of American planes were high, because pilots tended to use short routes that were soon lined with antiaircraft.

The bombing had been introduced in the hope of bringing Hanoi to the negotiating table within six weeks, but instead they became Hanoi's ostensible reason for refusing to negotiate. On May 12, the raids were suspended for five days, but resumed after the failure of North Vietnam to respond to new American peace overtures. That same year, the bombings were again suspended on December 23 as part of another American "peace offensive," but they were resumed on January 31, 1966, after these overtures were denounced by Ho Chi Minh.

Operation Sail As part of the nation's 200th birthday celebration, on July 4, 1976, sixteen square-rigged sailing ships from countries all over the world gathered in New York Harbor and sailed up the Hudson River to a point just north of the George Washington Bridge. The "tall ships" and an estimated 10,000 smaller craft that filled the harbor and the river were watched by over 6 million people who had gathered around the harbor and along the river banks to see the flotilla led by the U.S. Coast Guard ship *Eagle* ascend the river.

A naval review on the same day brought fifty-three warships from twenty-two countries to anchor in the Upper Bay and the Hudson River.

Operation Sandwedge Counterintelligence plan worked out by John J. Caulfield for use by the **Committee to Re-elect the President** (CREEP; CRP) during the 1972 presidential election campaign (*see* **Watergate Scandal**).

Caulfield, a former New York City policeman, had been Republican candidate Richard M. Nixon's personal bodyguard during the 1968 election. Hoping to eventually establish a private security firm if he could make proper use of his White House connections, in September 1971 he submitted to John W. Dean III, counsel to the President, a twelve-page memorandum outlining a half-a-million-dollar plan for gathering political intelligence that would be useful during the 1972 presidential campaign. Operation Sandwedge—sometimes erroneously referred to as Operation Sandwich—made provision for everything from convention security to undercover investigations. It was also unofficially made clear to Dean that electronic surveillance could be arranged for.

Operatives in the plan were to have included Joseph I. Woods, brother of the President's secretary Rose Mary Woods and former Cook County, Illinois, sheriff; Anthony T. Ulasewicz, a former detective and at that point an aide to Caulfield; and Roger Barth and Mike Acree, both of the IRS.

Based on their analysis of the 1968 campaign, members of the President's staff—such as speechwriter Patrick J. Buchanan—argued for the adoption of the "political hardball" tactics that had been, they claimed, used against Mr. Nixon by his opponents: staff infiltration, false rumors planted and leaked to the press, disrupted rallies, etc.

The necessity for a plan such as Operation Sandwedge seems to have been accepted by White House Chief of Staff H. R. Haldeman, Assistant to the President for Domestic Affairs John D. Ehrlichman, and Attorney General John N. Mitchell. The plan itself, however, was eventually scratched because both Mitchell and Haldeman lacked confidence in Caulfield and felt that any counterintelligence operation should come under the direct control of a lawyer.

A sandwedge is a club used in golf to dig the ball out of sand, deep weeds, or mud.

Operation Sunrise Sometimes considered the official name for the **Strategic Hamlet** program established in South Vietnam (see **Vietnam War**), this was actually the more limited operation suggested by the American Military Advisory Headquarters in Saigon. According to Roger Hilsman, who as Assistant Secretary of State for the Far East gave the strategic hamlet idea his complete endorsement, Operation Sunrise was "a total misunderstanding of what the program should try to do."

In order to cut the flow of communist recruits to the jungle area northeast of Saigon, it was proposed early in 1962 to construct strategic hamlets along the road from the South Vietnamese capital to the Tay Ninh Province in the Ben Cat region. This required the forcible relocation of whole hamlets. In addition, Operation Sunrise ignored the fundamental principle of proceeding outward from a secure base, because the Ben Cat road skirted one of the areas in which the Viet Cong were strongest.

Once the plan had been advanced, South Vietnamese leaders insisted upon it, and the Kennedy administration, fearing that the entire strategic hamlet program might be canceled, gave its reluctant approval. In spite of the fact that additional troops were assigned to guard the four main hamlets involved, these villages were overrun by the Viet Cong in 1964.

Operation Sunshine *See* **Strontium 90; U.S.S. Nautilus**.

Oppenheimer Affair In December 1953, while he was lecturing in England, where Oxford University bestowed an honorary degree on him, Dr. J. Robert Oppenheimer, special consultant to the **Atomic Energy Commission** (AEC), had his top-secret Q security clearance lifted as a result of orders from President Dwight D. Eisenhower, who had directed that a "blank wall" be placed between the scientist "and any information of a sensitive or classified character." The President had acted as a result of charges lodged with the FBI by William Borden, the former executive director of the staff of the congressional Joint Committee on Atomic Energy, that "more probably than not J. Robert Oppenheimer is an agent of the Soviet Union."

Dr. Oppenheimer had been instrumental in the development of the atomic bomb as director of the Los Alamos Scientific Laboratory during World War II. He had afterward been the chairman of the General Advisory Committee of the Atomic Energy Commission, but had resigned in 1952 to direct the Institute for Advanced Study in Princeton.

The reasons for Borden's charges at this time are obscure, but critics charged that they stemmed from Dr. Oppenheimer's opposition to the hydrogen bomb project. In any case, they caused FBI director J. Edgar Hoover to submit to the President, to AEC chairman Lewis Strauss, and to Secretary of Defense Charles Wilson, a digest of Oppenheimer's security file which greatly disturbed them. President Eisenhower called for an immediate investigation before a Personnel Security Board composed of Gordon Gray, president of the University of North Carolina; Thomas A. Morgan, former president of Sperry Corporation; and Dr. Ward V. Evans, Loyola University professor of chemistry. Known as the Gray Board, this group began hearings of Dr. Oppenheimer's AEC suspension in April 1954. It eventually rejected the charge of disloyalty, but, with Dr. Evans dissenting, voted to maintain the suspension of the security clearance in view of the fact that Dr. Oppenheimer's "associations have reflected a serious disregard for the requirements of the security system." The majority report also found his "conduct in the hydrogen bomb program sufficiently disturbing" to cast doubts on whether his continued participation in a program relating to national defense "would be clearly consistent with the best interest of security."

Dr. Oppenheimer was evidently given an opportunity to resign, but he chose to appeal the Gray Board decision to the AEC, which on June 29, 1954, upheld it four to one, a stong dissent having been entered by Henry D. Smyth. The majority decision cited Dr. Oppenheimer's "substantial defects of character and imprudent and dangerous associations, particularly with known subversives who place the interests of foreign powers above those of the United States. . . ." Although no charges of disloyalty were made, the decision noted that Dr. Oppenheimer had testified before the Gray Board that "from 1937 to at least 1942 he had made regular and substantial cash contributions to the Communist Party." However, these facts were not by and large new and had been known to the government when Dr. Oppenheimer had entered its service.

Some of the most important testimony against Dr. Oppenheimer had come from Dr. Edward Teller, an advocate of continued nuclear testing, who charged that Dr. Oppenheimer's lack of enthusiasm for the hydrogen bomb had delayed its development by several years (see **"Clean" Bomb Controversy**). The majority of the scientific community, however, defended Dr. Oppenheimer and attacked the procedures and humiliations to which he had been subjected. Their stand would seem to have been vindicated by the fact that in 1963 President Lyndon B. Johnson awarded Oppenheimer the Fermi Prize, the AEC's highest honor.

Opportunities Industrialization Center (OIC) *See* **10–36–50 Plan.**

Organization for Afro-American Unity Formed in March 1964 by the charismatic black leader Malcolm X after his suspension from the **Black Muslims** for having qualified the assassination of President John F. Kennedy (**November 22, 1963**) as a case of "the chickens coming home to roost," the group seemed to indicate a departure from his previously advocated black racist views. While it welcomed white cooperation, it did, however, reject whites as members.

As Malcom X explained: "I have these very deep feelings that white people who want to join black organizations are really just taking the escapist way to salve their consciences. . . . Where the really sincere white people have got to do their 'proving' of themselves is not among the black *victims*, but out on the battle lines of where America's racism really *is*—and that's in their own home communities. . . ."

Malcom X was assassinated on February 21, 1965, in Harlem.

See **The Autobiography of Malcom X.**

Organization for Economic Cooperation and Development (OECD) Replacing the 1948 Organization for European Economic Cooperation (OEEC), which had been designed to coordinate actions of nations receiving United States aid under the **Marshall Plan**, the Organization for Economic Cooperation and Development (OECD) was established in Paris on September 30, 1961. The function of the twenty-one-member group was to work together to improve their national economies and expand world trade. OECD's Development Assistance Committee was charged with coordinating aid to underdeveloped countries.

Member nations include the United States, Canada, Great Britain, France, Germany, Italy, Belgium, Luxembourg, the Netherlands, Austria, Denmark, Norway, Portugal, Sweden, Switzerland, Spain, Greece, Iceland, Ireland, Turkey, and Japan. Yugoslavia and Finland enjoy "special status" participation.

Working through the OECD, the United States hopes to distribute among the more advanced Western nations the burden of aid to nations under development. Other goals include a lowering of the continuing and rising U.S. trade deficit and an expansion of European markets by counteracting the discriminatory tariff systems introduced by the European Economic Community (EEC) and the European Free Trade Association (EFTA).

The Organization Man In this 1956 bestseller, William H. Whyte, assistant managing editor of *Fortune* magazine, analyzed some of the conflicts between the individual and the large-scale organization. Focusing on the decline of the "Protestant ethic" of work and thrift as a way to success, he deplored the attempt to use techniques derived from the physical sciences to create a "scientifically" administered group that would substitute for the individual in decision making and creativity. The decline of the basic sciences and liberal arts in American universities was seen as a result of the latter's eagerness to adapt to the supposed needs of the big corporation.

"In our attention to making the organization work," Mr. Whyte wrote, "we have come close to deifying it. We are describing its defects as virtues and denying that there is—or should be—a conflict between the individual and the organization. This denial is bad for the organization. It is worse for the individual. What it does, in soothing him, is to rob him of the intellectual armor he so badly needs."

The book's premise was that the essential problem is not the organization itself but our "worship" of it. One method advocated for fighting its scientific pretensions was to cheat on personality tests, which are seen as being essentially designed to weed out the individualistic entrepreneurial talent actually needed by the organization. This "cheating" is confined to giving testers the answers they want to hear.

In spite of the generally pessimistic facts and figures he presented, it was the author's "optimistic premise that individualism is as possible in our times as in others. I speak of individualism *within* organizational life."

Organization of American States (OAS) Formalization of the loose inter-American system established by the Rio de Janeiro Treaty of Reciprocal Assistance (September 2, 1947) (*see* **Rio Pact**) began with the Ninth International Conference of American States in Bogotá, March 1948. On May 2, 1948, the conference resulted in the signing of the Charter of Bogotá, which established the OAS as a regional organization—including the United States and all the Latin American nations—in conformity with the United Nations Charter. Canada has permanent observer status.

The United States did not ratify the charter until June 16, 1951, and the charter did not go into effect until December 13, 1951, when ratification by Colombia brought the percentage of nations having taken this action to the necessary two-thirds.

Intended to promote and defend hemispheric peace and solidarity, as well as to foster economic development, the OAS has as its key features a general secretariat—this role was assigned to the Washington-based Pan-American Union established in 1890—an executive council composed of one representative from each member state, and a number of economic, social, cultural, and juridical councils. Provision is made for regular inter-American conferences every five years, and the first of these was held in Caracas (1954). Threats to the peace and security of Western Hemisphere nations are dealt with by convoking consultative meetings of the foreign ministers of member nations.

The operational costs of the OAS are largely met by the United States, and that country's influence in the organization has been preponderant. In 1962 it secured the "suspension" of communist Cuba's participation in OAS activities. When in 1964 Venezuela requested OAS aid to prevent Cuban attempts to spread communist doctrine within its borders, the OAS responded by severing diplomatic and economic relations with Cuba. (Some nations delaying complying, and in 1975 all sanctions were lifted.)

Despite the fact that the United States violated the provisions of the Rio Treaty and the Charter of Bogotá by intervening unilaterally in the Dominican Republic (*see* **Dominican Intervention**) to prevent what it called a communist revolution (April 1965), the OAS backed the American position by creating an Inter-American Peace Force to which Brazil, Costa Rica, El Salvador, Honduras, and Nicaragua contributed token contingents that joined some 20,000 American troops dispatched to the island by President Lyndon B. Johnson.

Meeting in Washington, D.C. (June 21–July 1, 1978), the eighth annual General Assembly of the OAS heard charges that the governments of Chile, Paraguay, and Uruguay were involved in abuses of human rights including illegal arrest, torture, and murder. By a significant majority it passed resolutions urging these countries to cooperate in correcting the situation.

Organized Crime Control Act A major part of the Nixon administration's anticrime legislative program, the bill was passed by the Senate in January 1970, but remained in the House Judiciary Committee until the end of September, when it was released with amendments to create a special commission on individual rights and provisions to control explosives. Many liberals, including committee chairman Emanuel Celler (D.-N.Y.), considered that the bill contained constitutional infringements on personal rights. After passage by the House and approval by the Senate early in October, the amended bill was signed into law on October 15, 1970, by President Richard M. Nixon, who said it gave the federal government the means "to launch a total war against organized crime."

Among its provisions were the following: authorization of the imposition by federal judges of additional sentences of up to twenty-five years on "dangerous special offenders" whose offense was part of a pattern of criminal activity or of a conspiracy to engage in such a pattern; the creation of special grand juries empowered to issue reports on non-criminal misconduct by appointed government officials, if such conduct was related to organized criminal activity; the declaration that it was a crime to plot to obstruct state law by bribing government officials with a view toward establishing an illegal gambling business or using income from organized crime to acquire or set up businesses engaged in interstate commerce; the requirement that those engaged in manufacturing explosives or transporting them across state lines be licensed; the detention for up to eighteen months of witnesses unwilling to comply with court orders; the repeal of previous witness-immunity laws, and the authorization of legislative, administrative, and judicial bodies to grant witnesses limited immunity from prosecution based on their testimony; the authorization of federal protection for those testifying in cases concerning organized crime.

The special federal commission created by the act was to determine whether provisions of the act itself, or of any other laws authorizing activities such as "no-knock" searches and wiretapping, were in violation of human rights.

The Other America Published in 1962, Michael Harrington's compassionate study of poverty in the midst of affluence is generally considered to have influenced both Presidents John F. Kennedy and Lyndon B. Johnson in their attempts to make the abolition of poverty one of the major goals of their administrations (*see* **War on Poverty; The Great Society**).

Harrington points out that in addition to the fa-
miliar America that enjoys the highest mass standard of living the world has ever known and that worries about "learning to live decently amid luxury," there is an "invisible land" of 40 to 50 million citizens whose basic needs of food, clothing, and shelter are inadequately met. Crowded and segregated into urban slums—often by government-subsidized housing programs that concentrate on middle- and upper-class needs—they are generally politically invisible as well, because they "do not, by far and large, belong to unions, fraternal organizations, or to political parties." As a result, their sole representatives within the society are often social workers, who themselves have little political power.

A paradox of the "**welfare state**" that emerged from the 1930s, Harrington emphasizes, is that it benefits least those who need it most, since the lives, environments, and values of the millions of poor who over the generations have "proved immune to progress" do not permit them to take advantage of whatever new opportunities may have opened up. This new poor cannot be defined in simple statistical terms; their poverty is so constructed as to destroy "aspiration," the quality that characterized the immigrant poor, who although they "found themselves in slums" were not slum-dwellers. Shunted out of sight, the contemporary poor tend to lose their links with the rest of society and get caught in a vicious cycle that results in "a culture of poverty." Inadequately housed and badly fed, they are sick oftener than most Americans and tend to remain sick longer. As a result, they find it difficult to hold steady employment and therefore difficult to "pay for good housing, for a nutritious diet, for doctors"—all of which makes the cycle repeat itself.

Harrington's study is based on the ethical assumption that "in a nation with a technology that could provide every citizen with a decent life, it is an outrage and a scandal that there should be such social misery. Only if one begins with this assumption is it possible to pierce through the invisibility of 40 to 50 million human beings and to see the other America."

Writing in *The New Republic* (February 26, 1977), Harrington charged that the Congressional Budget Office (CBO), in a January report entitled "Poverty Status of Families Under Alternative Definitions of Income," took "a major step in turning the poor into non-persons. By an act of statistical legerdemain CBO eliminates the poverty of 3,628,000 families and doubles the rate at which the poor have been escaping from their fate since 1965."

"Our long national nightmare is over" On assuming the Presidency on August 9, 1974, following the resignation of President Richard M. Nixon (*see* **Watergate Scandal**), Gerald R. Ford won almost universal approval with an inaugural speech in which he pledged to conduct an administration of "openness and candor." He noted that he preferred to think of his speech as "just a little straight talk among friends" rather than an inaugural address.

Acutely aware that he had not come to the succession by way of the ballot, he asked that the nation confirm him with its prayers.

My fellow Americans, our long national nightmare is over.

Our Constitution works; our great Republic is a Government of laws and not of men. . . . As we bind up the internal wounds of Watergate, more painful and more poisonous than those of foreign wars, let us restore the golden rule to our political process, and let brotherly love purge our hearts of suspicion and hate.

Time magazine reported that "as Ford concluded there was an almost tangible lifting of spirits in the East Room and across the nation." That spirit was somewhat shattered when on September 8, the President granted Richard Nixon an unconditional pardon for crimes he "may have committed."

Outer Continental Shelf Lands Act *See* **Tidelands Oil Controversy**.

P

Project Apollo

NASA

Pachucos Movement The origins of *La Causa,* which brought Cesar Chavez to national prominence in the 1960s, can be found in the so-called Pachucos Movement of the 1950s.

Recruited by Fred Ross, a community organizer originally working with Saul Alinsky's Industrial Areas Foundation (IAF), Chavez was instrumental in getting the *pachucos,* or "toughs," of the San Jose *barrio* (Spanish-speaking quarter) to cooperate in community efforts to band together and fight discrimination against Mexican Americans.

Chavez, though not himself a *pachuco,* had considerable influence in the barrio, which was known as Sal Si Peudes ("get out if you can"). Ross's plan was to establish "house meetings" in which barrio residents could discuss their problems and organize for action. As these meetings increased in number and size they were to be absorbed into a Community Services Organization with chapters all over the area.

Originally hostile to Ross's intrusion into San Jose, Chavez was evidently won over after a personal encounter at which he realized that Ross "knew the problems as well as we did." In 1952, Chavez began working as a volunteer in a campaign to get barrio residents to register to vote. Initially, he supported himself by continuing to work as a lumber handler or a fruit picker, but eventually Ross was able to get IAF funds to hire him at $275 a month.

See La Huelga.

Pacific Council See ANZUS.

Pacific Doctrine On a stopover in Honolulu on December 7, 1975, on his return from Indonesia and the Philippines after four days of talks with leaders of the People's Republic of China (December 1–5, 1975), President Gerald R. Ford delivered a speech at the city's East-West Center in which he enunciated "a Pacific doctrine of peace with all— and hostility toward none." The new Asian policy declared by the President was a development of the so-called **Nixon Doctrine** announced by President Richard M. Nixon on July 25, 1969, at a news conference on Guam during a tour that took him from the Philippines to Great Britain.

"The first premise of a new Pacific Doctrine is that American strength is basic to any stable balance of power in the Pacific. We must reach beyond our concern for security. But without security, there can be neither peace nor progress," said the President, who went on to emphasize that the preservation of the sovereignty and independence of our friends and allies in the area remains a paramount objective of American policy.

We recognize that force alone is insufficient to assure security. Popular legitimacy and social justice are vital prerequisites of resistance against subversion or aggression. . . .

The second basic premise of a new Pacific Doctrine is that partnership with Japan is a pillar of our strategy. . . .

The third premise . . . is the normalization of relations with the People's Republic of China, the strengthening of our new ties with this great nation representing nearly one quarter of mankind. This is another recent achievement of American foreign policy. It transcends 25 years of hostility.

Commenting on his visit and talks with Chairman Mao Tse-tung and Vice Premier Teng Hsiao-ping, President Ford said that the results completed a process begun with the Shanghai Communiqué issued after President Nixon's visit to mainland China in February 1972 (*see* **Peking Summit**).

"A fourth principle of our Pacific policy is our continuing stake in the stability and security of Southeast Asia," he continued, making special reference to the Philippines and Indonesia.

"A fifth tenet of our new Pacific policy is our belief that peace in Asia depends upon a resolution of outstanding political conflicts," said the President, noting continuing tension in Korea and the necessity for "reciprocate gestures of good will" in Indochina and calling for information about or the return of the remains of Americans killed or missing in action there.

The sixth point of our new Pacific policy is that peace in Asia requires a structure of economic cooperation reflecting the aspirations of all the peoples in the region. . . . Our trade with east Asia now exceeds our transactions with the European community . . . increasing by more than 30 percent annually—reaching $46 billion last year.

The President concluded by emphasizing that we serve our highest national interests by strengthening the self-reliance of our friends and allies in the area.

During President Ford's visit in Peking, both he and Secretary of State Henry Kissinger reaffirmed in toasts with Chinese leaders the Shanghai Communiqué which acknowledged Chinese claims to Taiwan, but no new initiatives were announced and the issue was generally played down. Nationalist China's foreign ministry issued a statement attacking rapprochement with Red China as encouraging communist subversion in Asia. In Congress, Rep. Dawson Mathis (D.-Ga.) introduced a resolution calling on the Ford administration not to compromise Nationalist China's freedom in exchange for normalization of relations with the People's Republic of China.

Ending what his administration officials had described as "a thirty-year anomaly in international affairs," on December 15, 1978, President Jimmy Carter made a dramatic nationwide television broadcast in which he announced that the United States and China would establish diplomatic relations on January 1, 1979. "The United States recognizes the Government of the People's Republic of China as the sole legal Government of China. Within this context the people of the United States will maintain cultural, commercial and other unofficial relations with the people of Taiwan." He noted that both nations reaffirmed the principles agreed on in the Shanghai Communiqué and that this new step underscored "once again that both sides wish to reduce the danger of international military conflict." In closing, the President emphasized that "these events are the final result of long and serious negotiations begun by President Nixon in 1972 and continued under the leadership of President Ford."

Panama Canal Treaties Negotiations over terms under which the Panama Canal would eventually be turned over to Panama were initiated in 1964 after riots in the Canal Zone. In 1967, representatives of both Panama and the United States agreed on the drafts of three treaties under which Panama would participate in running the canal, the Canal Zone would be gradually integrated into Panama, and the United States was given the option of building a sea-level canal across Panama. These treaties were formally rejected in 1970 by the government of Brigadier General Omar Torrijos Herrera, who had assumed power after the overthrow of the elected Panamanian government in 1968.

In February 1974 a new basis for negotiations was established when Secretary of State Henry A. Kissinger and the Panamanian foreign minister, Juan Antonio Tack, reached agreement on eight guiding principles under which a date would be set for turning over the canal, with Panama sharing the revenues until the final transfer. However, negotiations were put off when the surrender of the canal was introduced in 1976 as a presidential campaign issue by California's former governor, Ronald Reagan, who was challenging President Gerald R. Ford's leadership of the Republican party.

Although Democratic candidate Jimmy Carter had said during the 1976 campaign that he would "never give up complete control or practical control over the Panama Canal Zone," after his triumph at the polls he made the achievement of a new canal

treaty the cornerstone of his administration's Latin American policy. Negotiations with Panama were resumed in February 1977, with a view toward transferring complete control of the canal in 1999. Among the major points of dispute was a provision that would allow the United States to defend the canal, if necessary, after the official transfer. In addition, Panama asked that—as compensation during the remaining years of American control—the United States make a down payment of $1 billion and annual payments of $500 million. (Final agreement was for annual payments up to $70 million from canal revenues.) On August 5, 1977, President Carter caused a temporary crisis in the talks when he called for an option that would permit this country to build a sea-level canal. This provision was unacceptable to Panama and did not figure in the final treaties signed by President Carter and General Torrijos in Washington on September 7, 1977.

In the months that followed, the Carter administration fought a hard battle to obtain Senate ratification of the treaties. On March 16, 1978, the Senate approved by a sixty-eight-to-thirty-two vote a Neutrality Treaty under which after the transfer of the canal both countries would have the right to defend it, if necessary. In case of an emergency, Panamanian and American vessels were to have the right to go to the head of the line for transit.

The Senate vote on the Panama Canal Treaty under which full responsibility for the canal would be turned over to Panama at noon December 31, 1999, did not take place until April 18, 1978. Again the vote was sixty-eight-to-thirty-two, one more than the required two-thirds majority. The previous day the Senate had adopted a measure allowing the United States to defend the canal unilaterally, if necessary. In addition, under the terms of the treaty the United States agreed to negotiate only with Panama for a possible sea-level canal across Central America. In turn, Panama agreed to undertake such a canal only with the United States.

Both treaties and their amendments were immediately accepted for Panama by General Torrijos. This acceptance includes a Senate amendment under which formal ratification of the transfer treaty would be delayed until the approval of implementing legislation, which had to be passed by March 31, 1979. Actual surrender of portions of the Canal Zone and a partial takeover of the canal itself will not begin until six months after formal ratification. Until complete transfer takes place, the canal will be operated by a Canal Commission including five Americans and four Panamanians. Integration of the Canal Zone into Panama is scheduled to take place within thirty months after formal ratification.

Paperback Revolution The origins of current techniques in the publishing and marketing of paperbacks go back to the formation of Pocket Books, Inc., in 1939 by Robert F. de Graff, M. Lincoln Schuster, Leon Shimkin, and Richard Simon. That company's first list of ten reprints including classics and bestsellers, e.g., *The Autobiography of Benvenuto Cellini* and James Hilton's *Lost Horizon*, launched the so-called "paperback revolution," which was only slightly delayed by paper rationing during World War II.

Paperback sales rose from only a few million in 1940 to 220 million by 1955, by which time Pocket Books had spawned a host of successful rivals and imitators. Ten years later there were 277 publishers producing paperbacks, and sales were said to be well over $300 million annually.

The original emphasis of paperback publishing was on inexpensive—the first ten were priced at twenty-five cents each—reprints of hardcover originals, but over the years the trend has been to more and more original publications with prices well over $2.00 and sometimes going higher that $10.

The industry obtained its own bibliographical reference publication when in 1955 R. R. Bowker Company issued the first volume of *Paperbound Books in Print*, listing more than 4,500 titles.

Parker Lynching On April 25, 1959, two days before he was to be tried on charges of raping a pregnant white woman, Mack Charles Parker, a twenty-three-year-old black, was pulled from a jail in Poplarville, Mississippi, by nine masked men and pushed screaming into a parked sedan. At Pearl River, the boundary between Mississippi and Louisiana, Parker was taken from the car and shot. His body was found in the river on May 4, 1959.

Although the detailed facts of the case were widely known and even discussed in print, an eighteen-member grand jury impaneled in Poplarville by Circuit Judge Sebe Dale on November 2, 1959, disbanded three days later without taking action. It had not requested a 378-page report on the lynching prepared by the FBI, and it had refused to hear FBI agents who offered to testify.

The judge, who in charging the jury had suggested that recent civil rights decisions in the Supreme Court might have incited the action, is quoted as saying: "I have an idea the nation may look down on Mississippi justice now, but I'm not apologizing."

Reopening the case as a federal proceeding, the Justice Department presented the FBI report to a grand jury made up of twenty local white men and one black. The jury was asked to return an indictment under an old civil rights act making it a crime to deprive a citizen of his constitutional rights; however, on January 14, 1960, the jury reported that it was "unable to arrive at any true bill," having found no basis for prosecution.

The victim of the rape, who had picked Parker out of a lineup of twenty blacks, was later reported to have said: "When I saw the man, I told these police that I wasn't positive it was him but it looked like him."

Parkinson's Law Title of a 1957 bestseller by British author and lecturer C. Northcote Parkinson in which he examines the vagaries of business administration. The first "law," which Professor Parkinson develops into a series of concomitant observations, is that "work expands to fill the time available for its completion." The book was originally published as a mock-serious essay in *The Economist* and, as Parkinson explains, "had various pieces of mathematics to show how scientific the whole thing was. . . . I was so encouraged by its reception that I expanded my researches in administration."

A "law of nature" that follows from the discovery of this first principle is the observation that any administrative organization increases its personnel at a given annual rate, regardless of the amount of work to be performed; in considering a financial agenda, Professor Parkinson notes that the time spent on any item is inverse proportion to the amount of money involved. . . .

Parrot's Beak *See* **Cambodian "Incursion."**

Participatory Democracy The term, which stood for both the goal and the means of action of many of the **New Left** movements of the 1960s, was first used in the **Port Huron Statement** of the **Students for a Democratic Society** (SDS). This manifesto called for "participatory democracy" and asked that "the individual share in those social decisions determining the quality and direction of his life, that society be organized to encourage independence in men and provide the media for their common participation."

New Left theorist Staughton Lynd emphasized that an important aspect of participatory democracy is the concept of parallel structure. For example, since the registration of blacks in the regular Democratic party was difficult if not impossible in

Mississippi, in 1964 civil rights activists established the **Mississippi Freedom Democratic Party** (MFDP). **Freedom Schools** which paralleled the public schools were another example, as were neighborhood organizations "challenging the legitimacy of the top-down middle-class 'community organizations' sponsored by urban renewal and anti-poverty administrators."

As Lynd saw it, the **Student Nonviolent Coordinating Committee** (SNCC; Snick) or SDS worker ought not to try to impose an ideology on such a parallel institution but to act as a "catalyst" helping local people to organize to express their wants. "There is an unstated assumption that the poor, when they find voice, will produce a truer, sounder radicalism than any which alienated intellectuals might prescribe," he noted.

Patman Committee   On October 3, 1972, the House Banking and Currency Committee rejected a proposal by Chairman Wright Patman (D.-Tex.) to probe matters related to the break-in of Democratic National Committee headquarters in Washington's Watergate complex the previous June for possible violations of banking laws. After the twenty-to-fifteen vote, Representative Patman accused the White House of having "engineered" the rejection of the probe. Had the resolution been accepted, the so-called Patman Committee was prepared to subpoena members of the **Committee to Re-elect the President** (CREEP; CRP) to give testimony.

Commenting on the squashing of the probe—which earlier in the month the Justice Department had said might jeopardize a fair trial for those arrested in connection with the break-in—Representative Patman predicted that "the facts will come out. When they do, I am convinced they will reveal why the White House was so anxious to kill the committee's investigation. The public will fully understand why the pressure was mounted."

See **Watergate Scandal.**

Payola   At hearings of the House Special Subcommittee on Legislative Oversight beginning on February 8, 1960, it was revealed that radio disc jockeys and radio stations themselves were receiving illegal payments for playing and plugging commercial recordings on the air. Popularly known as "payola," such payments were generally disguised as "consultant" fees or contributions to radio stations for "expenses." For example, a former KYW-Cleveland disc jockey testified that during 1958–1959 he had received $16,100 from various record companies for

judging the popularity potential of certain records, and the president of WMEX-Boston testified that his station had received $1,400 over the course of three months for featuring a record distributed by a local firm. (Complaints against a number of record firms had been issued on January 31, 1960, by the Federal Trade Commission.)

The "payola" scandal followed the 1958 revelations of rigged TV quiz shows (*see* **Twenty-One**) and led on August 30, 1960, to the passage of new legislation designed to curb such practices. Henceforth, radio and TV stations were required to reveal the receipt of money or other valuables for the broadcasting of material. The law also prohibited clandestine aid to quiz show contestants. Violations were punishable by maximum fines of $10,000 and one-year imprisonment. In addition, stations could have their licenses suspended for up to ten days for improper activities.

Pay Television   Efforts to establish an alternate form of television broadcasting—either over the air or by means of cable—first began in 1950 but met strong opposition from organized theater owners and representatives of advertising-supported television broadcasting. It was not until December 1968 that the Federal Communications Commission (FCC) authorized service selling programing directly to consumers, and even this move was blocked by court appeals until the U.S. Supreme Court definitively cleared the way for pay television on September 30, 1969, by refusing to review a lower court decision upholding the 1968 FCC permission.

FCC rules for pay-TV are intentionally restrictive and designed to protect the millions who have purchased television sets with the expectation of receiving free programing. Only markets already receiving four conventional televisions stations can be authorized a pay-TV outlet. The black-box devices used to unscramble pay broadcasts may not be sold to subscribers but only rented. In addition, pay stations must carry at least twenty-eight hours of free, unscrambled programs a week.

Among the more widely publicized fights against pay-TV was the November 1964 referendum by California voters making it illegal. By the time the referendum was declared unconstitutional by the courts, Subscription Television Inc., which had been fighting since 1962 for permission to operate pay-TV in Los Angeles and San Francisco, had gone into bankruptcy after losing $10 million.

By 1979 there were twelve pay-TV stations and applications for forty more were before the FCC.

PCP (Phencyclidine) Developed in 1956 by Parke, Davis and Company as an anesthetic, it was discontinued for use in humans because of postoperative symptoms of delirium and disorientation. As a street drug, it first emerged during the 1960s under such names as "angel dust," "hog," "goon," "tic," "tac," and "busy weed." Most commonly, PCP liquid or crystals is sprayed on tobacco, marijuana, mint, or parsley and then smoked, but the drug can also be injected, compressed into a pill, or inhaled.

Because even one-time use can bring about severe reactions—in 1977 some 4,000 users required emergency hospital care—PCP is considered the most pernicious drug to come along since heroin and LSD. It has been known to cause death in the user and to trigger psychotic reactions leading to suicide and homicide. Control of this drug presents a special law enforcement problem because it is said to be easily manufactured from ingredients legally available from most chemical supply houses.

Peace and Freedom Party (PFP) A predominantly white group, it was organized in California in the fall of 1967 by various independent radical groups, including members of the Independent Socialist Club. It won a place on the ballot for state and national elections and nominated **Black Panther** leader Eldridge Cleaver as its presidential candidate in 1968. The PFP also played an important role in the **"Free Huey!"** campaign organized for the defense of Black Panther leader Huey P. Newton, who was tried and convicted for the murder of an Oakland police officer in 1967 (*see* **Honkies for Huey**). The conviction was overturned on appeal.

Peace Corps Plans for this corps of volunteers who would devote their professional skills to improving conditions in underdeveloped nations were first made public on January 28, 1961, and the following March 1, President John F. Kennedy announced at a news conference that the Peace Corps had been established on a temporary basis by Executive order. That same day the President sent Congress a message urging the establishment of the corps on a permanent basis; the legislation he requested was signed into law on September 22, 1961.

Although the emphasis of the program was on youth, qualified Americans of all ages were welcomed in the corps. The initial focus was on teaching, agriculture, and health skills. Those participating would, said the President, "live at the same level as the citizens of the country which they are sent to, eating the same food, speaking the same language." Recruits were trained from six weeks to six months

in the culture of the country in which they would serve for periods of from two to three years. They received an allowance sufficient to "live simply and unostentatiously," and severance pay of $75 for each month of satisfactory service.

R. Sargent Shriver, the President's brother-in-law, who had helped with the original planning of the corps, was named director on March 4, 1961. (Mr. Shriver later said that he had been picked to organize the Peace Corps because no one thought it could succeed and it "would be easier to fire a relative than a political friend.")

The origins of the Peace Corps can probably be traced to President Franklin D. Roosevelt's Civilian Conservation Corps (CCC) of 1933, and in the 1950s Sen. Hubert H. Humphrey (D.-Minn.) and Sen. Henry S. Reuss (D.-Wis.) suggested similar ideas for sending trained American volunteers to overseas areas in need of their skills. Senator Humphrey sometimes even used the phrase "Youth Peace Corps," and in June 1960 he had introduced a bill to this effect into Congress.

Historian Arthur Schlesinger, Jr., who had served in the Kennedy administration, notes that President Kennedy "often envied the communist capacity to mobilize popular idealism, especially of the young. . . . He was sure there was a comparable fund of idealism among the youth of America; and the Peace Corps seemed a means of demonstrating the reality of this idealism to the world."

After 1971 the Peace Corps was administered by **ACTION**, the umbrella federal agency set up by President Richard M. Nixon to coordinate volunteer programs. By the mid-seventies some 50,000 had served in sixty-nine participating countries.

"Peace is hell" Summing up the troubles that had beset his administration following the end of World War II, President Harry S Truman told newsmen gathered on December 15, 1945, for the annual dinner of the Gridiron Club at which the Washington scene is satirized in songs and skits: "Sherman was *wrong*. I'm telling you I find peace is hell. . . ."

The President was referring to a speech reportedly made by Civil War General William Tecumseh Sherman in 1879, in which the leader of the famous March to the Sea summed up his experiences as follows: "I am tired and sick of war. Its glory is all moonshine. It is only those who have neither fired a shot nor heard the shrieks and groans of the wounded who cry aloud for blood, more vengeance, more desolation. War is hell."

Peace of Mind *See **The Power of Positive Thinking.***

"Peace with honor" In reply to those critics of the **Vietnam War** who demanded an immediate cessation of hostilities, President Richard M. Nixon called for "peace with honor." The President had apparently been inspired by his reading of a biography of the nineteenth-century British statesman Benjamin Disraeli, who had first used the phrase on his return from the Congress of Berlin in 1878.

Other echoes are to be found in President Woodrow Wilson's appeal for "peace without victory" in 1917, and President Dwight D. Eisenhower's Second Inaugural Address (January 21, 1957), in which he stated that it was his fixed purpose to build "a peace with justice in a world where moral law prevails."

(After having concluded the Munich Pact in 1938, British Prime Minister Neville Chamberlain spoke of "peace in our time.")

Peers Report *See **My Lai Massacre.***

Peking Summit On the invitation of Premier Chou En-lai of the People's Republic of China, President Richard M. Nixon and his wife, Patricia, visited there from February 21–28, 1972, accompanied by Secretary of State William Rogers and Assistant to the President Henry Kissinger.

The Nixon party visited sites of special interest in Peking, Hangchow, and Shanghai as part of this history-making trip that signaled the change in U.S. foreign policy first set in motion in 1969 when the United States unilaterally eased trade and travel restrictions with Red China. During the visit, the President also met with Mao Tse-tung, Chairman of the Chinese Communist Party. Additional talks on the normalization of relations between the United States and Red China were held with Premier Chou En-lai, and according to a joint communiqué issued in Shanghai on the final day of the visit, "The two leaders [Nixon and Mao] had a serious and frank exchange of views on Sino-U.S. relations and world affairs." (The text covering this exchange is generally known as the Shanghai Communiqué.)

The first part of this four-part, 1,800-word document was an overall account of the presidential visit. In the second part the United States and China issued separate statements on policy issues. The American statement supported an eight-point proposal made earlier in the year by itself and South Vietnam for ending the **Vietnam War.** The pro-posal envisaged "the ultimate withdrawal of all U.S. forces from the region consistent with the aim of self-determination for each country of Indochina." It said that the United States would maintain close ties with South Korea, advocated a continuation of the cease-fire in the India-Pakistan dispute and the withdrawal of all military forces to their own territories "and to their own sides of the cease-fire line in Jammu and Kashmir," and emphasized the importance of continually improved relations with Japan. (The Chinese supported a seven-point Viet Cong peace proposal, favored North Korean proposals for unification of Korea, opposed the "revival" of Japanese militarism, and favored the Pakistan government in its dispute with India, supporting "the people of Jammu and Kashmir in their struggle for the right of self-determination."

The third part of the communiqué noted differences between the systems and policies of the United States and Red China, but supported continued efforts of normalization in the relations between the two countries.

Separate statements on Taiwan composed the final section of the communiqué. The American part acknowledged that

. . . all Chinese on either side of the Taiwan Strait maintain there is but one China and that Taiwan is part of China. The U.S. government does not challenge that position. It reaffirms its interest in a peaceful settlement of the Taiwan question by the Chinese themselves. With this prospect in mind, it affirms the ultimate objective of the withdrawal of all U.S. forces and military installations from Taiwan. In the meantime it will progressively reduce its forces and military installations on Taiwan as the tension in the area diminishes.

The Chinese statement noted that the settlement of the Taiwan question was crucial to the normalization of U.S.-China relations. It also reaffirmed Chinese claims to the island and noted that its "liberation" was an internal Chinese affair.

No mention was made by either country of the 1954 treaty in which the United States committed itself to the defense of Taiwan against armed invasion, unless such treaty was canceled by either side after one year's notice.

The normalization of relations with China thus begun was continued under President Gerald R. Ford (*see* **Pacific Doctrine**) and culminated on December 15, 1978, when President Jimmy Carter announced that after 30 years diplomatic relations with China would be re-established on January 1, 1979. Recognizing the Government of the People's Republic of China "as the sole legal Government of China," the President said that the United States "acknowledges the Chinese position that there is but one China and Taiwan is part of China."

Pension Reform Act of 1974 Officially titled the Employee Benefit Security Act (September 2, 1974), the act established federal standards for private pension plans, of which by the middle of the decade there were more than 300,000 covering up to 35 million workers and representing assets of more than $160 billion. Eligibility, vesting, and funding of benefits were covered, and insurance against loss of benefits was to be provided by a Pension Benefit Guaranty Corporation set up within the Department of Labor with funding from premiums by companies with pension plans.

The act provides three alternatives for vesting or entitlement to benefits: 100 percent of pension rights after ten years of service; 25 percent after five years, with gradual increases to 100 percent after fifteen years; and 50 percent when a worker's age plus years of company service totaled forty-five, gradually increasing to 100 percent over five years.

See **Individual Retirement Account; Keogh Retirement Plan.**

Pentagon Papers Name given by the *New York Times* to a series of classified government documents—officially, "History of U.S. Decision-Making Process on Viet Nam Policy"—tracing the process by which the United States became involved in the **Vietnam War.** The documents were part of a forty-seven-volume study that had been commissioned in 1967 by Robert S. McNamara while Secretary of Defense under President Lyndon B. Johnson, and covered events from 1945 to 1968. (Increasingly disenchanted with what had once been known as **"McNamara's War,"** the secretary is reported to have told a friend: "You know, they could hang people for what's in that.")

Copies of the documents had been furnished the *Times* by Daniel Ellsberg, who as an employee of the Rand Corporation was one of the approximately forty scholars who contributed to the study. After an installment was published in the edition of June 13, 1971, the Nixon administration, acting through Attorney General John N. Mitchell, attempted to halt publication of the documents by informally suggesting to *Times* editors that they were laying themselves open to prosecution under the espionage statute. However, the following day, June 15, the newspaper not only published another installment but a story on the government threats it had received. It was not until several installments had been published that Justice Department law-

yers acting under Assistant Attorney General Robert Mardian obtained a temporary restraining order which would give the government time to show that injury to national interests and security could result from further publication. Although the *Times* obeyed the injunction, on June 18 the *Washington Post* began publication of additional documents. When the U.S. Court of Appeals issued a restraining order against the *Post,* the Pentagon Papers began appearing in the *Boston Globe.* Soon they were appearing in fourteen papers and were being carried on the wires of the Associated Press.

The case was brought to the Supreme Court, which granted certiorari and proceeded to rule six to three in favor of the *Times* and the *Post.* The court found that the government had failed to justify prior restraints against the two newspapers and that in obtaining the injunctions against them it had infringed against the guarantees of freedom of the press contained in the Constitution.

In a dissenting opinion, Chief Justice Warren Burger noted:

The newspapers make a derivative claim under the First Amendment; they denominate this as the public right-to-know; by implication the *Times* asserts a sole trusteeship of that right by virtue of its journalistic "scoop." The right is asserted as an absolute. Of course, the First Amendment right itself is not an absolute, as Justice Holmes so long ago pointed out in his aphorism concerning the right to shout of fire in a crowded theater.

The initial importance of the Pentagon Papers was their revelation of the means by which the war had constantly been deliberately escalated, even as the public was being reassured. For example, when in 1965 President Johnson told the press that he was aware of "no far-reaching strategy" concerning Vietnam, he had already decided to commit U.S. ground forces in the area.

However, the final importance of the Pentagon Papers may very well center on a newspaper's unilateral right to release classified government material. The *Times*'s position on this matter has not always been consistent. At the time of the **Cuban Missile Crisis** it had criticized newsmen Stewart Alsop and Charles Bartlett for a story that drew on secret conversations at a National Security Council Meeting: "The various positions of the members of the N.S.C. taken during deliberation must remain secret. . . ." (The *Times* has argued that the Pentagon Papers were overclassified and that since they stopped with events of 1968, the documents were of primarily historical value.)

Daniel Ellsberg and Anthony J. Russo, who as a member of the *Times* staff had helped him prepare the documents for publication, were indicted by the government and charged with espionage, theft, and conspiracy. However, the case against them was terminated in 1973 by U.S. District Judge William M. Byrne, Jr., on the grounds of government misconduct. It had come to light as a result of disclosures following the **Watergate Scandal** that a White House Special Investigations Unit—known in top administration circles, and eventually to the whole world, as **"the Plumbers"**—had on September 3, 1971, broken into the Beverly Hills, California, office of Dr. Lewis B. Fielding in an unsuccessful attempt to obtain the medical files covering the two-year analysis of Daniel Ellsberg. (This became popularly known as "The Ellsberg break-in.") In addition, Judge Byrne himself had been improperly approached by White House officials during the trial and sounded out on his willingness to accept an appointment as director of the FBI.

People United to Save Humanity (PUSH) After his 1972 split with the **Southern Christian Leadership Conference** (SCLC), whose **Operation Breadbasket** he had directed, Reverend Jesse L. Jackson formed the Chicago-based People United to Save Humanity (PUSH) to focus on economic issues by means of lobbying and educational approaches and through direct-action techniques such as marches and demonstrations. In March 1978, he announced that PUSH would open ten offices in South Carolina to fight the disfranchisement of black educators through the use of National Teacher Examinations prepared by the Educational Testing Service (ETS). These new offices would lobby for abandonment of the tests.

In 1975 minimal ETS scores for prospective teachers were raised from 975 to 1,165, with some differences depending on the curriculum. Following this, only 60 percent of both blacks and whites taking the examination were able to qualify for teaching positions in South Carolina. Only 3 percent of the black graduating college seniors who took the ETS examination qualified. The U.S. Court of Appeals for the Fourth Circuit ruled (April 1977) that the tests were not discriminatory in intent (*see* **Buckley Amendment**).

An offshoot of PUSH is Push-Excel (Push for Excellence), a program urging greater involvement by minorities in improving their education.

People's Coalition for Peace and Justice *See* **Mayday Tribe.**

People's Lobby A protest held in Washington, D.C., April 26–30, 1971, with the cooperation of the **Southern Christian Leadership Conference** (SCLC), the National Welfare Rights Organization (NWRO), and the National Action Group (NAG), a faction of the People's Coalition for Peace and Justice.

During that period, the "lobbyists" visited the offices of various federal agencies and presented a series of demands focusing on poverty, the draft, and taxes connected with the **Vietnam War.** The limited civil disobedience of the People's Lobby was largely confined to blocking the offices of members of Congress who refused to receive its representatives. The lobby was followed by four days of violence and mass arrests—which the courts later found had been illegally undertaken—when on May 2, 1971, Washington police broke up a demonstration by members of the **Mayday Tribe** who had sworn to make all activity in the nation's capital grind to a halt.

People's Park *See* **Battle of Berkeley.**

Peppermint Lounge *See* **Rock-and-Roll; the Twist.**

"Person-to-Person" *See* **"See It Now."**

Peterson v. Greenville On May 20, 1963, the U.S. Supreme Court sustained the right of Negroes to service at public lunch counters and prohibited state ordinances calling for segregated facilities. Along with *Garner v. Louisiana* (1961), the decision was important in upholding the **"sit-ins"** which spread through the South after beginning in Greensboro, North Carolina (January 31, 1960).

The petitioners were ten black young people who on August 9, 1960, had entered the S. H. Kress store in Greenville, South Carolina, and seated themselves at the lunch counter. The store manager promptly announced that the counter was closed and called the police, who arrested all the blacks after they insisted on remaining seated at the counter. They were subsequently sentenced to a fine of $100 or a prison sentence of thirty days. An appeal to the Greenville County Court was dismissed, and the Supreme Court of South Carolina affirmed the decision before the U.S. Supreme Court granted certiorari to "consider the substantial federal questions presented by the record."

The Kress store manager had testified that he had asked the petitioners to leave because integrated service was "contrary to local customs" of segregation at lunch counters and in violation of a city ordinance requiring racial separation in restaurants. There was testimony that the manager would have "acted as he did independently of the existence of the ordinance." In its ruling the Court declared that when a state agency, in this case the City of Greenville

. . . passes a law compelling persons to discriminate against other persons because of race, and the State's criminal processes are employed in a way which enforces the discrimination mandated by that law, such a palpable violation of the Fourteenth Amendment cannot be saved by attempting to separate the mental urges of the discriminators. *Reversed.*

PFP *See* **Peace and Freedom Party.**

Phase One Announcing a "new economic policy for the United States," on August 15, 1971, President Richard M. Nixon abruptly imposed a ninety-day freeze on wages, prices, and rents and also ended the convertibility of the dollar into gold at a fixed $35 an ounce. (By 1979 the price of gold was well over $200 an ounce.) Other parts of his program to fight inflation and unemployment included a 10-percent surcharge on dutiable imports, an almost $5 billion cut in federal expenditures, and a request for tax legislation that would supply new incentives for industry.

The price-wage freeze—the first since the ceiling imposed by President Harry S Truman on January 26, 1951—was a complete reversal of the economic policies of the Nixon administration, which had previously rejected any controls on the free play of the market place. It was accompanied by the creation of a Cost of Living Council (CLC) headed by Treasury Secretary John B. Connally, Jr., "to work with leaders of labor and business to set up the proper mechanism for achieving continued price and wage stability" once the freeze was over.

The administrative machinery for Phase Two was announced well in advance (October 7, 1971). It included a Price Commission of persons outside the government whose job it would be "to restrain prices and rent increases to the necessary minimum and to prevent windfall profits." A Pay Board including representatives of labor, management, and the public was to work with the Price Commission to achieve voluntary cooperation from business and labor. The work of the commission and the board was to be backed up by the CLC, which would have the power to invoke government sanctions "where necessary." Presidential Counselor Donald H. Rumsfeld was named full-time CLC director. In addition, Arthur Burns, chairman of the Federal Re-

serve Board, was appointed head of a Government Committee on Interest and Dividends. Although emphasis was on voluntary compliance, the President requested legislation providing "standby controls over interest rates and dividends."

Phase Three of the economic stabilization program began on January 11, 1973, and emphasized voluntary compliance with federal anti-inflation goals. The wage-price standards were to remain unchanged, but now they would be "self-administered" by labor and business to avoid what was called the mounting "burdens of a control system . . . in the coming period." Federal rent controls were abandoned, and both the Pay Board and the Price Commission were abolished. The CLC was retained—under the new direction of labor relations consultant John T. Dunlop—and a ten-person Labor-Management Advisory Committee to the CLC was appointed to advise on stabilization standards. AFL-CIO President George Meany, one of five labor representatives on the new committee, called Phase Three "a step in the right direction."

Acknowledging the essential failure of the voluntary compliance called for in Phase Three, on June 13, 1973, the President imposed a sixty-day freeze on retail prices, and promised "tighter standards and more mandatory compliance procedures" for Phase Four, which was announced July 18, 1973, and went into effect when the freeze expired. Meany called the new freeze "a failure of policy," because prices were fixed at their highest levels in twenty years. Essentially a return to features of Phase Two, Phase Four reinstituted mandatory controls. The June price freeze remained in effect in all sectors except food and health care—beef, however, remained under a March 29 ceiling until September 12, 1973—and prices were to be permitted to rise only in relation to cost increases since the end of 1972.

The largely unsuccessful four-phase economic program is sometimes known as "Nixon's NEP."

Philadelphia Plan A major and short-lived departure from the **Southern Strategy,** or voter-appeal approach, that characterized the Nixon administration, it is generally credited to Secretary of Labor George Shultz. Its name is derived from the fact that the Department of Labor first imposed the plan in Philadelphia, establishing a quota system under which construction unions working on federal contracts of $500,000 or more were required to make good-faith efforts to train black apprentices for full union membership. This was something even the most civil-rights-oriented Democratic administrations had never dared because of their close links with organized labor.

The unions fought the plan, and legislation outlawing it was passed by the Senate in 1969; but thanks to Shultz this legislation failed to win approval in the House. In January 1970 the Contractors Association of Eastern Pennsylvania asked that the courts declare the plan unconstitutional, claiming that it denied equal protection under the law because it was being applied only in Philadelphia. Their suit was rejected when Judge Charles R. Weiner ruled in Philadelphia's federal district court that the pilot job program did not violate the prohibition against racial quotas in the **Civil Rights Act of 1964.** In addition, Secretary Shultz announced that similar plans would be tried in eighteen other large cities unless they came up with plans of their own.

Although President Richard M. Nixon had fully backed the plan during the congressional struggle, he soon abandoned pressure on the unions. In June 1970, the Labor Department's Office of Federal Contract Compliance reported that contractors were abusing or disregarding the plan. "Unfortunately we dropped our pressure on construction unions too soon," wrote Nixon White House staff member William Safire.

See **Affirmative Action.**

Pike Committee Report Following charges that its presiding officer, Rep. Lucien N. Nedzi (D.-Mich.), had failed to act on information about illegal **CIA** activities, the House Select Committee on Intelligence was disbanded and a new and larger panel with similar authority was formed on July 17, 1975. The new panel's chairperson was Rep. Otis G. Pike (D.-N.Y.), Representative Nedzi having been dropped along with Rep. Michael J. Harrington (D.-Mich.), who had been criticized for his role in exposing testimony about CIA activities in Chile during the fall of the Allende government in 1973.

Late in 1975, the Pike Committee completed its investigation into controversial intelligence activities by federal agencies, but on January 29, 1976, the House voted overwhelmingly to accept President Gerald R. Ford's request that the panel's final report be suppressed until it could be stripped of classified information. Chairman Pike immediately charged that the Ford administration was trying to block his committee's report because it cast a dubious light on the activities of many government officials, including Secretary of State Henry Kissinger.

Meanwhile, much of the report's substance had already appeared in the *New York Times* and the *Washington Post* beginning on January 20, 1976.

Then on February 11, 1976, New York's *Village Voice* printed large excerpts from the report itself. The next day, Daniel Schorr, a CBS News correspondent, acknowledged that he was the source of the copy of the report. Having first denied responsibility for its publication, he now said that he had decided to arrange for the excerpts after being convinced that he was "possibly the sole possessor of the document outside the government" and could therefore "not be the one responsible for suppressing" its publication. (The original findings dealt, among other things, with CIA-media links, involvement in Angola, and financing of foreign political and military groups.)

In a television interview, CIA director George Bush said on February 22, 1976, that the publication of the Pike Committee report had injured national security. However, he refused to say exactly how, as that would only "make things worse." The following day, CBS News relieved Schorr of all reporting duties for an "indefinite period."

Appearing before a House ethics committee investigating the leak, on September 15, 1976, Schorr refused to identify his source for the classified report. Although the probe was dropped (September 22), a week later Schorr resigned from CBS, where he had been under considerable criticism for the manner in which he had originally denied furnishing the *Village Voice* with a copy of the Pike Committee report. Many charged that in originally focusing attention on the newspaper's introduction by journalist Arthur Latham, he had unfairly diverted suspicion onto the latter's close friend, CBS correspondent Leslie Stahl.

A final report by the House ethics committee on October 6, 1976, termed Schorr's conduct "reprehensible" and concluded that his unidentified source for the report was someone "on or very near" the Pike Committee itself. Secretary Kissinger had earlier castigated the leaks as "a new version of **McCarthyism.**"

The Pill Oral contraceptives that mimic the natural female reproductive cycle were developed in the late 1950s, and in May 1960 the Food and Drug Administration (FDA) formally approved the commercial distribution of Enovid 10, a "combination" birth control pill manufactured by G. D. Searle and Company. By the mid-1970s more than twenty-five different oral contraceptives were being marketed and 10 million American women were said to be "on the pill."

The most widely used variety are the "combination" pills which contain a mixture of estrogen and progestogen. Taken cyclically from the fifth to the twenty-fifth day of the menstrual cycle, they are said to provide absolute insurance against pregnancy. Somewhat less effective are the "sequential" pills, which contain only estrogen during the first fourteen to sixteen days of the menstrual cycle and estrogen plus progestogen for the remaining five to six days. This is thought to mimic the female hormonal pattern more closely.

"The pill" came into widespread use within two years of its commercial introduction and was said to have contributed to a revolution in American sexual mores. According to the National Catholic Family Life Bureau, it was being used regularly by many Catholic women in spite of the strong stand against contraception taken by Pope Paul VI, who in 1965 told the United Nations General Assembly that their task was "to make certain that there is enough bread at the banquet of life" and not that of "stimulating birth control by artificial means."

On July 30, 1968, the Pope, ignoring the advice of three papal commissions on birth control, issued the encyclical *Humanae Vitae*—expressed as a circular letter and not as dogma—which once more affirmed his opposition to artificial birth control. In response, 172 American theologians and other Catholics led by Father Charles Curran of Catholic University, Washington, D.C., rejected the encyclical as not binding on conscience. "We conclude that spouses may responsibly decide according to their conscience that artificial contraception in some circumstances is permissible and indeed necessary to preserve and foster the values and sacredness of marriage."

By the end of the decade there was some evidence that oral contraceptives could have unfortunate side effects and increase the incidence of heart attacks, blood clotting, and uterine cancer. In its July-August 1975 bulletin, the FDA advised doctors that women over forty who took "the pill" considerably increased their chances of heart attack and should be advised to use other forms of contraception.

Ping-Pong Diplomacy On April 6, 1971, during the world table tennis championships in Nagoya, Japan, Graham B. Steenhoven, president of the U.S. Table Tennis Association, received an invitation for the nine-man American team, four officials, and two wives to visit the Chinese mainland. The invitation was accepted the next day and a Chinese spokesman was quoted as saying that part of its purpose was "for the sake of promoting friendship between the peoples of China and the United States."

Reversing a policy in effect since 1949, the Chinese Communists also granted visas to seven Western newsmen so that they could cover the visit of the U.S. team.

At exhibition matches in Peking on April 13, the Americans were defeated. They were received the next day by Premier Chou En-lai—along with teams from Britain, Colombia, and Canada—who told them that "with your acceptance of our invitation, you have opened a new page in the relations of the Chinese and American people." Before leaving China, the American team in turn invited the Chinese team to visit the United States, and on his return home Mr. Steenhoven was assured by President Richard M. Nixon that he would cooperate in seeing to it that the necessary visas were expedited.

The "ping-pong diplomacy" thus initiated was to see a change in the relations between the two countries and the reemergence of policies first hinted at in the 1959 **Conlon Report.** Later that year Red China was admitted to the United Nations when the "two Chinas" approach urged by a United States resolution was defeated in favor of an Albanian resolution which called for the seating of Communist China and the expulsion of the representative of the Nationalist government in Taiwan. In February 1972, President Nixon visited the Chinese mainland for the **Peking Summit.** (He revisited China as a private citizen in February 1976.)

Relations between the United States and China continued to improve under the administration of President Gerald R. Ford (*see* **Pacific Doctrine**) and on December 15, 1978, President Jimmy Carter announced the resumption of normal diplomatic relations between the two countries—as of January 1, 1979—for the first time in thirty years.

Pinkville *See* **My Lai Massacre.**

Pioneer I Although *Pioneer I* went twenty-seven times higher than any previous man-made object, this unmanned space vehicle launched from Cape Canaveral on October 11, 1958, smashed into the atmosphere southwest of Hawaii after accomplishing only 79,243 miles of its intended 223,700-mile journey, at which point it was supposed to go into orbit around the moon. All three stages of the fifty-two-ton Thor Able-1 rocket designed to bring the instrumental payload within 50,000 miles of the moon fired on schedule, but the first stage produced a trajectory that was too steep to allow the rocket to accelerate to the required 35,350 feet a second.

This was the second unsuccessful American moon shot, an almost identical lunar probe having been tried on August 17, 1958. (A Soviet effort aimed at landing on the moon rather than going into orbit failed on May 1, 1958.) However, Air Force officials expressed satisfaction with the effort, which sent back valuable data on radiation, the earth's magnetic field, and rocket acceleration.

After Air Force scientists realized that the lunar probe would not go into orbit around the moon, they tried by means of a retro-rocket in the *Pioneer* itself to shift it into orbit around the earth; but the retro-rocket would not respond to radio signals.

Subsequent unmanned craft of the Pioneer series monitored interplanetary space phenomena and investigated the space between Earth and Mars, Jupiter, and Venus. The original series concluded with *Pioneer 11* (April 6, 1973) which passed Jupiter on March 12, 1974, and is expected to be near Saturn in September 1979. *Pioneer Venus 1* and *2*, launched May 20, 1978, and August 8, 1978, respectively, are designed to study the Venusian atmosphere.

Plowshare Program Established by the **Atomic Energy Commission** (AEC) in the summer of 1957, the purpose of the program was to investigate peaceful and constructive uses of nuclear power in operations such as the excavation of harbors and canals, the shattering of oil-bearing rock to release its oil content, and the tapping of new sources of natural gas. The name is derived from the Biblical injunction in Isaiah II:4: ". . . and they shall beat their swords into plowshares, and their spears into pruning hooks; nation shall not lift up sword against nation, neither shall they learn war any more."

By the middle of the 1970s, the federal government had invested over $160 million on the program and there had been close to thirty nuclear explosions.

The most advanced phase of Plowshare was the use of underground explosions to stimulate natural gas flow. In Operation Gasbuggy, the El Paso Natural Gas Company, the Department of the Interior, and the AEC participated in a joint experiment in which a nuclear charge was lowered into a 4,240-foot drill hole near Farmington, New Mexico, and detonated on December 10, 1967. Similar efforts were made in the Rocky Mountain area in succeeding years, but were halted by growing concern over health and environmental damage, as well as by indications that such efforts might not prove economically beneficial. In November 1974, Colorado voters approved a ban on additional tests in the state until there could be a new referendum on the question. Shortly afterward, the Energy Research and Development Administration (ERDA)—which had replaced the AEC—began consideration of the use of hydrogen bombs detonated in a salt mine so that they could release steam to power electric generators.

PLP *See* **Progressive Labor Party.**

"The Plumbers" In a statement to the press on May 22, 1973, President Richard M. Nixon noted that during the week following the publication of the **Pentagon Papers,** he had

. . . approved the creation of a Special Investigations Unit within the White House—which later came to be known as the "Plumbers." This was a small group at the White House whose principal purpose was to stop security leaks and to investigate other sensitive security matters. I looked to John Ehrlichman for the supervision of the group.

On July 17, 1971, Ehrlichman turned over direction of the Special Investigations Unit to Egil Krogh, Jr., a member of his own staff, and David R. Young, Jr., a young lawyer who had previously been on the staff of National Security Advisor Henry A. Kissinger. Soon afterward, E. Howard Hunt, Jr., and G. Gordon Liddy (see **Watergate Scandal**) were recruited to the group.

The name "Plumbers" is said to have become attached to the group after a relative of Young's wrote to him saying that she had seen a newspaper report indicating that he and Krogh were working on "leaks." She noted that his grandfather, who had been a plumber, would have been proud of him. Shortly afterward, Young had put up on the door of Room 16 in the Executive Office Building adjacent to the White House, a sign that read: "Mr. Young—Plumber."

In an attempt to gather evidence to discredit Daniel Ellsberg—an employee of the **Rand Corporation** who had helped compile the Pentagon Papers and later made a copy of them available to the *New York Times*—the "Plumbers" planned to break into the Beverly Hills, California, office of his former psychiatrist, Dr. Lewis B. Fielding. For this project, which had been approved by Ehrlichman— "if done under your assurance that it is not traceable"—Hunt and Liddy recruited Eugenio R. Martinez, Bernard Barker, and Felipe DeDiego, all anti-Castro Cubans. The actual break-in took place on September 1, 1971, and was done by the three Cubans while Hunt and Liddy kept watch outside both Dr. Fielding's office and home. Nothing of any significance was found, and the office was partly ransacked to make the burglary look like the work of addicts. (Dr. Fielding subsequently claimed that two batches of notes on Ellsberg, some sixty-five pages in all, looked as though they had been gone through.) Ehrlichman later refused permission for a break-in of Dr. Fielding's home, where the "Plumbers" felt they might find the material they were looking for.

The Special Investigations Unit went into action again later that year when on December 14 Washington columnist Jack Anderson (see **ITT Affair**) published excerpts from the minutes of the **Washington Special Action Group** (WASAG) dealing with the conflict raging between India and Pakistan. This information undercut the President's stance of neutrality by quoting National Security Advisor Kissinger as saying that President Nixon favored Pakistan.

The investigation of the "leak" was handled this time by Krogh and Young, who soon located the source of Anderson's information as Navy Yeoman First Class Charles E. Radford, a clerk in the Joint Chiefs of Staff liaison office with the National Security Council. Since it also turned out that Radford, under the instructions of his Navy superiors, was supplying information to Pentagon officials, no prosecution was ever undertaken, probably lest the prosecution of the case against Ellsberg and *Times* reporter Anthony Russo, who had helped Ellsberg prepare the papers for publication, be weakened by these revelations.

Several of those involved in the "Plumbers" were later to play a role in the break-in of Democratic National Committee headquarters at the Watergate complex on June 17, 1972.

Point Four   President Harry S Truman's inaugural address of January 20, 1949, contained four major foreign policy guidelines:

1. Support for the United Nations.

2. Continuation of the economic recovery policy embodied in the **Marshall Plan**.

3. Strengthening the noncommunist world against potential aggression as indicated in the **Vandenberg Resolution**.

4. The scientific and industrial improvement of underdeveloped areas.

The latter item—soon popularly known as "Point Four"—was suggested for the address by the President's Counsel, Clark Clifford. Although it immediately captured the attention of the public and the press, it was not until a year or so later that Congress appropriated the first funds—$34 million. Soon 350 technicians were at work on 100 cooperative technical projects in twenty-seven nations.

Dean Acheson has pointed out that in presenting the technical assistance program, President Truman tended to arouse greater expectations among the underdeveloped countries than there would be funds available to fulfill. This caused some bitterness when the program was finally explained at the United Nations Economic and Social Council.

As the President explained at a news conference:

The origin of Point Four has been in my mind and in the minds of the government, for the past two or three years, ever since the Marshall Plan was inaugurated. It originated with the Greece and Turkey proposition. Been studying it ever since. I spend most of my time going over to that globe back there, trying to figure out ways to make peace in the world.

"Point of Order!"   *See* **McCarthyism.**

POL   An acronym used by the U.S. military to designate "petroleum, oil and lubricants." For example, during the 1962 **Cuban Missile Crisis** it was argued that a POL blockade turning back tankers bound for Cuba would cause a collapse of that nation's economy.

Polaris   *See* **Intercontinental Ballistic Missiles.**

Poor People's Campaign   As the **Vietnam War** continued to drain off funds once designated for President Lyndon B. Johnson's **War on Poverty,** in the autumn of 1967 the **Southern Christian Leadership Conference** (SCLC), under the leadership of Dr. Martin Luther King, Jr., began planning a Poor People's Campaign which would demand from government agencies that an amount equal to that spent on arms ($70 billion in 1967) be devoted to obtaining jobs, housing, food, and public assistance for the nation's poor. After the assassination of Dr. King on April 4, 1968, Reverend Ralph D. Abernathy took over direction of the SCLC; the coordinator of the campaign was Hosea Williams.

Beginning in about the second week of May 1968, "poverty pilgrims" began arriving in the nation's capital on foot, in buses, by car, and in wagons often drawn by mules named for opponents of civil rights such as Alabama's Governor George Wallace. They established a fifteen-acre campsite near the Lincoln Memorial and named it Resurrection City. Heavy rains soon turned the area into a semibog, compounding problems created by bad planning that had resulted in inadequate housing and sanitation facilities. By mid-May food committees had been able to raise less than a third of the $90,000 that had been estimated would be required to feed 3,000 inhabitants of Resurrection City (ZIP Code 20013) for a month. Most of the protesters were southern blacks, and there was some tension at the campsite with other groups. "Black militants have taken over, and nobody else gets a chance to talk," complained Reis Lopez Tijerina, leader of a group of 200 Mexican-Americans (see **Alliance of Free City-States**).

On June 23, 1968, the Department of Interior's permit for the campsite expired and Resurrection City closed down, but not before some of those reluctant to leave had been routed by police using tear gas.

Unlike the 1963 March on Washington which had drawn some 200,000 demonstrators in a hopeful mood, the Poor People's Campaign had a dispirited turnout of some 55,000—sufficient, however, to have a bipartisan ad hoc committee of members of Congress (May 23) help the protesters present their demands to government agencies. As a result, Secretary of Agriculture Orville Freeman agreed to speed up food relief programs in more than 200 of the nation's poorest counties. In addition, the **Office of Economic Opportunity** (OEO) agreed to contribute an additional $25 million for various programs such as **Head Start,** and the Department of Labor presented a plan to create 100,000 new jobs. This was far from what Reverend Abernathy had hoped to obtain, however.

Columnist I. F. Stone noted in his newsletter **(I. F. Stone's Weekly)**:

To see the Poor People's March on Washington in perspective, remember that the rich have been marching on Washington ever since the beginning of the Republic. They came in carriages and they come on jets. They don't have to put up in shanties. Their object is the same but few respectable people are untactful enough to call it handouts.

Pop Art Its origins firmly rooted in a fascination with commercial art and modern technology, Pop Art first emerged as a force in New York in the mid-1950s when Jasper Johns and Robert Rauschenberg applied abstract techniques to the depiction of the every day objects in the world around them. Eventually commercial techniques themselves began showing up in Roy Lichtenstein's blowups of comic-strip panels, Andy Warhol's canvases of Campbell's soup cans and three-dimensional wooden reproduc-

tions of Brillo cartons, and Claes Oldenburg's outsized and gaudily painted plaster ice cream sundaes and hamburgers.

Two exhibitions of major influence were held at the prestigious and trend-setting Martha Jackson Gallery: "New Forms, New Media" (1960) and "Environments, Situations, Spaces" (1961). In March 1963 New York's Solomon R. Guggenheim Museum gave Pop Art—the word derives from "popular"—its official blessing by sponsoring the first major exhibition of the movement. The show moved on to several large cities later that year and helped establish Pop Art as a major American art movement.

In addition to those mentioned above, artists generally associated with Pop Art include George Segal, James Rosenquist, and Tom Wesselmann in the East. On the West Coast the movement in a somewhat relaxed form centered about the work of Al Benston, Mel Ramos, and Edward Kienholz. Reflections are also to be found in the productions of such European artists as Winfred Gaul, Laurence Alloway, Eduardo Paolozzi, Valerio Adami, and Peter Klasen.

Pop Art is interpreted by some critics as a satirical comment on twentieth-century machine-made mass-produced objects on which a new focus is obtained by showing them in a new context.

The Population Bomb Within two years of its publication, in 1968, by demographer Paul R. Ehrlich, there were 2 million copies of this book in print. Noting that the world's population was increasing at a faster rate than the food supply, it predicted that there would be water rationing in the United States by 1974 and food rationing by the end of the decade.

Ehrlich pointed out that only the United States, Canada, Australia, Argentina, France, New Zealand, Burma, Thailand, Rumania, and South Africa were then growing more food than was needed by their populations. The world food problem, he argued, was aggravated by a deteriorating environment. "Too many cars, too many factories, too much detergent, too much pesticide, multiplying contrails, inadequate sewage treatment plants, too little water, too much carbon dioxide—all can be traced easily to *too many people.*"

He foresaw only two "solutions": the first depended on some means of effectively lowering the birth rate—he rejected family planning on the grounds that people were currently planning for too many children; another possibility was a "death rate solution" in which population and food supply would be balanced by war, famine, or pestilence. *See The Limits of Growth.*

Pork Chop Hill When in April 1951 President Harry S Truman relieved General Douglas MacArthur of his command during the **Korean War** (see also **"Old soldiers never die"**), efforts to keep the war from spreading into a global conflagration reduced the conflict to a seesaw battle for control of important terrain features near the **38th parallel.** During the fighting in the hill country, readers of American newspapers were soon being informed of the desperate struggle going on in places which embattled GIs had nicknamed Pork Chop Hill, Old Baldy, and T-Bone Hill.

Pork Chop Hill became the title of a 1959 movie directed by Lewis Milestone and starring Gregory Peck. The movie dealt with a battle that was taking place while, only seventy miles away at Panmunjom, efforts were being made to set up peace negotiations. It ended with the following voice-over commentary: "So Pork Chop Hill was held, bought, and paid for at the same price we commemorate in monuments at Bunker Hill and Gettysburg. . . . Those who fought there, know what they did . . . and the meaning of it. Millions live in freedom today because of what they did."

Three months after it had been successfully held, the American forces ceded the hill back to the Chinese, feeling it was no longer "worth the price of a squad or a man."

Pornography Commission *See* **President's Commission on Obscenity and Pornography.**

Portal-to-Portal Pay On June 10, 1946, the U.S. Supreme Court upheld a 1942 U.S. District Court decision in a suit by the CIO United Pottery Workers against the Mt. Clemens (Michigan) Pottery Co. The result was to validate a union claim to back pay for more than 1,000 employees who had been required to be in the pottery plant and ready for work before the paid working day officially began. By December 1946 unions all over the nation had filed more than $1.5 billion in claims for "portal-to-portal pay." (Miners, for example, were to be paid, the Court said, for the time spent traveling from the portal of the mine to the working face.)

On May 1, 1947, Congress passed a bill outlawing nearly all such suits. The Portal-to-Portal Act signed by President Harry S Truman on May 14, 1947, invalidated all portal claims not specifically covered in labor contracts and put a two-year limit on future claims. It also provided that "preliminary and postliminary" activities of the working day were not to be counted unless they were part of the principal activities for which the employee was hired.

President Truman, who many feared would veto the bill, took the opportunity on signing it to urge Congress to raise the minimum wage from forty to sixty cents an hour and to extend the coverage of the wage-hour law.

Port Huron Statement In June 1962, 59 members of the **Students for a Democratic Society** (SDS) attended a convention at the United Auto Worker's (UAW) Franklin D. Roosevelt AFL-CIO Labor Center in Port Huron, Michigan. It was at this convention that the SDS emerged as a significant force in the **New Left** and issued the Port Huron Statement, the ideas of which were to provide a common denominator for the student protests that began on the Berkeley campus (*see* **Battle of Berkeley**) in 1964 and culminated with the "**siege of Morningside Heights**" at Columbia University in 1968.

"We are people of this generation, bred in at least modest comfort, housed now in the universities, looking uncomfortably to the world we inherit," runs the preamble. Largely the work of Tom Hayden, who had been elected president of the convention, the manifesto placed its emphasis on ethical concerns and attacked the contradictions in American life—the concern for liberty coupled with the lack of civil rights for blacks, the overall wealth that nevertheless permitted "poverty and deprivation to remain an unbreakable way of life for millions," the proclamation of peaceful intent accompanied by growing militarization. It called for **"participatory democracy,"** attacked the **"military-industrial complex,"** challenged the attempt by university authorities to enforce the practice of *in loco parentis*, and called for a shift in government spending from what it saw as an unnecessary defense buildup to the relief of poverty in this country and the support of underdeveloped nations in Africa, Asia, and Latin America.

While deploring the absence of civil liberties in the Soviet Union, it challenged the claim that the intentions of the U.S.S.R. were expansionist and argued that in any case the risks involved were worth taking since "the American military response had been more effective in deterring the growth of democracy than communism."

As a result of the Port Huron Statement, the SDS's parent organization, the League for Industrial Democracy (LID), summoned Tom Hayden and National Secretary Al Haber to hear charges that led to the suspension of salaries for the SDS staff and a ruling against publishing position pamphlets.

America and the New Era, issued at the June 1963 SDS convention, is generally considered a revision and updating of the Port Huron Statement. Largely the work of Richard Flacks, this document claimed that under the Presidency of John F. Kennedy society in America was being "engineered" to eliminate debate and dissent. "It is clear that, in the present situation, the **New Frontier** cannot solve the three most pressing needs of our time: disarmament, abundance with social justice, and complete racial equality."

Portnoy's Complaint Philip Roth's verbal wit and sexual explicitness made this (1969) novel into an immediate bestseller. The "complaint" in the title is used both in the sense of "lament" and of "complex," a description of which is given in a fictious medical note which precedes the story: "A disorder in which strongly-felt ethical and altruistic impulses are perpetually warring with extreme sexual longings, often of a perverse nature."

The device used by Roth is to have his protagonist, Alex Portnoy, a thirty-three-year-old Jewish lawyer involved in liberal causes, tell his story to a psychoanalyst. Front and center in the initial chapter—entitled "The Most Unforgettable Character I've Met" to ironically echo perennial articles of a similar title in the *Reader's Digest*—is probably the most hilarious, corrosive, and affectionate portrait of the "Jewish Mother" to appear in American fiction: Mrs. Portnoy.

Roth's mastery of the vernacular style kept the novel from ever turning into pornography in spite of the detailed descriptions of boyhood masturbation and adult sexual excesses.

Many feminist writers found the treatment of women in the novel particularly objectionable. Wrote critic Marya Mannes in a dissenting review: "Her use, and her interest, reside in one place only, and that place is certainly not mind or spirit. As on today's stage she is stripped naked, not merely of clothes—which after all, are not conventions so much as comforts in cold climates and decorations in hot ones—but of every quality that makes a whole woman."

In 1972 the novel was made into a particularly inept movie starring Richard Benjamin as Portnoy.

Poseidon Submarines Until the beginning of the decade, the U.S. Navy's fleet of more than forty nuclear-powered submarines carried single-target Polaris missiles. Since then the greater number have been equipped with the Poseidon missile capable of carrying ten **multiple independently targetable reentry vehicle** (MIRV) warheads.

Converted Poseidon submarines weigh 7,000 tons and are capable of twenty knots on the surface and thirty knots submerged. Each of the approximately 425-foot submarines carries two 145-man crews who alternate going on patrols that last two months. A special feature of these submarines is the inertial navigational system, which is based on a sophisticated working relationship between gyroscopes and accelerometers.

See **Intercontinental Ballistic Missile.**

Postal Reform Act Signed by President Richard M. Nixon on August 12, 1970, the act replaced (July 1, 1971) the 181-year-old U.S. Post Office Department with an independent agency that was free of congressional authority. The new United States Postal Service under Postmaster General Winton M. Blount was divided into five regions: New York (including southern Connecticut and northern New Jersey), East, Central, South, and West. As control shifted to these regions, the headquarters operations department in Washington, D.C., was eliminated. The Regional Postmasters report to a Deputy Postmaster General who has three Senior Assistant Postmasters in charge of mail handling ("manufacturing"), sales and deliveries ("retailing"), and support activities such as finance, planning, and housekeeping.

The postal reform was spurred by the first postal strike in American history, which began in New York City on March 18, 1970, and spread to various other sections of the country before it was ended on March 24. (In New York, some militants held out an additional day.)

Under the new setup, the Postmaster General was no longer included in the order of succession to the Presidency.

See **Presidential Succession Act of 1947.**

Potsdam Conference On July 17, 1945, President Harry S Truman, Prime Minister Winston Churchill, and Premier Josef Stalin began meeting in Potsdam, Germany, to discuss treaties with the defeated Axis powers, to plan the coming war crimes trials, and to call for the unconditional surrender of Japan. (Halfway through the meetings, which lasted until August 2, Churchill was replaced at the conference table by the new British prime minister, Clement Attlee, head of the United Kingdom's new Labour Government.) Similar meetings were held by Secretary of State James F. Byrnes, British Foreign Secretary Anthony Eden (eventually replaced by Ernest Bevin), and the U.S.S.R.'s Foreign Minister Vyacheslav Molotov.

Truman listed the achievements of the conference as the establishment of a Council of Foreign Ministers as a consultative body; the adoption of a reparations formula; and a compromise on Polish frontiers—"which was the best we were able to get"—to be finally approved by a peace treaty.

The most urgent reason for the President's trip to Potsdam, was not, however, announced in the communiqué issued at the end of the conference: viz., Stalin's personal reaffirmation of Russia's entry into the war against Japan.

President Truman found the Russians "relentless bargainers, forever pressing for every advantage for themselves," but was not completely surprised to find that their attitude toward future peace was conditioned by a belief that the Western world was heading for a major depression that could be exploited to advantage. "Force is the only thing the Russians understand. And while I was hopeful that Russia might someday be persuaded to work in cooperation for peace, I knew that the Russians should not be allowed to get any control of Japan." With this in mind, he was determined to see to it that General Douglas MacArthur would be given complete command and control in Japan once that country was defeated.

The regulations concerning the Council of Foreign Ministers were established in the "Protocol of the Proceedings of the Berlin Conference," dated August 1, 1945 (Potsdam Protocol). The first meeting was scheduled to be held in London no later than September 1, 1945, and the Council's primary task was to

. . . draw up, with a view to their submission to the United Nations, treaties of peace with Italy, Rumania, Bulgaria, Hungary, and Finland, and to propose settlements of territorial questions outstanding on the termination of the war in Europe. The Council shall be utilized for the preparation of a peace settlement for Germany to be accepted by the Government of Germany when a government adequate for the purpose is established.

For these tasks the Council was to be composed of representatives of states that signed the terms of surrender for the enemy state concerned. For Italy, however, France was to be regarded as a signatory to the Italian surrender terms.

"Poverty Palace" *See* **Office of Economic Opportunity.**

The Power Elite Published in 1956, this influential work by sociologist C. Wright Mills, author of *White Collar* (1951), argued that the nation's formal political processes carried out by men responsible to the people are no longer contemporary America's decision-making centers. A new power elite had arisen as a result of what he felt is the fact that our economy "is at once a permanent-war economy and a private-corporation economy. American capitalism is now in considerable part a military capitalism, and the most important relation of the big corporation to the state rests on the coincidence of interests" as defined by the "warlords and corporate rich" which strengthens both of them and subordinates the role of the politician. Not politicians but corporate executives sit with the military and plan the organization of their effort. Mills's focus on a seeming triumvirate in power was modified by the fact that both the military and political elites were seen as being dependent on the corporate elite.

Mills rejected the term "ruling class" and insisted on defining "class" as being limited to economics. He argued that power did not adhere in individuals but rather in the economic circumstances of a given society. The successful "economic man, either as propertied manager or manager of property, must influence or control those positions in the state in which decisions of consequence to his corporate activities are made." As a result, the tendency since the 1930s of business and government to become "intricately and deeply involved in each other has reached a new point of explicitness. The two cannot now be seen clearly as two distinct worlds." Not the politicians of

. . . the visible government, but the chief executives who sit in the political directorate, by fact and by proxy, hold the power and the means of defending the privileges of their corporate world. If they do not reign, they do govern at many of the vital points of everyday life in America, and no powers effectively countervail against them, nor have they as corporate-made men developed any effectively restraining conscience.

An increasingly bitter critic of American society—and especially of American policy toward Castro's Cuba—Mills is reported to have said at the time of his death in 1962 that he was "ashamed to be an American, ashamed to have John F. Kennedy as his President."

The Power of Positive Thinking This "spiritual" guide to self-help, published in 1952 by Norman Vincent Peale, pastor of New York's Marble Collegiate Church on Fifth Avenue, remained on the best-seller list for well over two years. It was in many ways a restatement of the views of Emile Coué, the French psychotherapist whose teachings were much in vogue during the 1920s and can best be summed up in his famous autosuggestive: "Day by day, in every way, I am getting better and better."

Dr. Peale's book used anecdote and spiritual exercise to convey a central message of "prayerize, picturize, actualize." Although it emphasized the necessity for prayer, the thrust of the book was a demonstration of how religion rewards in terms of material prosperity. It outlines a "perfect and amazing" method for arriving at positive action by simply willfully eliminating doubts and fears from the mind. This enviable state, Dr. Peale claimed, could be achieved by "mind-emptying at least twice a day." In one exercise the reader is urged: "Collapse physically. . . . Let go every muscle in the body. Conceive of yourself as a jellyfish, getting your body into complete looseness. Form a mental picture of a huge burlap bag of potatoes. . . . What is more relaxed than an empty burlap bag?"

In another exercise, the reader is exhorted to expel any negative thoughts in his mind "by increasing the positive affirmation. Affirm aloud: 'God is now giving me success. He is now giving me attainment.' "

In defending his "spiritual" message against attacks that it was in essence a formula for material success, Dr. Peale wrote in 1956: "I never preached that material success would come to anyone through the practice of the Gospel. But it is a fact that if one conditions his life to right thinking, right doing, right relationships with other people, he develops the characteristics and principles and type of personality to do his job well."

The relationship between spiritual purity and material success was not always as clear in Dr. Peale's mind. On assuming the pastorate of his church in 1932 during the Depression, he demanded that bankers and corporate leaders get down on their knees and pray that their sins be forgiven. His congregation at that time numbered about 200; by the 1950s it was close to 4,000, and his church ran a clinic staffed by seven psychiatrists.

Although he has insisted on the separation of church and state, in 1948 he took part in a MacArthur for President movement, and in 1960, Dr. Peale, a personal friend of Richard M. Nixon, led a group of Protestant ministers who issued a statement expressing doubt that a Catholic president could ever be entirely free of the influence of the Roman hierarchy.

Dr. Peale had been preceded in print by two other divines who contributed to establishing what hostile critics termed the "cult of reassurance" based on the tranquilizing power of prayer and positive thinking. In 1946 Rabbi Joshua Liebman published his bestselling *Peace of Mind* and three years later Monsignor Fulton J. Sheen offered *Peace of Soul.*

PPA *See* **Progressive Party of America.**

"Power to the People" *See* **Black Panther Party.**

Presidential Succession Act of 1947 On assuming office in April 1945, following the death of Franklin D. Roosevelt, President Harry S Truman became concerned that under the Presidential Succession Act of 1886 then in force, in the event of his death his own successor would be Secretary of State Edward R. Stettinius, Jr., who had never held elected office. He strongly felt that anyone who stepped into the Presidency "should have held at least some office to which he had been elected by a vote of the people." It was partly because of this, he noted, that he determined to make James F. Byrnes, who had been the Senator from South Carolina from 1931 to 1941, his new Secretary of State.

In addition, President Truman almost immediately tried to obtain a change in the 1886 law.

I felt that the Speaker of the House of Representatives most nearly represents selection by the people, because, as a member of the House, he is elected to the Congress by the voters of his district, and as Speaker, he is chosen by a majority of the representatives from all the states.

This recommendation was incorporated in a bill which was approved by the House on June 29, 1945, but failed to pass the Senate. On July 18, 1947, however, President Truman was able to put his signature to the current law governing presidential succession. It provides that in the absence of a vice president the Presidency was to go to the Speaker of the House. Those next in line are the president *pro tempore* of the Senate, the Secretary of State, and Cabinet members according to rank.

This order of succession became extremely important when in October 1973 Spiro Agnew resigned from office and the country was left without a vice president until President Nixon's appointment of Rep. Gerald R. Ford (R.-Mich.) was confirmed by Congress on November 27, and he took the oath of office on December 6, 1973.

In the early days of the republic, succession was

established by the Presidential Succession Act of 1792, under which the order was vice president, president *pro tempore* of the Senate, and Speaker of the House.

The Constitution's Twenty-Fifth Amendment, ratified on February 10, 1967, deals with procedure and succession in the event of presidential disability.

President's Commission on Campus Unrest *See* **Scranton Commission.**

President's Commission on Obscenity and Pornography To cope with some of the problems caused by changing American attitudes toward sex, on January 2, 1968, President Lyndon B. Johnson appointed William B. Lockhart, dean of the University of Minnesota Law School, to head an eighteen-man commission charged with investigating methods of dealing with the rising flood of pornography in films, books, and sexual gadgetry. Approximately $2 million was spent on the project which on September 30, 1970, resulted in a twelve-man majority report that was strongly attacked by dissenting commission members and rejected by the Nixon administration.

Although major emphasis in the more than 600-page report was given to the need for massive sex education efforts to create healthy sexual attitudes that would "provide a sound foundation for our society's basic institution of marriage and family," critical fire was centered on the commission's assertion that it found "no evidence that exposure to or use of explicit sexual materials play a significant role in the causation of social or individual harms such as crime, delinquency, sexual or nonsexual deviancy or severe emotional disturbances." While urging legislation to prohibit the sale of some types of sexual materials to young people, the majority recommended the repeal of laws preventing adults from having free access to sexually explicit materials.

Dissent from the majority opinion was spearheaded by Charles H. Keating, Jr., founder of Citizens for Decent Literature, Inc., who was President Richard M. Nixon's only appointee.

Even before the majority report had been approved or released, the White House leaked a draft of the document to the House Post Office and Civil Service subcommittee, which under the chairmanship of Rep. Robert N. C. Nix (D.-Pa.) began hearings on it (August 11-12, 1970). During the course of these hearings, the subcommittee released letters in which Commissioner Keating warned the President that the commission planned to recommend

the repeal of pornography laws where adults were concerned. While insisting that there was "no intent to prejudge the findings of the report," Press Secretary Ronald L. Ziegler announced that the President's feelings were at variance with its recommendations.

After the final report's official release, one of its strongest critics was Vice President Spiro Agnew, who noted that "as long as Richard Nixon is President, Main Street is not going to turn into Smut Alley." On October 13, 1970, a Senate resolution sponsored by Sen. John L. McClellan (D.-Ark.) denounced the report as "slanted and biased in favor of protecting the business of obscenity and pornography which the commission was mandated to regulate."

Commenting on President Nixon's criticism of the report's "morally bankrupt conclusions," Dean Lockhart said that the President was outraged because "scientific studies do not support the assumptions congenial to his viewpoint."

President's Commission on the Status of Women *See* **National Organization for Women.**

President's Committee on Civil Rights *See To Secure These Rights.*

Primal Scream Therapy In his widely read *The Primal Scream* (1970), Arthur Janov, a psychiatric social worker–psychologist, argued for a therapy that forces patients to relive core experiences that were painful enough to induce neurotic behavior as a defense and a refuge. The therapeutic approach is based on three weeks of individual work with the patient in sessions lasting as much as three or more hours daily. By means of what Janov called "direct talk" to the sources of primal pain—the denial of physical contact, food, warmth, etc., by an authoritarian father or overprotective mother intent on his or her own needs—the patient reexperiences key life episodes and reacts by releasing a "primal scream" which dissipates the stored pain. This moment is often accompanied by other intense physical actions such as shuddering, writhing, and sweating.

Critics claimed that Janov's focus on infantile deprivation as the origin of neurosis was new only in that it introduced a new terminology. The subtitle of his book—*Primal Therapy: The Cure for Neurosis*—was attacked as an indication of the dogmatism and authoritarianism with which he rejected all other therapeutic approaches.

Profiles in Courage Written by Sen. John F. Kennedy (D.-Mass.) while he was convalescing from a spinal operation, this 1956 bestseller concentrated on the careers of eight members of the Senate who in spite of enormous pressures from their constituents and colleagues had followed the dictates of their conscience in supporting and voting on major issues that had confronted the nation during its history. They included: John Quincy Adams, who though elected as a Federalist from Massachusetts in 1803 allied himself with Jeffersonian Republicans and was forced to resign in 1808 after supporting the Embargo of 1807 against British goods; Massachusetts's Daniel Webster, who sacrificed his presidential ambitions to support Henry Clay's Compromise of 1850; Missouri's Thomas Hart Benton, who lost his Senate seat after defying the South and voting against the same Compromise that extended slave territory within the nation; Sam Houston, who as a Senator from Texas voted against the repeal of the Missouri Compromise of 1820—which would have permitted slavery in the territory from Iowa to the Rockies—and was dismissed from his seat by the Texas Legislature in 1857; Edmund G. Ross, who as a Kansas Republican defied his party and voted against the impeachment of President Andrew Johnson in 1868 and sacrificed his political career; Lucius Quintus Cincinnatus Lamar, who as a Mississippi Senator from 1877 to 1885 enraged his constituents by supporting reconciliation between the North and South; George W. Norris, who as Senator from Nebraska temporarily defeated President Woodrow Wilson's Armed Ship Bill (1917), which he felt would force the country into World War I, by staging a filibuster; and Ohio's Robert A. Taft, who took an unpopular stand against the Nuremberg Trials by arguing that the condemnation of German war criminals was a violation of the "fundamental principle of American law that a man cannot be tried under an *ex post facto* statue."

Senator Kennedy did not argue for the rightness or the wrongness of any of the actions described but merely focused on the courage that was required by these men when they took stands based on a "deep-seated belief in themselves, their integrity and the rightness of their cause."

During the struggle against **McCarthyism,** Eleanor Roosevelt, widow of President Franklin D. Roosevelt, criticized Senator Kennedy for his own failure to take a firm stand and suggested that he show less profile and more courage.

John F. Kennedy was elected the country's first Catholic President in 1960. He was assassinated in Dallas on **November 22, 1963,** by Lee Harvey Oswald.

Program Evaluation and Review Technique (PERT)
Robert S. McNamara was one of several Army Air Force statistical-control experts who joined the Ford Motor Company following World War II and, as the "whiz kids," were largely responsible for the managerial and product changes that led to the company's resurgence in the postwar era. After fifteen years with Ford, during which he showed particular strength in the areas of statistical analysis, scientific management, and finance, he joined the Kennedy administration in 1961 as Secretary of Defense, bringing with him a team skilled in advanced managerial techniques. Among these techniques was PERT, a computerized method for indicating the most efficient means by which new weapons systems could be evolved. Many Pentagon officials felt that the McNamara team was "pert" indeed and in instituting new ways of doing things arrogantly overrode and overruled traditionalists.

"Progressive jazz" *See* **"Cool jazz."**

Progressive Labor Party (PLP) Founded in 1962, the PLP is a Marxist-Leninist organization with a strong Maoist orientation. Unlike many factions of the **New Left,** it completely rejected the drug and sex orientation of the **counterculture** of the 1960s. Because of its highly disciplined and puritanical revolutionary stance, it has sometimes been called "the Salvation Army of the Left."

The PLP broke with the Communist Party at the time of the Sino-Soviet split in the 1960s. Beginning in 1966, many of its members also belonged to the **Students for a Democratic Society** (SDS) and formed a tightly run caucus advocating a "Student-Worker Alliance." When this group won control at the June 1969 SDS annual meeting, in protest against the "wooden, mechanical Marxists" the SDS split into the Revolutionary Youth Movement I—which eventually became the ultraleftist **Weatherman** faction—and Revolutionary Youth Movement II, which was formed along more traditional left-wing lines.

By the end of the decade, the PLP had an estimated 1,000 members. In 1978 the group participated in demonstrations against American corporations doing business with South Africa.

Progressive Party of America (PPA) Following his resignation in 1946 as Secretary of Commerce under President Harry S Truman, former Vice President Henry A. Wallace became increasingly critical of the Truman administration's foreign policy. Finally, on December 29, 1947, he made a formal declaration of his intention to head a new political party in the 1948 presidential elections.

Wallace's candidacy was endorsed in January 1948 by the Progressive Citizens of America (PCA), an amalgamation of left-wing political action groups, and in March a National Wallace for President Committee was formed. The following May, the committee issued a call for a convention to be held in Philadelphia, July 23–25, 1948. It was here that the Progressive Party—actually Progressive Party of America (PPA)—was born and that Wallace and his running mate, Sen. Glen Taylor (D.-Id.), were nominated by acclamation and a party platform adopted with almost no dissent from the more than 3,000 delegates. The ticket was endorsed by the Communist Party at its New York convention early in August. (The 1948 Progressive Party should not be confused with national parties of the same name that had former President Theodore Roosevelt as presidential candidate in 1912, and nominated Robert La Follette for President in 1924.)

Campaigning on a platform that called for domestic reform, the repeal of conscription, the destruction of all atomic bombs, and improved relations with the Soviet Union—one popular slogan was "Wallace or War"—the former vice president hoped to attract 6 million votes from the Democratic column in crucial states. (Bitterly contested court battles won the PPA a place on the ballot in every state except Illinois, Nebraska, and Oklahoma.) Given the fact that earlier in July right-wing elements of the Democratic party opposed to President Truman's civil rights stand had selected South Carolina's Governor J. Strom Thurmond and Mississippi's Governor Fielding L. Wright to head the ticket of the newly formed **States' Rights Democrats,** or Dixiecrat Party, this seemed to assure the election of Republican presidential candidate Thomas E. Dewey of New York.

In the event, hard campaigning by President Truman resulted in a victory backed by over 24 million popular votes and 304 electoral votes. Wallace received well over a million popular votes but got no electoral votes. Soon after the election, Wallace broke with the PPA and returned to private life.

Writing in 1956, President Truman noted that while "some honest and well-meaning agitators for peace with Russia at any price found in Wallace a spokesman for their point of view," there had been a "sinister aspect to the Wallace movement" which provided "a front for the Communists to infiltrate the political life of the nation and spread confusion."

Project Apollo In his 1961 State of the Union message, President John F. Kennedy called on America to achieve "the goal before this decade is out of landing a man on the moon and returning him safely to earth." With this public commitment, the President gave the backing of his office to an already progressing moon-landing plan devised by the **National Aeronautics and Space Administration** (NASA) in 1960. Project Apollo was the third and final step in the program that was to fulfill the presidential pledge (with five months to spare) at a cost of over $26 billion.

Apollo called for an entirely new space technology. The first two programs—Mercury and Gemini—had carried into orbit just one and two men at a time, respectively. But the Apollo craft had to carry three men to the moon, towing with it a Lunar Module (LM) that would take two of the astronauts to the lunar surface and bring them back to the spacecraft. The resulting size of the "payload," or cargo to be boosted into space, was so staggering that no rocket in use at the time could have done the job. A thirty-six-story missile, the Saturn 5, had to be specially designed and constructed (many times over—once for each Saturn 5 flight).

When the brave new designs took form in hard steel, however, disaster struck almost immediately. *Apollo 1*, scheduled to lift off and orbit the earth in January 1967, tragically burned on the launch pad during a countdown rehearsal. Astronauts Virgil I. ("Gus") Grissom, Edward H. White (the first American to walk in space), and Roger B. Chaffee were asphyxiated when an electrical fire broke out and spread rapidly in the capsule's pure-oxygen atmosphere.

During the following long period of investigation and redesign, NASA launched three unmanned Apollo missions to test the capsule, the LM, and the Saturn 5 itself. The first manned Apollo flight did not come until October 1968. An earth-orbit test, the flight went well, and the program proceeded, picking up new momentum that December when *Apollo 8* became the first manned spaceship to break the bonds of orbital flight. Passing through the Van Allen radiation belt, the ship carried astronauts Air Force Colonel Frank Borman, Navy Captain James A. Lovell, Jr., and Air Force Major William A. Anders on a flawless path into lunar orbit. During a Christmas Eve telecast from the craft, the three touched the hearts of America as they read the first verses of the Book of Genesis from a distance of 230,000 miles.

Apollo 9 provided an earth-orbit checkout of the LM and how men would interact with it, and

Apollo 10 took three astronauts tantalizingly close to the moon, as a test of the LM in lunar orbit brought the craft to within 9.4 miles of the surface.

Launched on July 16, 1969, *Apollo 11* climaxed the lunar-landing program. Neil A. Armstrong, a civilian, commanded a crew consisting of Air Force Colonel Edwin E. ("Buzz") Aldrin and Air Force Lt. Col. Michael Collins. Aldrin and Armstrong descended in the LM and reported at 4:17:40 P.M. on July 20: "The *Eagle* [the code name they had given the LM] has landed." Six-and-a-half hours later, at 10:56:20, Armstrong stepped onto the lunar surface, saying, "That's **one small step for man, one giant leap for mankind.**" The landing had been in the area known as the Sea of Tranquility and the base established was called Tranquility Base.

Apollo 11 was spectacularly successful, as were *Apollos 12, 14, 15, 16* and *17* (all returns to the lunar surface). Only *Apollo 13* ran into trouble, when an exploding oxygen tank brought the craft close to disaster. The mission was aborted, and the men returned safely to earth.

The program closed in December 1972 with *Apollo 17*, which carried among its crew civilian geologist Harrison Schmitt, who uncovered important evidence relating to the question of lunar volcanic activity. Project Apollo then expired as a moon-landing program and gave way to the **Skylab Program** and the July 1975 linkup between *Apollo 18* and the Soviet Union's *Soyuz XIX*. Work on a space "shuttle" is now taking place, and no further manned lunar or planetary exploration is planned by the United States until the 1980s.

Project Bluebook *See* **Unidentified Flying Objects.**

Project Gemini The first of a series of flights designed to show that spacecraft could be maneuvered for docking purposes took place on March 23, 1965, when the 7,000-pound *Gemini 3* was launched from Cape Kennedy, Florida, with Air Force Major Virgil I. ("Gus") Grissom, the command pilot, and Navy Lt. Cmdr. John W. Young, the copilot. Nicknamed the *Molly Brown*, the craft was carried into orbit by a two-stage solid-fueled Titan 2 rocket. It was the first U.S. spacecraft to carry two men and it provided the first known opportunity for astronauts to shift orbits during flight. These maneuvers were made possible by thirty-two small rockets affixed to the approximately 18½-foot craft.

Gemini 3 had been preceded into space on March 18, 1965, by the Soviet spaceship *Voskhod* (*Sunrise*) *2*, one of whose two crew members (Alex-

éi Leonov) was the first man to step out of a spacecraft—to which he was attached by a sixteen-foot line—for what came to be known as Extravehicular Activity (EVA). Five months earlier, the *Voskhod 1* had carried three Soviet cosmonauts into space.

Four other successful Gemini flights were made during 1965. *Gemini 4* (June 3-7) was marked by the first American EVA when Air Force Major Edward H. White took a twenty-minute spacewalk.

The following year, *Gemini 8*, launched on March 16, 1966, proved that vehicles could rendezvous in space when it temporarily docked with an Agena-D target in the first such operation ever achieved. Four more Gemini flights completed the program, which ended with the launching of *Gemini 12* on November 11, 1966. As it circled the earth fifty-nine times, the two astronauts aboard practiced docking and undocking with the Agena target, completing four such operations successfully and keeping their craft attached to the target overnight.

The estimated cost of the Gemini project was $1.4 billion. In twenty months it put ten 2-man crews safely into orbit.

Project Mercury The first U.S. program to put a man into space, it was to be followed by Project Gemini and Project Apollo. Its somewhat uncertain origins go back to the establishment of the **National Aeronautics and Space Administration** (NASA) by President Dwight D. Eisenhower in April 1958. By the following September a NASA memorandum called for a project whose objectives were "to achieve at the earliest practicable date orbital flight and successful recovery of a manned satellite, and to investigate the capabilities of man in this environment."

In April 1959, NASA announced the selection of seven astronauts—military test pilots chosen from a candidate list of 110—from whom the first American to voyage into space would be chosen. These men—Navy Lt. Cmdr. Malcolm S. Carpenter; Marine Corps Lt. Col. John H. Glenn, Jr., Air Force Captain Leroy G. Cooper; Air Force Captain Virgil I. Grissom; Navy Lt. Cmdr. Walter M. Schirra, Jr.; Navy Lt. Cmdr. Alan B. Shepard, Jr.; and Air Force Captain Donald K. Slayton—were to undergo two years of intensive physical and scientific training, during the course of which they would contribute to the development of the Mercury space capsule.

Project Mercury, which was to cost $384 million and require the combined efforts of more than 2 million people, included a master control station at Cape Canaveral, Florida, and sixteen tracking stations around the world. The eventual launching vehicle for the 3,000-pound, cone-shaped capsule was a modified Atlas **Intercontinental Ballistic Missile** (ICBM) having two "boosters" capable of 150,000 pounds of thrust and a "sustainer" capable of 60,000 pounds.

The first Mercury capsule was launched into suborbital flight on May 5, 1961, when Navy Lt. Cmdr. Alan B. Shepard, Jr., was rocketed 116.5 miles above the earth in the *Freedom 7* and safely recovered in the Atlantic some 300 miles from Cape Canaveral. (On April 12, 1961, the Soviet Union's Major Yuri Gagarin became the first man to travel in space when the *Vostok I* returned to earth after circling the globe once.) A similar safe flight was made on July 21 by Air Force Captain Virgil I. ("Gus") Grissom, but his capsule, *Liberty Bell 7*, was lost in the ocean when a hatch was prematurely opened.

The first American orbital flight was made on February 20, 1962, when Marine Lt. Col. John H. Glenn, Jr., returned to earth safely after circling the planet three times. On May 24, 1962, Navy Lt. M. Scott Carpenter repeated the feat, but an error in manual retrofire during reentry caused a 250-mile landing overshoot. The next Mercury flight was by Navy Lt. Cmdr. Walter M. Schirra (October 3, 1962) in what was considered the most nearly perfect performance to date. After completing six orbits during an 8¾-hour flight, he landed his capsule in the Pacific within five miles of the splashdown target.

The Mercury series came to an end on May 16, 1963, after Air Force Captain Leroy Gordon Cooper returned safely to earth having completed twenty-two orbits and become the first American to spend more than twenty-four hours in space.

Project Pursestrings *See* **Hatfield-McGovern Amendment.**

Project Rebound Initiated by the Mid-Manhattan Branch of the National Association for the Advancement of Colored People (NAACP) in November 1971, it was part of an overall effort to help prisoners reestablish themselves in the community. The pilot project sparked similar programs by NAACP branches in Cleveland; Detroit; Hartford, Connecticut; Flint, Michigan; and Louisville, Kentucky. By the end of 1977 plans were underway to open offices in Atlanta; Durham, North Carolina; and Houston. Branches have also been established in eleven prisons.

Project Rebound is a two-part program which aims at both immediate job placement and on-the-job training in which federal funds obtained under the **Comprehensive Employment and Training Act** (CETA) are used to reimburse employers with up to $150 of a trainee's weekly salary for a maximum of twenty-six weeks.

Clients must be at least twenty-one years old, and they may not be current users of drugs or methadone.

Project Sentry Conceived in the 1950s to test the military applications of satellites put into orbits passing over both poles, Project Sentry split into three separate projects: Discoverer, Midas, and Samos.

Discoverer 1 was launched February 28, 1959, and though no signal was received, radar showed that it was in orbit. Because of its low perigee (ninety-nine miles), the orbit quickly decayed and the satellite reentered on March 5, 1959. *Discoverer 2* followed on April 13, 1959, and achieved a perigee of 142 miles and an apogee of 220 miles. Researchers hoped to develop a retrievable capsule, but this was not accomplished until *Discoverer 13* (August 10, 1960), whose capsule was ejected "backward"—so that there would be immediate entry—and retrieved from the Pacific the following day. The capsule of *Discoverer 14* was retrieved at an altitude of 8,500 by an aircraft equipped with two booms between which a rope was stretched. An unusual feature of *Discoverer 21* was a control mechanism which allowed the engine of the Thor-Agena-B rocket to be restarted while in orbit.

Midas (Missile Defense Alarm System) satellites were equipped with infrared sensors capable of detecting a missile launch by registering heat radiation, data on which were transmitted to air defense stations. *Midas 2* went into orbit on May 24, 1960, and was succeeded by a number of successful launchings, one of which signaled the firing of a Titan missile from Cape Canaveral, Florida, within ninety seconds of lift-off. After *Midas 4* the project was classified.

The initial Samos (Satellite and Missile Observation System) launch in October 1960 was a failure, but on January 31, 1961, *Samos 2* was put into polar orbit. Little information about it was released other than the fact that it was capable of photographing the earth and returning film in capsules recovered in midair off Hawaii, thanks to techniques developed during the Discoverer program.

Limited details on the Samos released by the government in 1964 revealed that it was equipped with electronic ferret devices capable of providing data on radio and radar facilities. The Samos satellites photographed the U.S.S.R. repeatedly each day.

Project Skylab *See* **Skylab Program**.

Project Vanguard Plans for launching small earth satellites capable of making scientific measurements during the **International Geophysical Year** (IGY, July 1957–December 1958) got underway in August 1955 when a committee of eight civilian consultants assembled by the Department of Defense recommended a Navy satellite-equipment program. The launch vehicle—to be called Vanguard—was to be a three-stage rocket in which an enlarged Viking was the first stage, an Aerobee the second stage, and a solid rocket the third.

Project Vanguard did not attract major interest until the national ego was stung when the Soviet Union launched the 184-pound *Sputnik I* on October 4, 1957. *Vanguard I*, a six-inch sphere weighing only 3.25 pounds, was launched into space on March 17, 1958, and went into a looping orbit 405 to 2,462 miles in altitude. It was the second American space satellite, having been preceded by the thirty-one-pound *Explorer I* on January 31, 1958.

Despite its small size, *Vanguard I* was to prove one of the most scientifically useful satellites. It provided evidence that the configuration of the earth is slightly pear-shaped, and thus permitted geophysicists to obtain new evidence on continental drift and the convection-cell theory of sea-floor spreading. For over six years its tiny radio enabled scientists to measure atmospheric density at a variety of orbits, record changes in atmospheric pressure during periods of solar activity, and estimate the influence of solar radiation pressure on an orbiting satellite.

Estimated at $11 million, Project Vanguard was to cost ten times that. It was during the program that Cape Canaveral, Florida, was converted from a rattlesnake-infested missile-test site to a sophisticated base for launching space satellites.

Proposition 13 Spearheading the 1978 "taxpayers' revolt" was a California ballot initiative calling—among other things—for the state property tax rate to be cut from 3 to 1 percent of market value. Despite opposition from Democratic Governor Jerry Brown and associations of teachers, firemen, policemen, etc., on June 6, 1978, 65 percent of the state's voters gave it their backing, peremptorily cutting an estimated $7 billion in annual taxes from the state budget.

Proposition 13 was largely the work of retired Republican businessman Howard Arnold Jarvis, who was also the $17,000-a-year director of the Apartment Association of Los Angeles. Collecting 1.3 million signatures to get his initiative on the California ballot, Jarvis recruited tax-cut advocate and former real-estate man Paul Gann, hired a consultant firm to manage the campaign, and blunted the charge of "kookiness" directed against the "Jarvis-Gann amendment" by critics when he obtained the endorsement of Milton Friedman, the Nobel Prize-winning economist.

There was some talk among opponents of a court challenge to Proposition 13. California's constitution requires that a ballot initiative be limited to one subject, and Proposition 13 not only limits the tax rate but requires that new taxes be agreed to by two-thirds of the state legislature. In addition, provisions of the amendment calling for a property tax roll-back to 1976 levels if property has not changed hands in the interval are seen by some as a possible violation of the Constitution's "equal protection" clause.

In November 1978 referendums calling for limits on state spending received voter approval in Arizona, Hawaii, Illinois, Michigan, and Texas. Meanwhile the co-authors of Proposition 13 would seem to have split. Mr. Gann has warned that though a property tax slash was relevant in California, it would be of no help in states where property taxes were low or where there were no other significant sources of state revenue. He and economist Friedman have joined in urging a Constitutional amendment that would tie Federal spending to the growth of the gross national product.

Psychohistory The application of the combined methods of psychoanalysis and history to the study of individual and collective life. The term is often associated with psychoanalyst Erik H. Erikson, whose *Young Man Luther* (1958) is an important example of the approach. Writing in 1974, however, Dr. Erikson began to look upon the use of the term as perpetuating the split in methodology that it was meant to deny. Practitioners in the two fields, he argued, must build bridgeheads on each side so that the completed bridge permitted "unimpeded two-way traffic; and once this is done, history will simply be history again, but now a history aware of the fact that it has always indulged in a covert and circuitous traffic with psychology which can now be direct, overt, and aware." At present, he noted, because of the clinical origin of psychoanalysis, "what is now called psychohistory often tends to resemble a case history."

Public Broadcasting Act of 1967 Signed by President Lyndon B. Johnson on November 7, 1967, it established the Corporation for Public Broadcasting (CPB) to aid and encourage individuals, noncommercial stations, or other groups to produce educational radio and television programs. The fifteen CPB directors were to be appointed by the President and confirmed by the Senate; no more than eight could be from the same political party and no one could be appointed for more than two consecutive terms of six years each. Among the first appointments announced by President Johnson was that of the distinguished American educator and diplomatist Milton Eisenhower, who had served the government during the administrations of his brother, President Dwight D. Eisenhower, and of President Harry S Truman.

CPB, for which Congress authorized $9 million in fiscal 1968, was prohibited from owning or operating a TV or radio system. In addition, noncommercial stations were barred from taking a stand on candidates for political office.

Under this new legislation, the Educational Television Facilities Act of 1962, which provided aid for building educational TV facilities, was extended for three years and broadened to include radio facilities. The act authorized $38 million for this purpose in fiscal 1968-1970.

In April 1971, National Public Radio, which had been incorporated in 1969, began offering a nationwide educational programming service, and by the middle of the decade, it was using CPB funds to supply close to 180 public radio stations with informational and cultural programs.

Public Law 4 *See* **Formosa Resolution**.

Public Law 480 *See* **Agricultural Trade and Development Act of 1954; Food for Peace**.

Pueblo Incident "If I had to pick a date that symbolized the turmoil we experienced throughout 1968, I think January 23 would be the day—the morning the U.S.S. *Pueblo* was seized," President Lyndon B. Johnson has noted.

An intelligence ship crammed with advanced electronic equipment that enabled it to gather data from the mainland, the *Pueblo* had for some time been cruising the Sea of Japan off the coast of North Korea. The communists were well aware of the true mission of this "environmental research ship," but there seemed little they could do about it as long as the *Pueblo* remained in international waters. Such electronic snooping was by no means confined to the United States and had come to be "accepted" among nations.

It is unsure whether on that morning the *Pueblo* had drifted within the twelve-mile limit, or whether the incident was deliberately provoked by the North Koreans. The ship's captain, Commander Lloyd M. Bucher, was used to harassment, but by the time he realized that the North Korean submarine chaser and the three patrol boats circling his ship actually meant to board and seize her it was too late to call for help. In the action that followed three Americans were injured and one killed. The ship and its complement of eighty-two men were seized, but not before the crew had destroyed much of the equipment.

In an attempt to obtain the immediate release of the ship and crew, Washington appealed to Moscow to intervene but met with a chilly refusal. On January 25, President Johnson called up 14,000 Navy and Air Force reserves to strengthen American forces in Korea without weakening them in Vietnam. Meanwhile, on the diplomatic front United Nations Ambassador Arthur Goldberg brought the matter before the Security Council, but failed to obtain action. While there was some saber rattling in Congress, the cooler heads prevailed and efforts to obtain the release of the crew—now threatened by North Korea with being brought to trial as criminals—went ahead through negotiations at Panmunjom.

It was, however, December 23 before Commander Bucher and his crew were released after a face-saving maneuver in which U.S. authorities simultaneously admitted and denied responsibility for the incident. Secretary of State Dean Rusk stated at the time:

After ten months of negotiations, during which we made every sort of reasonable offer, all of which were harshly rejected, we had come squarely up against a painful problem: how to obtain the release of the crew without having this government seem to attest to statements which simply are not true. Then, within the past week, a way which does just that was found, and a strange procedure was accepted by the North Koreans. Apparently the North Koreans believe there is propaganda value even in a worthless document which General [Gilbert H.] Woodard publicly labeled false before he signed it.

But the agony of the *Pueblo* crew was not over even after their return to these shores and the revelation that they had been tortured. Some members of the Pentagon attempted to bring Commander Bucher to court martial for a "confession" he had signed under duress, but this move was rejected by Secretary of the Navy John H. Chafee.

The *Pueblo* seizure occurred at the time of numerous incidents at the North Korean border, and there is some reason to assume that it was provoked by the communists in an attempt to draw off U.S. and South Korean forces from Vietnam, where the **Tet offensive** was soon to be launched, by creating fears of a new invasion from North Korea.

In 1978 the *Pueblo* was still in North Korean hands and was said to be anchored at Wonsan Harbor, where it was used as a museum. There had been no negotiations since December 1968 to obtain the return of the ship.

"Puff the Magic Dragon" Sometimes considered a children's song, in the 1960s it became associated with the marijuana cult, for obvious reasons.

During the **Vietnam War** the C-47 was armed with electrically powered 7.62 mm miniguns which fired one tracer in five rounds. Because of this, the gunship was often referred to as "Puff the Magic Dragon."

Pugwash Conferences The name given to a series of international scientific conferences on nuclear energy, the first of which was held in Pugwash, Nova Scotia, on July 11, 1957. Sponsored by British philosopher Bertrand Russell, the conferences were attended by some twenty leading nuclear experts from eleven countries, including the Soviet Union. At the conclusion, a warning was issued that abuse of nuclear power could lead to the extinction of human life on earth.

A second "Pugwash" conference, held in Beauport, Quebec, in the spring of 1960, urged that action be taken to ban nuclear tests or to establish test and weapons quotas.

According to a Senate Internal Security Subcommittee staff study, the first five conferences were financed by Cleveland industrialist Cyrus Eaton, who donated $100,000. Afterward, the conferences attracted foundation money.

Pumpkin Papers *See* **Alger Hiss Case**.

Punta del Este *See* **Alliance for Progress**.

PUSH *See* **People United to Save Humanity**.

Q

Quinlan Case

Quadriad Beginning with the Kennedy administration, this term was used to denote the President's chief economic advisers: the Secretary of the Treasury, the chairman of the Federal Reserve Board (FRB), the director of the **Office of Management and Budget** (OMB), and the chairman of the **Council of Economic Advisers** (CEA). Originally, the four were called the Fiscal and Financial Advisory Group, but this designation was found too "cumbersome" by CEA chairman Walter Heller, at whose suggestion the change was made. Minus the FRB chairman, the group becomes known as the Troika. (Not to be confused with the use of the term in 1960 by Soviet Premier Nikita Khrushchev, who suggested that United Nations Secretary General Dag Hammarskjöld be replaced by a "troika" of secretaries general who would represent the communist, capitalist, and neutralist states in the international organization.)

Quantico Panel When a summit conference on disarmament and other matters was scheduled to be held in Geneva in July 1955, Nelson A. Rockefeller set to work on a dramatic peace plan that President Dwight D. Eisenhower could present to the delegations from the United Kingdom, France, and the Soviet Union. Organizing a staff of technical experts, researchers and "idea men," he moved them to the Marine Base in Quantico, Virginia. Part of his purpose in selecting this site seems to have been to get them away from any possible influence of John Foster Dulles's State Department, where the notion of disarmament was received with considerable skepticism.

Apprehensive about the secrecy that surrounded the proceedings at Quantico, Secretary Dulles complained to Presidential Assistant Sherman Adams: "He seems to be building up a big staff. He's got them down at Quantico, and nobody knows what they're doing."

Eventually, the Quantico Panel came up with the **Open Skies** proposal that President Eisenhower was to present at Geneva in the hopes that it would provide a breakthrough in the disarmament stalemate. Secretary Dulles was predictably unenthusiastic about the plan, but his objections were based mainly on the belief that the Russians would not accept any realistic disarmament proposal. They did, in fact, reject Open Skies, but the proposal was generally considered a propaganda coup in the **Cold War.**

After the Geneva meeting, a second round of conferences sometimes referred to as Quantico II produced a forty-one-page classified document which was said to offer a "master plan" for future conduct of the Cold War; it called for an expenditure of $18 billion during the next six years.

Quemoy and Matsu When in August 1954, Red China's Prime Minister Chou En-lai warned that his government would "liberate" Formosa from the control of Nationalist Chinese forces under Generalissimo Chiang Kai-shek, President Dwight D. Eisenhower replied that any invasion of Formosa "would have to run over the Seventh Fleet." The Communist threat then shifted to a string of small Nationalist-held islands—the Tachen, Matsu, and Quemoy groups—off the coast of the mainland; on September 3, 1954, they began shelling the Quemoys, and an invasion appeared imminent.

On December 2, 1954, the United States and the Republic of China signed a Mutual Defense Treaty in which it was stated that an attack on the West Pacific territories of either nation would be considered dangerous to the peace and safety of the other. However, neither by this treaty nor by a later clarification was the United States necessarily obliged to act in the case of the offshore islands. When on January 18, 1955, the Communists invaded the island of Yikiang, eight miles from the Tachens, the Eisenhower administration announced that they considered neither Yikiang nor the Tachens as essential to the defense of Formosa. Nevertheless, at the request of the President, on January 28, 1955, Congress passed the **Formosa Resolution,** which authorized him to employ the Armed Forces to protect Formosa and the Pescadores against attack. The language of the resolution was vague about the Matsu and Quemoy islands. In February 1955, the Nationalist forces evacuated the Tachens and the Communists took over. The immediate crisis seemed over.

In August 1958, however, the Communists renewed their shelling of Quemoy, but this time the Eisenhower administration made it clear that it would protect Quemoy and Matsu, to which the Nationalists had now committed large forces. The Chinese Communists, however, relaxed their pressure on Quemoy after a pledge from the United States to seek a reduction of Nationalist forces on the island and to abstain from support of any attempted invasion of the mainland. (The Communists reserved the right to shell the island on alternate days of the week.)

In October 1960, Quemoy and Matsu once more were in the news when during the course of the

Kennedy-Nixon debates Vice President Richard M. Nixon denounced as "woolly thinking" Senator John F. Kennedy's contention that U.S. defense in the Pacific should be based only on Formosa itself. When in June 1962 the Communists again seemed to be threatening these islands, President Kennedy announced that American policy on Formosa had not changed since 1955.

Quiet Brain Trust In December 1963, historian Eric F. Goldman was summoned to Washington from Princeton University by President Lyndon B. Johnson and appointed Special Consultant to the President of the United States. His task, Goldman was told, was to form a group of "best minds" to suggest administration goals and programs.

It was Presidential Aide Walter Jenkins who in discussing the steps to be taken dubbed the group the "quiet brain trust." Some of the better known members recruited and eventually approved by President Johnson were: David Riesman (Harvard University), Eugene V. Rostow (Yale Law School), Clinton Rossiter (Cornell University), John Kenneth Galbraith (Harvard University), Richard Hofstadter (Columbia University), and Margaret Mead (American Museum of Natural History).

This group was also sometimes known as the "domestic affairs group." At President Johnson's request, both Goldman's connection to the White House and the existence of the "quiet brain trust" were kept secret until February 3, 1964. In May, Bill Moyers was given the major part of Goldman's responsibility in this area, and in August 1966, Goldman resigned.

The name had obvious echoes of the Brain Trust of the Roosevelt administration: Rexford G. Tugwell, Adolf A. Berle, Jr., Raymond Moley, Sam Rosenman, and Basil O'Connor.

Quinlan Case After having accidentally mixed barbituates and alcohol, twenty-one-year-old Karen Anne Quinlan, a resident of New Jersey, had gone into a coma. For the next eleven months it seemed as though only the mechanical respirator to which she was attached was keeping her alive. Assured by physicians that their daughter had experienced massive brain damage and could never recover, Mr. and Mrs. Joseph Quinlan sought legal permission to have the respirator turned off so that Karen Anne might die with "grace and dignity." On March 31, 1976, the New Jersey Supreme Court ended a complicated legal battle by ruling in favor of the Quinlan seniors, and Karen Anne was removed from the machine on May 22, 1976; however, she continued to breathe normally and was fed intravenously. Regularly administered antibiotics prevented infection.

More than two years later, Karen Anne Quinlan was still alive and her breathing was considered adequate to her limited needs.

The widely publicized Quinlan Case, and the moral controversy it evoked, stimulated interest in so-called right-to-die legislation under which "living wills" made out by individuals could limit the amount of medical treatment they would receive should they become terminally ill.

Although in 1977 such legislation was introduced in thirty-eight states, by the end of the year it was successful only in Idaho and California.

Quiz Show Scandals *See "Twenty-One."*

New York Daily News

Rosenberg Case

Radical Chic The June 8, 1970, issue of *New York* magazine was largely devoted to an article in which **"New Journalist"** Tom Wolfe acidly described a party given earlier that year (January 14, 1970) by composer Leonard Bernstein and his wife, Felicia, for members of the **Black Panthers.** "Radical Chic: That Party at Lenny's," spotlighted a growing tendency at the tail end of the tumultuous 1960s of the rich and famous to endorse radical causes in a manner that in no way exposed them to the risk of losing social status.

According to Wolfe, the development of Radical Chic could be traced to a party given by Andrew Stein, a member of the New York Assembly, in his father's fashionable Southampton "cottage" on June 29, 1969, in support of the California grape strike led by Cesar Chavez (*see* **La Causa**). This "epochal event" was preceded by a party given in support of the strike by Carter Burden and his then wife, Amanda (*see* **Jet Set**), and followed by a party given by the fashionable Jean vanden Heuvel for the **Chicago Eight.**

The Bernstein party focused on in the article brought Radical Chic to a more or less abrupt halt when two days later an editorial in the *New York Times* denounced it as "elegant slumming that degrades patrons and patronized alike." Similar parties that had been planned were said to have been quickly cancelled.

The impulse behind Radical Chic is traced by Wolfe to two underlying beliefs in certain segments of the fashionable world. "One rule is that *nostalgie de la boue* —i.e., the styles of romantic, raw-vital Low Rent primitives—are good; and *middle class*, whether black or white, is bad." He notes that the New York pacesetters tended to favor the Chicano grape workers not only because they were "exotic" but because they were 3,000 miles away and therefore unlikely to "come back next weekend and knock on the door." A second "rule" for Radical Chic is seen as the conviction "that no matter what, one should always maintain a proper address, a proper scale of interior decoration, and servants." While Wolfe does not doubt the sincerity of the party givers, he notes that "at the same time they feel quite sincerely about their social position. They want to keep things going on both tracks."

Radical Education Project (REP) Established in 1966 as an arm of **Students for a Democratic Society** (SDS), REP evolved into an independent organization that flourished during the late 1960s. Its goal was to fulfill what it identified as three basic needs: the need to educate the student activists

drawn to the radical movement on "single issues" such as the **Vietnam War** or poverty, or on "gut reaction" against the basic inequalities in American society; the need for competent research on the issues of **New Left** programs and theory; and the need to extend the movement beyond students to the professions, faculties, churches, and unions.

Radic-Lib *See* **John Birch Society.**

Railpax *See* **Amtrak.**

RAM *See* **Revolutionary Action Movement.**

RAND Corporation Founded in 1943 by the Army Air Force, for which it was operated by the Douglas Aircraft Company as a research organization or "think tank" in which scientists assigned to solve technological problems and make feasibility studies could operate in a civilian atmosphere congenial to them. The name is an acronym for *Research and Development.*

In the spring of 1946, RAND—sometimes described as a "university without students"—issued a study entitled *Preliminary Design for an Experimental World-Circling Space Ship*, in which it predicted that a man-made satellite with appropriate instrumentation could be a potent scientific tool which would "inflame the imagination of mankind and would probably produce repercussions in the world comparable to the explosion of the atomic bomb." The report added that "one can imagine the consternation and admiration that would be felt if the United States were to discover suddenly that some other nation had already put up a successful satellite." On October 4, 1957, the Soviet Union launched *Sputnik I*, a 184-pound satellite that orbited the earth every 96.1 minutes.

It was as a RAND employee that Daniel Ellsberg helped prepare a study of American involvement in the **Vietnam War** (see **Pentagon Papers**).

Ranger Program This trouble-plagued $270-million program was designed to provide photographs of the lunar surface that would help the scientists involved in **Project Apollo** determine the design of a lunar module, possible landing spots, and whether or not the lunar surface could indeed support the weight of a spacecraft. *Rangers 1* and *2*—launched August 26 and October 18, 1961, respectively—were not intended to fly to the moon but only to test the parking-orbit mode of launching and to see how well the automatic controls functioned. Both vehicles failed to be lifted out of earth orbit. *Rang-*

ers 3,4,5, and 6 were fully instrumented vehicles, but failed to send lunar photographs back to the earth either because they were off target or because the cameras failed to operate correctly. *Ranger 7* was launched on July 28, 1964, and crashlanded in the Mare Nubium (Sea of Clouds) on July 31, 1964, after transmitting more than 4,300 photographs. *Ranger 8* was launched on February 17, 1965, and on February 20, 1965, landed in the western side of Mare Tranquillitatis (Sea of Tranquility) and transmitted more than 7,000 photographs. *Ranger 9* was launched on March 21, 1965, and crashed into the moon's Alphonsus crater on March 24, 1965, after sending close to 6,000 photographs during the last nineteen minutes of flight.

Although the program had begun dismally, the more than 17,000 pictures obtained from the final three launchings brought it to a brilliantly successful conclusion. However, it was still not possible to determine with certainty that the lunar surface was of sufficient hardness to support a landing vehicle.

See **Surveyor I.**

Rat Pack   In the mid-1950s, this informal group of Hollywood celebrities, whose acknowledged leader was actor Humphrey Bogart, attracted considerable attention in the news media. Columnist Earl Wilson later described the group as "a do-nothing organization devoted to nonconformity and whiskey-drinking." The group—which included Frank Sinatra, Judy Garland, Paul Douglas, Joey Bishop, Peter Lawford, and Irving Lazar—was accidentally given its name by Bogart's wife, actress Lauren Bacall, who on one occasion referred to it as a "rat pack."

La Raza   Term often used to denote the linguistic and cultural unity of Americans of Mexican, Puerto Rican, and Cuban origin. In 1966, *Newsweek* magazine called this enormous community "the best kept secret in America." Armando M. Rodriquez, director of the Office of Spanish-Speaking Affairs of the Department of Health, Education, and Welfare, estimated in 1970 that *La Raza* included 10 million Americans.

RB–47 Incident   *See* **U-2 Flights.**

Reapportionment   *See* **Baker v. Carr; Reynolds v. Sims; Wesberry v. Sanders.**

Rebel Without a Cause   This 1955 film directed by Nicholas Ray made young James Dean a symbol of his generation. The "pathetic aggression" that char-

acterized his portrayal of a youngster alienated from parents who fail to provide understanding or moral support made him—at a time when fundamentally idealistic teenagers were beginning to warn that they would not conform to the role models furnished by the adult world—every girl's dream and every teenage boy's sulky vision of himself. After only a year in Hollywood, the twenty-four-year-old Indiana farmhand was killed in a sports car crash on September 30, 1955. His tragic death and the release of *Giant* the following year completed his elevation to the status of a cult hero. Twenty years afterward, fan mail was still being directed to him.

Set in the high-school of an affluent Los Angeles area, *Rebel Without a Cause* contrasts graphic presentations of switchblade duels and "chicky runs" in stolen automobiles with wistfully poignant encounters between Dean and actress Natalie Wood as adolescent exiles from their overly comfortable homes. To a lesser extent, the film also established the reputation of Sal Mineo, who played a youngster abandoned by his parents to the care of a maid.

Dean, who had previously been directed by Elia Kazan in *East of Eden* (1955), had many of the mannerisms of Marlon Brando, but in his final film he showed his own peculiar genius in mastering, as *Time* magazine put it, "the wry little jerks and smirks, tics and twitches, grunts and giggles that make up most of the language of a man who talks to himself a good deal more than he does to anyone else."

Red Channels   First published on June 22, 1950, it was an index listing 151 writers, actors, singers, dancers, producers, and radio and TV executives with "dubious" political associations. Edited by a group of former FBI agents and issued by American Business Consultants, it was in essence an expansion of *Counterattack*, a weekly newletter issued by the same organization, whose stated purpose was "to expose the Communist menace." American Business Consultants investigated cases for clients on a professional basis.

The names listed in *Red Channels* were culled from the files of the **House Committee on Un-American Activities** (HUAC), the Tenney Committee of California, the Attorney General's subversives list, and the files of various state and local investigations into subversive activities. The *Daily Worker* was also used as a source to show that an individual listed had done something which won the praise of the Communist Party.

Red Channels neither vouched for the facts contained in such public records nor made any attempt to consult with the persons involved before including their names on the index.

One of the more famous cases of a person who lost employment as a result of being listed in that publication involved Jean Muir, an actress with more than twenty years of experience, who was listed as having been associated with a number of organizations said to be communist-oriented. Miss Muir was to have appeared on August 27, 1950, in NBC–TV's "The Aldrich Family," but as the result of a telephone campaign organized against her she was replaced. She denied ever having been a member of most of the groups her name had been associated with, and pointed out that she had resigned from one of them when she discovered that it was procommunist. However, she received no backing from NBC, and the program's sponsor, General Foods Corporation, after suavely agreeing that she was a loyal American, insisted that she had unfortunately become "controversial."

Theodore Kirkpatrick, coeditor of *Counterattack,* described two methods by which a person might have his or her name removed from *Red Channels:* (1) join or work for organizations which colleagues considered pro-American; (2) appear before HUAC and make public confession. It would have been difficult, however, for many of the persons listed to know just what it was they were expected to confess.

See **Fund for the Republic.**

"Red Herrings" *See* **Turnip Congress; Alger Hiss Case.**

"Redlining" On April 26, 1976, ten civil rights and housing organizations filed suit charging that the Federal Reserve Board, the Office of the Comptroller of the Currency, the Federal Deposit Insurance Corporation, and the Federal Home Loan Bank Board had failed to prevent mortgage lenders from barring loans for houses located in center-city, largely nonwhite neighborhoods—a practice known as "redlining." Under the terms of an out-of-court settlement, in March 1977, the Federal Home Loan Bank Board, which has regulatory authority over savings and loan associations, agreed to step up efforts against racial and sexual discrimination in home-mortgage lending by placing civil rights specialists in its field offices. Later that year it proposed to require written guidelines for processing loans and a review by savings and loan associations of their operations and procedures to ensure that they served the entire community.

The 1977 Community Reinvestment Act (CRA) tacked on to that year's Housing and Community Development Act by Sen. William Proxmire (D.-Wis.) required the four regulatory agencies named above to judge an institution's lending record before making any decision on applications for federal charters, mergers, or the establishment of new branches.

In June 1978 the **Department of Housing and Urban Development** (HUD) issued a report charging that in many large cities property owners were being denied access to the voluntary fire and property insurance market. It noted that "redlining has an undeniable racial component, whereby redlined areas often coincide with nonwhite neighborhoods," extending "far beyond blighted urban areas into many otherwise healthy neighborhoods." The report charged that often insurance companies redlined on an arbitrary basis by merely checking the zip codes.

Reed v. Reed Acting unanimously on November 22, 1971, the U.S. Supreme Court for the first time in its history overturned legislation in which a distinction based on sex was made. In question was an Idaho law giving men preference as estate executors. The decision, however, did not make all laws incorporating a sexual bias "suspect."

On January 21, 1975, the Court upheld a lower court ruling on a Louisiana law when it decided that women may not be systematically excluded from jury duty—or given automatic exemption—if the result is a selection of predominantly male panels. Later in the year, it struck down a Utah law under which for the purposes of child support and marriage without parental consent women reached their majority at eighteen and men at twenty-one. States with similar laws were not affected.

Re-examinationists *See* **The Great Debate.**

Reitman v. Mulkey In a five-to-four ruling that overrode contradictions in two previous 1966 decisions, the U.S. Supreme Court on May 29, 1967, declared unconstitutional an amendment to the California constitution which had been used as the basis for racial discrimination in private housing by giving property owners "absolute discretion" in both resale and renting.

The decision upheld a California Supreme Court ruling in two distinct cases, one involving a Mr. and

Mrs. Lincoln W. Mulkey and the other a Mr. and Mrs. Wilfred J. Prendergast, who had brought suit against apartment house owners in Los Angeles and Santa Ana for refusing to rent to them because of their race. Justice Byron R. White's majority opinion noted that the voter-approved amendment had in effect repealed California's fair housing legislation and created "a constitutional right to discriminate on racial grounds."

Relay 1 *See* **Telstar.**

"Released time" By the end of the 1940s, well over 2,000 communities in the United States had instituted the practice of releasing public school children from their regular studies in order to give them time to attend classes on religion given by outside teachers within the school building. Ruling on one such program established in Champaign, Illinois, the U.S. Supreme Court decided in **Illinois ex re McCollum v. Board of Education** (1948) that such a program was contrary to the First Amendment of the Constitution, which prohibited any law "respecting an establishment of religion." In delivering the opinion of the Court, Justice Hugo Black noted:

Here not only are the state's tax-supported public school buildings used for the dissemination of religious doctrine. The State also affords sectarian groups an invaluable aid in that it helps to provide pupils for their religious classes through use of the state's compulsory public school machinery. This is not separation of Church and State.

Justice Stanley F. Reed, who cast the only dissenting vote, directed attention

. . . to the many instances of close association of church and state in American society . . . recalling that many of these relations are so much a part of our tradition and culture that they are accepted . . . . Devotion to the great principle of religious liberty should not lead us into a rigid interpretation of the constitutional guarantee that conflicts with accepted habits of our people. This is an instance where, for me, the history of past practices is determinative of the meaning of a constitutional clause not a decorous introduction to the study of its text.

Four years later, in *Zorach v. Clauson*, the Court ruled favorably on a New York City "released time" program. In this later case, the religious instruction was given at some place outside the school buildings.

In a case antecedent to the two discussed above, *Everson v. Board of Education* (1947), the Court ruled five to four that the state of New Jersey had not breached the "high and impregnable" wall separating church and state in providing for the payment of the bus fares for pupils attending a Catholic parochial school. This opinion was cited by Justice Black in the *McCollum* case:

The majority in the *Everson* case, and the minority . . . agreed that the First Amendment's language, properly interpreted, had erected a wall of separation between Church and State. They disagreed as to the facts shown by the record and as to the proper application of the First Amendment's language to those facts.

Financing, administration, and instruction under "released time" programs are the responsibility of the various religious denominations. When parents request that their children be excused for an hour of religious instruction, the pupils are transported from the school building to the place where they are given instruction in the Bible or on some aspect of religion.

Engel v. Vitale (1962) is often discussed in relation to those cases testing to see whether the First Amendment prohibition to breaching the wall between Church and State had been broken. In the *Engel* case, the Court found that the reading in New York public schools of a nondenominational prayer composed by the New York Board of Regents was unconstitutional.

The Reliable Source A humorous and often scurrilous publication put out at national political conventions in recent years by prankster and sometime consultant Richard Tuck. Convention delgates find it slipped under their hotel door in the morning, but during the four-year interval between conventions it vanishes from the political scene.

At the Democratic National Convention in New York, July 1976, Mr. Tuck created considerable confusion by printing bogus invitations to an RSVP party to which *Rolling Stone* magazine invited entertainment celebrities and selected delegates to meet with the campaign staff of presidential hopeful Jimmy Carter. As a result, the party was packed by gate-crashers, and most of those bearing authentic invitations were denied entrance.

During the investigations following the **Watergate Scandal,** there was an attempt by some to justify the **"Dirty Tricks"** of the Nixon team during the 1972 presidential campaign by pointing to the precedents established by prankster Tuck (*see* **Nixon's the one**).

Mr. Tuck assumed the roll of gadfly in the 1950s after losing a race for the California state senate. At the time, he conceded defeat by announcing humorously: "The people have spoken—the bastards!" This line was used again in 1976 by Rep. Morris Udall (D.-Ariz.), who had unsuccessfully entered more than twenty state primaries for the Democratic presidential nomination.

Reorganization Act of 1949 *See* **Hoover Commission.**

REP *See* **Radical Education Project.**

Republic of New Africa (RNA) At the National Black Government Conference held in Detroit in April 1968, it was proposed to establish a separate black nation within the United States. The RNA was to consist of five southern states: Mississippi, Georgia, South Carolina, Alabama, and Louisiana. Robert F. Williams, a black militant who in 1961 had fled to Cuba and then to Tanzania (1966) to escape FBI charges of kidnapping, was designated RNA's president. Its vice president and actual leader in the United States was Milton R. Henry.

A formal demand for the territory of the future RNA was presented to the U.S. State Department in May 1969 along with a demand for $200 billion in "reparations" due to black Americans. In August 1969 a four-day conference was held in Washington D.C. to establish an "official" RNA governmental structure. It was proposed to take over the five states by making a "conquest" of them at the ballot box. Federal interference, "Vice President" Henry declared, would result in black guerrilla action in the nation's major cities.

Meanwhile, in December 1969, Robert F. Williams returned to the United States and began to fight against extradition to North Carolina. When he resigned as "president," he was succeeded by Richard Henry, brother of the "vice president," who took the name Imari Obadele, moved RNA offices to Jackson, Mississippi, and attempted to found his capital, El Malik, in the vicinity.

Richard Henry soon became embroiled in a legal squabble over the acquisition of a twenty-acre farm. In August 1971, while FBI agents and local police were attempting to serve fugitive warrents on several RNA members, an officer was killed. Obadele and ten other "citizens" of RNA were arrested and charged with murder and treason.

Republican Cloth Coat *See* **Checkers Speech.**

Reserve Clause Hotly disputed, it gave a professional baseball club the right to invoke the terms of an expired contract with a player for an additional year when and if a new contract had not been agreed upon by a specific date. Since the same clause would appear in the new contract, the reserve clause was self-perpetuating and bound a player to a club for his entire career. Although the club had the right to trade his contract to another team, the player himself could make no move on his own initiative.

In 1970, Curt Flood refused to report to Philadelphia after being traded by the St. Louis Cardinals. His challenge in the courts was later rejected by the Supreme Court (1972) on the grounds that previous decisions has exempted baseball from antitrust laws. In December 1975, however, a three-member arbitration panel ruled that Andy Messersmith of the Los Angeles Dodgers was right when he insisted that he should become a "free agent" by playing out his option year. This ruling was upheld in February 1976 by a U.S. district court in Kansas City and again the following month by a three-judge panel of the U.S. Court of Appeals for the Eighth Circuit, St. Louis.

A new agreement arrived at with the clubs (1976) permitted the player to become a free agent once he had played out his reserve year. Six-year veterans were given a fifteen-day period following the World Series when they could become free agents by notifying their teams of such intentions; five-year veterans could demand to be traded and designate six teams they considered unacceptable. (They become free agents if not traded by March 15 of the following season.)

Nine months later, in November 1976, in a draft of free agents, Reggie Jackson signed a five-year contract valued at $2.9 million with the New York Yankees.

Resurrection City *See* **Poor People's Campaign.**

Retired Senior Volunteer Program (RSVP) One of the fastest growing programs administered by **ACTION**, the umbrella agency established by President Richard M. Nixon in July 1971 to coordinate volunteer programs, RSVP was designed to enable retired persons to offer part-time services in social welfare agencies, schools, museums, libraries, hospitals, and nursing homes. Participants are paid only for their transportation costs and on-site meals.

Revenue Sharing In his State of the Union Message of Janurary 22, 1971, President Richard M. Nixon called for an at-least-16-billion-dollar annual program "to reverse the flow of power and resources from the states and communities to Washington and start power and resources flowing back from Washington to the states and communities and, more important, to the people all over America." Citing "six great goals" in domestic legislation also touching on welfare reform, full-employment, environmental cleanup, national health insurance, and federal reform, he announced a "New American Revolution" that would be "as exciting as the first revolution almost two hundred years ago."

Automatic grants to the states and cities to administer at their own discretion were intended to promote "the **New Federalism**" by checking the growth of central power and increasing the responsibility of local communities in the areas of health, housing, welfare, and education. Since they would also tend to sap the power of various congressional committees, there was considerable opposition from the legislators; however, public enthusiasm for the program, as well as pressure from the governors and mayors of both the Republican and Democratic parties, resulted in legislation (October 20, 1972) under which more than $30 billion in federal tax revenues would be used to supplement state and local revenues over a five-year period.

Additional legislation approved by Congress on September 30, 1976, provided $25.6 billion for general revenue sharing from January 1, 1977 to September 30, 1980. The act eliminates previous limitations on local uses of the money, which can now be spent on any high-priority program. Many critics have attacked the legislation as a "handout" backed by no overall policy.

To a ban on bias based on race, national origin, or sex, the General Revenue Sharing bill of 1976 added the prohibition of discrimination because of age, religion, or a handicap. A state or locality found to be in violation of the antidiscrimination rules can lose all of its general revenue-sharing allotment.

First proposed in the 1950s by Rep. Melvin R. Laird (R.-Wis.) revenue sharing had also been advocated under the Johnson administration by Walter Heller, presiding officer of the **Council of Economic Advisers**. Pressure from organized labor was said to have caused its rejection by President Lyndon B. Johnson at that time (1964).

"Reverse discrimination" *See* **Affirmative Action**.

"Revolt of the Admirals" Secretary of Defense Louis A. Johnson, who had succeeded James V. Forrestal in March 1949, announced on April 22 that construction of the 65,000-ton supercarrier *United States* was to be abandoned only five days after the keel had been laid at Newport News, Virginia, in the face of opposition by the Air Force, which favored the use of B-36 land-based, long-range bombers. In protest, Secretary of the Navy John L. Sullivan resigned three days later.

Meanwhile, on March 5, 1949, President Harry S Truman had requested legislation revising the **National Security Act** of 1947, the weaknesses of which had led to interservice rivalry that had caused Forrestal, broken in health, to resign. Navy proponents began alleging irregularities in the Air Force's B-36 procurement program and to raise questions of the bomber's combat effectiveness.

"Some newspapers and radio," wrote President Truman in 1956, "were used to level insinuations of improper conduct against almost everyone who favored unification policies that in any way restricted the Navy." With Secretary Sullivan's resignation, the battle took on "the aspects of a revolt of the entire Navy." To restore discipline, the President replaced Admiral Louis E. Denfeld as Chief of Naval Operations.

On August 10, 1949, President Truman signed into law the National Security Act Amendments of 1949 under which the National Military Establishment was renamed the Department of National Defense. The new legislation increased the authority of the Defense Secretary and reduced the Department of the Navy from Cabinet to departmental rank.

Revolutionary Action Movement (RAM) This group of black militants first began attracting attention in 1963. Espousing a basic program of terrorism and assassination, it despised nonviolence as nonproductive and emasculating. It took a Marxist-Leninist orientation from Robert F. Williams, who though he had fled to Cuba in 1961 to escape FBI kidnapping charges remained an important intellectual leader among black revolutionaries and was later to become the president *in absentia* of the **Republic of New Africa** (RNA).

RAM hoped to build a "black liberation army" based on guerrilla groups to be formed in urban ghettos. In June 1967 its leaders were arrested in New York and Philadelphia, the police haul netting weapons and communications equipment, as well as a quantity of heroin. A few months later, more RAM members were arrested in Philadelphia; they had in their possession 300 grams of potassium cyanide with which, police charged, they had planned to poison the local water supply.

When RNA was established in 1968, it absorbed those RAM members still at liberty.

Reynolds v. Sims Helped to establish the principle of "one man, one vote" by holding that both legislative houses of states must be apportioned according to equal population. The suit was originally brought in an Alabama federal district court by M. O. Sims and others against a probate judge (Reynolds) and others responsible for administering Alabama election laws. Contrary to state law, which required a reapportionment of the legislature every ten years, there had been no substantial reapportionment during a sixty-year period in which Alabama's population—especially in urban areas—has approximately doubled. Sims and the other plaintiffs came from highly urbanized counties and they contended that they had been the victims of serious discrimination. At issue were existing apportionment provisions and two new plans which failed to provide for apportionment on the basis of population. After the district court ruled all three schemes unconstitutional, the case went to the Supreme Court on direct appeal.

Reynolds v. Sims and other apportionment cases in 1964 brought the so-called **Warren Court** into serious conflict with Congress, as many legislators saw that the doctrine expounded by the Court in these decisions could jeopardize their seats by bringing about a shift in power from rural areas to urban centers. In that year, the House of Representatives passed a bill designed to nullify the Court's reapportionment rulings by revoking the jurisdiction of federal courts in redistricting cases. After the failure of a compromise Senate bill that would have postponed federal court proceedings on redistricting until January 1966, Congress passed a watered-down resolution requesting that states be given a minimum of one legislative session plus thirty days to meet the one man, one vote requirement enunciated by the Supreme Court.

See Baker v. Carr, Wesberry v. Sanders.

Ridgway-Gavin Report After the fall of Dien Bien Phu in 1954 and the crushing defeat of the French in Indochina, Vietnam was divided at the 17th parallel and Ho Chi Minh became president of North Vietnam. (A year later Premier Ngo Dinh Diem became president of South Vietnam.)

Army Chief of Staff General Matthew Ridgway and Army Chief of Plans and Development Lt. General James Gavin made a study for President Dwight D. Eisenhower on the feasibility of American action in Indochina. Their report pointed out that modern military forces could not operate efficiently in the area without an engineering and logis-

tical effort that would dwarf the cost of the war in Korea. The factors they pointed out are said to have confirmed the President's feelings about the inadvisability of intervention.

"Right-to-Die" Legislation *See* **Quinlan Case**.

"Right to Know" *See* **Pentagon Papers**.

"Right-to-Work" Laws *See* **Taft-Hartley Act**.

Rio Pact "With the North Atlantic Treaty and the corresponding Western Hemisphere arrangement concluded at Rio de Janeiro," wrote President Harry S Truman, "we gave proof of our determination to stand by the free countries to resist armed aggression from any quarter."

Signed at the conclusion of the Inter-American Defense Conference in the Brazilian capital on September 2, 1947, the Inter-American Treaty of Reciprocal Assistance was the world's first regional defense and peace-keeping alliance under Articles 51-54 of the United Nations Charter. It fulfilled the treaty pledge of the **Act of Chapultepec** (March 3, 1945) by which all of the American republics except Argentina adopted a regional security agreement that was binding for the duration of World War II.

The terms of the Rio Pact, signed by 103 delegates of the nineteen nations meeting in Rio de Janeiro, provided for peaceful settlement, before reference to the United Nations, of disputes between the signatory nations, and emphasized that in uniting for mutual defense against aggression these nations agreed that an armed attack against one American state was to be considered an attack against all American states. Should fighting break out between American states, the nation which rejected pacifying action would lay itself open to the charge of aggression. Article 9 covered regions "under the effective jurisdiction of another state" and thus made the treaty apply to interests beyond the Western Hemisphere.

Nations included in the pact were: the Dominican Republic, Guatemala, Costa Rica, Peru, El Salvador, Panama, Paraguay, Venezuela, Chile, Honduras, Cuba, Bolivia, Colombia, Mexico, Haiti, Uruguay, Argentina, Brazil and the United States. Provision was made for later adherence by Nicaragua, Ecuador, and Canada. Before signing, President Truman told the final session of the conference that their meeting strengthened the fabric of the United Nations and made it "clear to any possible aggressor that the American Republics are determined to support one another against attacks. . . ."

RNA *See* **Republic of New Africa.**

Robin Hood Incident In 1953, with **McCarthyism** and anticommunist hysteria at its height, Mrs. Thomas J. White, a member of Indiana's State Textbook Commission, asserted that "there is a Communist directive in education now to stress the story of Robin Hood. They want to stress it because he robbed the rich and gave it to the poor. That's the Communist line. It's just a smearing of law and order."

Indiana's Governor George Craig refused to comment on Mrs. White's charge, but the State Superintendant of Education promised to reread the children's classic with her points in mind.

Rock-and-Roll A musical style that came into prominence in the 1950s, it was a combination of country, folk, and blues played at driving rhythms and high amplification that became the despair of the "older generation." Originally associated with black musicians and audiences, it was baptized "rock 'n roll" by white disc jockey Alan Freed, who featured it on his nightly "Moondog Rock 'n Roll Party" aired from Cleveland and, after 1954, from New York. Freed, who successfully filed for a copyright on the term "rock 'n roll," became a center of controversy after a 1958 Boston riot at one of his presentations. He was later to figure prominently in the 1960 "**payola**" scandals centering on the recording and broadcasting industries.

(*American Hot Wax*, a 1978 movie directed by Floyd Mutrux, offered a manicured version of Freed's career by presenting him—in 1962 he received a six-month suspended sentence for accepting $30,650 in bribes from record companies—as the victim of racist machinations.)

Rock-and-roll was given a boost by the enormous success of the "Heartbreak Hotel" recording made by Elvis Presley late in the decade. The rise of groups such as the Beatles and the Rolling Stones also contributed to the trend.

Texts, often sung in a combination of speech and falsetto, generally focused on the sentimental problems of the young, but sometimes dealt with social problems. After 1960, rock-and-roll was associated with dances such as "The Twist"—invented by black pop singer Chubby Checker (*see* **Peppermint Lounge**) and taken up by the **Jet Set**.

Rock-and-roll was eventually known simply as "rock," of which the various subcategories were the "folk rock," exemplified by Bob Dylan and emphasizing poetic ballads of social protest and emotional despair; "acid rock," characterized by the emotional intensity of electronic instruments; "raga rock," which highlighted the use of exotic instruments such as the Indian sitar; and "hard rock," in which the focus was on a strong beat.

Rockefeller Commission An eight-member blue-ribbon panel chaired by Vice President Nelson A. Rockefeller, it was appointed on January 5, 1975, by President Gerald R. Ford, and assigned to investigate whether the **CIA** had, in the course of its domestic activities, exceeded its statutory authority; to determine whether existing safeguards precluded agency activities that might go beyond its authority; and to make appropriate recommendations for necessary safeguards and changes. In its final report, made public on June 10, 1975, the commission concluded that while the "great majority" of the CIA's domestic activities since its establishment in 1947 had been in compliance with its statutory authority, it had on occasion engaged in practices that were "plainly unlawful and constituted improper invasions upon the rights of Americans." The report included thirty recommendations—ranging from restructuring the internal organization of the CIA to strengthening congressional and executive supervision—designed to prevent and check on any possible future excesses.

The commission focused particular attention on the fact that in August 1967 the CIA had violated its charter by establishing a Special Operations Group (*see* **Operation Chaos**) "to collect information on dissident Americans from CIA field stations overseas and from the FBI." It also charged that at various times between 1952 and 1974 the CIA had illegally opened the mail of American citizens, undertaken unlawful wiretaps and electronic surveillance, planned and executed criminal break-ins, and planted its agents in a number of domestic political groups. Taking note of "numerous allegations" of CIA participation in the assassination of President John F. Kennedy (*see* **November 22, 1963**), the report stated that "on the basis of the staff's investigation, the commission concludes that there is no credible evidence of CIA involvement."

Because he felt that the data were "incomplete and extremely sensitive," President Ford, to whom the commission's report had been submitted on June 6, did not make public that section dealing with charges that the CIA had been involved in assassination plots against foreign leaders and heads of states. However, the report as released did contain information on a drug-testing program in which the agency's Directorate of Science and Technology administered hallucinogens such as LSD to persons who were unaware that they were being tested. In at least one case, the report disclosed, a psychotic reaction by the subject being tested led to his death (1953).

Attention was also focused by the report on the CIA's Office of Security, which is charged with providing safety to persons who have defected to the United States. While most defectors were "processed and placed into society in a few months," the commission noted, in one case a man was kept for three years "in solitary confinement under spartan living conditions."

The report also disclosed that during his term in office President Richard M. Nixon had made use of the CIA to obtain data of potential use against his political opponents. In addition, at the request of the White House, in 1970 the CIA contributed $38,655 to the cost of replying to those who wrote the President after the **Cambodia "incursion."**

Members of the Rockefeller Commission included: John T. Connor, chairman of Allied Chemical Corp. and Secretary of Commerce under President Johnson; Douglas Dillon, managing director of Dillon, Read & Co. and Secretary of the Treasury during both the Kennedy and Johnson administrations; Erwin N. Griswold, Solicitor General in both the Kennedy and Johnson administrations; Lane Kirkland, Secretary-Treasurer of the AFL-CIO; General Lyman L. Lemnitzer, former Chairman of the Joint Chiefs of Staff in the Kennedy administration; Ronald Reagan, former actor and former governor of California; and Edgar F. Shannon, Jr., former president of the University of Virginia. Liberals complained that the panel was not an adequate cross section of the country.

Rockefeller Foundation "To promote the well-being of mankind throughout the world," this organization, established by John D. Rockefeller in 1913 with the help of Baptist clergyman and administrator Frederick Taylor Gates, had by the mid-seventies paid out more than $1.25 billion in income and principal. Initially concerned primarily with medical advances and public health—it joined the National Research Council in supplementing the funding that led to the *Kinsey Report* in 1948—it now makes study awards available to those work-

ing in the fields of education and the arts as well. In addition to making its own grants, it supports other agencies working in these fields. It was with funds from the foundation that in 1954 the Louisville (Kentucky) Orchestra began commissioning original compositions by contemporary musicians.

Since World War II, the foundation has focused mainly on the solution of scientific problems confronting the developing nations.

Roots This 1976 bestseller by black writer Alex Haley (see *The Autobiography of Malcolm X*) is a somewhat fictionalized account of the journey of his ancestor, Kunta Kinte from that portion of Africa which is currently Gambia, to a life of slavery in the United States. The book was awarded a Pulitzer Prize and was the basis of an eight-part television series early in 1977 which attracted audiences of up to 36,380,000.

Defended by Mr. Haley as "a symbolic history of a people," *Roots* attracted two plagiarism suits from novelists who claimed that it had infringed on their copyright. In April 1977, Margaret Walker Alexander, a professor at Mississippi's Jackson State College (*see* **Jackson State Tragedy**) filed a suit claiming that portions of the book were based on her 1966 novel *Jubilee*, a fictionalized account of her great grandmother's life as a slave in Georgia. The suit was dismissed in September 1978 on the grounds that the similarities between the two books were insignificant. A suit by Harold Courtlander, who claimed that portions of *Roots* were taken from his novel *The African* (1966), was settled out of court in December 1978 when Mr. Haley conceded that three passages, apparently supplied by student researchers who aided him, came from the earlier novel.

In February 1979, the television sequel *Roots II*—seven two-hour episodes—attracted a total audience of 110 million as against 130 million for *Roots*.

Rosenberg Case When Igor Gouzenko, a cipher clerk in the Russian Embassy in Ottawa, Canada, defected to the West in September 1945, he took with him documentary evidence of a nuclear spy ring. This information led to the arrest in England first of Allan Nunn May (March 1946), who in 1943 and after had been a member of the British team of atomic physicists in Canada, and then of Klaus Fuchs (February 1950), head of the British Atomic Energy Centre at Harwell. In his confession to the British authorities, Fuchs, who had been active on the Manhattan Project at Los Alamos until mid-

1946, identified Harry Gold, a Philadelphia chemist, as a courier for the spy ring. From Gold the trail led to David Greenglass, who in 1944–1945 had been an army sergeant assigned to Los Alamos. Greenglass, in turn, implicated his sister, Mrs. Ethel Rosenberg, and her husband, Julius, who he said had recruited him as a spy and directed his activities. The FBI arrested Julius Rosenberg in New York City in July 1950, and his wife was taken into custody the following month.

The Rosenbergs were tried in New York in March 1951 and, having been found guilty of espionage, were sentenced to death (April 5, 1951) by U.S. District Judge Irving R. Kaufman, who said: "By your betrayal you undoubtedly have altered the course of history to the disadvantage of our country." (Gold, Greenglass, and another member of the ring, Morton Sobell—all of whom, unlike the Rosenbergs, confessed—had received prison terms.) The trial and sentencing received international attention, and there were accusations that the Rosenbergs had been framed. Even many who were convinced of their guilt argued that the sentence was unusually harsh and that the information passed by them—of particular importance were drawings of a high-explosive lens used for detonation—had merely hastened the inevitable Soviet acquisition of the atomic bomb, since the Russians already possessed the basic theoretical data.

During the next two years there were four stays of execution as all legal resources were exhausted. The convictions were upheld by the U.S. Court of Appeals in February 1952, and several fruitless attempts were made to have the Supreme Court intervene. Meanwhile, pro-Rosenberg sympathizers all over the world held protest meetings and staged anti-American demostrations.

On several occasions appeals for executive clemency were made to President Dwight D. Eisenhower, who though he found it went "against the grain to avoid interfering in the case where a woman is to receive capital punishment," nevertheless decided against the Rosenbergs. On February 11, 1953, he issued a statement saying that the "nature of the crime for which they have been found guilty and sentenced far exceeds that of the taking of the life of another citizen; it involves the deliberate betrayal of the entire nation and could very well result in the death of many, many thousands of innocent citizens . . ."

On May 25, 1953, the Supreme Court refused to hear an appeal, and on June 15 it denied a plea to once again stay execution. A stay was, however, granted by Justice William O. Douglas on June 17 to consider a point of law. Defense attorneys charged that the Rosenbergs had been tried under the Espionage Act of 1917 and should have been tried under the **Atomic Energy Act of 1946**, which would have allowed the judge to impose the death penalty only if it had been recommended by the jury. No such recommendation had been made.

However, on June 19, 1953, the Supreme Court voted six to two to vacate the stay of execution. (Justice Felix Frankfurter declined to vote since he felt that the Court had not taken sufficient time to review the issue.) On that same day the Rosenbergs became the first Americans ever to be executed for treason. The execution touched off a series of anti-American riots reminiscent of those that followed the execution of Sacco and Vanzetti in 1927.

Gold, Greenglass, Sobell, and the Rosenbergs had been part of a major Soviet spy ring operated in the United States by Major Anatoli A. Yakovlev during World War II when the two countries were allies. Yakovlev had been Soviet vice-consul in New York.

Rostow-Taylor Mission *See* **Taylor-Rostow Mission**.

Roth v. United States The fundamental constitutionality of obscenity legislation was upheld by the U.S. Supreme Court on June 24, 1957. With Justices Hugo Black and William O. Douglas dissenting and Chief Justice Earl Warren concurring only in the result, the Court found that such legislation was not inconsistent with the guarantees of free speech in the First Amendment. The Court declared that the test of obscenity was "whether to the average person, applying contemporary community standards, the dominant theme of the material taken as a whole appeals to prurient interest."

The new ruling rejected the historic *Regina v. Hicklin* case (1868) in which the test for obscenity given was whether "the tendency of the matter charged . . . is to deprave and corrupt those whose minds are open to such immoral influences, and into whose hands . . . [it] may fall."

Under the *Roth* ruling, the Court later (March 21, 1966) upheld (five to four) the five-year conviction of Ralph Ginzburg, publisher of *Eros* magazine and *The Housewife's Handbook of Selective Promiscuity*, finding that the intent and the promotion of the material had to be taken into account. Dissenting, Justice Douglas noted that under such an interpretation works such as the Bible's *Song of*

Solomon could lose the Court's protection by being incorrectly advertised. He observed that the ruling "condemns an advertising technique as old as history." In his dissent, Justice Black said that "the Federal Government is without power whatever under the Constitution to put any type of burden on speech and expression of ideas of any kind . . ."

On the same day it handed down the Ginzburg ruling, the Court upheld the three-year prison sentence of Edward Mishkin, who had been convicted of violating New York obscenity laws by publishing "sadistic and masochistic" material; however, by six to three it reversed a Massachusetts court ruling that John Cleland's *Memoirs of a Woman of Pleasure* (an eighteenth-century novel popularly known as *Fanny Hill*) was obscene. In all three cases the majority opinion was written by Justice William J. Brennan and cited the 1957 *Roth* decision. In reversing the lower court's ruling against *Fanny Hill*, Justice Brennan noted that the Court's decision might have been otherwise if the book had been "exploited by panderers."

Critics have found the *Roth* decision confusing because of the vagueness of such concepts as "the average person," "contemporary community standards," and "prurient interest." In the *Mishkin* case there was less ambiguity, apparently, because the Court found that the material was designed for "a clearly defined deviant sexual group, rather than the public at large . . ."

Rowe-Ramspeck-DeCourcy Committee In December 1949, Secretary of State Dean Acheson, who had been vice-chairman of the 1947 **Hoover Commission**, appointed another former member, James H. Rowe, Jr., to head a committee that was to advise him on how to put into force the commission's recommendations dealing with the amalgamation of the State Department and the Foreign Service. The committee, made up of Rowe, Robert Ramspeck, chairman of the Civil Service Commission, and Foreign Services Ambassador William S. DeCourcy, reported in August 1950, endorsing a unified service and recommending that it be established by law. Additional points in its report dealt with the recruitment of personnel.

Only some of the minor recommendations were followed; Secretary Acheson explained this by pointing to the pressure that both the Foreign Service and the State Department were under due to attacks by Sen. Joseph R. McCarthy (R.-Wis.). It was not until after the **Wriston Committee** in 1954 that some degree of amalgamation was achieved.

RSVP *See* **Retired Senior Volunteer Program**.

Ruby II *See* **Dirty Tricks**.

S

Silent Spring

Sabin Vaccine *See* **Salk Vaccine.**

SAC *See* **Strategic Air Command.**

Sacred Cow The name given to the C-54 that served as the special plane of President Harry S Truman. It was objected to by some as being offensive.

During Christmas 1945, President Truman insisted on taking off from Washington National Airport for Kansas City, Missouri, although all commercial planes had been grounded by rain and sleet. The *Sacred Cow* was one hour and nineteen minutes late and the entire country spent a nervous afternoon. Later, Lt. Colonel Henry T. Myers, the plane's pilot, pointed out that the presidential C-54 had considerably more power and a higher operating ceiling than most commercial airliners.

Safeguard ABM System *See* **Antiballistic Missile System.**

Safe Streets Act *See* **Johnson Crime Commission.**

St. Lawrence Seaway Since the early days of the century, attempts had been made to pass legislation that would permit cooperation with Canada in a project designed to deepen the St. Lawrence River so that seagoing ships could sail from the Atlantic, through the Great Lakes, and into the heart of the Middle West—a distance of more than 2,000 miles. One such treaty had fallen short of Senate approval by twelve votes, and seaway bills had been bottled up in committee in 1948 and 1952. However, when in January 1953 President Dwight D. Eisenhower once more proposed such a bill, Congress had to face the fact that failure to pass the necessary legislation would result in Canada's building the seaway on her own side of the border, thus leaving the United States without a voice in its control and operation.

The President had long favored such a project, and as Chief of Staff of the Army (1945-1948) he had argued that it would strengthen the security of both nations. He now felt that "while certain interests, primarily Eastern seaports and the railways of that region, might suffer some disadvantages," the nation would benefit on the overall. He insisted, however, that the seaway pay for itself through tolls.

On May 13, 1954, he signed into law the Wiley-Dondero bill authorizing him to set up the St. Lawrence Seaway Development Corp., which was to be financed by a 105-million-dollar bond issue. The

seaway, to be built in cooperation with Canada, would develop the 114-mile stretch of the St. Lawrence between Montreal and Ogdensburg, New York, so that it could be navigated by seagoing vessels. Canada was to build five locks, the U.S. two—Bertrand D. Snell Lock and the Dwight D. Eisenhower Lock—as well as other improvements. Responsibility for an at-least-twenty-five-foot-deep seaway from Duluth, Minnesota, to the Atlantic was to be Canada's share of the project.

Informally opened to shipping in April 1959, the St. Lawrence Seaway was officially inaugurated June 26, 1959, when President and Mamie Eisenhower joined Great Britain's Queen Elizabeth and Prince Philip on a five-hour cruise through the first three sets of locks. Afterward, the Queen and her party continued the voyage to the Eisenhower Lock and disembarked in New York.

Closely associated with the seaway project was the construction of a hydroelectric development between Cornwall, Ontario, and Ogdensburg, New York, capable of generating 1.8 million kilowatts for use in both the United States and Canada. (Only Washington's Grand Coulee Dam had a greater capacity—1.947 million kilowatts.) The international power pool was established with contributions from the Hydro-Electric Power Commission of Ontario and the Power Authority of the State of New York, each of which gave approximately $300 million.

The total cost of the seaway itself was $470 million, of which the United States paid $130 million. Before the opening of the seaway the annual volume of cargo carried along its stretch was 13 million tons; in the first year of the improved seaway's operation cargo tonnage climbed to nearly 21 million.

Salk Vaccine In 1953, Dr. Jonas E. Salk reported on the development of a triple vaccine for the prevention of poliomyelitis. It consisted of a mixture of three types of polio virus that had been separately cultivated in monkey tissue and then inactivated with formaldehyde. Administration was by means of three injections at intervals of up to six months, followed by annual booster shots.

A program of inoculating school children was begun in Pittsburgh on February 23, 1954, and by April 1955 tests in most states had proved the effectiveness of the vaccine, which is said to provide a 90-percent-effective protection against paralyzation.

An orally administered live vaccine developed by the Russian-born American researcher Dr. Albert B. Sabin in 1953 is said to give longer-lasting protection and provide complete immunity with absolute safety. A safeguard against both infection and paralysis, it is widely used in the Soviet Union.

SALT *See* **Strategic Arms Limitations Talk.**

SAM *See* **Surface-to-Air Missile.**

Samos Satellites *See* **Project Sentry.**

San Antonio Formula "The United States is willing to stop all aerial and naval bombardment of North Vietnam when this will lead promptly to productive discussion. We, of course, assume that while discussions proceed, North Vietnam would not take advantage of the bombing cessation or limitation."

Speaking before the National Legislative Conference in San Antonio (September 29, 1967) during the **Vietnam War,** President Lyndon B. Johnson made public an offer that had been conveyed to North Vietnamese representatives in Paris through French intermediaries. One of several efforts made by the Johnson administration to bring the North Vietnamese to the negotiating table as the unpopular war dragged on, it softened a proposal made and rejected earlier in the year. As President Johnson later wrote, the United States was no longer asking Ho Chi Minh to restrict his military actions as the price for a bombing halt. In addition, once the bombing had been terminated the North Vietnamese were not required to stop all military action but merely not to increase it. "All we asked was that a cessation of the bombing would lead promptly to peace talks and that those talks would be 'productive.'"

After the failure of United States efforts to obtain satisfactory peace talks, the bombing of Hanoi and the surrounding area, which had halted on August 24, 1967, was resumed on October 23, 1967.

In January 1968, the North Vietnamese launched their famous **Tet offensive** in South Vietnam.

Saturday Night Massacre By May 1, 1973, the **Watergate Scandal** had assumed such proportions that a bipartisan group of Senators endorsed a resolution calling for a Special Prosecutor whose job it would be to bring suit against anyone found to have been involved in criminal activities during the 1972 presidential campaign. To fill this office, Attorney General Elliot L. Richardson named Archibald Cox, one of his former law professors at Harvard University.

Cox and the White House came into conflict when on July 25, 1973, Presidential Counsel J. Fred Buzhardt, Jr., rejected a subpoena for nine of the so-called **Nixon tapes**. The Special Prosecutor pushed his demand before Judge John J. Sirica, who on August 29 rejected the White House pleas that to surrender the tapes would be an infringement of "executive privilege." This district court decision was taken to the court of appeals in Washington, which on October 12, after trying to arrange for some compromise that would avoid a clash, ordered that the tapes be turned over to Judge Sirica by October 19.

Cox rejected a White House compromise under which an "authenticated summary" of the tapes would be supplied, and President Nixon then ordered the Attorney General to fire him. But Richardson, having pledged to both the Senate and Cox that the latter could not be removed except for "extraordinary improprieties," refused to follow this executive order—and Cox refused to resolve the situation by resigning. As Richardson saw it, he had no alternative but to resign himself, which he did on Saturday, October 20, 1973. The White House then called upon Deputy Attorney General William D. Ruckelshaus to fire Cox, but he too refused and resigned in protest. The same instructions were then given Solicitor General Robert H. Bork, who as Acting Attorney General fired Cox.

The resignations of Richardson and Ruckelshaus, the firing of Cox, the temporary elimination of the office of Special Prosecutor, and the sealing of all records by the FBI were announced by the White House that same evening. Much to President Nixon's surprise, a "firestorm" of protest swept the nation, and the White House and Congress were deluged by telegrams condemning what almost immediately came to be known as the "Saturday Night Massacre." In addition, the nation's leading newspapers called for the President's resignation or impeachment. When Leon Jaworski was named Special Prosecutor to replace Cox, he continued to press for the tapes, and on July 24 the U.S. Supreme Court unanimously ordered President Nixon to surrender all tapes and other subpoenaed material to Cox. After the tapes revealed that shortly following the Watergate break-in President Nixon had ordered a halt to an FBI probe of the incident, on August 9, 1974, Richard M. Nixon became the first U.S. President to resign and Vice President Gerald R. Ford was sworn into office.

SCAP *See* **Supreme Commander for Allied Powers.**

SCLC *See* **Southern Christian Leadership Conference.**

Scope Code name assigned to a program under which the FBI wiretapped the Israeli embassy in Washington during the administrations of Presidents Lyndon B. Johnson and Richard M. Nixon. The program was first exposed in *The New York Times* on May 22, 1973.

SCORE *See* **Service Corps of Retired Executives.**

Scranton Commission In the wake of the tragedies at Ohio's **Kent State** University and Mississippi's **Jackson State** College, on June 13, 1970, President Richard M. Nixon established a special nine-member President's Commission on Campus Unrest headed by William W. Scranton, former governor of Pennsylvania. Reporting to President Nixon on September 26, 1970, the Scranton Commission emphasized that "campus unrest reflects and increases a more profound crisis in the nation as a whole. . . . Much of the nation is so polarized that on many campuses a major domestic conflict or an unpopular initiation in foreign policy could trigger further violent protest and, in its wake, counter-violence and repression."

The commission noted that campus protest had been focused on three major questions: "War, racial injustice and the university itself." While emphasizing the right to peaceful protest, it criticized student militants for "a growing lack of tolerance, a growing insistence that their own views must govern, an impatience . . . of liberal democracy, a growing denial of the humanity and good will of those who urge patience and restraint, and particularly of those whose duty it is to enforce the law." At the same time, it felt that "many Americans have reacted to this emerging [student] culture with an intolerance of their own. They reject not only that which is impatient, unrestrained and intolerant in the new culture of the young, but that which is good. Worse, they reject the individual members of the student culture." Warning against both "a nation that has lost the allegiance of part of its youth" as well as against young people who have "become intolerant of diversity, intolerant of the rest of [a nation's] citizenry, and intolerant of all traditional values simply because they are traditional," the report emphasized that "violence must end. . . . Reconciliation must begin."

On October 1, 1970, in a special report on the killing of two black students at Jackson State College the previous May fourteenth, the Scranton Commission found: "Even if there were sniper fire at Jackson State—a question on which we found conflicting evidence—the 28-second barrage of lethal gunfire partly directed into crowded windows of Alexander Hall was completely unwarranted and unjustified." Jackson State officials were urged to develop plans and procedures for dealing with campus disorders. At the same time, the report emphasized, students had to recognize that the use of obscenities and derogatory terms such as "pigs" and "honkies" may trigger "a violent—if unjustifiable—response by peace officers. . . ."

A third report, issued by the commission on October 4, 1970, covered the killing of four students at Kent State University on May 4, 1970—when National Guardsmen opened fire on a student demonstration against the **Cambodian "incursion"** announced by President Nixon several days earlier—and noted while the "conduct of many students and nonstudent protesters at Kent State on the first four days of May, 1970, was plainly intolerable," the Guardsmen should not have been "able to kill so easily in the first place. The general issuance of loaded weapons to law-enforcement officers engaged in controlling disorders is never justified, except in the case of armed resistance. . . ." No evidence of a sniper attack on the Guardsmen was found. "The Kent State tragedy must surely mark the last time that loaded rifles are issued as a matter of course to Guardsmen confronting student demonstrators."

SDS *See* **Students for a Democratic Society.**

The Search for Bridey Murphy National newspaper syndication of this account by Colorado business executive Morey Bernstein of hypnotism and reincarnation made this 1956 bestseller a topic of widespread speculation by both believers and debunkers. The book is based on tape recordings said to have been made during six occasions when housewife Ruth Simmons—the name is a pseudonym—was placed under hypnosis by self-taught practitioner Bernstein. In a state of trance Mrs. Simmons was said to be able to recall events from a previous life as one Bridey Murphy in Cork, Ireland, some 100 years ago. Efforts were also made by the author-hypnotist to have her recall a life in New Amsterdam at an even earlier period.

Although Ruth Simmons had been raised by Scandinavians, it was later discovered that both her parents and foster parents had Irish backgrounds. Skeptics suggested that in this way she might have unconsciously imbibed the details of Irish local color that made her trance sessions so convincing. Said Yale University psychologist John Dollard: "We may be reasonably sure . . . that a searching psychological study of the subject would take all the 'mystery' out of this case. It would also reveal the remarkable power of the unconscious mental life to bilk not only a naïve hypnotist, but also the subject."

SEATO *See* **Southeast Asia Treaty Organization.**

Sedan Chair "After that fall [1971] we set up our 'Sedan Chair' program of harassment against Democratic contenders," wrote Jeb Stuart Magruder, deputy director of the **Committee to Reelect the President** (CREEP; CRP). He noted that the plan to forward the reelection of President Richard M. Nixon in 1972 by sabotaging the campaigns of his potential Democratic opponents grew out of talks with presidential appointments secretary Dwight L. Chapin, who was fascinated with "black advances," or what came to be known as **"dirty tricks."** The first part of the plan, the code name of which derived from a military exercise in which Herbert L. ("Bart") Porter, CREEP scheduling director, participated while a marine, consisted of hiring Roger Greaves—a friend of Ronald Walker, the President's chief advance man—to create incidents at the campaign rallies of aspirants for the Democratic presidential nomination (Sedan Chair I). Later, Michael McKinoway, a former Kentucky detective, worked briefly in the Philadelphia headquarters of Hubert H. Humphrey (Sedan Chair II).

According to Magruder, the Sedan Chair operation lasted three months and cost $3,800.

"See It Now" Adapting his popular radio news show "Hear It Now" to television in 1951, veteran reporter Edward R. Murrow joined with Fred Friendly—later president of CBS News—in producing "See It Now," a provocative weekly news program based on the premise that it was the journalist's role to bring problems in American society to the attention of the general public. Establishing a bold style for a medium that considered its principal function to be noncontroversial entertainment, Murrow was the first to report on the relationship between cigarette smoking and cancer, and in December 1952 he brought his cameras to the front in the **Korean War.** In October 1953, "See It Now" reported on the case of Milo Radulovich, a University of Michigan senior who after years of active service in the Air Force Reserve was forced to resign his lieutenant's commission after charges—whose source and substance were never revealed—that he had been in close association with Communists or

Communist sympathizers. (Secretary of the Air Force Harold E. Talbott restored Radulovich's commission several weeks later.) Probably the most famous broadcast took place on March 9, 1954, when Murrow focused on the threat to American civil liberties posed by the activities of Wisconsin's Senator Joseph R. McCarthy (*see* **McCarthyism**), who later refused an opportunity to reply to the charges. That episode, which in New York and San Francisco caused a flood of phone calls to CBS supporting Murrow's presentation by a fifteen-to-one margin, is often credited with having significantly contributed to the Senator's downfall.

Because of its controversial nature, "See It Now" made television executives uncomfortable, and in 1958 it was converted into a series of specials entitled "CBS Reports," which men in the broadcast media bitterly dubbed "See It Now and Then."

During the Kennedy administration, Murrow, who had denounced the television industry for encouraging "decadence, escapism and insulation from the realities of the world," left CBS to become director of the **U.S. Information Agency** (USIA), a position which he held until 1964, one year before his death from lung cancer. (He smoked a minimum of three packs a day.)

Murrow made his international reputation with a series of dramatic but accurate broadcasts from Nazi-blitzed London during World War II, many of the events of which he and Fred Friendly included in a series of phonograph recordings which in 1948 began appearing under the title "I Can Hear It Now." Two years after launching "See It Now," he inaugurated the popular and profitable television interview program known as "Person-to-Person," in which the camera took viewers on a guided tour of the homes of such celebrities as Elizabeth Taylor or the Duke and Duchess of Windsor.

Select Committee on Presidential Campaign Activities Popularly known as the Ervin or Watergate Committee, it was established by a Senate vote on February 7, 1973, to investigate events stemming from the break-in of the Washington offices of the Democratic National Committee on June 17, 1972 (*see* **Watergate Scandal**). The seven-member committee, which held televised public hearings from May 17 to August 7 and again from September 24 to November 15, was chaired by Sen. Sam J. Ervin, Jr. (D.-N.C.), and included Sen. Howard H. Baker, Jr. (R.-Tenn.), Sen. Herman E. Talmadge (D.-Ga.), Sen. Daniel K. Inouye (D.-Hawaii), Sen. Joseph M. Montoya (D.-N. Mex.), Sen. Edward J. Gurney (R.-

Fla.), and Sen. Lowell P. Weicker, Jr. (R.-Conn.). On July 13, 1974, they issued a final three-volume, 2,299-page report covering seventeen months of investigation. Although this document noted that the 1972 presidential campaign had been "characterized by corruption, fraud, and abuse of official power," it failed to assign individual responsibility for the situation because it had not been the committee's purpose "to determine the legal guilt or innocence of any person or whether the President should be impeached." (Senator Ervin informally noted that "some people draw a picture of a horse and then write 'horse' under it. We just drew the horse.")

The report contained more than thirty legislative proposals for reforming campaign practices, but the majority of the panel expressed opposition to publicly financed federal election campaigns. Strong recommendation was made for the creation of a permanent office of a "public prosecutor," who would function as an ombudsman and have both access to executive records and authority to investigate apparent misconduct by an administration in power.

Adding fuel to the growing campaign to impeach President Richard M. Nixon were the charges that from 1968 to 1972 his millionaire businessman friend Charles G. ("Bebe") Rebozo had, through a complex set of financial maneuverings, made more than $50,000 available to the President for his personal use. The report also charged that in 1972 the President had used $4,562 in campaign funds for the purchase of platinum-and-diamond earrings given Mrs. Nixon on her birthday.

Highlights of the Ervin Committee's public hearings include:

May 18: Convicted Watergate conspirator James W. McCord, Jr., said that he had been offered executive clemency by persons connected with the White House in exchange for his silence about the Watergate break-in.

June 14: Jeb Stuart Magruder, deputy director of the **Committee to Re-elect the President** (CREEP; CRP), implicated his boss, the former Attorney General John N. Mitchell, in the original break-in and the subsequent cover-up.

June 25: John W. Dean III, former presidential counsel, charged in a dramatic six-hour statement that President Nixon had been part of the Watergate cover-up for as long as eight months. The following day he revealed the existence of a **"White House enemies list"** of persons to be harassed by government investigators.

July 10: John N. Mitchell, former Attorney General and director of CREEP, said that he had kept from the President details of the Watergate break-in and the **"White House horror stories,"** but rejected Magruder's charges against him as a "palpable, damnable lie."

July 16: Alexander P. Butterfield, a former presidential deputy, revealed that since March 1971 the President had recorded his conversations in the White House and the Executive Office Building (*see* **Nixon Tapes**).

July 24: John D. Ehrlichman, former Assistant to the President for Domestic Affairs, designated Dean as the culprit in the cover-up following the Watergate break-in. He denied that either he or the President had authorized the burgling of Dr. Daniel Ellsberg's psychiatrist's office in September 1971, but said that such an action would have been within the President's constitutional duties and prerogatives (*see* **Pentagon Papers**).

July 30: H. R. Haldeman, former presidential Chief of Staff, confirmed earlier charges by Ehrlichman that Dean had misled the President about the Watergate affair.

Selective Patronage Program In 1960, Reverend Leon Sullivan, of the Zion Baptist Church in Philadelphia, joined with some 400 black ministers in organizing a series of boycotts designed to bring pressure on some of the city's major businesses and convince them of the necessity of hiring skilled black labor. Reverend Sullivan had drawn his inspiration from programs undertaken by Dr. Martin Luther King, Jr.'s **Southern Christian Leadership Conference** (SCLC), but it was the success of the Selective Patronage Program that caused Dr. King to invite Reverend Sullivan to Atlanta to discuss the program with local black ministers in 1962. Later the SCLC launched **Operation Breadbasket,** a program conceived along similar lines.

Sullivan claimed that by 1963 he had opened 2,000 new jobs for blacks in Philadelphia.

In March 1977, Reverend Sullivan was instrumental in getting twelve major American corporations—including IBM, General Motors, and Citicorp—to agree to support six principles aimed at ending segregation and promoting fair employment practices at their plants and other facilities in South Africa. The agreement included a pledge by these corporations to initiate training programs that would prepare blacks and other nonwhites for supervisory, administrative, clerical, and technical jobs.

"Selective Tolerance" *See* **Marcusean Revolution.**

Selma-Montgomery March After arbitrary qualification procedures, police brutality, and intimidation had defeated two years of efforts by **Southern Christian Leadership Conference** (SCLC) volunteers to add a significant number of black voters to the registration lists in Selma, Alabama, Dr. Martin Luther King, Jr. (*see* **Montgomery Bus Strike**), decided to lead his followers on a dramatic five-day, fifty-four-mile protest march from Selma to the state capital in Montgomery.

On March 21, 1965, following two previously unsuccessful attempts that focused national attention on the situation in Selma, Dr. King and more than 3,000 sympathizers started on the road to Montgomery under the protection of Alabama National Guardsmen, who had been federalized by President Lyndon B. Johnson, and U.S. Army troops. By the time they reached the capital, their number had swelled to 25,000, and among their ranks were such internationally known figures as United Nations Undersecretary Ralph J. Bunche. Along the way they had been entertained and encouraged by Harry Belafonte, Joan Baez, Sammy Davis, Jr., and Leonard Bernstein.

Dr. King carried with him a petition to Governor George C. Wallace which said: "We have come not only five days and fifty miles but we have come from three centuries of suffering and hardship. We have come . . . to declare that we must have our freedom NOW. We must have the right to vote; we must have equal protection of the law and an end to police brutality."

Although the governor agreed to receive a delegation immediately after the rally in front of the Capitol building, it was not until March 30 that a group led by Reverend Joseph E. Lowery of Birmingham gained access to him and received his assurances that he would give "careful consideration" to the petition.

The march itself had been free of violence, but on the evening it ended, Mrs. Viola G. Liuzzo, a white woman who had been active in Selma, was shot and killed as she was transporting demonstrators back to that city. Earlier that month, James J. Reeb, a Boston Unitarian minister, had died as a result of a beating from enraged local segregationists.

The first attempt to march from Selma to Montgomery had been made on March 6, but on the advice of Attorney General Nicholas Katzenbach, SCLC deputy Hosea Williams had substituted for Dr. King. After some 500 protesters were turned back on "Black Sunday" in a police free-for-all in which more than sixty blacks were hospitalized, Dr.

King immediately announced that he himself would lead a new march the following Tuesday. Some 1,500 black protesters and their white sympathizers started from Selma, but once more the marchers were turned back, this time because Dr. King felt that local authorities had set a trap for his followers a little beyond a bridge leading from Selma.

The civil rights leader came under severe criticism from militants such as Eldridge Cleaver, who felt that if he had ignored police orders and caused authorities to use force to turn back "all those nuns, priests, rabbis, preachers, and distinguished ladies and gentlemen" the ruthlessness employed would have publicly exposed the brutal methods to which segregationists were willing to resort.

See **Williams v. Wallace.**

Senator Sam North Carolina's senior Democratic senator, Sam J. Ervin, Jr., became familiar to millions of Americans as "Senator Sam" when on January 11, 1973, he agreed to become chairman of the Senate **Select Committee on Presidential Campaign Activities** which investigated the **Watergate Scandal.**

A conservative who consistently opposed civil rights legislation as an abridgement of constitutional freedoms, he had during a Senate career dating back to 1954 been unfriendly to organized labor and a firm supporter of the stand of both the Johnson and Nixon administrations during the **Vietnam War.** Nevertheless, the manner in which he conducted the Watergate investigation won the approval of the liberal community. He often disguised his outrage at statements made by Nixon officials involved in the Watergate break-in and subsequent cover-up by insisting that he was just a "country lawyer" and needed things explained to him in simple terms that he could understand. He was seventy-five when the investigation began, and though he sometimes appeared to stammer and pause, his questions tended to cut through the obfuscation of many witnesses and get right to the point they seemed to be avoiding.

As chairman of the Senate Judiciary Committee's Subcommittee on Constitutional Rights, he had before Watergate established a reputation as a strong defender of the Constitution—a copy of which he was said to have with him at all times—and a man who could be counted on to protect the rights even of those whose views he did not share. Previous to joining the Senate, he had been an Associate Justice of the North Carolina Supreme Court (1948–1954).

Sentinel ABM System *See* **Antiballistic Missile System.**

"Separate but Equal" *See* **Brown v. Board of Education of Topeka.**

Service Corps of Retired Executives (SCORE) Established in 1964 to bring the expertise of retired business executives to small business enterprises at no cost, it has since 1971 operated as part of **ACTION,** the umbrella agency set up by President Richard M. Nixon to coordinate a variety of volunteer programs. Its approximately 5,000 volunteers offer individual counseling on administrative and financial problems.

Sexual Behavior in the Human Male *See* **Kinsey Report.**

Shanghai Communiqué *See* **Peking Summit.**

SHAPE *See* **North Atlantic Treaty Organization.**

Sharon Statement *See* **Young Americans for Freedom.**

Shelley v. Kramer Covenants under which a person buying a house in a "restricted" neighborhood agreed never to sell the house to persons of specified ancestries—generally Negroes and Jews—were voided by the U.S. Supreme Court in May 1948 as being contrary to the "equal protection clause" of the Constitution's Fourteenth Amendment. During the 1960s, this ruling was to play an extremely important role in the litigation surrounding **"sit-ins"** at lunch counters. Civil rights lawyers argued that there was no distinction between a court's using its power to enforce racial discrimination and using it to enforce the now prohibited racially restrictive covenants governing the resale of property.

Sick Humor *See* **Black Humor.**

Siege of Morningside Heights In protests sparked by student and community opposition to a new $10 million gym New York's Columbia University planned to build in Morningside Heights Park on land leased from the city for $3,000 a year, black militants supported by members of the left-wing **Students for a Democratic Society** (SDS) seized several university buildings beginning on April 23, 1968, and held them until evicted by the police on April 30.

After first attempting to enter the Low Library,

where President Grayson Kirk had his offices, protesters marched to the proposed gym site and tore down the fences before taking over Hamilton Hall, headquarters of Columbia College. Soon five university buildings were in the hands of the militants, and three university officials, including Acting Dean Henry S. Coleman, were being held as "hostages." Although the latter were released after twenty-four hours, militants refused to meet with university officials until they had been given guarantees of amnesty. Meanwhile, an emergency faculty committee had met and recommended the suspension of plans to construct the gym.

Although protesters chanted "Gym Crow Must Go," the university had from the beginning announced that pool and gym facilities in the new construction would be made available free of charge to Harlem residents. But the issue went deeper than that, for there was vast resentment against the university, which—as the owner of more than $200 million in real estate—was accused of being one of the city's biggest slumlords. In addition, SDS militants led by their president, Mark Rudd, were demanding that Columbia break its ties with the Institute for Defense Analysis (IDA), which had been established on some dozen national campuses to conduct federally funded military research.

Black and white protesters had originally acted in unison, but the members of Rudd's predominantly white SDS group were soon expelled from Hamilton Hall by militants of the Students' Afro-American Society. Further splits in student ranks were demonstrated when a group of student athletes, in an unusual outburst of concern for an academic year that seemed to be going down the drain, offered to expel those occupying university property. ("If this is a barbarian society, then it's the survival of the fittest—and we're the fittest.") University officials sensibly declined the offer.

But since the occupiers refused to budge until granted amnesty, something which President Kirk felt he could not do without destroying "the whole fabric of the university community," police were called in on April 30. Through the intercession of lawyers and black community leaders, the black militants occupying Hamilton Hall left peacefully. The other buildings were cleared by 1,000 police who charged through a protective barrier formed by some of the younger faculty members in front of the Low Library—which during the occupation by militants had been renamed "Rudd Hall." Calm was restored to the campus, and SDS leader Mark

Rudd and some seventy others were suspended for a year. Some 180 students were injured and more than 600 arrested.

(In 1970, Rudd, who had joined the **Weathermen,** jumped bail in New York City with four charges stemming from 1968 still being held against him. He surrendered in September 1977 and the following month was given an unconditional discharge after pleading guilty to criminal trespassing in a pre-arranged plea bargain.)

University officials, and President Kirk in particular, were severely criticized in many quarters for their handling of the protests and their eventual decision to call in the police. Although critical of the direct-action techniques of militants, anthropologist Margaret Mead, who had been connected with Columbia for almost half a century, accused its officials of high-handedness in dealing with student demands to share in the running of the university. "We can no longer have privately endowed universities governed by boards of trustees that are not responsive to anyone but themselves," she noted angrily.

See **Cox Commission.**

Silent Generation Despairing editorial writers gave this name to the student generation that inhabited American campuses in the post-World War II years. Unlike the students of the 1960s, these young people seemed to have rejected active involvement in national and campus issues and fixed their sights almost exclusively on careers that would enable them to participate advantageously in the material benefits of American middle-class life. Social commentator John Brooks wrote in *The Great Leap* (1966):

They were in college at a time of many crucial and controversial happenings—the early bomb tests, the reconstruction of Europe, the expansion of corporations, the rise of television, the **Korean War,** the erosion of civil liberties by Communist witch hunts—yet in retrospect it almost seems that from 1945 through the McCarthy era American youth had lost its voice.

Writing in *The Nation* in 1957, poet and teacher Stanley Kunitz complained that the only liberal or speculative voices heard in classrooms were those of the professors. As for the students, they matriculated cautiously, "wanting above all—so well conditioned are they by the prevailing social climate—to buy security for themselves in the full knowledge that the price is conformity."

Silent Majority With protest against the continuing and unpopular **Vietnam War** becoming increasingly active and vocal (*see* **Moratorium Day**), on November 3, 1969, President Richard M. Nixon presented his case against dissent in a nationally televised address:

If a vocal minority, however fervent its cause, prevails over reason and the will of the majority, this Nation has no future as a free society. Let historians not record that when America was the most powerful nation in the world we passed on the other side of the road and allowed the last hopes for peace and freedom of millions of people to be suffocated by the forces of totalitarianism. And so tonight—to you, the great silent majority of my fellow Americans—I ask for your support.

The phrase "silent majority" was immediately picked up and highlighted by the news media, which had ignored it when it was first used by Vice President Spiro Agnew on May 9, 1969:

It is time for America's silent majority to stand up for its rights, and let us remember the American majority includes every minority. America's silent majority is bewildered by irrational protest—and looking at the sullen, scruffy minority of student protesters, probably feels like saying: "If you prefer the totalitarian ideas of Mao or Ho Chi Minh, why stay here and destroy our freedoms?"

Some historians trace the first use of the phrase to isolationist Charles A. Lindbergh, who at a pre-World War II rally in New York spoke of "that silent majority of Americans who have no newspaper, or newsreel, or radio station at their command," but who nevertheless were opposed to American involvement in the war unleashed against European democracies by Nazi Germany and Fascist Italy.

In his November 1969 television address—sometimes known as his "Silent Majority" speech, the President for the first time also used the expression **"Nixon Doctrine"** to refer to a change of American policy in Asia first outlined at an informal press conference on the island of Guam on July 25, 1969. He noted that while the United States would keep its treaty commitments in the area, it would avoid entanglements such as the Vietnam War by looking "to the nation directly threatened to assume the primary responsibility of providing the manpower for its defense." At the end of 1969, this country had 475,200 men in Vietnam.

Silent Majority Institute In December 1969, Lyn Nofziger, a former newspaper reporter employed at that time by the Nixon administration as a writer, circulated among the White House staff a detailed proposal for what he called an "Institute for an Informed America." To be budgeted at $1 million annually, the institute would have its own staff of writers, researchers, moviemakers, and public-relations experts who would work in close but informal contact with the White House "to ensure that the American people have access to all sides of significant issues. Implicit here is the understanding that the media already gives (*sic*) emphasis to *one* side."

Nofziger, a hard-line conservative who had been press secretary of California's Governor Ronald Reagan, suggested that the institute could function as a "rightwing Brookings Institution." His proposal was reportedly given top priority by President Richard M. Nixon and approved by White House Chief of Staff H. R. Haldeman and Special Presidential Counsel Charles W. ("Chuck") Colson. Both men, however, suggested that advantage be taken of the publicity given the so-called **Silent Majority** and that the institute be named the Silent Majority Institute, or possibly Silent Majority, Inc.

As director of the proposed institute, Colson suggested E. Howard Hunt, a former **CIA** agent. When the latter was interviewed for the position by Jeb Stuart Magruder, Special Assistant to President Nixon, he added to Nofziger's original conception the suggestion that the institute could also be used for covert political activity. Alarmed, Magruder objected to Hunt's "cloak-and-dagger orientation" and told Colson that he felt "we needed a scholar, an elder statesman to promote conservative ideas."

Writing in 1974, Magruder noted that this was the first introduction into White House circles of Hunt, who was to figure prominently in the **Watergate Scandal.** The institute was never in fact established, but Magruder retrospectively records his disagreement about the name change proposed by Haldeman and Colson. "Institute for Informed America had a certain dignity to it, but Silent Majority Institute sounded like a think tank full of hard hats. Neither Haldeman nor Colson was noted for his light touch."

Silent Spring An instant bestseller when it was first published in 1962, Rachel Carson's now classic study examines the disastrous effects on the ecology of the indiscriminate use of pesticides, especially chlorinated hydrocarbons such as DDT.

There was once a town in the heart of America where all life seemed to live in harmony with its surroundings. . . . Then a strange blight crept over the area and everything began to change. Some evil spell had settled on the community: mysterious maladies swept the flocks of chickens; the cattle and sheep sickened and died. . . . There was a strange stillness.

In the less than two decades since their introduction, Miss Carson argued, synthetic pesticides have altered the balance of nature and become so thoroughly disseminated throughout the "animate and inanimate world" that they are stored even in the bodies of most human beings, occurring in mother's milk and the tissues of the unborn child. The result is an increased danger of leukemia, cancer, and hepatitis, as well as emphysema and other respiratory diseases from poisons in the very air.

As a result of *Silent Spring,* severe restrictions were placed on the use of DDT by the federal government, and Congress eliminated loopholes through which the manufacturer of products challenged by the Department of Agriculture could continue production and sale.

The petrochemical industry has fought against Carson's arguments with charges of hysteria and by insisting that only pesticides will make it possible to feed the world's growing population. It has also been pointed out that synthetic pesticides have eliminated or controlled diseases such as typhus, yellow fever, and malaria in many areas of the world.

Silent Spring urges that insects and weeds can be controlled by increased—but expensive—biological research to find means to promote their natural enemies, or by developing nonchemical means such as sex lures, light traps, and the sterilization of male insects by radiation. Miss Carson concludes:

The concepts and practices of applied entomology for the most part date from the Stone Age of science. It is our alarming misfortune that so primitive a science has armed itself with the most modern and terrible weapons, and that in turning them against the insects it has also turned them against the earth.

A victim of cancer in 1964, the author was an aquatic biologist with the U.S. Bureau of Fisheries from 1936 to 1952. Her other books include *Under the Sea Wind* (1941), *The Sea Around Us* (1951), and *The Edge of the Sea* (1955).

Sit-Ins This form of civil rights protest was born on January 31, 1960, when Joseph McNeil, a black student at North Carolina Agricultural and Technical College, was refused service at a segregated lunch counter in the Greensboro, North Carolina, bus terminal. The next day he and classmates Ezell Blair, Jr., Franklin McCain, and David Richmond took seats at the lunch counter of the local Woolworth store and asked for service. When refused, they remained sitting quietly until closing time, but they returned the next morning with five friends, and on the following days more and more blacks came.

When the wire services picked up the story of what had been baptized a "sit-in," the idea spread like wildfire to other nearby cities, and then to over fifteen cities in five states. One of the most important such demonstrations took place early in February at the lunch counter of the Woolworth store in Nashville, Tennessee, where forty students took over a lunch counter. When refused service, they returned each day and tension began to mount. Soon seventy-six students were in jail and the nation was watching the demonstration on television. Those arrested preferred to stay in prison rather than pay their fines, and the home of Z. Alexander Looby, their chief defense lawyer, was all but demolished by a bomb. But the sit-ins continued, and on May 10 the lunch counters in six Nashville stores were desegregated; by the end of the month seven cities in the state had followed suit.

Meanwhile, sit-ins continued to spread throughout the South, and in the North branch stores of Woolworth and other chains were being picketed by civil rights adherents. By the end of the year an estimated 70,000 blacks and their sympathizers had staged similar demonstrations in over 100 communities. Several hundred lunch counters had been desegregated because young people had had the courage to stand their ground while screaming segregationists tossed lighted cigarettes at them or pulled them from their seats and began to pummel them.

In Greensboro, where it all began, the lunch counters in Woolworth and Kress were not integrated until July 25. The movement was to be a turning point in the struggle to desegregate public facilities throughout the South. The U. S. Supreme Court upheld the sit-ins in *Garner et al. v. Louisiana* (1961), *Peterson v. Greenville* (1963), *Shuttleworth v. Birmingham* (1963), and *Lombard v. Louisiana* (1963).

Six Crises This account by former Vice President Richard M. Nixon of the major turning points in his political career—which many observers assumed was over—appeared in 1962, six years before he acceded to the Presidency after defeating Democratic challenger Hubert H. Humphrey in 1968, and twelve years before, in August 1974, he became the first president to resign from office (*see* **Watergate Scandal**).

The first "crisis" deals with Mr. Nixon's pivotal role in the 1945 **House Committee on Un-American Activities** (HUAC) hearings into possible Communist associations of former State Department employee Alger Hiss. At the time, Mr. Nixon was a Republican Representative from California (*see* **Alger Hiss Case**).

The next section of the book deals with the revelation in September 1952 that Mr. Nixon—then a California Senator and the Republican nominee for the Vice-Presidency—had been the beneficiary of a political "slush fund" established by some seventy California businessmen (*see* **Checkers Speech**).

The third "crisis" deals with the author's controversial role as Vice President in the two-month period following President Dwight D. Eisenhower's heart attack on September 23, 1955.

I had long been the whipping boy for those who chose not to direct their political attacks against Dwight D. Eisenhower, the most popular President in recent history. The nation's attention would be focused on the sickbed in Denver, but many eyes would be watching to see whether I became brash or timid in meeting the emergency. My job was to be neither.

In May 1958, Vice President Nixon made a goodwill tour of South America during which there were anti-American riots in Lima, Peru, and Caracas, Venezuela. His car was surrounded and stoned by screaming mobs, and President Eisenhower dispatched four companies of Marines and paratroopers into Caribbean bases to guarantee his safety. In discussing this major incident of his career, Mr. Nixon notes:

I walked directly into the mob. . . . There were only a few leaders—the usual case-hardened, cold-eyed Communist operatives. The great majority were teen-age students. And what struck me about them was not the hate in their eyes, but the fear . . . the very fact that we dared to walk toward them seemed to strike fear into their hearts.

The fifth of the six crises discussed is the famous debate with Premier Khrushchev during Vice President Nixon's visit to the U.S.S.R. in July 1959 (*see* **Kitchen Debate**).

The book concludes with an account of the Vice President's unsuccessful 1960 campaign for the Presidency, with special emphasis on the televised debates with his Democratic challenger, Sen. John F. Kennedy (D.-Mass.) (*see* **Kennedy-Nixon Debates**). In this section, the former Vice President notes that because he represented the incumbent administration he was forced into a defensive position.

In a later edition of *Six Crises*, the author noted: "The Chinese have a symbol for the word 'crisis'. One brush stroke stands for danger. The other brush stroke stands for opportunity. We must recognize the danger, but we must seize the opportunity. . . ."

Psychiatrist David Abrahamsen emphasizes in *Nixon vs. Nixon* (1978) that the fact that these crises are described "as political rather than emotional in nature is important. . . . We know that crises do occur in the maturing process, but in Nixon's case these crucial events did not seem to change him. He gained no insight; his consciousness was not expanded. He viewed these events as external to himself."

"$64,000 Question" *See* "Twenty-One."

Skokie *See* **American Nazi Party.**

Skylab Program A nine-month, $2.5 billion space program that spanned most of 1973 and part of 1974, it began a new phase in America's exploration of space.

Designed to provide a link between the Apollo moon program and possible future interplanetary expeditions, the Skylab program provided data on human adaptability to long periods of weightlessness and, to some extent, kept alive interest in the space program (*see* **Project Apollo**).

During the Skylab program, three crews of three men each rode the familiar Apollo space capsule, slightly modified for their voyages, to a rendezvous and docking with an orbiting eighty-four-ton laboratory/space station launched into orbit May 14, 1973. This 9,550-cubic-foot laboratory housed experiments of four basic types: medical tests to be performed on the men themselves to determine their responses to extended stays in a zero-g environment; solar astronomy experiments designed to yield information on solar flares; technology experiments which demonstrated the feasibility of welding in a weightless environment—a crucial ability if large new interplanetary vessels are to be built in space itself; and finally, earth-resources experiments, which produced ample data on our planet's natural resources and weather systems.

Deployment failure of the orbiting laboratory's solar-power wings delayed the launch of the *Skylab 1* crew of Navy men—Captain Charles Conrad, Jr., Commander Joseph P. Kerwin, and Commander Paul J. Weitz—until May 25, 1973. They returned to earth June 22, having repaired damage caused during boost and accomplished most of their assigned missions. *Skylab 2* was launched July 28, 1973, and returned to earth September 25, 1973. For a time it was feared that Navy Captain Alan L. Bean, Marine Major Jack R. Lousma, and solar

physicist Dr. Owen K. Garriott might have to be rescued in space because trouble had developed in a set of small thruster rockets in the Apollo ferry craft. The final *Skylab 3* crew—Marine Lt. Colonel Gerald P. Carr, plasma physics scientist Dr. Edwin G. Gibson, and Air Force Lt. Colonel William R. Pogue—was launched November 16, 1973, and returned to earth on February 8, 1974, after a record stay in space of eighty-four days, one hour, and seventeen minutes. During the mission, the crew was able to make observations and take photographs of the comet Kohoutek.

In all, the three Skylab crews spent 171 days in the orbiting laboratory and, by their excellent performance, demonstrated beyond any doubt that man can function for extended periods in space. The astronauts responded well to life aboard the laboratory, which gave them more work and living room than any previous project had been able to, and produced nearly 30 percent more scientific data—including thousands of solar telescope photographs of the sun—than had originally been anticipated.

In 1978 the abandoned *Skylab* was still in orbit more than 200 miles up, but gradually losing altitude and expected to fall to earth in 1979 or 1980. The **National Aeronautics and Space Administration** (NASA) announced on December 18, 1978, that it was abandoning attempts to keep the laboratory in orbit for use by the upcoming space-shuttle program. There had previously been some hope in scientific circles that a manned space shuttle might be used to attach a small rocket that would have boosted *Skylab* to a higher orbit and thereby extended its life. An alternative plan called for a controlled re-entry over a remote ocean area.

SLA *See* **Patty Hearst Kidnapping.**

Slochower v. New York City Higher Education Board In a landmark case involving a former professor at New York's Brooklyn College, the U.S. Supreme Court found on April 9, 1956, that public servants may not be excluded from the protection of the Constitution's Fifth Amendment, which holds that "no person . . . shall be compelled . . . to be a witness against himself. . . ." The Court also noted that the exercise of this constitutional privilege is not to be construed as a confession of guilt.

Smith Amendment A change proposed by Rep. Howard W. Smith (D.-Va.) in the Johnson administration's 1965 Education Bill (*see* **Elementary and Secondary Education Act**) to allow a private citizen to challenge its constitutionality. Smith, the chairman of the powerful House Rules Committee, felt that this change was necessary because in 1923 the Supreme Court had ruled in *Frothingham v. Mellon* that no individual could challenge in the courts the manner in which the expenditure of funds was provided for in federal law. The amendment was defeated in the House.

Representative Smith had previously opposed so many educational bills that his fellow members of Congress had coined a special slogan for the octogenarian: "No rules for schools." The man who had fought the **Economic Opportunity Act** as a devious way to introduce "integrated camps" and even, possibly, nudist camps, marshalled all his congressional power to fight a bill which would use tax funds to promote integration. He also resented the extension of federal activity and the use of public funds to aid parochial schools.

The threat posed by the amendment to the success of the education bill was that it seemed destined to break up the coalition which President Lyndon B. Johnson had contrived for the bill's support. There was absolutely no doubt, for example, that those opposed to the use of federal funds to support religiously oriented parochial schools would under the provision proposed by Representative Smith challenge such use in the courts. Because of this, the National Catholic Welfare Conference had plainly indicated that if the Smith Amendment was accepted, it would withdraw its support for a bill which also improved the educational opportunities of poor minority groups.

Smoking and Health The rising U.S. death rate from lung cancer, arteriosclerotic heart disease, chronic bronchitis, and emphysema led Surgeon General Luther L. Terry in October 1962 to appoint a federal advisory committee to investigate the links between these diseases and cigarette smoking. *Smoking and Health*, the committee's final report, was issued on January 11, 1964, and startled a nation of 70-million cigarette smokers by announcing "cigarette smoking as a much greater causative factor in lung cancer than air pollution or occupational exposure."

The report was based on the evaluation and reprocessing of existing studies and statistics covering experiments with animals, clinical and autopsy studies, and seven population studies involving a random sampling of 1,123,000 men, of whom 37,391 were observed until their deaths.

Some of the results reported were as follows:

1. The death rate from all causes was 68 percent higher for smokers than for nonsmokers.

2. The number of cigarettes smoked daily, the age at which the habit started, and the degree of inhalation had an effect on the death rate.

3. The death rate of men who smoked fewer than five cigars a day was almost the same as for nonsmokers.

4. Cigarette smoking was a causative factor in lung cancer.

5. Smoking was a habit rather than an addiction, but nicotine substitutes were ineffective in dealing with it.

6. There was no evidence of a substantial link between nicotine and disease.

7. Pipe smoking was linked to lip cancer.

8. Smoking during pregnancy resulted in smaller babies.

Smoking and Health received national publicity and demands rose in Congress for immediate antismoking legislation, though some members—mostly those from tobacco-raising states—called the results inconclusive and recommended additional research. On June 24, 1964, the Federal Trade Commission ruled that beginning in 1965 all cigarette packaging and advertising must carry the following: "Warning: The Surgeon General has determined that cigarette smoking is dangerous to your health."

In 1967 a Public Health Services survey reported that 72 percent of those who smoke more than two packs a day suffer from at least one of the following: bronchitis, sinusitis, peptic ulcers, emphysema, and heart disease. Although it did not claim that there was a firm link between these diseases and smoking, it reported that only 53 percent of the nonsmokers suffer from any of these chronic ailments.

After 1971, cigarette advertising on television was banned.

An even stronger condemnation of smoking was contained in a new report issued by the Surgeon General on January 11, 1979. A digest of some 30,000 research papers focusing on medical, social, and psychological aspects of smoking, it greatly emphasized the hazards to women, particularly pregnant women. The 1,200-page document reported that of the 54 million Americans who smoke, 75 percent acquired the habit before they were twenty-one.

In 1978, domestic consumption of cigarettes dropped by .03 percent, or 2 billion cigarettes.

"Smoking Pistol" Critics of President Richard M. Nixon felt that in spite of his frequent denials he had been involved in an attempt to quash investigations subsequent to the break-in of Democratic National Committee Headquarters in Washington, D.C., on June 17, 1972, by men linked to the White House staff and the **Committee to Re-elect the President** (CREEP; CRP) (*see* **Watergate Scandal**). They were convinced that there must exist somewhere evidence linking the President to an attempted cover-up as incontrovertibly as the smoking pistol in an assassin's hand links him to a murder.

Such evidence was eventually found in three tape-recorded conversations (*see* **Nixon Tapes**) between President Nixon and former White House Chief of Staff H. R. Haldeman on June 23, 1972. These tapes showed that the President had been lying when on August 29, 1972, and subsequently, he had stated that he had no knowledge of involvement by White House staffers in the break-in. They also showed that less than a week after the Watergate break-in he had directed Haldeman to have the **CIA** step in to attempt to bring a halt to FBI investigations of the incident.

President Nixon: . . . Say, "Look, the problem is that this will open the whole, the whole **Bay of Pigs** thing, and the President just feels that"—ah, without going into the details. Don't, don't lie to them to the extent to say that there is no involvement, just say, "This is a comedy of errors," without getting into it, "the President believes that it is going to open the whole Bay of Pigs thing up again." And, ah, "Because these people are plugging for keeps," and that they should call the FBI in and say that we wish for the country, "Don't go any further into this case, period!"

As the result of an eight to zero decision against him (July 24, 1974) by the U.S. Supreme Court, President Nixon reluctantly released the transcript of these tapes on August 5, 1974. This evidence that the President had been lying when he claimed not to have known of the involvement of his staff before March 21, 1973, as well as the evidence that he had indeed attempted to halt an FBI investigation of the affair, crumbled his remaining support in the House Judiciary Committee, which on July 27, 1974, voted (twenty-seven to eleven) to impeach him for having "engaged personally and through his subordinates and agents in a course of conduct designed to delay, impede, and obstruct the investigation" of the break-in.

On August 9, 1974, Richard M. Nixon became the first United States President ever to resign from office. In a nationwide television and radio broadcast he had announced the previous night that he intended to resign because he "no longer had a strong enough political base" that would enable him to continue.

SNAP-10A Developed by the Atomic International Division of North American Aviation, Inc., for the U.S. Air Force and the **Atomic Energy Commission** (AEC), this 250-pound nuclear reactor was launched into polar orbit from Vandenberg Air Force Base, California, on April 3, 1965, by means of a two-stage Atlas-Agena rocket. The mission of the cone-shaped satellite designed to develop 500 watts of power was to see whether a unit of this design could withstand launching and space conditions and continue to produce power for a year.

SNAP-10A was powered by a pound of U-235 whose heat was transformed into electric current by germanium-silicone thermocouples. Shortly after launching, it was found to be producing from 620 to 668 watts instead of the anticipated 500.

Some of SNAP-10A's power was absorbed by a second experiment carried by the man-made satellite: a 2.2-pound nonnuclear ion engine that produced thrust by the electrical vaporizing of cesium. Although it could produce only $\frac{1}{500}$-pound of thrust, in constant operation such an engine could theoretically accelerate a spaceship to speeds of 100,000 mph.

"Snatched defeat out of the jaws of victory" In a reversal of the traditional expression, this is the way one political commentator described Republican candidate Thomas E. Dewey's upset defeat by President Harry S Truman in 1948. Dewey's victory had been forecast by the major public-opinion polls in the nation, and the *Chicago Tribune* had actually printed and distributed an issue announcing: "Dewey Defeats Truman."

In 1944, Dewey had been defeated by President Franklin D. Roosevelt. Alice Roosevelt Longworth, the daughter of President Theodore Roosevelt and the doyenne of Washington society, summed up this new defeat by noting: "You can't make a soufflé rise twice."

See **Whistle-Stop Campaign.**

SNCC *See* **Student Nonviolent Coordinating Committee.**

Snick (SNCC) *See* **Student Nonviolent Coordinating Committee.**

Soil Bank System The Eisenhower administration's **Agricultural Trade and Development Act of 1954** had aimed at gradually lowering government price supports in order to make farm prices more responsive to supply and demand. In January 1956, a new attack on the problem of farm surpluses was proposed. The main features of this approach were a two-part "soil bank system." Under an "acreage reserve" program, farmers would be paid for reducing the acreage of crops such as wheat, cotton, corn, and rice that were in serious surplus. In addition, a "conservation reserve" program would be instituted under which farmers would be compensated for voluntarily shifting acreage into use for forage, trees, and water storage.

To the President's dismay, "the Senate Agricultural Committee promptly tacked on [the bill] a provision for the return to 90 percent rigid price supports. They are completely indifferent to the fact that this feature, designed to provide an incentive for increased immediate production, is in direct conflict with the rest of the bill."

On April 16, 1956, the President vetoed the resulting legislation, explaining in a nationally televised address that while he was "happy that the administration's soil bank was still in it . . . other provisions of the bill would have rendered the soil bank almost useless."

Legislation that the President considered "reasonably satisfactory" was finally signed by him on May 28, 1956. However, though farmers set aside several million acres annually under the soil bank system, bumper crops during the next four years made the problem of surpluses as serious as ever.

Although the acreage reserve program was allowed to lapse after 1958, the conservation reserve program was expanded. Under it, farmers took almost 29 million acres out of production in 1960. This program was cancelled by the Food and Agriculture Act of 1965, which established the Cropland Adjustment program, a long-term land-retirement policy.

Sokolniki Summit *See* **Kitchen Debate.**

Soledad Brothers *See* **Angela Davis Trial.**

"Son of Sam" A year-long killing spree that terrorized New York City and resulted in the deaths of five women and one man ended on August 10, 1977, when police arrested David Richard Berkowitz, a 24-year-old Yonkers postal worker. Berkowitz, who captured national media attention with messages signed "Son of Sam," used a .44 caliber revolver to attack young women sitting with their escorts in parked cars on quiet residential streets. Found competent to stand trial, on May 8, 1978, he pleaded guilty and claimed to be acting on instructions from a 6,000-year-old demon incarnated in a neighbor, Sam Carr.

Berkowitz was sentenced (June 13, 1978) by a special panel of three judges from local jurisdictions to a total of more than 500 years, including individual sentences of from twenty-five years to life on each of the murder charges. Though in imposing the sentence Bronx Supreme Court Justice William Kapelman said that it was the court's "fervent wish that this defendant be imprisoned until the day of his death," under New York's penal law the "Son of Sam" may be eligible for parole after serving twenty-five years. If released from custody on the murder charges, he could face prosecution for arson as the result of some 2,000 fires to which he confessed and for which no indictment was sought at the time.

Songmy *See* **My Lai Massacre.**

South Asia Resolution *See* **Gulf of Tonkin Resolution.**

Southeast Asia Treaty Organization (SEATO) With the fall of Dien Bien Phu on May 7, 1954, French influence in Indochina came to an end, and the United States, faced with the alarming prospect of the unchecked spread of communism in that corner of the world, sought to establish some means to stabilize the area. According to President Dwight D. Eisenhower, it was Prime Minister Winston Churchill who first recommended a SEATO that would be patterned after the NATO alliance in Western Europe.

The Southeast Asia Collective Defense Treaty was signed in Manila on September 8, 1954, and is commonly known as the Manila Pact. In it the eight signatories—France, Britain, Australia, New Zealand, Thailand, the Philippines, Pakistan, and the United States—proclaimed that any attack within the treaty area, which included South Vietnam, Laos, and Cambodia, was to be construed as aggression against all, and they mutually pledged to come to one another's aid. Reaffirming the Charter of the United Nations, the parties to the pact proclaimed that "they uphold the principle of equal rights and self-determination of peoples," and declared that "they will earnestly strive by every peaceful means to promote self-government and to secure the independence of all those countries whose peoples desire it and are able to undertake its responsibilities." Formosa was not included in the treaty area. A treaty of this type had first been referred to by President Eisenhower in an address to newspaper editors on April 16, 1953. The President and Secretary of State John Foster Dulles conceived of it as a shield against communist encroachment, but most of the Southeastern Asia nations had the more limited view of a defense of their national borders, and this attitude delayed the treaty's realization. Consideration of SEATO was also sidetracked for some time by the urgent French desire to find some way out of their involvement in the war in Indochina.

In 1972, Pakistan withdrew from SEATO after the loss of Bangladesh, and the following year France withdrew, although it remained a signatory of the defense treaty. In May 1975, both Thailand and the Philippines recommended that SEATO be phased out, and the organization came to a formal end on June 30, 1977.

SEATO never included Singapore and Malaysia—both of which were British colonies at the time the organization was formed—or Indonesia, which pursued an independent policy under President Sukarno. Although never invoked in any major incident, SEATO did develop important economic, medical, and cultural projects only peripherally related to defense. Assistance from the United States was expected to allow some of these projects to continue.

SEATO headquarters was in Bangkok.

Southern Christian Leadership Conference (SCLC)

Founded in January 1957 by a group of black Baptist ministers—chief among whom were Dr. Martin Luther King, Jr., and Ralph Abernathy, who had both come into national prominence with the **Montgomery Bus Strike** (December 1955–December 1956)—the SCLC, under the direction of Dr. King, was one of the driving forces behind the nonviolent civil rights protests of the 1960s. ("Some of you have knives, and I ask you to put them up. Some of you may have arms, and I ask you to put them up. Get the weapon of nonviolence, the breastplate of righteousness, the armor of truth, and just keep marching.")

SCLC participated in the **March on Washington** on August 28, 1963, when more than 250,000 blacks and their white sympathizers gathered in the nation's Capital to dramatize Negro demands for jobs and civil rights. It was on this occasion that Dr. King made his moving **"I have a dream . . ."** speech

to crowds peacefully assembled before the Lincoln Memorial.

On March 21, 1965, after two years of efforts by SCLC volunteers to register black voters had been defeated by intimidation from local authorities in Selma, Alabama, Dr. King led some 3,000 sympathizers on a five-day protest march from Selma to the state capital in Montgomery, where he presented a petition to Governor George C. Wallace. As they marched along under the protection of U.S. Army troops and the Alabama National Guard—federalized by President Lyndon B. Johnson—the protesters were joined by more than 20,000 sympathizers.

Among the more successful SCLC campaigns was **"Operation Breadbasket,"** undertaken in Chicago in 1966 to pressure companies operating in Negro neighborhoods to hire more blacks, make use of black service companies, and deposit a percentage of their profits in black-run banks.

Planning for the **"Poor People's Campaign"**—beginning in May 1968 many thousands of blacks from all over the nation began arriving in Washington, D.C., to demand that the federal government speed up programs for jobs, housing, and public assistance—was begun under Dr. King. After his assassination on April 4, 1968, direction of the SCLC was taken over by Reverend Abernathy, and Hosea Williams was made coordinator of the Washington protest.

With Dr. King gone, the SCLC seemed to founder and lose direction. However, on May 19, 1970, SCLC vice president Hosea Williams led a march from Perry, Georgia, to Atlanta to protest the deaths of students at Kent State University and Jackson State College (*see* **Kent State Tragedy** and **Jackson State Tragedy**) and of six blacks who had been killed by police during riots in Augusta on May 11. In one of the largest civil rights demonstrations in the South since 1965, 10,000 people marched in Atlanta from Dr. King's tomb to Morehouse College. The so-called "March Against Repression" was in many ways the last gasp of the old civil rights coalition.

In 1972, Reverend Jessie Jackson, who had been in charge of Operation Breadbasket, left the SCLC after a dispute to form **People United to Save Humanity** (Operation PUSH). In July 1973, Reverend Abernathy temporarily resigned from SCLC because of the lack of financial support and conflict with Coretta King, who had been using her fund-raising power for the Martin Luther King Jr. Center for Social Change. His resignation was "rescinded" by SCLC delegates at their annual convention.

In 1976 Reverend Joseph Lowery took over leadership of SCLC. Reverend Abernathy made an unsuccessful attempt in March 1977 to win the congressional seat of Rep. Andrew Young (D.-Ga.), whom President Jimmy Carter had appointed U.S. representative at the United Nations.

Southern Manifesto of 1956 Signed by 101 Senators and Representatives from the states of the old Confederacy, this document captured newspaper headlines in March 1956 with its denunciation of the U.S. Supreme Court decision in **Brown v. Board of Education of Topeka** (1954). In that case—involving school segregation on the basis of race—the Court, speaking through Chief Justice Earl Warren, found: "We conclude that in the field of public education the doctrine of 'separate but equal' has no place. Separate educational facilities are inherently unequal."

The signers of the Manifesto called this decision an abuse of judicial power in which the justices had substituted their personal political and social ideas for "the established law of the land." They argued that in *Lum v. Rice* (1927) the Supreme Court had unanimously decided that the "separate but equal" principle originally expressed in *Plessy v. Ferguson* (1896) was "within the discretion of the state in regulating its public schools and does not conflict with the Fourteenth Amendment."

While the Manifesto did not call for the use of illegal force to avoid the implementation of the *Brown* decision in the South, by arguing that this decision was "unconstitutional," it seemed to suggest that it was all right to fall back on violent resistance. Having thus encouraged opposition to the enforcement of desegregation, the Manifesto ended as follows:

"In this trying period, as we all seek to right this wrong, we appeal to our people not to be provoked by the agitators and troublemakers invading our states and to scrupulously refrain from disorder and lawless acts."

Among the signers were Sen. J. William Fulbright (D.-Ark.) and Sen. John J. Sparkman (D.-Ala.); the latter had been vice presidential candidate on the Democratic ticket headed by Adlai Stevenson in 1952. The only Southern Senators not to sign were Lyndon B. Johnson (D.-Tex.), Estes Kefauver (D.-Tenn.), and Albert Gore (D.-Tenn.).

Southern Strategy The phrase first began to be used widely to describe the campaign strategy of Sen. Barry Goldwater (R.-Ariz.) in his 1964 fight for the Presidency. As employed by Democrats and liberals, it suggested that Senator Goldwater's stand on school desegregation and related issues was meant to appeal to the Southern voter. However, writing in 1971, the Senator noted that the strategy stemmed from the 1950s, when as leader of the Senate Campaign Committee he had ordered an in-depth survey of voting trends in the United States and that the results had shown that only in the Southwest was the Republican party making any gains. "For that reason we decided to put more emphasis on that part of the nation. . . . That is the so-called 'Southern strategy.' It has nothing to do with busing, integration, or any other of the so-called closely held concepts of the Southerner."

The Southern Strategy is said to have dominated the 1968 campaign of Republican presidential candidate Richard M. Nixon, when attempts were made to lure potential supporters of George C. Wallace by soft-pedaling desegregation in the South. Critics charged that eventually the same approach was used to appeal to those voters in Northern urban areas who were strongly opposed to **busing,** government-sponsored low-cost housing in nonghetto areas, and similar issues.

During the Nixon administration, the Southern Strategy was most often associated with John N. Mitchell, but it was worked out in detail by Kevin Phillips, a lawyer and ethnic voting-pattern expert who detailed it in *The Emerging Republican Majority* (1969), which outlined a plan for preempting **Middle America** for the Republican party. (Phillips had worked for Mitchell in the New York offices of the Nixon headquarters during the 1968 campaign.)

As Attorney General during the Nixon administration, Mitchell was influential in softening the guidelines of the **Civil Rights Act of 1964,** under which school districts that had taken no steps toward desegregation were faced with a loss of federal funds. It was Harry Dent, a protégé of segregationist leader Sen. Strom Thurmond (D.-S.C.), who was supposedly charged with working out the practical details of the strategy.

An interesting departure from this voter-appeal approach was the **Philadelphia Plan,** which though short-lived received the support of President Nixon.

Spacewalks The first instance of a spacewalk by an American took place on June 3, 1965, when Air Force Major Edward H. White, copilot of the *Gemini 4,* stepped outside the space vehicle during the third of sixty-two orbits around the earth for a record twenty minutes of **Extravehicular Activity** (EVA)—just double the time Soviet cosmonaut Alexei Leonov had remained outside the spaceship

Voskhod (*Sunrise*) *2* on March 18, 1965. During his EVA, Major White wore a 31½-pound space suit costing $26,000 and made up of eighteen layers of felt, Dacron, and aluminized Mylar plastic to protect him from meteoroids and temperatures ranging from −150°F to 250°F. A scheduled second spacewalk during the flight (June 3-7, 1965) had to be canceled when on reentering the capsule White experienced difficulty fastening the hatch.

The second American spacewalk was taken by Navy Lt. Comdr. Eugene A. Cernan on June 5, 1966, during the flight of *Gemini 9*. Programmed to last two hours and twenty-five minutes, it was cut back to one hour and twenty-six minutes when Cernan's helmet visor began to fog. Air Force Major Michael Collins, pilot of *Gemini 10* (July 18-21, 1966), was forced to curtail the EVA from fifty-five to thirty-five minutes when fuel trouble developed. Spacewalks were also made by Navy Lt. Comdr. Richard F. Gordon, Jr., on September 13, 1966, during the orbital flights of *Gemini 11*, and by Air Force Major Edwin E. ("Buzz") Aldrin, Jr., on November 12, 1966, during the flight of *Gemini 12*. On that same orbital voyage, Major Aldrin stepped outside the vehicle again on November 13 to tackle the problem of working in free fall. He established a record EVA of two hours and nine minutes, and left behind him in space pennants reading "Nov. 11—Vets Day"—in honor of the *Gemini 12* launching—and "Go, Army—Beat Navy." He performed a third EVA on November 14 by standing up in his seat with the hatch open for an hour.

Spirit of Camp David Accepting an invitation from President Dwight D. Eisenhower, in September 1959 Soviet Premier Nikita Khrushchev made a thirteen-day cross-country tour of the United States and concluded his visit with intensive conferences with the President at his Camp David, Maryland, retreat (September 25-27, 1959). Whereas only a few months before, both nations seemed on the brink of war as a result of the Soviet November 1958 ultimatum, which threatened to deny the Western powers access to Berlin, the joint communiqué issued at the end of this meeting stressed that all outstanding international problems were to be settled through peaceful means and that Berlin "negotiations would be re-opened with a view to achieving a solution which would be in accordance with the interests of all concerned and in the interest of the maintenance of peace." Another paragraph of the joint statement noted that general disarmament was the most important problem facing the world and that "both governments will make

every effort to achieve a constructive solution of this problem."

On September 28, President Eisenhower announced that the two leaders had agreed to remove the Soviet ultimatum on Berlin as a prelude to a possible summit meeting.

The "Spirit of Camp David" characterized the short-lived period of good feeling that followed and came to an abrupt halt with the disclosure in May 1960 of American **U-2** espionage flights over Soviet territory. An immediate casualty of the incident was the Paris Summit meeting held later that month. In addition, President Eisenhower's projected visit to the U.S.S.R. in June 1960 was canceled.

In June 1961, Premier Khrushchev renewed his threats over Berlin during a meeting with President John F. Kennedy in Vienna (*see* **Berlin Crisis of 1961).**

Built as a presidential retreat in 1939, the camp was originally called Hi-Catoctin and later renamed Shangri-La by President Franklin D. Roosevelt. In 1953, President Eisenhower renamed it after his grandson.

When Premier Khrushchev was first told that his 1959 itinerary in the United States included Camp David, he thought it must be "the sort of place where people who were mistrusted could be kept in quarantine."

Camp David was also the site (September 17, 1978) of "accords" between Israeli Prime Minister Menachem Begin and Egyptian President Anwar Sadat designed to lead to a peace treaty between those nations by the following December 17. The treaty was not signed until March 26, 1979.

Spirit of Geneva Shortly before his departure for the Geneva "summit" conference (July 18-23, 1955)—in which he was to meet with British Prime Minister Anthony Eden, French Premier Edgar Faure, and Soviet Premier N. A. Bulganin to discuss problems of disarmament and German reunification—President Dwight D. Eisenhower noted in a broadcast to the nation that "for the first time, a President goes to engage in a conference with the heads of other governments in order to prevent wars, in order to see whether in this time of stress and strain we cannot devise measures that will keep from us this terrible scourge that afflicts mankind."

At the opening of the Geneva meeting, he warned that while the assembled leaders could not be expected to solve all the problems to peace then and there, they could "perhaps, create a new spirit that will make possible future solutions of problems which are within our responsibilities. . . ."

It was at this meeting, on July 21, 1955, that President Eisenhower, as a gesture of a desire to seek accommodation, proposed a mutual aerial inspection plan that would serve as a basis for disarmament (see **Open Skies**).

The Geneva meeting, though concluded in a spirit of friendship, reached no agreements other than a directive to the foreign ministers of all the powers concerned to meet again in October and discuss the agenda agreed upon. Nevertheless, the President felt that "the personal contacts—in some cases, the friendships—that were developed there alone made the trip worthwhile."

On his return to the United States, he expressed the hope that if the spirit in which earlier international conferences had been conducted had been changed, "We will have taken the greatest step toward peace. . . ."

On August 25, 1955, in a talk on "The Spirit of Geneva" to the American Bar Association, the President said: "Whether or not such a spirit as this will thrive through the combined intelligence and understanding of men, or will shrivel in the greed and ruthlessness of some, is for the future to tell."

When the foreign ministers of the four nations met in Geneva (October 27–November 16, 1955), the President's hopes were to be disappointed. The meeting concluded without any agreements having been reached. British Foreign Minister Harold Macmillan noted that "once more we are back in a strange nightmare where men use the same words to mean different things."

"Spiro Who?"   Richard M. Nixon's choice of Governor Spiro T. Agnew of Maryland as his running mate on the Republican ticket in the 1968 presidential campaign was an obvious gesture toward Sen. Strom Thurmond (D.-S.C.), who had been influential in securing Nixon's own nomination against challenges from California's Governor Ronald Reagan and New York's Governor Nelson A. Rockefeller. Although the border-state governor, whose candidacy was to further the emerging **Southern Strategy,** declared himself "stunned" by his nomination, it could not have come as a complete surprise. Several months earlier, he had publicly switched from the Rockefeller to the Nixon camp, and *Time* magazine had already reported that Mr. Nixon was "dropping hints that he might look to Annapolis for a running mate."

However, the voters of the nation were truly stunned and began humorously asking one another, "Spiro *who?*" As the candidate himself admitted: "Spiro Agnew is not a household word." He had, in fact, never held elective office until the 1960s. As governor, his handling of that office had been generously described as "competent," but following his angry outburst at black leaders after the Baltimore riots of 1968, one civil rights leader was to note that "Agnew is the kind of guy who can't be described in terms of good or bad. He is a sort of nonentity."

The nation was destined to know him better. During the 1968 election campaign he was responsible for so many verbal indiscretions that in Washington one critic greeted him with a sign that read: "Apologize now, Spiro, it will save time later." Among the things that the vice-presidential candidate had to apologize for was the use of such expressions as "fat Jap" and "Polack." When he announced that Democratic presidential nominee Hubert H. Humphrey was "squishy soft" on communism, the uproar and accusations of **McCarthyism** were such that he was forced into an ambiguous retraction. Humphrey noted at the time that Agnew must have gotten "hold of one of Nixon's old speeches."

As "Zorba the Veep"—a name inspired by his Greek ancestry—after his election the Vice President often seemed to speak out in terms which President Nixon had abandoned in favor of a new and moderate image. In November 1969, presumably with President Nixon's approval, he opened an attack on the news media by telling a Des Moines, Iowa, audience that he deplored the power of a "small band of network commentators."

In his attacks, Vice President Agnew showed an increasing fondness for alliteration that bordered on obsession. For example, the nation heard dissidents described as "parasites of passion," "effete snobs," or "**nattering nabobs of negativism.**"

Vice President Agnew's career came to an abrupt end during his second term when on October 10, 1973, he resigned from office and several hours later pleaded nolo contendere to a charge of income tax evasion. As part of a plea-bargain agreement, the grand jury made public information that indicated that both as Governor of Maryland and as Vice President of the United States Agnew had accepted payoffs from construction company executives. President Nixon, who was himself to resign the following year as the result of the mounting **Watergate Scandal,** appointed Rep. Gerald R. Ford (R.-Mich.) to succeed him in office.

Spock Generation   Conservative critics of the student protests that spread across American campuses in the 1960s blamed the rebelliousness of the young people at least partly on Dr. Benjamin Spock, author of *The Common Sense Book of Baby and Child Care.* Published in 1946, the book immediately became the "bible" of most middle-class young parents, who responded to its apparently relaxed attitude toward the problems of child-raising. It was the "permissively" raised children of these parents who were now "troubling" the campuses with antiwar demonstrations, the seizure of faculty buildings (*see* **Siege of Morningside Heights**) and draft-card burnings.

In January 1968, the baby doctor himself was charged with "conspiring to counsel, aid and abet" draft evaders, and in June of that year he and Yale University chaplain William Sloane Coffin, Jr., were among four found guilty of that charge in Boston's Federal District Court. Dr. Spock's conviction was reversed on the grounds of insufficient evidence in July 1968.

With the rise of Women's Liberation in the 1970s, Dr. Spock was once more under fire—this time by feminists who objected to the "sexist attitudes" built into his counseling. In a second edition of his book published in 1968, the pediatrician had already defensively noted: "I want to apologize to the mother and father who have a girl and are frustrated by having the child called *him* through this book. It's clumsy to say *him* or *her* every time and I need *her* to refer to the mother." Nevertheless, he felt it necessary to revise the book again in 1976. "The main reason I'm revising it," he noted, "is because I came to recognize that the earlier editions showed common sexist attitudes that contributed to the build-up of discrimination against girls and women." Less permissive than was commonly thought ("He was a stern person," said his estranged wife in 1976), he was also concerned by the rise of violence in American life.

The third edition carries a full-page dedication to his wife in which he acknowledges the importance of her contribution to the original book, which in spite of the criticisms directed against it at various times went through 208 printings and 28 million copies in thirty years.

Spring Mobilization Committee Organized by pacifist David Dellinger and others, it sponsored giant New York and San Francisco parades on April 15, 1967, to protest the continuing **Vietnam War.** The success of these protests led to the establishment of the **National Mobilization Committee to End the War in Vietnam** (Mobe).

SPU *See* **Student Peace Union.**

Sputnik On October 4, 1957, Soviet scientists participating in the **International Geophysical Year** (IGY, July 1957–December 1958) startled the world by launching into space *Sputnik I,* a 184-pound man-made satellite that orbited the earth every 96.1 minutes. *Sputnik* carried two radios that sent out a beeping signal as it sped through space, and nowhere was that beep heard more loudly than in Washington.

Exactly one month later, the Soviet Union capped its scientific—and political—coup by sending into orbit *Sputnik II,* which carried a dog named Laika. Although Laika was destined to die in space because reentry procedures were still beyond the grasp of science, she did prove that it was possible to survive the shock of launching and the state of weightlessness.

Jolted into action, the lagging American space program that was to place the first men on the moon in 1969 (*see* **Project Apollo**) made a modest debut on January 31, 1958, when a Jupiter-C rocket placed a thirty-one-pound satellite (*Explorer I*) into an earth orbit. The space race was launched, but once more the Soviet Union scored a scientific triumph when on May 15, 1958, it launched into orbit *Sputnik III,* an almost 3,000-pound space laboratory.

The term Sputnik means "traveling companion" and had been coined by the pioneer Soviet space scientist Konstantin Tsiolkovsky, who died in 1953 after almost a half-century of investigation into rocket theory and fuels. His first scientific article appeared in 1903, but he was largely ignored until after World War I, when his earlier writings were republished. The launching of *Sputnik I* was planned for the celebration of the 100th anniversary of his birth in 1857. Tsiolkovsky's importance in Soviet rocket science parallels that of Robert Goddard in the United States.

SST *See* **Supersonic Transport.**

"Star Trek" Created by Gene Roddenberry, this television science-fiction series focusing on the interstellar voyages of the space ship U.S.S. *Enterprise* was launched by NBC on September 8, 1966, and continued with indifferent success for seventy-eight episodes until the series was cancelled after March 29, 1969. Although during the original runs the program failed to attract a mass audience, it was awarded an Emmy by the National Academy of TV Arts and Sciences, the television equivalent of the Academy of Motion Picture Arts and Sciences that makes the annual Oscar awards for films.

Thanks to the loyal support of cultist fans, whose letter-writing campaigns had kept the original program on the air for three seasons, "Star Trek" has had an amazingly vigorous afterlife. By 1972 the books, magazines, model kits, pendants, and posters based on the show had developed into a multimillion-dollar industry controlled by Star Trek Enterprises. Reruns began in 1973 and a variety of national Star Trek societies began drawing "Trekkies" to annual conventions at which there was brisk trading in mementos of the show. In addition, the Smithsonian Institution in Washington, D.C., acquired a copy of the pilot script and several of the props used in filming the show, which is even now being shown in fifty-five foreign countries.

The most popular members of the *Enterprise* crew were the indomitable Captain Kirk (William Shatner) and Mr. Spock (Leonard Nimoy), a "Vulcan" with pointed ears and a logical mind immune to the distortions of human emotion.

States' Rights Democrats Five days after the Democrats, meeting in Philadelphia on July 12, 1948, had adopted a strong civil rights platform and nominated Harry S Truman and Alben W. Barkley as the party's presidential and vice-presidential candidates, 6,000 segregationist Southerners from thirteen states met in Birmingham, Alabama, and "nominated" South Carolina's Governor, J. Strom Thurmond, and Mississippi's Governor, Fielding L. Wright, to run against the regular Democratic ticket. Assailing President Truman's civil rights program as an attempt "to make Southerners into a mongrel, inferior race by forced intermingling with Negroes," the rump convention adopted a platform stressing states' rights and condemning the platform of the Democratic party. "We stand for the segregation of the races and the racial integrity of each race; the constitutional right to choose one's associates; to accept private employment without government interference, and to earn one's living in any lawful way. We oppose the elimination of segregation. . . ."

Addressing the rebellious Southerners, Governor Thurmond, known for his anti-poll tax and anti-lynching stand, accused President Truman of having "betrayed" the South and warned that "we have just begun to fight." Although the convention called for the defeat of both President Truman and Republican nominee Thomas E. Dewey, its actions seemed designed to assure a Republican victory at the polls by draining votes away from the regular Democratic ticket, already threatened by Henry Wallace's **Progressive Party of America.**

On July 24, the steering committee of the Southerners who had deserted the Democratic party met in Atlanta and adopted the name States' Rights Democrats for their new party. The committee announced that Governors Thurmond and Wright would be officially notified of their nomination at a rally in Houston on August 11. In the subsequent 1948 national election the "Dixiecrats," as they were popularly known—the name was thought up by William Weisner, a staff member of the Charlotte, North Carolina, *News*—polled 1,169,021 popular votes and the thirty-eight electoral votes of Alabama, Louisiana, Mississippi, and South Carolina. (In addition, a single Tennessee elector later refused to cast his vote for the Democratic ticket which had carried the state.)

Governor Thurmond disapproved of the Dixiecrat label and felt that it was "a five-yard penalty" in talking to non-Southerners.

Status of Forces Treaty *See* **Girard Case; Bricker Amendment.**

The Status Seekers In 1959, Vance Packard, who two years earlier in **The Hidden Persuaders** had investigated the application of "motivational research" techniques to advertising, turned his attention to "an exploration of class behavior in America and the hidden barriers that affect you, your community, your future." Although sociologists and anthropologists objected to his "tabloid presentation" and his lack of professional competence in the field, the book immediately began climbing the bestseller lists.

With suitable, but inadequately documented, references to scholarly studies, the author records in journalistic vernacular snobbish attempts to use "status symbols" such as occupations, homes, voting patterns, education, the use of leisure, religious affiliations, and purchasing power to keep prosperity and technological change from blurring formerly clear-cut distinctions between the middle and lower classes, and the middle and upper classes. He puts special emphasis on the recent emergence of a "diploma elite" based on education.

Concentrating on anecdote, the book focuses almost exclusively on the middle-income groups in America and, with a sentimental democratic nostalgia, avoids analysis of the relationship between class stratification and economic or political power.

Steady State Theory *See* **Big Bang Theory.**

Stennis Plan As the result of a bipartisan Senate resolution on May 1, 1973, calling for the appointment of a special prosecutor to prosecute those involved in criminal activities related to the break-in of Democratic National Committee headquarters in 1972 (*see* **Watergate Scandal**), Harvard law professor Archibald Cox was appointed to that post by Attorney General Elliot L. Richardson. In July, Cox and the White House came into conflict when the latter rejected the subpoena for nine tapes relating to Watergate (*see* **Nixon Tapes**). When on October 12, 1973, the Washington Court of Appeals ordered that the tapes be surrendered to Judge John J. Sirica by October 19, the men surrounding President Richard M. Nixon tried to work out a compromise under which edited transcripts of the tapes would be furnished after they had been verified by a single witness who would have had access to the tapes themselves.

Senator John Stennis (D.-Mo.), the man selected to do the verifying, was seventy-two years old and in feeble health because of a mugging attack eight months earlier. Under the impression that he would verify the transcripts for the Senate Watergate Committee rather than for the courts, he reluctantly accepted the job. After some hesitation and attempts to work out a further compromise, Special Prosecutor Cox rejected the Stennis Plan. On October 19, President Nixon announced that he would edit a summary of the tapes for the courts, but the following day Cox announced at a televised news conference that he would secure a judicial ruling stating that the President had violated a specific court order to release the tapes themselves.

These events led to the **Saturday Night Massacre** in which Attorney General Richardson resigned rather than follow the President's order to fire Cox. When Deputy Attorney General William D. Ruckelshaus also resigned after refusing to follow the same order, Solicitor General Robert H. Bork was appointed Acting Attorney General and he fired Cox.

The President's effort to meet the crisis over the tapes by firing the Special Prosecutor is sometimes known as the "Bickel option," because it was inadvertently suggested by an article by Yale law professor Alexander M. Bickel which appeared in the September 29, 1973, issue of *The New Republic*. In it Professor Bickel pointed out that "Mr. Cox has no constitutional or otherwise legal existence except as he is a creature of the Attorney General, who is a creature of the President."

"Stonewalling" The word came into prominence during the disclosures subsequent to the break-in of Democratic National Committee headquarters at the Watergate Hotel complex in Washington, D.C., on June 17, 1972. It was used in secret conversations between President Richard M. Nixon and members of the **Committee to Re-elect the President** (CREEP; CRP) of the White House staff to mean preventing the disclosure of information by failing to answer questions and otherwise blocking investigative procedure. In British parliamentary terminology it means using obstructive tactics for the purpose of consuming time, i.e., filibuster. In football, a "stonewall defense" is a strong team.

Probably the most notorious use of the word came to light following the release of some of the recordings (*see* **Nixon Tapes**) of conversations between the President and his associates. On March 22, 1973, President Nixon was recorded as saying: "I don't give a shit what happens. I want you all to stonewall it. Let them plead the Fifth Amendment, cover up or anything else that will save the plan. That's the whole point."

On edited transcripts of tapes released by the White House on April 30, 1974, the expression "expletive deleted" was substituted for obscenities.

See **Watergate Scandal**.

Strategic Air Command (SAC) The largest of the U.S. Air Force's thirteen major commands, the Strategic Air Command (SAC) was activated on March 21, 1946. Two years later its headquarters was shifted from the vicinity of Washington, D.C., to Offutt Air Force Base, Omaha, Nebraska.

SAC's primary mission is the organization, training, equipment, administration, and preparation of strategic air forces for combat. This includes bombardment, missile, special mission, and strategic reconnaissance units.

A similar mission in tactical air operations is assigned to the Tactical Air Command (TAC), which is the Air Force component of the U.S. Readiness Command and the U.S. Atlantic Command. Along with the other services, TAC participates in the development of doctrine, procedures, tactics, techniques, training, and equipment for joint operations.

The **"massive retaliation"** doctrine enunciated by Secretary of State John Foster Dulles on January 12, 1954, was predicated on the ability of SAC to deliver "instant, massive retaliation" against a potential aggressor "at times and places of our own choosing."

Strategic Arms Limitation Talks (SALT) As the result of meetings held in Helsinki and Vienna in 1969 and 1970, the United States and the Soviet Union agreed in 1972 on a treaty limiting each nation to the deployment of no more than two **antiballistic missile systems** (ABMS) and on executive agreement—scheduled to expire in October 1977—limiting offensive weapons to those already in existence or under construction. The treaty was ratified by the Senate on August 3, 1972. Although the executive agreement did not require congressional approval, the Nixon administration submitted it to both houses in the form of a resolution, which was adopted with minor amendments on September 25, 1972.

Compliance with what became known as the SALT I accords is generally considered satisfactory, although some critics have insisted the U.S.S.R. has not lived up to the spirit of them, especially as concerns the interpretation of exactly what constitutes a "heavy missile."

Although SALT II talks began soon after the conclusion of the original accords, the basic framework for them was not set until President Gerald R. Ford met with U.S.S.R. General Secretary Leonid I. Brezhnev in Vladivostok (November 1974). The result was an *aide-mémoire* which limited each nation to 2,400 "strategic launchers." Of that number, no more than 1,320 could be armed with **multiple individually targetable reentry vehicles** (bomb clusters known as MIRVs).

No formal SALT II accords were reached, and in 1977 further progress seemed stalled by failure to obtain agreement on two outstanding issues.

Was the Soviet Backfire bomber to be considered a "strategic" weapon along with **intercontinental ballistic missiles** (ICBMs), submarine-launched ballistic missiles (SLBMs), and long-range bombers? If not, the Soviet cutback to reach the 2,400 figure agreed on in 1974 would be small. The U.S.S.R. had insisted that the Backfire was designed to attack targets on its periphery and not in the United States.

The second point at issue concerned limitations or a ban on nuclear **cruise missiles,** which were no longer the cumbersome and inaccurate weapons they had been in the 1950s. The problem is complicated by the fact that while air-launched cruise missiles (ALCMs) could be spotted by the reconnaissance satellites used to check on other strategic weapons, sea-launched cruise missiles (SCLMs) could be borne undetected upon a variety of naval craft.

SALT II talks were still stalled in spring 1979.

Strategic Hamlet Plan Adopted in March 1962 as a means of combatting communist guerrilla forces in the **Vietnam War,** it was first suggested by Robert K. G. Thompson, head of the British Advisory Mission in Saigon.

Thompson, who had had considerable experience fighting terrorists in Malaya, pointed out that the main thrust of the Viet Cong was concentrated in trying to gain administrative control over the 16,000 South Vietnamese hamlets and that fighting between regular troops was considered as secondary. The guerrillas in the area, he argued, could maintain themselves as long as they had either the voluntary or enforced support of the peasants. Given such circumstances, they were free to choose the conditions and moment of combat.

Under the strategic hamlet program, villages enclosed behind barbed wire and moats were armed so they could hold out against marauders until reinforcements could be sent. (Outlying habitations were relocated within this fortified area, and in some cases entire villages were uprooted.) In addition, civic action teams were to be sent out to supply the hamlets with basic government services, educational facilities, and agricultural extension loans.

Under the plan as originally conceived, the strategic hamlet area was to spread "oil blot" fashion from the sea toward the mountain and jungle strongholds of the communists. Villagers were given identity cards, curfews were set up, and checkpoints established.

Although security was to be the main focus of the program, Thompson felt that by means of revolutionary political, social, and economic changes within the hamlets the villagers could be won over to the government cause. He considered this aspect of the program an important war measure in that it could help isolate the guerrillas and cut them off from information and supplies.

When after the fall and assassination of President Ngo Dinh Diem in October 1963 villagers were allowed to leave the strategic hamlets if they so desired, there was a mass exodus. The program collapsed, even though on paper the statistics presented the American forces by the Diem regime had appeared excellent. It was learned that of the 8,600 strategic hamlets said to have been established, only 20 percent met the standards originally prescribed. In addition, the "oil blot" principle had been ignored and hamlets were often established in completely isolated areas.

As one South Vietnamese general put it, since

Secretary of Defense Robert S. McNamara loved statistics, they were manufactured to please him.

See **Operation Sunrise.**

Strategy of Peace Speaking at American University, Washington, D.C., on June 10, 1963, President John F. Kennedy announced that this nation would refrain from nuclear testing in the atmosphere so long as other nations did so too. Rejecting the notion that war was inevitable, he urged that both the United States and the Soviet Union reassess their basic attitudes toward one another and find a way out of the "vicious and dangerous cycle" of **cold war.**

In an age when great powers can maintain relatively invulnerable nuclear forces and a single nuclear weapon contains almost ten times the explosive force delivered by all the Allied air forces in World War II, the idea of total war could no longer be entertained, he noted. "It makes no sense in an age when the deadly poisons produced by a nuclear exchange would be carried by wind and water and soil and seed to the far corners of the globe and to generations yet unborn."

Announcing forthcoming discussions in Moscow on a treaty to outlaw nuclear tests, he said that the United States did not despair of success in eliminating war. "Confident and unafraid, we labor on—not toward a strategy of annihilation but toward a strategy of peace."

Beginning on July 15, 1963, the representatives of the United States, Great Britain, and the Soviet Union in Moscow participated in discussions that led on August 5, 1963, to a treaty under which their nations agreed not to test nuclear weapons in the atmosphere, in outer space, or underwater. Underground testing was permitted.

See **Nuclear Test Ban Treaty.**

Streaking A spring 1974 campus fad that seemed a welcome return to more traditional student lunacy after the turbulence of the late 1960s, streaking consisted of racing through a public area clad only in sneakers and a smile. There seemed to be no end to the varieties of streaking, which might involve either one brave soul or as many as 1,543 (University of Georgia). Honors for the most extended streak went to a group of students at Texas Tech, Lubbock, whose sprinting continued for five hours. In Lima, Ohio, a middle-aged couple too old to run was arrested for "snailing" through a public square in their birthday suits. In Paris, a dozen American students bared their all in the shade of the Eiffel Tower before a mixed group of delighted and en-

raged spectators who had their eyes peeled. Protesting nudists in Florida turned the process and the word around by "gnikaerts" fully clothed, and at the University of Alaska sixteen students in below-zero temperatures turned into blue streaks. The passion for streaking even hit West Point, where several dozen cadets were reported completely out of uniform. TV viewers watching the 1974 Academy Awards presentation saw a male streaker upstage the debonair David Niven.

Psychologists and social commentators called on to explain the phenomenon were unembarrassed by the problem. Marshall McLuhan, expert on the communications media, considered it "a form of assault," but psychologist Joyce Brothers confidently assured worried parents and university officials that "there's nothing at all sexual about streaking. If a beautiful woman stopped a streaker and told him 'You've won me,' he wouldn't react sexually. He would slink away embarrassed."

There were no reports of this theory having been put to the test.

Strontium-90 A radioactive isotope, strontium-90 is one of the major hazards of atomic fallout resulting from the testing of nuclear devices in the air. Possessing a half-life of twenty-five years, it is chemically similar to calcium and when deposited on the soil is readily taken up into plant and animal life. Once absorbed into food products such as milk and meat, it settles in the bones, causing cancer and leukemia, especially in children.

When on March 1, 1954, the **Atomic Energy Commission** (AEC) began a new series of tests and exploded its second hydrogen bomb at its Pacific proving grounds in the Marshall Islands, meteorologists had predicted a strong northward breeze, but instead the fallout blew the radioactive dust south and beyond what was considered the danger zone. As a result, twenty-three Japanese fishermen on a trawler named *Lucky Dragon Five* were caught in a radioactive shower. All had to be hospitalized and one eventually died.

Scientific records of the concentration of strontium-90 in humans date from 1953, and by the end of the decade it was estimated to have increased by 50 percent a year as nuclear testing continued. One-year-old infants were shown to have absorbed 2.6 units, adults 0.3. It was estimated that if testing in the air continued, by the 1970s the health of people everywhere would be affected as traces of the radioactive isotope were picked up in rainfall in the United States and Europe, in addition to heavier concentrations in Japan and Australia. However,

Rear Admiral Lewis A. Strauss, chairman of the AEC, felt that such predictions were "alarmist" on the basis of the findings of his own technicians, who were carrying on investigations all over the world in what he called "Operation Sunshine."

In 1956 strontium-90 became an issue in the presidential campaign when Democratic nominee Adlai Stevenson charged that the fallout from H-bomb tests was causing bone cancer, sterility, and other diseases. President Dwight D. Eisenhower asked the AEC and other scientific agencies to report to him on these dangers. It was later announced that in the opinion of the National Academy of Sciences the amount of strontium-90 absorbed by most people as a result of nuclear testing was only a fraction of the amount they would be most likely to absorb during the average lifetime of X-ray testing.

See **"Clean" Bomb Controversy.**

Student Nonviolent Coordinating Committee (SNCC; Snick) Meeting in Raleigh, North Carolina, in April 1960, the black students who had taken part in **sit-ins** earlier that year formed the Temporary Student Nonviolent Coordinating Committee. (It was not until later in the year that the committee was made permanent and became known as SNCC.)

Instrumental in its creation was Ella Baker, a black woman working with the **Southern Christian Leadership Conference** (SCLC) set up by the Reverend Martin Luther King, Jr., after the successful **Montgomery Bus Strike.** The organization was for several years run by John Lewis. In its founding statement, SNCC noted: "We affirm the philosophical or religious ideal of nonviolence as the foundation of our purpose, the presupposition of our belief, and the manner of our action."

It was under the guidance of the nonviolence principle that SNCC became the focus of civil rights actions in the early 1960s. "Field secretaries" living on $10 a week spread out into the Deep South and, in spite of being beaten and jailed by local authorities, were successful in getting blacks to form grass-roots movements and band together in defense of their constitutional rights. In the exciting years that followed, SNCC participated in **freedom rides,** voter-registration drives, the formation of the **Mississippi Freedom Democratic Party,** (MFDP), and the **Selma-Montgomery march** of 25,000 to protest discrimination against the registration of black voters. Decisive roles were played by John Lewis, chairman, and James Forman, executive secretary.

But after the failure of the 1964 Democratic National Convention to seat delegates of the MFDP, SNCC's orientation began to shift from nonviolence, and the committee more and more often came into conflict with the longer-established groups such as SCLC and **Congress of Racial Equality** (CORE). *Student Voice*, its original newsletter edited by Julian Bond, was replaced by the more strident *Nitty Gritty*, and in 1966 Stokely Carmichael was elected SNCC president. Nonviolence gave way as a slogan and principle to H. Rap Brown's cry for **Black Power.** As a result of this changed orientation, SNCC's financial support from white liberals crumbled. By 1968, the committee was moribund.

At its height it had 250 full-time workers. In Mississippi in the summer of 1964, more than 1,000 SNCC members and their supporters were arrested, eight were severely beaten, and six were murdered. But the demonstrations led by SNCC were helpful in bringing about the public accommodations laws of that year and the **Voting Rights Act of 1965.**

In November 1976, former members of SNCC held a reunion in Atlanta, Georgia. ("Stylish Clothes Replace Old Denim at Reunion of 1960's Group" ran *The New York Times* head on the story.) Among the items on the agenda was consideration of whether or not to bring suit againt the FBI for illegal spying against members in the 1960s. Conspicuously absent from the reunion were Stokely Carmichael and H. Rap Brown.

Student Peace Union (SPU) Formed in Chicago in 1959, the Student Peace Union (SPU) was probably the first student political association with national representation. In 1961 it adopted a "third camp" position in its fight for world peace. Some of its goals are indicated in the following excerpt from a widely distributed pamphlet:

We urge:

—that America not heed the hysterical cry of those who would duplicate the criminal act of the Soviet Union by testing in the atmosphere;

—immediate cessation of all testing, followed by further American initiatives towards peace;

—settlement of the Berlin crisis by the creation of a nuclear-free and disarmed zone in Central Europe—both Germanies must be taken out of the **Cold War;**

—investigation of alternative use of the huge sums spent for ineffective "defense" measures, in order to cut the tie of our economy to the Cold War;

—massive aid to the economically underdeveloped countries;

—the building of a strong U.N. with increased responsibilities in the field of arbitration of crisis situations.

The SPU was dissolved following its decline in 1963.

Students for a Democratic Society (SDS) The radical spearhead of the student protest movement of the 1960s, Students for a Democratic Society (SDS) had its roots in the Student League for Industrial Democracy (SLID), which had played a similar role in the mid-1930s. The name first appeared when in 1960 the League for Industrial Democracy (LID) determined to relaunch its student division under the name Students for a Democratic Society, an organization which remained essentially inactive until some thirty students met in Ann Arbor, Michigan, December 28–31, 1961, to establish the executive structure of a founding convention to be held the following year. The leaders of the group were three University of Michigan students: Tom Hayden, Al Haber, and Bob Ross.

Less than sixty students—only forty-three of whom had votes—representing eleven SDS chapters convened on June 15, 1962, at the FDR Labor Center, a United Automobile Workers (UAW) summer camp in Port Huron, Michigan. It was there that they adopted "as a document with which the SDS officially identifies" the so-called **Port Huron Statement,** a manifesto of principles which was largely the work of Tom Hayden. A controversial section condemning American "paranoia about the Soviet Union" caused a dispute with the strongly anticommunist LID which was settled largely through the intercession of Socialist leader Norman Thomas.

In addition to participating in the civil rights drive and the demonstrations against the **Vietnam War** that characterized the 1960s, the SDS launched community organization projects in the **"participatory democracy"** called for in the Port Huron Statement by organizing groups such as Chicago's Jobs or Income Now (JOIN) and the Economic Research Action Project (ERAP) under the direction of Rennie Davis. ERAP got its start when in April 1963 Tom Hayden, the first SDS president, wrote UAW's Walter Reuther requesting funds with which to finance an "education and action program around economic issues." Reuther sent $5,000. In spring 1965, the program was dissolved.

By 1966, SDS claimed some 5,500 members—most of them white and middle class—distributed among 151 chapters spread through most of the country. It was governed by a thirty-five-member National Council and maintained national headquarters in Chicago. Carl Oglesby, who had been president since 1965, noted that at its best, SDS was

. . . SNCC translated to the North and trained on a somewhat different and broader set of issues. . . . We work to remove from society . . . the inequity that coordinates with injustice to create plain suffering and to make custom of distrust. Poverty. Racism. The assembly line universities of this Pepsi Generation. The ulcerating drive for affluence. And the ideology of anti-communism, too, because it smothers my curiosity and bribes my compassion.

Originally, SDS took a nonviolent stand, but as the decade wore on, it more and more became identified with violent protest such as the **Siege of Morningside Heights** in April and May 1968. During this period, *Time* magazine called it "a loosely formed amalgam of some 35,000 young people who boast chapters on at least 250 campuses and, if anything, shy away from organization." This membership figure seems unlikely because, while many students may at one time or another have sympathized with SDS aims, even at its height SDS had little more than 7,000 paying members affiliated with the national office.

By the end of the decade, factional disputes caused SDS to split into the Revolutionary Youth Movement I—which became known as the **Weathermen**—and Revolutionary Youth Movement II.

SUB *See* **Guaranteed Annual Wage.**

Submerged Lands Act *See* **Tidelands Oil Controversy.**

Suez Crisis As a result of Secretary of State John Foster Dulles' abrupt cancellation of a promised $56 million to finance the Aswan High Dam project, Egypt's President Gamal Abdel Nasser, who had also failed to negotiate loans from Great Britain, seized the Suez Canal on July 26, 1956. Since the annual income from the canal was $100 million, he announced, "We shall rely on our own strength, our own muscle, our own funds."

Then on October 29, Israeli armed forces suddenly moved into Egyptian territory on the Sinai Peninsula on the east side of the Suez Canal. They had support and encouragement from the British and French, who had been cut off by the seizure of the canal from their chief sources of petroleum. Since the Tripartite Declaration of 1950 gave these nations the right to intervene militarily in the event of a breakdown in peace between Israel and Egypt, they dispatched invasion and bomber forces to the area.

The Soviet Union immediately proposed to the United States joint military action to halt the invasion, but the suggestion was indignantly rejected by President Dwight D. Eisenhower, who pointed out that at that very moment the Russians were brutally suppressing an anticommunist revolt in Hungary. However, in a nationwide television address, the President declared his opposition to this attempt to take over the canal by force. "There can be no peace—without law. And there can be no law—if we were to invoke one code of international conduct for those who oppose us—and another for our friends."

Soviet threats of unilateral intervention and pressure from the United States caused Great Britain and a more tenacious France to agree to a United Nations cease-fire after French infantry had landed on the east side of the canal—which the Egyptians had blocked with sunken ships—and British troops had taken over the west side at Port Said.

Summer of Love In 1967, the Haight-Ashbury section of San Francisco became a magnet that attracted thousands of young people who felt alienated from their middle-class backgrounds. Temporarily, at least, they found acceptance and satisfaction in a variety of communes and crash pads. Music, drugs, and sex—the news media informed the sensation-hungry nation—abounded. For a while it was less obvious that promoters, pushers, and prostitutes were beginning to outnumber the genuine "flower children." By autumn, however, disillusion had begun to set in and the Summer of Love came to a symbolic end with a "funeral" held in Buena Vista Park. The "deceased" was "Hippie, devoted son of Mass Media."

The San Francisco scene had its counterpart in New York's East Village.

Sun Day Patterned after the 1970 **Earth Day** observance, special activities across the nation on May 3, 1978, were designed to educate the general public about the potential of solar energy and to encourage federal support for its use. Solar energy exhibits, tours of homes and factories making use of solar energy, and sunrise ceremonies were held in all fifty states, and similar events were scheduled in many nations abroad. The national program was coordinated by Solar Action Inc., a Washington, D.C., organization formed with $250,000 in contributions from private individuals, foundations, industry, and universities.

Speaking in Golden, Colorado, President Jimmy Carter announced that in the next year the federal government would spend an additional $100 million "for expanded efforts in solar research, development and demonstration projects, and the development of commercial uses such as windmills. . . ." He also said that he had instructed his Cabinet to formulate a "national solar strategy," and he announced that during the next three years solar energy equipment would be installed in a variety of federal buildings, including the White House, which would get a solar hot-water-heating system.

Stressing the need to reduce the costs of solar energy conversion through mass production, the President noted that "nobody can embargo sunlight. No cartel controls the sun. Its energy will not run out. It will not pollute our air or poison our waters. It is free from stench and smog. The sun's power needs only to be collected, stored and used."

See **Energy Crisis.**

Sunday Night Massacre In a surprise move on Sunday, November 2, 1975, President Gerald R. Ford dismissed Secretary of Defense James R. Schlesinger and CIA Director William Colby. In addition, he requested Secretary of State Henry A. Kissinger to relinquish his post as White House national security adviser, a position in which he had served for seven years.

On November 3, the President also announced that he would nominate Elliot L. Richardson, recently appointed Ambassador to Great Britain, to succeed Rogers C. B. Morton as Secretary of Commerce. The following day, Vice President Nelson A. Rockefeller added to the upheaval in Washington by announcing that he would not run on the Ford ticket in 1976. He later noted that his decision, apparently neither sought nor opposed by the President, had been brought on by "party squabbles."

The removal of Secretary Schlesinger, who had opposed cuts in defense spending, was interpreted by most critics as a victory for Secretary Kissinger's policy of "détente." Although the publicized disagreement between the two men was originally denied by the President as being behind the dismissal, a few days later he conceded that it had indeed influenced his decision.

White House Chief of Staff Donald H. Rumsfeld was nominated to succeed to the post of Secretary of Defense, and George Bush, head of the United States Liaison Office in Peking, was designated to succeed as CIA Director. The moves were described by the President as an attempt to provide "closer liaison and cooperation" on matters of foreign policy and national defense. The Air Force's

Lt. General Brent Scowcroft, deputy general of the National Security Council, was appointed the President's adviser on national security.

The name given by the press to these abrupt changes in Washington echoes both the famous **"Saturday Night Massacre"** of the Nixon administration and the **"Thanksgiving Massacre"** of the Kennedy administration.

Supersonic Transport (SST) When in June 1963 President John F. Kennedy recommended for congressional consideration a federally funded supersonic transport (SST) project, he noted that it might have to be revamped or halted if supersonic transport proved economically infeasible, if technological problems could not be solved, and if sonic boom overpressures resulted in public nuisances.

The deadline for the detailed design phase was to be 1965, but it was not until 1969, when the Nixon administration was in power, that the Federal Aviation Administration (FAA) accepted from the Boeing Company a final design that included the "swing-wing," by means of which it was hoped that a moderate-size SST with an acceptable sonic boom could be economically built. The following year, however, Boeing admitted that its design could not be made to work in practice. Faced with an option between a larger plane or no plane, the FAA settled for something more than twice as big as what President Kennedy had originally considered—and with a correspondingly greater sonic boom.

But beginning in 1967, segments of public opinion had already been aroused by warnings of the environmental danger posed by supersonic transport. This was chiefly due to the efforts of Dr. William A. Shurcliff, who founded the Citizens League Against the Sonic Boom (CLASB).

When President Richard M. Nixon assumed office in 1969, he immediately established a governmental SST Review Committee and a President's Science Advisory Committee composed of independent experts headed by Richard Garwin to evaluate the SST proposals. Both committees turned in negative recommendations from technical, economic, and environmental points of view—it was considered that SST exhaust gases could seriously affect the upper atmosphere—but these reports were kept from the public.

Ignoring the recommendations of the committees he had established, the President, in September 1969, asked Congress for additional SST appropriations and received them, thanks in some measure to the fact that the Senate fight was led by Democratic Senators Warren Magnuson and Henry Jackson, both from the state of Washington, the home of the Boeing Company. However, by 1970, CLASB had brought public sentiment against the SST to such a pitch that a new appropriations bill was defeated in the Senate in December and shortly afterward both houses agreed to kill the project permanently.

In the interval a major national debate had raged with leading figures such as New York's Governor Nelson A. Rockefeller vowing to keep the SST out of his state, and Senators Magnuson and Jackson overwhelmed by an opposition led by Sen. William Proxmire (D.-Wis.), Sen. J. William Fulbright (D.-Ark.), and Sen. Gaylord Nelson (D.-Wis.). Thanks to the efforts of Rep. Henry Reuss (D.-Wis.), the damaging SST Review Committee reports were made public in 1969, but the so-called Garwin Report—which explicitly said: "We recommend the termination of the development contracts and the withdrawal of Government support from the SST prototype program"—did not become public until August 17, 1971.

Supplemental Unemployment Benefits *See* **Guaranteed Annual Wage.**

Supreme Commander for Allied Powers (SCAP) Hostilities in World War II came to a formal close on August 14, 1945, when the Japanese surrendered on condition that Emperor Hirohito be allowed to retain his throne. General Douglas MacArthur, who had been Supreme Allied Commander in the Southwest Pacific since February 1942, was appointed Supreme Commander of the Allied Powers—generally referred to as SCAP—and in the weeks following, set up the American occupation of Japan. Profiting from what were at that time seen as "mistakes" in organizing the occupation of Germany and Austria, President Harry S Truman refused the Soviet demand for the right to occupy a portion of the island of Hokkaido. As a result, though the military occupation was technically undertaken by the Allied Powers, it was for all practical purposes an American operation. Some Soviet objections to the situation were met in December 1945 by the creation of an eleven-nation Far Eastern Commission that had its headquarters in Washington, D.C. In addition, SCAP was advised on occupation matters by a Four-Power Council made up of the United States, Great Britain, China, and the Soviet Union; however, neither the commission nor the council were ever to play a decisive role in the occupation. SCAP's goals were the demilitarization of Japan and the establishment of a social basis for democracy.

General MacArthur was replaced in Japan by General Matthew Ridgway after April 10, 1951, when President Truman relieved the former of all his Far Eastern commands (*see* **Korean War** and **"Old soldiers never die; they just fade away"**). In April 1952, after the ratification of the Treaty of San Francisco (September 8, 1951), which was signed by the United States and forty-seven of Japan's former enemies—but not the U.S.S.R., India, and Nationalist China—the occupation of Japan came to a formal end.

Surface-to-Air Missile (SAM) In the years following World War II, the greatest emphasis in guided missile development was placed on the surface-to-air missile (SAM), an antiaircraft missile designed for use against high-speed aircraft and missiles relatively immune to conventional weaponry. Among the better known varieties in use by the U.S. Army are the Chaparral, a mobile air defense adaptation of the U.S. Navy's Sidewinder, an air-to-air missile (AAM); the Hawk, for use against low-flying aircraft; the Nike-Hercules, a continental air defense weapon; and the Redeye, a twenty-pound, shoulder-fired antiaircraft missile. U.S. Navy fleet air defense missiles include the Talos, the Terrier, and the Tartar. Among the better known Soviet SAMs are the Guideline (SA-2), a land-based air defense weapon; the GOA (SA-3), a land- and ship-based guided weapon; and the Galosh, an antiballistic missile.

Surrender on Morningside Heights Shortly after defeating Sen. Robert A. Taft (R.-Ohio) in a hard-fought fight for the 1952 Republican presidential nomination, General Dwight D. Eisenhower paid an unprecedented courtesy call on the man who "up to this moment, I thought [had] every right to think of himself as the logical candidate of the Republican party." This was the first step in healing party unity after the bitterness of the preconvention struggle.

The second step took place when, at the invitation of his former rival, Senator Taft visited General Eisenhower on September 12, 1952, at Eisenhower's Morningside Heights residence, which he occupied as president of Columbia University. After a two-hour breakfast talk, Senator Taft read to the press a prepared text which had been "gone over" by the Republican presidential candidate. "I have tried to state here the basic principles in do-

mestic policy which I think General Eisenhower and I agree on 100 percent." The concentration of the statement was on the need to reduce government spending from the then annual rate of $74 billion. "General Eisenhower has also told me that . . . he abhors the left-wing theory that the Executive has unlimited power . . . that he believes in the basic principles of the **Taft-Hartley Law** . . . and is opposed to its repeal." While he did not accept all the general's views on foreign policy, the Senator concluded that it was "fair to say that our differences are differences of degree."

Democrats and some liberal Republicans immediately attacked the statement as a capitulation to the "ultimatum" Senator Taft had supposedly earlier issued from his vacation retreat in Murray Bay, Canada. It was said that Senator Taft had refused to support the ticket unless he was given these written assurances by his triumphant rival.

Writing in 1963 about Senator Taft's prepared text and remarks, former President Eisenhower professed to see nothing remarkable in them.

Some journalists and the Democratic nominee, however, seemed to think that here was raw drama. The opposition saw in this meeting a great "surrender on Morningside Heights." The fact was that Senator Taft and I had agreed emphatically on the need for fiscal sanity in government, as on most other issues, long before the breakfast talk. In the succeeding weeks he evidenced his enthusiasm for our common cause by a rugged round of campaigning which included more than thirty speeches in nineteen states.

Surveyor I On June 1, 1966, *Surveyor I* became the first of a series of Surveyor spacecraft to achieve a "soft touchdown" on the surface of a celestial body. The U.S.S.R.'s *Luna 9* of February 3, 1966, had made a hard landing, though like *Surveyor I* it was able to send back photographs of the moon's surface.

An advance scout for the men who were to land on the moon as part of **Project Apollo**, *Surveyor I* had crushable aluminum honeycombed landing pads. The soft landing just south of the lunar equator in the Ocean of Storms (Oceanus Procellarum) was considered more important than the lunar photographs sent back because it proved the success of the craft's design. At the time of the landing the six-year-old Surveyor program was running three years behind schedule.

The more than 11,000 photographs transmitted confirmed, among other things, that the lunar surface was firm enough to support a spacecraft landing and the weight of a man walking about. Some theories had maintained that the moon was covered with several feet of fine dust, or that the surface was a fragile froth unable to support weight.

See **Ranger Program.**

Survival Sunday *See* **Clamshell Alliance.**

Swann v. Charlotte-Mecklenburg *See* **Busing.**

Swine Flu Imported into France by Chinese laborers, this virus was brought to the United States by returning soldiers after World War I. It was transferred to pigs and dubbed "swine" virus when later identified in the animals.

When some scientists warned of a possible flu outbreak in the fall of 1976 that would duplicate the 1918–1919 pandemic, President Gerald R. Ford ordered a massive vaccine preparation program as a precautionary step (March 24, 1976). However, on December 16, 1976, the government called a halt to its swine-flu inoculation program because of reports of paralysis in persons who had been given the flu vaccine. At that time only about one-third of the nearly 140 million doses of vaccine produced had been administered. (Worth $40 million, the entire output of the four drug producers involved has been bought up by the government.)

The paralysis, known as the Guillain-Barre syndrome or "French polio," was reported in eighteen states, and by mid-1977 was said to have caused twenty-three deaths in cases where it reached the respiratory system. In most of the approximately 500 cases reported, recovery was rapid and complete.

Few documented cases of swine flu actually appeared and those only in farmworkers who had had close contact with pigs. There was no evidence of person-to-person spread of the disease. However, by May 1977 there was an epidemic of more than $100 million in swine-flu suits against the federal government. (At the time the program had been launched, insurance companies, citing the haste in which it had been undertaken, refused to extend liability protection to the four pharmaceutical companies involved. As a result, the entire program had been placed under the Tort Claims Act which made the government solely responsible for suits alleging negligence.) In Philadelphia, the Andrews Publication Company began publishing a special newsletter for attorneys involved in flu litigation.

On December 4, 1978, the U.S. Supreme Court declined to review the dismissal of a constitutional challenge to the Swine Flu Act of 1976, under which vaccine manufacturers were shielded from liability. The case stemmed from a $2.5 million suit brought by a Louisiana woman who had been partially paralyzed as a result of a vaccine injection. She contended that the law violated her right to due process of law.

Symbionese Liberation Army *See* **Patty Hearst Kidnapping.**

Synanon Founded in 1958 in Ocean Park, California, by Charles E. Dederich, Synanon attracted widespread attention by using a combination of communal living and group therapy in the treatment of alcoholics and drug addicts. It rapidly developed a network of clinics and enjoyed a tax-exempt status as a nonprofit organization.

A basic feature of the therapeutic approach is the "Synanon Game," a no-holds-barred encounter group in which participants are encouraged to act out their hostilities and thereby get at the root of their problems. Membership under Dederich's somewhat authoritarian direction rose to a peak of approximately 10,000 in the early 1970s and thereafter began to decline (an estimated 1,000 in 1978) as the emphasis seemed to switch from rehabilitation to experiments in new life styles at communes in California. *Time* magazine reported (December 26, 1977) in a highly critical article that the corporation had an income of almost $9 million in 1976 and had assets worth $30 million.

"We are in the people business," said Dederich, "just exactly as if we were building Chevrolet axles."

Given the apparently lessening emphasis on rehabilitation, many critics, including disenchanted former Synanon residents, have questioned the corporation's continuing tax-exempt status. The various businesses owned by the group are said to have produced revenues of more than $13 million annually, and in 1977 Dederich was given a $500,000 "retirement bonus."

In December 1978, Dederich was among those charged with the assassination attempt against Paul Morantz, a Los Angeles lawyer who had recently won for a client a $300,000 lawsuit against Synanon. The previous October, Mr. Morantz had been bitten by a rattlesnake placed in his mailbox and soon afterward Los Angeles police arrested two Synanon members and charged them with the crime. The trail led to the Synanon founder after defectors from the group stated in affidavits that he had urged members to "get" Morantz.

Syncom After the creation of the Communications Satellite Corporation (Comsat) in August

1962, a decision had to be made as to whether the basis of a system of commercial communications satellites would be medium- or synchronous-altitude satellites. A medium-altitude relay system would have required up to fifty satellites, but the Syncom project undertaken by the Hughes Aircraft Company under a contract awarded by the **National Aeronautics and Space Administration** (NASA) called for the positioning of three synchronous satellites over the equator to cover the major part of the globe.

The seventy-nine-pound Syncom constructed by Hughes with the guidance of the Goddard Space Flight Center was to be lifted into space by a three-stage Delta rocket and then placed in a twenty-four-hour orbit by a solid-fuel rocket motor attached to the satellite. *Syncom I* was launched on February 14, 1963, but several hours later it ceased sending telemetry symbols and was presumed lost until it was sighted on February 20, 1963, having all but achieved the first synchronous orbit of the space age.

After several reschedulings for a NASA-ordered modification of the electronic system, *Syncom II* was launched on July 26, 1963. Following corrections for an eastward drift, on August 15 it was brought into synchronous orbit.

Syncom III was launched on August 19, 1964, and having been allowed to drift for three weeks went into orbit over the international date line on September 11, 1964. The following month, it transmitted television pictures of the Olympics in Japan to California. After the construction of microwave relay towers over the Atlantic and Pacific Oceans in 1965 and 1966, Comsat was ready to provide commercial service.

The name Syncom is an acronym for *synchronous communication*.

T

38th Parallel

TA *See* **Transactional Analysis.**

TAC *See* **Strategic Air Command.**

Tactical Air Command *See* **Strategic Air Command.**

Taft-Hartley Act Popular name for the Labor Management Relations Act of 1947. A major modification of the Wagner Act of 1935, it was bitterly fought against by organized labor, which called it the "slave labor law." Nevertheless, it became law on June 23, 1946, after Congress overrode the veto of President Harry S Truman three days earlier. Passage of the act had been facilitated by the fact that labor-management strife—particularly in the coal mining and railroad industries—had led to the loss of over 100 million man-days in 1946.

Under the provisions of the act, the closed shop was banned, though the union shop was permitted under rigidly controlled circumstances; employers could sue labor unions for breach of contract or secondary strike damage; the automatic check-off system under which union dues were deducted from pay checks was terminated unless an employer had written permission from an employee; unions were forbidden to contribute to political campaigns; unions were required to make financial statements public and to file with the Secretary of Labor copies of their constitutions and bylaws; and union officials—though not employers—were required to file noncommunist affidavits. Where national safety or health was concerned, the federal government was empowered to obtain an eighty-day injunction—a "cooling off" period—against strikes. A similar cooling-off period was imposed on employers, who had to submit to a newly established Federal Mediation and Conciliation Service a sixty-day notice of their desire to terminate a contract. Section 14b of the act permitted states to pass so-called right-to-work laws, which prohibit the requirement of membership in a union as a condition of employment. (Within ten years, nineteen states eager to attract new industry had passed such legislation.)

The Taft-Hartley Act was the result of a Senate-House conference committee combination of two separate but similar bills: the one submitted by Rep. Fred A. Hartley, Jr. (R.-N.J.), and the other by Sen. Robert A. Taft (R.-Ohio). In his veto message, President Truman argued that taken as a whole the bill would "reverse the basic direction of our national labor policy, inject the Government into private economic affairs on an unprecedented scale, and conflict with important principles of our democratic society." He felt that the provisions of the act would only increase the number of strikes and be "a dangerous stride in the direction of a totally managed economy."

Nevertheless, the President invoked the act's injunction provisions during a coal strike on February 6, 1950, despite a protest from the head of the United Mine Workers union John L. Lewis that "to use the power of the state to drive men into the mines . . . is involuntary servitude." Later, President Dwight D. Eisenhower ordered an eighty-day injunction (October 21, 1959) during a national steel strike that had been in progress since mid-July. (His injunction was upheld by the Supreme Court on November 7, 1959, and the 116-day strike—the longest in the country's history—collapsed.)

The **Landrum-Griffin Act** (1959) repealed the Taft-Hartley provision requiring union officials to file noncommunist affidavits. It also revised the ban on secondary boycotts, extending it to include union pressure to force employers to stop doing business with firms on strike.

By spring 1978 the Taft-Hartley Act had been invoked thirty-four times, and in all but five cases injunctions were issued.

Taylor-Rostow Mission Considered by many one of the turning points in American involvement in the **Vietnam War,** it was dispatched to Saigon by President John F. Kennedy on October 11, 1961, after he had received from President Ngo Dinh Diem a request for increased military aid. It consisted of General Maxwell D. Taylor, the President's military advisor, and Walt W. Rostow, deputy to McGeorge Bundy, Special Assistant for National Security Affairs. They were accompanied by a team of advisors whose job it was to determine how this country might further assist South Vietnam.

The final report contained a series of demands for political and administrative reforms by the Saigon government; a recommendation that American support for South Vietnam be shifted from advice to limited partnership in the war by furnishing the material and technical aid for a counterguerrilla program; a proposal for creation of **"Farmgate" squadrons** of U.S. Air Force units designed to assist in small-scale, guerrilla warfare. It also proposed sending 10,000 regular U.S. ground troops to South Vietnam and envisioned that eventually six full divisions might be required. At the time, President Kennedy accepted the recommendations for insistence on reform, increased aid, and the formation of the "Farmgate" squadrons, but he made no decision about the commitment of American ground troops. According to Department of Defense figures, there were 3,200 American advisors in Vietnam at the end of 1961. By the following year the number had risen to 11,300, and at the time of President Kennedy's assassination there were over 16,000. The U.S. **Military Assistance Advisory Group** (MAAG) had been upgraded to the Military Assistance Command, Vietnam (MACV) and put under the command of General Paul D. Harkins, who had been General George Patton's deputy chief of staff during World War II.

Among the members of the Kennedy administration to oppose General Taylor's recommendations concerning the commitment of ground forces were Chester Bowles, W. Averell Harriman, and George W. Ball. When the latter suggested to the President that such a commitment could eventually escalate to 500,000 troops, the possibility was dismissed as an absurdity. (By 1968 there were 536,100 American troops in Vietnam.) However, President Kennedy himself resisted the idea of such a commitment, and pointed out that the war in Vietnam could only be won if the South Vietnamese made it their war. He told Arthur M. Schlesinger, Jr., that if it were converted into a "white man's war," we would lose, just as the French in Indochina had lost a decade earlier.

In September 1963, General Taylor returned to Vietnam with Secretary of Defense Robert S. McNamara to once more survey the situation. The public report on the **McNamara-Taylor Mission** issued on October 2, 1963, stated that the military program in South Vietnam had made progress "and is sound in principles, though improvements were being energetically sought." It predicted that "the major part of the U.S. military task can be completed by the end of 1965" and that by the end of 1963 the training program for South Vietnamese "should have progressed to the point where 1,000 U.S. Military personnel assigned to South Vietnam can be withdrawn."

See **Vietnam War.**

Teacher Corps *See* **Higher Education Act of 1965.**

Teach-Ins An early response of the peace movement to the escalation of the **Vietnam War** during the Johnson administration were the teach-ins which began at the University of Michigan, Ann Arbor. Originally, militants had planned a one-day moratorium in which students would abandon the classrooms to hear analyses of the situation by sym-

pathetic professors. Eventually, it was decided to have an all-night meeting instead on March 24, 1965.

The idea spread like wildfire across the nation's campuses. At Berkeley more than 10,000 students attended a two-day session at which they heard talks by pacifist Dr. Benjamin Spock (*see* **Spock Generation**), novelist Norman Mailer, columnist I. F. Stone (*see* **I. F. Stone's Weekly**), socialist leader Norman Thomas, and many others.

By May, the Johnson administration, which had steadfastly tried to ignore this new antiwar development, was forced to take cognizance of it and begin sending three-man "truth teams" on tours of Midwestern campuses. They met with only indifferent success and were soon abandoned.

The "teach-in" movement began to fade away after a National Teach-in at the Sheraton Park Hotel in Washington, D.C., on May 15, 1965. Nevertheless, in July 1966, the Inter-University Committee for Debate on Foreign Policy, which had proposed March 21–26, 1966, as a National Week of Teach-Ins, reported that so far that year it had contributed to over 100 teach-ins across the country.

Attacking the "teach-ins" in an article in the *New York Herald Tribune* (October 24, 1965), Sen. Barry Goldwater (R.-Ariz.) claimed that they were actively procommunist.

The right of these people to yammer ahead with their almost obscene support of a regime that is actually at war with the United States is not in question. . . . We cannot complain that it is being abused by those who hate America and love Communism if we do not take advantage of it ourselves.

Telstar Following a heated congressional debate over the use by private industry of the results of government research, on January 19, 1961, the Federal Communications Commision (FCC) authorized the American Telephone and Telegraph (AT&T) Company and its Bell Telephone Laboratories to develop and maintain ownership of the first communications satellite with a solar-powered receiver and transmitter.

Telstar 1 was sent into orbit from Cape Canaveral, Florida, by a three-stage Thor-Delta booster rocket—for which AT&T is said to have paid the government $3 million—on July 10, 1962. On that same day it successfully began the transmission of TV pictures from the United States to both England and France, and on the following day it transmitted pictures from these countries to the United States.

The 170-pound, 34 1/4-inch satellite, powered by 3,000 solar cells, cost AT&T an estimated $50 million at the time of launching. Because of unexpectedly high radiation levels, it stopped obeying signals from the ground on November 23, 1962; however, by January 3, 1963, technicians had managed to diagnose the problem and transmit a cure based on the periodic cutting off of battery power in order to eliminate the voltage that had concentrated the ionization.

On that same day *Relay 1*, which had been built by the Radio Corporation of America for the **National Aeronautics and Space Administration (NASA)**, was also restored to service. *Relay 1* had been launched in December 1962, but almost immediately failed to function properly because of an unexplained power drain. By January 3, the solar panels managed to produce sufficient power to relay a test pattern from Andover, Maine, and back.

Following additional tests, the satellite began full-scale two-way transatlantic transmission of TV programs.

The experience gained from *Telstar 1* led to the launching on May 7, 1963, of *Telstar 2*, which had greater radiation resistance. Its higher orbit made it possible to exchange signals with Europe during three hours, or nearly twice the amount of time provided by *Telstar 1*.

A *Relay 2* was launched on January 21, 1962, and was in use until the fall of 1965.

10-36-50 Plan An outgrowth of the **Selective Patronage Program** launched by Reverend Leon Sullivan of Philadelphia's Zion Baptist Church in 1960. Sometime in 1962, Reverend Sullivan persuaded fifty members of his black congregation to pledge a $10 monthly contribution, for thirty-six months, to an investment cooperative. Eventually, hundreds of members of the congregation were participating in what became Zion Investment Associates, which in the 1960s acquired an apartment building, a shopping center, and several garment manufacturing plants.

Reverend Sullivan established the Opportunities Industrialization Center (OIC), which provided training for members of minority groups. From Philadelphia the OIC spread and became a national movement in which some 100 similar centers were receiving millions of dollars in federal aid from various government agencies, including the **Department of Health Education, and Welfare,** the **Office of Economic Opportunity,** and the Department of Labor.

Tet Offensive On January 30, 1968, the first day of the thirty-six-hour Tet (Chinese Lunar New Year) truce agreed to by the opposing communist and allied forces in the **Vietnam War,** Viet Cong and North Vietnamese forces launched a heavy and coordinated attack against major cities, airfields, and army bases in South Vietnam. Scenes of the heaviest fighting were Hue, Dalat, Pleiku, Danang, Quang Tri, Kontum, Nytho, and Cantho. In Saigon a Viet Cong suicide squad briefly occupied the compound of the U.S. Embassy.

Speaking to newsmen on February 2, President Lyndon B. Johnson announced that the Tet offensive was a "complete failure" militarily and psychologically, but critics of the administration's stance in Vietnam were quick to point out that "if taking over a section of the American embassy, a good part of Hue, Dalat, and major cities of the 4th Corps area constitutes complete failure, I suppose by this logic if the Viet Cong captured the entire country the administration would be claiming their total collapse" (Sen. Eugene McCarthy [D.-Minn.]).

On February 12, General William C. Westmoreland, U.S. Commander in Vietnam, sent the Pentagon the following assessment of the situation:

Since last October, the enemy has launched a major campaign signaling a change of strategy from one of protracted war to one of quick military/political victory during the American election year. His first phase, designed to secure the border areas, has failed. The second phase, launched on the occasion of Tet and designed to initiate public uprising, to disrupt the machinery of government and command and control of the Vietnamese forces, and to isolate the cities, has also failed. Nevertheless, the enemy's third phase, which is designed to seize Quang Tri and Thua Thien provinces has just begun.

Critics of the Vietnam War claimed that U.S. forces had been taken by surprise by the Tet offensive. However, just before it began, aware of a communist buildup around Khe Sanh, the United States and South Vietnam had canceled the truce for five of the northern provinces. According to President Johnson, General Westmoreland revised his plans to meet what he saw as a new threat; he is also said to have urged the South Vietnamese to make similar arrangements, "but they were more relaxed about leaves, and as a result many South Vietnamese soldiers were at home with their families when the first blows of the Tet offensive fell."

U.S. estimates were that about 45,000 of the 84,000 men the Communists sent into their attacks were dead by the end of February.

On March 21, *The New York Times* published a story which indicated that General Westmoreland had in fact been taken completely by surprise by the Tet offensive. This was denied by the Johnson administration, which announced the next day that General Westmoreland had been appointed Army chief of staff, with duties in Washington. (On June 10, 1968, General Westmoreland turned over his Vietnam command to General Creighton W. Abrams, of whom *Time* magazine said that he "could inspire aggressiveness in a begonia.")

Writing in 1971, President Johnson charged that there had been "a great deal of emotional and exaggerated reporting of the Tet offensive in our press and on television." He insisted that given the high communist casualties and the failure of the enemy to rally the South Vietnamese people to their cause, the offensive was "by any standard, a military defeat of massive proportions for the North Vietnamese and the Viet Cong." He went on to note that though the United States commanders had known that

. . . a show of strength was coming; it was more massive than we had anticipated . . . we did not believe they would be able to carry out the level of coordination they demonstrated. We expected a large force to attack; it was larger than we had estimated. Finally, it was difficult to believe that the Communists would profane their own people's sacred holiday.

TFX Controversy Beginning in 1959, the Tactical Air Command (TAC) wanted to develop a fighter-bomber capable of high-altitude flight at slow speeds and low-altitude flight at supersonic speeds. A solution suggested by researchers of the **National Aeronautics and Space Agency** (NASA) was a plane with a variable sweep that would allow it to meet the needs of both flight conditions. The design was dubbed the TFX (Tactical Fighter, Experimental).

The situation was complicated by the fact that the Navy was at the same time looking for a new plane that could perform a fleet defense role by loitering at high altitudes and thus guarding ships against aerial attack. Therefore, in the early days of the Kennedy administration, Defense Secretary Robert S. McNamara ordered studies of the possibility of building a single fighter-bomber, based on the TFX, that would meet the needs of both services. On September 1, 1961, despite the fact that neither service was happy about a joint fighter-bomber, Secretary McNamara issued a memorandum stating that "a single aircraft for both the Air

Force tactical mission and the Navy fleet air defense mission will be undertaken. The Air Force shall proceed with the development of such an aircraft." Only minimal changes in the Air Force version were to be made to accommodate Navy needs.

During the remainder of 1961 and for most of 1962, both Boeing and General Dynamics submitted proposals, which were constantly being revamped, for a variable-wing plane. Military experts were said to favor giving the contract to Boeing, but despite this, in late November 1962, at the insistence of Secretary McNamara, the Pentagon awarded a $439 million contract for the development of twenty-two prototype TFXs to General Dynamics.

There was an immediate outcry, and critics complained that the contract had in essence gone to General Dynamics—which was on the verge of bankruptcy—because it was located in Texas, a state whose twenty-five electoral votes had gone to President John F. Kennedy in 1960. (Boeing had its headquarters in Washington and Kansas, and the seventeen electoral votes of these states had gone to Republican presidential candidate Richard M. Nixon.) Secretary McNamara was to insist that General Dynamics had been awarded the contract because of its experience with the supersonic F-102 and F-106 fighters and the B-38 bomber, and because its designs offered greater commonality between the Air Force and Navy versions of the TFX that were respectively to be known as the F-111A and the F-111B.

Hearings on the contract award were opened on February 26, 1963, by the Senate's Permanent Subcommittee on Investigations, chaired by Sen. John L. McClellan (D.-Ark.). Although it was originally thought that they would last only five or six days, the hearings dragged on until November 20, 1963. After the assassination of President Kennedy in Dallas two day later, they were dropped.

The first F-111A was rolled out in special ceremonies on October 15, 1964, at the General Dynamics plant in Fort Worth. The cost per unit had zoomed from $2.4 million to approximately $6 million. If the 1,700 planes projected were to have been built, the total production costs would have risen from 6.5 billion to more than 15 billion dollars.

Test planes began flying in 1965, and a high rate of failure was reported, though the Pentagon insisted that the accident rate was consistent with all new advanced planes. The first six F-111s used in the **Vietnam War** were all lost within a few weeks. Senator McClellen continued his criticism of the plane even though there were no more hearings by his subcommittee.

A few weeks after Secretary McNamara resigned from office in February 1968—he was increasingly disenchanted with the Vietnam War, which had once been known as "**McNamara's War**"—Congress killed the F-111 production program with the concurrence of the Pentagon. McNamara is said to have ultimately felt that the F-111 had been undertaken without a clear demonstration of need and that it did not increase existing capabilities sufficiently to justify the costs involved.

The aircraft—especially a short-lived FB-111 bomber version—is sometimes known as "McNamara's Folly." Many Republicans called the TFX the "LBJ."

Thalidomide Developed in West Germany, where in 1957 it was marketed under the trade name Contergan, this "ideal sedative" was found in 1961 to have been the cause of an increasingly high incidence of phocomelia, a condition in which infants are born with missing or deformed limbs. Three years of research by Dr. Widukind Lenz, a Hamburg University pediatrician, ended in the attribution of these tragic births to the fact that the mothers had taken thalidomide during the first months of pregnancy.

Although it was removed from the German market in November 1961, thalidomide continued to be sold elsewhere in Europe under a variety of trade names for some time, and it was not until early 1962 that it was prohibited in Canada.

Thanks to the watchfulness of Dr. Frances Oldham Kelsey, a Food and Drug Administration medical officer, thalidomide was never sold in the United States, though an application for its introduction under the name Kevadon was made to the FDA in September 1960 by William S. Merrell Co., Cincinnati, which described the drug as "very safe and effective" for the treatment of nervous tension. For more than a year Dr. Kelsey continued to deny appeals from the American producer, insisting that there had been no adequate demonstration of its harmlessness. Although never marketed here, the Department of Health, Education, and Welfare reported in August 1962 that samples had been made available to doctors in most states and had been taken by more than 200 pregnant women.

In August 1962, Dr. Kelsey was awarded a gold medal for distinguished federal service and cited by President John F. Kennedy for her courageous resistance to "very rigorous" attempts to market thalidomide here. On October 4, 1962, Congress passed new and stricter laws covering the commercial release of new drugs on the American market.

Some 7,000 deformed births have been traced to the drug, most of them in West Germany.

Thanksgiving Massacre The swiftness with which President John F. Kennedy reorganized the State Department in November 1961 led Washington observers and the press to dub the action the "Thanksgiving Day Massacre."

While the President was politically indebted and personally sympathetic toward Under Secretary Chester Bowles, he had long been dissatisfied with the latter's apparent inability to cope with the careerists in the department and bring them into line with **New Frontier** policy. In addition, he apparently bore a grudge against Bowles from the time when, after the **Bay of Pigs** disaster, the press carried stories that Bowles had been opposed to the operation from the very beginning.

President Kennedy had apparently been prepared to replace Bowles in July 1961, but *The New York Times* carried a story that he intended to ask for the Under Secretary's resignation. The story, the President felt, transformed a "personnel question" into a political one. At a press conference, therefore, he reaffirmed his confidence in Bowles.

On that late November weekend, however, Bowles, who had been attending the Harvard-Yale game at the Yale Bowl in New Haven, received an urgent phone call from Secretary of State Dean Rusk asking that he come to Washington the next morning. Upon his arrival in the Capital he was informed that his job was being given to George W. Ball, the former Under Secretary of State for Economic Affairs. Bowles was given a face-saving assignment as the President's Special Representative and Adviser on African, Asian, and Latin American Affairs.

In related moves, Walt Rostow was appointed Assistant Secretary for Policy Planning and W. Averell Harriman was made Assistant Secretary for Far Eastern Affairs. Transfers from the White House staff to the State Department also included Frederick G. Dutton as Assistant Secretary for Congressional Relations and Richard N. Goodwin as Deputy Assistant Secretary for Latin American Affairs. To the latter was to go prime responsibility for getting the **Alliance for Progress** moving.

See **Chet Set.**

"That Was the Week That Was" (TW3) After a successful thirteen-month run on British television, this irreverent weekly news summary, which made a star of David Frost, was introduced on American television in January 1964 for a celebrated but brief run. According to Frost, TW3 was designed to "attack what is currently ludicrous and pernicious," even when it did not seem to be in the show's own best interests to do so.

NBC executives began by promising that "there would be no editing of this show by clients," but soon they were emphasizing that TW3 was essentially "an entertainment show." Leland Hayward, the Broadway producer who had acquired the show for American television, cautiously began to note that while he hoped politics would be used, it would be "not so much the issues as the people involved." On the very first show, Frost's annotated rundown of statements by Sen. Barry Goldwater (R.-Ariz.), frontrunner for the 1964 Republican presidential nomination, was canceled by the network for fear of possible libel.

David Frost's popularity on American television was to outlast the show's short life, and he later created the *David Frost Show*. In May 1977 he scored a television coup when he began a series of ninety-minute interviews with former President Richard M. Nixon, who on August 9, 1974, as the result of revelations following the break-in of Democratic National Headquarters at the Watergate complex in Washington (June 17, 1972), became the first President to resign from office.

See **Watergate Scandal.**

"Third-rate Burglary" *See* **Watergate Scandal.**

Third World The expresion is a translation of *tiers monde*, often used by France's President Charles de Gaulle in the 1950s to describe his country's position on the international scene as a noncommunist force which was also independent of American policy. (In 1966, this independence was to be definitively demonstrated when France withdrew all its forces from the command of the **North Atlantic Treaty Organization** [NATO]). Sometimes given as "third force," it was eventually used to indicate the so-called nonaligned nations and also the underdeveloped and "emerging" nations of the world which were often benefiting from American foreign-aid programs such as President Harry S Truman's **Point Four.** During the 1960's, **New Left** militants in the United States were strongly drawn to "third-world revolutionaries" such as Cuba's Che Guevara and Martinique's Frantz Fanon.

See ***The Wretched of the Earth.***

38th Parallel Dividing line established at the end of World War II between what eventually became North and South Korea. During the Korean War, U.S. Marines landed at Inchon Harbor in September 1950, forcing the North Koreans to retreat behind that line. UN forces under General Douglas MacArthur followed, and China's Premier and Foreign Minister Chou En-lai warned that his country would not "supinely tolerate seeing their neighbors being savagely invaded by imperialists."

At a meeting on Wake Island on October 15, 1950, General MacArthur assured President Harry S Truman that the chances of Chinese intervention were minimal. However, when on November 24, 1950, General MacArthur launched a general offensive, "human waves" of Chinese "volunteers" began to pour across the frozen Yalu as thirty-three communist divisions—300,000 men—began a massive counteroffensive. As American forces were being driven back, General O. P. Smith said: "Retreat, hell! We're just fighting in another direction."

See **Korean War; Yalu River Offensive.**

The Thousand Days Summoning the nation to the task of self-renewal in his inaugural address on January 20, 1961, President John F. Kennedy outlined the task before it and warned: "All this will not be finished in the first one hundred days. Nor will it be finished in the first one thousand days, nor in the life of this Administration, nor even perhaps in our lifetime on this planet. But let us begin."

At forty-three, President Kennedy was the youngest person ever elected to that office. His administration ended 1,037 days later when he was cut down by an assassin's bullet in Dallas on **November 22, 1963.** In his first address to Congress, President Lyndon B. Johnson pledged himself to continue his predecessor's international and domestic programs (*see* **"Let us continue"**).

A Thousand Days (1965) was the title given by historian and presidential aide Arthur M. Schlesinger, Jr., to his account of the Kennedy administration. Mr. Schlesinger recalls that in the early days of his administration President Kennedy objected to his staff's recording the daily discussion in the White House. However, after the **Bay of Pigs** (April 1961), he asked Mr. Schlesinger if he had kept a full account of the fiasco. "You can be damn sure," he said, "that the CIA has its record and the Joint Chiefs theirs. We'd better make sure we have a record over here. So you go ahead." Mr. Schlesinger did just that.

President Kennedy's speech and Professor Schlesinger's title stirred echoes of the initial days of the

Roosevelt administration in 1933, the "Hundred Days" in which President Franklin D. Roosevelt took dramatic and innovative steps to deal with the nation's economic crisis.

Thresher **Disaster** On April 10, 1963, the U.S. Navy announced that the atomic-powered U.S.S. *Thresher* with 129 men aboard had been lost early that morning after a deep dive in the North Atlantic some 200 miles east of Cape Cod, Massachusetts. The first of its class, the submarine had been built at a cost of $45 million and launched in July 1960. At the time of its loss, there were two similar ships in operation: the *Permit* and the *Plunger.* The Navy announced that there was no indication that the disaster had been caused by failure of the ship's atomic reactor, and Vice Admiral Hyman G. Rickover, director of nuclear propulsion in the Bureau of Ships, was quoted as saying that there was no danger of radioactive contamination.

Because of the 8,400-foot depth of the water in which the submarine had disappeared, no rescue operations were possible. However, between June 24 and September 5 the bathyscaphe *Trieste* made ten dives in a search for the missing submarine before having to call off further efforts because of worsening weather. On August 24, it had recovered a portion of the *Thresher*'s ventilating system.

Meanwhile, after eight weeks of hearing testimony, a Navy court of inquiry had concluded on June 20, 1963, that the disaster had "most likely" been due to the flooding of the engine room as the result of a piping system failure. On January 9, 1965, the Joint Congressional Atomic Energy Committee charged that the *Thresher*'s last voyage had been made in spite of known deficiencies in vital equipment. It was said that an overhasty overhauling operation had not allowed for a check on all the joints of the salt-water piping system which had previously been found to be "below standard." More than a year before the sinking, Admiral Rickover had complained that the ship's deballasting system was inadequate and that the Portsmouth (New Hampshire) Naval Shipyard, where the *Thresher* had been stationed, was also guilty of unsatisfactory workmanship on the atomic submarine the U.S.S. *Tinosa.* The committee endorsed Admiral Rickover's belief that the disaster proved that the Navy needed "to change its way of doing business to meet the requirements of modern technology."

Tidelands Oil Controversy "The special interests probably never worked harder on any legislation than on the Senate joint resolution which reached

my desk late in May of 1952," President Harry S Truman noted a few years later. "It was designed to make an outright gift of the offshore resources of the country to three states at the expense of the other forty-five. There was little question as to what action I would take on the bill. . . ." On May 29, 1952, he vetoed it; in addition, before leaving office in January 1953, President Truman issued an Executive order setting aside the submerged lands of the continental shelf as a naval petroleum reserve.

Reversing the policy of his predecessor, on May 22, 1953, President Dwight D. Eisenhower, who had campaigned on the issue, signed the Submerged Lands Act (also known as the Tidelands Oil Act), which gives coastal states off-shore oil lands within the three-mile limit. In the cases of Texas and Florida, the limit was made 10.5 miles in deference to the conditions under which those states had been admitted—in the case of Florida, readmitted after the Civil War—to the Union. The Outer Continental Shelf Lands Act (August 7, 1953) later gave the federal government rights to resources between the limit legislated to the states and the beginning of international waters.

President Truman claimed that the controversy was clouded by the intentional misuse of the word "tidelands," which he defined as land uncovered by low tide; he pointed out that their ownership by the states was never in dispute until the Supreme Court had ruled in *United States v. California* (1947) that submerged coastal lands were the property of the federal government. The confusion resulting from any definition of the limit of state title other than the low-tide mark would inevitably lead to inequities, he argued. Louisiana had by 1952 already enacted legislation extending its boundaries twenty-seven miles into the Gulf of Mexico.

Because of the loose wording of the Submerged Lands Act, the courts were deluged with disputes until 1960, when the Supreme Court ruled that Alabama, Louisiana, and Mississippi offshore rights extended three miles, and those of Texas and Florida to 10.5 miles, in recognition of the claims of those states under previous treaty obligations. In 1963, the Justice Department ruled that offshore islands created after a state had been admitted to the Union were under the control of that state.

Sticking to his own definition of the tidelands, President Truman noted several years after leaving office that it had always been his

. . . firm conviction that it would be the height of folly for the United States to give away the vast quantities of oil contained in the continental shelf and then buy back this same oil at stiff prices for use by the Army, Navy, and Air Force in the defense of the nation.

President Eisenhower felt that recognition of state claims within their historically recognized boundaries was "in keeping with basic principles of honesty and fair play," and he deplored federal encroachment on these rights. The Submerged Lands Act was hailed as a victory for those who opposed the "socialistic super-state" by Leonard W. Hall, National Chairman of the Republican party, who noted that until the "New Deal Supreme Court in 1947 ruled otherwise, it had on 53 occasions upheld states rights to offshore mineral resources."

In 1975 (*United States v. Maine*) the Supreme Court denied the claim of eleven Atlantic coast states to land beyond the three-mile limit, noting that the paramount rights of the federal government had been "embraced" by the Submerged Lands Act. The state claims had been advanced on the basis of colonial charters.

Emmett Till Lynching Because he had allegedly whistled at, embraced, and obscenely insulted the wife of a white storekeeper, fourteen-year-old Emmett Till, a Chicago Negro who was visiting with relatives in the vicinity of Money, Mississippi, was on August 28, 1955, kidnapped from his uncle's house by three white men. Three days later his badly decomposed body was found in the Tallahatchie River.

Roy Bryant, husband of the woman who claimed to have been insulted, and his half-brother J. W. Milam, were arrested and charged with the kidnapping. At a trial beginning on September 21, 1955, in Sumner, Mississippi, police officers testified that both men had admitted taking young Till from his uncle's home, but claimed that they had released him when they found he was not the person they wanted. Carolyn Bryant testified that a Negro with a "northern brogue" had entered the Bryant store on August 24, 1955, proposed a "date," taken her by the waist, and "wolf-whistled" at her as he was being pulled from the store by another Negro. She did not identify Till as the man who had done these things.

On September 23, the all-white jury hearing the case acquitted Bryant and Milam, basing their verdict on a defense contention that the body recovered from the river and identified by members of Till's family had been too badly decomposed for positive identification. Following the trial, Till's uncle, who had been a prosecution witness, announced his intention to move to Albany, New York. Another black prosecution witness, nineteen-year-old Willie Reed, returned to Chicago with Emmett Till's mother, Mrs. Mamie Bradley. Mississippi governor Hugh White, who had appointed a special prosecutor to assist the district attorney in the prosecution, said that the authorities had done "all we could do" to ensure a fair trial.

Tiros Meteorology entered the space age on April 1, 1960, when a 270-pound weather satellite was launched into orbit and its two television cameras 450 miles above the earth's surface began sending back photographs of approaching storms in the Middle Western and New England areas of the United States. *Tiros 1*—the name is an acronym for Television and Infra-Red Observation Satellite—was the prototype of the satellites that were soon providing around-the-clock information on weather conditions all over the earth. Because its stabilization in space required that a spinning motion be imparted to the satellite, the cameras on board were pointed at the earth's surface only during brief but predictable periods during each 100-minute orbit across the equator. Its swing covered a latitude 50° north and south. Later satellites in a near-polar orbit gave entire-globe coverage.

At the time of the *Tiros 1* launching, the U.S. operational earth satellites included *Explorer 1, Vanguard I, Vanguard II, Explorer VI, Vanguard III,* and *Explorer VII.* The only Soviet earth satellite still operating was *Sputnik III.*

The initial Tiros program ended with *Tiros 10.* The first of a new Tiros Operational Satellite (TOS) system began with the launching on February 3, 1966, of *Essa I,* financed and operated by the Environmental Science Services Administration (ESSA), created in 1965 through a merger of the Weather Bureau, the Coast and Geodetic Survey, the National Environmental Satellite Center, the Environmental Data Service, and the Environmental Research Laboratory. (The new administration's function was to study and report on the earth, oceans, and atmosphere.)

Essa 1 went into a near-polar, sun-synchronous orbit, and its two television cameras, equipped with wide-angle (104°) lenses, were designed to provide complete global weather coverage daily. *Essa 1* had cost $2.5 million to build and $3.6 million to launch. Power for its operation was provided by the more than 9,000 solar cells encrusted in the eighteen-sided satellite. *Essa 1* allowed for local-station readout.

The Essa series came to an end in 1969 after the launching of nine satellites. In 1970, the duties of

ESSA were taken over by the **National Oceanic and Atmospheric Administration** (NOAA), which began launching an improved TOS. In the NOAA series, advanced infrared instruments made it possible to obtain temperature profiles of any spot on the globe at any hour of the day.

TM *See* **Transcendental Meditation.**

"To err is Truman" Assuming the presidency after the death of Franklin D. Roosevelt in April 1945, Harry S Truman had the nation solidly behind him, but this support began to disintegrate with the end of World War II, and by the fall of 1946 the above summation—said to have been the response of Martha Taft, wife of the Republican Senator to the President's 1948 assertion that the spy scare caused by the **Alger Hiss Case** was a "red herring"—could have symbolized his status with many.

On his first coast-to-coast address the President nervously forgot to wait until he had been introduced by the Democratic Speaker of the House and was heard nationally to be admonished by Sam Rayburn: "Wait, Harry, until I introduce you."

"Sometimes the frailties of the human get the better of me," admitted the President in 1950 after he had fired off a racy rebuke to Paul Hume, *Washington Post* music critic, who had been less than enchanted with Margaret Truman's debut as a singer. ("Some day I hope to meet you," wrote the President. "When that happens you'll need a new nose, a lot of beefsteak for black eyes, and perhaps a supporter below.")

But the President had been making what his critics labeled "mistakes" of a more serious nature. He lost some labor support when he disciplined the railroad workers and miners during strikes in the spring of 1946; the farm-labor coalition broke, and farmers returned to their "traditional" Republican stance; liberals deserted him when he fired Secretary of Commerce Henry A. Wallace in a foreign policy dispute.

By the time President Truman began campaigning against Thomas E. Dewey in the 1948 presidential election, both houses of Congress had been captured by the Republicans, whose nominee was considered a shoo-in. "To err is Truman" was picked up and given wide national circulation by Republican campaign workers. But to the surprise of the pollsters, who were to err so seriously in their election predictions, President Truman beat his challenger by a popular vote of 24,106,000 to 21,069,000.

Togetherness A promotional campaign launched by *McCall's* magazine in May 1954, caught national attention by emphasizing the benefits the American family receives by doing things as a unit. Noting the post-World War II change in the quality of American life, the magazine expressed its conviction that "the most impressive and the most heartening feature of this change is that men, women and children are achieving it *together*. They are creating this new and warmer way of life not as women *alone* or men *alone*, isolated from one another, but as a *family* sharing a common experience." *McCall's* readers were told that whereas previously the publication had been edited with special sensitivity "to your needs *as women first*," henceforth the magazine would stress the needs and interest "of all of you who are or wish to be partners in this [new] way of life—the life of *McCall's*."

"Togetherness" as a theme caught the attention of editorial writers all over the country. As a result, it was reflected in advertising throughout the 1950s. Many social critics were less than enchanted by what they saw as the tyranny of "togetherness." Nevertheless, *McCall's* noted in January 1957, "the few men who resisted Togetherness as a concept agreed . . . that it is increasing under present social and cultural pressures. . . ."

Tom Swifties A verbal—or rather, adverbial—game that had a national vogue in 1963, it was based on the once popular series of Tom Swift boys' books by Victor Appleton which first began appearing in the early 1900s. The hero of *Tom Swift and His Motor-cycle* and similar adventures with a motorboat, airship, submarine, electric runabout, etc., was rarely recorded as having simply "said" something without an adverb such as "soberly," "slowly," or "thoughtfully" being tacked on as a modifier. Remembering this verbal tic of one of the favorite authors of his childhood, Minneapolis advertising man Earl Pease developed it into a party stunt sometime in the 1950s. Some ten years later, his son, Paul Pease, by then an advertising executive in San Francisco, revived the game, which proved so successful that in 1963 he put together a book entitled *Tom Swifties*. Soon the whole country was adding variations. Typical examples included:

"You have the charm of Venus," Tom murmured disarmingly.

"I feel like a king," Tom said leeringly.

In Washington, sophisticates of the Kennedy administration added variations of their own.

"My administration has plans for the South," JFK said darkly.

"Too old to cry" As an addendum to his formal concession statement after the victory of his Republican presidential rival, Dwight D. Eisenhower, at the polls on Novermber 4, 1952, Democratic presidential candidate Adlai Stevenson added an anecdote. He told how someone had once asked Abraham Lincoln how it felt to lose a political campaign. "He said," noted Stevenson, "he felt like a little boy who stubbed his toe in the dark. He was too old to cry, and it hurt too much to laugh."

To Secure These Rights The wartime Fair Employment Practices Commission (FEPC) having been dismantled by Congress, on December 5, 1946, President Harry S Truman established the President's Committee on Civil Rights with instructions to discover how "current law enforcement measures may be strengthened and improved to safeguard the civil rights of the people." *To Secure These Rights*, the committee's report, was released on October 29, 1947. Although it spotlighted a variety of problems, its primary focus was on racial discrimination.

In the field of education, it found that though "the United States has made remarkable progress toward the goal of universal education for its people . . . we have not finally eliminated prejudice and discrimination from the operation of either our public or our private schools and colleges." This was particularly true in the failure to "provide Negroes and, to a lesser extent, other minority group members with equality of educational opportunities in our public institutions, particularly at the elementary and secondary school levels."

In housing too, the committee found that "today, many of our citizens face a double barrier when they try to satisfy their housing needs." After encountering a general housing shortage, they then run up against "prejudice and discrimination based upon race, color, religion or national origin, which places them at a disadvantage in competing for the limited housing available."

President Truman later noted ten important recommendations by his fifteen-man committee: (1) the establishment of a permanent Commission on Civil Rights, a joint Congressional Committee on Civil Rights, and a Civil Rights Division in the Department of Justice; (2) the reinforcement of existing civil rights legislation; (3) federal protection against lynching; (4) improved protection of the right to vote; (5) the establishment of a permanent Fair Employment Practices Commission; (6) modification of federal nationalization laws to prevent discrimination against applicants on the basis of race, color, or national origin; (7) the provision of home rule and suffrage in presidential elections for District of Columbia residents; (8) statehood for Hawaii and Alaska, and more self-government for U.S. possessions; (9) equalizing the opportunities of all U.S. residents to become citizens; (10) settlement of the evacuation claims of Japanese-Americans.

In his message to Congress on February 2, 1948, President Truman requested legislation incorporating these recommendations, and took the opportunity to urge the abolition of segregation in the use of transportation facilities. Later he incorporated his recommendations in the 1948 Democratic platform.

Total Woman (TW) In the mid-1970s, TW seminars were being given in sixty cities across the country by teachers who had been trained by Marabel Morgan, author of *Total Woman* (1973) and *Total Joy* (1977). Similar to the also popular **Fascinating Womanhood** (FW) theory, TW puts greater emphasis on a woman's need to remain sexually stimulating to her husband—"You can become a Rembrandt in your sexual art or you can stay at the paint-by-numbers stage"—and draws more heavily on the Bible for inspiration.

In a nutshell, where most **Women's Liberation** adherents most likely thought it belonged, Mrs. Morgan's philosophy can be summed up by her warning to wives that only when they surrender their lives to their husbands, revering and worshipping them, do they become truly beautiful. Then a wife becomes "a priceless jewel, the glory of femininity, his queen!"

To charges that she advises women to be manipulative with their husbands, Mrs. Morgan replied: "The word I use for a wife is not subservient but submissive. One is voluntary. But if I do something because I want to, because it gives joy, I'm not being manipulative at all. It's a struggle to submit, but it's worth it." She saw no reason why her theories as expressed in her books and in the $15 seminars they inspired should be considered a threat to Women's Liberation, which she favored to the extent that it opened up more options for women. "But marriage and children is also an option. When I share with other women what happened to me, I give them hope."

TW enthusiasts are said to range in age from eighteen to sixty-four. Approximately one-third of them have jobs or careers, and their educational background goes from near-illiterates to Ph.Ds. More than 3 million copies of *Total Woman* had been sold by 1977.

Trade Expansion Act of 1962   Figuring importantly in the Kennedy administration's program, the Trade Expansion Act of 1962 was signed into law on October 11, 1962, and authorized the President to cut tariffs by as much as 50 and 100 percent, if 80 percent of the world trade in the goods involved was accounted for by the United States and the European trading bloc. As passed by the Senate, the bill would have included exports from Great Britain in that 80 percent, but the final version included Britain and six other potential European Economic Community members in that 80 percent only if they eventually joined the Common Market.

The President was given discretionary powers to retaliate against foreign import restrictions on American goods. He was also required to withdraw from both Yugoslavia and Poland "as soon as practicable" the tariff concessions extended these communist nations under the most-favored-nation trading policy.

The bill as passed retained a Senate amendment under which the cost of unemployment and retraining of workers necessitated by the trade adjustment assistance program would be borne by the federal government; originally, it had been planned to make some use of state unemployment compensation funds.

See **Kennedy Round.**

Tranquility Base   *See* **Project Apollo.**

Transactional Analysis (TA)   A form of psychotherapy focusing on interpersonal relationships, it was popularized in Eric Berne's *Games People Play* (1969) and Thomas Harris's *I'm OK—You're OK* (1969). It is based on the theory that social hungers such as the need for stimulation and recognition contribute to human motivation. These hungers are satisfied either positively or negatively by "stroking," i.e., any form of activity which acknowledges the presence of another person.

According to the theory, individuals early in life develop "scripts" which include a number of ways of structuring time so as to obtain a maximum number of "strokes." The safest is withdrawal from others and dependence on "stored" strokes from previously satisfying situations; the most satisfying is the open give and take of an intimate relationship. Games are seen as social transactions in which there is satisfactory communication.

Therapy is generally conducted on a group basis, and the therapist takes an active role in directing the client's three aspects of personality: Child, Parent, and Adult, or impulse aspect, critical aspect, and mature aspect. Care is taken to assure that in exchanges between persons the same aspect of their personalities is to the fore. Attempts are made to avoid self-destructive "scripts" and to encourage progress toward open give and take.

Transcendental Meditation (TM)   By the mid-1970s, more than 350,000 Americans were practicing the yogic discipline introduced into this country by the Maharishi Mahesh Yogi, who makes his headquarters in Switzerland. The "Science of Creative Intelligence"—or TM as it is generally called—is designed to allow disciples to reach a "higher consciousness" through a meditation technique that consists of repetition of a "mantra"—usually words or syllables drawn from the Hindu Vedas—until the meditator's mind "transcends" the divided consciousness of day-to-day life and experiences the soothing "pure awareness" which is said to be the source of all creative energy and intelligence.

The technique is taught in over 200 centers in this country by some 4,000 teachers trained by the Maharishi. They emphasize the fact the TM is not a religion and requires of the practitioner not a lifestyle or set of beliefs but only the consecration to it of some twenty minutes in the morning and evening. Its special popularity in the United States is attributed by the Maharishi to the fact that "creative intelligence can only be appreciated in a country that is more evolved," and that the "U.S. is the most creative country in the world."

Of the organizations set up by the Maharishi, the largest is the International Meditation Society (IMS), which has been invited by many business and industrial corporations to teach TM techniques to employees and their wives. Credit courses in TM are also available at many major universities, including the University of California at Los Angeles and Harvard. Research sponsored by the National Institute of Mental Health has indicated that TM can reduce the desire for alcohol, tobacco, and hard drugs; it has therefore sometimes been recommended by both the U.S. Army and the U.S. Bureau of Prisons as an alternative to drug abuse.

Treaty of Rio de Janeiro   *See* **Rio Pact.**

TRICAP   *See* **Airmobile.**

Trieste   New ocean diving records were established when U.S. Navy Lt. Donald Walsh and Jacques Piccard descended in the bathyscaphe *Trieste* to 24,000 feet in the Pacific Marianas trench, sixty miles off the coast of Guam, on January 7, 1960.

On January 23, 1960, even this record was surpassed when the *Trieste* descended to 37,800 feet.

Jacques Piccard is the son of the bathyscaphe's inventor, the Swiss physicist August Piccard, who began work on it in 1946 to provide a vessel which could explore the ocean depths. An unmanned dive was made in 1950, and in 1953 father and son achieved a record dive of 10,330 feet.

Unlike the bathysphere in which Otis Barton and the American naturalist Charles William Beebe made a 3,028-foot record descent off Bermuda in 1934, the bathyscaphe, once towed to the diving area, is self-propelled under water.

See **Thresher Disaster.**

Trinidad Plan *See* **Bay of Pigs.**

Troika *See* **Quadriad.**

"Trollope Ploy" *See* **Cuban Missile Crisis.**

Truman Doctrine By 1947, Soviet expansionist pressure was posing a threat to Turkey and providing support for communist insurgents in a civil war in Greece. Great Britain had supplied the Greek government with considerable financial aid, but at that time it was itself in a financial crisis, and in February 1947 it informed the U.S. State Department that all financial aid to Greece and Turkey would cease the following month.

After consulting with congressional leaders from both parties, President Harry S Truman decided that this country would have to step in to fill the vacuum created by the British political retreat. Acting on the advice of Sen. Arthur H. Vandenberg (R.-Mich.), who suggested that he go before Congress "and scare hell out of the country," on March 12, 1947, President Truman appeared before a joint congressional session and asked for an initial $400 million in military and economic aid for Greece and Turkey, for the period ending June 1948. He went on to say:

At the present moment in world history nearly every nation must choose between alternative ways of life. The choice is too often not a free one. . . . I believe that it must be the policy of the United States to support free peoples who are resisting attempted subjugation by armed minorities or by outside pressures. I believe that our help should be primarily through economic and financial aid, which is essential to economic stability and orderly political processes.

The stand was attacked by Henry Wallace—who had been dismissed on September 20, 1946, as Secretary of Commerce for his public opposition to administration foreign policy—as bypassing the United Nations; in the UN General Assembly it was denounced by the Soviet bloc as "warmongering."

On May 22, 1947, Truman signed the congressional bill allocating the initial sum he had requested. He later wrote: "With this enactment by Congress of aid to Greece and Turkey, America had served notice that the march of communism would not be allowed to succeed by default." His stand became known as the Truman Doctrine.

Truth-in-Lending Act Signed into law by President Lyndon B. Johnson on May 29, 1968, the Truth-in-Lending Act standardized procedures by which credit enterprises such as banks and credit-card companies stated their interest charges. It required that interest data and lending terms be disclosed to potential borrowers previous to the signing of any loan agreement.

It had taken a ten-year struggle by consumer advocates to obtain such a law from Congress. In mid-1977, the Truth-in-Lending Act was back in the news because of congressional efforts to "simplify" it so as to avoid the many suits which had sprung from the interpretation of technicalities. (Critics such as Carl Felsenfeld, consumer affairs counsel to Citibank, claimed that there had to date been "in excess of 10,000 lawsuits, most of which have comparatively little to do with real consumer understanding of credit terms. . . .")

Efforts to simplify the law were attacked by consumerists as designed to essentially weaken the law. However, there was widespread agreement that the law had not, as had been hoped, led to shoppers selecting a source of credit on the basis of the information furnished them in advance. Nevertheless, consumerists insisted that in view of a congressional report stating that in 1975 violations of the law had cost borrowers almost $7 million, what was needed was not a simplification of the law but an addition of provisions for stricter government enforcement. It is the lack of such enforcement, critics maintained, that resulted in the many lawsuits, which they see as the only means of bringing pressure to bear on financial institutions.

Among the many bills to amend the act was one by Sen. William Proxmire (D.-Wis.), who was the sponsor of the original legislation. His amendment called for certain disclosures by creditors, but required that federal agencies enforcing the law seek restitution for consumers when violations are discovered.

"Truth-in-Packaging" Law   In proposing legislation for the reform and control of the packaging industry, President Lyndon B. Johnson noted on March 21, 1966: "Free consumer choice—indeed our free enterprise—must rest on a firm foundation of reliable information on the costs and contents of the products we buy." On November 3, 1966, the President was able to sign the Fair Packaging and Labeling Act, which covered some 8,000 food, drug, and cosmetic products and required that their packaging carry precise statements of ingredients and amounts. The so-called Truth in Packaging law banned the use of such misleading advertising phrases as "a giant quart," "a jumbo ounce," etc. The legislation also barred "slack filling" practices and deceptively large containers that made consumers think they were getting more of a product than they actually were. As journalist and social commentator Marya Mannes complained at one congressional hearing, the American taxpayer was already paying enough for outer space, without having to pay for inner space as well.

Turnip Congress   In accepting the presidential nomination at the 1948 Democratic Convention in Philadelphia, President Harry S Truman told wildly enthusiastic delegates that in order to test "whether the Republican platform really meant anything or not" he would call the Republican-controlled Eightieth Congress into special session to pass legislation of which their platform theoretically approved and which was "essential to the welfare of the country."

On the twenty-sixth day of July, which out in Missouri we call "Turnip Day," I am going to call Congress back and ask them to pass laws to halt rising prices, to meet the housing crisis—which they are saying they are for in their platform.

At the same time, I shall ask them to act upon other needed measures, such as aid to education, which they say they are for; a national health program; civil rights legislation, which they say they are for; extension of the Social Security coverage and increased benefits, which they say they are for; funds for projects needed in our program to provide public power and cheap electricity. By indirection, this Eightieth Congress has tried to sabotage the power policies the United States has pursued for fourteen years. That power lobby is as bad as the real estate lobby which is sitting on the housing bill.

The Turnip Congress was part of Truman's strategy in his campaign for a second term of office. He later noted: "Of course, I knew that the special session would produce no results in the way of legislation." It did not, and after two weeks Congress adjourned to "go out and run for office," something it obviously considered its primary function. But national attention had been focused on the "achievements" of the "do-nothing" Congress. Critics have noted that this was a calculated effort—inspired by aide Clark Clifford—to win over liberals by emphasizing legislative issues Republicans would oppose.

It was in the course of his "Turnip Congress" speech that the President indicated that Republicans would "dodge their responsibilities" by dragging "all the red herrings they could across this campaign. . . ." The "red herring" phrase was to surface again in a somewhat altered context during the **Alger Hiss Case.**

TV Quiz Show Scandals   *See "Twenty-One."*

TV Wasteland   Speaking before the National Association of Broadcasters on May 9, 1961, Newton Minow, the recently appointed chairman of the Federal Communications Commission (FCC), decried the excess of violence on television and called for an increase in educational public service programs. He invited the communications executives present to sit before their TV sets without a book, newspaper, profit and loss sheet, or rating book to distract them and to keep their eyes glued to the screen until their stations signed off.

I can assure you that you will observe a vast wasteland. You will see a procession of game shows, violence, audience participation shows, formula comedies about totally unbelievable families, blood and thunder, mayhem, violence, sadism, murder, western badmen, western good men, private eyes, gangsters, more violence, and cartoons. And endlessly, commercials—many screaming, cajoling, and offending. . . .

Gentlemen, your trust accounting with your beneficiaries is overdue. Never have so few owed so much to so many.

Toward the end of his speech, Mr. Minow backed up his criticism with the threat of corrective action. In the past, he warned, licenses were renewed pro forma. This would no longer be the case. "There is nothing permanent or sacred about a broadcast license."

The FCC chairman showed himself skilled in using his office to aid noncommercial television. For example, when in 1961 National Telefilm Associates, licensee for WNTA-TV (Channel 13 in metropolitan New York) wanted to transfer its license to another commercial group, he forced the sale to National Educational Television (NET) by scheduling an inquiry on the desirability of securing noncommercial stations in New York and Los Angeles.

Twenty-One

Because this inquiry threatened to drag on interminably, with the funds from commercial bidders tied up in escrow, National Telefilm Associates finally accepted an NET bid.

Minow also persuaded Congress to require that all TV sets manufactured after January 1963 be equipped to receive UHF channels. Because many manufacturers of television equipment also owned licenses for VHF stations, they had been loath to increase their own competition. The FCC chairman's firm support by President John F. Kennedy is said to have kept the television industry constantly aware of Minow's warning that "it is not enough to cater to the nation's whims—you must also serve the nation's needs." In 1962, he received the Peabody Award for his efforts to "rescue the wasteland from the cowboys and private eyes." He resigned as FCC chairman in 1963, and was succeeded by E. William Henry.

"Twelve Grayhaired Guys Named George" "The men suggest cool competence rather than passion or brilliance. They are problem solvers rather than idea brokers. There are no blooded patricians in the lot, just strivers who have acted out the middle-class dream."

It was with these words that a December 1968 issue of *Time* magazine described the Cabinet of President-elect Richard M. Nixon. The men had been introduced to the nation in an unprecedented half-hour TV "spectacular." Washington wits were soon pointing out that the lack of passion or brilliance in his selection tended to create an impression of sameness in the new Cabinet: "Twelve grayhaired guys named George."

They were, in fact: Secretary of State, William P. Rogers; Secretary of Health, Education, and Welfare, Robert Finch; Secretary of Transportation, John Volpe; Secretary of the Interior, Walter Hickel; Secretary of Housing and Urban Development, George Romney; Secretary of Agriculture, Clifford Hardin; Secretary of Labor, George P. Shultz; Secretary of Commerce, Maurice H. Stans; Attorney General, John N. Mitchell; Postmaster General, Winton Blount; Secretary of the Treasury, David Kennedy; and Secretary of Defense, Melvin R. Laird.

"Twenty-One" One of the most popular television shows in late 1956 and 1957 was this weekly NBC quiz show, and by far the most popular contestant to appear on that program was Charles Van Doren. A member of a distinguished literary family, the young Columbia University instructor won

$129,000 during fourteen weeks as the nation watched him sweat and struggle in a glass-walled isolation booth before coming up with answers to an amazing variety of questions. When he finally lost out to another contestant, he was given a $50,000 job as a commentator on the "Today" show.

Then in mid-1958, Herbert M. Stempel, an "unpopular" contestant who had been eliminated by the erudite Van Doren after racking up $49,500 in prize money, contacted Manhattan District Attorney Frank Hogan and the editors of a New York newspaper with the information that the show had been rigged, that the contestants had been coached on the questions and answers as well as on their on-camera behavior, and that he, Stempel, had been ordered by the show's producers to take a dive for Van Doren. The latter angrily denied the charges both to the press and under oath to a New York grand jury. Since no proof could be offered by Stempel, that seemed to end the matter—temporarily.

But in October 1959, a congressional subcommittee on legislative oversight received from another "Twenty-One" contestant, James Snodgrass, a series of sealed registered letters containing questions, answers, and "acting" instructions for shows that had been aired in May 1957. The letters had been postmarked several days before the actual broadcast.

Van Doren had originally volunteered to appear before the special subcommittee, but when the time came he had dropped out of sight. When he surfaced in New York on October 17, he claimed that he hadn't known—in spite of national headlines—that he had been wanted, and he accepted the subpoena. On November 2, 1959, he appeared before the subcommittee and admitted the fraud—begun with his first appearance on the program, which the network had long since canceled.

"I would give almost anything I have to reverse the course of my life in the last three years," he testified. "I cannot take back one word or action, the past does not change for anyone. But I have learned a lot about good and evil." Van Doren resigned from his Columbia post and was summarily fired from his lucrative commentator job on NBC. Paradoxically enough, he won the sympathy of many Americans—"I've been getting just wonderful letters from wonderful people"—who insisted that "anyone" would have done the same thing.

On October 17, 1960, Van Doren and thirteen others were arrested and charged with perjury. He pleaded guilty to the charge in 1962 and was given a suspended sentence.

In a related scandal, the same congressional subcommittee heard testimony (November 2, 1959) from contestants on the CBS "$64,000 Challenge" that they had been coached previous to their appearances on the show. Testifying for thirteen-year-old actress Patty Duke, her manager said that she had been given the answers in advance. In addition, the former producer of "$64,000 Challenge" and "$64,000 Question" said that an executive of Revlon, Inc., which sponsored both quiz programs, would indicate at weekly meetings which contestants the company would prefer to win. "We always did our best to carry out their wishes," said Mert Koplin, the producer.

See **Payola.**

"Twenty Years of Treason" *See* **McCarthyism.**

The Twist A dance launched in Philadelphia in 1960 by Chubby Checker, a black pop singer and recording artist. "My two brothers, Tracy and Spencer, got together with me and made a dance from a record that was five years old called 'The Twist.' " Facing partners scarcely moved their feet, concentrating instead on erotic shoulder and hip movements while their arms worked like pistons.

The Twist became a national dance craze the following year when Igor Cassini, who under the name "Cholly Knickerbocker" wrote society news for the *New York Journal-American,* reported that members of the smart set could be seen nightly gyrating to its rhythms at the Peppermint Lounge on the city's unfashionable West Side

As Checker commented in 1973:

The Twist is every dance that anyone's doing right now. When it first made it big, everything was going along really great. . . . People were very happy. It was Reconstruction the second time around, I think, for our country. John F. Kennedy at that time, Martin Luther King, Robert Kennedy. So many things were happening. . . . It was a really good time for America, the whole country.

Two-Chinas Policy A shift in long-standing American opposition to the admission of Red China to the United Nations began to surface when in March 1971 the Nixon administration ended a twenty-year trade embargo with the People's Republic of China and terminated restrictions on travel in that country by U.S. citizens. The month that followed saw a general relaxation of relations between the two nations, and so-called **ping-pong diplomacy** was initiated when on April 14, 1971, an American table tennis team visited the Chinese mainland on the invitation of Premier Chou En-lai.

On September 27, 1971, the United States submitted to the UN General Assembly a resolution calling for the seating of Red China on the Security Council and the retention of the Taiwan Republic of China in the General Assembly. Secretary of State William P. Rogers supported that resolution in a speech before the UN General Assembly on October 4, 1971, that attacked an Albanian counterresolution which called for the admission of Red China and the expulsion of the Taiwan government. He argued that it was unrealistic to expel a country which governs a population "greater than the populations of two-thirds of the 130 UN members." On October 18, 1971, U.S. delegate George Bush noted that the UN Charter was "flexible enough to allow for representation of Byelorussia, the Ukraine and the U.S.S.R.," and should, therefore, be able "to accommodate this situation." Nevertheless, on October 25, 1971, the General Assembly voted overwhelmingly to admit Communist China to the United Nations and "to expel forthwith the representative of Chiang Kai-shek from the place they unlawfully occupy at the United Nations."

There were rumbles in Congress, and among the remnants of the "China Lobby"—which in 1953 had formed the **"Committee of One Million** Against the Admission of Communist China to the United Nations"—about possible withdrawal of the United States from the United Nations. However, the crisis passed and Sino-American relations continued to improve. On the invitation of Premier Chou En-lai, President Nixon visited Red China early in 1972, and the resultant **"Peking Summit"** closed with a joint communiqué calling for further contacts eventually leading to a normalization of relations.

In a dramatic television broadcast on December 15, 1978, President Jimmy Carter announced the establishment of diplomatic relations between the United States and the People's Republic of China as of January 1, 1979. Said the President: "The Government of the United States of America acknowledges the Chinese position that there is but one China and Taiwan is part of China." As a candidate for the Presidency, Mr. Carter had seemed to favor a "two-Chinas policy."

TW3 *See* **"That Was the Week That Was."**

Tydings Committee On February 20, 1950, Sen. Joseph R. McCarthy (R.-Wis.) read into the congressional record what he said was a copy of the speech on "Communists in Government" which he had delivered in Wheeling, West Virginia, on February 9, 1950 (*see* **McCarthyism**). As a result, the Senate Committee on Foreign Relations established a subcommittee headed by Sen. Millard Tydings (D.-Md.) which began hearings to investigate these charges on March 8, 1950. Members of the committee included Sen. Brien McMahon (D.-Conn.), Sen. Theodore Francis Green (D.-R.I.), Sen. Henry Cabot Lodge, Jr. (R.-Mass.), and Sen. Bourke B. Hickenlooper (R.-Iowa).

On March 30, 1950, Senator McCarthy, having failed to produce names of any communists in the State Department, charged that Dr. Owen Lattimore, director of the Johns Hopkins School of International Relations, was the "architect" of the Truman administration's foreign policy and that he was a communist propagandist. It was soon established, however, that Dr. Lattimore was not a member of the U.S. State Department but only an occasional consultant. He was, in any case, cleared of all charges by the committee, whose report, signed by the three Democrats, was adopted by the Senate.

"We are fully satisfied," stated the majority report, which was issued after four months of testimony, ". . . on the basis of our study of the loyalty files that the State Department has not knowingly retained in its employ individuals who have been disloyal." The report also noted that the Wheeling speech as read in the Senate had been sufficiently altered so as to constitute a "misrepresentation of the true facts to the Senate."

In conclusion, the majority report noted that it was constrained to "fearlessly and frankly call the charges, and the methods employed to give them ostensible validity, what they truly are: A fraud and a hoax perpetrated on the Senate of the United States and the American people."

Senator Lodge issued a minority report in which he conceded that the charges brought by Senator McCarthy had not been proved; he nevertheless called the committee's investigation of these charges superficial and inconclusive. Senator Hickenlooper, though sympathetic to McCarthy, refused to sign either the majority or minority reports.

U

Unidentified Flying Objects

Wide World Photos

UFOs *See* **Unidentified Flying Objects.**

UFW *See* **United Farm Workers.**

The Ugly American Said to be based on true incidents, this 1958 fictional indictment by reporters William J. Lederer and Eugene L. Burdick of the shortcomings and basic inefficiency of Americans on government service in Southeast Asia echoed a note previously struck by British novelist Graham Greene in his acid *The Quiet American* (1955). *The Ugly American* quickly became a bestseller, and the phrase "an ugly American" entered the language as a synonym for Americans basically unsympathetic to the problems being experienced by foreign nations. Paradoxically, the "ugly American" of the title is one of the few Americans in the book who is convinced of the need for a new approach in fighting communism in an area already becoming engulfed in what was to be the **Vietnam War.**

In 1963, the book was the basis of a movie starring Marlon Brando.

UMT *See* **Universal Military Training and Service Act.**

Uncle Corn Pone Said to have been the contemptuous way in which many members of the inner circle of President John F. Kennedy's administration referred to Vice President Lyndon B. Johnson. On a whistle-stop campaign through the South during the 1960 presidential elections, the then Texas senator had named his train "The Corn Pone Special."

"Uncle Shylock" *See* **Marshall Plan.**

Understanding Media In his 1964 bestseller, Canadian sociologist Marshall McLuhan argued that new mass media had changed or destroyed traditional intellectual and aesthetic standards and that it is the form of any medium rather than its content that determines what is being communicated. Succinctly put, this becomes the theory that "the medium is the message." For example, Professor McLuhan cites the electric light as "pure information"; i.e., a medium without a message, unless that light is being used to spell out an advertisement. It therefore follows, according to the maverick sociocultural theorist, that the use of the light for night baseball rather than brain surgery is a matter of indifference; both activities are in some manner the content of electric light since they could not exist without it. From the same point of view, a television comedy would be considered as nourishing as a good production of a Greek tragedy.

The medium is the message because it shapes and controls the intensity and "patterning of human association." Examples of how media affect our response are given in art, photography, movies, printing, radio, television, and simple speech. Technology is treated as an extension of the human organism and the central nervous system.

McLuhan's often eccentric judgments led critics to accuse him of intellectual megalomania, though there was general agreement that the book was stimulating, if occasionally infuriating. Critic Dwight Macdonald called the book—which became a campus favorite of a generation raised on television—"impure nonsense . . . adulterated by sense."

In his previous work, *The Gutenberg Galaxy* (1962), McLuhan had argued that the printing press had encouraged individualism and specialization, as well as mass production and nationalism.

Unidentified Flying Objects (UFOs) After more than twenty years of investigation into reports of flying saucers popularly assumed to be space vehicles of extraterrestrial origin, on December 17, 1969, the U.S. Air Force issued its final report on what was known as Project Bluebook. Prepared under the direction of Edward U. Condon of the University of Colorado, it covered more than 12,000 reported UFO "sightings" and declared that while several could not be explained there was no evidence at all of extraterrestrial intervention. With the end of Project Bluebook, the federal government ceased to concern itself with UFOs. (Among the UFO citings in 1969 was one by peanut farmer Jimmy Carter, Plains, Georgia, who reported a UFO near a Lions Club in nearby Leary.)

Toward the end of 1977, however, there was a new outbreak of sightings and Dr. Frank Press, White House Science Adviser, felt it necessary to ask the **National Aeronautics and Space Administration** (NASA) to consider reopening investigations. Increased reports of UFOs were generally attributed to the popularity of science-fiction movies such as *Star Wars* (1977) and *Close Encounters of the Third Kind* (1977). The Committee for the Scientific Investigation of Claims of the Paranormal, a group of scientists and others attempting to counteract increased public acceptance of the pseudoscientific and paranormal, attributed the new rash of UFO reports to a form of muted mass hysteria. Nevertheless, at the suggestion of the delegation from the Caribbean island nation of Grenada, in

December 1977 a Special Political Committee of the United Nations' General Assembly began debates on a proposal to establish a United Nations agency to investigate UFO sightings.

Most scientists attribute reports of UFOs to hoaxes, or to the layman's misunderstanding of conventional phenomena such as meteors and fireballs, or to the misidentification of aircraft and anticollision lights.

Unification Church Established in Seoul, South Korea, in 1954 by Reverend Sun Myung Moon, the Holy Spirit Association for the Unification of World Christianity made its first major bid for American converts when its crypto-Messiah visited the United States in October 1973. After a brief return to Korea—where the Park regime is said to look with special favor on the Unification Church, its more than 360,000 members, and its various financial enterprises worth some $15 million—Reverend Moon toured all fifty states preaching the true meaning of the Bible's "coded message" as revealed to him in private conversation by Jesus, who also warned him that Americans "must love Richard Nixon" (*see* **Watergate Scandal**).

On September 18, 1974, he held a mass meeting in New York City's Madison Square Garden at which he announced: "The time of the Second Coming of Christ is near, and America is the landing site."

Although "Master" Moon's public message is ecumenical and Christian, he has been reported to have insisted in private that he was "greater than Jesus himself" and that "God is now throwing Christianity away and is now establishing a new religion, and this new religion is Unification Church."

Meanwhile, the attention of IRS investigators has been drawn to his vast financial holdings in this country—in 1975 he acquired New York's Columbia Club as a $1.2 million headquarters for the Unification Church, which is said to own land worth $10 million in California and real estate worth $3 million in New York's Hudson Valley—which in 1973 gave him an income of $7 million. Some if not all of it is said to result from the sale in city streets of ginseng tea, flowers, peanuts, and candles by disciples who are often referred to in the press as "Moonies." Estimates of worldwide membership in the Unification Church have ranged from 600,000 to as high as several million.

Recently, Reverend Moon has run into opposition from parents both here and in Japan who claim that their children were psychologically coerced into remaining with the Unification Church. There have been various instances of children being kidnapped by their parents and subjected to "deprogramming." One of the better known deprogramming centers is the Freedom of Thought Foundation established in Tucson, Arizona, by Michael Trauschit. Its basis is a plan under which parents sue for thirty-day "conservatorship" even over children who have reached their majority. In April 1977 at hearings in California Superior Court the Unification Church lost a test case challenging the plan when Judge S. Lee Vavuris ruled that the parent-child tie is "never-ending," even if "the parent is 90 and the child 60."

United Farm Workers (UFW) *See La Causa.*

United States Information Agency (USIA) In the words of Edward R. Murrow, who was director of the USIA from 1961 to 1964, the function of the agency was "to develop abroad an understanding of America's national goals and way of life. It conducts this effort throughout the world by the most modern communications techniques."

Established on August 1, 1953, under Reorganization Plan 8 as a branch of the executive, the USIA maintained more than 200 posts in over 100 countries. Its libraries and reading rooms abroad were visited by millions annually. Among its communications facilities was the **Voice of America** (VOA), which broadcast news about the United States in more than thirty languages. In addition, the USIA placed hundreds of television programs with foreign stations and networks and made movie documentaries about the United States available in more than 100 foreign nations.

During the **Cuban Missile Crisis,** the USIA was important in bringing the American point of view about the "quarantine" of Cuba to the far corners of the globe even as the event was happening. (By law, it was prohibited from disseminating information for domestic consumption.)

On April 3, 1978, the USIA was replaced by a new International Communication Agency, which in addition to carrying on the USIA's traditional functions is responsible for arranging international cultural exchanges.

United States v. California *See* **Tidelands Oil Controversy.**

United States v. Maine *See* **Tidelands Oil Controversy.**

United States v. Richard M. Nixon Charged with responsibility in criminal proceedings against those involved in a cover-up of the Watergate break-in (*see* **Watergate Scandal**), on April 16, 1974, Special Prosecutor Leon Jaworski petitioned Judge John J. Sirica of the U.S. District Court for the District of Columbia, to direct that President Richard M. Nixon turn over tape recordings and documents relating to sixty-four conversations between himself and four of his former top aides: John W. Dean III, H.R. Haldeman, John D. Ehrlichman, and Charles W. Colson. When the President rejected the subpoena issued and appealed on the grounds of "executive privilege," the U.S. Supreme Court decided on May 31, 1974, to accept the Special Prosecutor's petition for a writ of certiorari that would make it possible to bypass the Court of Appeals and bring the case before it on an expedited schedule. Justice William H. Rehnquist disqualified himself from taking part in the proceedings because he had served in the Justice Department under former Attorney General John N. Mitchell, now a defendant in *United States v. Mitchell et al.*, the Watergate cover-up trial. In a historic decision issued on July 24, 1974, the Court ruled eight to zero against the President, who was directed to turn over the tapes. Within hours, the President, who had challenged the Court's jurisdiction over him, issued a statement declaring: "While I am of course disappointed in the result, I respect and accept the Court's decision, and I have instructed [my special counsel, James D. St. Clair] to take whatever measures are necessary to comply with that decision in all respects."

The decision read by Chief Justice Warren E. Burger, a Nixon appointee, covered several main features. To begin with, it rejected the argument by the President's counsel that Judge Sirica had lacked jurisdiction to issue the subpoena because the matter was an intrabranch dispute between a subordinate and superior officer of the executive branch. "It would be inconsistent," the decision stated, "with applicable law and regulation, and the unique facts of this case, to conclude other than that the Special Prosecutor has standing to bring this action and that a justiciable controversy is presented for decision. . . ." It also noted that the Special Prosecutor had made a sufficient showing to justify a subpoena for production *before* trial, that the materials subpoenaed were not available from any other source, and that their examination and processing should not await trial in the circumstances shown.

The decision also rejected the contention that the subpoena should have been quashed because it demanded "confidential conversations between a President and his close advisors" and was therefore inconsistent with the public interest. It rejected the President's challenge to its own jurisdiction in the matter, noting that *Marbury v. Madison* (1803) and subsequent decisions had held that it was the "province and duty of the judicial department to say what the law is."

Finally, the justices decided that

. . . when the ground for asserting privilege as to subpoenaed materials sought for use in a criminal trial is based only on the generalized interest in confidentiality, it cannot prevail over the fundamental demands of due process of law in the fair administration of criminal justice . . . accordingly we affirm the order of the District Court that subpoenaed materials be transmitted to that court. . . .

The Court failed to act on the President's petition to expunge the grand jury's citation of him as a coconspirator in the Watergate cover-up.

Although there had been reports in the news media that the case before them had involved the Justices in considerable internal dispute, a Court press officer later announced that there had been only one conference of the Justices between the close of argument and the final decision.

The release of the tapes destroyed the last vestiges of congressional opposition to the impeachment of President Nixon, who officially resigned from office on August 9, 1974, and was succeeded by President Gerald R. Ford. On September 8, 1974, President Ford granted former President Nixon an unconditional pardon for all federal crimes he "committed or may have committed" while in office.

"Uniting for Peace" A veto-proof plan against aggressor nations conceived by Secretary of State Dean Acheson and introduced into the United Nations General Assembly by U.S. representative John Foster Dulles in the fall of 1950. On November 3, 1950, shortly before a massive Chinese Communist counteroffensive against UN forces engaged in the **Korean War,** the plan was approved of by the UN General Assembly with only the five-nation Soviet bloc voting against it (Argentina and India abstained, Lebanon was absent).

Under what is sometimes called the "Acheson Plan," a special General Assembly session may be called to deal with a breach of peace if Security Council action is prevented by a veto; a special fourteen-nation Peace Observation Commission was established to investigate and report on developments threatening peace; every member nation of the United Nations was asked to maintain units ready to fight for the United Nations on short notice when peace enforcement action was ordered by either the Security Council or the General Assembly; and a fourteen-nation Collective Measures Committee was established to report on ways to strengthen standby forces and improve collective security measures. In a final section—supported by the U.S.S.R. during a preliminary section-by-section vote—the United Nations was urged to take stronger action to secure "fundamental freedoms for all" and "conditions of economic and social well-being in all countries."

Although originally designed to circumvent Soviet use of the veto in the Security Council, the "Uniting for Peace" resolution was used during the 1956 **Suez Crisis** when Great Britain and France vetoed American and Soviet resolutions calling on Israel and Egypt to cease fighting and on Israel to withdraw her military forces from Egyptian territory.

Universal Military Training and Service Act (UMT)
President Harry S Truman, citing the Chinese intervention in the **Korean War,** declared a national emergency on December 16, 1950, and announced an increase of the armed forces to 3.5 million men. On June 19, 1951, UMT legislation passed by Congress made all men between the ages of 18½ and twenty-six liable for training and periods of service up to twenty-four months, afterward becoming subject to call up in the reserve for a maximum of six years. High school students in good standing could be deferred until after graduation or the age of twenty. The deferment of college students was subject to certain restrictions. UMT provisions of the legislation were administered by a five-man National Security Training Commission appointed by the President.

The legislation was extended in 1955, 1959, 1963, 1967, and 1971, at which point steps were taken toward establishing an all-volunteer army by raising military pay and increasing benefits. By the time UMT expired in June 1973, the U.S. Armed Forces were once again—the last time had been 1948—on an all-volunteer basis.

Unsafe at Any Speed Published in 1965, Ralph Nader's bestseller noted that while for over half a century the "automobile has brought death, injury, and the most inestimable sorrow and deprivation to millions of people," the industry behind it has never been called to account to the public. This was so, he argued, first because the public had never been

supplied with necessary information—which Nader then proceeded to do—and second because it had never been offered the "quality of competition to enable it to make effective demands through the marketplace and through government for a safe, nonpolluting and efficient automobile that can be produced economically." While the situation is still far from perfect, it underwent a rapid change when, as a result of Nader's book, Congress passed on September 9, 1966, the Traffic Safety Act, which established production safety standards that were to be included in all automobile models after 1968, and the Highway Safety Act, which provided federal funds for the improvement of road safety.

Following his investigation of the automobile industry, Ralph Nader was in turn investigated by General Motors (GM), whose Chevrolet Corvair had been the particular object of his attention and criticism—"one of the nastiest handling cars ever built." James Roche, GM president, later apologized for his company's attempt to harass Nader by investigating his austere private life, and GM made a more than $250,000 settlement of Nader's $26 million suit for invasion of privacy. This money was used for the consumer activism of hundreds of students and lawyers who operated from Nader's Center for Study of Responsive Law which was established in Washington, D.C., in 1969. Known as "Nader's Raiders" as the result of a *Washington Post* headline following Nader's testimony before the Federal Trade Commission (FTC) in November 1968 concerning FTC operations, they compiled reports on the meat packing industry, banks, the Interstate Commerce Commission, the Food and Drug Administration, and bureaucracy in general. They also developed data on such national problems as care for the elderly, the use and abuse of natural resources, and occupational safety.

"Naderism" soon entered the language as a noun signifying protest against defective consumer goods.

Upward Bound Part of the **War on Poverty** devised by the **Office of Economic Opportunity** (OEO) in 1965, it is a federally funded program designed to encourage economically disadvantaged high school students to go on to post-secondary education. Estimates are that it spends $44 million annually to provide these students with tutoring, counseling, cultural enrichment programs, and other forms of aid designed to improve scholastic opportunity and motivation. Participants in the program often spend up to two months of the summer living on a college campus and participating in both formal courses and counseling sessions.

An evaluation of the Upward Bound program released in December 1977 found that of the 194, 337 students who had participated, 71 percent went on to some form of post-secondary education. This was contrasted with only 47 percent of nonparticipating students from similar economic backgrounds. The sample was based on 3,710 students involved in fifty of the 333 projects operating during the 1973–1974 school year.

The average annual cost of the program was seen as $5,000 for each student who elected to continue his or her studies after graduation from high school. More than 80 percent of those who have taken advantage of the program have come from minority groups.

Urban Development Bank *See* **Urbank.**

Urban Renewal An all-inclusive term used to describe efforts to eliminate, correct, and prevent the decline of metropolitan areas, it was first heard during the administration of President Franklin D. Roosevelt, when under the Housing Act of 1937 the federal government began providing assistance to local governments for use in slum clearance and low-rent public housing. During World War II, other national needs gained the ascendancy, but under the Housing Act of 1949, 810,000 housing units were to be built in six years. Although Congress subsequently reduced this figure, the years that followed saw the mushrooming of categorical programs such as housing for the aged. In the 1950s the number of urban-renewal projects continued to climb, and the better-known ones today include the Penn Center and Independence Square projects in Philadelphia, the Charles Center in Baltimore, the Lincoln Center in New York, and the Golden Triangle Development in Pittsburgh.

However, though many of these projects cleared away slum and near-slum conditions, they did little to help those who had formerly dwelt in the area. Among black militants, it was increasingly said that "urban renewal means Negro removal."

The Omnibus Housing Act of 1965 included a rent-supplement program for low-income families, the aged, the physically handicapped, and those displaced by government action. It extended urban-renewal programs for four years with $675 million on enactment (August 10, 1965), $725 million in fiscal 1967, and $750 million dollars in each of the following two years. It doubled the $50 million for rehabilitation loans under the Housing Act of 1964,

and provided that up to 35 percent of capital grant authorizations for urban renewal could be employed in predominantly residential projects.

November 1966 saw the birth of President Lyndon B. Johnson's much talked about **Model Cities** program aimed at the decentralization of urban planning and the diversion of a fairer share of a city's resources to inner-city residents. Applications for funds under the program could be submitted by any city to the recently established **Department of Housing and Urban Development** (HUD). Described by the President as "one of the major breakthroughs of the 1960s," the Model Cities program came to an end as a separate federal program in 1974. Under the **Housing and Community Development Act** that year, locally administered block grants for community development substituted for categorical aid plans.

On March 27, 1978, President Jimmy Carter revealed his administration's long-awaited plan for a "new partnership" of federal, state, and local government in fighting urban blight. Among other things, what he described as his "tough, no-nonsense program" would: eliminate a tangle of federal regulations that impedes the flow of funds to state and municipal governments; provide $1 billion annually for public works projects in which 50 percent of the work force would come from the ranks of the hardcore unemployed hired under the **Comprehensive Employment and Training Act** (CETA); establish a "national development bank" which would over three years make $11 billion in private loans available to businesses willing to establish themselves in distressed areas; provide a $200-million fund from which states aiding troubled local communities could draw; provide $150 million annually in low-interest, long-terms loans used for inner-city housing rehabilitation; offer employment tax credits to businesses that hire the hardcore unemployed; make $200 million annually available in the form of advantageous loans to be used in efforts to improve mass transit; finance community groups involved in revitalization projects.

The approximately thirty elements in the program had to win congressional approval—in some instances state and local approval was also required.

Urbank (Urban Development Bank) First proposed in 1968 by Harvard Law Professor Charles Haar as a federal agency that would help communities build needed facilities. Later, the idea surfaced as a means for cities in financial distress to borrow money when the traditional municipal bond market was closed to them.

In 1977, the Carter administration revived the idea as a means of making long-term loans available at favorable interest rates to employers willing to bring plants into distressed cities, or willing to remain in the area if already in operation. It would be part of a developed system of tax credits designed to help save or rebuild deteriorating communities. *See* **Urban Renewal.**

USIA *See* **United States Information Agency.**

U.S. Military Assistance Advisory Group (MAAG)
The growth of MAAG's size and importance in the **Vietnam War** began with the decision by President Dwight D. Eisenhower that the support of the beleaguered French in Indochina was in the national interest. On June 1, 1953, he sent Lt. General John W. O'Daniel to Saigon to confer with French military leaders there. By September, the Eisenhower administration had obtained legislation that made it possible to announce a commitment of $385 million up to the end of 1954 "in addition to other aid funds already earmarked for the prosecution of the war."

General O'Daniel was MAAG chief at the time of the French collapse at Dien Bien Phu. He offered a plan for the relief of the city, which, President Eisenhower noted, "was considered but never attempted by the French high command." This may have been due to what the President called the "sensitivities" of France's General Navarre, who did not allow himself to be intimidated by a report in the French National Assembly in March of that year that the United States was absorbing 78 percent of the cost of the fighting in Vietnam.

When after the Geneva Conference of 1954 Vietnam was "temporarily" partitioned at the 17th parallel into South and North Vietnam, MAAG, still under General O'Daniel, assumed responsibility for training the South Vietnamese army. The decision of Premier Ngo Dinh Diem not to allow the reunification elections called for by the Geneva agreements was followed by an increase in guerrilla activity and a corresponding increase in American aid and personnel.

When President John F. Kennedy assumed office in 1961, there were probably under 1,000 American "advisers" in Vietnam. By the end of the year that number had grown to 3,200, including specialists whose mission it was to train Vietnamese soldiers in counterinsurgency methods.

During most of the Kennedy administration, the head of MAAG was General Paul D. Harkins, who took over in February 1962. A determinedly optimistic man who called the daily situation appraisals he sent to Washington "The Headway Report," General Harkins tended to delete from them setbacks which he saw as reflecting on himself. **Operation Sunrise,** launched under his command, aroused such enthusiasm in Washington that President Kennedy authorized the increase of American forces from 11,300 at the end of 1962 to 16,300 at the end of the following year. In addition, MAAG was upgraded to the Military Assistance Command, Vietnam (MACV). In 1964 General William C. Westmoreland replaced General Harkins as the American commander in Saigon. By the end of that year there were 23,000 American soldiers in Vietnam. The number steadily increased to a maximum of 536,100 in 1968.

U.S.S. *Nautilus* The world's first atomic-powered submarine, it was commissioned by the U.S. Navy on September 30, 1954. Because its power plant obtained all necessary energy from the fission of nuclear fuel, no air was required for combustion and there was no necessity to rise to the surface at frequent intervals for the recharging of batteries. The long life of the nuclear fuel was another factor enabling the ship to travel at high speed and remain submerged for extended periods.

Successful testing of the *Nautilus* led to the launching of the U.S.S. *Seawolf* and then the U.S.S. *Skate* in 1957. On August 1, 1958, under Commander William R. Anderson, with 116 officers and men aboard, the *Nautilus* submerged near Point Barrow, Alaska, during a nineteen-day voyage from Hawaii to Portland, England, crossing the North Pole under ice in a secret maneuver known as Operation Sunshine. The world first learned of the achievement—sometimes considered the United States's technological answer to the U.S.S.R's ***Sputnik***—ninety-six hours later when on August 5, 1958, the *Nautilus* emerged from the edge of the ice pack in the Greenland area. Nine days later, the *Skate*, on a round-trip voyage from Groton, Connecticut, to the North Pole, actually surfaced in the pole area.

The *Nautilus* had been an experimental vessel, but the *Skate* was a prototype of a new model such as the attack submarines U.S.S. *Skipjack* and U.S.S. *Plunger*, and the U.S.S. *George Washington*, which was launched in June 1959 and was the first submarine designed around the **Polaris** ballistic-missile weapons system. The *George Washington* was created to provide a mobile undersea missile base as a safeguard against a sneak **intercontinental-ballistic-missile** (ICBM) attack.

On October 6, 1958, the *Seawolf* had successfully completed a sixty-day submersion. By 1960, the submarine U.S.S. *Triton*—which had two nuclear power plants—navigated the world under water, "breaching" only twice in the eighty-four-day voyage (February 16–May 10).

The *Nautilus* was named for the forerunner of the modern submarine successfully operated in France by the American inventor Robert Fulton on the Seine and at Le Havre in 1800 and 1801. Fulton was unable to interest any government in his craft.

U.S.S. *Triton*   *See* **U.S.S.** *Nautilus.*

U-2 Flights   The Soviet rejection of the **Open Skies** program proposed in Geneva in 1955 led President Dwight D. Eisenhower to agree the following year to the establishment of an information-gathering program in which high-altitude planes known as U-2s made regular photoreconnaissance flights over U.S.S.R. territory from bases in Turkey. Since the U-2s flew at altitudes of 60–70,000 feet, they were considered safe from fighter interception or accurate spotting by radar. Because of their special construction, it was thought that should they crash the planes would be virtually disintegrated. In addition, special self-destruct mechanisms had been built in to destroy all evidence of the planes' use for espionage purposes. Pilots who flew these missions were aware that under the circumstances their chances for surviving a crash were minimal.

For four years this top-secret program produced critical intelligence information—some of it, the President later noted, proving that the so-called bomber and missile gaps "were nothing more than imaginative creations of irresponsibility." Then on May 1, 1960, a U-2 flight from Adana, Turkey, was reported as missing and probably lost; it had been about 1,300 miles within the U.S.S.R. The moment was a tense one, and the President, preparing at the time for a meeting in Paris with Premier Nikita Khrushchev, Prime Minister Harold Macmillan, and President Charles de Gaulle, awaited news from the Soviet Union.

Then on May 5, speaking before the Supreme Soviet, Khrushchev announced that a photoreconnaissance plane had been downed over the U.S.S.R. On the advice of those around him, the President released a previously arranged "cover story": a weather plane making flights from Turkey was missing, and it was considered possible that after the failure of the oxygen equipment the plane's automatic pilot could have carried it deep into the U.S.S.R. But on May 6, Khrushchev announced that the uninjured pilot, Francis Gary Powers, and much of the plane's equipment were in Soviet hands. Powers had confessed to his mission.

With the cover story destroyed, President Eisenhower now admitted the real purpose of the flight and the fact that the U-2 program had been in operation for several years. Khrushchev, who seems to have left room for the President to have pleaded ignorance of the program, was infuriated when the latter took full responsibility for the U-2 flights, though the President did agree to their cessation. (The U-2 had in any case shown itself unreliable because of improved radar and ground-to-air rocketry, and progress had been made in photography from earth satellites.) President Eisenhower's invitation to visit the U.S.S.R. in June was canceled, and because of anti-American demonstrations in Japan a projected visit there was also shelved. Another casualty was the Paris Summit, which on May 17, one day after it had begun, broke up in mutual recriminations between the East and West.

The captured American pilot was tried and condemned to ten years in prison in the Soviet Union (August 1960), but in February 1962, in a tacit admission that the espionage was reciprocal, the Russians agreed to exchange him for Colonel Rudolf Abel, the master Soviet spy captured in this country.

In a related incident a U.S. RB-47 reconnaissance plane was shot down over Soviet territory on July 1, 1960, while it was on a flight to the Barents Sea. Two survivors were imprisoned but were released by the Russians in January 1961.

V

Wide World Photos

Vietnam War

Vandenberg Resolution In January 1948, the U.S. State Department was informed that Great Britain was planning to propose to France, Belgium, the Netherlands, and Luxembourg a series of bilateral defense agreements which would offer some protection against potential aggression. British Foreign Secretary Ernest Bevin sounded out Secretary of State George C. Marshall on the United States attitude toward such agreements and was informed that the United States would do all it could to help bring them about.

With this encouragement, Bevin went to work and the result was the Brussels Pact, a regional arrangement which, at the suggestion of Belgian Foreign Minister Paul Henri Spaak, was substituted for the originally proposed bilateral agreements. President Harry S Truman was eager to find some way of endorsing what was known here as the Western Union without attempting to obtain a military alliance from the Republican-controlled Eightieth Congress. Keeping in mind President Woodrow Wilson's disastrous failure to obtain congressional endorsement for his policies after World War I, Truman turned for help to Sen. Arthur H. Vandenberg (R.-Mich.), who in 1945 had completely reversed his former isolationist stance. The result was a Senate resolution adopted on June 11, 1948, and popularly known as the Vandenberg Resolution. It favored United States participation in regional security agreements within the framework of the United Nations, calling for:

1. Voluntary agreement to remove the veto from all questions involving pacific settlements of international disputes and situations, and from the admission of new members.

2. Progressive development of regional and other collective arrangements for individual and collective self-defense in accordance with the purposes, principles, and provisions of the Charter.

3. Association of the United States, by constitutional process, with such regional and other collective arrangements as are based on continuous and effective self-help and mutual aid, and as affect its national security.

4. Contributing to the maintenance of peace by making clear its determination to exercise the right of individual or collective self-defense under Article 51 should any armed attack occur affecting its national security.

5. Maximum efforts to obtain agreements to provide the United Nations with armed forces as provided by the Charter and to obtain agreement among member nations upon universal regulation and reduction of armaments under adequate and dependable guarantee against violation.

6. If necessary, after adequate effort toward strengthening the United Nations, review of the Charter at an appropriate time by a general conference called under Article 109 or by the General Assembly.

Though without legal force, the resolution indicated to those who still feared American isolationism that the United States could be depended on for aid in the case of aggression.

Vanguard I *See* **Project Vanguard.**

Vesco Affair Under investigation by the Securities and Exchange Commission (SEC) for having "looted" a mutual funds complex named Investors Overseas Services of $224 million, New Jersey financier Robert L. Vesco went to Washington, D.C., in March 1972 and, seeking out Maurice H. Stans, former Secretary of Commerce and at that time the chairman of the Finance **Committee to Re-elect the President** (CREEP; CRP), offered a $250,000 cash contribution to the 1972 campaign of President Richard M. Nixon. This contribution was said to have been made with the understanding that the Nixon administration would do what it could to halt the SEC investigation.

Stans is said to have asked that the contribution be made before April 7, 1972, because that was the date on which the legislation signed by President Nixon earlier in the year was to go into effect as a replacement for the loophole-ridden Federal Corrupt Practices Act of 1925. Since the old law expired on March 10, 1972, the period before April 7, 1972, was covered by no legislation at all and there was therefore no need to reveal contributors.

However, it was not until April 10 that Laurence B. Richardson, Jr., president of the Vesco-controlled International Controls Corporation, and Harry L. Sears, the corporation's associate counsel, delivered $200,000 in $100 bills to Stans, who decided to consider the money as "pre-April 7 funds because it had been committed to us before that date." The additional $50,000 was later paid.

On the same day the money was delivered, former Attorney General John N. Mitchell is said to have arranged a meeting for Sears with SEC chairman William J. Casey and SEC counsel Bradford Cook. Several additional meetings were held and Vesco contributed an additional $250,000, but the SEC continued to prosecute. Eventually, Vesco fled to Costa Rica to avoid possible imprisonment.

On April 28, 1974, a jury found Mitchell, Stans, and Sears innocent of the charges in a federal indictment that they had participated in a conspiracy to have the SEC charges against Vesco quashed in exchange for a contribution to CREEP.

Vesco remained in Costa Rica, which has no extradition treaty with the United States, and was said in 1977 to have become a citizen of Italy until such time as he would complete a five-year residence requirement that would allow him to become a citizen of Costa Rica.

"Victory has a hundred fathers" *See* **Bay of Pigs.**

Vicuña Coat Scandal *See* **Adams-Goldfine Scandal.**

Vietnam War When during World War II the Japanese occupied the French protectorate of Indochina, Vietnamese nationalists led by the Soviet-trained Ho Chi Minh formed the Vietminh (Independence) League to organize resistance. Following the war, these nationalists determined to reject the return of French rule, and for a time they seemed to have the limited sympathy of the U.S. government. In 1945, Ho Chi Minh proclaimed the Democratic Republic of Vietnam—comprised of the Indochinese states of Tonkin, Annam, and Cochin China—and in March of the following year the French agreed to a limited autonomy for Vietnam by recognizing it as a "free state within the French Union." Subsequent disagreements led the Vietminh to attack the French in Hanoi; thus began a more than seven-year period of intense warfare that ended with the defeat of the French at Dien Bien Phu on May 7, 1954, after a fifty-five-day siege by communist forces under General Vo Nguyen Giap.

In the interval, the French had in June 1949 created the State of Vietnam, which was to be led by Bao Dai, a former emperor of Annam, and have Saigon as its capital. After the cessation of hostilities, the Geneva Accords of 1954 divided Vietnam by establishing a Demilitarized Zone (DMZ) at the 17th parallel and creating two nations: to the north of the DMZ Ho Chi Minh's Democratic Republic of Vietnam (North Vietnam), to the south Bao Dai's State of Vietnam (South Vietnam). The Geneva agreements, signed by neither the Bao Dai government nor the United States, called for reunification elections by no later than July 1956. Bao Dai appointed the Catholic leader Ngo Dinh Diem premier of South Vietnam in 1954, and in October 1955 Diem overthrew the emperor and established the Republic of Vietnam, of which he became the first president. The United States quickly recognized the Diem government.

A change in American attitude toward Vietnamese nationalism had been underway ever since it became apparent in 1950 that the Chinese Communists were supplying the Vietminh with arms. Beginning in May 1950, the United States began supplying the French in Indochina with military and economic aid. After the Communist forces of North Korea invaded South Korea on June 25, 1950 (see **Korean War**), President Harry S Truman stepped up this aid as part of a larger struggle for the containment of communism and sent a military mission to work with the French. He did this by invoking the **Mutual Defense Assistance Act** of 1949, which was interpreted as making it necessary to aid France in Indochina as part of an effort to maintain her as an effective **NATO** ally in Europe. From 1950 to 1954, such assistance cost the United States $500 million annually.

When Dien Bien Phu fell, President Dwight D. Eisenhower was in office, and though he disliked the Geneva Accords he felt that they were probably the best that could have been obtained under the circumstances, since as Undersecretary of State Walter Bedell Smith put it: "Diplomacy has rarely been able to gain at the conference table what cannot be gained or held on the battlefield." The **U.S. Military Assistance Advisory Group** (MAAG)—some 300 men—took over the training of the South Vietnamese army in 1955, doubling in number the following year to replace French advisers who had since been withdrawn. When in 1956 the Diem government refused to permit the reunification elections called for in the Geneva Accords, the Eisenhower administration concurred.

Although Ho Chi Minh had abstained from interference while Diem was establishing a surprisingly stable government, the rejection of elections quickly led to a terrorist campaign against the Diem regime by Communist guerrilla fighters. (A U.S. State Department "white paper" published in 1965 was to note that when Vietnam was partitioned in 1954

. . . thousands of carefully selected party members were ordered to remain in place in the South and keep their secret apparatus intact to help promote Hanoi's cause. Arms and ammunition were stored away for future use. Guerrilla fighters rejoined their families to await the party's call. Others withdrew to remote jungle and mountain hideouts. The majority—an estimated 90,000—were moved to North Viet-Nam.

After 1954, an estimated 800–900,000 refugees, most of them Catholics, flowed into South Vietnam from the north.)

In 1960, the Communist government in Hanoi openly avowed its support for the guerrilla terrorists—known as Viet Cong—by creating the **National Liberation Front** (NLF) of South Vietnam to direct activities dedicated to the overthrow of the Diem regime and the ousting of its American advisers. When President John F. Kennedy assumed office in 1961 there were said to be 900 Americans in Vietnam; within a year the number had risen to 3,200, according to Department of Defense figures. A counterinsurgency program was launched under American guidance, and American helicopters began supporting units of the Army of the Republic of Vietnam (ARVN).

In 1962, MAAG was reorganized into the Military Assistance Command, Vietnam (MACV) under General Paul D. Harkins, and troop levels rose to 11,300. Meanwhile, insurgent activity increased as men and materials flowed south from North Vietnam to aid the NLF. The Diem regime responded with intensifying repressive measures that increasingly alienated support from various segments of the South Vietnamese population. Of particular importance was the brutal repression of the Buddhist demonstrations in Saigon and Hue in the latter half of 1963. Said to have been undertaken by Diem with the encouragement of his brother, Ngo Dinh Nhu, and the latter's wife—whom the United States press had christened the **Dragon Lady**—they were a contributing factor in the overthrow of Diem by a military junta, and to the assassination of both him and his brother. (In 1971, members of the administration of President Richard M. Nixon tried to "prove" President Kennedy's complicity in these events by forging the famous **Diem Cables.**) The collapse of the Diem regime also brought with it the end of the **Strategic Hamlet Plan,** established in March 1962 to combat guerrilla activities by herding thousands of Vietnamese into protected and barbed-wire-enclosed villages.

At the time of President Kennedy's assassination in Dallas on **November 22, 1963,** American troop levels in Vietnam had risen to 16,300. By the end of the first year which saw President Lyndon B. Johnson in office, this figure had risen to 23,300.

A turning point of American involvement in Vietnam came in August 1964 when the U.S.S. *Maddox*, a destroyer assigned to intelligence operations in the Gulf of Tonkin, was attacked by North Vietnamese PT boats while it was reported to be in international waters. As a result of this never adequately explained incident, President Johnson obtained from an outraged and overhasty Congress the **Gulf of Tonkin Resolution,** which gave him advance approval to "take all necessary steps, including the use of armed force, to assist any member or protocol state of the **Southeast Asia Collective Defense Treaty** [SEATO] requesting assistance

in defense of its freedom." (The resolution was eventually repealed by an embarrassed Congress in December 1970.)

American troops were committed in combat for the first time in June 1965—in a "search and destroy" mission at Dong Xoai—by General William C. Westmoreland, who had the previous year replaced General Harkins as commander of MACV. (American planes had begun bombing North Vietnam in February of that year after Viet Cong attacks had resulted in the deaths of thirty-one Americans at Pleiku and Qui Nhon.) Under his urgings for a major commitment, troop levels in Vietnam began to rise astronomically: 184,300 by the end of 1965 and more than double that number by the close of the following year. At the end of the Johnson administration there were 536,100 Americans in Vietnam.

In an effort to cut the flow of men and equipment into South Vietnam, U.S. planes began bombing the Ho Chi Minh Trail, a network of Communist supply routes passing through Laos to South Vietnam. In addition, retaliatory air strikes against North Vietnam were authorized by President Johnson, who suspended them from time to time in the vain hope of forcing the Communists to negotiate. Meanwhile, as MACV feverishly built airfields and improved the harbor facilities in South Vietnam, American combat troops fought in the Central Highlands to stave off a Communist attempt to cut South Vietnam in two. A major North Vietnamese buildup within the DMZ was concealed by a siege of a U.S. Marine base at Khe Sanh begun on January 21, 1968, in an atmosphere that ominously recalled the siege of Dien Bien Phu, and General Westmoreland hastily arranged for an airlift of additional men and supplies.

Meanwhile, opposition to the war had begun to build up in the United States. On April 15, 1967, some 100,000 antiwar protesters marched in a New York City demonstration organized by the **National Mobilization Committee to End the War in Vietnam** (Mobe), and a similar protest took place in the nation's capital on October 21, 1967.

The "**credibility gap,**" which since 1965 had been widening between the Johnson administration's optimistic pronouncements on the progress of the war and mounting casualty figures as the situation required the commitment of more and more American troops, became a veritable chasm when on January 30, 1968, the Communists launched their **Tet offensive,** which resulted in record casualties for both sides during attacks on the provincial capitals of South Vietnam. Hue was held for twenty-five days—during which time the Communists executed 3,000 civilians—and the U.S. Embassy in Saigon was briefly occupied. Total American casualties that year were 14,589 dead and 46,796 wounded.

On March 31, 1968, President Johnson announced that he would not be a candidate for re-election later that year. Proclaiming a bombing halt over most of North Vietnam, he asked that both sides proceed to peace negotiations. (They began in Paris the following May, but were for a long time unproductive.)

Continuing protests against the war marred the Democratic National Convention in Chicago (*see* **Battle of Chicago**) and helped assure the election of Republican candidate Richard M. Nixon. Under his administration, withdrawal of combat troops from Vietnam began on July 8, 1969, and by the end of the year the troop level in that battered country was down from the high of 1968 to 475,200. As the war continued under the command of General Creighton Abrams, who in 1968 had replaced a somewhat dispirited General Westmoreland, who now felt that a military victory was unlikely, the nation learned with horror of the **My Lai Massacre,** in which American soldiers were responsible for the slaughter of unarmed Vietnamese civilians. In "**Moratorium Day**" demonstrations on October 15 and November 19, 1969, thousands of Americans turned out to protest the continuation of the most unpopular war in the nation's history.

In a television broadcast on November 3, 1969, President Nixon stated that "in the previous Administration we Americanized the war in Vietnam. In this Administration we are Vietnamizing the search for peace." Appealing for the support of the "**silent majority**," he announced a secret timetable for the withdrawal of all American combat forces from Vietnam as quickly as their duties could be taken over by revitalized ARVN forces. The thousands of letters the White House received in support of this stand were later revealed as part of an organized Republican program. To gain time for "Vietnamization," he authorized the **Cambodian "incursion"** in which combined U.S. and South Vietnamese forces invaded neutral Cambodia with a view to destroying Communist supply bases in sanctuary areas along the border. Student protests against this extension of the war on April 30, 1970, resulted in the **Kent State Tragedy** (May 4, 1970) in which four demonstrators were killed when National Guardsmen opened fire on a protest group.

Although the number of American troops in Vietnam were down to 156,800 by the end of 1971,

the war dragged on as the President continued his efforts to establish "**peace with honor.**" In June 1971, presidential assistant Henry A. Kissinger had begun secret negotiations with the Communist leader Le Duc Tho. However, after the North Vietnamese launched a major offensive in March 1972, the bombing of North Vietnam was resumed. Before this new invasion across the DMZ could be brought to a standstill, Quang Tri, the capital of South Vietnam's most northern province, was in Communist hands (May 1). On orders from President Nixon, the harbors of Haiphong and other Communist ports were mined.

There were 24,200 American troops in Vietnam by the end of 1972, but no combat troops. Meanwhile, the publication of the **Pentagon Papers** (June 1971) tracing the course of American involvement in the Vietnam quagmire had completed the nation's disenchantment with a war that had so far brought it only shame, dissension, and dishonor. In addition, the White House caught itself increasingly entangled in events stemming from the break-in of Democratic National Headquarters at the Watergate complex in Washington (June 17, 1972). It had also become increasingly difficult to defend association with the repressive government of President Nguyen Van Thieu, who had risen to power after the fall of the Diem regime. (Returning from a trip to Vietnam in early 1968, Sen. Edward Kennedy (D.-Mass.) had stated: "The government of South Vietnam is infested with corruption. Government jobs are bought and paid for. Police accept bribes. Officials and their wives run operations in the black market.")

Secret peace talks that were said to have reached tentative agreement in October 1972 collapsed in December when it proved impossible to get President Thieu to accept a draft of the settlement.

Around-the-clock bombings of North Vietnam by B-52s began again on December 18, 1972, and continued until December 30, 1972. On January 8, 1973, the Communists returned to the negotiating table, and on January 24, 1973, a reluctant President Thieu joined with President Nixon in announcing the agreement that three days later was signed in Paris by representatives of the United States, South Vietnam, North Vietnam and the Provisional Revolutionary Government of the Viet Cong. A separate agreement between the United States and North Vietnam provided for the release of American POWs in Communist hands and for the withdrawal of all American forces from Vietnam within sixty days.

It was in violation of the four-party agreement that in January 1975 North Vietnam once more massed troops within the borders of South Vietnam and began a major offensive that ended with the collapse of the Thieu regime on April 21, 1975. (In an amendment to an appropriations bill, Congress had prohibited funds for combat actions in Southeast Asia after August 15, 1973.) Only hours after American embassy personnel and many South Vietnamese who were probably marked for death by the Communists were airlifted from Saigon, Viet Cong and North Vietnamese troops entered the city on April 30, 1975.

Official Department of Defense figures put the number of Americans killed in Vietnam from 1961 through the time of the emergency airlifts of 1975 at 46,370; hospitalized wounded rose to 153,316 for the same period. In addition, there were over 10,000 deaths from causes other than combat, and more than 1,300 men were reported as missing. The estimated cost of the war is approximately $140 billion. Among the casualties were President Kennedy's **New Frontier,** President Johnson's **Great Society,** and President Nixon's **New American Revolution.**

Viking 1 and 2 In a mission conceived in 1968 to determine the possibility of life on Mars, two Viking unmanned spacecraft were launched from Cape Canaveral, Florida, the first on August 20, 1975, and the second the following September 9. After completing an elliptical flight of more than 500 million miles, *Viking 1* arrived in orbit around the planet on June 19, 1976. A 1,300-pound landing vehicle detached itself from the orbiting "mother" craft on July 20 and settled on the planet's surface after a 12,170-mile descent, during which it sent back reports on the atmosphere at different altitudes. Although suppositions that most of Mars's atmosphere was carbon dioxide were confirmed, findings of nitrogen (3 percent) and argon (less than 2 percent) suggested that at one time, at least, the planet might have supported some form of life. The two cameras on the lander unit began sending back color and black-and-white photographs of the surface that reminded some scientists of the Arizona or Utah deserts.

Viking 2 arrived on Mars September 3, 1976, and settled down at a landing site some 4,600 miles northeast of the first lander in order to see if this supposedly moister terrain would prove more hospitable to life. Photographs sent back showed a rock-strewn plain, surprising scientists who had expected to find rolling dunes.

The Viking project, which had been expected to cost $364 million, actually came closer to costing $1 billion. It was managed by the **National Aeronautics and Space Administration** (NASA) through its Langley Research Center, Hampton, Virginia. NASA's Jet Propulsion Laboratory at Pasadena, California, controlled the mission.

VISTA *See* **Volunteers in Service to America.**

VOA *See* **Voice of America.**

Voice of America (VOA) Established on February 24, 1942, to combat Axis propaganda and explain the goals of the United States during World War II, VOA beamed 2,500 broadcasts a week to war-torn Europe and Asia. On January 27, 1948, President Harry S Truman signed legislation making the VOA permanent under the Department of State. Its function in the propaganda war against communism is to present objective news and a comprehensive view of American thought and official U.S. policy. It is on the air twenty-four hours a day, and its broadcasts in about forty languages are said to reach a weekly audience of 50 million.

In 1953, VOA became a part of the **United States Information Agency** (USIA), which was in turn replaced in April 1978 by the International Communication Agency. Unlike the Munich-based Radio Free Europe and Radio Liberty established by the **Central Intelligency Agence** (CIA) in 1950 and 1953, respectively, to beam news about developments in their own countries to citizens in Soviet-bloc nations, the VOA continues to concentrate on American culture and the international goals of the United States. (Radio Free Europe and Radio Liberty were separated from the CIA in 1971, and since 1973 have been under the supervision of the Board for International Broadcasting.)

Volunteers in Service to America (VISTA) Established under the **Economic Opportunity Act** of 1964, VISTA provides volunteers to help solve problems in poverty communities. In 1971 its activities were placed under the control of **ACTION,** an umbrella agency established by President Richard M. Nixon to coordinate volunteer programs that had previously been separately administered.

VISTA assignments can be made under the sponsorship of either public or private nonprofit organizations dealing with problems in health, housing, education, and social service. By 1978 there were over 4,500 volunteers in the program, and its fiscal budget was over $26 million.

Voting Rights Act of 1965 Addressing a joint session of Congress on the bill before them on March 15, 1965, President Lyndon B. Johnson said: "There is no constitutional issue here. The command of the Constitution is plain. There is no moral issue. It is wrong—deadly wrong—to deny any of your fellow Americans the right to vote in this country. There is no issue of states' rights or national rights. There is only the struggle for human rights. . . . This time, on this issue, there must be no delay, no hesitation, and no compromise with our purpose."

Debate on the Voting Rights bill began on April 22, 1965, and on May 25 the Senate imposed cloture on additional debate; it later passed the Act by a seventy-seven-to-nineteen vote. After a House version was passed on July 9 by 333-85, a conference committee adjusted the differences between the two bills. Threatened with federal action, Alabama, Arkansas, and Mississippi had already relaxed restrictions on voting rights.

On August 6, 1965, the President was finally able to put his signature to a bipartisan bill of which the importance in the area of political rights is comparable only to the Fifteenth Amendment. It suspended all literacy tests and other devices "in all states and counties where less than 50 percent of the voting age population was registered to vote in 1964"; it gave the Attorney General the right—but not the obligation—to use federal examiners to register voters and it authorized him to send federal observers to polling and vote-counting places in those states and counties; it also prevented the denial or abridgment of the right to vote by an alteration in voting qualifications and procedures in force in 1964. The areas primarily involved were the states of Alabama, Alaska, Georgia, Louisiana, Mississippi, South Carolina, Virginia, and portions of North Carolina and Arizona.

By August 10, federal inspectors were looking into registration and voting procedures used in parts of the South to keep black voters from the polls. Exactly one year later, the Justice Department announced that in five Deep South States Negro voter registration had increased by 50 percent.

But if the struggle for black voting rights was eased, it was not won. "Millions of Negroes are frustrated and angered because extravagant promises made less than a year ago are a shattered mockery today," said Martin Luther King, Jr., in 1966. He noted that fewer than forty federal registrars had been appointed "and not a single federal law officer capable of making an arrest was sent to the South. As a consequence the old way of life—economic coercion, terrorism, murder, and inhuman contempt—continue unabated."

Voyager Launched from Cape Canaveral, Florida, on September 1, 1977, the 1,820-pound *Voyager 1*, an unmanned spacecraft on a scientific mission, set off on a 400-million-mile journey destined to bring it within some 174,000 miles of Jupiter. It had been preceded into space by *Voyager 2* which had a somewhat troubled launching (August 20, 1977) and whose science boom failed to lock properly into place. *Voyager 2* was nevertheless already sending back information about low-frequency radio emissions from earth.

Equipped with a variety of instruments as well as closeup and wide-angle cameras, early in March 1979, the drum-shaped *Voyager 1* began justifying the $400-million project by sending back photographs that captured the front pages of the nation's newspapers. Among the color transmissions were magnificent shots of Jupiter's Great Red Spot, a permanent hurricane which at places is three times as wide as the earth's diameter. The craft also provided us with our first real information about the largest of Jupiter's moons: Callisto, Ganymede, Europa, and Io.

Sometime in mid-1980, *Voyager 1* will be catapulted toward Saturn. In 40,000 years it should pass its first star. The craft carries a copper record that includes a variety of earth music and sounds, including the voice of President Jimmy Carter.

W

Watergate Scandal

Walker Report Officially entitled *Rights in Conflict*, this 233-page report was the work of a special panel charged by the National Commission on the Causes and Prevention of Violence with investigating clashes between antiwar demonstrators and police during the Democratic National Convention in Chicago in August 1968. The 212-member study team assembled by Daniel Walker, president of the Chicago Crime Commission, began hearings on September 27, 1968, and issued its findings on December 1, after having heard 1,410 eyewitnesses and reviewed films, photographs, news reports, and more than 2,000 statements provided by the FBI.

Sharply critical of the Chicago police for the use of brutality in controlling demonstrators, it charged that at times the situation had deteriorated into a "police riot" more violent than the demonstrations that had apparently provoked it.

During the week of the Democratic National Convention the Chicago police were the targets of mounting provocation by both word and act. It took the form of obscene epithets and rocks, sticks, bathroom tiles and even human feces hurled at police by demonstrators. Some of these acts had been planned; others were spontaneous or were themselves provoked by police action. Furthermore, the police had been put on edge by widely published threats of attempts to disrupt both the city and the Convention.

That was the nature of the provocation. The nature of the response was unrestrained and indiscriminate police violence on many occasions, particularly at night.

That violence was made all the more shocking by the fact that it was often inflicted upon persons who had broken no law, disobeyed no order, made no threat. These included peaceful demonstrators, onlookers, and large numbers of residents who were simply passing through, or happened to live in, the areas where confrontations were occurring.

The report noted the influence of press and TV reporters on both the demonstrators and the Chicago police, and charged that as many as sixty-three reporters and photographers had been subjected to police violence. It ascribed police behavior as due at least in part to the belief that violence against demonstrators would be condoned by Mayor Richard J. Daley, who earlier that year had established the pattern by his controversial "shoot to kill" orders during the riots that followed the assassination of civil rights leader Martin Luther King, Jr., on April 4.

The accounts given of confrontations between Chicago police and the demonstrators reproduced the language used so faithfully that the Government Printing Office asked that obscenities be censored; however, Mr. Walker insisted that the language be reproduced since it was a contributing factor in the riots.

Issued by the special panel's sponsoring commission without evaluation or comment, the report was attacked by radicals as a "whitewash." **Students for a Democratic Society** (SDS) leader Tom Hayden charged that though some incidents in Chicago may have been due to "policemen breaking orders and going berserk," the overall response was "generated by official policies that deliberately created the major episodes of police violence in Chicago."

See **Chicago Eight; Battle of Chicago.**

"Wallace or War" *See* **Progressive Party of America.**

Wanna-Go-Home Riots The origin of these can probably be traced to Manila, where in January 1946 service-weary GIs reacted angrily to the announcement that Army demobilization schedules following the end of World War II had been reduced from 800,000 to 300,000 men a month. Protesters meeting in the city's Rizal Stadium booed a soothing message from Lt. General W. D. Styer, Commander of the Armed Forces in the Western Pacific, and the story was picked up by the wire services and headlined by newspapers.

Soon there were crowds of GI protesters in Tokyo, London, Paris, and even occupied Germany. Members of Congress, flooded with protest mail—stamped "No boats, no votes"—from GIs and their families, were quick to back up these demands. As a result of rapid demobilization and declining reenlistments, the U.S. Army began shrinking at such a pace that General Dwight D. Eisenhower—who may have contributed to the riots with an amiable comment that men overseas should be discharged as quickly as possible—began to fear that America's commitments abroad would be taken over by "some other country."

War on Poverty In his first State of the Union address to the Congress on January 8, 1964, President Lyndon B. Johnson announced: "This administration today, here and now, declares unconditional war on poverty in America. . . . It will not be a short or easy struggle, no single weapon or strategy will suffice, but we shall not rest until that war is won." In an appeal to fiscally minded conservatives he noted that this "war" was not only morally justified but economically sound in that "one thousand dollars invested in salvaging an unemployable youth today can return forty thousand dollars in his lifetime."

On February 1, 1964, the President appointed **Peace Corps** director R. Sargent Shriver to the task of working out a legislative program to back up the "war." Among the many who aided him was Adam Yarmolinsky, who left his job as special assistant to Secretary of Defense Robert S. McNamara to do so. Six weeks later, the program they assembled was approved by the President and sent to Congress on March 16, 1964, with a special message noting that since we have "the power to strike away the barriers to full participation in our society . . . we have the duty."

The heart of the war on poverty was the Economic Opportunity Act passed by Congress on August 11, 1964. Its initial $947.5 million authorization financed only the first year of a program which included a **Job Corps** to provide remedial education and job training at camps and residential centers for 40,000 young men and women; another basic feature of the act was the establishment of **Volunteers in Service to America** (VISTA), whose members would function as a **Domestic Peace Corps**, receiving $50 a month and living expenses for working in poverty areas and mental hospitals, and on Indian reservations. Provision was also made to help communities fight poverty by setting up local slum clearance, remedial education, and guidance projects. Other aspects of the act established work-study and work-training programs to provide financial assistance to both high school and college students. In addition, provision was made for a loan program to help the small farmer and businessman.

On April 28, 1964, a comprehensive program dealing with increasing and endemic poverty in the eleven-state Appalachian area was proposed; however, it was not until March 6, 1965, that President Johnson was able to sign the Appalachia Aid Act. Of the $1,092,400,000 in aid authorized, up to $36.5 million was to go into reclamation necessitated by the ravages of strip mining; $17 million into soil maintenance and erosion control; $840 million in federal funds—or 70 percent of the total cost—into highway and road construction; and $28 million for hospital construction. Funds were also allocated for sewage treatment systems, school construction, a water-resources study, and general research and development.

As part of the war on poverty, the **Office of Economic Opportunity** (OEO) established under the Economic Opportunity Act envisaged a five-year plan with a total budget of $3.5 billion, but there was a drastic change in the mood of Congress beginning in 1966—partly due to the fiscal drain of the continuing **Vietnam War**—and only $1.625 billion was appropriated by Congress.

See **The Great Society**.

Warren Court Considered by many the most controversial judge of his time, Earl Warren, former Republican governor of California, was appointed Chief Justice of the U.S. Supreme Court in September 1953 and retired in June 1969. His fifteen years in office spanned the administrations of Presidents Eisenhower, Kennedy, and Johnson, and under his guidance and influence the Court handed down major decisions in civil rights (**Brown v. Board of Education of Topeka,** 1954), reapportionment (**Reynolds v. Sims,** 1964), and criminal justice (**Miranda v. Arizona,** 1966).

Its extreme dedication to protecting the rights of the individual made the term "Warren Court" a term of opprobrium in some quarters, and there were constant calls in conservative circles to "Impeach Earl Warren." In 1968, the year in which the Chief Justice announced his decision to retire at the end of the 1968–1969 term, Alabama's segregationist Governor George C. Wallace accused him of having done "more to destroy constitutional government in this country than any one man," and President Eisenhower, who had appointed him, is said to have considered that appointment the "biggest damfool mistake I ever made."

The civil libertarian bloc on the Court led by Warren included Justices Hugo L. Black, William O. Douglas, William J. Brennan, Arthur J. Goldberg, and his successor Abe Fortas. Justice Felix Frankfurter, who retired in 1962, led Justices Tom C. Clark, Potter Stewart, Charles E. Whittaker, and John M. Harlan in urging "judicial self-restraint."

Chief Justice Warren's decision to announce his retirement during the final months of President Johnson's term in office was said to have been motivated by his fear that Richard M. Nixon would be elected President in November of that year. He had intended to give President Johnson the opportunity to name a new Chief Justice who would follow what he considered a liberal, activist tradition. However, when President Johnson named Associate Justice Fortas to the post in June 1968, a Senate filibuster by Southerners opposed to the nomination caused Justice Fortas to ask that his name be withdrawn (October 1968) during confirmation proceedings. In May 1969, President Nixon named District of Columbia Court of Appeals Judge Warren E. Burger to the post, and he was confirmed by the Senate the following June.

Warren Report Only one week after assuming office, on November 29, 1963, President Lyndon B. Johnson issued Executive Order No. 11130 which established a special investigative commission "to ascertain, evaluate, and report about the facts relating to the assassination of the late President John F. Kennedy." It was headed by Chief Justice Earl Warren and therefore popularly referred to as "the Warren Commission." Other members included Sen. Richard B. Russell (D.-Ga.), Sen. John Sherman Cooper (R.-Ky.), Rep. Hale Boggs (D.-La.) Rep. Gerald R. Ford (R.-Mich), former **CIA** director Allen Dulles, and John J. McCoy, former U.S. High Commissioner for Germany.

Chief Justice Warren had been reluctant to accept the assignment but had done so on the insistence of the President. ("Mr. Chief Justice, you were once in the Army, weren't you? Well, I'm calling you back in.")

The commission had hoped to complete its work within three months, but it was not until September 24, 1964, that what has become known as "the Warren Report" was submitted to President Johnson. It basically concluded that there was no evidence to support the rumors that President Kennedy had been the victim of an assassination conspiracy. "The shots which killed President Kennedy and wounded Governor Connally were fired from the sixth-floor window at the southeast corner of the Texas School Book Depository . . . by Lee Harvey Oswald. . . ." The report further concluded that there was no evidence to link Oswald to Jack Ruby, the nightclub operator who had in turn gunned the assassin down in the Dallas county jail on November 24, 1963. The motives for the Presidential assassination, it stated, were to be found in the killer himself, but the commission had been unable to make any "definitive determination" of them.

It has endeavored to isolate factors which might have influenced his decision to assassinate President Kennedy. These factors were:

(a) His deep-rooted resentment of all authority which was expressed in a hostility toward every society in which he lived;

(b) His inability to enter into meaningful relationships with people, and a continuous pattern of rejecting his environment in favor of new surroundings;

(c) His urge to try to find a place in history and despair at times over failures in his various undertakings;

(d) His capacity for violence as evidenced by his attempt to kill General [Edwin A.] Walker [on April 10, 1963];

(e) His avowed commitment to Marxism and communism, as he understood the terms and developed his own interpretation of them; this was expressed by his antago-

nism toward the United States, by his defection to the Soviet Union, by his failure to be reconciled with life in the United States, even after his disenchantment with the Soviet Union, and by his efforts, though frustrated, to go to Cuba.

Senator Russell had objected to the categorical rejection of the possibility of conspiracy and had originally been unwilling to go beyond the statement that it had indeed been Oswald who had fired the shots that killed the President and wounded Governor John Connally. He had desired to append a dissent to the report, but was eventually won over by Chief Justice Warren, who was insistent that the report be unanimous.

When it was made public on September 27, 1963, the report was generally accepted by the public and the press. But rumors of a conspiracy continued to come from critics of both the left and right. One of the more sober appraisals of the commission's work was in Edward Jay Epstein's *Inquest* (1966), but the thrust of its criticisms was on the commission's procedures and omissions, rather than on its conclusions.

It soon became obvious that the Warren Report had not silenced speculation about a possible conspiracy, and in 1967 a Harris Poll showed that 66 percent of those questioned doubted its validity.

In recent years the Warren Report has come under increased criticism for its heavy reliance on information supplied to it by federal agencies such as the FBI and the CIA. In September 1975, it was revealed that the FBI had withheld from the commission the fact that shortly before the assassination Oswald had delivered to its offices a letter threatening to blow up the Dallas police station. The withholding of this evidence—and its subsequent destruction—raised additional doubts about the evidence on which the Warren Report was based.

See **November 22, 1963**.

WASAG *See* **Washington Special Action Group**.

Washington Confidential A 1951 best-seller by newsmen Jack Lait and Lee Mortimer, it purported to give a behind-the-scenes view of life in the nation's capital. Critics charged that it was largely a collection of unsupported statements from unidentified sources. The same authors were also responsible for similar sensational "exposés" such as the previously published *New York Confidential* and *Chicago Confidential*, both of which were popular with mass audiences.

Washington Merry-Go-Round Title of an influential syndicated Washington column read by millions throughout the country and originally written by veteran newsmen Drew (Andrew) Pearson and Robert S. Allen. It came from a 1931 book of the same name on which both men had collaborated to provide an irreverent exposé of American politics. After 1942, Pearson conducted the column by himself, frequently engaging in controversy with leading politicians. (In 1951, he was assaulted by an enraged and drunken Sen. Joseph R. McCarthy [R.-Wis.] [*see* **McCarthyism**]). One of Pearson's more notorious pieces was one written in advance but published the day after the upset victory in 1948 of President Harry S Truman over Republican presidential contender Thomas E. Dewey. It began: "I have surveyed the close-knit group around Tom Dewey, who will take over the White House 86 days from now."

Pearson's column was a training ground for some who went on to become top-notch Washington reporters of national fame. Among them is one-time legman Jack Anderson. When in 1958 the latter was caught bugging the offices of the public relations man for industrialist Bernard Goldfine (*see* **Adams-Goldfine Scandal**), Pearson refused to fire him. Echoing President Dwight D. Eisenhower's defense of Sherman Adams, he said: "I need him."

Washington Special Action Group (WASAG) A special crisis panel first constituted when on April 15, 1969, North Korean Migs shot down an unarmed U.S. reconnaissance plane in the Sea of Japan, approximately 100 miles off the Korean coast. Headed by National Security Advisor Henry A. Kissinger, it included General Earle G. Wheeler, Chairman of the Joint Chiefs; Marshall Green, Assistant Secretary of State for Far Eastern Affairs; David Packard, Deputy Secretary of Defense; and U. Alexis Johnson, Under Secretary of State for Political Affairs.

See "**The Plumbers.**"

Watergate Committee *See* **Select Committee on Presidential Campaign Activities**.

Watergate Scandal While making his rounds at the Watergate hotel-office complex in Washington, D.C., on June 17, 1972, night watchman Frank Wills noticed that two doors connecting the main part of the building to an underground garage had been taped to prevent them from locking. He removed the tapes, but when a half hour later he found they had been replaced, he telephoned the police to say that someone had made an illegal entry into the building.

That simple phone call started a chain of events that was to lead to criminal procedures against more than fifty individuals and some twenty leading American corporations; it resulted in prison sentences for a former Attorney General and several leading members of the White House staff; and it brought about the resignation from office of a President of the United States, who until he was pardoned by his successor for all offenses he had "committed or may have committed or taken part in" during his term in office lived under the threat of a prison sentence.

At 2:30 A.M., members of the tactical squad of the Washington Metropolitan Police, who had responded to the call in an unmarked car, arrested five men who were attempting to bug the phones in the sixth floor offices of the Democratic National Committee (DNC); they were equipped with cameras and had obviously been going through the files. They refused to say what they were doing in the DNC headquarters, and when booked they all gave aliases. Investigation soon proved them to be James W. McCord, Jr., a former **CIA** operator who was now the security coordinator of the **Committee to Re-elect the President** (CREEP; CRP), and four members of the anti-Castro Cuban community in Miami: Bernard L. Barker, Eugenio R. Martinez, Virgilio R. Gonzalez, and Frank A. Sturgis. Among their belongings were $2,300 in consecutively numbered $100 bills—which were eventually traced to CREEP funds. When police searched their rooms at the Watergate Hotel, they found an additional $4,200 and an address book with the notation "E. Hunt—W.H." This eventually led to the arrest of E. Howard Hunt, Jr., a former CIA agent and now CREEP security chief, and G. Gordon Liddy, a former FBI officer who was now a staff member of the White House Domestic Council. (Unknown to the police, both Hunt and Liddy had been in the Watergate at the time of the break-in, but they had managed to escape after being warned of police intervention by a confederate posted in a hotel facing the complex.)

When the White House connections of several of the men had been established, President Richard M. Nixon's press secretary, Ronald L. Ziegler, refused comment and referred to the break-in as a "third-rate burglary attempt," predicting that "certain elements may try to stretch this beyond what it is." As pressure built up, however, President Nixon stated in a press conference on August 29, 1972, that he could "state categorically" that the investigation he had ordered made by John W. Dean III, chief White House counsel, "indicates that no one in the White House staff, no one in this Administration, presently employed was involved in this very bizarre incident. . . . What really hurts is if you try to cover it up." (Dean was later to say this was the first he had heard of this report. Meanwhile, on July 1, 1972, former Attorney General John N. Mitchell had resigned as CREEP chairman after citing "family" difficulties as the cause.)

On September 15, 1972, all seven men arrested in connection with the Watergate break-in were indicted on charges including wiretapping, planting electronic eavesdropping devices, and stealing documents. That same day the Justice Department announced: "We have absolutely no evidence to indicate that any others should be charged." Meanwhile, Vice President Spiro T. Agnew asserted that "someone set up these people and encouraged them to undertake this caper to embarrass them and to embarrass the Republican party."

Two weeks later, the *Washington Post* featured a story by investigative reporters Bob Woodward and Carl Bernstein indicating that while Mitchell was Attorney General he had controlled a secret fund that was used to finance espionage operations against the Democratic party. Later stories by the two reporters—they became popularly identified as "Woodstein" and in 1974 published an account of their investigation in the bestselling *All the President's Men*—linked specific espionage operations to the White House, and Press Secretary Ziegler responded with charges of "character assassination" and "shoddy journalism." (In 1973 Woodward and Bernstein received the George Polk Memorial Award for their coverage of the Watergate scandal, and the *Washington Post* was given the Pulitzer Prize. Their book was later made into a popular movie starring Robert Redford [Woodward] and Dustin Hoffman [Bernstein].)

On January 30, 1973, after a sixteen-day trial during which sixty-two witnesses were heard in the court of Judge John J. Sirica, chief judge of the U.S. District Court for the District of Columbia, the "Watergate Seven"—the five burglars and Hunt and Liddy—were found guilty on a variety of charges by a jury that had required only ninety minutes to reach a decision. Judge Sirica stated that he was "not satisfied" that the full Watergate story had been disclosed, and early in February it was learned that Gordon C. Strachan, former assistant to the President's Chief of Staff, H. R. Haldeman, had in February 1972 been a contact between Liddy's intelligence operations and a political sabotage

campaign undertaken by Donald H. Segretti, who had been hired by the President's appointments secretary, Dwight L. Chapin (*see* **Dirty Tricks**). The Senate voted on February 7 to form a seven-member **Select Committee on Presidential Campaign Activities**, and Sen. Sam J. Ervin (D.-N.C.) was named chairman.

On February 28, 1973, at hearings before the Senate Judiciary Committee to confirm the nomination of L. Patrick Gray III as director of the FBI, there were indications that Dean had received FBI cooperation in covering up the involvement of White House aides in the break-in. Citing "executive privilege," Dean refused to testify. (Gray resigned as acting director of the FBI on April 27, his nomination as permanent director having been previously withdrawn on his request.) A policy statement by President Nixon (March 12) cited executive privilege as grounds on which present and former members of his staff "normally shall . . . decline a request for a formal appearance before a committee of the Congress," but pledged that such privilege would "not be used as a shield to prevent embarrassing information from being made available. . . ."

At the sentencing of the Watergate Seven on March 23, 1973—President Nixon was later to say (April 17 and 30, 1973) that two days earlier new charges brought to his attention had caused him to initiate "intensive new inquiries" into the break-in—Judge Sirica revealed a March 19 letter in which defendant McCord said that all those involved had been under "political pressure" to remain silent and plead guilty. The letter also indicated that others involved should have been indicted. (Although Attorney General Richard G. Kleindienst had pledged on August 28, 1972, that his investigation would be extensive and thorough, he had sought no new indictments.)

As pressure mounted, Press Secretary Ziegler announced that all previous White House statements on Watergate were "inoperative" (*see* **Ziegles**). In a nationwide television address on April 30, 1973, the President noted that he had "repeatedly asked those that conducted the [Watergate] investigation whether there was any reason to believe that members of my administration were in any way involved. I received repeated assurance there were not. . . . Until March of this year, I remained convinced that the denials were true and that the charges of involvement by members of the White House staff were false."

He also announced that he had accepted the resignations of Haldeman and John D. Ehrlichman, his domestic affairs advisor, "two of my closest associates in the White House . . . two of the finest public servants it had been my privilege to know." In addition, the President said that Kleindienst would be replaced as Attorney General by Elliot L. Richardson, who would be directed "to do everything necessary to insure that the Department of Justice has the confidence and the trust of every law abiding person in this country." The resignation of John Dean—who had publicly denied that the President had ever ordered him to investigate the possibility of a Watergate cover-up—was announced without comment.

Three days earlier, Federal Judge W. Matthew Byrne, Jr., before whom Daniel J. Ellsberg and *New York Times* reporter Anthony J. Russo, Jr., were being tried on charges of espionage and theft (*see* **Pentagon Papers**), had disclosed a Justice Department memorandum which revealed that the office of Ellsberg's psychiatrist had been burglarized on September 3, 1971, by Liddy and Hunt, who were in search of information damaging to the defendant. On May 11, 1973, Judge Byrne—who on April 7, 1973, had been approached by Ehrlichman with the information that he was being considered by the White House as director of the FBI—dismissed the charges against both men when he learned that in 1969 and 1970 there had been wiretaps on Ellsberg's phone and that the tape recordings made were no longer available.

Televised hearings by the Ervin Committee (Select Committee on Presidential Campaign Activities) began on May 17, 1973, and drew a nationwide audience as a parade of witnesses revealed what Senator Ervin called a "Gestapo mentality" in the Nixon administration. Jeb Stuart Magruder (June 14), deputy director of CREEP, implicated Mitchell in the planning and approval of the Watergate break-in; Dean (June 25–29), to whom Judge Sirica had granted immunity before the committee but not before a grand jury hearing testimony, implicated the President, Haldeman, and Ehrlichman in the subsequent cover-up and revealed the existence of a **"White House Enemies List,"** and of **"the Plumbers,"** whose job it was to "plug" press leaks that were plaguing the Nixon administration; and Mitchell (July 10-12) testified that he had kept from the President information about the break-in and the subsequent **"White House Horrors."** The former Attorney General labeled Magruder's charge that he had approved the Watergate break-in as a "palpable, damnable lie," and he implicated both Ehrlichman and Haldeman as having taken part in "a design not to have the stories come out." (He

had earlier noted his own efforts to "limit the impact" of Watergate on the coming elections.)

The existence since March 1971 of a "bugging" system to record the President's conversations in the White House and the Executive Office Building was revealed by Alexander P. Butterfield, a former presidential deputy assistant who made a surprise appearance before the Ervin Committee on July 16, 1973 (*see* **Nixon Tapes**).

Access to the tapes immediately became a focus of legal maneuvering as the President cited "executive privilege" in refusing to turn them over either to the committee or to Archibald Cox, who on May 18, 1973, had been appointed Watergate Special Prosecutor. Cox's perseverance led President Nixon to order Attorney General Richardson to "fire" the Special Prosecutor, but both Richardson and his deputy, William D. Ruckelshaus, resigned on October 20, 1973, rather than carry out this order, which was complied with by the new Acting Attorney General, Solicitor General Robert H. Bork (*see* **Saturday Night Massacre**). In the "firestorm" that followed the intense public reaction to this maneuver, impeachment proceedings against President Nixon were introduced into the House, whose Judiciary Committee, chaired by Peter W. Rodino, Jr. (D.- N.J.), began preliminary investigations on October 30, 1973, and commenced closed hearings the following May 9. Meanwhile, in an effort to comply with a subpoena for the tapes, President Nixon turned over to it 1,308 pages of edited transcripts.

On November 1, 1973, the President had appointed Sen. William B. Saxbe (R.-Ohio) Attorney General, and Houston lawyer Leon Jaworski replaced Cox as Special Prosecutor, having received assurances that his independence would not be limited and that he could proceed against anyone, including the President. A few days later Sen. Edward W. Brooke (R.-Mass.) became the first Republican to call for President Nixon's resignation, and editorials urging this course of action appeared in *Time*, the *New York Times*, and the *Detroit News*.

Judge Sirica had ordered the President (May 20, 1974) to turn over to Special Prosecutor Jaworski sixty-four tapes of Watergate-related conversations, and on May 31 the U.S. Supreme Court agreed to bypass the court of appeals and rule on the President's right to withhold evidence of possible crimes.

The House Rules Committee having voted to approve live radio and TV coverage of the Judiciary Committee's impeachment proceedings, the nation watched the debate; and beginning on July 27, 1974, three articles of impeachment were recommended: (1) for having hindered the Watergate investigation; (2) for having abused his authority as President in violation of the Constitution; (3) for having defied the committee's subpoenas.

By an eight-to-zero decision, on July 24 the Supreme Court had ruled that the President was obliged to hand over to Judge Sirica the sixty-four tapes; although the ruling acknowledged a constitutional basis for executive privilege, it declared that "it cannot prevail over the fundamental demands of due process of law in the fair administration of justice."

Transcripts of three conversations the President had had with Haldeman only six days after the Watergate break-in were released on August 5, 1974. These tapes made it clear that the President had—unknown to his lawyers and his supporters on the House Judiciary Committee—ordered an end to the FBI investigation of the incident (*see* **"smoking gun"**). With impeachment now an absolute certainty, on August 8, 1974, President Nixon told a nationwide television audience: "I shall resign the Presidency effective at noon tomorrow." At 12:03 the following day Vice President Gerald R. Ford became the thirty-eighth President of the United States. A month later President Ford gave his predecessor an unconditional pardon for all federal crimes that he committed or may have committed or taken part in during his term in office.

See **United States v. Richard M. Nixon; ITT Affair; Milk Fund.**

Water Quality Act of 1965 President Lyndon B. Johnson considered this one of the most important conservation measures of his administration. As signed into law on October 2, 1965, it required all states to set antipollution standards by July 1, 1967. Under its provisions the federal government could establish such standards if a state failed to comply, or if its standards were not approved by the **Department of Health, Education, and Welfare** (HEW). A conference board made up of HEW employees and representatives of all states involved was empowered to review federal action. Before action could be brought in federal court, those involved would have to be given 180 days in which to comply voluntarily.

Other provisions created a Federal Water Pollution Control Administration within HEW and authorized $20 million annually in fiscal 1966-1969 for federal matching grants to aid in the development of antipollution projects by states or groups of states, as well as municipalities. The grant authorization for 1966 and 1967 community sewage-treatment facilities was increased from 100 to 150 mil-

lion dollars, and project ceilings were doubled: $1.2 million for a single project, and $4.8 million for a multicommunity project.

At a special signing ceremony, President Johnson noted that "there is no excuse—and we should call a spade a spade—for chemical companies and oil refineries using our major rivers as pipelines for toxic wastes. There is no excuse for communities to use other people's rivers as a dump for their raw sewage." He praised the new act, but called for "bolder" legislation in the future.

On November 3, 1966, President Johnson signed the **Clean Water Restoration Act of 1966**, which authorized $3.908 billion in fiscal 1967-1971 for water pollution control projects. Of that sum, $3.55 billion was to go for grants to aid in the construction of community sewage-treatment plants. More than $3 million was authorized for a variety of research-and-development projects.

In 1970, the **Environmental Protection Agency** (EPA) took over responsibility for "restoring the nation's water."

Watkins v. United States By ruling that the First Amendment cannot be abridged in legislative inquiries, on June 17, 1957, the U.S. Supreme Court voided a contempt of Congress conviction of John Thomas Watkins, a United Auto Workers official, who had refused at a **House Committee on Un-American Activities** (HUAC) hearing in April 1954 to identify former communist associates, though he had testified freely about himself. In writing the majority (six to one) decision, Chief Justice Earl Warren agreed that Watkins was within his First Amendment rights (free belief) as "there is no Congressional power to expose for the sake of exposure." He contended that HUAC's authorizing resolution was overly vague and that the "kind of investigation that the committee was directed to make" could not therefore be deduced. In addition, the Court held that HUAC had failed to demonstrate the pertinency of the questions and had therefore not met the statutory test for contempt. However, the Chief Justice insisted that the decision in no way prevented Congress from obtaining information necessary to it "for the proper fulfillment of its role."

In a dissenting opinion, Justice Tom C. Clark held that the Court's requirements for the operation of the committee inquiry system were both unnecessary and unworkable. In addition, he argued that Watkins had sought to use the First Amendment to "vindicate the rights, if any, of his associates" and that the Constitution could not so be invoked to protect the rights of another. "The right of free belief has never been extended to include the withholding of knowledge of past events."

Watts Riots A minor incident in which police attempted to arrest a black for drunken driving in the Watts district of Los Angeles on August 11, 1965, led to almost a week of rioting and looting in which thirty-four people were killed, more than 1,000 injured, and property damages were estimated to be from 40 to as high as 200 million dollars. Before calm had been largely restored on August 16, the almost-all-black ghetto was being patrolled by 12,364 National Guardsmen, 1,430 Los Angeles policemen, 1,017 county sheriff's deputies, and 68 California highway patrolmen.

The apparently spontaneous outbreak of violence was ascribed by community leaders to resentment against poverty, unemployment, de facto school segregation, and "police brutality," all brought to a boil during the prevailing heat wave. At times as many as 10,000 young blacks were said to have poured out into the streets, sniping at law enforcement officers, attacking white motorists, and looting local stores, which were largely owned by whites. Many black-owned businesses were also attacked, but signs such as "Brother," "Blood," or "Black owned" were reported to have saved some from being sacked by the mob.

Although it was widely felt that only a fraction of the 90,000 Watts residents had participated in the riot, University of California social scientists who made a study of the Watts outbreak reported that more than 15 percent of the community had participated in it and that 62 percent had approved of the outbreak as an effective means of drawing attention to local problems and demands. Nevertheless, the chief sufferers from the disturbances were the residents of Watts themselves, twenty-nine of whom had died.

Responsible black leaders such as Martin Luther King, Jr., condemned the outbreak as a "blind and misguided revolt against authority and society." Dr. King noted that he had visited the area six weeks before the trouble and had recommended a civil rights march as a means of expressing local frustrations. "But the white leadership encouraged the Negro leaders not to march," he noted. Although he had endorsed the use of police power to restore calm, he pointed out that "police power can only bring a temporary halt," and that what was needed was a full program of aid to blacks.

When Dr. King toured Watts on August 18, he was shouted down by angry groups as he attempted to speak in the Westminster Community Center. During the rioting, black comedian Dick Gregory had been shot in the thigh as he pleaded with rioters to "get off the streets."

In many ways, Watts seemed an unlikely place for the racial outbreak. In March 1965, *Ebony* magazine had reported that more than 10 percent of the black families in Los Angeles earned at least $10,000 a year and that as much as a fourth of the municipal employees were black.

A special commission appointed by Governor Edmund G. ("Pat") Brown and headed by John McCone issued a report later that year (the McCone Report) which rejected charges that the rioting had been incited by outside leadership and carried out according to a preestablished plan.

Weathermen Factionalism began to seriously tear the **Students for a Democratic Society** (SDS) apart when at an annual meeting in June 1969 one group presented a program entitled "You Don't Need a Weatherman to Know Which Way the Wind Is Blowing"—a line from Bob Dylan's "Subterranean Homesick Blues." This program called upon white radicals to support all liberation movements both at home and abroad. When the program was rejected after a struggle with the **Progressive Labor Party** (PLP), the group withdrew from the SDS and took the name Revolutionary Youth Movement (RYM).

But this splinter group soon splintered in turn into an RYM I—which began calling itself Weathermen—and a more traditionally oriented faction called RYM II.

Largely white and middle class themselves, the Weathermen tried to attract the alienated and disfranchised among America's young by the novel method of picking fights to demonstrate that they were as tough as anybody on the street.

A confrontation with the Chicago police was planned for October 1969 and the Weathermen hoped to attract 5,000 adherents to that city, where the **Chicago Eight** were on trial. Only some 300 Weathermen and Weatherwomen showed up for the Days of Rage (October 9–11) and formed a "New Red Army," which was soon running through the streets shouting "Bring the War Home" and inaugurating the revolution by tossing a rock through the window of the Chicago Historical Society, shattering windshields, and indulging in pitched battles with the police, who eventually arrested 290 of them.

Their ranks depleted, the Weathermen at some point became the Weather Underground and were "credited" with a variety of bomb explosions in the offices of leading banks and corporations.

Among the more spectacular events associated with them was the explosion on March 6, 1970, in a townhouse on West 11th Street in New York City, in which three of the group were killed, apparently as the result of an accident while five Weathermen were making bombs. The house had belonged to the father—who was off on a Caribbean holiday—of Cathlyn Platt Wilkerson; she and Kathy Boudin, daughter of radical lawyer Leonard B. Boudin, survived the explosion, originally attributed to a leaky gas main, and disappeared before they could be questioned by the police. Both women were out on bail after indictment for having participated in the Days of Rage. They were due to appear for trial in Chicago on March 16, and when they failed to do so they were listed as wanted by the FBI.

"We came in peace for all mankind" Message engraved on a plaque attached to one of the legs of the *Eagle*, the lunar module used for travel on the moon's surface during the successful *Apollo 11* mission that was one of the high points of **Project Apollo.** Civilian pilot Neil A. Armstrong, who commanded the mission, unveiled the plaque before beginning his two-hour, thirteen-minute lunar walk.

"The Week That Changed the World" Also known as the **Peking Summit**, this was the meeting in Red China between President Richard M. Nixon, Secretary of State Henry A. Kissinger, and Communist leaders Mao Tse-tung and Chou En-lai in February 1972.

Weight Watchers Since its inception in May 1963, Weight Watchers International, Inc., founded by Jean Nidetch, is said to have helped more than 9 million members (as of 1977) "lose weight and learn how to keep it off through a program that consists of a nutritionally sound, scientifically developed diet together with a behavior modification program called the 'Personal Action Plan.'" In other words, sensible diet is reinforced by weekly classes at which members have their weight checked while the rest of the group looks on approvingly or disapprovingly.

Approximately 14,000 individual classes of Weight Watchers are held weekly throughout the world at company-owned or franchised operations. The inspirational message is reinforced in this country by *Weight Watchers Magazine*, a monthly publication with a circulation of about 800,000. In 1966, Ms. Nidetch published the first *Weight Watchers Cookbook*, which is said to have sold over a million and a half copies and is constantly being updated. Several firms have been licensed to sell a variety of Weight Watcher products such as frozen foods and dairy items. In addition, several summer camps have been licensed to accept overweight adolescents. All in all, the operation suggests that helping America take it off can be big business. In November 1978 Weight Watchers was sold to H. J. Heinz Company, a major producer of canned food products.

Welfare and Pension Fund Disclosure Act With an estimated 80 million people in the United States relying to some extent on private welfare and pension funds, on August 28, 1958, President Dwight D. Eisenhower signed legislation effective the following January and requiring that such plans be registered with the Department of Labor, which was to be supplied with both a description and an annual financial report. The President noted that while the act established a precedent for federal responsibility in the area, it contained "no provision for dealing directly with the most flagrant abuses, such as embezzlement and kickbacks, once they are uncovered." Critics considered the legislation entirely inadequate.

Although the House Committee on Education and Labor had reported on July 28, 1958, that estimates of existing welfare and pension plans varied from 500,000 to in excess of 1.25 million, by the early 1970s less than 35,000 such funds had been registered. They represented an accumulation of more than $135 billion in assets. Small labor welfare and pension funds were exempt under the act, which is sometimes known as the Douglas-Kennedy-Ives Act.

See **Pension Reform Act of 1974.**

Welfare State *See* "Creeping socialism."

Wesberry v. Sanders In a controversial case which contributed to the increasing "one man, one vote" tendency, the U.S. Supreme Court ruled six to three on February 17, 1964 that Congressional districts within a state must be as nearly equal in population as is practicable. The case originated in Atlanta when James P. Wesberry, Jr., brought suit claiming that population disparities in Georgia congressional districts deprived him of the constitutional right to have his votes for congressman given the same weight accorded to other qualified voters in the state. While the average population of the ten Georgia congressional districts was 394,312, the population of the Atlanta district was 823,680. Wesberry asked that Georgia's Governor Sanders and the state secretary of state be enjoined from conducting elections under the Georgia districting statute. He claimed that Atlanta voters were deprived of the Due Process, Equal Protection, and Privileges and Immunities Clauses of the Fourteenth Amendment.

Relying on the Supreme Court decision in *Colegrove v. Green*, the federal district court in which the Wesberry case was originally tried dismissed the complaint by a two-to-one vote on the ground that challenges to congressional district apportionment were not justifiable because they raised only "political" questions. (The dissenting judge based his opinion on *Baker v. Carr*.)

As a result of the late Supreme Court ruling, the heavily populated Atlanta district was divided and given two congressmen; other state districts were redrawn to be nearly equal in population.

"We Shall Overcome"   Civil rights song that was often heard at demonstrations of the 1960s and was especially associated with the 1963 **March on Washington** and the 1965 **Selma-Montgomery March.**

According to an unpublished Howard University dissertation, "The Role of Music in the Civil Rights Movement," by Bernice Regan, it was originally an old Black spiritual entitled "I Will Overcome." In the late 1940s, striking members of the Food, Tobacco and Agricultural Union in Charleston, South Carolina, brought the song to the Highlander Folk School, Monteagle, Tennessee. Here Zilphia Horton changed the words and music into "We Shall Overcome." She later sang it at a Carnegie Hall concert of Pete Seeger, who also recorded it. Guy Carawan, the music director at Highlander, introduced it into the civil rights movement.

> We shall stand together, we shall stand together
> We shall stand together—now.
> Oh, deep in my heart I do believe
> We shall overcome someday.

On March 15, 1965, in an address before a joint session of Congress in which he requested support for the legislation that eventually became the **Voting Rights Act of 1965,** President Lyndon B. Johnson echoed the words of that song when he noted that "it is not just Negroes, but really it is all of us who must overcome the crippling legacy of bigotry and injustice. And . . . we . . . shall . . . overcome."

West Coast II   Launched from the West Coast on May 9, 1963, this experimental satellite released 400 million copper needles in a polar orbit. They were intended to reflect long-distance radio signals.

"What's good for General Motors is good for the country"   A widespread misquotation of remarks made by Charles E. Wilson, former president of General Motors, at Senate hearings beginning on January 15, 1953, on his confirmation as Secretary of Defense in the new administration of President Dwight D. Eisenhower.

Mr. Wilson—popularly known as "Engine Charlie"—had been reluctant to dispose of the large blocks of GM stock owned by himself and his wife. He argued before the Senate Armed Services Committee that the tax penalty would be too great. When questioned about possible conflict-of-interest, he replied: "For years, I thought what was good for the country was good for General Motors and vice versa." Opponents of the incoming administration quickly twisted it around to the form quoted above. Adlai Stevenson, President Eisenhower's Democratic rival in the November 1952 elections, was shortly afterward quoted as saying: "I for one do not believe the story that the general welfare has become a subsidiary of General Motors."

On January 22, 1953, Mr. Wilson announced that he would dispose of his GM stock, and the following day his nomination was confirmed by the Senate. He continued to show a remarkable propensity for foot-in-the-mouth statements, however. For example, in defending the Pentagon against charges of excessive spending, he noted: "I didn't come down here to run a grocery store." In the fall of 1954, when unemployment was a problem, he was quoted as saying: "I've always liked bird dogs better than kennel-fed dogs myself—you know one who'll get out and hunt for food rather than sit on his fanny and yell." This was his way of suggesting that it behooved working men to migrate from economically depressed areas such as Flint, Michigan—where unemployment was over 20 percent—to areas in which there were supposed labor shortages. Secretary Wilson later apologized for "bringing up those bird dogs at the same time I was talking about people."

"What's My Line?"   This popular CBS quiz show was a national television favorite from February 1950 to October 1967. Its format consisted of a master of ceremonies (John Daly) and four panelists, whose job it was to question an unidentified guest in an attempt to determine his or her occupation. The panelists who established the reputation of the show were publisher Bennett Cerf, actress Arlene Francis, Broadway columnist Dorothy Kilgallen, and gag writer Hal Block. When the latter dropped out, his spot was at various times taken over by such celebrities as comedians Fred Allen, Henry Morgan, Mort Sahl, Ernie Kovacs, Steve Allen, and actor Peter Ustinov. A special feature of the show was a celebrity "mystery guest" whose identity the blindfolded panelists tried to establish. Over the years, those who appeared on the show were Mrs. Eleanor Roosevelt, Buster Keaton, Gracie Allen, Jack Benny, and Gypsy Rose Lee.

Tapes of the show are still a standard television rerun.

"Which clause" *See* **Bricker Amendment.**

Whistle-Stop Campaign The practice had long been a part of American political history when, amid deepening Democratic gloom about his candidacy, President Harry S Truman in June 1948 began an extended railroad tour on his sixteen-car Presidential Special in his campaign to win the Democratic presidential nomination in the forthcoming election. Similar tours had been undertaken, he later noted, by President Andrew Johnson in his search for support for his post-Civil War reconstruction plan, and by President Woodrow Wilson, who hoped to win support for the League of Nations.

Traveling from Washington, D.C., to the West Coast and back, President Truman made more than seventy speeches in "the cities, towns, and villages along the way." Occasionally appearing on the train platform in his bathrobe and pajamas, at every stop he tore into the legislative record of the Republican-controlled Eightieth Congress, which he was to christen the **"Do-Nothing Congress."** His ostensible purpose was to explain to the American people the workings of U.S. foreign policy and the status of the then current domestic issues.

While the President was en route, Sen. Robert A. Taft (R.-Ohio), speaking before the Union League Club of Philadelphia, sourly complained that the President was making a spectacle of himself "blackguarding Congress at whistle-stops all across the country." He soon had cause to regret his petulance, as Howard McGrath, chairman of the Democratic National Committee, joined forces with publicity man Jack Redding to exploit the casual slur. Wiring the mayors of the small cities at which the President had spoken, they asked if these men agreed with Senator Taft's characterization of their community. The tart denials were soon being featured in newspapers and on radio broadcasts across the nation. Upon his arrival in Los Angeles, the President gleefully greeted the waiting crowd with: "This is the biggest whistle-stop!"

After his renomination by the Democrats in July, President Truman—considered by many political experts a "gone goose"—began another extended railway tour in September. Ignoring the major public-opinion polls that predicted his defeat by the Republican nominee, New York's Governor Thomas E. Dewey, he conducted one of the most remarkable campaigns in American political history. "The technique I used at the whistle-stops was simple and straightforward," he later wrote. "There were no special 'gimmicks' or oratorical devices. I refused to be 'coached.' I simply told the people in my own language that they had better wake up to the fact that it was their fight."

He was helped considerably by the uninspired campaign of Governor Dewey, who in the words of one wit **"snatched defeat out of the jaws of victory."**

Harry Dexter White Affair Speaking before the Executives Club of Chicago on November 6, 1953, Attorney General Herbert Brownell, Jr., touched off a national controversy when he accused former President Harry S Truman of having in 1946 appointed Harry Dexter White the United States Executive Director of the International Monetary Fund (IMF), in spite of an FBI report accusing him of espionage for the Soviet Union.

The accusations were immediately denied by Truman, who said that at the time he nominated White he knew of no FBI report: "As soon as we found White was wrong, we fired him." (White had been allowed to resign on April 3, 1947.) However, former Secretary of State James F. Byrnes insisted that on the day White's nomination had been confirmed by the Senate, he had drawn the FBI charges to the President's attention and suggested that the confirmation be reconsidered.

On November 10, 1953, Rep. Harold H. Velde (R.-Ill.), Chairman of the **House Committee on Un-American Activities** (HUAC), subpoenaed the former President to appear before HUAC. The subpoena was rejected by Truman as setting an unconstitutional precedent, but he nevertheless said he would appear to answer questions limited to "any acts as a private individual before or after my Presidency and unrelated to any acts as President." No attempt was made to follow up the subpoena.

The Attorney General's speech had been made with the knowledge and consent of President Dwight D. Eisenhower, who later seemed to backtrack on the charge and said that it was inconceivable that a President would knowingly damage the United States. Brownell himself modified his charge and said that his purpose had been to expose "laxity" in the Truman administration rather than to impugn "the loyalty of any high official." However, Sen. Joseph R. McCarthy (R.-Wis.) said that President Truman lied when he denied the charges and that he had "deliberately, knowingly and without regard for the interests of the country, appointed, promoted, and advanced a Communist."

Assistant Secretary of the Treasury at the time of his IMF appointment, White was a leading authority on international monetary affairs. He and British economist John M. Keynes (*see* **Keynesianism**) established the principles of the IMF at the 1944 Bretton Woods Conference.

In 1948, White had apppeared before a New York Federal Grand Jury and denied that he was a Communist. Although the jury indicted twelve leading Communists in the country, it refused to indict White, who died on August 16, three days after repeating his denials to HUAC. The charges had been made by former Communist agents Whittaker Chambers and Elizabeth Bentley.

Writing in 1969, Dean Acheson, who was Undersecretary of State during the time of White's nomination to the IMF, expressed his belief in White's innocence, though he noted that there was often strong disagreement between them. "I have often been so outraged by Harry White's capacity for rudeness in discussion that the charges made against him would have seemed mild compared to expressions I have used . . . time has mellowed me for the harsher side of his nature. . . ."

"White Backlash" Term generally applied during the 1960s to white resentment against some aspects of the black civil rights protests, especially "affirmative action" demands which would bring blacks into sectors of the job market previously the exclusive preserve of whites.

Writing in 1965, Arthur Schlesinger, Jr., former aide to President John F. Kennedy, said of the national atmosphere in June 1963, when the President submitted his civil rights bill to Congress: "We were first beginning to hear this summer about the phenomenon of the 'white backlash.' "

When in August 1964 the newly formed **Mississippi Freedom Democratic Party** (MFDP) attempted to have its delegation seated at the Democratic National Convention in Atlantic City, New Jersey, millions of television viewers heard MFDP delegate Dr. Aaron Henry argue against the use of the term "backlash" to describe a minority reaction to a majority trend in Mississippi. Fear of "white backlash" at the polls caused the convention to oust the MFDP delegation. This resulted in a split between liberal and radical forces in the civil rights movement, which came increasingly under the control of radicals and militants.

Brad Cleaveland, a founding member of the **Free Speech Movement** (FSM) born on the Berkeley campus of the University of California in September 1964, angrily noted that the real meaning of "white backlash" was "Don't bug me nigger . . . you're buggin' me with that civil disobedience . . . ."

"White backlash" is generally credited with the strong showing made in the 1964 Democratic presidential primaries by Alabama segregationist Governor George C. Wallace. On May 5, 1964, an unpledged slate backed by him in Alabama won a five-to-one victory over a slate pledged to President Lyndon B. Johnson. Although Governor Wallace lost in Indiana, on that same day he got a surprising 30 percent of the vote. Two weeks later he received 43 percent of the vote in the Maryland Democratic presidential preference primary. By the time Governor Wallace—satisfied that he had "conservatized" both major parties—withdrew as a presidential candidate in July, he had been committed to run in sixteen states. Some thought he stood a good chance of depriving either major candidate of a majority, thus forcing the election into the House of Representatives.

White Citizens' Councils Designed to combat desegregation and the growing Negro demand for civil rights by organizing economic reprisals and mass demonstrations against blacks, the first of these councils was formed in Indianola, Mississippi, in June 1954 when a group of fourteen white business executives met to discuss possible responses to the recent ***Brown v. Board of Education of Topeka*** case in which the U.S. Supreme Court ruled that segregation in the public schools was unconstitutional. The spread of these groups throughout the South in the years that followed—by 1957 there were a sufficient number to merit the establishment of an Association of Citizens' Councils—coincided with a revival of the once moribund Ku Klux Klan, which tended to attract segregationist whites of a lower economic class.

Anthony Lewis has noted in his *Portrait of a Decade* (1964), an account of the civil rights movement, that the White Citizens Councils were "designed to make bigotry respectable." In Mississippi, for example, they included most white business leaders and other prominent community members and were operated like chambers of commerce or civic clubs. Since they dominated the state legislature, they were able to obtain appropriations for a television program entitled Citizens Council Forum, which preached the biological inferiority of blacks and argued that integration was the work of Communists.

Although the councils themselves were theoretically nonviolent, violence was often their result. For example, rioting broke out in New Orleans following a mass rally on November 16, 1960, in which more than 5,000 White Citizens' Council members and others opposed to school desegregation were told: "This is total war. . . . We must use every weapon at our command." At another meeting, segregationist oil millionaire Leander Perez told his audience: "Don't wait for your daughter to be raped by these Congolese. Don't wait until the burr-heads are forced into your schools. Do something about it now."

Following the 1963 **March on Washington** organized by Dr. Martin Luther King, Jr., and other proponents of nonviolent resistance, **Black Muslim** leader Malcolm X jeeringly noted: "If they have the Ku Klux Klan nonviolent, I'll be nonviolent. If they make the White Citizens' Councils nonviolent, I'll be nonviolent."

In some areas of the South, effective leadership by white moderates was able to combat the influence of the White Citizens' Councils. For example, in Atlanta, a "city too busy to hate," the leadership of Mayor William B. Hartsfield and Ralph McGill, editor of the *Atlanta Constitution*, effectively established a white-black dialogue that spared the city the violence that gripped many parts of the South. Nevertheless, it was due to a great extent to the resistance organized by White Citizens' Councils that in 1964—a decade after the historic *Brown* decision which reversed the separate but equal decision in *Plessy v. Ferguson* (1894) by ruling that "separate educational facilities are inherently unequal"—only 1 percent of the South's black children were attending even partially integrated schools.

Resistance by the White Citizens' Councils was also important in delaying other forms of desegregation. During the 1955-1956 **Montgomery Bus Strike,** organized by Dr. King, Mayor W. A. Gayle and several city leaders ceremoniously joined the White Citizens' Council as a public expression of their determination not to give in to black demands that the city's bus service be desegregated.

White Collar Said by many to be one of the most important books on American sociology since Thorstein Veblen's *The Theory of the Leisure Class* (1899), this 1951 study by C. Wright Mills examines the emergence in the United States of the "new middle classes": salespersons, teachers, intellectuals, accountants, supervisors, personnel managers, journalists, technicians, entertainers, bookkeepers, nurses, receptionists, and lawyers. "The white-collar people slipped quietly into modern society. Whatever history they have had is a history without events; whatever common interests they have do not lead to unity; whatever future they have will not be of their own making." This new middle class was under pressure from wage earners over whom it enjoyed an educational advantage.

Mills argues that by their rise to numerical importance, the white-collar people overturned nineteenth-century predictions that society would eventually be split between entrepreneurs and wage workers. He explains "the uneasiness, the malaise of our time" by the absence in this new class of "any order of belief," arguing that "white-collar man has no culture to lean upon except the contents of a mass society that has shaped him and seeks to manipulate him to its alien ends."

According to Mills, "when white-collar people get jobs, they sell not only their time and energy but their personalities as well. They sell by the week or month their smiles and their kindly gestures, and they must practice the prompt repression of resentment and aggression" because these traits are of "commercial relevance and required for the more efficient and profitable distribution of goods and services."

Whereas previously rationality was identified with freedom, now it has its seat, says Mills, "not in individual men, but in social institutions which by their bureaucratic planning and mathematical foresight usurp both freedom and rationality . . . ." As a result, white-collar people are "the interchangeable parts of the big chains of authority that bind the society together." The liberal ethos developed early in the century by men such as historian Charles Beard and philosopher John Dewey is seen as "often irrelevant," and the popular Marxist views of the 1930s as "inadequate." The problems that now concern American society, he argues, border on the psychiatric, and it is the social scientists' duty "to describe the larger economic and political situation in terms of its meanings for the inner life and the external career of the individual," taking into account how he "often becomes falsely conscious and blinded."

Hard hit by the inflationary spiral of the 1960s, it was to a large extent from the new middle class described by Mills that President Richard M. Nixon later drew his **"silent majority."**

*See **The Power Elite.***

White House Conference on Education Supported by a congressional appropriation of $900,000, some 2,000 educators and representatives of various business, professional, labor, and community groups met in Washington, November 28-December 1, 1955, to discuss ways of meeting the nation's educational needs. The conference had been prepared for by fifty-three state and territorial meetings, which had in turn been prepared for by a variety of local and regional meetings in what President Dwight D. Eisenhower described as "the greatest citizen study of our country's public schools—the most comprehensive analysis of their needs—in the history of the United States."

The delegates were welcomed in a filmed address by the President in which he advocated federal aid to schools without the creation of "any central authority." Following a series of meetings, the procedure for which was criticized by a caucus of 100 AFL and CIO delegates as designed to "stack the meeting" in favor of Eisenhower administration policies, the conference adopted a report calling for federal funds for public schools, opposing the allocation of federal funds for private schools, and proposing a variety of means for attracting and increasing the number of qualified teachers.

The disputed procedure worked out by a White House Conference Committee of thirty-four educators and laymen was as follows: the overall agenda was first discussed by delegates broken down into 180 groups selected by a computer to assure a representative cross section; after a two-hour meeting, the leaders of the original groups were broken down into eighteen groups to further refine the discussion; these eighteen leaders were then broken down into two groups of nine to prepare summaries; finally, the leaders of the previous two groups met to prepare a final report that was to reflect majority opinion.

A delegate demand that there be a full conference vote on the final report was rejected by Conference Chairman Neil H. McElroy, president of Procter and Gamble.

White House Enemies List On August 16, 1971, John W. Dean III, counsel to the President during most of the Nixon administration, submitted to Lawrence M. Higby, assistant to the President's Chief of Staff, H. R. Haldeman, a memorandum entitled "Dealing with Our Political Enemies."

This memorandum addresses the matter of how we can maximize the fact of our incumbency in dealing with persons known to be active in their opposition to our Administration. Stated a bit more bluntly—how we can use the available federal machinery to screw our political enemies.

After reviewing this matter with a number of persons possessed of expertise in the field, I have concluded that we do not need an elaborate mechanism or game plan, rather we need a good project coordinator and full support for the project. In brief, the system would work as follows:

—Key members of the staff . . . would be requested to inform us of who they feel we should be giving a hard time.

The project coordinator should then determine what sorts of dealings these individuals have with the Federal Government and how we can best screw them (e.g., grant availability, federal contracts, litigation prosecution, etc.). . . .

As a next step, I would recommend that we develop a small list of names—not more than ten—as our targets for concentration. . . . I feel it is important that we keep our targets limited for several reasons; (1) a low visibility of the project is imperative; (2) it will be easier to accomplish something real if we don't overexpand our efforts; and (3) we can learn more about how to operate such activity if we start small and build.

The original list then worked up for Dean by Charles W. Colson, special counsel to the President, included twenty names ranging from Eugene Carson Blake, General Secretary of the World Council of Churches, to Mary McGrory, a columnist for the *Washington Star News.* Later the list of "Political Opponents" was expanded to include ten Democratic Senators, eighteen Representatives—including all twelve black House members who were given a special category of their own—some fifty newspaper and television reporters considered unfriendly to the Nixon administration, and other prominent figures in the worlds of entertainment, business, education, and political action.

In his testimony before the Senate **Watergate Committee** in June 1973, Dean stated that the list was maintained and kept updated; he related incidents of harassment utilizing such federal services as the FBI, the IRS, and the Secret Service.

White House Festival of the Arts and Humanities On June 14, 1965, some 400 persons including poets, painters, theatrical performers, musicians, novelists, critics and museum curators attended a thirteen-hour festival at the White House at the invitation of President Lyndon B. Johnson and his wife, Lady Bird. The event featured exhibitions of art and photography, poetry and prose readings, and musical and ballet performances.

In addressing his guests, the President noted that much of what artists do is "profoundly political," adding that they worked toward peace by helping "dissolve the barriers of hatred and ignorance."

The hastily planned event was somewhat marred when on June 2, 1965, Pulitzer Prize-winning poet Robert Lowell rejected an invitation to participate because of his "dismay and distrust" of American foreign policy. "We are in danger of imperceptibly becoming an explosive and suddenly chauvinistic nation," he said in a letter to President Johnson. "Every serious artist knows that he cannot enjoy public celebration without making subtle public commitments," he noted in an indirect reference to the continuing **Vietnam War.**

In introducing the event in which Lowell was to have participated, Mark Van Doren noted that his fellow poet "may or may not have been correct" and that he did not "commit any of the writers present here to agreement or disagreement with it." Before beginning to read from his *Hiroshima*, an account of the aftermath of the atomic bombing of that Japanese city during World War II, novelist John Hersey dedicated his participation to "the great number of citizens who have become alarmed by seeing fire beget fire." He warned that "the step from one edge of violence to the next is imperceptibly taken and cannot easily be taken back."

"White House Horrors" Testifying on July 10, 1973, before the Senate **Select Committee on Campaign Activities** set up to investigate charges stemming from the 1972 break-in of Democratic National Committee (DNC) headquarters in Washington's Watergate complex, John N. Mitchell, former Attorney General and Director of the **Committee to Re-elect the President** (CREEP; CRP) stated that he had kept from President Richard M. Nixon information about the break-in, subsequent cover-up stories, and "White House horror stories." Although conceding that he had attempted to "limit the impact" of Watergate on the 1972 presidential campaign, he denied that he had approved the original break-in operation. In his second day of testimony, Mitchell implicated White House Chief of Staff H. R. Haldeman and Assistant to the President for Domestic Affairs John D. Ehrlichman in "a design not to have the stories come out."

The "White House Horrors" are generally considered to include the break-in and electronic surveillance of the DNC; the establishment of a secret fund controlled by White House consultant Gordon C. Strachan to obtain the silence of those in-

volved in the break-in; the burglarizing of the office of Dr. Lewis Fielding, former psychiatrist to Daniel J. Ellsberg (see **Pentagon Papers**); and the **"dirty tricks"** operations of Donald H. Segretti.

Mitchell was the last of the men sentenced to prison for their role in Watergate to be released on parole (January 19, 1979).

See **Watergate Scandal.**

Whiz Kids *See* **Program Evaluation and Review Technique.**

Whole Earth Catalog Originally conceived of as "an evaluation and access device," it first appeared in late 1968 as a 128-page compilation of some 300 items—tools, looms, hardware, simple furniture, musical instruments, natural foods, books (how-to and ecological), posters, etc.—that could be ordered directly from the manufacturer or from the Whole Earth Truck Store in Menlo Park, California. Both the catalog and the store were the brainchildren of Stewart Brand, who once lived two years with American Indians, and who earlier that year had toured New Mexico's hippie communes "to find out what the kids" wanted, needed, and were willing to buy.

The first print order of the catalog, which contains no paid advertising, was 2,000 copies, but by the third edition in Spring 1970 some 160,000 copies were being run off and the book had acquired a reputation as an underground bestseller. Items were included in the catalog only if they were "useful as a tool, relevant to independent education, high quality or low cost, and easily available by mail." In a somewhat strangely worded statement of purpose prefacing the catalog, Brand noted:

We are as gods and might as well get good at it. So far remotely done power and glory—as via government, big business, formal education, church—has succeeded to point where gross defects obscure actual gains. In response to this dilemma and to these gains a realm of intimate, personal power is developing—power of the individual to conduct his own education, find his own inspiration, shape his own environment, and share his adventure with whoever is interested. Tools that aid this process are sought and promoted by the WHOLE EARTH CATALOG.

Brand's publication became widely distributed in bookstores and began to show an "embarrassing" profit. The May 1971 issue was originally intended to be the last, but was followed in 1974 by the *Whole Earth Epilog*. "The last *Whole Earth Catalog*," Brand explained, "continued to sell 5,000 copies a week with increasingly outdated information, and the North American economy began to lose its mind, putting more people in need of tools for independence and the economy as a whole in need of greater local reliance."

The catalog and its oversize, cheap paper format has been widely imitated.

"Whole Hog Mentality" *See* **Dixon-Yates.**

"The Whole World Is Watching" *See* **Battle of Chicago.**

Wiggins Amendment *See* **Equal Rights Amendment.**

The Wild One Directed by Laslo Benedek and starring Marlon Brando, this 1953 film focused on the phenomenon of the motorcycle gangs that had sprung up in California following World War II. In it the camera graphically records the language, costumes, and attitudes of a "wolf pack" of cyclists intent on terrorizing a small town. The portrait of alienated and frustrated young people finding compensation in association with a cult and a gang which allow them to express their resentment of discipline and their contempt for the established order of things was a convincing one; less so was a contrived ending in which Brando is shown as being summoned to redemption by a local, clean-living beauty.

The success of this film and the focus of news media attention on the **Hell's Angels** cyclists in the 1960s led to a number of "motorcycle movies." Among the worst were *Motorcycle Gang* (1957) and *Devil's Angels* (1967). The best and only truly accurate portrait was Kenneth Anger's noncommercial *Scorpio Rising* (1966). Somewhat related to these was Dennis Hopper's *Easy Rider* (1969), which launched the film careers of Peter Fonda and Jack Nicholson. In the words of one critic, "the film [*Easy Rider*] nearly ruined Hollywood when every studio tried to duplicate its success."

Wilderness Areas Act After a three-year battle begun under the Kennedy administration, on August 20, 1964, Congress approved legislation permanently placing some 9.1 million acres of federally owned land under a National Wilderness Preservation System. Similar legislation had originally been approved by the Senate in September 1961, but strong opposition from the mining industry had caused it to be shelved. In the bill signed into law by President Lyndon B. Johnson on September 3, 1964, current mining rights within the system were to be permitted only until the end of 1983.

The system as originally established included fifty-four national forest areas in thirteen states; individual "wilderness" areas of a minimum 100,000-acre size in Arizona, California, Idaho, Montana, New Mexico, Oregon, Washington, and Wyoming; "wild" areas of from 5,000 to 100,000 acres in Arizona, California, Colorado, Montana, Nevada, New Hampshire, New Mexico, North Carolina, Oregon, and Washington; and an 886,673-acre Minnesota "canoe" area near the Canadian border.

The act permitted a ten-year review of "primitive" national forest areas, roadless national park areas, and wildlife refuges for possible inclusion in the system—to which, despite opposition from cattle, mining, and lumbering interests, an additional 1.9 million acres had been added by 1973.

Williams v. Wallace The **Selma-Montgomery** protest march led by Dr. Martin Luther King, Jr., on March 21, 1965, was made possible after two unsuccessful attempts only after action against Alabama's Governor George C. Wallace had been brought in federal court by **Student Nonviolent Coordinating Committee** (SNCC; Snick) deputy Hosea Williams, who had substituted for Dr. King on the first attempt to march on March 6, 1965. The case came before Judge Frank Johnson, whose decision on March 17, 1965, found for Williams and the other plaintiffs after outlining the history of harassment and intimidation in Selma. In a historic opinion, Judge Johnson noted:

This Court finds the plaintiffs' proposed plan to the extent that it relates to a march along U.S. Highway 80 from Selma to Montgomery, Alabama, to be a reasonable one to be used and followed in the exercise of a constitutional right of assembly and free movement within the state of Alabama for the purpose of petitioning their state government for redress of their grievances. . . . The wrongs and injustices inflicted upon these plaintiffs and the members of their class . . . have clearly exceeded—and continue to exceed—the outer limits of what is constitutionally permissible.

Wilmington Ten After a week of racial violence in Wilmington, North Carolina, ten civil rights activists, including Reverend Ben Chavis, field director of the United Church of Christ's mission for racial justice, were arrested and charged with the firebombing on February 6, 1971, of a grocery store opposite the church in which the group had taken refuge from roving white bands. A year later all ten were convicted of arson and most received sentences ranging from twenty-nine to thirty-four years. (The only white person involved, a woman, was given a shorter sentence and was subsequently paroled.)

The case was appealed through the state courts, and in May 1977, at a postconviction hearing, three black prosecution witnesses testified that their original testimony had been extracted from them by means of threats and promises of favors. Nevertheless, the hearing judge declined to grant a new trial or to explain the reasons for his decision.

The controversy surrounding the Wilmington Ten attracted worldwide attention and has been treated in the Communist press as an example of this country's duplicity in its insistence on the guarantees of human rights contained in the 1975 **Helsinki Accord**. Among those calling for the release of the civil rights militants, whom it has designated as "prisoners of conscience," is the London-based organization Amnesty International, winner of the 1976 Nobel Peace Prize.

Rejecting the criticism of "those from outside," on January 23, 1978, North Carolina's Governor James B. Hunt, Jr., affirmed his belief in the guilt of the prisoners, but reduced the sentences of most by one third, making them eligible for parole in the latter part of that year. Reverend Chavis' sentence was reduced to from seventeen to twenty-one years, making him eligible for parole in January 1980.

According to Amnesty International, as of February 1979 one of the ten was still imprisoned.

"With all deliberate speed" Phrase used in the U.S. Supreme Court's implementing decision of May 31, 1955, one year following its historic decision in **Brown v. Board of Education of Topeka**, which struck down racial segregation in public school education. Responding to a brief in which the federal government requested that segregation cases be remanded to the trial courts to work out local problems, the Court noted that the lower courts must require of school authorities "a prompt and reasonable start toward full compliance." In a phrase first used by Justice Oliver Wendell Holmes, Jr., in 1911 and often after by Justice Felix Frankfurter, the Court directed that the process of desegregation was to proceed "with all deliberate speed." It did not, as the Justice Department had suggested, direct that it was the responsibility of the lower courts to make local school authorities present concrete plans for desegregation within a given time.

A paragraph personally inserted in the government brief by President Dwight D. Eisenhower suggested that just as the Court had previously noted the importance of the psychological impact of segregation upon children, in a similar fashion it should take cognizance of the fact that psychological and emotional factors were involved "in the alterations that must now take place in order to bring about compliance with the Court's decision." The same paragraph noted that segregation had not only had "the sanction of decisions of this Court but has been fervently supported by great numbers of people as justifiable on legal and moral grounds."

Women Strike for Peace (WSP) WSP was born on November 1, 1961, when some 50,000 women in sixty communities throughout the nation took part in demonstrations urging "End the Arms Race—Not the Human Race." The "strike" action had been planned in Washington, D.C., the previous September by a small group —led by Mrs. Dagmar Wilson—who spread the word by means of chain letters and telephone calls. Participants were required to commit themselves to no political position except a firm opposition to nuclear war. The demonstrations planned by various communities took different but simultaneous forms: marching, lobbying with local government representatives, advertisements in the press, and letters and telegrams to Washington—particularly to Jacqueline Kennedy, wife of President John F. Kennedy.

In the nation's capital, as many as 1,500 women joined in a walk from the Washington Monument to the White House and the Soviet Embassy to deliver a letter from "the women of America" urging Mrs. Kennedy and Madam Khrushchev to join them in the struggle for the survival of the human race.

A week after the first "strike," WSP leaders agreed that the organization would remain unstructured. There were to be "no national organization, no membership, no dues, no board: women [would] stay in touch informally and raise their own funds locally for local projects." The absence of a national board gave local groups complete autonomy.

WSP joined in demonstrations for peace before the United Nations during the **Cuban Missile Crisis** in October 1962. It took an increasingly strong stand against the **Vietnam War** and participated in "Stop-the-Draft Week" demonstrations (December 4-8, 1967); the **Moratorium Day** protests (October 15, 1969); and the picketing of the House of Representatives (January 18, 1973) with signs demanding that Congress "Censure Nixon, the Mad Bomber" for the air strikes against Hanoi.

Women's Liberation Having assumed productive and active roles in the American economy during World War II, many women only reluctantly yielded to pressure and returned to their traditional domestic pursuits following general demobilization. Although on the surface the 1950s seemed a period of quiescence in the feminist movement, the discontents seething underneath came to a boil in the 1960s.

In 1963, the **President's Commission on the Status of Women,** established two years earlier under the chairwomanship of Eleanor Roosevelt, reported that women were earning as much as 40 percent less than men for comparable jobs.

The subtle limitations imposed by custom are, upon occasion, reinforced by specific barriers. . . . Some of these discriminatory provisions are contained in common law. Some are written into statute. Some are upheld by court decisions. Others take the form of practices of industrial, labor, professional or governmental organizations that discriminate against women in apprenticeship, training, hiring, wages and promotion.

That same year Betty Friedan published her bestselling **The Feminine Mystique,** which pointed out the discrepancy between the lives led by women and the image to which they were trying to conform. Charging that women too often attempted to live vicariously through their husbands and children, she asked: "Who knows what women can be when they are finally free to become themselves?" (Other prominent feminist writers of the decade included Ti-Grace Atkinson, Gloria Steinem, Kate Millet, and Shulamith Firestone.)

As the result of growing pressure from women's groups and their male sympathizers, Title VII of the **Civil Rights Act of 1964** also prohibited discrimination by employers or unions on the basis of sex. It was because officials of the Third National Conference of Commissions on the Status of Women refused to bring to the floor a resolution urging the Equal Employment Opportunity Commission (EEOC) to ensure that this provision was enforced that the **National Organization for Women** (NOW) came into being in June 1966. Often described as a NAACP for women, NOW went from 300 charter members to more than 1,200 in less than two years, and there was a heavy concentration of educators, lawyers, and sociologists. (By the end of the decade NOW had some 8,000 members.) The founder and driving force behind NOW in the early years was Ms. Friedan.

The attention of the news media was attracted to the group by outrageously staged stunts: public bra burnings, picketing the Atlantic City Miss America pageant as sexist, and invading an EEOC hearing on sex discrimination with signs such as "A Chicken in Every Pot, A Whore in Every Home." Adopting some of the techniques of the **New Left,** militant women's groups set up their own publications—*Off Our Backs, Up From Under, Everywoman,* etc.— and guerrilla theater troupes such as Robin Morgan's Women's International Terrorist Conspiracy from Hell (WITCH). However, the alliance of feminists and the often "macho" oriented New Left was sometimes an uneasy one. As early as 1964 Stokely Carmichael had informed feminists that "the only position for women in SNCC is prone," and women assigned housekeeping duties during the occupation of Columbia University by radical students in April 1968 (see **Siege of Morningside Heights**) had to stage a revolt within a revolt by announcing firmly that "Free women do not cook."

In the late 1960s and early 1970s, feminist groups campaigned for a liberalization of abortion laws and a series of legislative measures designed to equalize career opportunities for men and women. Thanks in large measure to their efforts, the **Equal Rights Amendment** (ERA) was finally presented to the states for ratification in 1972, almost a half century after it was first introduced into Congress. By mid-1979 it had still not been ratified by the required thirty-eight states, and Congress had extended the deadline to June 30, 1982. One of its most formidable opponents was the antiliberationist women's group known as STOP ERA, which was founded by Illinois conservative Phyllis Schlafly. (Other antiliberationist movements of the 1970s were the commercially oriented **Fascinating Womanhood** seminars of Helen Andelin and the **Total Woman** seminars of Marabel Morgan.)

"Women's Lib" captured national headlines with the **Women's Strike for Equality** sponsored by a coalition for feminist groups which urged women to cease their daily occupations on August 26, 1970, and demonstrate "against the concrete conditions of their oppression." In July 1971, some 200 women's leaders met in the nation's capital to form the **National Women's Political Caucus** (NWPC) to support political candidates of both sexes who would join in the struggle against "sexism, racism, violence and poverty."

Pressures within the women's movement began to develop in the 1970s as many radicals rejected its original, essentially civil rights orientation and argued that the unique needs of women called for the feminine equivalent of "black separatism." Others argued that there could be no true liberation of women under capitalism and urged that groups such as NOW move "out of the mainstream, into the revolution." There was also a small, openly lesbian component of the movement, which received a disproportionate amount of attention from the communications media.

Women's Strike for Equality On August 26, 1970, the fiftieth anniversary of the ratification of the Nineteenth Amendment to the Constitution, which gave them the right to vote, thousands of women all over the United States went on a twenty-four hour general strike. Sponsored by a coalition of women's groups, the idea had originated with Betty Friedan, author of *The Feminine Mystique* and founder of the **National Organization for Women** (NOW). Housewives, secretaries, waitresses, editors, actresses, and corporate executives were called upon to cease their daily occupations and unite in a demonstration "against the concrete conditions of their oppression."

In the major cities across the nation, they and some male sympathizers paraded down the main streets. In New York City, the demonstration drew 15,000 marchers; in Boston, the Common was crowded with costumed suffragettes who flew balloons calling for legalized abortion; and in Washington, D.C., members of Federally Employed Women (FEW)—forbidden by law to strike—held a lunchtime rally in front of the White House. The demands most frequently heard were for equal opportunity in education and jobs, legalized abortion, and free day-care centers for the children of working mothers. In the words of Ms. Friedan's revolutionary anthem "Liberation Now!" the participants in the strike wanted it generally known that they were "more than mothers and wives/With secondhand lives."

Amid the general enthusiasm and rejoicing, a few sour notes were sounded. Said Ti-Grace Atkinson, founder of the Feminists—a splinter group of NOW—from which she had recently resigned: "Radical feminism is almost dead. People in the movement now are only concerned with day care, abortion, and job discrimination. . . . The real gut issues of love, sex, and marriage have fallen away. We need a revolution within a revolution."

"Woodstein" *See* **Watergate Scandal.**

Woodstock Festival Acid-rock music festival held in Bethel, New York, on White Lake, August 15-17, 1969. Its name derives from the fact that promoters Michael Land and John Roberts—both of whom were only twenty-four—originally advertised the festival for the Woodstock area, but had to change sites when a local zoning board backtracked and

refused permission. Land and Roberts, who had invested $2.5 million in the venture, leased a 600-acre dairy farm instead, and the crowds of young people began rolling in from all parts of the country to set up tents, geodesic domes, and open-air campsites. Although the sponsors had counted on selling 50,000 $7 tickets, some 200,000 packed the natural amphitheater where they listened to Joan Baez, Janis Joplin, Jimi Hendrix, the Jefferson Airplane, and other heroes of the rock movement. Unfortunately for Land and Roberts, few of those who attended actually bought tickets, and the festival ended up $2 million in the red.

Culturally—or "counterculturally"—it was a great success, however—in spite of downpours that turned the site into a muddy swamp. Some 400,000 young people "participated" in some aspect of the event during the three days the "Woodstock nation" lasted. *The New York Times*, which had originally condemned the festival as a "colossal mess," eventually reconsidered and decided that it was "essentially a phenomenon of innocence." The crowd was good-naturedly determined to demonstrate to a "materialistic" older generation which had permitted the horrors of the **Vietnam War** that love and cooperation were possible as well as desirable. Such policing as there was was supplied by members of the Hog Farm, a New Mexico hippie commune. Nevertheless, three people died—at least one from an overdose of drugs—and hundreds of youngsters suffered "bad trips" as the result of the low-grade **LSD** that was being openly peddled. Fifty doctors were flown in from New York City as the result of a "health emergency" stemming from the bad weather and a variety of accidentally caused wounds and bone breaks.

The success of the festival led to imitations, but the luster was somewhat lost after the **Altamont Death Festival** in California in December.

In 1970, *Woodstock*, a documentary film shot during the festival, was awarded an Oscar.

Workfare *See* **Family Assistance Plan.**

Work Incentive Program (WIN) Jointly administered by the Departments of Labor and Health, Education, and Welfare, WIN was authorized by the Social Security Amendments of 1967 and 1971 to help persons receiving Aid to Families with Dependent Children (AFDC) become self-supporting. With some exemptions, AFDC applicants are required to register with a WIN sponsor, such as a state employment agency, for employment and workforce services. Existing employment training programs and WIN-funded activities are used to place such applicants in unsubsidized jobs. Under the Revenue Act of 1971, private employers are given an incentive in the form of a tax credit for hiring WIN registrants. The current emphasis of the program is immediate employment rather than training.

The Work Incentive program is not to be confused with the abortive and much-ballyhooed Whip Inflation Now (WIN) program launched under the Ford administration. A mixture of tax recommendations and pleas for restraint in consumer buying, the latter WIN was scuttled by deepening recession in 1976.

Wounded Knee On February 27, 1973, some 200 armed supporters of the American Indian Movement (AIM) occupied the hamlet of Wounded Knee on the Oglala Sioux reservation, South Dakota, and demanded government investigations of the Bureau of Indian Affairs (BIA) and of the 371 treaties between the United States and various Indian nations. The raiders took weapons and supplies from the Wounded Knee trading post and then barricaded themselves in a Roman Catholic church, defying the more than 250 law enforcement officers who soon surrounded the area to either negotiate or attack and wipe them out. (In 1890, more than 300 Indian men, women, and children were massacred by a U.S. cavalry unit attacking an Indian village at Wounded Knee.)

The occupation of Wounded Knee continued until May 8, 1973, during which time federal agents arrested some 300 persons who attempted to either enter or leave the area. Some 120 remaining occupiers surrendered in compliance with a May 5, 1973, agreement, according to which the government agreed to investigate charges of broken treaties and the uncompensated expulsion of Sioux from lands once ceded to them. The break in the seventy-day stalemate between government and Indian representatives is said to have come after the former received a letter in which Leonard Garment, counsel to President Richard M. Nixon, reaffirmed an earlier offer to have White House representatives participate in talks in which Indian demands and charges would be considered.

Some fifteen persons were arrested at the time the occupation came to an end; although AIM leader Dennis Banks managed to slip past government road blocks, he surrendered shortly after. On September 16, 1974, a federal district court judge dismissed charges of assault, conspiracy, and larceny brought by the government against Banks and Rus-

sel Means, another Indian militant. The judge charged Chief Prosecutor R. D. Hurd with having several times misled the court and committed errors of judgment and negligence; he also said that the FBI had "stooped to a new low" in dealing with witnesses and evidence. Documentation showing that testimony of a prosecution witness was false, was proved to have been suppressed by the FBI.

The Wretched of the Earth Translated into English in 1965, this clinical examination, by the Martinique-born political theorist Frantz Fanon, of the oppressive and dehumanizing treatment of colonized peoples by Western nations immediately caught the attention of young black militants who were growing increasingly disenchanted with the nonviolence of Dr. Martin Luther King, Jr. Along with *The Autobiography of Malcolm X* (1964), it is said to have been a major influence on the thinking of Huey P. Newton and Bobby Seale, cofounders of the **Black Panther Party** (BPP), who were struck by Fanon's identification of the United States as an oppressor of the "colonized" American blacks.

Fanon warned against nonviolence as a compromising weakness, "an attempt to settle the colonial problem around a green baize table, before any regrettable act" had been committed. Using a combination of Marxist, psychoanalytic, and sociological approaches, he argued that justice could be brought to the colonized "wretched of the earth" only when they carried out a violent revolution that would destroy the physical and psychological shackles created by their racist oppressors. Violence, he felt, could by means of a "collective catharsis" create a new culture which rejected the traditional European values. "At the level of individuals, violence is a cleansing force. It frees the native from his inferiority complex and from his despair and inaction; it makes him fearless and restores his self-respect."

Eldridge Cleaver wrote that the passions racking black militants were incoherent and unconnected until they read Fanon. "Then many things fell together for us, harmonizing our attitudes and making it possible for us to organize into a political organization."

After service in the French Army during World War II, Fanon studied medicine and psychiatry in France. His first book, *Black Skin, White Masks* (1952), probed the social and psychological processes by which blacks were alienated from their own culture. From 1954 to 1956 he secretly aided the revolutionaries of Algeria's National Liberation Front, later openly becoming one of the movement's leading ideologists and developing a theory of anticolonial **"third world"** struggle. He served as the Algerian provisional government's ambassador to Ghana in 1960 before it was discovered that he had leukemia. After seeking treatment in the U.S.S.R, he came to the United States, where he died in 1961, the year in which *The Wretched of the Earth* was published with an introduction by Jean-Paul Sartre.

Wriston Committee In 1954, President Dwight D. Eisenhower appointed a committee headed by Dr. Henry Wriston to study the reform and reorganization of the U.S. State Department. As a result of its recommendations, about 2,400 State Department specialists of various kinds were made Foreign Service officers. The ranks of the Foreign Service were tripled from 1,200 to 3,600 in spite of objections from critics who argued that this addition of personnel without essential services abroad further sapped morale of Foreign Service officers already hard-pressed by attacks from Sen. Joseph R. McCarthy (R.-Wis.), who rumbled obscurely about "Communist infiltration." The swollen Foreign Service ranks were said as a result of "Wristonization" to have developed a "Wriston Bulge" made up of "Wristonees."

To a large extent, the work of the Wriston Committee had been anticipated and prepared by the **Hoover Commission** (1947) and the **Rowe-Ramspeck-DeCourcy Committee** (1950).

"The wrong war, at the wrong place, at the wrong time and with the wrong enemy" Statement made by General Omar Nelson Bradley, chairman of the Joint Chiefs of Staff, defending the decision by President Harry S Truman to relieve General Douglas MacArthur of his various Far Eastern commands on April 10, 1951. The dismissal came about as a result of the dispute between the President and General MacArthur over the conduct of the **Korean War.** After the failure of the **Yalu River Offensive** in November 1950, Chinese "volunteers" poured into North Korea. General MacArthur blamed the defeat of his troops on Washington's prohibition against extending the air war across the Manchuria-North Korean border. General Bradley supported the President's decision against extending the war with North Korea into a possible war against China.

See **"Old soldiers never die; they just fade away."**

WSP *See* **Women Strike for Peace.**

XYZ

Yippies

X-1 Work on a rocket-powered plane to exceed the speed of sound was proposed at a seminar of the National Advisory Commission for Aeronautics (NACA) in the spring of 1944 when German jets began appearing over Great Britain. In 1945, Congress appropriated $500,000 for preliminary studies of a rocket airplane.

The first result of this effort was the X-1 built by Bell Aircraft Corporation, and news of its successful testing at Muroc Air Base, California, was first broken by *Aviation Week* magazine in December 1947. Secretary of the Air Force W. Stuart Symington immediately sought legal means of clamping down on the unauthorized use of such information.

On June 10, 1948, after being informed by Attorney General Tom C. Clark that such censorship and prosecution of the magazine was impossible under peacetime law, Secretary Symington confirmed that the X-1—originally called XS-1—had many times flown "much faster than the speed of sound . . . since last October." At about the same time, it was revealed that a Soviet DFS 346 jet based on German plans had flown at speeds of 745 mph.

The X-1 piloted by war ace Captain Charles E. Yeager was announced as having flown at an altitude of 35,000 feet, where sound travels at 660 mph. (Later sources gave the speed as 700 mph, or Mach 1.06 at 43,000 feet.) A beefed-up copy of a captured German plane brought to the United States in 1945, it was taken aloft by a B-29 and then released for independent flight. Its fuel supply—a combination of alcohol, distilled water, and liquid oxygen—was sufficient for 2½ minutes.

In September 1956, a Bell X-2 established a world speed record of 2,094 mph at Edwards Air Force Base, California, but its pilot, Air Force Captain Milburn Apt, was killed when for reasons never established he failed to use his parachute.

Testing in the series ended with the X-15—conceived in 1954 and developed by North American Aviation, Inc.—which on August 4, 1960, set a new world record for manned flight in a test which achieved a speed of 2,196 mph. A week later the X-15 established a new altitude record at 136,500 feet. On both flights it was towed aloft from Edwards Air Force Base, California, by a B-52.

Throughout the decade the X-15 continued to establish new records.

YAF *See* **Young Americans for Freedom.**

Yalu River Offensive Communist China had rejected a United Nations invitation to explain its position in the **Korean War**, but on November 24, 1950, a Chinese delegation did arrive in New York with the stated mission of presenting charges that the United States had been guilty of aggression against Formosa. There seemed some possibility that contact might be opened for settlement of the fighting in Korea. But on that very day, General Douglas MacArthur, commander of the UN forces in Korea, launched an all-out offensive north to the Yalu River. Two days later, 300,000 Chinese—massed in North Korea and pouring across the frozen Yalu separating it from Manchuria—launched an offensive that split General MacArthur's 10th Corps from the Eighth Army. Due to faulty intelligence, the general had been convinced that there were no more than 60,000 Chinese regulars and "volunteers" in the area.

Yates v. United States In 1951, the U.S. Supreme Court had found in **Dennis et al. v. United States** that the conviction of eleven Communist leaders found guilty under the Smith Act (1940) of advocating the violent overthrow of the government did not abridge any constitutional guarantees. The following year, fourteen minor Communist leaders—including an Oleta Yates—were convicted under the conspiracy provisions of the 1940 legislation. In reversing that conviction by a five-to-two vote on November 25, 1957, the Court found that caution had to be exercised in interpreting the Smith Act and the *Dennis* decision.

The ruling was based on two grounds: (1) the Communist Party in the United States had been disbanded in 1944 and reorganized in 1945. This meant that under the three-year statute of limitations prosecution under the Smith Act for organizing to advocate the overthrow of the government had to be undertaken by no later than 1948. The government contention that the act's words "to organize" should be construed in a "continuing" sense was rejected by the Court. (2) Yates et al. had also been prosecuted for conspiracy to teach and advocate, but the decision by Justice John Marshall Harlan made a distinction between instruction in the abstract doctrine and advocacy of "concrete action."

As amended in June 1962, the Smith Act provided that the term "organize" was to include new recruiting, the setting up of additional units, or the expansion of existing units. Nevertheless, given the Yates decision, prosecution for conspiracy to teach or advocate became a practical impossibility.

"Yellow Submarine" *See* **LSD.**

Yippies In February 1968, Abbie Hoffman, Jerry Rubin, Ed Sanders, and Paul Krassner formed the Youth International Party (YIP), whose members, known as Yippies, soon captured the attention of the press and the nation by merging "revolutionary" political tactics with surface aspects of the lifestyle of the hippies. "With our free stores, liberated buildings, communes, people's parks, dope, free bodies and our music, we'll build our society in the vacant lots of the old, and we'll do it by any means necessary," explained Hoffman.

At the "life festival" they planned during the 1968 Democratic National Convention in Chicago, the bearded and sandaled Yippies entered into an uneasy alliance with militants of **Students for a Democratic Society** (SDS) to demonstrate against the continuing **Vietnam War**. But their lack of discipline was in many ways a disaster for the radical cause. "I am my own leader," said Hoffman. "I make my own rules. The revolution is wherever my boots hit the ground. If the Left considers this adventurism, fuck 'em. They are a total bureaucratic bore."

The official 1968 presidential candidate of the Yippies was Sen. George McGovern (D.-S.Dak.); however, they arrived in Chicago with their first choice for president, Pigasus, a live hog, and settled down in Lincoln Park, from which they were eventually expelled by police, who charged, swinging their nightsticks. The events of these days are covered in the **Walker Report**.

A Yippie manifesto called for an Election-day demonstration in which tribute would be paid to "rioters, anarchists, Commies, runaways, draft dodgers, acid freaks, snipers, beatniks, deserters, Chinese spies. . . . And then on Inauguration Day . . . we will bring our revolutionary theater to Washington to inaugurate Pigasus . . . and turn the White House into a crash pad. They will have to put Nixon's hand on the Bible in a glass cage."

The best summary of the "principles" of the Yippies is contained in Abbie Hoffman's *Steal This Book* (1971), which advocated nonpayment for "food, clothes, housing, transportation, medical care, even money and dope"—everything including the $1.95-book itself.

At the 1972 national conventions held in Miami Beach by both leading political parties, Rubin and Hoffman began to lose their influence with their followers and were both later expelled from YIP for preventing demonstrations called for by the "Crazies" among them and for failing to share their lecture fees with the organization. In 1974, Hoffman dropped out of sight after being indicted on the charge of selling cocaine to undercover government agents.

Yobo System Sometimes used to denote the relations GIs stationed in South Korea establish with local women. *Yobo* stems from the Korean word for "honey." For a fixed monthly rate, depending on army grade and salary, a yobo will not only become a GI's sexual companion but also keep house for him, sometimes maintaining even his army gear in order. Army authorities are said to shut their eyes to the elaborate "yobo culture" because it provides an approximation of home life for men generally unable to have their families with them, and because it helps keep down venereal disease.

Yom Kippur Statement On October 4, 1946, the eve of the Jewish Day of Atonement holiday (Yom Kippur), President Harry S Truman issued a statement calling on Great Britain to allow 100,000 Jewish refugees into Palestine immediately. The President pledged American aid in transporting the immigrants and said that a plan to partition the British mandate between Arabs and Jews "would command the support of public opinion in the United States." He also urged, as he had done in the past, that Congress liberalize immigration laws to permit more displaced persons to find a home in this country (*see* **Displaced Persons Act**).

The statement was attacked at the time—congressional elections were only a month away—as a play for the Jewish vote in Ohio, Pennsylvania, Illinois, and especially New York, where advance information indicated that its Governor, Thomas E. Dewey, was said to be preparing an attack on the Truman administration's handling of the refugee problem. (Shortly afterward, Governor Dewey followed the President's lead and called for the immigration of several hundred thousand Jews into Palestine.) However, there seems little doubt that the President was sincerely concerned about the fate of these refugees and, in June 1945, had sent Earl G. Harrison, dean of the University of Pennsylvania, to Europe to investigate the fate of "non-repatriables." The Harrison Report, submitted to him, stated that "if there is any genuine sympathy for what these survivors have endured, some reasonable extension or modification of the British White Paper of 1939 ought to be possible without too serious repercussions. For some of the European Jews, there is no acceptable or even decent solution for their future other than Palestine."

At the time, Dean Acheson, who was Under Secretary of State, approved of the Yom Kippur Statement, but he later wrote that on reconsideration it "seems to have been of doubtful wisdom." Authorship of the statement itself was attributed in some quarters to David K. Niles, the President's assistant for minority groups.

Young Americans for Freedom (YAF) While student activism in the 1960s was generally marked by liberal or radical tendencies, that same period saw the birth and development of YAF, a conservative student movement which grew from a nucleus group of about 100 to 50,000 by the end of the decade. YAF was formed September 9-11, 1960, when representatives of forty-four colleges met at the home of journalist William Buckley, Jr., in Sharon, Connecticut, and issued a 400-word manifesto that is sometimes known as the Sharon Statement. Reflecting the organization's strong emphasis on the democratic importance of a free-market economy, the manifesto noted that government interference "tends to reduce the moral and physical strength of the nation; that when [the government] takes from one man to bestow on another, it diminishes the incentive of the first, the integrity of the second, and the moral autonomy of both. . . ." The document stressed international communism as the greatest single threat to liberty, and urged that the United States strive for "victory over, rather than coexistence with this menace. . . ."

In its "activist" efforts to combat liberalism on campus, YAF often foreshadowed the disruptive tactics of the radical groups that were to dominate the 1960s. Critics found this particularly true of the efforts to take over the liberally oriented **National Student Association** (NSA) at that organization's fourteenth annual congress at Madison, Wisconsin, in August 1961. YAF also played a significant role in the presidential campaign of Sen. Barry Goldwater (R.-Ariz.) in 1964.

Among the recipients of YAF awards "for contributions to American Conservatism and the youth of the nation" were Buckley, the **House Committee on Un-American Activities** (HUAC), and the Republic of China. The group sponsored frequent showings of *Operation Abolition*, a documentary supporting FBI charges that protests against the May 1960 HUAC hearings in San Francisco were communist-inspired.

Young Turks At the 1948 Democratic Convention in Philadelphia, this was the name given to the determined band of "radicals" led by the young mayor of Minneapolis, Hubert H. Humphrey, and including Paul Douglas and Adlai Stevenson, respectively the Democratic senatorial and gubernatorial candidates in Illinois, who demanded that the party platform include planks backing specific civil rights legislation, public housing, an increased minimum wage, and national health insurance. Although President Harry S Truman had himself requested civil rights legislation in his message to Congress on February 2, 1948, it is likely that faced with the loss of votes to Henry A. Wallace, who was to be nominated as presidential candidate of the **Progressive Party of America** later that month, he might have preferred a more ambiguously worded civil rights plank that would have avoided alienating Southern delegates and later Southern voters. But the civil rights plan was put before an open convention and after three hours was accepted by a vote of 651½ to 582½. The **Dixiecrats** withdrew from the convention on July 14, and three days later nominated South Carolina's Governor J. Strom Thurmond for president.

The expression Young Turks originally referred to a strongly reformist movement that flourished in Turkey at the turn of the century. It has several times in American history been applied to any reformist group within a political party.

Youth International Party *See* **Yippies.**

"You won't have Nixon to kick around any more." *See* **Nixon's Last Press Conference.**

Zemel v. Rusk In a six-to-three decision, with Justices William O. Douglas, Arthur J. Goldberg, and Hugo L. Black dissenting, the U.S. Supreme Court on May 3, 1965, upheld the State Department's right to restrict travel of U.S. citizens in designated areas. At issue was a Department policy, initiated January 16, 1961, which authorized visits to Communist Cuba only by those whose travel there would be in the best interests of this country. In effect, that meant reporters or business executives.

The suit was brought against Secretary of State Dean Rusk by Louis Zemel, Middlefield, Connecticut, after he was refused authorization to visit Cuba in order to "satisfy [his] curiosity" about conditions there. In his majority opinion, Chief Justice Earl Warren held that Secretary Rusk was justified in imposing restrictions because the Castro regime was seeking to use visitors as a means of exporting revolutionary ideas.

Restrictions against travel to Cuba were lifted in 1977.

Zero Population Growth (ZPG) Incorporated by its founders (Paul Ehrlich, Charles Remington, and Richard Bowers) on December 9, 1968, as a nonprofit organization advocating the international reduction of population growth to zero, by the mid-1970s ZPG had more than 8,000 members, sixty active chapters and state lobbying groups, and a national staff of twenty-two at its headquarters in Washington, D.C. It supports extended research in contraception, urges the repeal of antiabortion legislation, calls for the establishment of more birth-control clinics and services, and fights for the elimination of current pronatalist implications in tax and insurance laws. The family replacement level per fertile married woman is seen as 2.54 children—not including illegitimate births.

ZPG maintains a Washington lobby and its representatives testified in regional hearings on the 1978 Presidential Report on Urban Growth and Economic Development and at state-level hearings preliminary to the 1978 White House Conference on Balanced National Growth and Economic Development. Its Population Education Project works with public school systems to give children and teen-agers an understanding of the dynamics and effects of population change.

Ziegles Among the special gifts brought to the White House by the men surrounding President Richard M. Nixon was a tortuous sentence structure that almost appeared intended to obscure communication rather than to further it. Ronald Ziegler, the President's official press secretary, seemed to have perfected a technique of briefing reporters without informing them. An example of one such "ziegle," as the journalists called it, is the following exchange reported by Dan Rather and Gary Paul Gates in *The Palace Guard* (1974):

Question: Is General Hershey's replacement under consideration by the White House?

Ziegler: There is no information that I have that would lead me to respond to that question in the affirmative.

Statements previously affirmed by the White House and subsequently proved to be false were said by Ziegler to have become "inoperative."

Zion Investment Associates *See* **10-36-50 Plan.**

Zorach v. Clauson *See* **"Released time."**

ZPG *See* **Zero Population Growth.**

Index of Names in the News